Fire in My Soul

FIRE IN MY SOUL

Essays on Pauline Soteriology and the Gospels in Honor of Seyoon Kim

edited by
SOON BONG CHOI,
JIN KI HWANG,
and MAX J. LEE

◆PICKWICK *Publications* • Eugene, Oregon

FIRE IN MY SOUL
Essays on Pauline Soteriology and the Gospels in Honor of Seyoon Kim

Copyright © 2014 Wipf and Stock Publishers. All rights reserved. Except for brief quotations in critical publications or reviews, no part of this book may be reproduced in any manner without prior written permission from the publisher. Write: Permissions, Wipf and Stock Publishers, 199 W. 8th Ave., Suite 3, Eugene, OR 97401.

Pickwick Publications
An Imprint of Wipf and Stock Publishers
199 W. 8th Ave., Suite 3
Eugene, OR 97401

www.wipfandstock.com

ISBN 13: 978-1-62564-110-6

Cataloging-in-Publication data:

Fire in my soul : essays on Pauline soteriology and the gospels in honor of Seyoon Kim / edited by Soon Bong Choi, Jin Ki Hwang, and Max J. Lee.

xxiv + 350 p. ; 23 cm. —Includes bibliographical references and index(es).

ISBN 13: 978-1-62564-110-6

1. Paul, the Apostle, Saint—Views on salvation. 2. Bible. Gospels—Criticism, interpretation, etc. 3. Kim, Seyoon. I. Title.

BS2655 S25 F62 2014

Manufactured in the U.S.A.

cover image: "St. Paul Preaching in front of the Areopagus" by Marià Fortuny
© MNAC Museu Nacional d'Art de Catalunya, Barcelona
Photographers: Calveras/Mérida/Sagristà

Dr. Seyoon Kim

Scholar, Teacher, and Pastor

Contents

Foreword by Won Lee | ix
Contributors | xi
Abbreviations | xiii
Introduction by Soon Bong Choi, Jin Ki Hwang, and Max J. Lee | xix

Part One: Essays on Pauline Soteriology and Paul's Gospel

1 Greek Words and Roman Meanings, Part 1:
   (Re)mapping Righteousness Language in Greco-Roman Discourse | 3
   —Max J. Lee

2 Greek Words and Roman Meanings, Part 2: A Prolegomenon to Paul's
   Use of Righteousness Language in His Letters | 29
   —Max J. Lee

3 The Occasion and Purpose of Romans Revisited | 53
   —Hae-Kyung Chang

4 Universal Sinfulness and Paul's Reading of the Old Testament
   in Rom 3:9–18 | 77
   —Kyoung-Shik Kim

5 The Antithesis between the Law and Grace in Gal 5:4 | 95
   —Hung-Sik Choi

6 The Internal Integrative Motive Running
   through 2 Cor 11:23—12:10 | 115
   —Chulhong Brian Kim

Part Two: Essays on the Gospels and Gospel Hermeneutics

7 Matthew's Use of the Septuagint and Its Implications | 131
   —Jin Ki Hwang

8 The Understanding of στηρίζειν τὸ πρόσωπον in Luke 9:51 | 148
   —Soon Bong Choi

9 Re-examining the Ironical Interpretation of the Parable of the Unjust Steward in Luke 16 | 159
   —Chang Wook Jung

10 Forgiveness, Faith, and the Lordship of Jesus: A Contextual Reading of Luke 17:1–10 | 184
   —Yon-Gyong Kwon

11 Was Johannine Christianity Sectarian? | 202
   —Dongsoo Kim

12 The "Son of Man" in Johannine Eschatology | 212
   —Stephen E. Young

13 The Bilingualism of the Hebrews and the Hellenists in the Jerusalem Church | 231
   —Sang-Il Lee

14 "The Word of God" as a New Testament Term: An Investigation into Its Terminological Origin | 254
   —Sung-Jong Oh

15 Methodological Similarity between *Xunguxue* and Biblical Exegesis | 277
   —Hyeon Woo Shin

Dr. Seyoon Kim: A Comprehensive Bibliography | 299
Epilogue: Words of Appreciation from Former Students and Colleagues of Dr. Seyoon Kim | 305
Subject Index | 313
Author Index | 317
Ancient Document Index | 325

Foreword

A few words would not be sufficient to capture the impact and scope of Professor Seyoon Kim's career which has spanned over three decades in three continental contexts. Nonetheless, all of his achievements can be summed up with a single word: *exceptional*.

I begin with his exceptional presence. Anyone who has heard him preach or teach knows that Dr. Kim has a deep, baritone voice that immediately commands the attention of his listeners. Even more powerful are his insights into God's word and his exhortations to God's people. Dr. Kim works with an unwavering diligence, penetrating the mystery of the Word for all learners, fitting its complex meanings into one simple truth of the gospel, and manages to deliver prophetic challenges with such passion and clarity. His preaching and teaching have uplifted desperate souls and stretched the hearts of the already-committed toward greater service for God's kingdom. Yet, Dr. Kim's presence is also inviting, never intimidating. He is well loved by students and colleagues in North America, Europe, and Korea. Before leaving classrooms or conferences, he takes time to ponder questions and objections seriously. He invites students to lunch, coffee, and on occasion a glass of wine (or a carefully brewed German beer) to share their thoughts, their burdens, and almost always, to pray with them.

Dr. Kim is exceptional, not simply because of his presence, but also because of his scholarship. For the better part of his academic career, his scholarship has been fueled by a fire and passion for understanding Paul. His arguments for Paul's Damascus Road experience as the foundation of his apostleship and mission to the Gentiles has fueled debate and intense discussion for the past three decades since the debut of *The Origin of Paul's Gospel* (1981). Instead of psychologizing the Damascus Road experience, it is, for him, a historical event providing an explanation of how and why Paul converted from Pharisaism to become a Christian herald. Paul's vision of Jesus as divine Wisdom and the very image of God provides the theological framework for all Pauline teachings on justification, reconciliation, the transformed life, and new creation. It is a thesis that has remained convincing despite the attempts of many to derail its arguments.

A quick glance at his bibliography, however, also demonstrates that Dr. Kim's research has expanded well beyond his early work on Paul's Christophany. In his *Paul and the New Perspective* (2001), Dr. Kim offers a spirited debate with proponents of the New Perspective and persistently defends a traditional Protestant Reformation view of Paul. He has consistently worked on Paul's knowledge of Jesus' sayings and is convinced of the coherence between Paul and Jesus despite the objections of many critics. Dr. Kim never shies away from hard questions nor skillful opponents. He is a committed evangelical scholar with a pastoral commitment to the church's mission. No other scholar of Korean descent has achieved as many milestones in Pauline studies for the church and the international academic community as Dr. Kim.

Lastly, Dr. Kim is an exceptional mentor and model for his students. His presence and scholarship have inspired a rising generation of young scholars. He constantly encourages his students to aim at making substantial contributions to the guild through their work. In fact, Dr. Kim with other colleagues helped found the Korean Biblical Colloquium (KBC) to promote scholarly advancement and networking among Korean professors and graduate students in the field of biblical studies. From his personal relationships with students and through the auspices of KBC, Dr. Kim has demonstrated a tireless advocacy for the maturity and continual support of a new wave of Korean scholars who will influence the academy and serve the church.

The essays in this volume clearly convey the deep influence Dr. Seyoon Kim has had, and continues to make, on his former students and present colleagues. But don't just take my word for it. Read the essays and especially the words of appreciation in the epilogue. Or, better yet, take the time to meet Dr. Kim. Talk with him. Get to know who he is and what he has done. You, too, then, will discover what an exceptional scholar, pastor, and person he truly is!

Won W. Lee
Professor of Old Testament at Calvin College
President of the Korean Biblical Colloquium

Contributors

Hae-Kyung Chang (DTh, Eberhard–Karls–Universität in Tübingen) is Professor of New Testament at Asian Center for Theological Studies and Mission, Yangpyoung, Korea.

Hung-Sik Choi (PhD, Durham University) is Associate Professor of New Testament at Torch Trinity Graduate University, Seoul, Korea.

Soon Bong Choi (DTh, Eberhard–Karls–Universität in Tübingen) is Professor of New Testament at Kwangshin University, Gwang-Ju City, Korea.

Jin Ki Hwang (PhD, Fuller Theological Seminary) is Assistant Dean for Korean Doctor of Ministry Program and Assistant Professor of New Testament at Fuller Theological Seminary, Pasadena, California.

Chang Wook Jung (PhD, Free University in Amsterdam) is Professor of New Testament at Chongshin University, Seoul, Korea.

Chulhong Brian Kim (PhD, Fuller Theological Seminary) is Associate Professor of New Testament at Presbyterian College and Theological Seminary, Seoul, Korea.

Dongsoo Kim (PhD, Cambridge University) is Associate Professor of New Testament at Pyeongtaek University, Pyeongtaek, Korea.

Kyoung-Shik Kim (PhD, Aberdeen University) is Assistant Professor of New Testament at Westminster Graduate School of Theology, Yongin, Korea.

Yon-Gyong Kwon (PhD, King's College London) is Associate Professor of Christian Studies at Soongsil University, Seoul, Korea.

Max J. Lee (PhD, Fuller Theological Seminary) is Associate Professor of New Testament at North Park Theological Seminary, Chicago, Illinois.

Sang-Il Lee (PhD, Durham University) is Assistant Professor of New Testament at Chongshin University, Seoul, Korea.

Sung-Jong Oh (DTh, Eberhard–Karls–Universität in Tübingen) taught as Associate Professor of New Testament at Calvin University, Seoul, Korea, until his retirement in 2012.

Hyeon Woo Shin (PhD, Free University in Amsterdam) is Assistant Professor of New Testament at Chongshin University, Seoul, Korea.

Stephen E. Young (PhD, Fuller Theological Seminary) is Assistant Professor of New Testament at Fuller Theological Seminary, Houston, Texas.

Abbreviations

AASF	Annales Academiae scientiarum fennicae
AB	Anchor Bible
ABD	*The Anchor Bible Dictionary.* Edited by David Noel Freedman. 6 vols. New York: Doubleday, 1992.
ABR	*Australian Biblical Review*
ABRL	Anchor Bible Reference Library
AcOr	*Acta orientalia*
ANRW	*Aufstieg und Niedergang der römischen Welt.* Edited by H. Temporini and W. Haase. New York: de Gruyter, 1972–
ANTC	Abingdon New Testament Commentary
ANTF	Arbeiten zur neutestamentlichen Textforschung
AR	*Archiv für Religionswissenschaft*
ATANT	Abhandlungen zur Theologie des Alten und Neuen Testaments
BAGD	Bauer, Walter, et al. *Greek-English Lexicon of the New Testament and Other Early Christian Literature.* 2nd ed. Chicago, 1979.
BBR	*Bulletin for Biblical Research*
BDAG	Bauer, Walter, et al. *Greek-English Lexicon of the New Testament and Other Early Christian Literature.* 3rd ed. Chicago: University of Chicago Press, 2000.
BECNT	Baker Exegetical Commentary on the New Testament
BETL	Bibliotheca ephemeridum theologicarum lovaniensium
BHT	Beiträge zur historischen Theologie
Bib	*Biblica*

BKAT	Biblischer Kommentar, Altes Testament
BNTC	Black's New Testament Commentaries
BRev	*Bible Review*
BSac	*Bibliotheca sacra*
BWM	Bibelwissenschaftliche Monographien
BZAW	Beihefte zur Zeitschrift für die alttestamentliche Wissenschaft
BZNW	Beihefte zur Zeitschrift für die neutestamentliche Wissenschaft
CBET	Contributions to Biblical Exegesis and Theology
CBQ	*Catholic Biblical Quarterly*
CD	*Church Dogmatics*, by Karl Barth. Edited by G. W. Bromiley and T. F. Torrance. Translated by G. T. Thomson et al. Edinburgh: T. & T. Clark, 1936–1977.
CRINT	Compendia rerum iudaicarum ad Novum Testamentum
CTM	*Concordia Theological Monthly*
CTR	*Criswell Theological Review*
DPL	*Dictionary of Paul and His Letters*. Edited by G. F. Hawthorne and R. P. Martin. Downers Grove: IVP Academic, 1993.
EDNT	*Exegetical Dictionary of the New Testament*. Edited by H. Balz and G. Schneider. 3 vols. Grand Rapids: Eerdmans, 1990–1993.
EKK	Evangelisch-katholischer Kommentar zum Neuen Testament
EvQ	*Evangelical Quarterly*
EWNT	*Exegetisches Wörterbuch zum Neuen Testament*. Edited by H. Balz and G. Schneider. 3 vols. Stuttgart: Kohlhammer, 1981–1983.
ExpTim	*Expository Times*
FAT	Forschungen zum Alten Testament
FRLANT	Forschungen zur Religion und Literatur des Alten und Neuen Testaments
HeyJ	*Heythrop Journal*
HibJ	*Hibbert Journal*
HNT	Handbuch zum Neuen Testament

HNTC	Harper's New Testament Commentaries
HRCS	Hatch, E., and H. A. Redpath. *Concordance to the Septuagint and Other Greek Versions of the Old Testament*. 2 vols. Oxford, Clarendon: 1897. Supplement, 1906. 2nd. ed., 2 vols. in 1, Grand Rapids: Baker Academic, 1988.
HSM	Harvard Semitic Monographs
HTKNT	Herders theologischer Kommentar zum Neuen Testament
IBC	Interpretation: A Bible Commentary for Teaching and Preaching.
ICC	International Critical Commentary
Int	*Interpretation*
JBL	*Journal of Biblical Literature*
JETS	*Journal of the Evangelical Theological Society*
JJS	*Journal of Jewish Studies*
JSNT	*Journal for the Study of the New Testament*
JSNTSup	Journal for the Study of the New Testament: Supplement Series
JSOT	Journal for the Study of the Old Testament
JSOTSup	Journal for the Study of the Old Testament: Supplement Series
JTS	*Journal of Theological Studies*
KEK	Kritisch-exegetischer Kommentar über das Neue Testament (Meyer-Kommentar)
KENTS	*Korean Evangelical New Testament Studies*
KNTS	*Korean New Testament Studies*
LCL	Loeb Classical Library
LNTS	Library of New Testament Studies
LSJ	Liddell, H. G., R. Scott, and H. S. Jones. *A Greek-English Lexicon*. 9th ed. Oxford: Clarendon, 1996.
MM	J. H. Moulton and G. Milligan. *The Vocabulary of the Greek Testament: Illustrated from the Papyri and Other Non-Literary Sources*. 1930. Reprint, Peabody, MA: Hendrickson, 1997.
MNTC	Moffatt New Testament Commentary

NAC	New American Commentary
Neot	*Neotestamentica*
NewDocs	*New Documents Illustrating Early Christianity.* Ed. G. H. R. Horsley and S. Llewelyn. Ancient History Documentary Research Centre, Macquarie University, 1981–
NIB	*The New Interpreter's Bible*
NIBC	New International Biblical Commentary
NIBCNT	New International Biblical Commentary on the New Testament
NICNT	New International Commentary on the New Testament
NICOT	New International Commentary on the Old Testament
NIDNTT	*New International Dictionary of New Testament Theology.* Ed. C. Brown. 4 vols. Grand Rapids: Zondervan, 1975–1985.
NIGTC	New International Greek Testament Commentary
NovT	*Novum Testamentum*
NovTSup	Novum Testamentum Supplements
NPNF	*Nicene and Post-Nicene Fathers of the Christian Church.* Ed. and trans. P. Schaff et al. New York: Scribner's Sons, 1904.
NTAbh	Neutestamentliche Abhandlungen
NTG	New Testament Guides
NTL	New Testament Library
NTS	*New Testament Studies*
OBT	Overtures to Biblical Theology
OTL	Old Testament Library
RB	*Revue biblique*
RNT	Regensburger Neues Testament
RTR	*Reformed Theological Review*
S&I	*Scripture and Interpretation*
SBAB	Stuttgarter biblische Aufsatzbände
SBLDS	Society of Biblical Literature Septuagint Dissertation Series
SBLSBS	Society of Biblical Literature Sources for Biblical Study
SBLSCS	Society of Biblical Literature Septuagint and Cognate Studies
SBT	Studies in Biblical Theology

SE	*Studia evangelica*
SNT	Studien zum Neuen Testament
SNTSMS	Society for New Testament Studies Monograph Series
SP	Sacra Pagina
SR	*Studies in Religion*
Str-B	Strack, H. L., and P. Billerbeck. *Kommentar zum Neuen Testament aus Talmud und Midrasch.* 6 vols. Münich: Beck, 1922–1961.
TDNT	*Theological Dictionary of the New Testament.* Ed. G. Kittel and G. Friedrich. Trans. G. W. Bromiley. 10 vols. Grand Rapids: Eerdmans, 1964–1976.
THAT	*Theologisches Handwörterbuch zum Alten Testament.* Ed. E. Jenni, with assistance from C. Westermann. 2 vols. Münich: Kaiser: 1971–1976
THKNT	Theologischer Handkommentar zum Neuen Testament
ThViat	*Theologia viatorum*
TLNT	*Theological Lexicon of the New Testament* by C. Spicq. Trans. and ed. J. D. Ernest. 3 vols. Peabody, MA: Hendrickson, 1994.
TLZ	*Theologische Literaturzeitung*
TNTC	Tyndale New Testament Commentaries
TS	*Theological Studies*
TWNT	*Theologische Wörterbuch zum Neuen Testament.* Ed. G. Kittel and G. Friedrich. 10 vols. Stuttgart: Kohlhammer, 1932–1979.
VC	*Vigiliae christianae*
VTSup	Vetus Testamentum Supplements
WBC	Word Biblical Commentary
WUNT	Wissenschaftliche Untersuchungen zum Neuen Testament
ZNW	*Zeitschrift für die neutestamentliche Wissenschaft und die Kunde der älteren Kirche*
ZTK	*Zeitschrift für Theologie und Kirche*

Introduction

SOON BONG CHOI, JIN KI HWANG, and MAX J. LEE

In 2004, Professor Seyoon Kim was voted in a poll conducted by the national newspaper *Dong-A Ilbo* as Korea's most important theologian for the twenty-first century. This volume pays tribute to his legacy and a lifetime of teaching, scholarship, and service to the church. It is our distinct pleasure and honor to present this Festschrift to Dr. Kim in the year of his retirement from full-time teaching at Fuller Theological Seminary (2012–2013) and on the occasion of his sixty-eighth birthday.

The title *Fire in My Soul* is taken from the words of Jeremiah ("His word is in my heart like a fire . . . I am weary of holding it in. Indeed I cannot!"; Jer 20:9) and from a well-known maxim that has been paraphrased from Plutarch ("The soul is not a vessel to be filled but a fire to be ignited"; *On Listening to Lectures* 48C). We editors wanted a title that would duly recognize Dr. Kim's fire and passion for preaching but also his ability as a mentor to ignite and inspire his students. Dr. Kim has left an indelible mark on a rising generation of theological educators who have learned from him how to participate in the mission of the church through serious biblical scholarship and teaching pastorally. This collection of essays was written mostly by past Korean students and colleagues of Dr. Kim who are now established professors in leading universities, Christian colleges, and seminaries in Korea and North America. Perhaps on his seventieth or seventy-fifth birthday, we can enlarge the range of essayists to include those from Europe and more prominent voices in the academy. But for now, we hope that the work presented here by those who have been discipled by Dr. Kim in one way or another will reflect the deep gratitude and admiration we have for a beloved teacher, mentor, and friend.

Part 1 of this volume focuses on a theme dear to the heart of Dr. Kim: Paul's soteriology and gospel. The first two chapters are written by Max Lee, who, in a two-part study on righteousness language in Greco-Roman discourse and Paul's letters, provides an alternative taxonomy of semantic classifications for the δικ(αιο)- lexical group (ch. 1) and applies this new lexicon to Paul's own use of δίκαιος, δικαιοσύνη, and δικαιόω in the Letter to the Romans (ch. 2). Lee argues that the forensic dimensions of Paul's soteriology fit well within the discourse of Greco-Roman juridicial texts and need not appeal to the idiolect of the Septuagint.

In ch. 3, Hae-Kyung Chang revisits the Romans debate and offers a proposal for the main purpose(s) that occasioned Paul's letter to Rome. Chang seeks to resolve the tension between Paul's plans to start the Spanish mission and his pastoral aim to resolve the Jewish-Gentile conflict within the Roman church. Chapter 4 by Kyoung-Shik Kim addresses the intertextual connections between Rom 3:9-18 and Isa 59. He argues that even though the original context of Isa 59 makes a distinction between the righteous and unrighteous within Israel, there is still a "hermeneutical seed" in Isa 59 which allows Paul to develop from the Old Testament a concept of universal sinfulness.

In ch. 5, Hung-Sik Choi takes a fresh look at the classic dialectic between the law and grace in Paul's Letter to the Galatians. Choi posits that the saving sufficiency of χάρις, anticipated by the Abrahamic blessing to all nations (Gen 12:3; 18:18), not only stands in opposition to the covenantal nomism of some Jewish-Christian agitators at Galatia but also brings about the justification of the Gentiles through the gifting of God's Son and Spirit. Chapter 6 by Chulhong Brian Kim argues for the coherence of 2 Cor 11:23—12:10 by uniting the seemingly disparate sections—i.e., Paul's suffering catalogue (11:23-30), the story of his escape from Damascus (11:31-33), his vision of the third heaven (12:1-4), and his experience of a thorn in the flesh (12:5-10)—against the backdrop of OT traditions describing the true vs. false prophet. Paul takes the idea of illness as judgment against the false prophet and transforms it into a theology of weakness, which identifies an authentic apostle.

Part 2 contains essays on the gospels and gospel hermeneutics. This section moves from focused exegetical treatments of select passages in the canonical gospels to larger hermeneutical issues in the New Testament. In ch. 7, using Philo's practice of quoting Scripture as an analogue for Matthew, Jin Ki Hwang offers a comprehensive analysis of Matthew's use of the Septuagint and not only demonstrates that Matthew's practices align well the citation methods of other Hellenistic Jews like Philo, but also Matthew's Gospel might be directed to Greek-speaking Jews of the Diaspora who would appreciate the transliteration of Hebrew or Aramaic words.

Chapter 8 by Soon Bong Choi analyzes the origin of the phrase "to set one's face against" (στηρίζειν τὸ πρόσωπον) in Luke 9:51 and concludes that Jesus employed the idiom from the OT prophetic oracles in the Septuagint (especially Ezekiel's) to pronounce a message of repentance and judgment against the city of Jerusalem. In ch. 9, Chang Wook Jung argues that the parable of the unjust steward (Luke 16:1–9) ends with an ironic turn of phrase: τὰς αἰωνίους σκηνάς ("eternal tents"). A disciple of Jesus, therefore, should *not* rely on earthly wealth or relationships as the unjust steward did but only upon the teachings of Jesus if one wants to enter eternal habitations. Yon-Gyong Kwon, in ch. 10, provides a contextual reading of Luke 17:1–10 which focuses on the command to forgive, so that the eschatological σκάνδαλον is a (self-righteous) act that prevents sinners from experiencing God's forgiveness and faith is exercising unconditional forgiveness toward others.

In ch. 11, Dongsoo Kim argues against Käsemann's thesis that the Johannine community was a heretical sect outside of a larger Christian orthodoxy but insists, both sociologically and theologically, that John's church was not sectarian and instead functioned as prophetic voice *within* early Christianity to correct an institutionalizing tendency among other churches. Stephen Young, in ch. 12, re-examines in the Gospel of John the identity of Jesus as the (Danielic) Son of Man and his role as the locus of God's revelation, eschatological judge, present Savior, and the one who guarantees the final glorification of his disciples. The Son of Man texts are the literary junctures for interweaving coherently the realized and future eschatologies of the Fourth Gospel.

Beginning with the essay by Sang-Il Lee, we move away from focused exegetical treatments of the gospels to larger historical, theological, and hermeneutical themes. In ch. 13, Lee provides a comprehensive treatment on the nature of ancient bilingualism in Luke-Acts. Starting with the identification of "the Hebrews" and "the Hellenists" of Acts 6, Lee describes the former as Aramaic-matrix speakers who also spoke Greek and the latter as Greek-matrix speakers who also spoke Aramaic. He refuses to isolate either the Hebrews or the Hellenists to a specific geographic location or ethnicity.

Among the polyvalent meanings for the phrase "word of God" in the New Testament, Sung-Jung Oh, in ch. 14, focuses on the particular technical use of the term, which equates God's word with the gospel message. Oh concludes that the origin of the phrase comes from the historical Jesus himself and particularly his interpretation of Isa 40:3–11, which is recorded in Mark's Gospel (1:1–15; 4:14–20) and, in turn, bears its influence on

1 Pet 1:23–25, Rom 10:5–17, and other NT texts. In the final chapter of the volume, Hyeon Woo Shin offers a comparative study of the gospels with the long-standing history of critical exegesis in China called *Xunguxue*. Among other insights, Shin argues that the parallelism found in ancient Chinese literature—e.g., *huwen* (synonymous parallelism), *duiwen* (antithetical parallelism), *hexu* (AA'BB' word order), and other rhetorical devices—might provide better analogues for studying parallelism in the Gospels than Western literary conventions. Even larger hermeneutical principles as "scripture interpreting scripture" have equivalent practices (like *yijingzhengjing*) in the literary criticism of *Xunguxue*. Chapter 15 illustrates well how one methodological approach can serve as a comparative foil for another to reveal the strengths and weaknesses of both hermeneutical models.

A brief word is needed here about the conventions used in this book. In order to make this volume available in e-book format, the editors have chosen to transliterate the Hebrew according to the general-purpose style outlined in the *SBL Handbook of Style*. Primary source abbreviations follow the *SBL Handbook* and the *Oxford Classical Dictionary*. For all other secondary sources, an abbreviations table is provided.

Lastly, a word of appreciation is owed to many who generously gave their time, energy, and resources to the publication of this Festschrift. Among the editors, Soon Bong Choi, who was the primary organizer of the project, contacted each essay writer and gathered the initial drafts of their work. Despite health challenges, he not only saw the project through to its conclusion but provided leadership in all correspondence with authors residing in Korea. Jin Ki Hwang compiled the comprehensive bibliography of Dr. Kim's works, organized the epilogue of reflections by the authors, and as a bilingual was the main liaison between scholars in Korea and North America. Max Lee was primarily responsible for editing and revising the essays in their final form for publication.

Special thanks are due to the teaching assistants of the editors. Kerry Herdegen and Luke Oliver were of invaluable help to Dr. Lee in the editing process and helped compile the abbreviations table, indices, and essay bibliographies. Dr. Hwang would like to thank Beom Jin Jeon, a doctoral candidate at Fuller, who helped him build a comprehensive bibliography of Dr. Seyoon Kim's publications.

The editors would also like to thank the following individuals for their participation and support in bringing the Festschrift to print: Dr. Won Lee, Professor of Old Testament at Calvin College and current President of the Korean Biblical Colloquium, wrote an inspiring foreword to this volume. Dr. Lida Nedilsky, Professor of Sociology at North Park University, offered sage guidance on how to best transliterate the Chinese to English for one of the essays. Rev. Tae Geun Song of Samil Church (Seoul, Korea), one of Dr. Kim's DMin students and a Fuller alumnus, gladly sponsored the Festschrift project financially by providing funds for the typesetting fees and other expenses. Dr. Yea Sun Eum Kim, wife of Seyoon Kim and Professor of Family Counseling and Korean Family Studies at Fuller Theological Seminary, provided needed biographical information and advice. Her support for the Festschrift is especially appreciated.

Thanks are also owed to the home institutions of the editors: Kwangshin University, Fuller Theological Seminary, and North Park Theological Seminary for providing the space, time, and human resources to complete the project.

The editors and contributors would like to thank the following *publishers for permission to reprint* material copyrighted or controlled by them:

The journal *Korean Evangelical New Testament Studies* (*KENTS*) of the Korean Evangelical Society of New Testament Studies for the articles by Hae-Kyung Chang, "Occasion and Purpose of Romans: Reflected in Its Distinctive Features," *KENTS* 12, no. 1 (2013) 57–89; Chang Wook Jung, "Reexamination of the Ironical Interpretation of the Parable of the Unjust Steward in Luke 16," *KENTS* 11, no. 4 (2012) 793–828; Yon-Gyong Kwon, "Forgiveness, Faith, and the Lordship of Jesus: A Contextual Reading of Luke 17:1–10," *KENTS* 11, no. 3 (2012) 613–42; and Hyeon Woo Shin, "Methodological Similarity between Traditional Chinese Exegesis and Western Biblical Exegesis," *KENTS* 11, no. 3 (2012) 553–86.

The journal *Korean New Testament Studies* of the New Testament Society of Korea for the article by Kyoung-Shik Kim, "Paul's Reading of Isaiah 59 in Romans 3:9–18," *KNTS* 19, no. 3 (2012) 937–79.

The journal *Scripture and Interpretation* (*S&I*) of the Torch Trinity Center for Biblical Research for the article by Hung-Sik Choi, "The Antithesis between the Law and Grace in Galatians 5:4," *S&I* 2, no. 1 (2008) 120–39.

The journal *Kwangshin Nondan* of Kwangshin University for the article by Soon Bong Choi, "The Understanding of 'στηρίζειν τὸ πρόσωπον' in Luke 9:51," *Kwangshin Nondan* (2011) 83–94.

The publisher Walter de Gruyter for chapter 5 of the monograph published by Sang-Il Lee, *Jesus and Gospel Traditions in Bilingual Context: A Study in the Interdirectionality of Language*, BZNW 186 (Berlin: de Gruyter, 2012).

Finally, our heartfelt thanks to the fantastic editorial team and staff of Pickwick Publications at Wipf and Stock Publishers, but especially co-founder John Wipf, editor Chris Spinks, and assistant managing editor Christian Amondson for their unwavering encouragement and support from beginning to end.

PART ONE

Essays on Pauline Soteriology and Paul's Gospel

1

Greek Words and Roman Meanings, Part 1

(Re)mapping Righteousness Language in Greco-Roman Discourse

MAX J. LEE

INTRODUCTION: DO GREEK WORDS ONLY HAVE HEBREW MEANINGS?

THOSE FAMILIAR WITH DAVID Hill's classic study on soteriological terms in the biblical corpus will immediately recognize the appreciative nod that the title of this essay gives to his pioneering work. In *Greek Words and Hebrew Meanings*, Hill argues that the Greek words (i.e., ἱλάσκεσθαι, λύτρον, δικαιοσύνη, ζωή, and πνεῦμα) the Apostle Paul and other New Testament authors employ in their writings basically function as linguistic shells for new polysemous definitions. These definitions are atypical of normal Hellenistic usage and are derived from Hebrew words Paul translates through the Septuagint to Greek.[1] When Paul, for example, utilizes the δικ(αιο)- word group, he does not use these words as they are commonly understood in

---

1. Hill, *Greek Words and Hebrew Meanings*, 294–96.

Greco-Roman discourse but has the Hebrew meanings of *tsedaqah* / *tsedeq* in mind. By quoting or alluding to the Septuagint's translations of *tsedaqah* / *tsedeq*, Paul redeploys the δικ(αιο)- word innovatively through bilingual interference. The Hebrew meanings of *tsedaqah* / *tsedeq* introduce new classifications well beyond the normal definitions of the Greek δικ(αιο)- lexemes.[2] In short, Hill claims that though we read Greek words in Paul's letters, these words essentially have Hebrew meanings.

This essay challenges the validity of Hill's thesis. An artificial wall has been placed between Paul's (Septuagintal) definitions of the δικ(αιο)- word group and their normal or Κοινή meanings in everyday discourse. Greek words have (Greco-)Roman meanings. Greek words are not empty shells into which the meanings of their Hebrew correlatives are infused. Much of the forensic dimensions of δικαιοσύνη and its cognates, for instance, that are attributed by past scholars to the Old Testament and Paul's rereading of these OT texts,[3] can also be found in the juridical and legal literature of the wider Roman Mediterranean world during the early imperial period. While Paul certainly contributes some unique usages of the δικ(αιο)- word group, for the most part, the uniqueness of Paul's righteousness language in his letters has been exaggerated. Paul cannot use Greek words in such an innovative fashion that he becomes incomprehensible to the Greco-Roman readers of his day. He must have been coherent and his use of Greek understandable.

In what follows (i.e., a two-part study which comprises chapters 1 and 2 of this volume), I offer a detailed study of δικ(αιο)- lexemes as they were commonly deployed in Greco-Roman discourse and make suggestions how this study can inform our understanding of Paul. In this chapter (= Part 1), I first give a short description of early Homeric to Hellenistic usages of the δικ(αιο)- word group. This diachronic study is followed by an more extensive synchronic analysis of the semantic classifications or polysemous definitions of δίκαιος, δικαιοσύνη, δικαιόω, and δίκη during early imperial period of Rome. In Chapter 2 (= Part 2), I examine Paul's (re)deployment of these terms in his Letter to the Romans (3:21–26 in the main). I suggest that Paul's particularly forensic (and non-forensic) use of the δικ(αιο)- lexical group fits well within the semantic range of Greco-Roman social, legal and juridical discourse and does *not* require an appeal to the idiolect of the Septuagint.

---

2. Ibid., 160–61.

3. See, e.g., Moo, *The Epistle to the Romans*, 73–75, who not only acknowledges Paul's indebtedness to the LXX and Jewish concepts of righteousness but in Paul's rereading of Scripture also claims that: "His theology also leads him to develop the idea of righteousness as an enduring, judicial status far beyond anything found in the OT" (74).

Part 2 functions as a prolegomenon to a more comprehensive and future study of Paul's use of righteousness language throughout his letter corpus.

MAPPING JUSTICE AND RIGHTEOUSNESS LANGUAGE LEXICALLY: THE UNMARKED AND MARKED MEANINGS OF THE ΔΙΚ(ΑΙΟ)- LEXICAL GROUP IN GRECO-ROMAN DISCOURSE

A Diachronic Perspective: From Homer to Hellenism

From a diachronic perspective (spanning from Homer ca. ninth to eighth century BCE, through the classical and Hellenistic periods, to Dio Cassius in the second century CE), the δικ(αιο)- word group has a long standing history as meaning the "rightness" of something in reference to a given standard or norm.[4] Homer understands the adjective δίκαιος to mean what is "right," "fitting," "customary," or "obligatory" according to the rules which governed an ordered community (*Od.* 6.120–21; 9.172–76; 13.209–12; 14.89–92).[5] In one of its oldest Hesiodic meanings, doing what is right is personified as the cosmic principle Justice (Δίκη) who is at constant war with Violent Rage (Ὕβριος), the latter of whom deceived men like Perses to make wrong judgments instead of right ones (δίκῃσιν; *Op.* 213–24). According to Seifrid, it is this definition of δίκη as justice which influenced all further conceptions of righteousness language.[6]

The noun δίκη and adjective δίκαιος constitute the earliest Homeric and Hesiodic usages of the δικ(αιο)- lexical group. The addition of -συνη to the δικ(αιο)- stem represents a later abstraction of the δικ(αιο)- word group in the fifth century BCE.[7] The verbal form δικαιόω (originally meaning "deem right / suitable," or sometimes "set right") is also a latter development corresponding to the appearance δικαιοσύνη in the classical period.[8] The first documented occurrence of δικαιοσύνη is Herodotus's description of

---

4. LSJ, s.v. δίκαιος, δικαιοσύνη, 429; Schrenk, "δίκη, δίκαιος, δικαιοσύνη, κτλ.," 192–93; BDAG, s.v. δίκαιος, 246; Seebass, "Righteousness, Justification," 352–56; Kerteleges, "δικαιοσύνη," 326; Reumann, "Righteousness: Greco-Roman World," 742–45.

5. Seebass, "Righteousness, Justification," 353; BAGD, s.v. δίκαιος, 246.

6. Seifrid, "Paul's Use of Righteousness Language against its Hellenistic Background," 45; see also Spicq, "δίκαιος, κτλ.," 318.

7. Havelock, "*Dikaiosune*," 51; and also noted by Seifrid, "Paul's Use of Righteousness Language against its Hellenistic Background," 45; Seebass, "Righteousness, Justification," 353; Reumann, "Righteousness: Greco-Roman World," 743.

8. See, e.g., Plato's famous quotation of Pindar (Fr. 16.9) in *Gorg.* 484B; Hill, *Greek Words and Hebrew Meanings*, 101–2; Schrenk, "δίκη, δίκαιος, δικαιοσύνη, κτλ.," 211.

the Median Deioces (*Hist.* 1.96) who, in contrast to the lawlessness (ἀνομία) rampant in other surrounding villages (ἐν τῇσι ἄλλῃσι κώμῃσι), practiced justice (δικαιοσύνην ἤσκεε) by judging rightly according to the conventions of his township (κατὰ τὸ ὀρθὸν δικάζων). He was considered a discerning judge (δικαστής) who was both honest and just (ἰθύς τε καὶ δίκαιος). Here, when Deioces "practiced justice," the text defines δικαιοσύνη as the exercise and maintenance of political, social, and civic order. Also, δίκαιος does not refer so much to an inner quality or characteristic, but rather Deioces's ability to make right and fair verdicts for each lawcourt case.

From the classical and Hellenistic periods onward, the meaning of righteousness language starts to broaden. From its initial denotation of rightness in reference to laws or customs, the δικ(αιο)- word group develops ethical connotations.[9] On one hand, Aristotle, can use δικ(αιο)- language to demarcate conformity to legal norms and define δίκαιος as what is lawful (νόμιμος) and equitable (ἴσος).[10] In the lawcourt, what is just (τὰ δίκαια) and unjust (τὰ ἄδικα) is whatever the laws (of the city) say it is (οἱ νόμοι λέγουσιν).[11] But elsewhere, Aristotle defines δικαιοσύνη as a moral virtue (ἠθικὴ ἀρετή)[12] or a disposition (ἕξις).[13] So Aristotle incorporates both the legal and ethical senses of δικ(αιο)- terms in his treatise on justice (*Nicomachean Ethics*, Bk. 5). The just person is impartial, equanimous, and upright in character (the ethical sense), but he or she does what is right and fitting according to the customs, decorum, and rules of the community (the social, legal, and political sense).[14]

---

9. Reumann, "Righteousness: Greco-Roman World," 742–45.

10. See, e.g., *EN* 1129a34–1129b1: "Now it is clear that the law-abiding person (ὁ νόμιμος) and the fair person (τὸ ἴσος) will both be just (δίκαιος). Therefore, 'the just' (τὸ δίκαιον) means that which is lawful (τὸ νόμιμον) and what is equal or fair (τὸ ἴσον), and 'the unjust' (τὸ ἄδικον) means that which is illegal (παράνομον) and what is unequal or unfair (τὸ ἄνισον)" (ET follows Rackham, LCL, 257).

11. See *EN* 1137a10–12; also *EN* 1136b32—1137a4: "Again, although if a judge has given an unfair judgment in ignorance, he does no injustice (οὐκ ἀδικεῖ) nor is the judgment unjust (ἄδικος ἡ κρίσις ἐστίν) in the legal sense (κατὰ τὸ νομικὸν) of justice" (ET follows Rackham, LCL, 311).

12. See, e.g., *EN* 1138b10–11: "So much may be said concerning justice (δικαιοσύνης) and other moral virtues (ἠθικῶν ἀρετῶν)" (ET follows Rackham, LCL, 323).

13. See, e.g., *EN* 1129a6–9: "Now we observe that what everybody means by justice (δικαιοσύνην) is that moral disposition (ἕξιν) which renders people apt to do just things (δικαιοπραγοῦσι), which causes them to act justly (πρακτικοὶ τῶν δικαίων) and to wish what is just (τὰ δίκαια)" (ET follows Rackham, LCL, 253). Here justice is what a person is (ἕξις) and what one does (πρᾶγμα).

14. See also Aristotle, *Politics* 1291a26–29 on how "judicial justice" (δικαιοσύνη δικαστική) contributes to the "work of politics" (πολιτκῆς ἔργον).

Similar to Aristotle, Demosthenes defines "the just citizen" (δίκαιος πολίτης) as one who has taken up "the salvation of the state" (τὴν τῶν πραγμάτων σωτηρίαν) above everything else (*Or.* 3.21). Such a citizen "upheld one's [civic] duties" (ᾤετο δεῖν) despite hardship. This person earned for oneself great happiness by good faith (πιστῶς) towards fellow Greeks, with piety (εὐσεβῶς) towards the gods, and with fairness (ἴσως) towards other citizens (*Or.* 3.26).[15]

As a specification of the legal sense, the δικ(αιο)- terms also took on juridicial and forensic meanings when used in civic disputes or tribunal contexts. For example, δίκαιος as a substantive could refer to a person's legal rights, entitlements, or claims. In one Hellenistic inscription,[16] the lawcourt scribe records a case concerning "those (defendants) who have some legal right" (τοίς ἔχουσιν τι δίκαιον) to a plot of land. According to the inscription, the defendants based their case on the premise that they owned and lived on the land for many years and the statute of limitations to claim back the property (some two to three years) had passed already without challenge from the plaintiff. Therefore, they had some right (τι δίκαιον) to continue residing on the land and claim it as their own.

In Thucydides's account of the Peloponnesian War (*Hist.* 2.71.2–4), a Plataean delegation to the Peloponnesian general Archidamus asked him "not to wrong the land of Platea" (γῆν τὴν Πλαταιίδα μὴ ἀδικεῖν; 2.71.4) nor "do injustice" (οὐ δίκαια ποιεῖν; 2.71.2) by seizing their property and enslaving them. The delegation drew on the previous legal verdict of Archidamus's predecessor Pausanias to make their case against enslavement. They asked Archidamus that he allow them "to live autonomously, exactly as Pausanias declared to be just and appropriate (ἐὰν δὲ οἰκεῖν αὐτονόμους καθάπερ Παυσανίας ἐδικαίωσεν)" (2.71.4). Here δικαιόω means to "declare as just, appropriate, and valid," or simply "judge as (in the) right." Also, the construction οὐ ποιεῖν + δίκαια ("to not practice just actions" or "to do injustice") can function as the syntactical equivalent of οὐ δικαιόω and points to another semantic classification of the verb. That is, while δικαιόω can refer to someone who "stands in the right" by law or custom (the more frequent use),[17] it can, on occasion, mean "to do right," or "to practice just actions or

---

15. See also Spicq, "δίκαιος, κτλ.," 320–21n7, who adds that, for Demosthenes, the "just citizen" (δίκαιος πολίτης) is "the citizen who carries out his[/her] legal obligations toward the state."

16. UPZ II 16 (= Wilcken, ed., *Urkunden der Ptolemäerzeit*, vol. 2), col. 7 lines 22–27 = Llewelyn and Kearsley, eds., *NewDocs* 7:154–55.

17. See also Demosthenes, *Or.* 44.4: "If we did not believe that we were in the right (ἐν μὴ τῷ δικαίῳ ἐπιστεύομεν)," we would never have come before you [= the court] at all [to plead our case]." Here, the meaning of δικαιόω as "declare [in the] right" is

justice" (the less frequent use, since the ποιεῖν / πράττειν + δίκαια construction was more often used).¹⁸

A Synchronic Perspective: The Early Imperial Period

By the time we reach the first century CE, the δικ(αιο)- word group denotes *iustitia distributiva* in its social, legal, and judicial senses. This is its primary and most widely understood use. The noun δικαιοσύνη comes to assume the same meaning and function that δίκη once did during the Homeric period: that is, "what is according to custom and law," or "what is just." While δίκη retains in a few select texts its older and more neutral meaning as "justice,"¹⁹ in the New Testament era δίκη has come to denote more punitive designations as "punishment" or "penalty."²⁰ For all practical purposes, δικαιοσύνη has replaced δίκη as the most commonly used term to denote *iustitia distributiva*.

The freed slave turned Stoic philosopher Epictetus, for example, in positing the legendary Heracles as the paradigm of a just king, so comments: "Heracles was ruler (ἄρχων) and governor (ἡγεμῶν) over all the land and sea, purging them of injustice and lawlessness (ἀδικίας καὶ ἀνομίας) and establishing justice and piety (δικαισύνης καὶ ὁσιότητος); and he did this naked and by himself."²¹ In a manner reminiscent of Aristotle's use of the δικ(αιο)- word group, Epictetus here defines δικαισύνη in contrast to ἀνομία. Justice is ordered social and political rule where its citizens are in right

---

rendered with the alternative construction πιστεύειν + δικαίῳ or "believe that one is in the right." One can also argue that the dative construction could use alternative verbs like λέγειν / ἀπαγγέλλειν + δικαίῳ ("say / announce [he or she is] in the right") to convey the same meaning as δικαιόω.

18. See, e.g., Polybius, *Hist.* 3.31.9, which reads: "It is by this means we shall often and in many situations find people who intervene mercifully, share our outrage, and do justice (δικαιώσοντα)" (ET my own, based on the LCL Greek text). Cf. BAGD, s.v. δικαιόω, 249, which translates δικαιώσοντα as "take up our just cause," or the ET by Paton as "avenge us" (LCL, 73).

19. See, e.g., Plutarch, *Princ. iner.* 780E: "Now justice is the aim and end of the law (δίκη μὲν οὖν νόμου τέλος ἐστί), but law is the work of the ruler, and the ruler is the image of God who orders all things" (ET by Fowler, LCL, 59). See also Plutarch, *Princ. iner.* 781B where Justice (Δίκη) is personified as a goddess (the daughter of Zeus) who along with the Law (Θέμις) stands on each side of Zeus as he rules the universe.

20. See, e.g., Epictetus, *Diss.* 3.24.4–5, which in its description of the fool (vs. the sage) says: "And therefore he [the fool] pays the penalty (δίκας) for his own folly" (ET by Oldfather, LCL, 185). Other translations of δίκη as punishment or penalty are catalogued by BAGD, s.v. δίκη, 250; Spicq, "δίκαιος, κτλ.," 318–20.

21. Epictetus, *Diss.* 3.26.32 (ET modified from Oldfather, LCL, 237).

relationship with one another. Framed at a cosmic scale, in the hymn Κόρη κόσμου recorded by Stobaeus, the god Osiris and his consort the goddess Isis are praised for each having gifted (ἐχαρίσατο) humanity with systems of justice. They were "the first ones who appointed just tribunals" in the universe (οὗτοι πρῶτοι δείξαντες δικαστήρια) and "filled the sum of all things with orderliness and justice" (εὐνομίας τὰ σύμπαντα καὶ δικαιοσύνης ἐπλήρωσαν).²² The reach of justice in this hymn has extended beyond the realm of human law and custom to include a divinely-ordained structure of retribution and reward which governs how the universe operates.

Like Osiris and Isis, Zeus is featured in another text as part of a wider Greco-Roman tradition on the divine origins of human justice. Diodorus Siculus, in his discussion of myth, tells us that Zeus surpassed all others in justice (δικαιοσύνη) when he started "to demonstrate for others concerning acts of injustice what was [truly] just" (καταδείξαι περὶ τῶν ἀδικημάτων τὸ δίκαιον ἀλλήλοις) and taught them "to refrain from doing something out of violence and to settle disputes by judgment and the lawcourt" (τοῦ βίᾳ τι πράττειν ἀποστῆσαι, κρίσει δὲ καὶ δικαστηρίῳ τὰς ἀμφισβητήσεις διαλύειν).²³ Diodorus, like the anonymous author of the Κόρη κόσμου hymn, posits a divine source to civic and political order. The gods gave humanity its system of laws and jurisprudence to maintain equity, fairness and orderliness. As Marcianus, the Roman jurist, notes in his *Institutes*, Bk. 1: "The law (ὁ νόμος) is king (βασιλεύς) over all things, divine and human. It ought to be the patron (προστάτην), ruler (ἄρχοντα), and governor (ἡγεμόνα) of both things noble and ignoble, and the standard of things just and unjust (καὶ κατὰ τοῦτο κανόνα τε εἶναι δικαίων καὶ ἀδίκων). For political creatures, [it is] by nature a prescription of what ought to be done and a proscription of what ought not to be done" (Justinian, *Dig.* 3.2 – SVF 3.314).²⁴

So, even in juridicial contexts, δικαισύνη continues to mean during the early imperial period what it meant during the Hellenistic era: that is, justice is whatever the courts declare as right and is in accordance to custom, law, and legal precedence. During a case before the magistrate Flavius Abinnaeus, one plaintiff charged that his neighbor "in a manner like a bandit . . . contrary to justice, came upon the [plaintiff's] sheep and snatched away the fully fleeced sheep, eighty-two in number" (λῃστρικῷ τρόπῳ . . . παρὰ

---

22. Stobaeus, *Ecl.* 1.49.44 (= Wachsmuth, p. 406, lines 5–15).

23. Diodorus Siculus, *Bibliotheca historica* 5.71.1 (ET modified from Oldfather, LCL, 289).

24. This excerpt is a quotation of the Hellenistic Stoic Chrysippus, reapplied to the Roman juristic context by Aelius Marcianus, and recorded here by Justinian in his *Digest* 3.2. The Latin and Greek texts are taken from Mommsen and Krueger, eds., *The Digest of Justinian*, vol. 1.

τὴν δικαιοσύνην ἐπῆλθεν τοῖς προβάτοις καὶ ἥρπασαι πρόβατα σύμποκα τὸν ἀριθμοῦ ὀγδοήκοντα δύο).[25] In the end, justice for this plaintiff meant recompense for the loss of stolen livestock. The outcome of the trial was unclear, but if the defendant was found not guilty of the crime, justice for the defendant would alternatively mean exoneration from paying any penalty.[26] Spicq cites other papyri in which δικαιοσύνη is used within lawcourt contexts to denote the justice or just verdicts of the magistrate (στρατηγός) as plaintiffs and defendants made their respective appeals to the courts.[27]

The adjective δίκαιος (including its adverbial forms) has likewise retained its social, legal, and juridicial meanings as "appropriate / fitting," "right," "just," or "fair / equitable." The examples are prolific,[28] and I list a few here. Diodorus Siculus (*Bibliotheca historica* 40.11.1–2), for instance, narrates the trial of Tiribazus who was accused of treason but was later exonerated before the Persian court. The judges (δικασταί) in the case were commended by King Artaxerxes as "ones who had judged justly" (ὡς δικαίως κεκρικότας; 40.11.2). "As each [judge] followed the principles of justice (δικαίοις προσσχὼν ἕκαστος; 40.11.1)," so continues Diodorus, it became clear that the charges against the defendant Tiribazus were contrived. The court therefore "pardoned the accused" (ἀπέλυσε τὸν κατηγορούμενον; 40.11.1) . . . "and concerning [the plaintiff] Orontes, he was condemned as one who had fabricated a false accusation (τοῦ δὲ Ὀρόντου καταγνοὺς ὡς ψευδῆ κατηγορίαν πεπλακότας; 40.11.2)." The acquittal of Tiribazus and the punishment of Orontes were all done "according to the laws and customs" (ταῖς νομιζομέναις; 40.11.2) governing the Persian judicial system.[29] Justice was the meting out of punishment for the guilty and restored honors (μεγίσταις τιμαῖς ἐκόσμησεν) for the innocent. Elsewhere Diodorus uses the neuter substantive to speak of "just actions" (τὰ δίκαια; *Bibliotheca historica* 19.85.4; 49.12.1) or "what is fair and right" (δίκαιον; 12.45.1).[30] The term

---

25. *P. Thead.* 23.9–11= Jouget, ed., *Papyri de Théadelphie*, 135; cited partially in MM, s.v. δικαιοσύνη, 162.

26. See the rest of the papyrus transcript: *P. Thead.* 23.12–21 (= Jouget, ed., *Papyri de Théadelphie*, 135).

27. See Spicq, "δίκαιος, κτλ.," 326n29, which lists: *BGU* 1138.4, 1824.30; *P. Oslo* 128.10; *P. Oxy.* 1873.15.

28. Ibid., 1.320–21; BAGD, s.v. δίκαιος, 246–47; Schrenk, "δίκη, δίκαιος, δικαιοσύνη, κτλ.," 182–85; Olley, "Righteousness" in the Septuagint of Isaiah, 32–43; Hill, *Greek Words and Hebrew Meanings*, 99–100; Ziesler, *The Meaning of Righteousness in Paul*, 48–51; Reumann, "Righteousness: Greco-Roman World," 743.

29. ET for Diodorus Siculus, *Bibliotheca historica* 40.11.1–2 is modified from Oldfather, LCL, 353–55.

30. See also Dio Cassius, *Roman History* 49.12.1, which reads: "Caesar, however, made no answer to these demands since it seemed he had all justice (πάντα τὰ δίκαια) on his side, as well as his weapons" (ET modified from Cary, LCL, 363).

has also retained its specialized use as a "legal right" or "duty."[31] In rare instances, δίκαιος can even mean "punishment."[32]

The verb δικαιόω typically means "to deem just" or "declare someone to be in the right." Dio Cassius, for example, tells the tale of how General Sextus Pompey took advantage of Antony's sudden withdrawal to Greece as a way to criticize Caesar. Pompey charged that Antony's failure to meet Caesar in Italy meant that "Antony did not deem him [Caesar] to be in the right" (μὴ δικαιοῦντος τοῦ Ἀντωνίου αὐτόν; *Roman History* 48.46.4).[33] Moulton and Milligan note several other papyri from the first century CE with similar meanings.[34] P. Giss. I.47.16, for instance, records the following reasons why a particular business transaction failed. The merchant refused to buy a girdle for two reasons: "The girdle was not found to be a genuine article (Παραζώνιον γὰρ πρὸς τὸ παρὸν γνησίον οὐχ εὑρέθη), but neither I did think it right to buy what cannot be accepted (ἀλλ' οὐδὲ ἐδικαίωσα ἀγοράσαι ἀποδοκιμασθῆναι δυνάμενον)."[35] In other words, the object was neither genuine nor in a good, acceptable condition. The merchant therefore felt justified to refuse to purchase it.

In another papyrus, P. Ryl. II.119.14–16 renders δικαιόω with the specialized juridicial meaning "to declare / pronounce a verdict."[36] This papyrus records a lawsuit made by Demetrius son of Aristomenes and his uncles against their creditor Musaeus son of Hermophilus. The former plaintiffs claimed: "we have been robbed in every way by this man [Musaeus]! . . . " (κατὰ πᾶν οὖν συνηρπασμένοι ὑπὸ τούτου; lines 28–30) when the defendant prematurely foreclosed on 83¼ *arurae* of land which Demetrius and his uncles had left to Musaeus as a security (ὑποθήκη) for a 4,800 *drachmae* loan (lines 1–14). Demetrius further explains that the juridicus (δικαιοδότης) Gaius Caecina Tuscus therefore "pronounced that we [Demetrius and his uncles] should repay the capital sum owed and recover the

---

31. P. Oxy. VI, 905.9 = Grenfell and Hunt, eds., *The Oxyrhynchus Papyri* 6:244. The texts reads: "Then let the married couple live with one another, keeping the duties / rights of marriage (τὰ τοῦ γάμου δίκαια), and might the husband according to his ability provide for the wife the things necessary to live" (ET my own). See also other references cited in by MM, s.v. δίκαιος, 162.

32. See, e.g., Dio Cassius, *Roman History* 40.19.2: " . . . by the punishments he [Augustus] was inflicting (πράττοντας δικαιῶν), he was now grieving the many who committed some acts contrary to his decrees . . . " (ET by Cary, LCL, 329).

33. Cary translates this as: "Antony did not think Caesar's conduct right," LCL, 319.

34. MM, s.v. δικαιόω, 162–63.

35. P. Giss I.47.14–17 = Kornemann and Meyer, eds., *Griechische Papyri zu Giessein* 1:64.

36. P. Ryl. II.119.14–16 = Johnson et al., eds., *Catalogue of the Greek Papyri in the John Rylands Library* 2:108.

mortgage" (ἐδικαίωσεν ἀποδοῦναι ἡμᾶς τὸ κεφάλαιον καὶ ἀνακομίσασθαι τὴν ὑποθήκην ἀπολύθῆναι; lines 14–15). Musaeus was allowed to keep any rent he had previously received since the time he foreclosed on the property (τε τὸν Μουσαῖον ὧν ἔφθη λαβεῖν ἐκφορίων; line 16).[37] Here, ἐδικαίωσεν, though simply translated "pronounced," means that the juridicus Tuscus had declared a verdict which he thought exacted justice for both the plaintiffs and the defendant: the plaintiffs received back their land but the defendant was allowed to keep the rent received from the land while it was held as security.[38]

In another juridical context, Dionysius of Halicarnassus—in his history of Roman consulship during the late Republic period—explains that in the days when neither the concept of "an equality of laws" (ἰσονομία) nor "an equality of rights" (ἰσηγορία) existed, and when "all the principles of justice" (ἅπαντα τὰ δίκαια) had not yet been committed to writing (*Ant. rom.* 10.2), it was the character and decisions of the consuls that determined what justice is (ἡ τοῦ δικαίου διάγνωσις; *Ant. rom.* 10.3). In short, "whatever was declared just or right by them [the consuls], this was law! (τὸ δικαιωθὲν ὑπ' ἐκείνων τοῦτο νόμος ἦν; *Ant. rom.* 10.2–3)."[39] In some rare cases, the definition of δικαιόω as "pronounce" or "declare right" can be extended to mean "pronounce as true," "verify," or "ratify," as when Dio Cassius explains: "The woman Dynamis was married to him [Polemon] only when Augustus clearly verified / sanctioned that these things can be (τοῦ Αὐγούστου δῆλον ὅτι ταῦτα δικαιώσαντος; *Roman History* 54.24.6–7).[40]

Given the above examples, we observe that in social contexts the verb δικαιόω mainly means to "deem just" or "regard someone as in the right," but in specifically legal or juridicial contexts δικαιόω is best understood as

---

37. ET modified from Johnson et al., eds., *Catalogue of the Greek Papyri in the John Rylands Library*, 2:109.

38. See also P. Tebt. II.444 = *The Tebtunis Papyri* 2:306, which is a small fragment describing a loan for a dowry. Concerning the capital sum of the loan, the papyrus states: "I owe and received the dowry amount of your wife Thaesios of Patyneos according to which she has, from the full (rights) of the marriage contract, the capital sums (of the dowry) fixed (= declared just) by the contract without (recourse to) punishment, judgment and every litigious argument . . . (ὀφ[ε]ίλω καὶ ἔλαβα φερνῆς τῆς γυναικὸς σου Θαήσιος τῆς Πατύνεος ἀκολούθως ἥ ἔχει τοῦ γάμου συνγραφῇ ἐκ πλήρους τὰ διὰ τῆς συνγραφῆς δετακιομέμα [l. δεδικαιωμένα] κεφάλαια ἄνευ δίκης καὶ κρίσεως καὶ πάσης εὐρησιλογίας . . . ; ET my own). Milligan and Moulton comment that δετακιομέμα or "fixed / determined" is equivalent in good vernacular Greek as δεδικαιωμένα "declared or pronounced [as the] just [amount]" (MM, s.v. δικαιόω, 162–63).

39. ET modified from Cary, LCL, 165; see also Olley, "*Righteousness" in the Septuagint of Isaiah*, 38.

40. ET modified from Cary, LCL, 345.

"declare just" or can even mean "pronounce (a) just (verdict)."⁴¹ However, these are not the only semantic classifications for the verb. A fascinating development in the Roman era is the semantic shift from the classical and Hellenistic meaning of δικαιόω as "set right," "do justice (for someone)," or "see that someone got his / her rights recognized"⁴² to a narrower definition of "punish" or "condemn (a guilty) person."⁴³ The specific translation of δικαιόω *in negativae* as "punish" probably arose when "to do justice" called for a penalty against the lawbreaker.⁴⁴ Perhaps the passive translation brings out best this extended definition: "They were brought to justice (ἐδικαιώθησαν)."⁴⁵ Dio Cassius records several uses of δικαιόω as "penalize," many of which occur in judicial contexts where retribution must be made to the wronged or injured party.⁴⁶

---

41. Cf. P. Oxy. III.653 = Grenfell and Hunt, eds., *The Oxyrhynchus Papyri* 3:289–90. The papyrus records a lawsuit held before the praefect L. Volusius Maccianus over a mortgage and seizure of property dispute. It records how the courts decide (δικαιοῦμεν) to summon the chiliarch Honoratus who had previously judged the trial to bear testimony in the case: "Maccinus said: '[Present before the court is] the chiliarch whom we [the courts] decide to summon'" (Μαικιανὸς εἶπεν· ὁ χιλίαρχος ὃν μεταπέμπειν δικαιοῦμεν). Here the verb δικαιόω extends its meaning to "pronounce a verdict" or "render judgment" to the idiom "decide" or "decide for."

42. See my discussion above on classical and Hellenistic uses of δικαιόω in Polybius, *Hist.* 3.31.9 and other texts. For an example from the Roman period, see Dio Cassius, *Roman History* 52.24.3–4, which reads: "The magistrates (ἄρχοντες) . . . have the power to put to death any of them who do wrong (θανατοῦν τοὺς ἀδικοῦντας αὐτῶν) . . . let those [magistrates] themselves *do* these [soldiers] *justice* (τούτους μὲν γὰρ αὐτοὶ ἐκεῖνοι δικαιούτωσαν), in order that the former [= the magistrates], having the authority to mete out punishment and honors to them [the soldiers] may be able to command their unwavering support" (ET modified from Cary, LCL, 135–37).

43. Seifrid, "Paul's Use of Righteousness Language against its Hellenistic Background," 45–49; Spicq, "δίκαιος, κτλ.," 337n70; Schrenk, "δίκη, δίκαιος, δικαιοσύνη, κτλ.," 211–12.

44. LSJ, s.v. δικαιόω, 429 [definition III.1 "chastise, punish"]; Seifrid, "Paul's Use of Righteousness Language against its Hellenistic Background," 45–46; Schrenk, "δίκη, δίκαιος, δικαιοσύνη, κτλ.," 211.

45. Dio Cassius, *Roman History* 41.28.4; see also 55.14.3 which reads: "And not even the punishment of those who are brought to justice (αἱ τιμωρίαι τῶν δικαιουμένων) serves to keep them in check!" (ET by Cary, LCL, 429).

46. Dio Cassius, *Roman History* 37.12.2 (ἐδικαιώθη; "he was punished"); 37.41.2 (ἐδικαιοῦντο; "they were convicted"); 38.11.3 (ἐδικαίου; "he punished"); 41.28.4 (ἐδικαιώθησαν; "they were brought to justice"); 43.24.4 (ἐδικαιώθη; "he was executed / punished"); 49.12.5 (ἐδικαιώθησαν; they were punished"); 54.15.4 (ὁ Αὔγυστος ἄλλους μέν τινας ἐδικαίωσε; "Augustus executed / punished some of them"); 55.14.3 (αἱ τιμωρίαι τῶν δικαιουμένων; "the punishment of those who are brought to justice"); 56.4.5 (μισήσαντες δ' ὑμᾶς ἂν δικαιώσειαν; "if they hate you, they would likely punish you").

In *Roman History* 49.12.5, for example, Dio Cassius records the overthrow of Marcus Aemilius Lepidus (one of the Second Triumvirate) by Octavian. Concerning cities previously ruled by Lepidus, Dio Cassius comments: "As for the cities, the ones who voluntarily conceded to Caesar were the ones who experienced pardon (συγγνώμης ἔτυχον), and the others who rebelled were punished (αἱ δ' ἀντάρασαι ἐδικαιώθησαν)."[47] In fact, later reflecting on this same event, Dio Cassius also states: "As for the time to which we are addressing, Augustus executed a fair number of men (ὁ Αὔγουστος ἄλλους μέν τινας ἐδικαίωσε), but in the case of Lepidus, however, although he hated the man . . . he [Augustus] did not want to kill him (οὐ μέντοι καὶ ἀποκτεῖναι ἠθέλησεν; *Roman History* 54.15.4).[48] In this last text, ἐδικαίωσε can be translated idiomatically as "execute" or "put to death" probably as a further extension of the idea that punishing the wrong-doer meant the death sentence. For Octavian, just punishment meant executing most revolutionists with the exception of Lepidus.

In his discussion of the different forms of divine chastisement (Τῶν δ' ἄλλων δικαιώσεων), Plutarch explains that when the goddess Justice (ἡ Δίκη) judges a criminal, she first brings this person in front of his own deceased relatives. Then, continues Plutarch, "he [the criminal] first sees them [his relatives] punished (κολαζομένους) and he is also seen by them; then he [the criminal] is disciplined for a long time . . . (δικαιοῦται πολὺν χρόνον)."[49] Here Plutarch clearly defines δικαιόω as "discipline" or "punish" when he pairs it with the synonymous term κολάζω.[50] Even the construct ποιεῖν / πράττειν + δίκαια, which is usually translated "to do justice" or "practice just actions," can sometimes mean "to inflict punishments" as in this text by Dio Cassius where he explains why there was an escalating resentment towards Octavian: "He [Octavian] was grieving many people who opposed some of his decrees because of the punishments he was inflicting [against them]" (καὶ συχνοὺς μὲν ἔξω τι τῶν τεταγμένων πράττοντας δικαιῶν ἐλύπει; *Roman History* 54.19.2).[51]

---

47. ET modified from Cary, LCL, 365.

48. ET modified from Cary, LCL, 319.

49. Plutarch, *Sera* 565B; ET modified from De Lacy and Einarson, LCL, 281.

50. Cf. Josephus, *Ant.* 20.135 (τῇ ἑαυτοῦ δικαιοσύνῃ τιμωρήσασθαι; "to punish with his own justice") who pairs δικαιοσύνη with τιμωρέω.

51. ET modified from Cary, LCL, 329. For other uses of the substantive form of δίκαιος as an object of a finite verb to connote the idea of retribution or punitive justice, see also Josephus, *Ant.* 14.288 (δίκαια πράξειν; "do punitive actions") and 15.233 (δίκαια πάσχειν; "suffer punishment"); as noted by Seifrid, "Paul's Use of Righteousness Language against its Hellenistic Background," 46.

Seifrid, likewise, has noted how Josephus repeatedly translates δικαιόω *in negativae* as "penalize," "chastise," or "execute."[52] In the famous scene where Herod the Great arrested two Jewish scholars (οἱ σοφισταί) Judas and Matthias who ordered their forty disciples to tear down the golden eagle from atop of the Jerusalem temple (*Ant.* 16.151–67), Josephus explains that "those who had pulled down the golden eagle had been punished / executed" (ἦσαν δὲ τῶν ἐπὶ καθαιρέσει τοῦ χρυσοῦ ἀετοῦ δεδικαιωμένων; *Ant.* 16.206). Elsewhere, Josephus comments that since a speedy trial was often a means "by which alleviation happened for the ones who were condemned to death" (ὑπὸ τοῦ δικαιωθεῖσι μὲν θανάτῳ κούφισιν γενέσθαι), Roman governors purposefully sought "the delay of the hearings of prisoners" (τῶν δεσμωτῶν τὴν ὑπερβολὴν τῆς ἀκροάσεως) to prolong the latter's miseries (*Ant.* 18.178). In the above two examples, the passive participles δεδικαιωμένων and δικαιωθεῖσι identify those who have been punished and executed as enemies of the state. Lastly, on the *lex talionis* in Exodus 21:23, Josephus comments: "If she [the wife] should die from a blow, he [the husband] should also die, since the law declares as just (punishment) to grant life for life" (ψυχὴν ἀντὶ ψυχῆς καταθέσθαι δικαιοῦντος τοῦ νομοῦ; *Ant.* 4.278).[53]

If we were to stop here in our lexical analysis, it would appear that the δικ(αιο)- word group delimits the semantic domain of justice–righteousness to purely social, legal, and juridicial meanings. This, however, would be a false assumption. While these meanings are certainly salient and even prototypical for δικαιοσύνη and its cognates, δικ(αιο)- lexemes nevertheless cannot be limited to only legal or forensic definitions. There is an increasing appearance of the δικ(αιο)- word group in moral discourse, where δικαιοσύνη goes beyond its commonly understood meaning of "distributive justice" to denote "just character," "moral uprightness," or "righteous integrity." Several past lexical studies have noted the widespread use of the δικ(αιο)- word group as ethical terminology.[54]

In several treatises, Greco-Roman philosophers identify δικαιοσύνη as one of four cardinal virtues exhibited by the wise person or ideal Roman

---

52. Seifrid, "Paul's Use of Righteousness Language against its Hellenistic Background," 46–47.

53. ET modified from Thackeray, LCL, 611.

54. Havelock, "*Dikaiosune*," 51–52; 59–60; Schrenk, "δίκη, δίκαιος, δικαιοσύνη, κτλ.," 192–94; Ziesler, *The Meaning of Righteousness in Paul*, 49–50; Olley, "*Righteousness*" *in the Septuagint of Isaiah*, 41; Hill, *Greek Words and Hebrew Meanings*, 100–101; Reumann, "Righteousness: Greco-Roman World," 743–45 [B. Plato–D. Stoicism]; Seifrid, "Paul's Use of Righteousness Language against its Hellenistic Background," 48–49; Spicq, "δίκαιος, κτλ.," 321–22; 321n7; Seebass, "Righteousness, Justification," 354; BDAG, s.v. δικαιοσύνη, 248 [definition 3a].

ruler.⁵⁵ Diogenes Laertius, for example, in his account on the Stoic Zeno of Citium, states: "Among the virtues (ἀρετῶν), some are primary and the others are subordinate to these. The primary virtues are: wisdom (φρόνησις), courage (ἀνδρεία), justice (δικαιοσύνη), and temperance (σωφροσύνη)."⁵⁶ Likewise Epictetus, in a longer virtue list, argues that to be truly human is to be "upright in character" (δίκαιος), high-minded, temperate, self-possessed, deliberate, free from deceit, modest, free, and all the rest."⁵⁷ Plutarch, in his description of the noted Roman general and consul Aemilius Paulus, described Paulus as a person "who was gaining for himself a reputation from his courage, just character, and loyalty" (τὴν ἀπ' ἀνδρείας καὶ δικαιοσύνης καὶ πίστεως δόξαν αὐτῷ περιποιούμενος; *Aem.* 2.6).⁵⁸ Epictetus's predecessor and teacher, Musonius Rufus, similarly employs δικαιοσύνη as the ethical characteristic of the wise person in several of his treatises.⁵⁹ In particular, Musonius asserts: "Concerning the soul, a person should expect that it be firmly habituated toward temperance and justice and in general most naturally-disposed toward virtue (ψυχὰς δὲ ἐπιτηδειοτάτας εἶναι νομιστέον τὰς πρὸς σωφροσύνην καὶ δικαιοσύνην καὶ ὅλως πρὸς ἀρετὴν εὐφυεστάτας)."⁶⁰

55. Reumann, "Righteousness: Greco-Roman World," 744–45.

56. Diogenes Laertius, *Lives* 7.92; ET modified from Hicks, LCL, 199. Cf. *Lives* 3.80.

57. Epictetus, Fr. 28b; ET modified from Oldfather, LCL, 473; see also *Diss.* 3.14.13–14; Fr. 14.

58. ET modified from Perrin, LCL, 361. See also Plutarch, *Virt. mor.* 440E–441B; *Comp. Dem. Cic.* 3.4.

59. See Musonius Rufus, Fr. 11: "What is there to prevent a student while he is working (in the harvest fields) from listening to a teacher speak about temperance, justice (δικαιοσύνης), or endurance?" (Lutz, p. 82, lines 30–33); Fr. 14: "For a person, evil consists of injustice (ἀδικία), cruelty, and indifference to the plight of a neighbor, while virtue (ἀρετή) is philanthropy, goodness and justice (δικαιοσύνη), and to show benefaction and concern for one's neighbor" (Lutz, p. 92, lines 29–33); Fr. 17: "On the whole, above all creatures on earth, humanity alone is the imitation of God (δὲ ἄνθρωπον μίμημα μὲν θεοῦ μόνον) and in Him has the same virtues (ἐκείνῳ δὲ παραπλησίας ἔχει τὰς ἀρετάς), since we can imagine nothing even in the gods better than wisdom (φρονήσεως), justice (δικαιοσύνης), courage (ἀνδρείας), and temperance (σωφροσύνης)" (Lutz, p. 108, line 2). Cf. Fr. 16: "His [Zeus's] command and law is that a person be just (δίκαιον), honest, beneficent, temperate (σώφρονα), high-minded, superior to pain, above pleasure, free from all envy and malice; but in order to put it simply, I say: the law of Zeus bids a person to be good (ἀγαθὸν εἶναι κελεύει τὸν ἄνθρωπον ὁ νόμος ὁ τοῦ Διός)" (Lutz, p. 104, line 33); and Fr. 38: "God has put some things in our control, others not in our control. In our control, he has put . . . (Lutz, p. 134, lines 23–24) . . . the power of using our impressions (τὴν χρῆσιν τῶν φαντασιῶν). For when this is correctly used, it means serenity, cheerfulness, and constancy; it also means justice (δίκη), law (νόμος), temperance (σωφροσύνη), and virtue as a whole (ξύμπασα ἀρετή)" (Lutz, p. 136, lines 1–3). The above ET are modified from Lutz, "Musonius Rufus 'Roman Socrates,'" 83, 93, 107, 109, 135–37. The above references are also noted by Spicq, "δίκαιος , κτλ.," 328.

60. Fr. 13B (Lutz, p. 90, lines 12–13); ET modified from Lutz, YCS 10, p. 91.

This last text from Musonius reminds the modern reader to think of δικαιοσύνη not so much as an innate quality that a person possesses as part of his or her disposition, but rather to conceptualize justice as a *practiced* virtue. The soul has to be habituated, shaped, or adapted toward (ἐπιτήδειος πρός) such virtues as temperance and justice. In other words, a person is just, upright, or righteous because the person practices and maintains justice. The just person consistently does the right, customary, and fair deeds which allows for orderly life in society. Justice is not so much a commodity to possess or own, it is rather a state of habitual action. The boundary between justice as an inherent attribute of one's personality and justice as the consistent performance of right ethical deeds in relation to his or her community is fuzzy, not discrete, and we have several texts in addition to Musonius's that demonstrate this blurring of boundaries between character and behavior.[61]

Take, for instance, the famous last will and testament of Augustus Caesar, known as the *Res Gestae Divi Augusti* ("The Deeds Accomplished by the Divinized Augustus"), originally read by Tiberius's son the Younger Drusus before the Roman Senate, later preserved by several inscriptions in Ancyra, Pisidian Antioch, and Apollonia from which the critical text is reconstructed, both in Latin and Greek.[62] Beginning from the very first three chapters of *Res Gestae* and culminating in ch. 34,[63] Augustus has been cataloguing one achievement after another as evidence of his fitness to rule and govern. He boasts:[64]

> I brought peace to the sea that was being subjected to piracy by renegade slaves . . . (θάλασσαν πειρατευομένην ὑπὸ ἀποστατῶν δούλων εἰρήνευσα; 25.1)
> I have enlarged the boundaries of all Roman provinces . . . I settled in peace (ἐν εἰρήνῃ κατέστησα) the regions of Gaul and Spain . . . I brought peace (εἰρηνεύεσθαι πεπόηκα) to the Alps

---

61. Besides the primary example of *Res Gestae* to be discussed below, see also Plutarch, *Curios.* 522B on "training / practice towards justice" (πρὸς δικαιοσύνης ἄσκησιν); and Diogenes Laertius, *Lives* 7.126 which describes δικαιοσύνη as the qualities of "equity" (ἰσότης) and "fair-mindedness" (εὐγνωμοσύνη) but also as "putting into practice what ought to be done" (πρατικὸν τῶν ποιητέων). In fact, elsewhere Plutarch adds that, while justice is a virtue, it requires that a person have the wisdom to know what is just and equitable as well as the power to put that wisdom into practice (καὶ ἡ δικαιοσύνη τῆς φρονήσεως δεῖται παρούσης; *Fort.* 87E).

62. The Greek and Latin text edition of *Res Gestae* comes from Cooley, *Res Gestae Divi Augusti*.

63. On the role of ch. 34 as the "capstone" of Augustus's career achievements, see the comments by Cooley in ibid., 256, and Lacey, *Augustus and the Principate*, 98.

64. ET modified from Cooley, *Res Gestae Divi Augusti*, 89, 91, 97, 99.

> ... but made war on no nation *unjustly* ... (οὐδενὶ ἔθνει ἀδίκως ἐπενεχθέντος πολέμου; 26.1–3)
>
> [Through Roman expansion] very many other nations experienced the good faith of the Roman people (δήμου Ῥωμαίων πίστεως) under my leadership, with whom the Roman people [previously] had no exchange of embassies and friendship (32.3).
>
> [Finally] in my six and seventh consulships, after I had extinguished the civil wars (μετὰ τὸ τοὺς ἐνφυλίους ζβέσαι με πολέμους) ... I was called *Sebastos* and my entranceway was publically crowned with laurels, and the oak wreath which is given for saving fellow citizens (δρύινος στέφανος ὁ διδόμενος ἐπὶ σωτηρίαι τῶν πολειτῶν) was set up above the gateway of my house, and [finally] a golden shield which was set up in the council chamber by the Senate and the people of Rome bore witness through its inscription to my virtue, clemency, justice and piety (διὰ τῆς ἐπιγραφῆς ἀρετὴν καὶ ἐπ[ι]είκειαν καὶ δικαιοσύνην καὶ εὐσέβειαν ἐμοὶ μαρτυρεῖ; 34.1–2).

This last paragraph is undoubtedly the climax of *Res Gestae*.[65] The long catalogue of achievements listed from the first chapter until the climatic thirty-fourth culminate in Augustus Caesar's ultimate claim in 34.2: that is, his accomplishments demonstrate his overall virtue (ἀρετή), clemency (ἐπιείκεια), justice (δικαιοσύνη), and piety (εὐσέβια). What I wish, however, to do here is focus upon what Augustus means by δικαιοσύνη (*iustitia* in the Latin inscriptions). In fact, the texts quoted above (25.1; 26.1–3; 32.3; 34.1) have been selected precisely because they narrate accomplishments which highlight the δικαιοσύνη or justice of Augustus.

By ending piracy and keeping the international trade routes safe throughout the Mediterranean Sea (25.1), by extending the boundaries of the Roman Empire and pacifying Gaul, Spain, and other western territories (εἰρηνεύεσθαι / ἐν εἰρήνῃ κατέστησα; 26.1–3), by establishing embassies and extending friendship even to nations who were once at war with Rome (32.3), and by definitively ending the civil wars which once threatened to tear the empire apart (ζβέσαι με πολέμους; 34.1), Augustus brought justice to all lands.[66] The political and social stability which he established was his way of "putting to rights" all that was disorderly and chaotic in the ancient world. What is more, Augustus alleged to have accomplished this peace and order "without waging war against any nation unjustly" (οὐδενὶ ἔθνει ἀδίκως

---

65. See the comments by Cooley on ch. 34 in her *Res Gestae Divi Augusti*, 256.

66. These claims by Augustus are exaggerated, of course, and Cooley catalogues some of the differences between *Res Gestae* and other Roman histories in ibid., 218–19.

ἐπενεχθέντος πολέμου; 26.3).⁶⁷ If violence was used, it was a necessary and just use of force. So the socio-political δικαιοσύνη that Augustus established for the Roman world was a public expression of his ethical just character. Justice is both what he did (= he established an orderly system of rule over all lands) and who he is (= he therefore demonstrated virtue and moral uprightness). There cannot be a hard distinction between the ethical quality of Augustus from the political, social, and legal acts that he performed to bring about justice. The latter is evidence for the former.

So far, we investigated the ethical uses of δικαιοσύνη / δίκαιος, but what about the verb δικαιόω? Does the verb δικαιόω ever mean "to make righteous" or "to become (ethically) just"? For the most part, the ethical use of δικαιόω appears to be absent from Greco-Roman discourse. Schrenk records one possible exception in the *Corpus Hermeticum*.⁶⁸ In Book 13, the disciple (with the alias *Tat*) asks his teacher (under the pseudonym *Hermes Trismegistus*, which is the Greek name for the Egyptian god *Thoth*) a series of questions concerning the "doctrine of new birth" (τὸν τῆς παλιγγενεσίας λόγον; *Corp. herm.* 13.1).⁶⁹ Hermes responds by telling Tat that "no one is saved without being born again" (γὰρ μηδένα δύνασθαι σωθῆναι πρὸ τῆς παλιγγενεσίας; 13.1) and that the process of rebirth involves an inner purging of bodily vices through the acquisition of divine wisdom or knowledge (γνῶσις θεοῦ; 13.8b). "Nullify the senses of the body," says Hermes, "and there will be the birth of divinity" (κατάργησον τοῦ σώματος τὰς αἰσθήσεις, καὶ ἔσται ἡ γένεσις τῆς θεότητος; 13.7a).

In the language of the mystery cults but without their rituals,⁷⁰ Book 13 describes a radical transformation whereby the initiate experiences the extirpation (καθᾶραι) of the irrational passions—twelve in all—and the attainment of their corresponding opposite virtues as divine *gnōsis* grips the person.⁷¹ Grief (λύπη), for example, is replaced by joy (χαρά), inconti-

---

67. Similarly, Appian comments that Roman citizens can trust the gods and the rationale of the war waged by Caesar; that is, the noble and just (δικαίαν) goal of the war is the defense of the Republic (*Bell. civ.* 2.8.51).

68. Schrenk, "δίκη, δίκαιος, δικαιοσύνη, κτλ.," 212, although he categories this use as "mystical" instead of ethical; see also BDAG, s.v. δικαιόω, 249 [def. 3]. Cf. Ziesler, *The Meaning of Righteousness in Paul*, 48.

69. The Greek text is taken from Scott, ed. and trans., *Hermetica*, 238, line 13. English translations, unless otherwise indicated, are modified from Copenhaver, ed. and trans., *Hermetica*.

70. Chlup has argued that the language of the Hermetic hymns themselves function to replace the rituals of the cults by performing through its words, verses, and language the kind of transformation that past rituals would have previously done for the convert; see Chlup, "The Ritualization of Language in the *Hermetica*," 133–59.

71. See the comments by Copenhaver, *Hermetica*, 180–84.

nence (ἀκρασία) replaced by self-control (ἐγκράτεια), desire (ἐπιθυμία) by endurance (καρτερία), and so on.⁷² Concerning the vice of injustice (ἀδικία), Hermes exclaims: "Behold how it [knowledge of justice] drove out injustice without judgment. With injustice gone, my child, we were made righteous / cleansed / transformed" (ἐδικαιώθημεν, ὦ τένον, ἀδικίας ἀπούσης). Here ἐδικαιώθημεν cannot mean "we were declared just" but rather "we were made (into) just (persons)." When vice is being replaced by virtue and the entire process is called a "rebirth," δικαιόω cannot be declarative but denotes an ethical transformation. Schrenk translates ἐδικαιώθημεν in *Corp. herm.* 13.9 idiomatically as "we have become sinless."⁷³ BDAG translates it as "we were made free / pure" or even "we became deified."⁷⁴

But this particular ethical use of δικαιόω must be seen as an exception. As Ziesler points out, the definition of δικαιόω as "make righteous" or "become a just person" is rare in secular Greek, and so the declaratory force should be given priority in translation unless there are strong reasons to the contrary.⁷⁵ What is more, it is still unclear if this particular tractate (= *Corp. herm.* 13) in the Hermetica is early enough to be of any real relevance for our study of δικ(αιο)- lexical usage during the first-century CE period. Book 13 could be as late as the third century CE and reflect Christian influence upon the text rather than being a true parallel to the New Testament corpus.⁷⁶ Hence the ethical dimensions of the δικ(αιο)- lexical group are limited to usages of the noun δικαιοσύνη and its adjectival correlative δίκαιος, but the verb δικαιόω predominantly delimits its semantics to non-ethical—i.e., social, legal, and juridicial—definitions.

---

72. See *Corp. herm.* 13.7b–9 (= Scott, pp. 242–44).
73. Schrenk, "δίκη, δίκαιος, δικαιοσύνη, κτλ.," 212.
74. BDAG, s.v. δικαιόω, 249 [def. 3].
75. Ziesler, *The Meaning of Righteousness in Paul*, 48.
76. Because the Hermetica are a loose anthology of disparate texts grouped together more because of the biases of Byzantine compilers than due to a traceable literary unity, these texts are notoriously difficult to date on an individual basis. Their final composition is probably the late third century CE, although parts of the collection could contain traditions as early as the Ptolemaic and Hellenistic periods. Concerning *Corp. herm.* 13 in particular, Dodd has long proposed that the tractate provides independent and "striking parallels" with the rebirth language in the Gospel of John; see his *The Interpretation of the Fourth Gospel*, 44–53. However, because the tractate contains religious and philosophical material found among later Greek Magical Papyri and the Nag Hammadi Library, it is more likely that the content of Book 13 reflects a second century CE date. See the discussions by Copenhaver, *Hermetica*, xxxiii, 180–82; and Scott, *Hermetica*, 8, 12.

SUMMATION OF RESULTS

A Polysemous Network for the Semantic Classifications of Δικ(αιο)- Lexemes

After having traced the diachronic history of the δικ(αιο)- word group and having catalogued its use during the early imperial period from a synchronic perspective, we can now make the case for the following unmarked and marked definitions of these lexemes. For what follows, I have re-cited in the notes the select texts that were discussed in the above sections and regrouped these text citations under the semantic classifications of each lexeme. Also, this study cites texts which best represent a given semantic classification or definition. This study does *not* claim to offer a statistical analysis for word usage. Unless otherwise noted, the quantity of citations in the notes for each entry is therefore *not* indicative of how frequent a particular use of a lexeme occurs in Greco-Roman discourse. Citations merely indicate the quality of representative texts which illustrate each definition.

There are two additional features worthy of mention for the alternative taxonomy of δικ(αιο)- lexemes mapped out below. First, definitions are ranked from unmarkedness to markedness.[77] The lower digit categories (1, 2, etc.) signify the lexeme's unmarked meaning(s) that are the least context dependent, while the higher digit categories (3, 4, etc.) indicate increasing semantic markedness. Subcategories (2.1, 2.2, etc.), however, represent specialized or marked uses of the lexeme regardless of ranking. Second, in keeping with some of the linguistic principles outlined in BDAG, English glosses (or what Danker calls "formal equivalents") are distinguished from the definitions or main semantic classifications of the lexeme by rendering the gloss in *italics*.[78]

---

77. Definitions for what constitutes "unmarked" (least context dependent) vs. "marked" (more context dependent) meanings are addressed in detail in part 2 of this study (= chapter 2 of this volume); see also Lakoff, *Women, Fire and Dangerous Things*, 59–61; Comrie, *Aspect*, 111–22.

78. See the "Forward to the Revised Edition" by Danker in BDAG, viii–ix. Danker renders English glosses or formal equivalents in bold italics but for the sake of style, my lexical categories feature the glosses in regular (unbolded) italics.

δίκαιος: (A1): in accordance with the expectations, customs or decorum of the community; *right, fitting, appropriate, customary*[A]
(A2): in accordance to the rules or civic laws which govern society; *just, equitable, fair, lawful*[B]
  (A2.1; as a substantive): the right to do something as guaranteed by law or custom; legal license or civic liberty; *right, freedom*[C]
  (A2.2; as a substantive): punitive action; *punishment*[D]
(A3): in accordance to moral integrity; *righteous, upright, honest*[E]
(A4): judged in the right; *justified*[F]
unattested [[(A4.1): judged innocent; *acquitted; innocent; free*]][G]

δικαιοσύνη: (N1): distributive justice (= the opposite of lawlessness); *justice, fairness; equitableness*[H]
(N2): just character; moral *uprightness; righteousness; honesty*[I]
(N3): act or state of setting something right; the administration of just order; the practice or exercise of justice; accomplishing social, civic and political orderliness; *rightifying activity, setting aright, putting to rights*[J]
(N4): juridicial justice; what the ruler or judge / lawcourt declares is just, fair, legal, and equitable; *justice, judgment, just verdict*[K]

δικαιόω: (V1): consider someone as having met the expectations and customs of the community; *deem right, regard as appropriate, consider fitting*; (passive) *be in the right*[L]
(V2): judge (as in the) right; *declare just; justify*[M]
  rare (V2.1): verify as true; *ratify; sanction*[N]
  unattested [[(V2.2) set free or liberate through a juridicial process; *acquit, release*]][O]
(V3): perform just actions; establish just order; *do justice* (for someone), *set right*[P]
  rare (V3.1) see that someone got his / her rights recognized; *vindicate* (an innocent person)[Q]
  (V3.2) bring someone to justice; exercise punitive penalties; *punish; penalize; condemn* (a guilty person); *execute*[R]
  rare? [(V4) make righteous; transform someone (into a just person); become (an) upright (person); *justify, transform, purify, deify*][S]

δίκη: (X1): castigation of a person for a crime or wrong done; *punishment, penalty*[T]
(X2): distributive *justice*; Justice (personified as a goddess)[U]

A. See Homer, *Od.* 6.120–21; 9.172–76; 13.209–12; 14.89–92. The social meaning of δίκαιος during the Hellenistic and Greco-Roman eras is well-attested, and here I depend mostly on the citations listed in Spicq, "δίκαιος, κτλ." 320–21; BAGD, s.v. δίκαιος, 246–47; Schrenk, "δίκη, δίκαιος, δικαιοσύνη, κτλ.," 182–85; Olley, "Righteousness" in the Septuagint of Isaiah, 32–43; Hill, *Greek Words and Hebrew Meanings*, 99–100; Ziesler, *The Meaning of Righteousness in Paul*, 48–51; Reumann, "Righteousness: Greco-Roman World," 743.

B. Aristotle, *EN* 1129a6-9; 1129a34-1129b1; Demosthenes, *Or.* 3.21; Thucydides, *Hist.* 2.71.2; Diodorus Siculus, *Bibliotheca historica* 5.71.1; 12.45.1; 19.85.4; 40.11.1-2; 49.12.1; Dionysius of Halicarnassus, *Ant. rom.* 10.2.

C. *UPZ* II 16 col. 7 lines 22-27; *P. Oxy.* VI, 905.9.

D. Dio Cassius, *Roman History* 40.19.2; 54.19.2; Josephus, *Ant.* 14.288; 15.213.

E. Herodotus, *Hist.* 1.96; Epictetus, *Diss.* 3.14.13-14; Fr. 14; Fr. 28b; Musonius Rufus, Fr. 16 (= Lutz, p. 104, line 33).

F. Demosthenes, *Or.* 44.4; Dionysius of Halicarnassus, *Ant. rom.* 10.2. Cf. Aristotle, *EN* 1137a10-12 (ἄδικος ἡ κρίσις ἐστίν).

G. The double brackets [[ ]] signify that definition of δίκαιος as "acquitted," "innocent," or "free" is unattested in Greco-Roman discourse. If found in Paul's letters, this semantic classification denotes a unique Pauline use atypical of its κοινή usage during the early imperial period of Rome. However, the substantive use of δίκαιος as "punishment" is attested, though rare (see above def. A2.2). The denotation of the verb δικαιόω as "punish / penalize" is much more frequent and *well* attested (see below def. V3.2).

H. Herodotus, *Hist.* 1.96; Epictetus, *Diss.* 3.26.32; Stobaeus, *Ecl.* 1.49.44 (= C. Wachsmuth, p. 406, lines 5-15).

I. Aristotle, *EN* 1129a6-9; 1338b10-11; Diogenes Laertius, *Lives* 7.92; Plutarch, *Aem.* 2.6; Musonius Rufus, Fr. 11 (= Lutz, p. 82, lines 30-33); Fr. 14 (= Lutz, p. 92, lines 29-33); Fr. 17 (Lutz, p. 108, line 2).

J. Herodotus, *Hist.* 1.96; Musonius Rufus, Fr. 13B (= Lutz, p. 90, lines 12-13); Augustus, *Res Gestae* 34.1-2.

K. Aristotle, *Politics* 1291a26-29; *P. Thead.* 23.9-11; *BGU* 1138.4; 1824.30; *P. Oslo* 128.10; *P. Oxy.* 1873.15.

L. Plato, *Gorg.* 484B (= Pindar, Fr. 16.9); Dio Cassius, *Roman History* 48.46.4; *P. Giss* I.47.16.

M. Thucydides, *Hist.* 2.71.4; *P. Ryl.* II.119.14-16; *P. Tebt.* II.444; Dionysius of Halicarnassus, *Ant. rom.* 10.2-3; *P. Oxy.* III.653. Cf. Demosthenes, *Or.* 44.4 (ἐν μὴ τῷ δικαίῳ ἐπιστεύομεν).

N. Dio Cassius, *Roman History* 54.24.6-7.

O. The double brackets [[ ]] signify that definition of δικαιόω as "acquit" or "release" is unattested in Greco-Roman discourse. If found in Paul's letters, this semantic classification denotes a unique Pauline use atypical of its κοινή usage during the early imperial period of Rome.

P. Polybius, *Hist.* 3.31.9; Dio Cassius, *Roman History* 52.24.3-4. Cf. Aristotle, *EN* 1129a6-9 (δικαιοπραγοῦσι); 1137a10-12 (οὐκ ἀδικεῖ); Thucydides, *Hist.* 2.71.2 (οὐ δίκαια ποιεῖν); 2.71.4 (γῆν τὴν Πλαταιίδα μὴ ἀδικεῖν).

Q. The closest text where δικαιόω might mean "vindicate" or "see someone's rights / privileges enforced" is Dio Cassius, *Roman History* 52.24.3-4 ("let those [magistrates] themselves see that the rights of these [soldiers] are fulfilled;" τούτους μὲν γὰρ αὐτοὶ ἐκεῖνοι δικαιούτωσαν) but the translation could alternatively be: "let those [magistrates] do justice to these [soldiers];" that is, the magistrates should provide lands and homes to retiring soldiers who have had faithfully fulfilled their military service. This text is ambiguous but certainly the idea of vindication would be a semantic extension of doing justice to someone.

R. Dio Cassius, *Roman History* 37.12.2; 37.41.2; 38.11.3; 41.28.4; 43.24.4; 49.12.5; 54.15.4; 55.14.3; 56.4.5; Plutarch, *Sera* 565B; Josephus, *Ant.* 4.278; 16.206; 18.178; 20.135.

s. *Corp. herm.* 13.9. The single brackets [ ] signify that the ethical use of the verb δικαιόω is either rare or altogether unattested in Greco-Roman discourse, given the uncertainty of how to date the Hermetica.

t. Epictetus, *Diss.* 3.24.4–5.

u. Hesiod, *Op.* 213–24; Plutarch, *Princ. iner.* 780E; 781B; *Sera* 565B; Musonius Rufus, Fr. 38 (= Lutz, p. 136, lines 1–3).

Given the above semantic mappings for each lexeme, I want to highlight a few observations to frame the next chapter (Part 2 of this study) on Pauline usages of the δικ(αιο)- word group.

First, the *unmarked* or prototypical meanings[79] for the δικ(αιο)- lexical group in Greco-Roman discourse are as follows:

1. The prototypical meaning of δίκαιος is its social use as "right, fitting, appropriate, customary" (A1). At times however, this definition overlaps with it legal use as "just, equitable, fair, lawful" (A2) since there is often a fuzzy boundary between the social expectations of a community and the rules or civic laws which govern society.

2. δικαιοσύνη prototypically means "justice" (*iustitia distributiva*) in its social and legal senses (N1).

3. δικαιόω prototypically means "deem right, appropriate, and fitting" or "be in the right" according to the social expectations and laws governing communal life (V1).

Second, frequently attested but *marked* in their meanings are the following semantic categories:

4. The ethical uses of δίκαιος (A3) and δικαιοσύνη (N2) are well-attested but are marked in specific contexts. When deployed in the moral discourse of philosophical writings or in the *encomia* of emperors, military generals or other heroic figures, δίκαιος can mean "just, righteous, upright, honest" as a moral quality, while δικαιοσύνη denotes "just and righteous character" as a moral disposition.

5. At times the distinction between distributive justice (N1) and just character (N2) are blurred (e.g., *Res Gestae* 34) where the latter is demonstrated only when the said person is able to establish the former. In such cases, δικαιοσύνη (N3) means "the act or state of setting something right" or "the administration or practice of justice." Here

---

79. Concerning semantic markedness as protypicality, see Lakoff, *Women, Fire and Dangerous Things*, 59–61; also Taylor, *Linguistic Categorization*, 59–65; Evans and Green, *Cognitive Linguistics*, 255–67.

δικαιοσύνη functions as the nominal equivalent of the verbal definition of δικαιόω (V3) as "set right," "do justice," or "perform just actions."

6. When judicial contexts are clearly marked by syntagmatic factors, the forensic meanings of the δικ(αιο)- group override their social and legal senses. Typically, where a lawcourt or tribunal context is evoked, the following are true:

   α) δίκαιος (A4) means "justified" or "judged in the right."

   β) δικαιοσύνη (N4) refers to the justice of the courts or what the ruler or judge declares is just, fair, legal, and equitable.

   γ) δικαιόω (V2) means "declare just," or "judge (as in the) right."

   Some of the syntagms which have marked a lawcourt context in Greco-Roman discourse include, but are not limited to, the following tags: judge (δικαστής), ruler (ἄρχων), or magistrate (στρατηγός); law or legal system (νόμος / νομία); judgment / verdict (κρίσις / κρίμα); penalize / punish (τιμωρέω / κολάζω); and pardon (ἀπολύω).

7. The unmarked definitions of the δικ(αιο)- lexemes can have extended marked definitions *in negativae*. The punitive definition of δίκαιος (A2.2) as "penalty" or "punishment" is not wide-spread, but the specialized use of δικαιόω (V3.2) to mean "punish," "penalize," "condemn," or even "execute" is very well-attested and is a viable translation option in punitive contexts.

Lastly, a word or two needs to be said concerning semantic gaps or *unattested* usages of the δικ(αιο)- lexical group that have been attributed in the past by scholars to Paul.

8. Though we have some scattered examples, on the whole, δικαιόω (V.3.1) rarely means "vindicate (an innocent person)." Instead, the extended use of δικαιόω (V.3) as "set right" and "do justice" usually takes a negative or punitive trajectory in Greco-Roman discourse to mean (V.3.2) "punish" or "penalize."

9. The extended meaning of δικαιόω (V2.2) as "acquit, release, set free" (and δίκαιος [A4.1] as "innocent / free") is unattested in Greco-Roman discourse. While δικαιόω in juridicial contexts does mean "declare just" or "judged in the right" (V.2), this is not the same as the acquittal of the innocent. The latter is an extended definition. If, therefore, Paul uses δικαιόω to mean "acquit" or "release" in his letters, it is likely that the intertextual semantic contribution of the Hebrew verb *tsadaq* enables Paul to extend the meaning δικαιόω in this direction, a direction

confirmed by the LXX translation of *tsadaq* in select places where "acquit" is the best translation option.[80]

10. The ethical use of δικαιόω (v4) as "make righteous" or "transform someone (into a just person)" is arguably non-existent in Greco-Roman discourse. One exception could be *Corp. herm.* 13.9, but as noted above, the dating of this text is so problematic that I would be hesitant to base an entire semantic classification to this one text. Therefore, δικαιόω must either mean "deem / set right" in its social use or "declared just" / "judged in the right" in its legal / juridicial usage unless again context and syntagmatic factors demand otherwise.[81]

Prelude to Part 2

Having mapped out the polysemous definitions of δίκαιος, δικαιοσύνη, δικαιόω, and δίκη during the synchronic period of early imperial Rome (Part 1), this essay sets the stage for an initial sounding on Paul's (re)deployment of these terms in his Letter to the Romans (Part 2). In what follows (Chapter 2), comparisons will be made between this study and the benchmark lexicon BDAG. I also analyze Rom 3:21–26 as a test case for evaluating the diverse positions of several Pauline scholars in the current debate on justification. Chapter 2 contends that Paul's vocabulary operated well within the polysemous network of the wider Greco-Roman world and need not be dependent on Septuagintal definitions except in a few select places.

BIBLIOGRAPHY

Appian. *Roman History*. 4 vols. Trans. H. White. LCL. Cambridge, MA: Harvard University Press, 1912–1913.
Aristotle. *Nicomachean Ethics*. Trans. H. Rackham. Rev. ed. LCL. Cambridge, MA: Harvard University Press, 1934.
———. *Politics*. Trans. by H. Rackham. LCL. Cambridge, MA: Harvard University Press, 1944.

---

80. Similarly Ziesler has argued that the semantic category "acquit" only arises when the LXX applies the δικαιόω ("declare just") to special circumstances where the declaration means not so much the condemnation of the guilty but the vindication of the innocent or righteous; see Ziesler, *The Meaning of Righteousness in Paul*, 48; 52–69.

81. Bird, for example, who is *almost* convinced by the wholly forensic use of δικαιόω as "declare just," finds that Rom. 6:7 (δεδικαίωται ἀπὸ τῆς ἁμαρτίας) might be the one text where a forensic translation is not possible and therefore Paul atypically uses δικαιόω in a transformative sense; see Bird, *The Saving Righteousness of God*, 17–18. See also Garlington, "Imputation or Union with Christ," 66–70.

Chlup, Radek. "The Ritualization of Language in the *Hermetica*." *Aries* 7 (2007) 133–59.
Cooley, Alison E. *Res Gestae Divi Augusti: Text, Translation, and Commentary.* Cambridge: Cambridge University Press, 2009.
Comrie, Bernard. *Aspect.* Cambridge Textbooks in Lingustics. Cambridge: Cambridge University Press, 1976.
Copenhaver, Brian P., ed. and trans. *Hermetica: The Greek Corpus Hermeticum and the Latin Asclepius in a New English Translation with Notes and Introduction.* Cambridge: Cambridge University Press, 1992.
Demosthenes. *Orations.* 7 vols. Trans. J. H. Vince et al. LCL. Cambridge, MA: Harvard University Press, 1930–49.
Dio Cassius. *Roman History.* 9 vols. Trans. E. Cary and H. B. Foster. LCL. Cambridge, MA: Harvard University Press, 1914–1927.
Diodorus Siculus. *Library of History.* 12 vols. Trans. W. A. Oldfather et al. LCL. Cambridge, MA: Harvard University Press, 1933–1967.
Diogenes Laertius. *Lives of Emminent Philosophers.* Vol. 2 of 2: Books 6–10. Trans. R. D. Hicks. LCL. Cambridg, MA: Harvard University Press, 1925.
Dionysius of Halicarnassus. *Roman Antiquities.* Vol. 6 of 7: Books 9–10. Trans. by E. Cary. LCL. Cambridge, MA: Harvard University Press, 1947.
Dodd, C. H. *The Interpretation of the Fourth Gospel.* Cambridge: Cambridge University Press, 1953.
Epictetus. *Discourses.* 2 vols. Trans. W. A. Oldfather. LCL. Cambridge, MA: Harvard University Press, 1925–1928.
Evans, Vyvyan, and Melanie Green. *Cognitive Linguistics: An Introduction.* Mahwah, NJ: Erlbaum, 2006.
Garlington, Don. "Imputation or Union with Christ: A Response to John Piper?" *Reformation and Revival Journal* 12, no. 4 (2003) 45–113.
Grenfell, B. P., and A. S. Hunt, eds. *The Oxyrhynchus Papyri.* Parts 3 and 6. Oxford: Oxford University Press, 1903–1908.
Grenfell, B. P., et al., eds. *The Tebtunis Papyri.* Part 2. Oxford: Oxford University Press, 1907.
Havelock, E. A. "Dikaiosune: An Essay in Greek Intellectual History." *Phoenix* 23, no. 1 (1969) 49–70.
Hill, David. *Greek Words and Hebrew Meanings: Studies in the Semantics of Soteriological Terms.* SNTSMS 5. Cambridge: Cambridge University Press, 1967.
Homer. *The Odyssey.* 2 vols. Trans. A. T. Murray. Rev. G. Dimock. LCL. Cambridge, MA: Harvard University Press, 1995.
Johnson, J. de M., et al., eds. *Catalogue of the Greek Papyri in the John Rylands Library.* Vol. 2, *Documents of the Ptolemaic and Roman Periods: Nos. 62–456.* Manchester: University Press, 1915.
Josephus. *Antiquities.* 9 vols. Trans. H. St. J. Thackeray et al. LCL. Cambridge, MA: Harvard University Press, 1930–65.
Jouget, Pierre, ed. *Papyri de Théadelphie.* Paris: Fontemoing & Cie, 1911.
Kertelege, K. "δικαιοσύνη." In *EDNT* 1:326–30.
Kornemann, E., and P. M. Meyer, eds. *Griechische Papyri zu Giessein.* Vol. 1/2, nos. 36–57. Leipzig: Teubner, 1910.
Lacey, W. K. *Augustus and the Principate: The Evolution of the System.* ARCA Classical and Medieval Texts, Papers and Monographs 35. Leeds: Cairns, 1996.

Lakoff, George. *Women, Fire and Dangerous Things: What Categories Reveal about the Mind*. Chicago: University of Chicago Press, 1987.
Llewelyn, R., and R. A. Kearsley, eds. *NewDocs 1982–83*. Vol. 7, *A Review of Greek Inscriptions and Papyri Published in 1982–83*. Ancient History Documentary Research Centre, Macquarie University. Marrickville, NSW: Southwood, 1994.
Lutz, Cora E. "Musonius Rufus 'Roman Socrates.'" *Yale Classical Studies*, ed. A. R. Bellinger, 10:3–147. New Haven: Yale University Press, 1947.
Mommsen, Theodor, and Paul Krueger, eds. *The Digest of Justinian*. Vol. 1. Trans. Alan Watson. Philadelphia: University of Pennsylvania Press, 1985.
Moo, Douglas. *The Epistle to the Romans*. NICNT. Grand Rapids: Eerdmans, 1996.
Olley, John W. *"Righteousness" in the Septuagint of Isaiah: A Contextual Study*. SBLSCS 8. Missoula, MT: Scholars, 1979.
Plato. *Lysis. Symposium. Gorgias*. Trans. W. R. M. Lamb. LCL. Cambridge, MA: Harvard University Press, 1925.
Plutarch. *Lives*. Vol. 6, *Dion and Brutus, Timoleon and Aemilius Paulus*. Trans. B. Perrin. LCL. Cambridge, MA: Harvard University Press, 1918.
———. *Moralia*. 14 vols. Trans. F. C. Babbitt et al. LCL. Cambridge, MA: Harvard University Press, 1927–76.
Polybius. *The Histories*. Vol. 2. Trans. W. R. Paton. LCL. Cambridge, MA: Harvard University Press, 2010.
Reumann, John. "Righteousness: Greco-Roman World." In *ABD* 5:742–45.
Schrenk, Gottlob. "δίκη, δίκαιος, δικαιοσύνη, κτλ." in *TDNT* 2:174–225.
Scott, Walter, ed. and trans. *Hermetica: The Ancient Greek and Latin Writings Which Contain Religious or Philosophical Teaching Ascribed to Hermes Trismegistus*. Oxford: Clarendon, 1924–1936. Reprint, Boston: Shambhala, 1993.
Seebass, H. "Righteousness, Justification." in *NIDNTT* 3:352–56.
Seifrid, Mark. "Paul's Use of Righteousness Language against its Hellenistic Background." In *Justification and Variegated Nomism*. Vol. 2, *The Paradoxes of Paul*, ed. by D. A. Carson et al., 39–74. Grand Rapids: Baker Academic, 2004.
Spicq, Ceslas. "δίκαιος, κτλ." In *TLNT* 1:318–47.
Stobaeus. *Anthologium*. 5 vols. ed. by C. Wachsmuth and O. Hense. Berlin: Weidmann, 1884–1912. Reprint, Berlin: Raabe, 1958.
Taylor, John R. *Linguistic Categorization: Prototypes in Linguistic Theory*. 2nd ed. Oxford: Oxford University Press, 1995.
Thucydides. *History of the Peloponnesian War*. Vol. 1 of 4: Books 1–2. Trans. C. F. Smith. LCL. Cambridge, MA: Harvard University Press, 1919.
Wilcken, U., ed. *Urkunden der Ptolemäerzeit*. Vol. 2, *Papyri aus Oberägypten: Nos. 151–229*. Berlin: de Gruyter, 1935–1957.
Ziesler, John. *The Meaning of Righteousness in Paul: A Linguistic and Theological Inquiry*. SNTSMS 20. Cambridge: Cambridge University Press, 1972.

2

Greek Words and Roman Meanings, PART 2

A Prolegomenon to Paul's Use of Righteousness Language in His Letters

MAX J. LEE

INTRODUCTION: APPLYING A NEW TYPE OF LEXICON TO PAULINE STUDIES

This essay comprises Part 2 of a two-part study on the polysemy of the δικ(αιο)- lexical group in Greco-Roman discourse and Paul's semantic remappings of these lexemes in his letters. In Part 1 (= Chapter 1 of this volume), I argued for an alternative taxonomy of semantic classifications for the δικ(αιο)- word group based on their occurrence in the literature of early imperial Rome. Here in Chapter 2, comparisons will be made between this taxonomy of definitions for δίκαιος, δικαιοσύνη, δικαιόω, and δίκη with those of the benchmark lexicon BDAG. BDAG, despite its major linguistic advances, is nevertheless too dependent on Septuagintal meanings for some of its major semantic classifications. The alternative polysemous network argued for in Chapter 1 provides a much better basis for evaluating Paul's use of δικ(αιο)- lexemes precisely because it is a network based on

Greco-Roman usages unencumbered by the bilingual interference stemming from the Hebrew which the Septuagint translates.

In Chapter 2, I use Rom 3:21–26 as a test case for evaluating the diverse positions of several Pauline scholars in the current debate on justification. The goal for Part 2 is not to resolve the debate but rather to provide methodological clarity for the way forward. I revisit the linguistic distinction between word and context, or lexical vs. syntagmatic meaning, and apply the semantic taxonomies of Chapter 1 against the exegetical arguments of select scholars in the debate. It will be shown that most of these scholars (re)define righteousness language in Paul's letters according to the intertextual ties that they find with the Septuagint. Yet this chapter contends that Paul's vocabulary operated well within the polysemous network of the wider Greco-Roman world and need not be dependent on Septuagintal definitions except in a few select places.

A FIRST ATTEMPT AT MISSION IMPOSSIBLE: SKETCHING THE DEBATE AND CLEARING UP THE METHODOLOGICAL FOG

The Debate on the Meaning of Righteousness Language in Paul

As we look at how Paul quotes from the Old Testament in Greek (e.g., Hab. 2:4 in Rom 1:17) or how the Greek Septuagint translates Hebrew passages (e.g., Ps 99:4–5; cf. Ps 9:1–20; 89:5–14; 97:1–12; 103:6; Jer 9:23–24), we observe that the Hebrew lexemes *tsedaqah* ("righteous act" or "vindicating act") and *tsedeq* ("righteousness," "justice," or "vindication")[1] are often translated into the Greek as δικαιοσύνη ("righteousness," "justice," or "uprightness").[2] It has been a long standing trend among NT scholars to define δικαιοσύνη in correlation with the terms *tsedaqah* / *tsedeq* as the OT and Jewish background to Paul's use of righteousness language in his letters.[3]

---

1. Seifrid makes the case for a distinction between *tsedaqah* and *tsedeq*, arguing that the feminine noun *tsedaqah* usually denotes a righteous act or vindicating action. So *tsedaqah* might be a nominalization of the hiphil stem (*hitsdiq*) of the verb and refers to something concretely done. In contrast, the masculine noun *tsedeq* is the more general and abstract term denoting "right order," or "that which is morally right." See Seifrid, "Righteousness Language in the Hebrew Scriptures," 428.

2. Reumann, *Righteousness" in the New Testament*, 13–22; Danker, s.v. δικαιοσύνη, *Concise-English Lexicon*, 97.

3. See, e.g., Cremer, *Die paulinische Rechtfertigungslehre*, 295–440; Moo, *The Epistle to the Romans*, 79–90.

The difficulty, however, begins when the interpreter stumbles upon the wide semantic range of both word groups and the significant semantic overlap between them. On one hand, *tsedeq* denotes the administration of a just standard or norm to establish order, but it can also mean behavioral uprightness, or a righteous disposition.[4] Likewise, the lexeme δικαιοσύνη can be defined as "distributive justice" (*iustitia distributiva*), but it can also mean "upright character." Certainly δικαιοσύνη is a Greek term that also has a wide semantic range like its Hebrew correlatives; therefore, δικαιοσύνη can cover *tsedeq*'s juridicial and ethical dimensions without assuming that both definitions are operative in any single use of the term.

As Bird has noted,[5] the debate on how to interpret these lexemes is divided along several fronts: 1) Does "righteousness" refer to a norm/standard or is it a relational term? 2) Is righteousness forensic or transformative?, and 3) Is it covenantal or creational? The arguments for and against a position at each level of questioning have become so complex, that Laato laments that no one paper could provide a completely thorough lexical study which interacts with the entire history of research on righteousness language and adequately engages each scholar's arguments. In fact, the task itself might be "mission impossible."[6]

The Semantic Relationship between Word and Context

Part of the problem contributing to the apparent impasse on how to define righteousness language in the biblical corpus lies in the fact that many scholars struggle to maneuver successfully through the overlap of lexical semantics and syntagmatic semantics. Or to put it simply, exegetes have been guilty of blurring a word's core or unmarked definition (lexical) with its specialized use in context (syntagmatic). A word can derive additional meaning apart from its inherent definition by the way it connects with other words and phrases in the discourse unit.[7] Attempts, for example, to define δικαιοσύνη strictly as forensic righteousness,[8] saving righteousness (*iustitia*

---

4. Seifrid, "Righteousness Language in the Hebrew Scriptures," 416–22; Bruckner, "Justice in Scripture," 18–22.

5. Bird, *The Saving Righteousness of God*, 7–39.

6. Laato, "God's Righteousness," 59.

7. Lyons, *Semantics*, 1:261–66; 2:512–20; Cruse, *Lexical Semantics*, 23–48, 49–50, 76–79; Murphy, *Lexical Meaning*, 108–9; Geeraerts, *Theories of Lexical Semantics*, 57–64; Taylor, *Cognitive Grammar*, 225–42.

8. Bultmann, *The Theology of the New Testament*, 272. Though more nuanced, Moo likewise insists on a strictly forensic sense: "For Paul, as in the OT, 'righteousness of God' is a relational concept. Bringing together the aspects of activity and status, we can

salutifera),⁹ covenantal faithfulness,¹⁰ and moral uprightness¹¹ are either partially or wholly guilty of confusing the specialized use of δικαιοσύνη with its base meaning.

So when Bultmann and those who follow him argue that Paul "did not consistently employ *dikaiosyne* in the senses in which that word was ordinarily understood by the Greek-speaking public of the first century . . . but more distinctively imparted to *dikaiosyne* a meaning which reflected his knowledge of the Hebrew Old Testament in Greek translation,"¹² these scholars draw out a Pauline conception of δικαιοσύνη whose particularly forensic, judicial, acquitting and declarative meaning finds its semantic source not in the lexeme itself but the specialized contexts or syntagmatic constructions where Paul deploys the word.¹³ Likewise in a similar fashion,

---

define it as *the act by which God brings people into right relationship with himself*. With Luther, we stress that what is meant is a status *before* God and not internal moral transformation—God's activity of "making right" is a purely forensic activity, an acquitting, and not an 'infusing' of righteousness . . . [italics author's own]." See Moo, *The Epistle to the Romans*, 74.

9. Käsemann, to his own chagrin, has been credited with championing the subjective genitive reading of δικαιοσύνη θεοῦ as "God's salvation-creating power" (*heilsetzende Macht*) exclusively, and in contradistinction to the traditional (Lutheran and Reformed) reading of righteousness as a gift; see his "God's Righteousness in Paul," 100–110. However, Way, in his book *The Lordship of Christ*, 193–202, is correct to insist that "Käsemann . . . holds a middle position which takes up [δικαιοσύνη θεοῦ as] both 'gift' [*genitivus auctoris*, or the genitive of origin] and 'power' [the subjective genitive]" (198). Other scholars who read δικαιοσύνη θεοῦ as mainly as "saving righteousness" include: Stuhlmacher, *Paul's Letter to the Romans*, 31–32; Stuhlmacher, *Gerechtigkeit Gottes bei Paulus*, 222–28; Bird, *The Saving Righteousness of God*, 12–18; Cremer, *Die paulinische Rechtfertigungslehre*, 23–34; Beker, *Paul the Apostle*, 262–64; Martyn, *Galatians*, 249–50.

10. Ironically, despite his own warnings to the contrary, Hill has read the covenantal context of *tsedaqah / tsedeq* language into his own definitions of righteousness; see his *Greek Words and Hebrew Meanings*, 96–98. On δικαιοσύνη as "covenantal faithfulness," see also Wright, *What Saint Paul Really Said*, 95–103; Gorman, *Inhabiting the Cruciform God*, 52–57; and selectively Ziesler, *The Meaning of Righteousness in Paul*, 39, 93–96.

11. See, e.g., VanLandingham, *Judgment and Justification*, 246–52; and Jüngel, *Justification*, 204–24. Cf. Ziesler, *The Meaning of Righteousness in Paul*, 212, who argues that the noun δικαιοσύνη and adjective δίκαιος forms are behavioral or ethical, but the verb δικαιόω is mainly forensic.

12. This is the position of the Bultmann school as summarized by Leland Jamison who himself argues against it in his article "*Dikaiosyne* in the Usage of Paul,"93; cf. Bultmann, *The Theology of the New Testament*, 272.

13. Ibid.; Moo, *The Epistle to the Romans*, 74; Laato, "God's Righteousness," 45–54, who likewise says: "In secular Greek the word 'righteousness' (*et alia*) was mainly an ethical term. It expressed what was morally acceptable and advisable. In the Old Testament emphasis lies elsewhere. There, justification is also and foremost a part of judicial

VanLandingham has argued for the opposite case that δικαιοσύνη and its cognates are non-forensic, ethical, and transformative terms by looking at select biblical and Jewish source material and drawing from them specialized usages of the δικ(αιο)- word group.[14]

This is not to say that the Bultmann school or VanLandingham are incorrect in their every exegetical assessment of Paul's use of justification terms. But it does make the task of working through their and others' work on justification more difficult when word and context are at times confused, and with this confusion there is also a blurring between Paul's conceptualization of righteousness (*Grundbegriff*) and the lexical definitions of righteousness terms. While New Testament lexicography has come a long way since Barr's *The Semantics of Biblical Language* and his famous critique of Kittel's *Theological Dictionary of the New Testament* as a horrible example of "illegitimate totality transfer,"[15] scholars nevertheless continue to err in mistaking the *Grundbegriff* or the overall concept with the actual meaning of its lexeme.[16]

A Modest Proposal on Method

What I propose in the limited space of this essay is to draw an artificial line between lexical and syntagmatic semantics, i.e., word and context, simply as a heuristic tool to sort out the various usages of righteousness language in the biblical texts. The separation between lexical and syntagmatic semantics is admittingly an artificial one since, as Louw points out, a word's meaning(s) can only be determined when it is used in context.[17] Nevertheless, because

---

language. He is righteous who is acquitted in a court of law ... Paul uses the same [OT] language [vis-à-vis the Greek ethical use]" (45).

14. VanLandingham, *Judgment and Justification*, 271–72, who concludes after a semi-detailed study on δικαιοσύνη, δίκαιος, and δικαιόω (243–71) that: "None of the δικαι- group of terms is intrinsically forensic" (271).

15. Barr, *The Semantics of the Biblical Language*, 218.

16. While faulting Cremer, Ziesler, Hill, and others for mistaking *Grundbegriff* (concept) with lexical definition (Seifrid, "Righteousness Language in the Hebrew Scriptures,"418–19, 422, 423n37), Seifrid in a subsequent essay admits that in any word study a certain amount of confusion between conceptualization and semantics may be unavoidable. See Seifrid, "Paul's Use of Righteousness Language against its Hellenistic Background," who candidly states: "[S]ynthetic judgments are unavoidable, particularly when dealing with the theological vocabulary of Scripture. Consequently, the danger of imposing foreign ideas on the biblical text cannot be avoided—nor can it be fully overcome" (39).

17. Louw, *Semantics of New Testament Greek*, particularly when he states: "[A] word does not have a meaning without a context, it only has possible meaning. When used in

the state of NT scholarship on the topic of righteousness language has been so riddled with theological controversy and debate,[18] methodologically it makes sense in the beginning, at least, to attempt a separation between a word's functional meaning(s) as a semantic classification from how the word might actually come to be translated in a sentence or passage when other contributing textual factors connected to the word are considered.

Take, for example, the phrase δεδικαίωται ἀπὸ τῆς ἁμαρτίας (Rom 6:7). Though the unmarked meaning of δικαιόω is simply "to justify," no commentator translates this phrase as "justified from sin." Dunn understands δικαιόω in this verse to mean "exonerate" and translates the phrase as "declared free from (responsibility in relation to) sin."[19] Moo, in contrast, understands δεδικαίωται ἀπὸ τῆς ἁμαρτίας to mean "set free from (the power of) sin."[20] In both cases, the translation reveals the exegetical and theological commitments of the interpreter.[21]

Thus, in arguing for unmarked meanings of *tsedaqah* / *tsedeq* or δικ(αιο)- language, I am not advocating a return to the problems of Kittel, nor am I trying to distill some general schema of a lexeme that somehow unites all polysemous meanings into a single gloss. Rather, I simply follow some of the linguistic principles outlined, for example, in BDAG: to distinguish the definition or formal equivalents of a word (what is in bold typeface or bold italics in BDAG) from its actual translations in context (what is in normal italics), since all translations are ultimately interpretations.[22]

This exercise is necessary because the definition of a lexeme provides the rules for how a word can be deployed in actual spoken or written discourse. As Ryle notes, "to know what an expression means involves knowing what can (logically) be said with it, and what cannot (logically) be said with it. It involves knowing a set of bans, fiats, and obligations, or, in a word, it is

---

a context, the situation and the syntactic environment contribute to the choice between the several possibilities of meaning" (40).

18. One only needs to look at the recent exchanges between Piper and Wright to appreciate how heated the arguments can become. See Piper, *The Future of Justification*, 1–25; and Wright, *Justification*, 1–37. See also the history of Protestant vs. Catholic disagreement and debate on imputed vs. imparted righteousness catalogued by Lane, *Justification by Faith*, 1–126.

19. Dunn, *Romans 1–8*, 320–21.

20. Moo, *The Epistle to the Romans*, 377, n. 129; see also Campbell's "forensic-liberative" interpretation of δεδικαίωται ἀπὸ τῆς ἁμαρτίας as "has been released from Sin('s imprisonment)" in his *The Deliverance of God*, 662–63, 826.

21. Garlington, "Imputation or Union with Christ?" 66–67.

22. See Danker, "Foreword to the Revised Edition," in BDAG, viii; also Danker, Preface to the *Concise Greek-English Lexicon*, vi–vii..

to know the rules of employment of that expression."²³ In short, words have a base meaning outside of their contextualized usage otherwise we would not know how to employ them in the first place. Therefore, the less context dependent a word's meaning is—or the less that syntagmatic factors contribute to a word's (specialized) translation in context—the more likely the definition is "unmarked." The more context dependent the word is—that is, the more a word's translation in context depends on contributing syntagmatic factors—the more "marked" the definition is.²⁴

Now let us return to the lexical semantics of righteousness language in the biblical corpus. The first question we seek to answer is: What were the common (κοινή) or unmarked meanings of δικαιοσύνη as it was employed in Hellenistic and Greco-Roman discourse? Secondly, we ask: Does Paul's deployment of δικαιοσύνη and its cognates in his letters constitute a specialized usage? If the usage is specialized, then what contextual factors or (OT and Jewish) traditions inform Paul's redeployment of these terms? The importance of asking the first question before the second cannot be overemphasized. To paraphrase A.T. Robertson, Paul did not create his own "Holy Ghost" language when he wrote his letters.²⁵ New Testament Greek is not its own distinct dialect, nor is it a variety of Septuagintal Greek.²⁶ The language and vocabulary of Paul's letters are part of the conversational Greek that was common to the wider Mediterranean world from the time of Alexander the Great to the beginnings of the Byzantine empire.²⁷ Whatever specialized use of righteousness language Paul employed, he did so within the range of what δικαιοσύνη and its cognates commonly meant in the every day discourse of Greco-Roman society.

Likewise, Ziesler has also warned the New Testament exegete against disassociating Paul's use of the δικ(αιο)- lexemes too quickly from their Hellenistic and Roman contexts:

---

23. Ryle, "The Theory of Meaning," 143; which is quoted by Winger in *By What Law?*, 19.

24. Again, while I agree with Louw that a word's meaning(s) can only be determined when it is used in context (see Louw, *Semantics of New Testament Greek*, 40), certain definitions or semantic classifications are less context dependent than others. I am not talking about the presence or absence of syntagmatic factors contributing to lexical semantics as much as *the degree* to which syntagmatic factors add to, or redefine, lexical meaning. Semantic markedness or unmarkedness is a matter of degree, not a question of whether syntagmatic factors affect lexical meaning because, as Louw points out, they do. See the discussion on markedness by Lakoff, *Women, Fire and Dangerous Things*, 59–61; cf. Comrie, *Aspect*, 111–22.

25. Robertson, *A Grammar of the Greek New Testament*, 77–78.

26. Ibid.; Deissmann, *Light from the Ancient East*, 62–63.

27. Wallace, *Greek Grammar Beyond the Basics*, 18–30.

> Much is sometimes made of the view that the Greek meaning of these words [δίκαιος, κτλ.] is a barrier to correct understanding of St. Paul's meaning. If pressed, this means that Paul was quite incompetent in having used the words at all. There must have been effective points of contact . . . unless we are to assume that when the early Christians entered their assemblies or read their literature, they put away the normal association of words, and adopted another set.[28]

Following Ziesler's warning, I am weary against placing a false wedge between Paul's use of righteousness terms and "the normal associations of [these] words." Whatever modifications to righteousness language that Paul made, they would not be so radically different from their normal use that Paul would become incoherent in his letters. It makes logical sense then to map first the common meanings of the δικ(αιο)- word group before exploring Paul's in-context redeployment of δικ(αιο)- terms, since the normal associations of words provide boundaries for any Pauline modifications.

A POLYSEMOUS NETWORK FOR ΔΙΚ(ΑΙΟ)- LEXEMES IN GRECO-ROMAN DISCOURSE AND COMPARISONS WITH BDAG

In Chapter 1, we already answered the first question posed by this study (i.e., what are the common or unmarked meanings of δικαιοσύνη and its cognates in Greco-Roman discourse?). The κοινή meanings for each of the δικ(αιο)- lexemes have since been organized into an alternative set of semantic classifications. This alternative taxonomy of definitions is reprinted here in the table below. Along with these results, the definitions of δικαιοσύνη and its cognates according to BDAG are presented in the right column for a side-by-side comparison. Note that the bold typeface that is typical of BDAG has been removed for the sake of style, so that major semantic classifications and their specialized usages in context are distinguished by Arabic numerals vs. lettering. Formal equivalents (or English glosses) are rendered in normal italics.[29] This slight change in convention provides for a better framework of comparison with my alternative taxonomy.

---

28. Ziesler, *The Meaning of Righteousness in Paul*, 48–49; 47.

29. Note that some of the entries in BDAG have been abridged for the sake of space but the main semantic categories are represented here in full (1, 2, 3, etc.). Specialized cases (a, b, etc., or α, β, κτλ.) have been selectively cited (especially if the cases reflect an over-reliance on the LXX) or omitted (where they represent extraneous information that is irrelevant to this study). See BDAG, s.v. δίκαιος, 246–47; BDAG, s.v. δικαιοσύνη, 247–49; BDAG, s.v. δικαιόω, 249; BDAG, s.v. δίκη, 250.

Lexeme	Greco-Roman Semantic Classifications	BDAG
δίκαιος:	(A1): in accordance with the expectations, customs or decorum of the community; *right, fitting, appropriate, customary* (A2): in accordance to the rules or civic laws which govern society; *just, equitable, fair, lawful* (A2.1; as a substantive): the right to do something as guaranteed by law or custom; legal license or civic liberty; *right, freedom* (A2.2; as a substantive): punitive action; *punishment* (A3): in accordance to moral integrity; *righteous, upright, honest* (A4): judged in the right; *justified* unattested [[(A4.1): judged innocent; *acquitted; innocent; free*]]	(1) pertaining to being in accordance with high standards or rectitude, *upright, just, fair* (a) of humans (α) In Gr-Rom. tradition a δίκαιος person upholds the customs and norms of behavior . . . In keeping with OT tradition . . . δίκαιος like *tsaddiq* = conforming to the laws of God and people (β) of things relating to human beings . . . αἷμα δικαίου (Jo 4:19; La 4:13 = Pr 6:17 αἷμα δικαίον) *blood of an upright*, or better, *an innocent man* (b) of transcendent beings (α) God and deities are *just* or *fair* in their judgments (β) of Jesus who, as the ideal of an upright person, is called simply ὁ δίκαιος *the upright one* (2) obligatory in view of certain requirements of justice, *right, fair, equitable*

Lexeme	Greco-Roman Semantic Classifications	BDAG
δικαιοσύνη:	(N1): distributive justice (= the opposite of lawlessness); *justice, fairness; equitableness* (N2 just character; moral *uprightness; righteousness; honesty* (N3): act or state of setting something right; the administration of just order; the practice or exercise of justice; accomplishing social, civic and political orderliness; *rightifying activity, setting aright, putting to rights* (N4): juridicial justice; what the ruler or judge / lawcourt declares is just, fair, legal, and equitable; *justice, judgment, just verdict*	(1) the quality, state, or practice of judicial responsibility with a focus on fairness, *justice, equitableness, fairness* (2) quality or state of juridicial correctness with focus on redemptive action, *righteousness* [which includes:] – God's equitableness, displaying judicial integrity in contrast to human beings' wrath – In Pauline thought, God's δικαιοσύνη is pardoning action. On the one hand, a way of sharing God's character with believers (δ. θεοῦ = *righteousness bestowed by God*; Ro 1:17, 3:21f, 25, 26, 5:17, 10:3; 1 Cor 1:30; 2 Cor 5:21; 1QS 11, 9–15; 1QH 4, 30–37), then they exhibit righteousness in a moral sense. In this area, it closely approximates *salvation* (cp. Is 46:13, 51:5) (3) the quality or characteristic of upright behavior, *uprightness, righteousness*

Lexeme	Greco-Roman Semantic Classifications	BDAG
δικαιόω:	(V1): consider someone as having met the expectations and customs of the community; *deem right, regard as appropriate, consider fitting*; (passive) *be in the right* (V2): judge (as in the) right; *declare just; justify* rare (V2.1): verify as true; ratify; sanction unattested [[(V2.2) set free or liberate through a juridical process; *acquit, release*]] (V3): perform just actions; bring just order; *do justice* (for someone); *set right* rare (V3.1) see that someone got his / her rights recognized; *vindicate* (an innocent person) (V3.2) bring someone to justice; exercise punitive penalties; *punish; penalize; condemn* (a guilty person); *execute* rare? [(V4) make righteous; transform someone (into a just person); become (an) upright (person); *justify, transform, purify, deify*]	(1) to take up a legal cause, *show justice, do justice, take up a cause* (2) to render a favorable verdict, *vindicate* (a) as activities of humans *justify, vindicate, treat as just* (b) of experience or activity of transcendent figures, esp. in relation to humans (α) of wisdom (β) of God *be found in the right, be free of charges.* Esp. δικαιοῦθαι *be acquitted, be pronounced and treated as righteous*—Rom 3:20 (Ps 142:2), 24, 28; 4:2; 5:1; 8:30, 33 (Is 50:8); 1 Cor 4:4; Gal 2:16f (Ps 142:2); 3:11, 24; 5:4; Tit 3:7; Phil 3:12. Acquittal in conjunction with God's activity promoting uprightness in believers—Rom 3:24 (cf. Ex 23:7; Is 5:23), 26, 30; 8:30, 33 (Is 50:8); Gal 3:8 (3) to cause someone to be released from personal or institutional claims that are no longer to be considered pertinent or valid, *make free/pure* (Ps 72:13; Sir 26:29; TestSim 6:1; Ac 13:38; Rom 6:7), *become pure* (1 Cor 6:6), *become deified* (Herm. Wr. 13, 9) (4) to demonstrate to be morally right, *prove to be right*
δίκη:	(X1): castigation of a person for a crime or wrong done; *punishment, penalty* (X2): distributive *justice*; Justice (personified as a goddess)	(1) punishment meted out as legal penalty, *punishment, penalty* (2) *Justice* personified as a deity

An exhaustive comparison between the above two lexical taxonomies is not possible within the scope of this essay, but a few important remarks are warranted.

First, BDAG is at its best when it classifies any case where the meaning of a δικ(αιο)- lexeme depends on its Hebrew equivalent as a *specialized* usage that is uniquely Septuagintal. These entries include:

δίκαιος (1-a-α): "conforming to the laws of God and people" (like *tsaddiq*)

δίκαιος (1-a-β): "innocent" (Joel 4:19; Lam 4:13; Prov 6:17 LXX)

δικαιόω (2-b-β): "be found in the right," "be free of charges," "acquit" (e.g., Rom 3:20 [Ps 142:2]; Rom 3:24 [cf. Exod 23:7; Isa 5:23])

When these specialized Septuagint-dependent cases are compared to my alternative taxonomy, we find that they are either unattested (A4.1, V2.2) or rare (V2.1, V3.1) in Greco-Roman discourse. But the Septuagint does not make up definitions in a vacuum. While unattested or rare, the definition of δίκαιος as "innocent"—or δικαιόω as "acquit, be free of charges"—are nevertheless *possible* as polysemous extensions of existing major semantic classifications (A4, V2, V3) in my network. We simply do not find such usages *common* or *extant* in Greco-Roman literature. As long as BDAG categorizes any semantic classification dependent on the Septuagint as a *specialized* case, its taxonomy finds many important parallels with mine.

However, BDAG becomes problematic when it labels specialized Septuagintal usages as *major* semantic classifications. Most troublesome are its definition (2) for δικαιοσύνη and definition (3) for δικαιόω. For the former, BDAG's most detailed and longest entry for δικαιοσύνη has no subcategories or subset definitions. Each citation is an example of the main semantic classification in operation which defines δικαιοσύνη [definition (2)] as a "quality or state of juridical correctness with focus on redemptive action" and renders its formal equivalent as *righteousness*. Relying upon several Septuagintal and Qumranic texts, as well as modern lexical studies by Reumann, Käsemann, and others,[30] BDAG creates a definition of δικαιοσύνη that is soteriologically framed. BDAG argues that for Pauline thought, δικαιοσύνη (especially God's) "closely approximates salvation."[31] I will make the case below in the next section that this definition (2) in BDAG should not stand as an unmarked semantic classification, nor a major one, but is marked and highly specialized. That Paul understands δικαιοσύνη as equivalent to salvation is a thesis to be argued for, subject to debate, not a definition to be

---

30. See BDAG, s.v. δικαιοσύνη, 247–48 for additional citations from the LXX and other Jewish literature not reprinted in the above table. See there also studies in addition to Reumann and Käsemann on which BDAG depends.

31. Ibid., 247.

readily incorporated in our standard lexicons. Much depends on how convinced a person is of Paul's use of select Septuagintal texts to remap the unmarked meanings of δικαιοσύνη and its cognates along soteriological lines.

Concerning BDAG's definition (3) for δικαιόω as *make free, purify*, and even *deify*, I have made the case in Chapter 1 that this semantic classification is virtually non-extant. Yet again, BDAG categorizes it as a major definition based on its marked use in Ps 72:13 LXX, Sir 26:29, *T. Sim.* 6:1, and (the very late) *Corp. herm.* 13.9. While it might be the case that the ethical use of the verb is possible for Rom 6:7, this usage is specialized and should *not* constitute a major semantic category on par with its other polysemous definitions.

To summarize, what is striking about BDAG is its overdependence on the Septuagint for some of its major semantic categories. I believe this overdependence to be a methodological mistake. It confuses context with meaning. In the next section, I apply my alternative taxonomy of δικ(αιο)-lexemes to Paul's redeployment of these same terms in his letters. It is my hope that this alternative lexicon for the δικ(αιο)- word group will provide one path through the current impasse in the justification debate among Pauline scholars.

A PROLEGOMENON TO PAUL: SKETCHING POSSIBILITIES IN ROM 3:21-26

We are now ready to address the second question of our study: compared to their κοινή usage, how does Paul redeploy the δικ(αιο)- lexemes in his letters (if at all), and what intertexts (OT and Jewish) inform Paul's specialized meanings of these terms?

In what follows, my goal is not to argue for a particular reading of Paul, but demonstrate that both traditional or Lutheran ways of interpreting Pauline vocabulary on justification, as well as New Perspective or Post-New Perspective ways, can be mapped according to the polysemous network argued for in Chapter 1 (and reprinted above). A good place to sketch the possibilities for Paul's use of righteousness language is Rom 3:21-26. Laato, in rearticulating a traditional Lutheran or Old Perspective interpretation of the text, has argued for the following translation. Note below that the semantic classification of each δικ(αιο)- lexeme is identified in parentheses and the resulting translation is also shown in italics.

> 21 But now *God's own righteousness* [δικαιοσύνη θεοῦ; (N2/N3? with θεοῦ as the possessive genitive], apart from the Law, has been made known, to which the Law and the Prophets testify:

> 22 that is, *the righteous status granted by God* [δικαιοσύνη θεοῦ; (N4) with θεοῦ as the objective genitive] through faith in Jesus Christ for all who believe. There is no difference,
>
> 23 for all have sinned and fall short of the glory of God,
>
> 24 and *are declared just*, freely by his grace [δικαιούμενοι (V2) δωρεὰν τῇ αὐτοῦ χάριτι], through the redemption that came by Christ Jesus.
>
> 25 God presented him as an atoning sacrifice through faith in his blood. He did this *as a demonstration of his distributive justice* [εἰς ἔνδειξιν τῆς δικαιοσύνης αὐτοῦ (N1)] because in his forbearance he had left the sins committed beforehand unpunished.
>
> 26 He did it to demonstrate *his justice* [δικαιοσύνης αὐτοῦ (N1)] at the present time, so as to be *just* [δίκαιον; in his judgments (A2)] and *the one who declares just* [δικαιοῦντα (V2)] those who have faith in Jesus.[32]

Laato's translation is a thoroughly forensic reading of Paul. According to Laato, Paul begins his description of justification in Rom 3:21–26 with a general understanding of δικαιοσύνη θεοῦ in v. 21 as "God's own righteousness," where θεοῦ is a possessive genitive and δικαιοσύνη is defined by the semantic classification (N2) as the "just character" or "moral uprightness" of God. As Laato says, "it can be stated that the concept of 'God's righteousness' [δικαιοσύνη θεοῦ] comprises centrally the notion of God's *own* righteousness. He is just. There is no iniquity in him."[33] Piper has similarly argued that δικαιοσύνη θεοῦ is God's righteous character but more narrowly as the inviolable nature of God to act for his name's sake and bring glory to himself.[34]

Yet Laato also goes on to claim: "It is not merely that he is righteous. He also creates righteousness. This is his saving *action* . . . righteousness and salvation are synonymous concepts . . . God's righteousness and his saving action are seen as parallel."[35] There seems to be some categorical confusion with this last statement. On one hand, Laato's qualifying remarks concerning θεοῦ as the possessive genitive correlates best with the interpretation

---

32. Laato, "God's Righteousness," 48–54. I have made a few modifications to Laato's translation in order to conform the translation to the polysemous network outlined in the previous section, while to the best of my ability preserving the substance of his arguments in his essay.

33. Ibid., 50; italics added.

34. Piper, "The Demonstration of the Righteousness of God," 2–32.; Piper, *The Justification of God*, 100, 140–47.

35. Laato, "God's Righteousness," 50; italics added.

of δικαιοσύνη as (N2): God's righteous character. Yet his understanding of this same righteousness as God's saving *action* would define it not under the semantic classification (N2) but rather (N3) as "the actions or active administration of someone to set something right or in just order."

Thus Laato appears to affirm that δικαιοσύνη θεοῦ is both God's character and activity, but our current lexicons lack a semantic classification to incorporate both senses.[36] The problem cannot be resolved by reference to the genitival θεοῦ. Wright, for example, in his discussion of the subjective and possessive genitive use of θεοῦ, concludes that while "the two [subjective and possessive genitive uses] shade into one another," they are nevertheless "still clearly distinguishable" so the interpreter must choose which is operative in any given text.[37] Yet Laato's struggle to define δικαιοσύνη as both attribute and action should not be dismissed as a misnomer. Wright himself has admitted the meanings "shade into one another," and other scholars have made similar observations. According to Moo, if the interpreter does not assume that divine attributes are ontological but rather experiential (that is, God's character is what Israel experiences when God acts on their behalf), then δικαιοσύνη θεοῦ can be called an "experienced attribute," that is, a reference to God's disposition to do what is right, establish right, and as a by-product of this activity put his people (in the) right.[38] While Moo makes his argument from Old Testament texts, I have argued for a similar category from Greco-Roman discourse without having to appeal to special Septuagintal usage.

My point, then, is that semantic classification (N3) explains Paul's use of δικαιοσύνη in v. 21. Definition (N3) focuses on the action of the agent to set something aright but also carries with it a sense of a practiced virtue. Texts outlined in Chapter 1 from Musonius Rufus, Plutarch, Diogenes Laertius, and Augustus Caesar demonstrate a semantic overlap between doing justice and being just, between one's just character and the demonstration of it by establishing a just order, between being right and making something right. Laato and Moo (and to a lesser degree, Wright) have opted for the possessive genitive to emphasize the character of God as the impetus for his actions. Other scholars (as Käsemann, Stuhlmacher, Wright in the main, Bird, and Campbell, to name just a few), however, understand θεοῦ as the subjective genitive to highlight the actions of God, which—in

---

36. Cf. BDAG, s.v. δικαιοσύνη, 247–49. Perhaps BDAG's definition 2: "quality or state of juridical correctness with focus on redemptive action" is the closest to my definition (n3), but the differences are acute primarily because BDAG focuses on the state or effect of the action, rather than the process or activity itself.

37. Wright, *Justification*, 65.

38. Moo, *The Epistle to Romans*, 84.

turn—demonstrate his character.³⁹ Both groups, in my opinion, make use of the same definition of δικαιοσύνη (N3).⁴⁰

However, in order for Paul to push the semantics of δικαιοσύνη (N3) beyond the act of setting something right socially or politically and modify it to mean *saving* action, there needs to be an intertextual or contextual syntagm that extends the base meaning of δικαιοσύνη. Laato has thus argued that the intertextual ties of Rom 3:21–26 (and 1:16–17) with Ps 98:1–5 (LXX) enable Paul to reinterpret δικαιοσύνη as saving and restorative.⁴¹ Without having stated it explicitly, Laato has effectively argued that the syntagms in the biblical text (i.e., in this case, the intertextual echoes of Ps 98:1–5 and other Isaianic texts where the concepts of "salvation" and "righteousness" are juxtaposed)⁴² have extended the semantic classification of δικαιοσύνη (N3) to mean more than the active administration of just order but the actions of God to arrange salvation for those who believe.

Equating salvation and righteousness as virtually synonymous terms is not an argument original to Laato. Other scholars (mentioned above) have made the same case, but they have turned to a different set of echoes and see Paul deploying them in different ways to produce alternative definitions for δικαιοσύνη θεοῦ. The most famous example is Käsemann and his understanding of δικαιοσύνη θεοῦ as God's apocalyptic power to recreate the fallen cosmos (including humanity).⁴³ Stuhlmacher has since further reinforced Käsemann's apocalyptic arguments by providing his own intertextual analysis of 1 QS 11.12–15, 4 *Ezra* 8:34–36, and Dan 9:16–28.⁴⁴

Wright, like Käsemann and Stuhlmacher, interprets δικαιοσύνη θεοῦ as δικαιοσύνη (N3) with the subjective genitive θεοῦ but removes the phrase, in part, from its specifically cosmic or creational framework. For Wright, God is about "putting to rights" what is wrong with our world, but God does it

---

39. Käsemann, "God's Righteousness in Paul," 100–10; Stuhlmacher, *Paul's Letter to the Romans*, 31–32; Wright, *What Saint Paul Really Said*, 100–103; Wright, *Justification*, 65, 178–81; Bird, *The Saving Righteousness of God*, 12–18; Campbell, *The Deliverance of God*, 687–88.

40. I should note here that Moo might possibly consider his definition of δικαιοσύνη closer to (n2) than (n3). But given his understanding of God's righteous character as an "experienced attribute," I think the classification which best encapsulates this experiential component is (n3). Clearly, however, Piper's definition of God's righteous character is better categorized as (n2), while Laato's juxtaposition of righteousness with salvation, or salvific activity, falls firmly under (n3).

41. Ibid., 46–48.

42. Ibid., 48. Laato cites Isa 46:13; 51:5–8; 56:1, 62:1; cf. 54:17; 61:10–11.

43. Käsemann, "Justification and Salvation History," 77n27; Käsemann, "God's Righteousness in Paul," 100–110.

44. Stuhlmacher, *Revisiting Paul's Doctrine of Justification*, 18–20.

by fulfilling his covenantal promises to Israel since the fulfillment of these promises include a plan for all humanity to experience his salvation. Reread through this covenantal framework (outlined in Deut 30 and Dan 9), Wright's definition of δικαιοσύνη θεοῦ as "the faithfulness of God" is possible if one sees Paul taking the basic definition δικαιοσύνη as "setting something right" but that "something," by use of intertextual echoes (e.g., Hab 2:4; Gen 15:6; cf. Ps 143:1–2), has been modified to mean explicitly God's covenantal relations with Israel.[45]

Campbell, on the other hand, employs a different set of intertextual echoes (i.e., texts from the Psalms, Isaiah, and 1 Kings which speak of the "right actions" taken by the king) to modify the subjective genitive reading of δικαιοσύνη θεοῦ to mean "the liberating, life-giving, eschatological act of God," or simply "the deliverance of God."[46]

I could go further, but it suffices to say: each of these scholars understands δικαιοσύνη θεοῦ on the whole to be Paul's umbrella term for "saving righteousness" (*iustitia salutifera*) but depending on *which* intertextual echoes and *how* the echoes are interpreted,[47] there is a diversity of opinion on how Paul extends and modifies the meaning of δικαιοσύνη (N3) and redeploys the term in his articulation of the gospel. In the remaining space of this essay, I will treat the rest of Rom 3:21–26 in brief, showing how my polysemous network categorizes Laato's and other scholars' interpretation of the remaining δικ(αιο)- lexemes.

According to Laato, Paul had previously introduced God's own righteousness in 1:17, and here in 3:21–26 sets out to explain more precisely how that righteousness has been revealed in the Christ event. For Laato, God's righteous character is at stake and when it is finally revealed, it takes on a particular form as "the righteous status granted by God," the second use of δικαιοσύνη (N4) in the passage, but with θεοῦ as an objective genitive (v. 22).[48] While I prefer to identify the θεοῦ as the genitive of origin, i.e., "the righteous status or declaration which comes from God," this is a minor criticism. More important is the specifically juridical context which

---

45. Wright, *Justification*, 57–71; also Gorman, *Inhabiting the Cruciform God*, 52–57.

46. Campbell, *The Deliverance of God*, 687–88; 690–700.

47. The different possible OT parallels for Paul's use of righteousness language are summed up well by Moo, *The Epistle to the Romans*, 81–86, who maps out when δικαιοσύνη is synonymous with salvation (e.g., Psalm 51:14; Isaiah 46:13), when it is an aspect of a gift or right standing experienced by the recipient (e.g., Psalm 25:27–28; 51:14), when it is not God's saving activity but the motivation behind his saving actions for his people (e.g., Psalm 31:1), when δικαιοσύνη is God's distributive justice (Psalm 119:7, 62, 106, 160, 54), and when it means God's vindication of his people (e.g., Daniel 9:17–19).

48. Laato, "God's Righteousness," 53.

accounts for Laato's thoroughly forensic reading of vv. 22–26. Laato and others have noted several contextual clues in Rom 3 that connote lawcourt proceedings.[49] Though not exact with what I have listed from the Greco-Roman juridicial texts (see Observation 6 in Chapter 1), I, too, think the following syntagms cannot be missed in Rom 3: judge/judgment (κρίνω [3X], vv. 4, 6–7; κρίμα, v. 8), law (νόμος [11X], v. 19, 20, 21, 27, 28, 31), witness (μαρτυρέω, v. 21), accuse (προαιτιάομαι, v. 9), pardon/clemency (πάρεσις, v. 25; ἀνοχή, v. 26), and release/redemption (ἀπολύτρωσις, v. 24). Fitzmyer adds βλασφημέω in v. 8 by translating it as "defame with a libelous charge."[50]

Recall that in Observation 6, I noted that when juridical contexts are clearly marked by syntagmatic factors in Greco-Roman discourse, the forensic meanings of the δικ(αιο)- group override their social and legal senses. Given this juridicial context, Laato has defined the second use of δικαιοσύνη in v. 22 as (N4): "what the ruler or judge/lawcourt declares is just, fair, legal, and equitable," and with the objective genitive (or better, the genitive of origin) this declaration comes from God as *the* Judge over all creation. Laato goes on to provide a thoroughly forensic reading of Paul: God could have meted out justice-fairness with a vengeance for sins committed beforehand, but God chose not to. Instead God demonstrated his *distributive justice* (N1) [δικαιοσύνης αὐτοῦ (2X), vv. 25, 26] and proved himself *just in his judgments* (A2) [δίκαιον, v. 26], not by condemning sinners but by presenting Christ as an atoning sacrifice for sin. He paved the way for sinful humanity to be *declared just* (V2) [δικαιούμενοι / δικαιοῦντα, vv. 24, 26] and in right relations with himself.

There have been both modifications and objections to the traditional (Lutheran and Reformed) readings of Rom 3:21–26, here epitomized by Laato's interpretation above. These alternative readings, however, have had to either qualify or explain away the clearly juridical context of the passage. Wright, for example, qualifies the lawcourt context of Rom 3 by arguing that the juridicial proceedings must be set within the covenantal relations of God with Israel.[51] Campbell makes a distinction between the forensic-retributive (or juridicial) language which describes the just verdicts of the judge vs. the forensic-nonretributive (or liberative) language which describes the righteous actions taken by the king.[52] For Campbell, it is the latter executive actions of the king that provide the immediate context of translating δικαιόω

---

49. Ibid., 45–46; Wright, *What Saint Paul Really Said*, 96–99; 105–10. Note especially the translation provided by Fitzmyer, *Romans*, 324, 333, 341.

50. Fitzmyer, *Romans*, 324.

51. Wright, *What Saint Paul Really Said*, 96–99; 105–10.

52. Campbell, *The Deliverance of God*, 658–65.

not as "declare in the right" (V2) but rather as "set right" (V3) which, by use of his intertextual echoes with the Psalter (e.g., Psalms 17 and 18; 5, 7, 10, 12, 16), can be semantically extended to mean "liberate," or "set free."[53]

I myself have a few qualifications to make concerning traditional readings on Paul, but for the sake of space, I only mention one of them here.[54] As noted above, in a juridicial setting, δικαιόω (V2) means "declare just; judge (as in the) right; justify." However, this is not the same as "acquit," (V2.2) or "vindicate (an innocent person)" (V3.1), the former of which is unattested, and the latter rare in the Greco-Roman discourse. In fact, the cases when the semantics of δικαιόω are extended, Greco-Roman writers often employ the verb *in negativae* to mean "punish" or "penalize" (V3.2), but not "acquit" or "release." Yet many exegetes clearly understand δικαιόω as acquittal or vindication in vv. 25–26.[55] While this interpretation is possible, it does require an appeal to Septuagintal usage. In Hebrew, the verb *tsadaq* can mean "acquit" (e.g., Exod 23:7; Deut 25:1; Job 11:2; 13:18; 1 Kgs 8:32; 2 Chr 6:23; Isa 50:8)[56] and "vindicate" (e.g., Ps 51:4 = Ps 50:6 LXX),[57] and so if an intertextual echo can be demonstrated (typically Ps 50:6 LXX quoted in Rom 3:5), then it could be argued that Paul's use of δικαιόω is a special case where he redeploys the word in the opposite direction of what a Greco-Roman reader would have expected: that is, instead of God's justification-punishment (V3.2) of the sinner, he justifies-acquits (V2.2) the ungodly on the basis of Christ's redeeming work (Rom 3:23–24; cf. 4:5).[58]

However, there are other possibilities for understanding how Paul redeploys the verb δικαιόω. The most difficult to defend is VanLandingham's, who interprets δικαιόω as definition (V4): "make righteous; transform someone (into a just person); become (an) upright (person)."[59] As discussed above, this is arguably a non-existent, hypothetical definition that represents a semantic gap in my polysemous network of δικ(αιο)- lexemes. While the network anticipates that definition (V4) *should be* attested in Greco-Roman literature, it is not, unless we were to depend on the problematic text *Corp. herm.* 13.9, which VanLandingham interestingly enough cites as support.[60]

---

53. Ibid., 663; 666–67; 690–94.

54. Another qualification: I prefer to translate δωρεάν in v. 24 as "as a gift" rather than "freely."

55. Moo, *The Epistle to the Romans*, 74; Dunn, *Romans 1–8*, 179–80.

56. Scullion, "Righteousness: Old Testament," 726–27.

57. Reumann, "Righteousness: New Testament," 766.

58. Ziesler, *The Meaning of Righteousness in Paul*, 47.

59. VanLandingham, *Judgment and Justification*, 320.

60. Ibid., 320n281.

His main argument is based on the causative hiphil *hitsdiq* translated by the Septuagint as δικαιόω (particularly Ps 72:13 LXX; cf. *T. Sim.* 6:1; Sir 26:29) but even VanLandingham says: "Admittedly, δικαιόω does not often have this sense."[61] While I believe that the *concept* of justification includes the process of transformation, the *words* of the δικ(αιο)- group do not necessarily include the semantic component of transformation. The transformation language comes elsewhere from Paul.

A better alternative for understanding the verb δικαιόω is to keep its original forensic meaning as "declare just; judge (as in the) right; justify," but not overly extend its definition to mean "acquit" or "vindicate," and instead think of the declaration as a kind of speech-act, what Peter Leithart has coined as a "deliverdict," where the word of declaration by God *does something* to the recipient.[62] The verb δικαιόω still denotes a verdict or declaration, but it is a verdict by God which, like the creating word in Genesis, changes reality. For Paul, the declaration that someone is just or (in the) right transfers the person who has faith from the dominion of sin to the dominion of God. Within the sphere of God's dominion, we are united with Christ by the Spirit and it is our union with Christ, who is righteousness (1 Cor. 1:30), that conveys to the believer a righteous status before God. Bird has called this model of justification "incorporated righteousness," or less elegantly as "the progressive Reformed view."[63] It has been known more widely among systematic theologians as the "union-in-Christ" model. Stephen Chester, Todd Billings, and the Finnish school on the "new Luther" have argued that the forensic and participationist categories this model weds together finds its support in both Luther's and Calvin's exegesis of the Pauline letters.[64]

The exegetical basis for the "union-in-Christ" model is a project worth exploring further as part of a larger study on Paul's righteousness language throughout his letters. For now, however, I simply note that in the examples cited above, whether it is the traditional readings by Laato, or Post-New Perspective interpretations by Campbell, all can be framed within the polysemous network outlined from the literature of the Greco-Roman world. In Rom 3:21–26, within the span of just six verses, Paul has used δικαιοσύνη

---

61. Ibid., 320.

62. Leithart, *The Baptized Body*, 75–76.

63. Bird, "Progressive Reformed View," 131–57; Bird, *The Saving Righteousness of God*, 60–87.

64. See Chester, *Righteousness in Christ*. I am grateful to Stephen for letting me read a draft of his chapter on Calvin prior to its prospective publication in 2014/15 with Eerdmans Press. See also Billings, *Calvin, Participation, and the Gift*, 14–23, 28–63; and Mannermaa, *Christ Present in Faith*, 39–42; 49–61.

(and its cognates δίκαιος and δικαιόω) several different ways as God's saving righteousness (N3), as distributive justice (N1), as God's righteous character or integrity (N2), as a forensic declaration (A2 / N4 / V2), and as the divine action which places the forgiven sinner in right relations with God (V3). The polysemous network outlines what readings are unmarked and marked. Where a New Testament scholar asserts a definition that is rarely attested (or unattested) in Greco-Roman discourse, the burden of proof falls on the exegete to show what intertextual or contextual syntagms are present in the biblical text that account for Paul's specialized redeployment of the δικ(αιο)- lexical group.

CONCLUSION AND PROSPECTUS

I began this two-part work by challenging Hill's 1967 thesis. According to Hill, the Greek words used by the writers of the New Testament have Hebrew meanings due to their dependence on Septuagintal echoes. It should be readily apparent now that Hill's thesis is overstated, and the NT writers' dependence on the Septuagint has been exaggerated by subsequent scholarship. Paul's use of the δικ(αιο)- word group fits well within the semantic range of the polysemous network outlined in the literature of the wider Greco-Roman world. Even Paul's modifications to the meanings of these terms by use of the Septuagint translation of *tsedaqah* / *tsedeq* demonstrate not unattested random usages but rather marked extensions of existing definitions. More rarely, *if* Paul does generate an unattested usage [e.g., δικαιόω (V4): "make righteous"], he does not do so haphazardly but fills in semantic gaps that have been anticipated from existing semantic classifications.

This essay not only illustrates the importance of remapping current semantic classifications for the δικ(αιο)- word group found in lexicons like BDAG, but it also sets the stage for a future study on Paul's (re)deployment of these terms throughout his letters. The prolegomenon on Rom 3:21–26 has hopefully illustrated that more precise lexical definitions can serve as a gauge to evaluate the diverse positions of scholars in the current justification debate by distinguishing between core definitions and syntagmatic factors. Even with a limited initial sounding in Romans, it is clear that Paul's vocabulary operated within the polysemous network of common (κοινή) Greek and yet his encyclopedic knowledge of the Septuagint also functioned to extend this network. It remains to be seen how Paul remaps the δικ(αιο)- lexemes for the rest of Romans and his other letters.

BIBLIOGRAPHY

Barr, James. *The Semantics of the Biblical Language*. Oxford: Oxford University Press, 1961. Reprint, London: SCM, 1983.

Beker, J. C. *Paul the Apostle: The Triumph of God in Life and Thought*. Philadelphia: Fortress, 1980.

Billings, J. Todd. *Calvin, Participation, and the Gift: The Activity of Believers in Union with Christ*. Oxford: Oxford University Press, 2007.

Bird, Michael. "Progressive Reformed View." In *Justification: Five Views*, ed. J. K. Beilby and P. R. Eddy, 60–87. Downers Grove, IL: IVP Academic, 2011.

———. *The Saving Righteousness of God: Studies on Paul, Justification, and the New Perspective*. Paternoster Biblical Monographs. Eugene, OR: Wipf and Stock, 2007.

Bruckner, James. "Justice in Scripture." *Ex Auditu* 22 (2006) 17–25.

Bultmann, Rudolf. *The Theology of the New Testament*. Trans. K. Grobel. New York: Scribner, 1951–1955. Reprint, Waco: Baylor University Press, 2007.

Campbell, Douglas. *The Deliverance of God: An Apocalyptic Rereading of Justification in Paul*. Grand Rapids: Eerdmans, 2009.

Chester, Stephen. *Righteousness in Christ: Paul, the Reformers, and the New Perspective*. Grand Rapids: Eerdmans, forthcoming 2014/15.

Comrie, Bernard. *Aspect*. Cambridge Textbooks in Linguistics. Cambridge: Cambridge University Press, 1976.

Cremer, Hermann. *Die paulinische Rechtfertigungslehre im Zusammenhange ihrer geschichtlichen Voraussetzungen*. Gütersloh: Bertelsmann, 1899.

Cruse, D. A. *Lexical Semantics*. Cambridge Textbooks in Linguistics. New York: Cambridge University Press, 1986.

Danker, Frederick. *The Concise Greek-English Lexicon of the New Testament*. Chicago: University of Chicago Press, 2009.

Deissmann, Adolf. *Light from the Ancient East*. Trans. L. R. M. Strachan. New York: Doran, 1927.

Dunn, James. *Romans 1–8*. Vol. 1. WBC 38A. Dallas: Word, 1988.

Fitzmyer, Joseph. *Romans*. AB 33. New York: Doubleday, 1992.

Garlington, Don. "Imputation or Union with Christ: A Response to John Piper?" *Reformation and Revival Journal* 12, no. 4 (2003) 45–113.

Geeraerts, Dirk. *Theories of Lexical Semantics*. Oxford Linguistics. New York: Oxford: Oxford University Press, 2010.

Gorman, Michael. *Inhabiting the Cruciform God: Kenosis, Justification, and Theosis in Paul's Narrative Soteriology*. Grand Rapids: Eerdmans, 2009.

Hill, David. *Greek Words and Hebrew Meanings: Studies in the Semantics of Soteriological Terms*. SNTSMS 5. Cambridge: Cambridge University Press, 1967.

Jamison, Leland. "*Dikaiosyne* in the Usage of Paul." *Journal of Bible and Religion* 21, no. 2 (1953) 93–99.

Jüngel, Ebehard. *Justification: The Heart of the Christian Faith*. Trans. J. F. Cayzer. Edinburgh: T. & T. Clark, 2001.

Käsemann, Ernst. "God's Righteousness in Paul." In *The Bultmann School of Biblical Interpretation: New Directions?*, ed. James Robinson et al., 100–110. Trans. W. F. Bunge. Journal for Theology and Church 1. New York: Harper & Row, 1965.

———. "Justification and Salvation History in the Epistle to the Romans." In *Perspectives on Paul*, 60–78. Trans. M. Kohl. Philadelphia: Fortress, 1971.

Laato, Timo. "'God's Righteousness'—Once Again." In *The Nordic Paul: Finnish Approaches to Pauline Theology*, ed. Lars Aejmelaeus and Antti Mustakallio, 40–73. LNTS 374. New York: T. & T. Clark, 2008.

Lakoff, George. *Women, Fire and Dangerous Things: What Categories Reveal about the Mind.* Chicago: University of Chicago Press, 1987.

Lane, Anthony N.S. *Justification by Faith in Catholic-Protestant Dialogue: An Evangelical Assessment.* London: T. & T. Clark, 2002.

Leithart, Peter. *The Baptized Body.* Moscow: Canon, 2007.

Louw, Johannes P. *Semantics of New Testament Greek.* Atlanta: Scholars, 1982.

Lyons, John. *Semantics.* 2 vols. Cambridge: Cambridge University Press, 1977.

Mannermaa, Tuomo. *Christ Present in Faith: Luther's View of Justification.* Ed. Kirsi Stjerna. Minneapolis: Fortress, 2005.

Martyn, J. Louis. *Galatians.* AB 33A. New Haven: Yale University Press, 1997. Reprint, 2004.

Moo, Douglas. *The Epistle to the Romans.* NICNT. Grand Rapids: Eerdmans, 1996.

Murphy, M. Lynne. *Lexical Meaning.* Cambridge Textbooks in Linguistics. New York: Cambridge University Press, 2010.

Piper, John. "The Demonstration of the Righteousness of God in Romans 3.25, 26." *JSNT* 7 (1980) 2–32.

———. *The Future of Justification: A Response to N.T. Wright.* Wheaton, IL: Crossway, 2007.

———. *The Justification of God: An Exegetical and Theological Study of Romans 9:1–23.* Grand Rapids: Baker, 1983.

Reumann, John. *"Righteousness" in the New Testament: "Justification" in the United States Lutheran-Roman Catholic Dialogue.* With responses by Joseph Fitzmyer and Jerome Quinn. Philadelphia: Fortress, 1982.

———. "Righteousness: New Testament." In *ABD* 5:745–73.

Robertson, A. T. *A Grammar of the Greek New Testament in the Light of Historical Research.* Nashville: Broadman, 1934.

Ryle, Gilbert. "The Theory of Meaning." In *Philosophy and Ordinary Language*, ed. C. E. Caton, 128–53. Urbana: University of Illinois Press, 1963.

Scullion, J. J. "Righteousness: Old Testament." In *ABD* 5:724–36.

Seifrid, Mark. "Paul's Use of Righteousness Language against its Hellenistic Background." In *Justification and Variegated Nomism*, ed. by D. A. Carson et al., 2:39–74. Grand Rapids: Baker Academic, 2004.

———. "Righteousness Language in the Hebrew Scriptures and Early Judaism." *Justification and Variegated Nomism*, ed. D. A. Carson et al., 1:415–42. Grand Rapids: Baker Academic, 2001.

Stuhlmacher, Peter. *Gerechtigkeit Gottes bei Paulus.* Göttingen: Vanderhoeck & Ruprecht, 1965.

———. *Paul's Letter to the Romans: A Commentary.* Trans. Scott J. Hafemann. Louisville: Westminster John Knox, 1994.

———. *Revisiting Paul's Doctrine of Justification: A Challenge to the New Perspective.* Trans. D. P. Bailey. With an essay by D. A. Hagner. Downers Grove, IL: IVP Academic, 2001.

Taylor, John R. *Cognitive Grammar.* Oxford Textbooks in Linguistics. New York: Oxford: Oxford University Press, 2010.

VanLandingham, Chris. *Judgment and Justification in Early Judaism and the Apostle Paul.* Peabody, MA: Hendrickson, 2006.

Wallace, Daniel. *Greek Grammar Beyond the Basics: An Exegetical Syntax of the New Testament.* Grand Rapids: Zondervan, 1996.

Way, David. *The Lordship of Christ: Ernst Käsemann's Interpretation of Paul's Theology.* Oxford: Clarendon, 1991.

Winger, Michael. *By What Law? The Meaning of* Νόμος *in the Letters of Paul.* SBLDS 128. Atlanta: Scholars, 1992.

Wright, N. T. *Justification: God's Plan and Paul's Vision.* Downers Grove, IL: IVP Academic, 2009.

———. *What Saint Paul Really Said: Was Paul of Tarsus the Real Founder of Christianity.* Grand Rapids: Eerdmans, 1997.

Ziesler, John. *The Meaning of Righteousness in Paul: A Linguistic and Theological Inquiry.* SNTSMS 20. Cambridge: Cambridge University Press, 1972.

3

The Occasion and Purpose of Romans Revisited[1]

HAE-KYUNG CHANG

INTRODUCTION

The Letter to Rome is marked not only by its past influence upon the formation of Christian theology, but also by its present impetus toward new research. Most research on Romans is concerned with its content. Its content is, however, organically related to the circumstances that occasioned this letter. Concerning Romans, the introductory questions about "when," "where," and "by whom" it was written have never been controversial. Nobody doubts that Paul wrote it in AD 56 or 57 from Corinth or somewhere nearby, while planning his final voyage to Jerusalem with the intention of going on thereafter to Rome and thence to Spain. But the question "why" is nowhere in the letter explicitly answered, and it has been an ongoing source of controversy in the so-called "Romans debate" for the past two centuries.[2]

---

1. This article was originally published in the journal *Korean Evangelical New Testament Studies* (2013) under the title: "Occasion and Purpose of Romans: Reflected in Its Distinctive Features." I am grateful to the editors of *KENTS* for permission to reprint this essay here in a revised form.

2. In 1991, Donfried, in the *Romans Debate*, brought together twenty-three essays by twenty authors discussing this issue. In addition to these, see also Baur, "Über Zweck

The present essay aims to review this debate in light of a growing tendency toward certain agreement in some of the most recent studies on Romans. First, it begins with an overview of the latest discussions on this topic, gathering up some vital points on which there seems to be an emerging general consensus. Then, on the basis of the results of this agreement, it will proceed to examine five distinctive features of Romans in the opening (1:1–15) and closing (15:14—16:27) sections of the letter, as well as the major body (1:16–15:13), in order to ascertain how each feature contributes toward the reconstruction of the letter's purpose(s).

MAJOR TRENDS AND OUTCOMES IN RECENT STUDIES

Why did Paul send such a heavy "tractate letter"[3] to the Christians of Rome who were mostly unknown to him? Numerous suggestions have been made in response to this question, and these suggestions can be classified into various categories.[4] Jervis, for example, groups the proposed solutions as follows: The purpose of Romans is: (1) "theological," stemming from Paul's desire to explain his gospel, perhaps in the light of his forthcoming trip to Jerusalem; (2) "missionary," stemming from Paul's concern about the extension of his missionary work; and (3) "pastoral," to set right certain errors either of doctrine or behavior among the Roman Christians.[5] Kruse also divides the various proposals into three groups but differently. He sees the proponents' views on the purpose(s) of Romans as either focusing on (1) a

---

und Veranlassung," 59–178; Grafe, *Über Veranlassung und Zweck des Römerbriefes*; Smith, "Address and Destination," 1–21; Drummond, "Occasion and Object," 787–804; MacRoy, "Occasion and Object," 21–32; Harder, "Der konkrete Anlass des Römerbriefes," 13–24; Schrenk, "Der Römerbrief als Missionsdokument," 81–106; Wood, "Purpose of Romans," 211–19; Minear, *Obedience of Faith*; Williams, "Paul's Purpose," 62–67; Suhl, "Der konkrete Anlass des Römerbriefes," 119–30; Wilckens, "Über Abfassungszweck und Aufbau des Römerbriefes," 110–70; Campbell, "Why Did Paul Write Romans?," 14–24; Campbell, "Romans Debate," 19–28; Kettunen, *Der Abfassungszweck des Römerbriefes*; Drane, "Why did Paul Write Romans?," 208–27; Jewett, "Romans as an Ambassadorial Letter," 5–20; Russell, "Alternative Suggestion," 174–88. Since 1991, other relevant works include: Smiga, "Romans 12:1–2 and 15:30–32," 257–73; Haacker, "Der Römerbrief als Friedensmemorandum," 25–41; Jervis, *Purpose of Romans*; Wedderburn, *Reasons for Romans*; Weima, "Preaching the Gospel in Rome," 337–66; Miller, *Obedience of Faith*; Gaventa, "'To Preach the Gospel,'" 179–95.

3. Carson et al., *Introduction*, 248.

4. So Dunn, *Romans 1–8*, liv–lviii, and others. For an older classification, cf. Guthrie, *New Testament Introduction*, 397–400, who introduced five different views on the purpose of Romans: (1) polemical; (2) conciliatory; (3) doctrinal; (4) to sum up Paul's present experience; and (5) to meet the immediate needs of the readers.

5. Jervis, *Purpose of Romans*, 10–28, esp. 14; similarly Edwards, *Romans*, 11–15.

situation existing in the Roman church; (2) a stage in Paul's apostolic career; or (3) a combination of both.[6]

A more convincing and comprehensive survey, however, is the one by Longenecker.[7] While having adopted much from Jervis, he observes only two opposing viewpoints that have dominated all past discussions: (1) that Paul's purpose(s) for writing must be seen as having originated principally from within his own consciousness and ministry—whether to introduce himself to an unknown audience, to seek support for a forthcoming mission to the western part of the Roman empire, to defend himself against criticism and misrepresentation, to assert his apostolic authority over a church he considered within the orbit of his Gentile ministry, or to set out his own understanding of the Christian gospel as something of a summary of his message or a "last will and testament;" or (2) that the letter was written primarily to address some particular problem or set of problems, or some identifiable circumstance or set of circumstances, that existed among the Christians of Rome—whether doctrinal or ethical or whether arising from outside the church or from within it.[8]

Subsequently, Longenecker describes the first viewpoint as "missionary" in nature, the second as "pastoral," and makes an additional remark that these two approaches are, though ostensibly quite different, not "mutually exclusive options."[9] His observation seems correct, in so far as the first two categories of Jervis ("theological" purpose and "missionary" purpose) can be accurately brought together in the first group of Longenecker. Both the "theological" and the "missionary" viewpoints are born from Paul's own circumstances and needs, while the "pastoral" viewpoint has a natural connection with the situation of Christians in Rome. Further, the former viewpoints do not methodologically conflict with the latter, as Kruse also noted with his third group: "a combination of both" (his first two categories).

Thus, a brief survey of the long history of interpretation about the purpose(s) of Romans would do well to follow the classification scheme of Longenecker. According to him, these two main positions have been advanced in roughly historical order and contain within them specialized areas of research.[10]

---

6. Kruse, *Romans*, 6–11.

7. Longenecker, *Introducing Romans*, 92–128.

8. Ibid., 92–93; similarly Carson, *Introduction*, 249–52; Moo, *Romans*, 16–22; Hultgren, *Romans*, 11–13.

9. Longenecker, *Introducing Romans*, 93.

10. For this survey, see Longenecker, *Introducing Romans*, 94–128; cf. Jervis, *Purpose of Romans*, 14–28.

Positions Based on Paul's Own Consciousness and Ministry

1. *A Theological Treatise*: Throughout the first eighteen centuries of the Christian church, Romans was usually treated as a "theological treatise" or "tractate" that sets out a relatively complete statement of Christian doctrine, or, at least, that clearly articulates the basic features of Paul's teaching. This understanding of Romans continues to have enduring influence upon many scholars today.

2. *A Summation of Earlier Teaching*: Romans was recognized as a "real letter" but as being different from all other letters of Paul since its content demonstrated a maturation of his earlier thoughts and experiences.

3. *A Circular Letter*: The first fourteen chapters of Romans were not originally written with any particular church in mind, but was meant as an encyclical letter for all of Paul's churches, or, at least, for his churches in certain provinces of the Roman empire. Romans 1–14 (minus the designation "at Rome" in 1:7 and 15) was the original composition, to which was later added the travel plan of 15:14–33 when sent to Christians at Rome and the greetings of 16:1–24 when sent to the Christians at Ephesus.

4. *A Final Literary Testament*: Romans was "the last will and testament" of Paul, for he wrote it to summarize and develop his thoughts and theology for the benefit of the Roman Christians, extending his apostolic ministry and anticipating the necessity to defend his message and the Gentile mission before the church leaders during his forthcoming visit to Jerusalem.

5. *A Brief Prepared Originally for Paul's Defense at Jerusalem*: The primary reason for Paul's writing Romans was the necessity of defending his gospel in Jerusalem, hence the letter, at least its central theological section (1:18—11:36), was first prepared for his imminent "collection speech" at Jerusalem. In fact, it was essentially a letter to Jerusalem since its "secret addressee" was Jerusalem.

6. *An Attempt to Establish an Apostolic Church at Rome*: Romans was written to provide the Roman church with an apostolic presentation of the gospel, which Paul said that he intended to do in person when he made his visit to Rome (1:13) because that church lacked an apostolic foundation.

7. *An Ambassadorial Letter of Self-Introduction Soliciting Support for Paul's Proposed Mission to Spain*: Romans was a unique fusion of the "ambassadorial letter" with several other epistolary subtypes, such as

the paraenetic letter, hortatory letter, and philosophical diatribe. Its purpose was to advocate in behalf of the "power of God" a cooperative mission to evangelize Spain.

8. *A Missions Document Soliciting Support*: Romans was a "missions document" that was written in order to engender support from the Roman Christians for Paul's anticipated mission to Spain. In this letter Paul explained at some length both who he was and what was the gospel that he had preached as an apostle to the Gentiles.

Positions Based on the Historical Situation among the Christians in Rome

1. *To Oppose Jewish Particularism and Proclaim Christian Universalism*: Romans was written to a group of Gentile Christians at Rome who were being opposed by certain Jewish Christians in the city who, because of their inherited Jewish values, were antagonistic to Paul's message. Paul sought to remove the last remnants of Jewish particularism and to proclaim the universalism of Christianity.

2. *To Counter the Claims of the Judaizers*: Romans, just like Galatians, was written for the same apologetic and polemical reason of contending against the Judaizers who called on all Christian believers, whether ethnically Jews or Gentiles, to observe the Torah, either in whole or in part. Thus, the same anti-Judaistic themes and arguments boldly sketched in Galatians also underlies Paul's statements in Romans, though in a more moderate and reflective manner.

3. *To Effect a Reconciliation between "the Strong" and "the Weak"*: At least one of Paul's purposes for writing Romans was to reconcile the division between two rival parties within the Roman church that is mostly explicitly seen in 14:1—15:12. There was a conflict between the law-observant Christian Jews who were called "the weak" and the law-free Gentile Christians who called themselves "the strong."

4. *To Counsel regarding the Relation of Christians to Civil Government*: The discussion of Rom 13:1–7 concerning the Christian attitude towards civil government and paying taxes to civic authorities, which is unique in Paul and breaks the continuity of the exhortations on love in 12:9–21 and 13:8–10, is to be understood as reflecting one of the purposes of Romans. Paul teaches here how the Christian church should respond to their particular situation of unrest at Rome during

the mid-50's regarding the aggressive practices of those who collected the city's revenues and tolls.

5. *To Defend against Criticisms and Misrepresentations*: A number of passing comments and veiled allusions and rhetorical questions in Romans give a broad hint that Paul in writing Romans intended from the outset to defend himself against certain criticisms of his person and/or various misrepresentations of his message among the Christians of Rome. Such instances are recorded in Rom 1:16a, 2:16, 3:8, 16:17–20 (signaled by rhetorical questions in e.g., 3:31; 4:1; 6:1, 15; 7:7, 12, 14).

6. *Separate Letters Written on Different Occasions for Different Purposes*: Romans was, as a few scholars insist, a composite of two separate letters that were originally written on different occasions for different purposes, but which later became somehow united into a single composition.

A historical review of research exhibits considerable diversity. The various interpretive methods include theological reflection, historical-critical reconstruction, rhetorical analysis, and a social scientific approach. In spite of these competing methodologies, one can perceive certain arguments converging together in agreement on some significant matters. In his "Introduction" to the 1991 revised edition of *the Romans Debate*, Donfried summarized five points of "consensus" that has emerged since 1977:[11]

(1) Romans addresses a specific situation in Rome (such as the polarization among house-churches)

(2) Paul had more than one purpose in mind in writing

(3) Romans 16 should be considered integral to the whole letter

(4) Paul's use of diatribe does not exclude his address to specific historical problems

(5) Romans 9–11 forms an integral part of the overall argument of the letter and is not simply a Pauline afterthought; a major concern of Paul in Romans is defining the relationship between Jew and Gentile in God's plan for salvation.

Since 1991, the purpose(s) of Romans has been incessantly treated in several monographs and articles,[12] with the result that their considerable outcomes have influenced the most recent commentaries on Romans. Having reviewed these works, it seems sufficient to add some additional points of general consensus concerning the purpose of Romans, though an overall

---

11. Cf. Donfried, "Romans Debate since 1977," lxix–lxx.
12. See n1 above.

agreement for the *communis opinio* has not been reached yet. In my opinion, the following additional points of consensus can be added to Donfried's:

(1) Hardly anyone doubts that Romans is directed to specific realities in the Roman congregations, yet at the same time it still constitutes a systematic presentation of Paul's theology.[13]

(2) Most interpreters speak of several purposes at a time, combining elements of two main positions but designating the one or two as primary, the remainder as subsidiary.[14]

(3) In ascertaining the purposes of Romans recent commentators tend to give primary attention to the epistolary frame of Romans (1:1–15; 15:14—16:27), while supplementarily taking certain sections from the letter body (1:16—15:13) into consideration.[15]

(4) Most commentators regard Paul's missionary consciousness and future plan (15:16–28) as an overriding purpose in writing Romans, from which other purposes derive.[16]

(5) With regard to the Roman recipients, there is today a wide-ranging agreement that:

> (a) ethnically they constituted both Jewish and Gentile Christians, though the latter group had become increasingly dominant since the Edict of Claudius exiled for the former in AD 49
>
> (b) theologically the church, after Jewish Christians had returned from exile to Rome since AD 54, experienced a great deal of friction as Jewish and Gentile Christians disagreed especially on matters of Torah-observance

---

13. Here Mohrlang is an exception: "Although it is popular today to emphasize the importance of understanding the letter in light of the specific problems facing the church or the author . . . the dominant focus is not on the problems of the church or the author per se but on the all-absorbing content of the Good News itself" (*Romans*, 6).

14. See e.g., Edwards, *Romans*, 15–17; Moo, *Romans*, 16–22; Schreiner, *Romans*, 15–23, esp. 19; Hultgren, *Romans*, 14–20; Longenecker, *Introducing Romans*, 158–59; Kruse, *Romans*, 10–11.

15. So e.g., Hultgren, *Romans*, 11–20; Longenecker, *Introducing Romans*, 147–160; Kruse, *Romans*, 10–11. Differently, Wright finds in 11:11–32 and 15:7–13 the "two main 'situational' aims" of Romans ("Letter to the Romans," 406–8).

16. See e.g., Edwards, *Romans*, 15–17; Moo, *Romans*, 20; Schreiner, *Romans*, 19–22; Haacker, *Theology*, 17–20; Keck, *Romans*, 30–31; Osborne, *Romans*, 18–19; Harrison and Hagner, *Romans–Galatians*, 24–25; Hultgren, *Romans*, 14–20; Longenecker, *Introducing Romans*, 158–59. Unusually Kruse ranks this missionary factor as "secondary" (*Romans*, 11).

(c) socially, the church members were no longer meeting in the synagogues, but gathered for worship and fellowship in the homes and tenement accommodations of various Christians throughout the city. The church at Rome grew into a loose association of separate congregations.[17]

Having rehearsed these additional points of current general consensus, we can now readdress the occasion and purpose of Romans. In light of the foregoing review, I suppose, the decisive question that remains unresolved but will provide a possible key towards the resolution of the Romans debate is: *How can we correlate and explain the deliberate theological character of Romans, the specific historical problems of the Roman church, and Paul's primary missionary purpose in writing?* Most interpreters, insofar as I have observed, acknowledge the significance of Paul's missionary consciousness, yet are divided about why he had to write and send such a comprehensive, systematic letter to Rome. Therefore, I shall probe the peculiar features of Romans in search for an answer to this particular question.

OCCASION AND PURPOSE REFLECTED IN THE SPECIFIC EPISTOLARY CONVENTIONS OF ROMANS

As mentioned above, I am methodologically convinced to preferentially treat the epistolary framework of the letter in ascertaining its occasion and purpose. For it is in the opening sections of the letter (i.e., "salutation,"

---

17. Claudius, who ruled Rome from AD 41 to 54, imposed in 41 a restraining order on the Jews, "forbidding them to meet together in accordance with their ancestral way of life" (Dio Cassius, *Roman History*, 60.6). In AD 49 he issued the edict reported both in Acts 18:2 and by the second century Roman historian Suetonius: "Since the Jews constantly made disturbance at the instigation of Chrestus (*impulsore Chresto*) he [Claudius] expelled them from Rome" (Suetonius, *Claud*. 25:4). This report is generally interpreted as a garbled reference to conflicts over the messianic identity of Jesus and as implying that Jewish Christians most likely existed in the early 40s in Rome (see Lampe, *From Paul to Valentinus*, 11–16). However, Rom 16:3 indicates that Prisca and Aquila, who had been expelled from Rome (Acts 18:2), could come back to the city, because, after the death of Claudius in 54, Jews and Jewish Christians were able to immigrate once again into the city. A plausible reconstruction well accepted by recent commentators reads: Christianity in Rome began among Jews (early 40s); the resulting conflicts within the Jewish community prompted Claudius to banish them (49). In their absence, Christianity became predominantly Gentile, perhaps primarily among those who had been "God-fearers" (49–54). When the Christian Jews began to return (since 54), they found themselves marginalized, and often at odds with Gentile believers over Torah-observance (cf. Brown, *Introduction*, 559–62; Edwards, *Romans*, 9–11; Schreiner, *Romans*, 11–14; Haacker, *Theology*, 12–13; Keck, *Romans*, 29–32; Hultgren, *Romans*, 3–4, 7–11; Longenecker, *Introducing Romans*, 133–36).

"thanksgiving," and "body opening"), together with the closing sections (i.e., "body closing," "final greeting," "admonition," and "personal subscription"), where Paul most explicitly articulates his concerns and purposes in writing.[18] In the letter's main body, however, such expressions are reasonably muted and implied.

Hence, in the case of Romans, the "salutation" (1:1–7) and the "thanksgiving" (1:8–15) at the beginning, together with the so-called "apostolic *parousia*" (15:14–33) and the "closing" (16:1–27) at the end, are the most important source material for determining Paul's major concerns and purpose. The content of the body of Romans (1:16—15:13) needs then to be carefully investigated with respect to: (1) how the body correlates with what can be determined from the letter's frame concerning the purpose of Romans, and (2) whatever else might be determined from the body of the life situation at Rome by means of a 'mirror reading.'[19]

In what follows, there are five areas of investigation that function as the focii of this study: the first three are found within the epistolary framework of Romans and the remaining two in the main body.

Paul's Self-Introduction to Unfamiliar Addressees in Rome

The first unusual feature of Romans is the unfamiliar relationship between Paul and his letter recipients. This is the only letter that Paul sent to a church he has not founded, nor visited.[20] Yet both partners might have been in no way ignorant about each other. As the opening of the letter indicates, Paul, conscious of his apostolic calling to the Gentiles (1:5), wanted to preach the gospel to the Roman Christians (1:15), and even had attempted to visit them several times (1:13; 15:22). Paul's reason to visit them was to garner support from them to extend the Gentile mission to Spain (15:23–24, 28). If he had thought their cooperation indispensable for his future ministry, he must have taken every means to grasp their past history and current situation.

---

18. Cf. Schubert, who first argued: "Each thanksgiving not only announces clearly the subject matter of the letter, but also foreshadows unmistakably its stylistic qualities, the degree of intimacy and other important characteristics" (*Pauline Thanksgivings*, 77). His thesis has been supported and clarified by O'Brien, *Introductory Thanksgivings*; Jervis, *Purpose of Romans*, 48–52, 86–109. As for the importance of "closings" of Pauline letters, see Deissmann, *Bible Studies*, 347; Jervis, *Purpose of Romans*, 52–55, 132–157; Weima, *Neglected Endings*, 177–78, 197.

19. So rightly Longenecker, *Introducing Romans*, 128–31.

20. Paul had never seen the Colossians (Col 2:1) either, but the church was probably established and overseen by Paul's coworker Epaphras (Col 1:7–8; 4:12–13).

According to 16:1–23,[21] Paul knew a fairly large number of persons in the Roman Christian community. There he sends greetings to 28 persons one by one (19 men and 9 women), addressing them by name except two anonymous women (16:13, 15). Among them at least two couples, i.e., Priscilla–Aquila (16:3) and Andronicus–Junia (16:7), could have been reliable sources of information for Paul concerning the Roman community as well as for the community about Paul.[22] Seeing that letter correspondence from Corinth to Rome by sea under favorable sailing conditions took about seven to eight days,[23] Paul could easily and frequently have been informed by his friends in Rome about conditions prevailing there.

The members of the Christian community in Rome could also have known, whether correctly or incorrectly, something about Paul in differing degrees. Their knowledge of him depends, however, solely on listening to others. Two groups of firsthand information about Paul can be deduced from the circumstances of that community during AD 49–56.[24] One group are the friends of Paul whose names are called in 16:1–23. Another are those Jewish Christians who had lived through or at least had heard about Paul's conflict in Galatia, Philippi, and Corinth but since AD 54 could have, like Priscilla and Aquila, returned or immigrated to Rome. It is very likely that the latter group might have formed a negative public opinion about Paul within the community because they could have encountered and assimilated the criticisms of Paul's enemies against his person and gospel during their expulsion from Rome under the Edict of Claudius.[25]

What, then, should be the first task for Paul in writing Romans? Beyond doubt: to introduce himself to the Christians of Rome. But this task

21. Hardly anyone questions today the integrity of the sixteen-chapter form of Romans. Consequently, the theories of the "Circular Letter" and "Separate Letters," which presuppose either the fourteen-chapter form or the fifteen-chapter form as being original, have few supports, if any. This change is due largely to the arguments of Gamble, *Textual History*, 56–129.

22. Especially Prisca (called Priscilla in Acts) and Aquila would have been prime sources of information between Paul and Rome, for they—after having been expelled from Rome due to the Edict of Claudius, met Paul at Corinth (Acts 18:1–3), and thence remained his faithful co-workers at Corinth and Ephesus (Acts 18:18, 26; 1 Cor 16:19)—subsequently returned to Rome and were already heading a house church there (16:5). Andronicus and Junia, who had been considered prominent among the apostles, i.e., "itinerant evangelists or missionaries" (Schreiner, *Romans*, 796) and been prisoners along with Paul (16:7), would have well informed the community about the person and preaching of Paul.

23. Cf. Pliny, *Natural History*, 19:1, 3–4.

24. See n17 above.

25. Stuhlmacher, "Purpose of Romans," 238–39, has properly pointed out this consequence of the Jewish return to Rome since AD 54.

was not as simple as painting a fresh self-portrait on *tabula rasa*. In Romans he had to introduce himself *and* correct any misunderstanding toward him. Paul therefore begins Romans with the longest salutation (1:1–7) among all his extant letters in order to explicate his apostleship and gospel. Moreover, he sends this letter in his name alone even though Timothy was with him at the time of writing (16:21).[26] This suggests that because Paul's customary mention of coworker(s) at the start of the letter would divert attention from his particular purposes in writing Romans, he omits mentioning Timothy until the very end of his letter.[27] The epistolary framework of Romans as a whole, compared to those of the other Pauline letters, speaks most often of Paul's own person, desires, and concerns by using the pronoun "I" dominantly.[28]

Paul's Explicit Presentation of His Apostleship and Gospel

Next, one needs to pay attention to the reason why the salutation of Romans (1:1–7) is atypically extended. It is because Paul has, between the units of the sender (v. 1) and the recipients (v. 7), inserted three relative clauses that explicate the "gospel" centering on Jesus Christ (vv. 2–4) and his "apostleship" for the Gentiles including the Roman Christians (vv. 5–6). Considering that the first verse already highlights his apostolic authority ("Paul . . . called by God to be an apostle, having been set apart for the gospel of God"), the two major themes dominating this section are Paul's "apostolic authority" and the "gospel" that he preaches. Here from the start Paul's concern is manifested to underscore his apostolic commission for the church at Rome. The relationship which he is interested in having with his readers involves their acceptance of his apostolic calling. His stress on such a calling probably indicates that he expected opposition to this self-presentation.[29]

Paul's apostolic self-consciousness is also reflected in his word "my gospel" (τὸ εὐαγγέλιόν μου) that appears in Romans twice (2:16; 16:25) but in his other letters never recurs. This designation of "*my* gospel" does not hint at theological pluralism, rather implies that God willed to reveal the gospel to him and through him (16:25–26) as an apostle for the Gentiles.[30]

---

26. Cf. 2 Cor 1:1; Phil 1:1; Col 1:1; 1 Thess 1:1; 2 Thess 1:1; Phlm 1:1, where Timothy appears as the cosender.

27. So Jervis, *Purpose of Romans*, 158; see further 29–68.

28. For the details, see Longenecker, *Introducing Romans*, 138–41.

29. So Jervis, *Purpose of Romans*, 69–79, 158.

30. The phrase τὸ εὐαγγέλιόν μου does not mean "my Gospel-preaching" but the "gospel preached by me;" cf. τὸ εὐαγγέλιον τὸ εὐαγγελισθὲν ὑπ' ἐμοῦ (Gal 1:11) or τὸ

Therefore, he is obliged to preach *his* gospel to the Christians at Rome also (1:14–15) since he was especially commissioned by God to do so. In Romans Paul, fully conscious of his apostolic commission and responsibility, envisages representing in his name the very gospel that has been proclaimed by himself over two decades among the Gentiles in Asia Minor, Macedonia, and Achaia. That is why he omitted the mention of any co-sender(s) in the opening formula against his custom. Paul represents his gospel first and foremost as rooted in the Jewish Scriptures of the Old Testament and as fulfilling what was promised there beforehand (1:2). This statement very likely takes on an apologetic tone, anticipating his arguments that his gospel is witnessed by the law and the prophets (3:21), establishes and fulfills the law (3:31; 8:4), and this is confirmed in the cases of Abraham (Rom 4) and of Israel (Rom 9–11).

It is of enormous significance that the closing doxology (16:25–27), which frames together with the opening salutation the entire letter as an *inclusio*, thematizes again Paul's apostleship and gospel in many parallel phrases.[31] Both sections focuses on the "gospel" that is committed to Paul (1:1, 16:25), that centers on Jesus Christ (1:3; 16:25), stems from the prophetic OT Scriptures (1:2; 16:26), and sets the goal of the obedience of faith among all the Gentiles (1:5; 16:26). The term "gospel" that is so intensively employed in the epistolary framework,[32] functions as the keyword in 1:16–17, the statement generally identified with the theme of the whole letter.[33] Here Paul begins his definition of gospel somewhat abruptly: "I am not ashamed of the gospel . . ." (v. 16a). This sentence, directly connected to v. 15 ("I am eager to preach the gospel to you also who are in Rome"), seems to make a reference to Rome as if he were saying: "I am not afraid to preach *this* gospel in Rome, even if there will be a confrontation that my gospel used to call forth in other cities."[34]

εὐαγγέλιον ὃ κηρύσσω (Gal 2:2).

31. Cf. Schreiner, *Romans*, 30; see further 810–18 for the authenticity and placement of 16:25–27.

32. See the noun εὐαγγέλιον in 1:1, 9, 16; 15:16, 19; 16:25 and the verb εὐαγγελίζεσθαι in 1:15; 15:20.

33. E.g., Wilckens, *Der Brief an die Römer*, 1:91; Weima, "Preaching the Gospel in Rome," 337–38; Moo, *Romans*, 27–30.

34. So Schmithals, *Römerbrief als historisches Problem*, 92: "Ich scheue mich nicht, *dies* Evangelium auch in Rom zu predigen . . . ich fürchte mich nicht vor der Auseinandersetzung, die meine Predigt auch in Rom mit sich bringen wird" (his italics); following him, Stuhlmacher, "Purpose of Romans," 239n20.

Paul's Detailed Explanation of His Apostolic Ministry and Missionary Travel Plan

Third, in Romans' thanksgiving section (1:8–15) and body-closing (15:14–33), Paul speaks almost entirely about his own desires and concerns in contrast to those parts of the other Pauline letters where he speaks about the issues and concerns of his recipients.[35] Especially these frame sections leave us in no doubt about Paul's intention to visit Rome and his purpose for it. Therefore, we can expect them to contain some clear notations about his purposes in writing the letter, insofar as this was sent as a preparation for his visit to Rome. It is here that we find the occasion of Romans most explicitly stated.

In Rom 1:10–13 Paul uses rather strong terms to assure the readers of his long-standing wish and even several definite plans to come to Rome. In 15:22–24, he reemphasizes these themes. Yet the purposes of visiting his readers have different nuances in their respective contexts. In the letter's address, *one* purpose is to "impart some spiritual gift (τι χάρισμα πνευματικόν) to stabilize you" (1:11) so that "you and I may be mutually encouraged by each other's faith" (1:12). This gifting and encouragement will result in spiritual fruit among the Roman Christians (1:13). Paul's desire to gift and encourage is not to be confined to his past plans but is also valid for his present and future purposes.[36] Most recent commentators construe the "spiritual gift" necessary for "stabilizing" the Roman Christians as referring to the "reminder" of Paul's gospel (15:15–16) which proclaims the unity of Jews and Gentiles in Christ.[37] Indeed Paul set forth "his own gospel" in Romans for unifying and stabilizing the discordant Roman congregations who, being composed of Jewish and Gentile members from various house churches, were disputing over the ethnic advantage (2:17–20, 3:1; 11:18) and demand for Torah-observance (14:1—15:13).[38]

---

35. With the exception of Ephesians that is regarded as having been composed as a circular-letter (see Carson et al., *Introduction*, 309–11).

36. Contra Stuhlmacher, "Purpose of Romans," 236–37; Zeller, *Römer*, 39; Byrne, *Romans*, 50–51, 58. See the counterarguments of Moo, *Romans*, 57–58; Fitzmyer, *Romans*, 251; Schreiner, *Romans*, 52–53.

37. So Edwards, *Romans*, 36; Schreiner, *Romans*, 54; Osborne, *Romans*, 36–37; Kruse, *Romans*, 62.

38. This understanding of "some spiritual gift" (τι χάρισμα πνευματικόν) in 1:11 is corroborated by the body-closing statement in 15:14–15 where Paul tells his intent of writing the letter ("I have written very boldly to you on some points, so as to remind you again"), implying that the whole content of main body has special relevance to his preceding admonition for the "strong" and the "weak" (14:1—15:13).

But there are *other* purposes which are articulated in the letter's closing (15:24). Among these purposes, Paul names: to "see you" and "enjoy your company for a while" (v. 24a, c) and then to "be sent on my way there [to Spain] by you" (v. 24b). The *former* desire (v. 24a, c), correlated with 1:11–15, tells us that Paul planned to spend some time in Rome to strengthen the church and have a harvest of souls by preaching the gospel there.[39] Seeing the Roman recipients within the orbit of his own Gentile ministry (1:5–6), Paul wanted to "preach the gospel" (εὐαγγελίζεσθαι) also to them (1:15), enlarging and extending their understanding of the gospel for a certain period of time in order to obtain "some fruit" among them (1:13).[40] The *latter* desire of being "sent on" (προπεμφθῆναι) to Spain by the receivers in Rome (v. 24b) obviously refers to a "missionary sending" with the church's support.[41]

The crucial statements of 15:22–24 that shed light on the primary purpose of Romans are located just in the middle of the so-called "apostolic *parousia*" (15:14–33). In closing his letter body, Paul first affirms his receivers, explains the grounds upon which he has written to them "quite boldly," and describes his apostolic mission of evangelizing the Gentiles in terms of the "priestly ministry of the gospel" (v. 14–16). Then, in vv. 17–21, he, looking *backward* upon his previous activity in the eastern Mediterranean, proudly rehearses what Christ has accomplished through him in various ways (v. 17–19a) and what has been his ambition all along: i.e., to be a pioneer of reaching, and even extending, the boundaries of the known world with the gospel (v. 20–21). In doing so, Paul visualizes the regions of his missionary work to encompass "a circle (κύκλῳ) from Jerusalem to Illyricum" and in reaching these areas, he claims: "I have completed (πεπληρωκέναι, literally: fulfilled) the gospel of Christ" (v. 19b). This claim is not an exaggeration, for his Old Testament-oriented ardor is to preach the gospel only in those important cities where Christ has not yet been confessed, i.e., where nobody has planted a church yet (v. 20–21). As a result, there is no more room for him to continue working in the eastern territory comprising Asia Minor, Macedonia, and Greece (v. 23a). That is why Paul has been longing for

---

39. So rightly Haacker, *Theology*, 18–19, and Osborne, *Romans*, 18, who argue against those holding the view that Paul considered Rome just a short stop on his way to Spain.

40. For a recent discussion on the meaning of εὐαγγελίζεσθαι in 1:15, see Gaventa, "'To Preach the Gospel,'" 184–89, who argues in special connection with 15:15 for a broad meaning of "ongoing apostolic activities of preaching and teaching."

41. The verb translated "to send on" (προπέμπειν) denotes "to assist someone in making a journey, send on one's way with food, money, by arranging for companions, means of travel, etc." (BDAG, s.v. προπέμπω, 873); cf. Radl, "προπέμπω," in *EDNT* 3:160: "equip for (further) journeys." For this word usage, see Acts 15:3; 1 Cor 16:6, 11; 2 Cor 1:16; Titus 3:13.

many years to start another pioneer missionary campaign toward Spain and as part of this plan he has been trying to visit Rome (v. 23b). Paul wants support and cooperation from the Roman house churches in his extending Gentile mission to Spain (15:24b), expecting from them the same role that his former sending church at Antioch of Syria had done in mission to Macedonia and Achaia.

However, in vv. 25–33 Paul switches to looking *forward* at the potential challenges to his mission in the near future. In addition to saying that he is going to the Jerusalem church with the collection raised among his Gentile churches in Macedonia and Greece (vv. 25–26), Paul urgently asks for the prayers of the Roman Christians that his travels in Judea will be safe and that the church at Jerusalem will accept the gift he brings (vv. 30–31). It is important for him that the collection be received as a sign of unity and fellowship between the mother church of Jerusalem in the East and his Gentile churches of the West.[42] Still, Paul is under no illusions about latent hostility of disobedient Jews awaiting him in Jerusalem. He has already escaped one plot on his life there (Acts 9:29–30), and omens of yet another awaited him (Acts 20:3b, 22–25; 21:10–13).[43] In going to Jerusalem Paul was risking his very life for the unity and equality of Gentiles and Jews in Christ. Thus the Roman church was asked earnestly to pray for himself, both for protection from his Jewish enemies and for the reception of the gift by the Jerusalem church.

The "Double Character" of the Letter to Rome

Every serious reading of Romans is supposed to be confronted with its bewildering "double character." This term is first used by Paul Feine ("Doppelcharakter")[44] for the seemingly contradictory character of Romans that this letter is, on the one hand, primarily addressed to Gentile Christians,[45] but engages, on the other hand, in a controversy over Jewish issues far more than any other letter. A cursory reading shows that Paul draws the attention of the Roman church to: the Mosiac law, circumcision,

---

42. In 2 Cor 8:4 and 9:13 Paul designates the collection for the Jerusalem church as a sign of "fellowship" (κοινωνία); cf. Georgi, *Remembering the Poor*, 33–42.

43. The Lukan report on Paul's arrival in Jerusalem (Acts 21:19–21) spells out how justified his apprehensions had been. At that time Paul was informed of a remarkable church growth in Judea: "Many thousands of Jews have become believers," but "all of them are zealous for the law" (v. 20). As such, they were all too ready to believe rumors spread about Paul as teaching apostasy among the Jews of the diaspora (v. 21).

44. Feine, *Römerbrief*, 1.

45. See Rom 1:5–6, 13–15; 11:13, 17–24, 28, 30–31; 15:7–9, 15–16, 18.

and the so-called "advantage" of Jews (ch. 2–3); the justification of Abraham (ch. 4); the function of the Mosaic law (ch. 7); the destiny and salvation of Israel (ch. 9–11); and the present conflict among Jewish and Gentile Christians regarding the Torah-observance (ch. 14–15).[46]

This unique feature of Romans was very likely occasioned by the situation of its addressees, which, in turn, prevented Paul from achieving the primary purpose of soliciting support for his anticipated mission to Spain. As depicted above, the Jewish Christians' return from exile to Rome since AD 54 brought an enormous change to the Roman Christian community in ethnical, social, and theological aspects. This change entailed conflicts of the congregation members over theological issues about food laws and observance of certain days as well as over their opinions about Paul himself. It is likely that Paul was well informed by his friends about the conflict between Jews and Gentiles in the Roman congregations. He would also have learned that doubts and questions had surfaced in Rome about his apostleship and his gospel, if he did not yet face actual opponents in Rome (cf. 3:8; 16:17–19).[47]

The differences of opinion between Jewish and Gentile Christians regarding Torah-observance are reflected in 14:1—15:13. The difficulties that arise between the "strong" (mostly Gentile Christians) and the "weak" (mostly Jewish Christians) in Rome, however, was rather typical of the kind of debates that occurred as the gospel spread throughout the Greco-Roman world. Paul could not arbitrate the debate simply by sharing his opinion on the matter. He felt it necessary to summarize the core content of the gospel he preached, particularly as it pertained to issues relating to Jews and

---

46. Longenecker (*Introducing Romans*, 128) touches upon this dual character in a broader sense, accentuating the necessity of "a proper method for determining Paul's purposes." He states: "In particular, a method needs to be established for resolving the tensions that have existed between (1) Romans as a letter directed to a particular group of Christians at Rome *and* Romans as a theological statement suitable for widespread distribution and use, (2) the epistolary nature of the frame of the letter *and* the expositional nature of its main body of material, and (3) the author's explicit and repeated references to his addressees as Gentile believers *and* his extensive use of what appears to be Jewish Christian argumentation" (his italics).

47. Stuhlmacher ("Purpose of Romans," 239) supposes that when Paul wrote Romans "there were living at Rome Christian opponents as well as friends of Paul" and sees the evidences of the former's existence in 3:8 and 16:17–19; similarly Campbell, "Determining the Gospel," 315–36. Though the warning against troublemakers in 16:17–18 is frequently taken as referring to a potential danger threatening the Romans Christians (Lampe, "Roman Christians," 221; Moo, *Romans*, 929; Schreiner, *Romans*, 801; Hultgren, *Romans*, 592), it looks impossible to identify those false teachers nor to decide whether the danger was potential or actual (Edwards, *Romans*, 358–59; Kruse, *Romans*, 576–77). Cf. the many parallels between 16:17–19 and Phil 3:17–21; Gal 6:11–16.

Gentiles. It is not surprising, therefore, that the Mosaic law and the place of Israel in salvation history are at the forefront of his discussion in Romans.

Paul also needed to explicate his gospel thoroughly because he had been the target of persistent attacks, especially by other Jewish Christians. We do not know exactly whether he feared that Jewish opponents would soon arrive in Rome and counter his gospel,[48] or if he even knew of actual opponents operating in the Roman congregations.[49] If he merely communicated his judgments on the controverted issues without providing a full exposition of his gospel, some would have rejected his advice instantly, adding also the criticism that Paul was under suspicion by some leaders in Jerusalem (cf. Acts 21:20–21). The apprehension about Paul's teaching in Rome could surely be alleviated if his gospel were thoroughly explained, particularly on issues relating to Jews and Gentiles. He was required to satisfy both Jewish and Gentile Christians that his stance on the Mosaic law, circumcision, and the place of Israel accords with the OT Scriptures.

We can see, therefore, why Paul wrote at such length and with such care, and why he took up the particular topics that we find in Romans. The reason for the astonishing detail of Paul's arguments in Romans is that he wanted to allay the arguments of his opponents and the slanderous rumors against him before his arrival. He had to prevent the Roman Christians, who were unfamiliar with him, from rejecting him, his gospel, and his cause. Paul's intention was to show his Jewish and Gentile readers that the gospel as he received it constitutes the true fulfillment of what the OT Scriptures teach about God's purpose to redeem humankind and all creation.

He felt free to omit some topics, such as the Lord's Supper, because there was no controversy over such matters in Rome. However, he did have to contend about justification, the Mosaic law, circumcision, new life in the Spirit, Christian obedience in view of the last judgment, and the role of Israel (and Gentiles) in salvation history. Paul's particular advice to the "strong" and the "weak" in Rom 14–15 would never be accepted if fundamental disagreement existed over his conception of the role of Jews and Gentiles in God's salvation plan. Thus, Romans took the shape of a "tractate letter," which contains an extended dialogue with the Jews but in no way excludes Gentile addressees from any part of it.[50]

---

48. Schreiner, *Romans*, 21.
49. Campbell, "Determining the Gospel," 315–36.
50. Becker, *Paul the Apostle*, 74–91.

Paul's Intensive Use of the Old Testament and Diatribe

Lastly, the distinctiveness of Romans is also manifested by Paul's intensive use of the Jewish Scriptures of the Old Testament and the Greek rhetorical device of diatribe. This letter contains significantly more quotations from Scripture than any of Paul's other letters. According to Koch, of the 89 explicit OT quotations in the Pauline corpus, fifty-one (or 57 percent) are in Romans.[51] According to Longenecker, of a total 83 explicit OT citations in all of the thirteen canonical Pauline letters, forty-five (or 54 percent) are in Romans.[52] Besides those citations, much of Paul's appeal to Scripture here appears in the form of allusions. The central theological vocabulary of the letter belong to these allusions.[53] However, it is remarkable that explicit quotations from Scripture in Romans are not dispersed evenly across the letter. Nearly a third of them are concentrated in ch. 9–11 and four-fifth's of them are clustered in four passages: 3:4–18; 4:1–25; 9:6—11:36; and 15:1–12.[54] At several points in the letter Paul develops a lengthy argument with little or no explicit reference to the Scripture (e.g., 1:18—2:29; 5:1—8:30; 12:1—14:23). Why then is the distribution of OT quotations in Romans so uneven?

We can find the reason in the fact that Paul unusually asserts in the opening salutation that "his gospel" is what God "promised beforehand through his prophets in the Holy Scriptures" (1:2). This assertion that his gospel is part of a larger OT prophetic tradition verifies Paul's apologetic purpose.[55] He emphasizes this point repetitively throughout the letter (1:17; 3:21, 31; 4:23–24; 9:6, 24–33; 10:16–21; 11:7–10, 25–27; 15:8–12; 16:25–26). Paul needed to establish in Romans that his gospel fulfilled what was written in the Scriptures. His teaching on the Mosaic law and others had already precipitated disputes in Galatia and Corinth. These debates were not confined to these localities, and before Paul could use Rome as a

---

51. See Koch, *Schrift als Zeuge*, 21–24.

52. Longenecker counts the OT quotations in Romans in a different way: "[There are] 55–60 biblical passages of about 100 passages total, if the conflated texts and dual sources are unpacked and counted separately" (*Introducing Romans*, 237). He counts the OT quotations in Paul's other letters: "[O]nly 15 in 1 Corinthians, 7 in 2 Corinthians, 10 in Galatians, 4 in Ephesians, 1 in 1 Timothy, and 1 in 2 Timothy, with none in 1 Thessalonians, 2 Thessalonians, Philippians, Colossians, Philemon, and Titus." Cf. Longenecker, "Prolegomena," 145–68; Smith, "Pauline Literature," 268–72.

53. So Seifrid, "Romans," 607–94, esp. 607: "Such terms as 'gospel,' 'promise,' 'faith,' 'calling,' 'son of God,' 'holy Spirit' have their roots in the Hebrew Scriptures and implicitly recall the contexts from which they are drawn."

54. The exceptions are Rom 1:17; 2:24; 7:7; 8:36; 12:19; 13:9a, 9b; 14:11; 15:21.

55. Contra Koch, *Schrift als Zeuge des Evangeliums*, 328–29. Against him Chang, *Knechtschaft und Befreiung*, 51–54; cf. Schreiner, *Romans*, 14–15.

bridge for bringing the gospel to Spain, he needed to show his addressees why his opponents' objections to his gospel, which had certainly reached Rome also, were unfounded. All the subsequent quotations from Scripture in Romans serve this purpose.

It was Paul's soteriology that *ab initio* aroused the vehement antagonism from his opponents.[56] It comprises a pair of ideas that are irreconcilably challenged with Jewish presuppositions: (1) justification of the ungodly through faith in Jesus Christ alone, independent of Torah-observance and (2) the non-differential calling of Jews and Gentiles into the one universal church of eschatological salvation. Paul not only cites Scripture most extensively just within these two subject areas of the letter (ch. 3–4, 9–11, 15), but also interweaves his rhetorical questions with the biblical citations that immediately follow. That Paul deals with the Scripture so intensely in those sections was not caused by a mere provisory frame of mind but by the subject matter he carefully articulates.[57]

In writing Romans Paul wanted to demonstrate (vis-à-vis Jewish objections) that his message of salvation absolutely corresponds with the "Holy Scriptures" of Israel and is adequately substantiated within them. He chose this basis of argumentation because the Scripture was the common "Mutterboden" on which both his own faith and that of his opponents find their origin and continued support. Furthermore, Scripture was the common source of divine authority and was also acknowledged by his opponents as such. Thus, Paul appealed to the "common basis of faith" that secured him an access to, and a favorable hearing with, the recipient congregations who, for the most part, scarcely knew him. On this common basis of faith he could also elucidate his gospel "in an objectifying way."[58]

Paul's use of the Greek "diatribe" (διατριβή, i.e., a dialogical style that makes use of direct address to an imaginary interlocutor, hypothetical objections, and false conclusions) enhances the purposefully systematic character of his argumentation in Romans.[59] Compared to the wider use of

---

56. See e.g., Acts 13:38–41, 45–50; 14:1–2, 19; 17:2–5; 21:17–28; 22:19–23.

57. See Chang, *Knechtschaft und Befreiung*, 50–51. Stanley (*Arguing with Scripture*, 142–43) indicates virtually the same point when he says: "Probably the most important clue to Paul's rhetorical purpose is to be found in the fact that all three passages (4:1–25, 9:6—11:36, and 15:1–12) center on a common theme: the plan of God to create a chosen people that would include both Jews and Gentiles."

58. Van der Minde, *Schrift und Tradition*, 191, 194.

59. Some diatribal elements are found in portions of Paul's letters (1 Cor 6:12–13; 15:35–38; and Gal 2:17; 3:21), but are most heavily utilized in Romans. It is particularly in 2:1–5 and 2:17–24 that they appear most prominently in the letter—probably also in 9:19–21 and 11:17–24; possibly in 3:1–8 (or 3:1–9); and perhaps in 3:27–31 (or 3:27—4:2) and 14:4–11.

diatribe in Greco-Roman literature, one of the major distinctives of Pauline usage is that he creates a fictive dialogue in which he writes both sides of the debate. This is particularly obvious with his use of rhetorical questions, where he guides the course of the argument by means of positing questions that he then answers.[60] Therefore, in Romans, two main subforms of diatribe predominate:

(1) *An address to an imaginary interlocutor* (e.g., 2:1–5, 17–24; 9:19–21; 11:17–24; 14:4, 10). Paul introduces a Jewish interlocutor who boasts over Gentiles (2:17–29) and subsequently dialogues with him (3:1–9; 3:27—4:2); or also a Gentile interlocutor who boasts over Jews (11:17–24).

(2) *Objections and false conclusions from Paul's arguments drawn by the interlocutor.* These often set forth possible misinterpretations of a point, correct them, and lead to other points in the argument. These are often rejected with the interjection: "May it never be!" (μὴ γένοιτο)[61] and given accompanying reasons for their rejection (3:1–9, 31; 6:1–3, 15–16; 7:7, 13; 9:14, 19–20; 11:1, 11, 19–20).[62]

Behind this extraordinary usage of rhetorical convention in Romans lies Paul's anticipation of long-standing problems with those who have misunderstood his gospel. Almost every objection and false conclusion from the mouth of imaginary interlocutors seems to be reflecting the typical questions and counterarguments he has confronted in his missionary enterprises. Thus a large number of rhetorical questions allude to criticisms and challenges from his Jewish Christian opponents as they spread from Asia Minor and Macedonia to Greece.[63] Paul intends to answer and refute them. The dialogue we are witnessing in Romans is a real one in which Paul is wrestling for the hearts and minds of the Christians in Rome.

---

60. Porter, "Diatribe," 296–98, esp. 298.

61. The phrase μὴ γένοιτο appears in Romans ten times (3:4, 6, 31; 6:2, 15; 7:7, 13; 9:14; 11:1, 11), but merely four times in the other letters of Paul (1 Cor 6:15; Gal 2:17; 3:21; 6:14—Gal 6:14 is not in a diatribal structure) and only once elsewhere in the New Testament (Luke 20:16).

62. See Watson, "Diatribe," 213–14; Schmeller, *Paulus und die 'Diatribe'*; Stowers, *Diatribe*.

63. See e.g., Hultgren, *Romans*, 85–86, 111–19, 126–32, 134–45, 362–68, 502–10. Take for example, Rom 3:31: "Do we, then, nullify the law by this faith?"; 4:1: "what then shall we say about Abraham, our forefather according to the flesh?"; 6:1: "Are we to continue in sin that grace might increase?"; 6:15: "What then? Shall we sin because we are not under law but under grace?"; 7:7, 12, 14: "What shall we say then? Is the Law sin? May it never be! . . . the law is holy, and the commandment is holy, righteous and good . . . We know that the law is spiritual."

SUMMATION AND CONCLUSION

It is an appropriate, cogent method to ascertain the occasion and purpose of Romans first and foremost within its epistolary framework (1:1–15 and 15:14—16:27). The reason for writing Romans most explicitly stated in 1:10 and 15:28–29, 32 where Paul explains his plan to visit the Roman recipients and shares his frustration that several past attempts have been unsuccessful (1:13; 15:22). Hence the letter's immediate occasion was to prepare his forthcoming visit to Rome.

Paul's purposes of visiting his addressees, which are carefully and plainly articulated in the epistolary frame, are binary: (1) Paul's gifting and encouragement of the Roman church (1:11–12), and (2) his effort to garner their support for a mission to Spain (15:24b). These two purposes of Paul's visit to Rome—the first *pastoral* and the second *missionary*—determined the unique qualities and features of the letter. They account for the five peculiarities we have probed in the latter part of this study.

As for the "double character" and the "intensive use of the OT and the diatribe-style" of the letter to the Romans, they become comprehensible when we situate both purposes into the circumstances of Paul's addressees. The ethnic, social, and theological change in the Roman congregations that was caused by the Edict of Claudius and the subsequent Jewish return to Rome compelled Paul to introduce himself and his gospel in a way which anticipated any antagonism towards him. Paul felt it necessary to elucidate the core content of his gospel in depth and so Romans took the shape of a "tractate letter."

Alternative proposals by other scholars in the Romans debate need not be competing with my own. Theories on Paul's purpose for Romans based upon the "conditions existing among the Christians at Rome," or "to counter the claims of the Judaizers," or "to effect a reconciliation between the strong and the weak (14:1—15:12)," or "to counsel regarding the relation of Christians to civil government (13:1–7)" could have been Paul's "secondary" or "subsidiary" purposes. Yet these concerns would hardly be identified with the original purposes of Paul. Lastly, my thesis and findings coalesce well with the words of Haacker, who says succinctly: "The character and purposes of this letter results from *who* Paul had become as an individual and *what* he believed was his commission, *when* in his life he wrote this letter and *where* he intended to go (Jerusalem – Rome – Spain)."[64]

---

64. Haacker, *Theology of Romans*, 20; author's own italics.

BIBLIOGRAPHY

Baur, F. C. "Über Zweck und Veranlassung des Römerbriefs und die damit zusammenhängenden Verhältnisse der römischen Gemeinde. Eine historisch-kritische Untersuchung." *Tübinger Zeitschrift für Theologie* 3 (1836) 59-178. Reprint, *Ausgewählte Werke in Einzelausgaben I: Historisch-kritische Untersuchungen zum Neuen Testament*, ed. K. Scholder, 147-266. Stuttgart: Frommann, 1963.

Beker, J. C. *Paul the Apostle: The Triumph of God in Life and Thought*. Philadelphia: Fortress, 1980.

Brown, R. E. *An Introduction to the New Testament*. ABRL. New York: Doubleday, 1997.

Byrne, B. *Romans*. SP 6. Collegeville, MN: Liturgical, 1996.

Campbell, D. A. "Determining the Gospel through Rhetorical Analysis in Paul's Letter to the Romans Christians." In *Gospel in Paul: Studies on Corinthians, Galatians and Romans for Richard N. Longenecker*, ed. L. A. Jervis and P. Richardson, 315-36. JSNTSup 108. Sheffield: Sheffield Academic, 1994.

Campbell, W. S. "The Romans Debate." *JSNT* 10 (1981) 19-28.

———. "Why Did Paul Write Romans?" In *Paul's Gospel in an Intercultural Context: Jew and Gentile in the Letter to the Romans*, 14-24. Studien zur interkulturellen Geschichte des Christentums 69. New York: Lang, 1991.

Carson, D.A., et al. *An Introduction to the New Testament*. Grand Rapids: Zondervan, 1992.

Chang, H.-K. *Die Knechtschaft und Befreiung der Schöpfung: Eine exegetische Untersuchung zu Römer 8,19-22*. BWM 7. Wuppertal: Brockhaus, 2000.

———. "Occasion and Purpose of Romans: Reflected in Its Distinctive Features." *Korean Evangelical New Testament Studies* 12 (2013) 57-89.

Deissmann, G. A. *Bible Studies: Contributions, Chiefly from Papyri and Inscriptions, to the History of the Language, the Literature, and the Religion of Hellenistic Judaism and Primitive Christianity*. Trans. A. Grieve. Edinburgh: T. & T. Clark, 1901.

Donfried, K. P. "The Romans Debate since 1977." In *The Romans Debate*, ed. K. P. Donfried, xlix–lxxii. Rev. exp. ed. Peabody, MA: Hendrickson, 1991.

Drane, J. W. "Why Did Paul Write Romans?" In *Pauline Studies: Essays Presented to Professor F.F. Bruce on his 70th Birthday*, ed. D. A. Hagner and M. J. Harris, 208-27. Exeter: Paternoster, 1980.

Drummond, J. "Occasion and Object of the Epistle to the Romans." *HibJ* 11 (1913) 787-804.

Dunn, James D. G. *Romans 1-8*. WBC 38A. Nashville: Nelson, 1988.

———. *Romans 9-16*. WBC 38B. Nashville: Nelson, 1988.

Edwards, J. R. *Romans*. NIBCNT 6. Peabody, MA: Hendrickson, 1992.

Feine, P. *Der Römerbrief. Eine exegetische Studie*. Göttingen: Vandenhoeck & Ruprecht, 1903.

Fitzmyer, J. A. *Romans: A New Translation with Introduction and Commentary*. AB 33. New York: Doubleday, 1993.

Gamble, H. Y. *The Textual History of the Letter to the Romans: A Study in Textual and Literary Criticism*. Grand Rapids: Eerdmans, 1977.

Gaventa, B. R. "'To Preach the Gospel': Romans 1,15 and the Purposes of Romans." In *The Letter to the Romans*, ed. U. Schnelle, 179-95. BETL 226. Leuven: Peeters, 2009.

Georgi, D. *Remembering the Poor: The History of Paul's Collection for Jerusalem*. Nashville: Abingdon, 1992.
Grafe, E. *Über Veranlassung und Zweck des Römerbriefes*. Tübingen: Mohr/Siebeck, 1881.
Guthrie, D. *New Testament Introduction*. 3rd ed. Downers Grove, IL: InterVarsity, 1970.
Haacker, K. *Der Brief des Paulus an die Römer*. THKNT 6. Leipzig: Evangelische, 1999.
———. "Der Römerbrief als Friedensmemorandum." *NTS* 36 (1990) 25–41.
———. *The Theology of Paul's Letter to the Romans*. New Testament Theology. Cambridge: Cambridge University Press, 2003.
Harder, G. "Der konkrete Anlass des Römerbriefes." *ThViat* 6 (1954) 13–24.
Harrison, E. F., and D. A. Hagner. *Romans–Galatians*. Vol. 11 of the *Expositor's Bible Commentary*. Rev. ed. Grand Rapids: Zondervan, 2008.
Hultgren, A. J. *Paul's Letter to the Romans: A Commentary*. Grand Rapids: Eerdmans, 2011.
Jervis, L. A. *The Purpose of Romans: A Comparative Letter Structure Investigation*. JSNTSup 55. Sheffield: Sheffield Academic, 1991.
Jewett, R. "Romans as an Ambassadorial Letter." *Int* 36 (1982) 5–20.
Keck, L. E. *Romans*. ANTC. Nashville: Abingdon, 2005.
Kettunen, M. *Der Abfassungszweck des Römerbriefes*. AASF. Dissertationes Humanarum Litterarum 18. Helsinki: Suomalainen Tiedeakatemia, 1979.
Koch, D.-A. *Die Schrift als Zeuge des Evangeliums: Untersuchungen zur Verwendung und zum Verständnis der Schrift bei Paulus*. BHT 69. Tübingen: Mohr/Siebeck, 1986.
Kruse, C. G. *Paul's Letter to the Romans*. Pillar New Testament Commentary. Grand Rapids: Eerdmans, 2012.
Lampe, P. *From Paul to Valentinus: Christians at Rome in the First Two Centuries*. Minneapolis: Fortress, 2003.
———. "The Roman Christians of Romans 16." In *The Romans Debate*, ed. by K. P. Donfried, 216–30. Rev. exp. ed. Peabody, MA: Hendrickson, 1991.
Longenecker, R. N. *Introducing Romans: Critical Issues in Paul's Most Famous Letter*. Grand Rapids: Eerdmans, 2011.
———. "Prolegomena to Paul's Use of Scripture in Romans." *BBR* 7 (1997) 145–68.
Miller, J. C. *The Obedience of Faith, the Eschatological People of God, and the Purpose of Romans*. SBLDS 177. Atlanta: SBL, 2000.
Minear, P. S. *The Obedience of Faith: The Purposes of Paul in the Epistle to the Romans*. SBT 2/19. London: SCM, 1971.
Mohrlang, R. *Romans*. Cornerstone Biblical Commentary 14. Carol Stream, IL: Tyndale House, 2007.
Moo, D. J. *The Epistle to the Romans*. NICNT. Grand Rapids: Eerdmans, 1996.
O'Brien, P. *Introductory Thanksgivings in the Letters of Paul*. NovTSup 49. Leiden: Brill, 1977.
Osborne, G. R. *Romans*. IVP New Testament Commentary Series 6. Downers Grove, IL: IVP, 2004.
Porter, S. E. "Diatribe." In *Dictionary of New Testament Background*, ed. C. A. Evans and S. E. Porter, 296–98. Downers Grove, IL: IVP, 2000.
Russell, W. B. "An Alternative Suggestion for the Purpose of Romans." *BSac* 145 (1988) 174–88.
Schmeller, T. *Paulus und die 'Diatribe'. Eine vergleichende Stilinterpretation*. NTAbh 19. Münster: Aschendorff, 1987.

Schmithals, W. *Der Römerbrief als historisches Problem*. SNT 9. Gütersloh: Mohn, 1975.
Schreiner, T. R. *Romans*. BECNT. Grand Rapids: Baker Academic, 1998.
Schrenk, G. "Der Römerbrief als Missionsdokument." In *Studien zu Paulus*, 81–106. ATANT 26. Zürich: Zwingli, 1954.
Schubert, P. *Form and Function of the Pauline Thanksgivings*. BZNW 20. Berlin: Töpelmann, 1939.
Seifrid, M. A. "Romans." In *Commentary on the New Testament Use of the Old Testament*, ed. G. K. Beale and D. A. Carson, 607–94. Grand Rapids: Baker Academic, 2007.
Smiga, G. "Romans 12:1–2 and 15:30–32 and the Occasion of the Letter to the Romans." *CBQ* 53 (1991) 257–73.
Smith, D. M. "The Pauline Literature." In *It Is Written: Scripture Citing Scripture: Essays in Honor of Barnabas Lindars, SSF*, ed. D. A. Carson and H. G. M. Williamson, 265–91. Cambridge: Cambridge University Press, 1988.
Smith, W. B. "Address and Destination of St. Paul's Epistle to the Romans." *JBL* 20 (1901) 1–21.
Stanley, C. D. *Arguing with Scripture: The Rhetoric of Quotations in the Letters of Paul*. New York: T. & T. Clark, 2004.
Stowers, S. K. *The Diatribe and Paul's Letter to the Romans*. SBLDS 57. Chico, CA: Scholars, 1981.
Stuhlmacher, P. "The Purpose of Romans." In *The Romans Debate*, ed. K. P. Donfried, 231–42. Rev. exp. ed. Peabody, MA: Hendrickson, 1991.
Suhl, A. "Der konkrete Anlass des Römerbriefes." *Kairós* 13 (1971) 119–30.
Van der Minde, H.-J. *Schrift und Tradition bei Paulus: Ihre Bedeutung und Funktion im Römerbrief*. Paderborner theologische Studien 3. Münich: Schöningh, 1976.
Watson, D. F. "Diatribe." In *DPL*, ed. by G. F. Hawthorne and R. P. Martin, 213–14. Downers Grove, IL: IVP, 1993.
Wedderburn, A. J. M. "The Purpose and Occasion of Romans Again." In *The Romans Debate*, ed. K. P. Donfried, 195–202. Rev. exp. ed. Peabody, MA: Hendrickson, 1991.
———. *The Reasons for Romans*. Edinburgh: T. & T. Clark, 1988. Reprint, Minneapolis: Fortress, 1991.
Weima, J. A. D. *Neglected Endings: The Significance of the Pauline Letter Closings*. JSNTSup 101. Sheffield: Sheffield Academic, 1994.
———. "Preaching the Gospel in Rome: A Study of the Epistolary Framework of Romans." In *Gospel in Paul: Studies on Corinthians, Galatians and Romans for Richard N. Longenecker*, ed. L. A. Jervis and P. Richardson, 337–66. JSNTSup 108. Sheffield: Sheffield Academic, 1994.
Wilckens, U. *Der Brief an die Römer*. 3 vols. EKK 6/1–3. Zürich: Benziger, 1978–1982.
———. "Über Abfassungszweck und Aufbau des Römerbriefes." In *Rechtfertigung als Freiheit: Paulusstudien*, ed. U. Wilckens, 110–70. Neukirchen-Vluyn: Neukirchener, 1974.
Williams, P. R. "Paul's Purpose in Writing Romans." *BSac* 128 (1971) 62–67.
Wood, J. "The Purpose of Romans." *EvQ* 40 (1968) 211–19.
Wright, N. T. "The Letter to the Romans: Introduction, Commentary, and Reflections." In *The New Interpreter's Bible*, ed. L. E. Keck et al., 10:393–770. Nashville: Abingdon, 2002.
Zeller, D. *Der Brief an die Römer*. RNT 6. Regensburg: Pustet, 1985.

4

Universal Sinfulness and Paul's Reading of the Old Testament in Rom 3:9–18[1]

KYOUNG-SHIK KIM

INTRODUCTION

This study looks into Paul's use of the Old Testament in Rom 3:9–18. Paul often develops his argument by citing or alluding to the OT texts. Paul uses Genesis (3x), Psalms (3x), Deuteronomy (3x), and Isaiah (16x).[2] Among these OT books, Isaiah is used 16x in Romans, which suggests how important the Isaiah text was for Paul in this letter.

This study focuses on the catena in Rom 3:10–18, highlighting Paul's reading of Isa 59 in connection with the theme of universal sinfulness. As mentioned above, Paul employs Isa 16x in Romans, and most of these uses of Isaiah are found in Rom 9–11.[3] When he uses Isaianic texts, Paul usually

---

1. This article was originally published in the journal *Korean New Testament Studies* (2012) under the title: "Paul's Reading of Isaiah 59 in Romans 3:9–18." I am grateful to the editors of *Korean New Testament Studies* for permission to reprint this essay here in revised form.

2. Oss, "Paul's Use of Isaiah," 106. According to Oss, Paul employs Exodus (2x), Hosea (2x), Joel (1x), Malachi (1x), 1 Kings (2x), 1 Samuel (1x), and Job (1x).

3. Ibid. Oss indicates that Paul uses Isaiah 11x out of 16 in Rom 9–11.

cites Isaiah just once or alludes to it.[4] But Paul's use of Isa 59 is different in that he employs the text more than once in Rom 3:15–17 and 11:26.[5]

Paul argues in Rom 3:9–18 that Jews and Gentiles are all sinful and in doing so, he appeals to the Old Testament to support his explanation of universal sinfulness. However, this apparently logical connection between Paul's claim of universal sinfulness and the support from the Old Testament is not transparent. Two questions are salient in the analysis of 3:9–18. First, do the long chains of the Old Testament that Paul uses really support Paul's claim that all human beings, Jews and Gentiles, are sinners? Second, does Paul respect the original context of the cited OT texts? In 3:9–18, Paul does not explicitly indicate whether he appeals to Isaiah, Psalms or any other OT books. He simply interweaves several OT passages without making any distinction among them and without specifying the sources of the texts. So, does Paul cite OT texts while taking into account the original context? Or does he simply use them as proof-texts? This study aims to answer these questions. Although it is necessary to deal with all the texts used in the catena of Rom 3:9–18, the focus of this study is Isa 59 and its tie to the main theme of universal sinfulness.

ROM 3:9–20 AND UNIVERSAL DEPRAVITY

After Paul asserts that Jews and Gentiles are all sinners in Rom 3:9, he cites the longest chain of the OT texts in vv. 10–18 by utilizing the citation formula καθὼς γέγραπται. There have been scholarly debates about the relation between Paul's argument for universal sinfulness and the role of the catena in 3:9–18. Does the catena really support the apostle's assertion that all human beings are under the power of sin? Many scholars would answers this question in the negative.

Davies pays attention to the fact that majority of the cited OT texts in vv. 10–18 is from the Psalter. On the basis of this observation, he looks into the broad context of the cited Psalm texts and Isa 59. His analysis of the OT texts reveals, according to him, that the Psalms show a coherent

---

4. Isaianic texts that are used twice or more are Isa 28 (2x), Isa 29 (2x), Isa 45 (2x), Isa 52 (3x). For a more comprehensive list of Pauline quotations of Isaiah, see Court, *New Testament Writers*, 107–10.

5. Isa 59 plays a crucial role in Paul's argument because of its placement in Romans. The text is utilized in the concluding section of Rom 1:18—3:20 in which Paul explains the wrath of God in a climactic manner and once more Isa 59 is employed in the concluding part of Rom 9–11 which deals with salvation of Israel and Gentiles. Considering the frequency of the use and placement in Romans, the importance of Isa 59 for Paul's argument in Romans becomes clear.

distinction between the righteous and the unrighteous. Davies maintains that depending on the contexts of each psalm, the righteous are indentified with Gentiles or the upright among Israelites. On the basis of his study, he concludes that the Psalm texts and Isa 59 do *not* support Paul's argument for universal sinfulness.[6] He asserts that the chain of the OT texts does not deal with the problem of universal sin. On the contrary, the cited OT texts highlight not the theme of total depravity but the theme that "there is no righteousness among the *wicked*."[7] Davies analyzes the original context of the Old Testament but his conclusion suggests that the logical relation between Rom 3:9 and Rom 10:18 is contradictory or, at the very least, irreconcilable. He tries to connect 3:10–18 not to 3:9 but to 1:17–18 and in so doing, relates the righteous human being to God's righteousness (1:17) and the unrighteous person to God's wrath (1:18). Consequently, Davies argues that there is a sharp distinction between the upright and the wicked throughout Romans.[8] Similarly Keck contends that the original contexts of the OT citations in Rom 3 do not support the apostle's claim of universal sinfulness among human race.[9]

Many scholars since Davies have argued that the cited OT texts *do* support Paul's argument for universal sinfulness among Jews and Gentiles, noting an important link between Rom 3:9 and 3:10–18. Dunn's discussion of this passage in Romans is attractive in that he finds a polemical setting behind 3:10–18. He maintains that Jews believed the wicked in the cited OT passages were identified with Gentiles in particular, excluding Jews, and God's wrath would be upon these Gentiles. According to him, these OT texts were originally used to support Jewish prerogative in which the righteous are identical with Israel and the wicked with the Gentiles.[10] He maintains that Paul redeploys these texts in a dramatic reversal to critique Jewish privileged status. Schreiner seems convinced by Dunn's thesis.[11]

Watson goes beyond Dunn by insisting that Paul has little interest in the original contexts of the OT texts and that the apostle changes the meanings of these texts in order to support his theology.[12] Watson insists that most of the Psalm texts cited in Rom 3:9–18 are related to David, who was considered righteous, and the Jewish people, over time, came to identity

---

6. Davies, *Faith and Obedience*, 89.
7. Ibid., 90.
8. Ibid., 94.
9. Keck, "Function of Rom 3.10–18," 146.
10. Dunn, *Romans 1–8*, 149.
11. Schreiner, *Romans*, 167.
12. Watson, *Paul and the Hermeneutics of Faith*, 63–64.

themselves with David and the promises of God made to him.[13] Seifrid, on the other hand, while insisting that the OT citations do support Paul's claim in 3:9, nevertheless focuses on how Paul modified the OT texts rather than their original contexts. He concludes that Paul combined Isaiah's verdict against Israel with the righteous' complaint against the wicked found in the Psalms to make his case for universal human sinfulness.[14]

Dunn, Schreiner, Watson, and Seifrid maintain the same thrust of argumentation that the OT texts used in Rom 3:10–18 are employed as scriptural proof to support Rom 3:9 in which Paul claims that all are sinners. Nevertheless, their shared view is that Paul modifies the OT texts for the convenience of his argument and that the apostle has little interest in the original contexts of the citations. Rather Paul borrows the phrases and expressions from the Old Testament and redeploys them for his own rhetorical ends.

ROM 3:9–18 AND THE OT TEXTS

Rom 3:9–18 contains the longest citations from the Old Testament in Romans and even in the whole of the Pauline letters. The citation from the Old Testament begins at v. 10 and ends at v. 18, with a set of rhetorical questions introducing the citation at v. 9. The citation from Isa 59:7–8 is found in vv. 15–17. Paul indicates in v. 9 that Jews and Gentiles are all under the power of sin (ὑφ' ἁμαρτίαν εἶναι). Paul's claim of universal sinfulness is given as the answer to the question in 3:1a which deals with the prerogative of Jewish people in the light of their place in redemptive history (3:1–8). Paul then introduces several OT texts with the citation formula. Rom 3:9–18 comprises of the Psalms and Isaiah as follows:

(1) Rom 3:11–12 = Ps 13:1–3 (LXX)

(2) Rom 3:13 = Ps 5:10 (LXX) + Ps 139:4 (LXX)

(3) Rom 3:14 = Ps 9:28 (LXX)

(4) Rom 3:14–17 = Isa 59:7–8 (LXX)

(5) Rom 3:18 = Ps 35:2 (LXX)

It shall be argued that the above passages cited from the Old Testament in Rom 3:10–18 are not randomly collected but contain the following flow of argument: (1) God's verdict is that the Gentiles are sinners, (2) there are the righteous and the unrighteous among Jews, (3) there is no righteous person

---

13. Ibid., 62.
14. Seifrid, "Romans," 615–17.

even among Jews, and (4) God does not show any favoritism to any person according to ethnic distinction.

Ps 13 (LXX) in Rom 3:10–12

First, v. 10 introduces the main idea in the passage. The claim that none is righteous provides the reason why God's wrath (Rom 1:18) should fall upon all human races. The original context of Ps 13 (LXX) cited in vv. 10–12 is concerned with the clear distinction between Israel and the Gentiles. Accordingly, the wicked who deserve God's judgment are Gentiles, the enemy of God's people. Ps 3:7 (LXX) shows that God will save his people, Jacob and Israel. The fool (v. 1), all those who practice lawlessness (v. 4), and those who "eat up my people" (v. 4) are none other than the Gentile nations.[15] Thus, in the first citation from Ps 13 (LXX), Paul indicates that all Gentiles are under God's judgment. Jews could agree to this view.

Ps 5 (LXX) and Ps 139 (LXX) in Rom 3:13

The second category of the citations that Paul employs in the catena contains the idea that there are both the upright and the wicked among Israel. This includes Ps 5 (LXX) and Ps 139 (LXX). Ps 5 (LXX) of which v. 10 is used in Rom 3:13a contrasts the righteous (v12) with the unrighteous that are referred to as "lawbreakers" (v. 6), "all those who speak the lie" (v. 7), "a bloodthirsty and deceitful man" (v. 7), and "my enemies" (v. 9). According to Ps 5 (LXX), the righteous one is identified with the speaker "I" and the "I" belong to all who hope in God (v. 12). The righteous one hopes to enter into God's house (v. 8). In contrast, the wicked ("lawbreakers" v. 6) are described not to "endure before your eyes." The phrase "before your eyes" could mean one's presence in temple worship and ultimately their verdict not to be vindicated at the final judgment before God. This leads us to argue that the wicked are those within Israel. The lawbreakers that God hates are not those outside Israel but those who embitter God as sinful members of the covenantal community (v. 11).[16]

Paul uses Ps 139:4 (LXX) in Rom 3:13 and the text compares the lips of the wicked to venom of vipers. Ps 139:2 (LXX) deals with the prayer of the righteous one that the Lord might rescue him from the wicked and then

---

15. Kissane, *Book of Psalms*, 54; Mowinckel, *Psalms in Israel's Worship*, 220.

16. Anderson, *Book of Psalms*, 1:81; Briggs and Briggs, *A Commentary on the Psalms*, 1:40. Oesterley, *Psalms*, 132.

v. 4 describes who the wicked are. Thus the psalm also contains the sharp distinction between the upright (v. 14) and the unrighteous (vv. 2, 5, 9). Who are the wicked according to Ps 139 (LXX)? The reference to "a day of battle" in v. 8 seems to suggest the righteous one is a kingly figure and the wicked are the Gentile armies who oppose him.[17] However, it is more likely that "a day of battle" is mentioned not as a present event but as a past one as the ground for the righteous one's confidence in God.[18] The reference to "a day of battle" should be taken figuratively along with the image of hunting as symbolizing persecution.[19] Accordingly, there is no compelling reason to see the phrase "a day of battle" as implying the Gentile wicked. Ps 139:12 (LXX) provides a clue to the identity of the wicked. The wicked according to v. 12 (LXX) will "not succeed in the land." Weiser indicates that this means the wicked will be excluded from the cultic community and thus they do not inherit their land in Israel.[20] The last verse of Ps 139 (LXX), "the upright shall live together with your presence" implies that this psalm is closely related to temple worship because "your presence" means temple.[21] Although there is no explicit indication about the identity of the wicked, it is more likely that the unrighteous are sinful Israelites in contrast to those who can participate in cultic ceremony in the temple.[22]

Ps 9:28 (LXX) in Rom 3:14

Ps 9 (LXX) quoted in Rom 3:14 supports Paul's argument that all people groups without distinction are sinful. While the MT of Pss 9 and 10 are separated, the Septuagint treats these two psalms as one unit. It is likely that the two separate psalms are originally one psalm on the basis of the following two reasons: (1) the initial verses of both psalms follow the Hebrew alphabetical order with some variations, and (2) Ps 10 (MT) does not have a title or heading for it.[23] What is important for our analysis is the fact that Ps 9 (MT) and Ps 10 (MT) are treated as one unit in the LXX.

---

17. Croft, *Identity of the Individual*, 32. Croft does not exclude Gentiles from the identity of the wicked. However, he contends that the main members of the wicked are sinful Israelites.

18. Weiser, *Psalms*, 809.

19. Allen, *Psalms 101–150*, 266.

20. Weiser, *Psalms*, 810.

21. Ibid. Weiser argues that the last verse of the psalm describes the righteous as participating in cultic ceremonies.

22. Anderson, *Book of Psalms*, 2:914; Oesterley, *Psalms*, 558.

23. Craigie, *Psalms 1–50*, 116; Weiser, *Psalms*, 149.

Paul usually prefers the Septuagint to the Hebrew text of the Old Testament and this suggests that Paul could have read Pss 9 and 10 as one psalm rather than two separated compositions. This possibility shows why Paul argues for universal sinfulness in Rom 3 on the basis of scriptural interpretation. The first part of Ps 9 (LXX), which is identical with the Hebrew text of Ps 9, indicates that the unrighteous in the psalm are Gentile nations, as v. 5 (LXX) shows. Verse 16 (LXX) designates the wicked more clearly as Gentiles:

> Nations got stuck in the corruption they produced; in this trap, which they hid, their own foot was caught (Ps 9:16; LXX)[24]

In addition, the wicked are identified as the Gentile nations throughout Ps 9:18, 20, 21 (LXX).

Then, who are the unjust in the last part (vv. 22–39) of Ps 9 in the Septuagint, which corresponds to the Hebrew text of Ps 10? Do we have to understand the wicked as the same Gentile nations as the earlier part of Ps 9? Psalm 9 LXX refers to Gentile nations in the context of God's kingship. The speaker of this psalm asks God to prevent Gentile nations from practicing wickedness by breaking their arms. Accordingly, it is likely that the wicked are the Gentile nations.[25] Nonetheless, it is also possible to include sinful Israelites in the wicked group because the references are made to the powerful men who did wickedness.[26] In Ps 10:4 (MT), the wicked are described as "cursing and renouncing God." Similarly, Ps 9:24 LXX (= Ps 10:4 MT) claims that the impious think that there is no God before him. Also, v. 34 (LXX) shows that the wicked provoked God. The expression "curse and renounce God" is easily applied to the sinful Israelites. Therefore, it is very likely that the wicked in Ps 9 (LXX) and its corresponding Hebrew text (Ps 9–10) are not only the Gentile nations but also the sinful Israelites within the covenant community.

In sum, the earlier section of Ps 9 (LXX) points out that the unjust are Gentile nations but the later section of Ps 9 (LXX) implies that there are also sinners among the Israelites. Thus, Ps 9 (LXX) could suggest to Paul that there is no partiality in God's judgment in dealing with both Jews and Gentiles.

---

24. Unless otherwise noted, all English translations of the LXX are by Pietersma and Wright, *New English Translation of the Septuagint*.

25. Kissane, *Book of Psalms*, 36.

26. Oesterley, *Psalms*, 145.

Ps 35:2 (LXX) in Rom 3:18

The last citation from the Old Testament in the longest catena (Rom 3:10–18) is Ps 35:2 (LXX). This psalm is characterized with the sharp contrast between the wicked's deeds and God's mercy.[27] Who are the wicked in Ps 35 (LXX)? Briggs understands the unjust not to be Gentiles but to be the sinful Israelites in the faith community.[28] The reason, as Davies argues, is that to fear God is the essential requirement for the covenant members of Israel. Accordingly, this psalm functions as a warning to unrighteous Israelites. Yet Ps 35 (LXX) also contains the idea that God is not only the Lord of Israel but also of the whole world. This is because vv. 6–7 show that God's mercy and truth reach the sky, and His righteousness and judgments are also extended not only to humans but also to animals (v. 7).[29] In other words, God is described as carrying out his righteousness and judgment toward the whole world. It is highly likely that Paul could understand this universal aspect of God's righteousness and judgment as embedded in the psalm when he argued universal sinfulness in Rom 3:9–18.[30]

PAUL'S READING OF ISA 59 IN ROM 3:15–17

Does Paul Use Isa 59?

It is only Paul among the NT writers that uses Isa 59. Considering his use of Isa 59 in other letters (1Thess 5:8; Eph 6:14, 17), it seems clear that his use of Isa 59 in Romans reflects Paul's unique understanding of Isa 59. Paul uses Isa 59 twice in Romans. His first use of Isa 59 in Romans is located in Rom 3:15–17.[31] The comparison between Rom 3:15–17 and Isa 59:7–8 (LXX) is necessary to confirm the presence of Isa 59 in this passage.

In Rom 3:15, every word except the first one is identical with Isa 59:7 (LXX). The apparently different word ὀξεῖς is conceptually similar to ταχινός because these words mean "fast" or "swift." Stanley contends that Paul prefers ὀξεῖς to ταχινός because the latter is not frequently used in Greek

---

27. Jacobson, "Psalm 36:5–11," 64.
28. Briggs and Briggs, *A Commentary on the Psalms*, 1:315.
29. Craigie, *Psalms 1–50*, 292.
30. It is also possible that Paul discovers God's impartial salvation to all humans without racial differences in Ps 35(LXX) when he cites the psalm in Rom 3:1–20 where the necessity for the wrath of God is explained. Ps 35 also mentions the theme of God's impartial mercy. Thus, Paul already has God's mercy in view even when he mentions divine wrath in Rom 3:1–20.
31. The second citation from Isa 59 is found in Rom 11:26.

literature whereas the former is a more commonly used word.³² Also, it is likely that Paul uses Isa 59:7b (LXX) in Rom 3:16 since every word in 3:16 is found in the Isaiah text. Lastly, there is a strong verbal similarity between Rom 3:17 and Isa 59:8a except the last word (ἔγνωσαν) in 3:17. These pieces of evidence suggest that Paul cites Isa 59:7–8 in Rom 3:15–17.

However, in spite of this strong verbal connection between these two texts, it has been maintained that Paul does not use the OT texts here but he simply employs a pre-composed texts which were available for Paul to utilize in Romans. One of the first proponents for this view is Keck. Jewett in his commentary on Romans follows Keck's argument while he pays more attention to how Paul redacted the composed text available to him.³³ It is necessary to interact more with Keck since he is probably the first scholar who has held the view of Paul's use of the pre-composed text in Rom 3:9–18.

The catena looks like, according to Keck, a pre-composition of non-Pauline authorship when taken from the context of Rom 3.³⁴ In addition, he has discussed that the comparison between Rom 3:10–18 with the previous context in Rom 1–3 shows a logical contradiction because the former does not support Paul's argument in the earlier section in Rom 1–3.³⁵ Accordingly, Keck concludes that the catena does not show Paul's theology or his interpretation of the Old Testament since it is not Paul's own composition. If Keck's argument is right, it is useless to look into the catena to understand Paul's reading of the Old Testament and Isa 59 in particular because the catena is not Paul's own use of the Old Testament. Not all scholars follow Keck's view in this matter.

Probably the most persuasive argument against Keck's thesis is Shum's view. Shum summarized Keck's argument as follows:

> First, the catena has its own internal structure and theme; second, the elements of Paul's arguments in Rom 1:18—3:8 do not appear in the catena; third, the catena is found to have something in common with other apocalyptic literature (like 2Esdr. 7:21ff; Assum.Mos 5:2–6; CD 5:13–17) and with later later Christian writings (like Justin's *Dial.* 27:3) and with later Christian writings (like Justin's *Dial.* 27:3).³⁶

After this summary, Shum argues against Keck's view point by point. First, he discusses that the intricate composition of the text in itself is not necessarily

32. Stanley, *Paul and the Language of Scripture*, 96.
33. Jewett, *Romans*, 254.
34. Keck, *Romans*, 97.
35. Keck, "Function of Rom 3.10–18," 146.
36. Shum, *Paul's Use of Isaiah*, 181.

a strong counter-evidence against the argument for Pauline authorship.[37] Against the second point above, Shum contends that Rom 3:10–18 has a different contextual function—i.e., to support Rom 3:9b—and thus does not summarize Rom 1:18—3:9, as Keck mistakenly argues. Finally, regarding the final point about the shared apocalyptic features, he points out that Rom 3:10–18 is characterized with elements which reflect Paul's own apocalyptic understanding, not that of a another Jewish (or Christian) apocalypticist.

Moreover, Seifrid argues against Keck that there is no instance in early Jewish literature nor early Christian literature which has the exactly same configuration of OT citations in a single text as in Rom 3:10–18. Therefore, he concludes that the catena is Paul's own composition.[38] Furthermore, it is also probable that the citation formula (καθὼς γέγραπται ὅτι) in Rom 3:10 is a clear evidence to support that the catena is Paul's. This citation formula is used three times in Romans (3:10; 4:17; 8:36). Apart from Rom 3:10, there are other uses of the same formula to introduce OT citation. Rom 4:17 uses Gen 17:5 with this phrase and also Rom 8:36 introduces Ps 43:23 (LXX). There is a shorter form (καθὼς γέγραπται) that is found in the Gospels and exclusively in Romans and 2 Corinthians. This shorter form is also used in early Jewish literature to introduce OT citations.[39] The evidence, accordingly, suggest that Paul does not employ a text composed earlier by someone else but he himself cites directly from the Old Testament.

There is another objection to the view that Paul cites Isa 59:7–8 (LXX) in Rom 3:15–17. Hüber suggests the possibility that Prov 1:16 is cited here together with Isa 59:7–8.[40] It is admitted that there is verbal similarity among Rom 3:15, Isa 57:7(LXX), and Prov 1:16 (LXX). However, it is unlikely that Prov 1:16 (LXX) is used here in Rom 3:15 for two reasons. First, Isa 59:7 is used not only in Rom 3:15 but also in 3:16. In addition to that, the next verse to Isa 59:7, i.e., 57:8, is also employed in Rom 3:17. To put it another way, Isa 59:7–8 are used in Rom 3:16–17 in the immediate context and thus it is more likely that Rom 3:15 also cites Isa 59:7, not Prov 1:16. Furthermore, Proverbs is used only once in Romans (Rom 12:20 = Prov 25:21–22) whereas Isaiah is more frequently cited. Also, Isa 59 which we examine here is used once more in Rom 11. The frequency of the use of Isa 59 as well as the frequent employment of Isaiah in Romans points to the probability that Paul uses not Prov 1:16 (LXX) but Isa 59:7 (LXX) in Rom 3:15.[41]

---

37. Ibid., 182.
38. Seifrid, "Romans," 616.
39. Ellis, *Paul's Use of the Old Testament*, 48–49.
40. Hüber, *Vetus Testamentum in Novo*, 2:54.
41. For more criteria to decide the presence of the Old Testament in the New, see

The Original Context of Isa 59

What is Paul's intention in using Isa 59 in the catena? Paul discovered the imbedded meaning of Jewish universal sinfulness, that is, all Jews are sinful without exception. Our close analysis of the text and context of Isa 59 will show that the text in Rom 3 functions in a more subtle manner than it appears. Isa 59 is an important text for Paul to develop his argument in Rom 3 that the indictment in Isa 59 is not targeted against Gentiles but Israel.

It is very clear that Isa 59 (LXX) deals with God's judgment against his own people.[42] Isa 59 (LXX) is composed of three parts. The first two parts can be divided on the basis of the change in personal pronouns and the last part can be discerned according to the shift in focus.[43] The first part (1–11a) is concerned with the verdict against Israel's sin and is mainly characterized with the use of second person plural pronouns ("you") to refer to the people of Israel as a whole. The second part (11b–15a) deals with confession of sin and interestingly first person plural pronouns ("we") replace second person plural pronouns which dominate the first part.[44] The last part (15b–21) of Isa 59 (LXX) highlights God in contrast with sinful Israel and yet God's saving activity for Israel. The structure of Isa 59 (LXX) is summarized as follows:

1–11a: Indictment against the sin of Israel ("you")

11b–15a: Israel's confession of sin ("we")

15b–21: God's salvation and the restoration of Israel

In Rom 3, Paul cites v. 7 from the first section of Isa 59. Accordingly, Paul supports the universal sinfulness without ethnic distinction by citing from the first section in which the people of Israel are charged with sinfulness. At first glance, Paul seems to misunderstand and thus to distort the original meaning of the text since the indictment in Isa 59:1–11a is closely related to sinful people in the covenant community rather than Gentiles or all human races. However, a closer look at the broad context of Isa 59 and the role of Isa 59 in Rom 3:9–11 shows that Paul interpreted Isa 59 in its literary and historical context, but he also uses the Isaianic text in a more nuanced way.

Kim, *God Will Judge Each One according to Works*, 34–36.

42. Watts, *Isaiah 34–66*, 280.

43. Most of scholars who analyze Isa 59 pay attention to the change of personal pronouns in this text. For example, Motyer, *Prophecy of Isaiah*, 484.

44. There is difference between the MT and the LXX. The MT first employs third person plural pronouns ("they") and then starts to use first person plural pronouns ("we") in v. 9. But the LXX utilizes first person plural pronouns ("we") in v11b. Cf. Oswalt, *Book of Isaiah 40–66*, 516n31.

Paul understands Isa 59 to deal with sin of Israel. As indicated above, most scholars agree that Isa 59 has to do with indictment against sinful Israel. Yet, our earlier analysis of the cited Psalm texts in Rom 3:10–18 reveals that within the Jewish view there are both righteous ones and wicked people within the covenant community of Israel. The Israelites believed that not all Israelites are righteous since only some of them will be punished on account of their wickedness, while the Gentiles as a whole are subject to God's punishment. This line of thought is found in the citations of Psalms from the catena of Rom 3.

However, Paul's uniquely reads Isa 59 as proving that there are no righteous ones in Israel at all. It is probable that the change in personal pronouns in Isa 59 enables Paul to uphold the view that all Jews are sinners without exception. The first section of Isa 59 (LXX) charges Israel with wickedness and in so doing it employs second person plural pronouns (you/your). The pronoun "you" in the context refers to other groups of sinful Israelites except the upright Israelites ("we"). Thus, the text seems to support Jewish thought that some are righteous and others are wicked among Israelites. Yet Paul's reading of the second section of Isa 59 (LXX) changes this view with which Paul could have consented. This is because the second part in Isa 59 (LXX) is concerned with the confession of sin by the upright who are referred to as "we" in the Isaianic text. The second section (11b–15a) describes the act of lawlessness and sins of the "we" who had been contrasted with the wicked ("they") in the first section of Isa 59 (LXX). The prophet Isaiah starts to speak of the sin of the righteous and their wickedness.[45] Consequently, he includes all the righteous Israelites among the sinful. He identifies the upright with the rest of the wicked in the second section. In other words, the text of Isa 59 (LXX) has an imbedded semantic potential in which there is no distinction between the righteous and the unrighteous because all are sinners before God. Although Paul cites from the first section of Isa 59, he also has in mind the second section.

What is more, Isa 59:15b–21 (LXX) emphasizes the situation in which all the people of God are totally unjust. This last section sharply contrasts God's salvation with the sinfulness of His people. What is underscored here is the hopeless condition in which the people of God cannot save themselves with their own power. Verse 16 is the clear evidence for this view.[46] God himself intervenes to save Israel on the basis of his mercy. The last

---

45. Oswalt, *Book of Isaiah 40–66*, 519; Brueggemann, *Isaiah 40–66*, 2:199.

46. There is a important difference between Isa 59:16 (MT) and its corresponding text in the LXX. In 59:16 (MT) God's righteousness is found but the LXX has God's mercy in place of it. Thus, the ground for God's salvation of His people is divine righteousness in the Hebrew Bible.

section (15b–21) of Isa 59 (LXX) transparently shows the total depravity of Israel and also indicates that God is the only source for salvation. To put it another way, Isa 59 (LXX) has a hermeneutical seed which suggests that not only Jews but also all human races are powerless for salvation and thus all are under the power of sin such that all human races can be saved only on the basis of divine mercy and righteousness. Paul probably develops this semantic potential imbedded in Isa 59.[47] All of these ideas are similar to Paul's argument in Romans as a whole. It is highly likely that on the basis of his reading of Isa 59 in which God is described as the only hope for salvation, Paul could confirm his view that all human races as well as all Israelites are sinners.

Our analysis of the catena in Rom 3:10–18 which includes Isa 59 shows how intricate and subtle Paul's use of the Old Testament is.[48] Paul does not distort the original meaning of the Old Testament for his own theological purpose(s) as proof-texts. Above all, Isa 59 in Rom 3:15–17 is a significant text to show that all Jews are totally depraved, which can be developed to mean universal sinfulness of all nations including Israel.

The Use of Isa 59 in Early Jewish Literature

Is Paul's reading of universal sinfulness in Isa 59 his own unique interpretation or is it dependent upon early Jewish reading(s) of the same text? In order to answer this question, it is imperative to look into early Jewish texts which employ Isa 59. Interestingly, Isa 59 is used several times in the Damascus Document (CD).[49] Campbell examined the use of the Old Testament in the Damascus Document and argued that Isa 59 plays a significant part in the document. He looked into the text of CD 1–8 and 19–20 and discerns two parts, namely, the historical sections and the midrashic sections. Then, he dealt with the citations of, and allusions to, the three parts of

---

47. The later part of Isa 59 indicates: there appears "a man" whom the Spirit of God is upon. This interpretation is supported by the change of personal pronoun from "they" to "you" in v. 21 (cf. Motyer, *Prophecy of Isaiah*, 492–93). Considering the whole context of Isaiah, the man is God's instrument and his "servant" who will save Israel. The early church identifies this servant with Jesus Christ.

48. Intriguingly, two texts (LXX) that Paul cites in Rom 3:15–17 share two common concepts: God's mercy and his righteousness (Isa 59:16–17; Ps 35:6–7).

49. It has been suggested that 4 Ezra (= 2 Esdras) 7:22–24 uses Isa 59. But there is no clear verbal similarity, just minimal conceptual similarity. Furthermore, 4 Ezra is dated to the late and as a result the text is not useful chronologically to shed light on our interpretation of Romans.

the Old Testament (*Torah, Neviim, Ketuvim*).[50] According to him, Isa 59:10, 12 is used in CD 1:1—2:1 and Isa 59:20 is employed in CD 2:2–13. Also Isa 59:20 is utilized in CD 2:14–4:12a and Isa 59:5 is found in CD 4:12b–5:15a. Furthermore, Isa 59:20 is present in CD 5:15b–6:11a, CD 6:11b–8:21 and CD 19:33–20:34.

On the basis of Campbell's examination, this study will focus on the use of Isa 59 in CD in the context of sin, depravity, and judgment in order to compare it with its employment in Rom 3. Campbell's investigation shows that Isa 59 is used 5 times in CD 1–8 and 19–20. What is intriguing is how Isa 59:20 is used in abbreviated forms rather than in the form of citations or allusions. By contrast, Isa 59:5, 10, 12 are used in a little longer form in the context of sin and its consequences.

CD 1:8b–9

CD 1:8b–9 utilizes Isa 59:10, 12, while Isa 59:10 is employed first in CD 1:9 and then Isa 59:12 is in CD 1:8. The broader context (CD 1:1–2:1) in which CD 1:8–9 are located treats God's judgment of Israel and God's election of the remnants among Israel. CD 1:3–12 are concerned with history from Israel's sinful deeds before exile to the appearance of the teacher of righteousness and his teaching of the truth.[51] In this context, the Damascus Document explains that Israel had experienced the exile as a result of God's judgment ("the period of wrath"; CD 1:5) before it makes reference to the beginning of the Qumran community to which the author(s) of CD belong(s).

The passage which employs Isa 59:10, 12 deals with the situation right before the appearance of the teacher of righteousness. Isa 59 is used in the context which describes the situation right after the return from the exile as the result of Israel's confession of wickedness and their subsequent repentance.[52] The people of Israel acknowledge their sin, repent, and seek God "with an undivided heart" (CD 1:10). The Damascus Document understands Isa 59 as being related to the confession and repentance of Israel and

---

50. Campbell admits that it is difficult to distinguish citations from allusions. Campbell, *Use of Scripture in the Damascus Document*, 176.

51. Davies, *Damascus Covenant*, 61. For the discussion of the teacher of righteousness, see Davies, *Sects and Scrolls*, 89–94.

52. Campbell views CD 1:1—2:1 as describing the situation before the exile to Babylon. Cf. Campbell, *Use of Scripture in the Damascus Document*, 67. However, It is more likely that the references to 390 years in CD 1:3–5 and to twenty years in CD 1:10 indicate that the period under our examination here is related to the period between the return from the exile and the appearance of the teacher of righteousness.

also describes sinful Israel as being 'like blind persons and like those who grope for a path' (CD 1:10). The same perspective is found here between the original context of Isa 59 and the understanding of Isa 50 in CD 1. Both texts deal with the sin of Israel.

However, Paul uses Isa 59 differently from the Damascus Document. Paul reads Isa 59 as describing universal sin among Israel: all are sinful without exception. By contrast, CD understands it as referring to the situation in which some Israelites are righteous (CD 1:4) and others are wicked. Also in the Damascus Document, God is described as sending the teacher of righteousness because the righteous ones sought God with all their hearts and God remembered his covenant. In sum, the context where Isa 59 is employed in the Damascus Document is concerned with Israel's blindness of "forsaking God" (CD 1:3) and its repentance. Thus, CD does not understand Isa 59 as describing universal sinfulness among Israelites whereas Rom 3 does.

CD 5:13-14

Isa 59 is also used in CD 5:13-14.[53] This passage describes the opponents of the Damascus community. The text employs two metaphors of a spider's web and viper's eggs to refer to the wicked deeds of the unrighteous. It is noteworthy that these two metaphors are also used in Isa 59 to depict the sinful behavior of Israel. The Damascus Document describes the wicked deeds with the metaphor from Isa 59, but it does not apply them to universal sinfulness among Israelites but to outsiders of the Qumran community. These outsiders are those who "have opened their mouth against the statutes of God's covenant" (CD 5:12). This shows that there is a difference between the use of Isa 59 in Rom 3 and its use in CD. The Document describes only the outsiders of the community as sinful. In contrast, Paul does not refer to a particular group of people as sinners but the whole of humanity. Paul's understanding of Isa 59 is not arbitrary because there is a hermeneutical seed imbedded in the text of Isa 59 that can be developed to argue for universal sinfulness, as our analysis above showed.

To summarize, there is a difference between the use of Isa 59 in Rom 3 and its use in CD. Unlike Paul who reads it as supporting the idea of universal sin, CD does not understand the text as arguing for universal sin. Although CD 1:8b-9 read Isa 59 as being related to the results of God's

---

53. Campbell argues that CD 5:13ff. combine Isa 59:5 and Isa 50:11 (*Use of Scripture in the Damascus Document*, 129). Our focus, however, is on the use of Isa 59 and therefore our analysis will not consider Isa 50.

judgment, which is similar to Paul's argument in Rom 3, the text does not understand Isa 59 to indicate universal sinfulness. Also, the use of Isa 59 in CD 5:13–14 is different from its use of Isa 59 in Rom 3. In reading Isa 59, CD 5 understands the righteous as referring to its community and views the wicked as the outsiders of the community. By contrast, Paul interprets Isa 59 as announcing that all are sinful and accordingly understands the Isaianic text as identifying the wicked with all nations without ethnic distinction. So Paul's reading of Isa 59 in Rom 3 is independent from early Jewish interpretations of the same text. Paul is also the only New Testament writer who employs Isa 59 in his discourse.

Paul indicates that Jews have no privilege over Gentiles in terms of sin and divine judgment. Furthermore, the apostle does not believe that there are some righteous Jews among Israel. On the basis of reading Isa 59, he argues that all Jews are sinners and consequently deserve God's judgment along with the rest of humanity. In addition, the following v. 19 after the text of Rom 3:10–18 clearly has a Jewish referent in Paul's longest of citations from the Old Testament. That all Jews are sinners is buttressed by Paul's reading and citation of Isa 59 in Rom 3:15–17 as well. It is likely that Paul's reading of Isa 59 also enables him to confirm his belief that human salvation is totally dependent upon divine sovereignty (Isa 59:16). Isa 59 contains the ideas of total depravity and divine initiative for human salvation with which Paul shares in Romans. Also, Isa 59 implies a figure that plays a crucial role in God's saving plan (vv. 20–21) and includes the idea of Gentiles' inclusion into God's people (v. 19). In sum, Isa 59 is a small 'the letter to the Romans' or Romans in a "nutshell."

CONCLUSION

Our analysis shows how intricate Paul's use of the Old Testament is in the catena in Rom 3:10–18. Of course, it is admitted that Rom 3:9–18 is clear as it stands without considering the original OT contexts. Gentiles who did not have sufficient knowledge of Israel's Scriptures could have understood the passages enough because Rom 3:9–18 has its own flow of argumentation within the literary context of Romans itself. However, their reading and studying of Isa 59 as well as other OT citations in their original contexts would have enhanced their understanding of Rom 3. The flow of argument in the long citations from Psalms and Isa 59 in Rom 3:11–18 develops as follows:

(1) Rom 3:11–12: Gentiles are sinners (Ps 13).

(2) Rom 3:13: Some Jews are righteous while other Jews are wicked (Ps 5; Ps 139).

(3) Rom 3:14: God judges both Jews and Gentiles (Ps 9 LXX).

(4) Rom 3:15–17: Even Jews are all sinners without exception (Isa 59).

(5) Rom 3:18: God is impartial in dealing with whole world (Ps 35).

Paul respects the original context and meaning of the Psalms and Isaiah. The several citations are tightly interwoven to support Paul's argument that all humanity is under the power of sin whether Jews or Gentiles. Yet, these citations do not shout independently from one another but unite their voices into one purpose to assert that all Jews are included in God's wrath against the nations. The logic of Paul's rhetoric moves from: (1) Gentiles are all sinners, to (2) some Jews are sinners, to (3) all Jews are sinners. Paul does not randomly collect several OT texts to support his theology without considering their original contexts, as our study has showed. Above all, Isa 59 is the most significant text which embeds a semantic potential from which Paul reads the idea that even the people of God are unrighteous and therefore all human races are depraved. The whole of humanity needs the deliverance of God.

BIBLIOGRAPHY

Allen, L. C. *Psalms 101–150*. WBC 21. Waco: Word, 1983.
Anderson, A. A. *The Book of Psalms*. 2 vols. New Century Bible Commentary. London: Oliphants, 1972.
Birkeland, H. *The Evildoers in the Book of Psalms*. Oslo: Dybward, 1965.
Briggs, C. A., and E. G. Briggs. *A Critical and Exegetical Commentary on the Book of Psalms*. Vol 1. ICC. Edinburgh: T. & T. Clark, 1907.
Brueggemann, Walter. *Isaiah*. Vol 2, *40–66*. Louisville: Westminster John Knox, 1998.
Campbell, Jonathan G. *The Use of Scripture in the Damascus Document 1–8, 19–20*. BZAW 228. Berlin: de Gruyter, 1995.
Court, John M., ed. *New Testament Writers and the Old Testament: An Introduction*. London: SPCK, 2002.
Craigie, Peter C. *Psalms 1–50*. WBC 19. Waco: Word, 1983.
Croft, Steven J. L. *The Identity of the Individual in the Psalms*. Sheffield: Sheffield Academic, 1987.
Davies, Glenn N. *Faith and Obedience in Romans: A Study in Romans 1–4*. JSNTSup 39. Sheffield: JSOT Press, 1990.
Davies, Philip R. *The Damascus Covenant: An Interpretation of the Damascus Document*. JSOTSup 25. Sheffield: JSOT Press, 1982.
Dunn, James D.G. *Romans 1–8*. WBC 38A. Dallas: Word, 1988.
Ellis, E. Earle. *Paul's Use of the Old Testament*. Repr. Eugene, OR: Wipf & Stock, 1981.

Hüber, Hans. *Vetus Testamentum in Novo.* Vol. 2, *Corpus Paulinum.* Göttingen: Vandenhoeck & Ruprecht, 1997.

Jacobson, Rolf A. "Psalm 36:5–11." *Int* (2007) 64–66.

Jewett, Robert. *Romans: A Commentary.* Hermeneia. Minneapolis: Fortress, 2007.

Keck, L. E. "The Function of Rom 3.10–18. Observations and Suggestions." In *God's Christ and His People,* ed. Jacob Jervell et al., 141–57. Oslo: Universites-forlaget, 1977.

———. *Romans.* Nashville: Abingdon, 2005.

Kim, Kyoung-Shik. *God Will Judge Each One according to Works: Judgment according to Works and Psalm 62 in Early Judaism and the New Testament.* BZNW 178. Berlin: de Gruyter, 2010.

———. "Paul's Reading of Isaiah 59 in Romans 3:9–18." *Korean New Testament Studies* 19, no. 3 (2012) 937–79.

Kissane, E. J. *The Book of Psalms.* Vol. 1. Dublin: Richview, 1953.

Motyer, J. A. *The Prophecy of Isaiah: An Introduction and Commentary.* Downers Grove, IL: IVP, 1993.

Mowinckel, S. *The Psalms in Israel's Worship.* Vol. 1. Oxford: Blackwell, 1982.

Oesterley, W. O. E. *The Psalms: Translated with Text-Critical and Exegetical Notes.* London: SPCK, 1939.

Oss, Douglas A. "A Note on Paul's Use of Isaiah." *BBR* 2 (1992) 105–12.

Oswalt, John N. *The Book of Isaiah 40–66.* NICOT. Grand Rapids: Eerdmans, 1998.

Pietersma, Albert and Benjamin G. Wright. *A New English Translation of the Septuagint.* Oxford: Oxford University Press, 2007.

Schreiner, Thomas R. *Romans.* BECNT. Grand Rapids: Baker Academic, 1998.

Seifrid, Mark A. "Romans." In *Commentary on the New Testament Use of the Old Testament,* ed. G. K. Beale and D. A. Carson, 607–94. Grand Rapids: Baker, 2007.

Shum, Shiu-Lun. *Paul's Use of Isaiah in Romans: A Comparative Study of Paul's Letter to the Romans and the Sibylline and Qumran Sectarian Texts.* WUNT 2/156. Tübingen: Mohr/Siebeck, 2002.

Stanley, Christopher. *Paul and the Language of Scripture: Citation Technique in the Pauline Epistles and Contemporary Literature.* SNTSMS 74. Cambridge: Cambridge University Press, 1992.

Wagner, J. Ross. *Herald of the Good News: Isaiah and Paul "in Concert" in the Letter to the Romans.* NovTSup 101. Leiden: Brill, 2002.

Watson, Francis. *Paul and the Hermeneutics of Faith.* London: T. & T. Clark, 2004.

Watts, John D. W. *Isaiah 34–66.* WBC 25. Waco: Word, 1987.

Weiser, A. *The Psalms: A Commentary.* London: SCM, 1962.

5

The Antithesis between the Law and Grace in Gal 5:4[1]

HUNG-SIK CHOI

INTRODUCTION

The Galatians were willing to depend on the law for their justification because they were persuaded by the agitators' teaching that Gentiles can be full and genuine members of the covenant community through Torah-observance, in particular circumcision. There is little doubt that the agitators argued for justification on the basis of the law (2:16, 21; 3:11, 18, 21). In Gal 5:4b and 5:4c Paul tackles the issue of justification saying: οἵτινες ἐν νόμῳ δικαιοῦσθε, τῆς χάριτος ἐξεπέσατε ("You who want to be justified in the sphere of the law have fallen away from grace").[2] Τῆς χάριτος ἐξεπέσατε denotes that the Galatians' attempt to depend upon the law has resulted in their separation from grace. Thus Paul contrasts the law with grace as two mutually exclusive foundations of justification.

---

1. An earlier version of this article was published in *Scripture and Interpretation* (2008). I am grateful to the editors of *S&I* for permission to reprint this essay here.

2. Unless otherwise noted, all English translations from the Greek are the author's own.

Paul attempts to solve the issue of justification by setting the law in antithesis with grace as two mutually exclusive soteriological sources for justification. The two terms (the law and grace) seem to represent larger complexes of belief and praxis and the larger complexes are summarized in the antithesis.[3] While many scholars have rightly observed this antithesis,[4] they have not satisfactorily expounded its force, function, and significance with special reference to the issues at stake in Galatia, in particular the Galatians' desire to accept the law for justification.

There are several questions for us: What does Paul intend to achieve through the antithesis? Why does Paul hold that grace is sufficient for justification of the Gentiles in Galatians? What is the significance of the antithesis both for Paul's opposition to the law as the soteriological basis of justification and for his critique of covenantal nomism? In order to answer these questions, it is first necessary to explain the meaning of χάρις.

THE MEANING OF ΧΑΡΙΣ

What did Paul have in mind when he says the Galatians have fallen from ἡ χάρις? Without attempting to investigate the full range of χάρις in Paul's letters,[5] it is sufficient to focus on Galatians not only because χάρις with the article (ἡ) probably refers back to that grace of God, of Christ, or both, which Paul explained to the Galatians in the previous section,[6] but also because ἡ χάρις seems to summarize Paul's previous argument about grace. In Galatians χάρις occurs seven times (1:3, 6, 15; 2:9, 21; 5:4; 6:18). It is proper to deal with each occurrence in order to clarify the meaning of ἡ χάρις in 5:4.

The word χάρις is employed in the opening salutation (1:3) and closing benediction (6:18) as in Paul's other letters.[7] When χάρις is used in

---

3. Moffatt notes the significance of the antithesis by saying: "Law and Grace are viewed as incompatible systems of religion. To toy with the former is to invalidate the latter" (*Grace in the New Testament*, 182).

4. This is properly pointed out by Betz, *Galatians*, 261; Burton, *Epistle to the Galatians*, 275, 277; Dunn, *Paul's Letter to the Galatians*, 269; Fung, *Epistle to the Galatians*, 223–24; Mußner, *Galaterbrief*, 349; Oepke, *Paulus an die Galater*, 119.

5. For the word study of χάρις in Paul, see Berger, "χάρις, ιτος, ἡ." 457–60; Conzelmann, "χάρις, κτλ.," 373–76, 387–402; Eastmann, "The Significance of Grace." For the central role of χάρις in Paul's theology, see Conzelmann, "χάρις, κτλ.," 393; Dunn, *Theology of Paul*, 319–20; Westerholm, *Israel's Law*, 165–69.

6. Burton, *Galatians*, 276.

7. χάρις ὑμῖν καὶ εἰρήνη ἀπὸ θεοῦ πατρὸς ἡμῶν καὶ κυρίου Ἰησοῦ Χριστοῦ (Rom 1:7; 1 Cor 1:3; 2 Cor 1:2; Gal 1:3; Phil 1:2; Phm 1:3; cf. Eph 1:2; Col 1:2; 1 Thess 1:2; 2 Thess 1:2; 1 Tim 1:2; 2 Tim 1:2; Titus 1:4); ἡ χάρις τοῦ κυρίου Ἰησοῦ μεθ' ὑμῶν (Rom 16:20;

relation to his greeting and benediction, it normally refers to the "favor" of God or Jesus Christ which sustains and empowers believers. So χάρις (1:3; 6:18) refers to God's or Christ's continuous mercy, spiritual benefit, and enabling for the edification of believers, not to God's past redemptive act in and through Christ.

What is the meaning of χάρις at 1:6? In order to clarify its meaning, it is necessary to define the meaning of the phrase ἐν χάριτι [Χριστοῦ]. First of all, we should decide what the original reading among the five variant readings is.[8] As Metzger indicates, "the absence of any genitive qualifying ἐν χάριτι has the appearance of being the original."[9] The absence of Χριστοῦ from P^{46vid} and some Western witnesses is hard to explain and may well indicate that copyists added the other readings.[10] In other words, transcriptional probability prefers the shorter reading.[11] Thus it is fair to say that ἐν χάριτι is original reading.[12] Secondly, it is necessary to clarify the meaning of the preposition ἐν. There are two possible renderings: 1) It may be taken in an instrumental sense (cf. 2 Thess 2:16) in light of Gal 1:15 where Paul says that God called him διὰ τῆς χάριτος αὐτοῦ,[13] or 2) It could be rendered in a locative sense,[14] which would mean that God called the Galatians to be in grace. The latter is preferable because when the expression καλέω ἐν occurs, ἐν is normally used in a locative sense. The preposition has as its object a state, such as peace (ἐν δὲ εἰρήνῃ κέκληκεν ἡμᾶς ὁ θεός; 1 Cor 7:15), holiness (ἐκάλεσεν ἡμᾶς ὁ θεὸς ἐπὶ ἀκαθαρσίᾳ ἀλλ ' ἐν ἁγιασμῷ; 1 Thess 4:7), one body (ἐκλήθητε ἐν ἑνὶ σώματι; Col 3:15), and hope (ἐκλήθητε ἐν μιᾷ ἐλπίδι; Eph 4:4).[15] It is thus fair to say that ἐν (1:6) should be understood in a locative sense,[16] and thus 1:6 probably means that God called the

---

1 Cor 16:23; 2 Cor 13:13; Gal 6:18; Phil 4:23; 1 Thess 5:28; Phm 1:25; cf. Eph 6:24; Col 4:18; 2 Thess 3:18; 1 Tim 6:21; 2 Tim 4:22; Titus 3:15).

8. See Metzger, *Textual Commentary*, 520.

9. Ibid.

10. Dunn, *Galatians*, 38.

11. Martyn, *Galatians*, 109; Matera, *Galatians*, 45.

12. Metzger mentions that a majority of the committee that worked on the UBS^3 was unwilling to adopt a reading that is supported by only part of the Western tradition, though Χριστοῦ was included with reservations due to its omission by P^{46vid} and other Western witnesses (*Textual Commentary*, 520). Cf. Mußner, *Galaterbrief*, 55.

13. Bruce, *Galatians*, 79; Longenecker, *Galatians*, 15; Matera, *Galatians*, 45; NIV.

14. Burton, *Galatians*, 21; Fung, *Galatians*, 44; Martyn, *Galatians*, 109; Mußner, *Galaterbrief*, 55; Schlier, *Brief an die Galater*, 37; Witherington, *Grace in Galatia*, 79.

15. See Burton, *Galatians*, 21.

16. Betz, *Galatians*, 48; Burton, *Galatians*, 21; Fung, *Galatians*, 44; Martyn, *Galatians*, 109.

Galatians to be "in the realm or state of God's grace," in which they now exist. Here χάρις is depicted as the realm in which God's grace rules and where Christians may find their existence and enjoy God's rule (cf. 2 Tim 2:1; Acts 13:43; 1 Pet 5:12; 2 Pet 3:18). This suggestion can be strengthened by Paul's understanding of grace as the realm of God's saving benevolence. This use is reflected, for example, in Rom 5:2 (δι' οὗ καὶ τὴν προσαγωγὴν ἐσχήκαμεν [τῇ πίστει] εἰς τὴν χάριν ταύτην ἐν ᾗ ἑστήκαμεν).

In 1:15 χάρις is used as the basis of Paul's own calling to apostleship among the Gentiles. In light of Isa 49:1 and Jer 1:5 Paul probably understood himself as the apostle to the Gentiles called and commissioned by God.[17] With a view to God's grace as the grounds for calling, "grace" in 1:15 probably refers to God's generous salvific act.

In 2:9 the "grace" given to Paul seems to refer to God's entrusting τὸ εὐαγγέλιον τῆς ἀκροβυστίας to Paul (2:7). When James, Cephas, and John recognised the "grace" given to Paul, they approved the gospel that Paul proclaimed among the Gentiles (2:9–10). What is the grace of God that "the pillars" (2:9) recognised in Paul? What is the grace of God that convinced them to approve the gospel? It seems that the grace recognised by the pillars refers to the grace of God manifested in Paul's successful missionary work among Gentiles with the gospel.[18] It does not, however, necessarily exclude God's commission of τὸ εὐαγγέλιον τῆς ἀκροβυστίας to Paul,[19] Paul's privilege of apostleship,[20] or Paul's own apostolic office (Rom 1:5; 15:15–16).[21]

What is the meaning of ἡ χάρις τοῦ θεοῦ in 2:21? Scholars are divided. Some claim that it refers to God's special gift of Torah to Israel.[22] For instance, Longenecker argues: "Probably the Judaizers were picking up on one of Paul's favorite terms, 'grace,' and turning it against him, asserting that his doctrine of grace apart from the law is really a denial of God's grace to the nation Israel."[23] Some argue that it refers to Paul's apostolic commission to the Gentiles.[24] For example, Dunn says: "[H]ere Paul obviously has in mind 'the grace of God' manifested in his calling and in his successful missionary

---

17. See Martyn, *Galatians*, 155–57; Mußner, *Galaterbrief*, 82. The concept of "grace" as the basis of God's calling is reflected in 2 Tim 1:9.

18. Burton, *Galatians*, 95; Dunn, *Galatians*, 147.

19. Gaventa, "Galatians 1 and 2," 316; Gordon, "Problem at Galatia," 35.

20. Bruce, *Galatians*, 121; Fung, *Galatians*, 99; Schlier, *Galater*, 78.

21. Betz, *Galatians*, 99; Matera, *Galatians*, 77; Mußner, *Galaterbrief*, 118.

22. Betz, *Galatians*, 126; Bruce, *Galatians*, 146; Burton, *Galatians*, 140; Fung, *Galatians*, 125; Schlier, *Galater*, 104.

23. Longenecker, *Galatians*, 94–95.

24. Dunn, *Galatians*, 147; Sampley, *Pauline Partnership in Christ*, 40.

work (1:15; 2:9)."[25] However, the majority of scholars think that it refers to God's salvific grace in Christ.[26] Notably, Lambrecht suggests: "God's grace is basically the gift of Christ, his person and all that he did, especially dying out of love."[27]

Although it is conceivable that Paul is answering the agitators' criticism (i.e., that he had destroyed God's grace manifested in God's giving of the law to Israel), the first view is unlikely because there is no clear indication that Paul is reacting to such an accusation here.[28] Rather it is most likely that Paul states his present position, in contrast to his past attempts as a Pharisee to destroy the early church (cf. 1:13, 23). Unlike Peter in Antioch and the agitators in Galatia who were nullifying the grace of God, Paul declares: "I do not nullify the grace of God" (2:21a). Although it is difficult to rule out the second view, in our opinion, the third view is preferable because the immediate context supports it: Paul's new life anchored in the Son of God who loved and gave himself for Paul (2:20); Christ's death which is considered by Paul as the central manifestation of God's grace (2:21). In a word, ἡ χάρις τοῦ θεοῦ refers to God's saving grace in Christ and through Christ's death, which justifies the Gentile believers.

What then is the reference of ἡ χάρις at 5:4c? It is uncertain whether it refers to the grace of God or the grace of Christ. It is probable that ἡ χάρις refers generally to God's salvific benevolence and act[29] in and through Christ and the Spirit in the light of the following observations:

1) With a view to "grace" as the foundation of the justification of the Gentiles at 5:4, χάρις denotes God's salvific act for the Gentiles which welcomes the Gentiles into the people of God (2:21).

2) If 5:4 summarizes Paul's previous argument, χάρις with the article (ἡ) refers back to God's salvific benevolence and act for the salvation of the Gentiles which Paul explained in the previous section (1:1—5:1).

3) God's calling the Galatians to be in the state of God's salvific grace (1:6) suggests that the grace from which the Galatians have fallen is God's saving favor in which they were called to be.

---

25. Dunn, *Galatians*, 147.

26. Betz, *Galatians*, 126; Bruce, *Galatians*, 146; Cole, *Galatians*, 126; Cousar, *Galatians*, 52; Guthrie, *Galatians*, 91; Lightfoot, *Galatians*, 120; Martyn, *Galatians*, 260; Mußner, *Galaterbrief*, 184; Witherington, *Grace in Galatia*, 192.

27. Lambrecht, "Transgressor by Nullifying God's Grace," 228.

28. Cf. Guthrie, *Galatians*, 91; Mußner, *Galaterbrief*, 184n80.

29. Cf. Bruce, *Galatians*, 231; Dunn, *Galatians*, 268; Martyn, *Galatians*, 471; Matera, *Galatians*, 182.

4) The antithesis between the law and the grace of God as two contrasting grounds of justification (2:21) suggests that "grace" set in opposition to the law (5:4) in terms of the basis of justification refers to God's salvific act for justification.

As it shall become clear below, God's grace in Galatians is described as a salvific power to redeem his people and to make the Gentiles God's own children.[30]

SOLA GRATIA: PAUL'S THEOLOGICAL RATIONALE FOR OPPOSITION TO JUSTIFICATION ON THE BASIS OF THE LAW

Paul argues that God's saving benevolence and act are the sufficient soteriological basis or source for the justification of the Gentiles. In order to appreciate the force and significance of this antithesis of grace vs. law, we must clarify what Paul intended his readers to understand by his summary reference to χάρις.[31] How does Paul attempt to convince the Galatians of the sufficiency of God's grace for justification? In order to answer this question, first we need to know what God's saving benevolence and activities for justification of the Gentiles are. The prominent salvific favor and activities of God appearing in Galatians are as follows:

1) God called the Galatians (1:6; 5:8; cf. 5:13).

2) God promised to bless the nations (3:8, 15–18, 21, 23, 29; 4:28).

3) God sent his Son in order to redeem those who were under the law (4:4).

4) God sent the Spirit to make the Gentiles God's children (4:6; cf. 3:5).

5) God knew the Galatians (4:9).

In what follows we shall investigate the significance of each saving activity of God both for Paul's persuasion of the Galatians not to depend on the law for justification and for his opposition to the agitators' message of justification on the basis of the law.

---

30. Dunn notes that "in Paul's usage it [grace] is not merely a disposition in God, but something dynamic, the generous output of his power to achieve what is best for his creation" (*Galatians*, 31). For χάρις as power, see Dunn, *Jesus and the Spirit*, 202–5; Martyn, *Theological Issues in the Letters of Paul*, 279–97; Nolland, "Grace as Power," 26–31.

31. As we shall see below, the term "grace" sums up what Paul said earlier about the saving benevolence and activity of God.

God's Calling

When he rebukes the Galatians' apostasy,[32] Paul says: Θαυμάζω ὅτι οὕτως ταχέως μετατίθεσθε ἀπὸ τοῦ καλέσαντος ὑμᾶς ἐν χάριτι Χριστοῦ εἰς ἕτερον εὐαγγέλιον (1:6). In 5:8 Paul seeks to persuade the Galatians to reject the agitators' gospel by saying that their gospel does not come from the one who calls them (τοῦ καλοῦντος ὑμᾶς; 5:8). There is little doubt that "the one who calls" refers to God.[33] Why is God's act of calling the Galatians so important for Paul when he tries to urge them to reject the agitators' message of justification on the basis of the law?

In order to answer this question, first we need to clarify the soteriological significance of God's calling.[34] Paul's understanding of God's calling of his people probably derives from the Old Testament, particularly from the striking language of Isaiah (Isa 41:8–9; 43:1; 45:3–4; 48:12, 15),[35] where God's calling is described as the soteriological cause of Israel's election. Presumably, it is with this background that Paul speaks of God's calling as the cause of salvation. This point can be substantiated by Paul's statement of God's calling in Romans. Paul understands that God summons Gentiles as well as Jews into the right relationship with himself (Rom 9:4–26; cf. 1 Cor 1:24). He regards God's calling of the Gentile believers as God's making of them as God's elected people (cf. 1 Cor 1:26–29). Paul understands God's calling of the Gentiles as the fulfillment of Hosea's prophecy (Rom 9:25–26; cf. Hos 2:23; 1:10). In Rom 8:28–30, he also emphasizes God's calling of all believers to salvation.[36] Moreover, God's call is the means of election (Rom 9:12). Most importantly, the divine call is closely related to God's justifica-

---

32. Oropeza understands the Galatians' apostasy as accepting the agitators' *faux* gospel that contradicts the essence of the true Gospel (*Paul and Apostasy*, 225).

33. Having translated ἀπὸ τοῦ καλέσαντος ὑμᾶς ἐν χάριτι as "from Christ who called you in grace," some older commentaries render Christ as the subject of calling. For a list of the older commentaries as they agree or disagree this position, see Burton, *Galatians*, 19. But Paul's general use of the verb καλέω encourages us to take God as the subject of τοῦ καλέσαντος (Gal 1:15; Rom 4:17; 8:30; 9:12, 24; 1 Cor 1:9; 7:15, 17; 1 Thess 2:12; 4:7; 5:24), following most commentators: e.g., Betz, Bruce, Burton, Dunn, Fung, Longenecker, Martyn, Matera, Mußner, Schlier. In particular, Martyn suggests that ὁ καλῶν virtually functions as a name for God (Gal 5:8; 1 Thess 2:12; 5:24; Rom 9:12; see his *Galatians*, 108).

34. In the Pauline letters God's calling is described in three different connections: God's calling of all believers (Rom 1:7; 8:28–30; 9:24; 1 Cor 1:2, 26; 1 Thess 2:12; 5:24), God's calling of Paul as an apostle (Gal 1:15; Rom 1:1; 1 Cor 1:1; 15:9), and God's calling of Israel (Rom 11:28–29; cf. 9:11). Cf. Kruse, "Call, Calling," 84–85.

35. Cf. Schmidt, "καλέω, κτλ.," 490; Dunn, *Galatians*, 40.

36. God's calling as the basis of salvation is indicated in 1 Thess 2:12; 2 Thess 2:14; cf. Eph 1:18; 1 Tim 6:12.

tion (Rom 8:30). Thus it may be reasonable to claim that for Paul God's calling is the cause of election and to be called by God means to be justified and to become the people of God.[37] In consideration of the close relationship between God's call and salvation (esp. election), it is clear, therefore, that God's calling of the Galatians denotes that God elected them to become members of the people of God and called them to salvation (cf. Rom 9:25–26; 1 Cor 1:9; 2:17). Once again the point is clearly expressed by God's calling of the Galatians to freedom (Ὑμεῖς γὰρ ἐπ' ἐλευθερίᾳ ἐκλήθητε; 5:13). This text means that the Galatians are not "the children of the slave" (Hagar) but "the children of the free woman" (Sarah), as is explicitly expressed in 4:31 (ἀδελφοί, οὐκ ἐσμὲν παιδίσκης τέκνα ἀλλὰ τῆς ἐλευθέρας). In other words, as a consequence of God's calling, the Galatians are the descendants of Abraham (4:28) who are free from the slavery of the law (5:1).

On the basis of the observations above, we can proceed to answer the question raised earlier. For Paul, just as Israel's own election was a consequence of God's calling so too is the election of the Galatians. God's gracious calling is available to Gentiles as well as Jews, not to Jews exclusively (cf. Rom 9:24–26; 1 Cor 1:24). Since God called them as God's people, in practice the Galatians do not have to undergo circumcision nor to observe the whole law in order to have membership within the people of God. This is one theological reason (among others; see below) by which Paul urges the Galatians to reject the agitators' message of a Torah-based justification. Because the identity of God's people is determined by neither circumcision nor the law but God's salvific act of calling (cf. Rom 9:10–12), justification on the basis of the law must be rejected.

God's Promise

Another significant aspect of God's justifying grace in Galatians is God's promise. In Galatians there are several texts where Paul argues that God's promise is primary and sufficient for justification (3:15–26; 3:29; 4:28). Before discussing the texts, however, we need to know what the reference of God's ἐπαγγελία is. In Galatians the word ἐπαγγελία is used 10 times (3:14, 16, 17, 18 [X2], 21, 22, 29; 4:23, 28). There is no consensus concerning the content of the promise.[38]

---

37. Martyn correctly notes that Paul's use of the verb καλέω describes the genesis of the church by God's election ("The Abrahamic Covenant, Christ, and the Church," 171; idem, *Galatians*, 109).

38. For the various views regarding the content of the promise, see Williams, "*Promise* in Galatians," 709n2.

There are two major views. The one is that the promise refers to God's blessing of the nations (Gen 12:3; 18:18) cited in 3:8.[39] The other is that the Spirit itself is the promise.[40] It is true that Paul understands the eschatological coming of the Spirit as the fulfillment of God's promise (Isa 32:15; 44:3; 59:21; Ezek 11:19; 36:26–27; 37:14; 39:29; Joel 2:28–29) in light of Christian tradition (Luke 24:49; Acts 1:4; 2:17, 33). But it is more probable that the content of the promise is primarily God's blessing of the nations for the following reasons.[41] First, although Paul does not use the term ἐπαγγελία at 3:8, the two words (προϊδοῦσα and προευηγγελίσατο) seem to indicate that he considered "all the Gentiles shall be blessed in you" as the promise of God which would be fulfilled in the future. Second, the fact that God made the promise before the law came (3:17) indicates that the promise is God's blessing to Abraham. Third, that the Gentile Galatians are heirs according to the promise (3:29) and children of the promise like Isaac (4:28) reflects that they become the heirs of the Abrahamic blessing because the promise that ἐνευλογηθήσονται ἐν σοὶ πάντα τὰ ἔθνη was fulfilled. Fourth, Paul's use of the word ἐπαγγελίαι (the plural of ἐπαγγελία; 3:16) seems to suggest that ἐπαγγελία refers to God's promise given to Abraham.[42] Fifth, if Gal 3:10—4:7 is Paul's elaboration of the promise of 3:8 and its implications,[43] this promise is likely the blessings of the nations through Abraham. Thus it

39. Following most commentators: e.g., Betz, Bruce, Burton, Dunn, Howard, Martyn, Mußner; but in particular Eckstein, *Verheißung und Gesetz*, 95, 97.

40. E.g., Williams suggests that promise "on the one hand . . . refers to the divine pledge to Abraham that he would have innumerable descendants. But since God keeps his word, fulfills his pledge, through the operation of his Spirit, the promise of many descendants is, at the same time, the promise of the Spirit—that is, the promise of the *means* by which sons of Abraham would be created out of people who had been enslaved" ("*Promise* in Galatians," 716). This is followed by Matera, *Galatians*, 143; Witherington, *Grace in Galatia*, 244.

41. God's promise to Abraham contains three primary strands: land, descendants, and blessing for the nations; see Wisdom, "Blessing for the Nations and the Curse of the Law," 27–49. In Galatians, however, the promise refers to God's blessing of the nations (Gen 12:3; 18:18), which Paul quotes in Gal 3:8. The reference to the land plays no part in Galatians (cf. Bruce, *Galatians*, 172). The promise of Abraham's innumerable descendants can be understood in association with Gentiles' justification as a result of the fulfillment of God's promise in Gen. 17:5: "I have made you a father of many nations," i.e., the blessing of the nations. Cf. also Rom 4:16–25.

42. The plural ἐπαγγελίαι (Gal 3:16, 21) probably refers to God's promise to bless the nations that God repeated several times in different occasions (Gen 12:3; 18.18; cf. Gen 22:18; 26:4; 28:14), not the three different blessings (i.e., land, descendants, and blessing for the nations). Cf. Martyn, *Galatians*, 339; *contra* Betz, *Galatians*, 156, 157, 159; Schilier, *Galater*, 143.

43. The term ἐπαγγελία appears in the section intensively (Gal 3:14, 16, 17, 18 [2X], 21, 22, 29; 4:23, 28); cf. Longenecker, *Galatians*, 125.

is fair to say that the ἐπαγγελία refers to God's promise to bless the nations (Gen 12:3; 18:18; cf. Gen 22:18; 26:4; 28:14; Pss 72:17; Jer 4:2),[44] which Paul quotes in 3:8. In light of the parallel between δικαιοῖ τὰ ἔθνη ὁ θεὸς and ἐνευλογηθήσονται ἐν σοὶ πάντα τὰ ἔθνη, it is probable that ἐπαγγελία refers to God's promise of justification of Gentiles (3:8).[45] Let us now turn to the passages where Paul deals with the theme of God's promise of justification of Gentiles.

In Gal 3:15–18, Paul elaborates upon how the justification of Gentiles is based not on the law but on God's promise. This is clearly summed up in 3:18 (εἰ γὰρ ἐκ νόμου ἡ κληρονομία, οὐκέτι ἐξ ἐπαγγελίας· τῷ δὲ Ἀβραὰμ δι' ἐπαγγελίας κεχάρισται ὁ θεός). It is widely recognized that with the antithesis between the law and God's promise,[46] Paul argues that not the law but God's promise is the sufficient means of the inheritance, i.e., Abrahamic sonship.[47] In view of the criticism from the side of traditional Jewish covenantalism that Paul treated the law of the covenant too lightly, Paul argues that the law does not nullify a covenant previously ratified by God (i.e., God's promise to Abraham). In other words, God's promise of the justification of Gentiles cannot be nullified by the law because God's promise to Abraham precedes the law which came 430 years later (3:17).[48] Paul makes the point that just as a human διαθήκη, once signed and witnessed, could not be set aside by another document claiming to represent the will of the testator and could not be added to by another authority (3:15), so with the covenant which God made with Abraham.[49]

---

44. See particularly Bruce, *Galatians*, 172.

45. Martyn, *Galatians*, 355.

46. See Betz, *Galatians*, 158; Lightfoot, *Galatians*, 144; Longenecker, *Galatians*, 134; Martyn, *Galatians*, 337; Matera, *Galatians*, 127; Mußner, *Galaterbrief*, 242; Witherington, *Grace in Galatia*, 245.

47. While Paul is not explicit about what the content of κληρονομία is, in the light of the argument of the letter, it is likely becoming Abraham's heir. Although κληρονομία is primarily concerned with land (Gen 15:7–8; 28:4; Deut 1:39, 2:12), the crucial Genesis passage includes the idea of being Abraham's heir (Gen 15:2–4; 21:10; cf. Dunn, *Galatians*, 186). Note that the territorial and material features of the Abrahamic inheritance are not mentioned here by Paul. Interestingly some suggest that it refers to the promised Spirit in 3:14 (Martyn, *Galatians*, 343; Mußner, *Galaterbrief*, 242; Matera, *Galatians*, 127; Williams, *Galatians*, 97). Ziesler thinks that it refers to both justification by faith and the gift of the Spirit (*Galatians*, 44). Betz says: the term "'inheritance' includes all the benefits of God's work of salvation" (*Galatians*, 159).

48. See Dunn, *Galatians*, 87–88; Hays, *Echoes of Scripture*, 109.

49. Nevertheless, according to Roman law, testators were allowed to cancel or modify their will at any point during their lifetime (Bruce, *Galatians*, 170–71; Longenecker, *Galatians*, 128–30).

What is more, the inheritance of Abraham's sonship is a matter of divine initiative and grace.[50] Paul's insistence on the priority of God's graceful promise effectively relativizes the idea that Gentiles can become the descendants of Abraham only through the observance of the law, in particular circumcision. In short, the point of Paul's argument in 3:15–18 is that since God always intended, from the time of the promise to Abraham, that the Gentiles are to be blessed,[51] the inheritance of Abraham's sonship (i.e., justification) comes to the Gentiles not from the law but from the gracious promise of God which cannot be modified or nullified by the law given subsequently.

In Gal 3:19–22, Paul continues to explain God's promise as the sufficient soteriological basis of justification. Without attempting to tackle the relationship between the law and the promise,[52] it is sufficient to focus on God's promise of justification of the Gentiles ἐκ πίστεως Ἰησοῦ Χριστοῦ, which was given to those who believe (3:22). Contrary to the agitators' ethnocentric covenantalism maintaining that righteousness comes through the law, Paul argues that the law has no function to "make alive" and thus righteousness cannot come through the law (3:21).[53] Although the law regulates life within the covenant for the people of Israel (e.g., Lev 18:5; Deut 6:24; Prov 3:1–2; 6.23; Sir 17:11; Bar 3:9; 4:1; *Pss. Sol.* 24:2), the law does not make one alive because God did not intend the law to play such a role.[54] From a Jewish perspective, rather, the role is ascribed to God (2 Kgs 5:7; Neh 9:6; Job 36:6; Ps 71:20; *Jos. Asen.* 8:3, 9; 12:1; 20.7; *Let. Arist.* 16; John 5:21; Rom 4:17; 1 Cor 15:22).

Paul also argues that the law is not the means of righteousness because the law cannot set everything (τὰ πάντα [3:22]—including all humanity [both Jews and Greeks]) free from the power of sin. In other words, Jews and Gentiles alike cannot be accepted by God on the basis of the law (2:16;

---

50. Dunn, *Galatians*, 187; Betz, *Galatians*, 160.

51. Dunn rightly argues that the "initial expression of God's covenant purpose was in terms of promise and faith and always had the Gentiles in view from the first" ("Theology of Galatians," 125).

52. Eckstein, *Verheißung und Gesetz*, 190–212; Kruger, "Law and Promise in Galatians," 311–27.

53. Here righteousness is used as the equivalent of "life." Cf. Sanders, *Paul and Palestinian Judaism*, 493–95.

54. The subject of the passive verb ἐδόθη is God (divine passive). Sanders argues: "God sent Christ; he did so in order to offer righteousness; this would have been pointless if righteousness were already available by the law (2:21); the law was not given to bring righteousness (3:21)" (*Paul, the Law, and the Jewish People*, 27). Hong likewise states: "The law was never planned to be the condition for entering the people of God at all" (*Law in Galatians*, 132).

cf. Rom 3:20) because the law cannot deal with the problem of sin which prevents anyone from approaching God (cf. Rom 3:23). This implies that the privileged status of righteousness is not automatically guaranteed for the people of Israel by means of the law because they are not exempt from the power of sin (cf. Rom 3:9; 11:32) to which the law provides no real answer. For Paul the solution to the problem of sin is God's promise. The promise as the embodiment of divine power defeats the power of sin.[55] It is thus fair to say that 3:22b means that God's unconditional promise, which precedes the law and breaks the power of sin, is given to those who believe, Jews and Gentiles without distinction ἐκ πίστεως Ἰησοῦ Χριστοῦ.[56] In short, Paul opposes justification through the law on the basis of God's promise to bless nations. Instead, salvation is given to Gentiles ἐκ πίστεως Ἰησοῦ Χριστοῦ.

In Gal 3:23–29, Paul develops his point (that not the law but God's gracious promise fulfilled in Christ and through πίστις is the soteriological basis for the justification of Gentiles) even further. In 3:23–25, Paul explains that before the coming and revelation of πίστις, Paul and the Galatians ("we") were imprisoned and guarded under the power of the law.[57] Paul implies that the coming of Christ and πίστις, and the revelation of πίστις, set them free from imprisonment of the law (cf. 5:1; Rom 7:6) and ended the interim role of the law as custodian. He also argues that πίστις came and was revealed so that Paul and the Galatians ("we") might be justified by πίστις (3:23–25).[58] After making the point that God's promise to justify the

---

55. Dunn, *Galatians*, 195.

56. For the discussion of the meaning of πίστις Ἰησοῦ Χριστοῦ, see Campbell, "Meaning of ΠΙΣΤΙΣ and ΝΟΜΟΣ," 91–103; Campbell, *Rhetoric of Righteousness*, 58–69, 214–18; Campbell, "Romans 1:17," 265–85; Choi, "ΠΙΣΤΙΣ in Gal 5:5–6," 467–90; Dunn, "Once More, ΠΙΣΤΙΣ ΧΡΙΣΟΥ," 61–81; Hays, *Faith of Jesus Christ*; Hays, "ΠΙΣΤΙΣ and Pauline Christology," 35–60; Hooker, "ΠΙΣΤΙΣ ΧΡΙΣΟΥ," 321–42; Matlock, "Detheologizing the ΠΙΣΤΙΣ ΧΡΙΣΟΥ Debate," 1–23; Matlock, "'Even the Demons Believe,'" 300–318; Wallis, *Faith of Jesus Christ*; Williams, "Again *Pistis Christou*," 431–47.

57. It is likely that "we" in 3:23–25 refers to both Jewish and Gentile believers (in particular Paul and the Galatians) on the basis of the following: 1) In 3:23–29 Paul is addressing not Jewish believers as in 2:15–17 but the Galatians. 2) The parallelism between 3:22 ("all things" [Jews and Gentiles] were imprisoned under the power of sin) and 3:23 ("we were imprisoned under the power of the law" hints that "we" includes both Jews and Gentiles). 3) Paul does not contrast "we" (Jews) with "you" (the Gentile Galatians) in 3:23–29 because no contrast can be ascertained in the sudden shift from "we" (4:5b, 4:6b) to "you" (4:6a, 4:7a). Rather Paul grounds a statement about "us" on a statement about "you" (3:25–26; 4:6) or "you" on "us" (4:6b–7). See Cousar, *Theology of the Cross*, 115–18; Howard, *Paul*, 59–62; Scott, *Adoption*, 155–57. *Contra* Donaldson, "'Curse of the Law,'" 94–112.

58. It is likely that "we" includes Gentile believers (cf. 5:5) because in 3:10–29 Paul elaborates God's justification of Gentiles by faith (3:8).

Gentiles through πίστις is the soteriological basis of justification, in 3:26–29 Paul argues that in Christ Jesus the Galatians are all children of God through πίστις. He further argues that there is neither Jew nor Greek, slave nor free, male nor female because the Galatians are one in Christ Jesus (3:28). In other words, Jewish and Gentile believers are full and equal members of the covenant community as one people of God.

Finally he concludes that if the Galatians belong to Christ, then they are Abraham's offspring and heirs according to the promise (3:29). Since the benefit of becoming Abraham's heirs was given to the Galatians by the promise, it did not come from the law. In short, the central point of Paul's argument in 3:23–29 is that by means of God's gracious ἐπαγγελία realized by the advent and revelation of πίστις, the Gentiles (e.g., the Galatians) have become heirs of Abraham (3:29).[59] Paul realizes that God's promise to bless the Gentiles which was given to Abraham (Gen 12:3; 18:18) has been fulfilled by God's justification of the Gentiles both in and through Christ and through the coming and revelation of πίστις.[60]

The point that Gentile believers can become the descendants of Abraham not by the law but by God's promise is reinforced in 4:28. To the Galatians who were eager to become Abraham's descendants through Torah-observance (4:21), in particular circumcision, Paul responds to the agitators' thesis that the Jewish people are the children of Abraham, in the pattern of Isaac (ὑμεῖς δέ, ἀδελφοί, κατὰ Ἰσαὰκ ἐπαγγελίας τέκνα ἐστέ; 4:28). Identifying the child of Hagar (i.e., Ishmael) with Gentiles (including the Galatians) and the child of Sarah (i.e., Isaac) with Jews, the agitators argued that the Galatians could become the descendants of Abraham through circumcision.[61] To the contrary, Paul identifies the Galatians with Isaac (not with Ishmael as the agitators do), who was the child of the free woman (Sarah) born through the promise (4:23). The Galatians are children of the promise (4:28; cf. Rom 9:8).

Paul's statement here is so radical as to deny traditional Jewish covenantalism which maintains the status of the Jews as the sole recipients of God's promise. Why does Paul attempt to make a totally different exegesis of Gen 16–21 from the agitators? Paul's complete "turn-around" exegesis is based on his conviction that God's promise of justification of Gentiles was fulfilled through Christ and the Spirit; therefore, the Galatians became the

---

59. So rightly Hansen, *Abraham in Galatians*, 136–39; Howard, *Paul*, 65.

60. While Söding takes πίστις (= the soteriological basis of justification) as the Christian's faith, he rightly notes that Paul discovers that what God has promised to Abraham has been fulfilled in God's justification of Jews and Gentiles ("Verheißung und Erfüllung," 150–61).

61. Barrett, "Allegory of Abraham," 1–16.

offspring of Abraham and heirs without their conversion to Judaism. Since the Gentile Galatians are children of the promise like Isaac and thus belong to the covenant community, they do not need to become Jewish converts through circumcision and depend upon the law for justification. This is a central point of the allegory of Hagar and Sarah (4:21–31).

To sum up, with a view to the priority and sufficiency of God's promise, Paul argues that Gentile believers receive adoption as sons of God and become the offspring of Abraham, the children of God (4:5–7), and the heirs of the promise (4:28), not through the law (3:11, 18, 21), but through Christ and the Spirit (3:14, 29; 4:4–6, 29). According to Paul, God's blessing promised to Abraham always had the justification of the Gentiles in view from the start. The gift of righteousness was for Gentiles as well as for the Jews. Since God's promise of justification of the Gentiles given to Abraham, which cannot be nullified by the law, was fulfilled at a preordained time by God's sending of his Son and the Spirit with the advent and revelation of πίστις, the Galatians have become the children of Abraham apart from Torah-observance and circumcision. Thus, for Paul, to maintain the law as the soteriological basis of justification means to deny the eschatological fulfillment of God's promise. In short, the fulfillment of the Abrahamic covenant (i.e., God's promise of justification of Gentiles) through Christ and the Spirit is Paul's theological foundation upon which he seeks to persuade the Galatians not to rely on the law for justification and to reject the agitators' message.[62]

God's Sending of His Son and the Spirit

Without attempting to investigate Gal 4:4–7 in detail,[63] it is sufficient to concentrate on the fact that God sent his Son and the Spirit so that believers receive redemption and adoption as sons [and daughters] through God (διὰ θεοῦ; 4:7).[64] Before the fullness of time (τὸ πλήρωμα τοῦ χρόνου)[65] had come, both Jewish and Gentile believers used to be under the power of τὰ στοιχεῖα τοῦ κόσμου (4:3). The precise meaning of the phrase has been disputed

---

62. So rightly Longenecker, *Triumph of Abraham's God*, 178–79.

63. For a detailed discussion, see Scott, *Adoption*, 121–86.

64. Martyn argues: "the sentence comprising 4:3–5 is nothing less than the theological center of the entire letter" (*Galatians*, 388). Martyn interprets God's sending of his Son and the Spirit as God's apocalyptic invasion into the cosmos.

65. In light of the parallel between τῆς προθεσμίας τοῦ πατρός (4:2) and τὸ πλήρωμα τοῦ χρόνου, the phrase means the time foreordained by God. Cf. Scott, *Adoption*, 161–62.

among scholars.⁶⁶ Since it is impossible to discuss it in detail here, it will suffice to say that 4:3b (ὑπὸ τὰ στοιχεῖα τοῦ κόσμου ἤμεθα δεδουλωμένοι) means that Jew and Gentile Christians were enslaved under the influence or dominion of certain primal and cosmic forces.⁶⁷

It is significant for our present study that as a result of God's sending of his Son, all the believers (Jewish and Gentile) receive the salvific benefits of redemption and adoption. Notably God sent the Spirit of his Son into the Galatians' hearts (cf. 3:2–5), crying "Abba! Father!" (4:6). Since God has given the Spirit of his Son to them, they are the children of God. In 4:7 Paul concludes that since God sent Christ and the Spirit of his Son, the Galatians are no longer slaves but sons and heirs through God. In short, the force of Paul's argument in 4:4–7 is that the salvific gifts of redemption, adoption as sons of God, and becoming God's children and heirs are given to Jewish and Gentile believers through God's saving act, that is, God's sending of his Son and the Spirit.

God's Knowing

It is important to note that Paul attempts to persuade the Galatians not to turn back again to τὰ ἀσθενῆ καὶ πτωχὰ στοιχεῖα by reminding them of the fact that they were known by God (γνωσθέντες ὑπὸ θεοῦ; 4:9). Paul's swift correction (μᾶλλ ον δὲ) from the Galatians' act of knowing God (γνόντες θεόν) to God's act of knowing them (γνωσθέντες ὑπὸ θεοῦ) stresses the divine initiative in the relationship between God and the Galatians. Why is it so crucial for Paul that God knew the Galatians when he discourages them from turning back again to τὰ ἀσθενῆ καὶ πτωχὰ στοιχεῖα and from keeping the festival law? There is little doubt that the verb γινώσκω here is employed not in the sense of either "to perceive" or "to acquire knowledge about" but in the biblical sense of "to experience."⁶⁸ Paul emphasizes God's act of knowing here on the basis of the idea that when God knows someone he or she engages in an intimate, personal relationship with God (e.g., Gen

---

66. Arnold, "Returning to the Domain of Powers," 55–76; Bandstra, *Law and the Elements of the World*; Longenecker, *Triumph of Abraham's God*, 47–58; Bundrick, "Ta Stoicheia tou Kosmou," 353–64; Schweizer, "Slaves of the Elements," 455–68.

67. Arnold, "Returning to the Domain of the Powers," 55–76; Dunn, *Galatians*, 213; Hong, *Law*, 162–66; Longenecker, *Triumph*, 46–58; Martyn, *Galatians*, 393–406.

68. It is widely accepted that despite the fact that this meaning is strange against the background of broad Greek usage, it is natural in light of the use of γινώσκω in the LXX to translate the Hebrew *yadʿ* when it denotes intimate relationship. For a discussion of this OT relational sense of *yadʿ*, see Bultmann, "γινώσκω," 697–98; Schmitz, "γινώσκω," 395–96.

18:19; Num 16:5; Ps 1:6; 37:18; 44:21; 94:11; 139; Jer 1:5; Amos 3:2). Most importantly, God's graceful act of knowing his people was the basis of the election of his people (e.g., Gen 18:19; Num 16:5; Jer 1:5; Amos 3:2).[69]

In light of this background Paul probably intends the Galatians to recognize that they became God's people and thus had come to the right relationship with God not through the observance of the law but by God's graceful act of knowing them personally. The point can be reinforced by Paul's use of God's knowing in the sense of election elsewhere in his letters (Rom 8:29; 11:2; cf. 1 Cor 8:3; 13:12; 2 Tim 2:19); for Paul to be known by God means to be elected and accepted by God.[70] Moreover, being known by God means having a loving relationship with God (1 Cor 8:3). Thus for Paul the Galatians' being known by God means that they became the elected people of God and that they are in a justified relationship with God.[71] It is on the basis of this point that Paul urges the Galatians not to turn back again to τὰ στοιχεῖα and not to observe the ritual calendar, which would mean to deny God's election. In short, for Paul God's gracious act of knowing Gentiles is part of Paul's theological rationale both for his persuasion of the Galatians not to observe the law and for his opposition to justification on the basis of the law.

CONCLUDING REMARKS

What Paul intends the Galatians to realize by the antithesis between the law and grace is that they do not have to undergo circumcision nor to observe the law in order to become full members of the covenant community. They became God's elected people by God's act of calling and knowing. They are heirs of Abraham and children of God by God's promise and his sending of Christ and the Spirit. In contrast to the agitators who argue that the identity of God's people is determined by the law and circumcision, Paul upholds that this identity depends upon God's saving activities, which includes God's calling, God's promise, God's sending of Christ and the Spirit, and God's knowing.

---

69. Gen 18:19: "for I have 'known' ['chosen'—NRSV, NIV] him [Abraham]"; Num 16:5: "God will know who is his" [where "know" is paralleled by "choose"]; Jer 1:5: "Before I formed you in the womb I 'knew' you" [where "know" is paralleled by "consecrate" and "appoint"]; Amos 3:2: "You [Israel] only have I 'known' ['chosen'—NIV] of all the families of the earth."

70. Cf. Bruce, *Galatians*, 202; Bultmann, "γινώσκω," 706; Mußner, *Galaterbrief*, 292; Schmithals, "γινώσκω," 250.

71. Compare Martyn (*Galatians*, 412) who states, "to be known by God is to know that there are no holy times."

For Paul to argue for justification through the law means to nullify and deny God's graceful saving acts which welcome the Gentiles into God's people apart from the law (2:21). For the agitators God's grace is for the Jews and proselytes, but for Paul God's grace is for both Jews and Gentiles.[72] The antithesis (i.e., justification through the law vs. justification by God's grace) is both a substantial feature of Paul's theology in Galatians and an interpretive clue to understanding Paul's theology in Galatians.[73] Justification *sola gratia* is a central content of Paul's gospel (Gal 2:21; 5.4; Rom 3:24; 5:15–17).

What is the significance of the antithesis between the law and grace for Paul's denial of the law as the soteriological basis of justification? The law requires the one who wants to share God's covenant to obey the works of the law. Against this idea, Paul argues that God's saving grace is the primary and sufficient soteriological basis of justification. Thus to add the observance of the law and circumcision for the salvation of the Gentiles to God's grace means a perversion of the gospel of Christ (1:7) and a denial of God's grace (2:21), which results in ἀνάθεμα (1:8–9). In short, Paul rejects the law as the soteriological basis of justification not only because the exclusivistic law prevents the Gentiles from enjoying the salvific effects of God's grace (e.g., righteousness, the Abrahamic blessing, sonship, election), but also because God's eschatological salvific deeds (e.g., God's calling, God's sending of Christ and the Spirit, God's knowing) brought these salvific blessings to the Gentiles without Torah-observance.

The antithesis between the law and grace is also significant for understanding Paul's critique of covenantal nomism. According to traditional Judaism, the Jewish privileges (e.g., righteousness, the Abrahamic blessing,

---

72. This is certainly Paul's point of view in Rom 3:29 (ἢ Ἰουδαίων ὁ θεὸς μόνον; οὐχὶ καὶ ἐθνῶν; ναὶ καὶ ἐθνῶν) and in Rom 4:9 (ὁ μακαρισμὸς οὖν οὗτος ἐπὶ τὴν περιτομὴν ἢ καὶ ἐπὶ τὴν ἀκροβυστίαν).

73. The antithesis seems to serve the same role in Paul's letter to the Romans. The antithesis is clearly expressed in Rom 3:20–24. In 3:20 Paul says, ἐξ ἔργων νόμου οὐ δικαιωθήσεται πᾶσα σὰρξ ἐνώπιον αὐτοῦ. In contrast to 3:20, Paul says in 3:24, δικαιούμενοι δωρεὰν τῇ αὐτοῦ χάριτι. The point of the antithesis is that for Paul a right relationship with God is wholly of God's grace, and thus justification through the works of the law must be rejected. The point is restated in Rom 11:6: εἰ δὲ χάριτι, οὐκέτι ἐξ ἔργων, ἐπεὶ ἡ χάρις οὐκέτι γίνεται χάρις. The antithesis between the human endeavor of Torah-observance and God's grace is embedded in Rom 9–11. Moreover, the antithesis between the law and grace as two antithetical salvific spheres or realms in Rom 6:14 (cf. 6:15) indicates that Paul understood the law and grace as two contrasting ways of salvation. Paul says, ἁμαρτία γὰρ ὑμῶν οὐ κυριεύσει, οὐ γάρ ἐστε ὑπὸ νόμον ἀλλὰ ὑπὸ χάριν. Paul means that sin will no longer have lordship over believers because they are not under the law but under grace. In light of the observations above, it is fair to say that Paul's argument of *sola gratia* (i.e., the right relationship with God is no longer dependent upon the law but upon God's salvific grace) is significant for the interpretation of Romans.

sonship, election) are restricted to Jews while proselytes and Gentiles are excluded from these prerogatives. On the contrary Paul argues that the blessings and God's grace are not exclusive to Jews and proselytes but inclusive of the Gentile believers. God's blessings and grace have been granted to Gentiles through God's saving activities through Christ and the Spirit. Paul rejected ethnocentric "covenantal nomism" because it denies God's grace which welcomes Gentile believers as the offspring of Abraham, God's children, and full membership into the people of God apart from the law (cf. Rom 3:21–26).[74] Furthermore, Paul denied covenantal nomism because it does not recognize that God's promise to bless all nations (i.e., the Abrahamic covenant) was already fulfilled eschatologically when God sent Christ and the Spirit. On the basis of the Abrahamic covenant, Paul refutes the covenant on Mt. Sinai and makes grace through faith the sole means of salvation.[75]

BIBLIOGRAPHY

Arnold, C. E. "Returning to the Domain of Powers: *Stoicheia* as Evil Spirits in Galatians 4:3, 9." *NovT* 38 (1996) 55–76.
Bandstra, A. J. *The Law and the Elements of the World*. Kampen: Kok, 1964.
Barrett, C. K. "The Allegory of Abraham, Sarah, and Hagar in the Argument of Galatians." In *Rechtfertigung: Festschrift für E. Käsemann zum 70. Geburtstag*, ed. J. Friedrich et al., 1–16. Tübingen: Mohr/Siebeck, 1976.
Berger, K. "χάρις, ιτος, ἡ." In *EDNT* 3:457–61.
Betz, H. D. *Galatians: A Commentary on Paul's Letter to the Churches in Galatia*. Hermeneia. Minneapolis: Fortress, 1989.
Bruce, F. F. *Commentary on Galatians*. NIGTC. Grand Rapids: Eerdmans, 1982.
Bultmann, Rudolf. "γινώσκω, κτλ." In *TDNT* 1:689–718.
Bundrick, D. R. "*Ta Stoicheia tou Kosmou* (Gal 4:3)." *JETS* 34 (1991) 353–64.
Burton, E. D. *A Critical and Exegetical Commentary on the Epistle to the Galatians*. ICC. Edinburgh: T. & T. Clark, 1921.
Campbell, Douglas A. "The Meaning of ΠΙΣΤΙΣ and ΝΟΜΟΣ in Paul." *JBL* 111 (1992) 91–103.

---

74. Dunn rightly states: "And what he [Paul] denies is that God's justification depends on 'covenantal nomism,' that God's grace extends only to those who wear the badge of the covenant" ("New Perspective," 194). Cf. Burton who notes the significance of the antithesis for Paul's opposition to first century Judaism as follows: "Grace, by virtue of which God accepts as righteous those who have faith, itself excludes, and is excluded by, the principle of legalism, according to which the deeds of righteousness which one has performed are accredited to him as something which he has earned" (*Galatians*, 277).

75. Sanders writes: "Paul in fact explicitly denies that the Jewish covenant can be effective for salvation" (*Paul and Palestinian Judaism*, 551).

———. *The Rhetoric of Righteousness in Romans 3,21–26*. JSNTSup 65. Sheffield: JSOT Press, 1992.

———. "Romans 1:17—A *Crux Interpretum* for the ΠΙΣΤΙΣ ΧΡΙΣΟΥ Debate." *JBL* 113 (1994) 265–85.

Choi, Hung-Sik. "The Antithesis between the Law and Grace in Galatians 5:4." *Scripture and Interpretation* 2, no. 1 (2008) 120–39.

———. "ΠΙΣΤΙΣ in Gal 5:5–6: Neglected Evidence for the Faithfulness of Christ." *JBL* 124 (2005) 467–90.

Cole, R. Alan. *The Letter of Paul to the Galatians: An Introduction and Commentary*. TNTC 9. 2nd ed. Grand Rapids: Eerdmans, 1989.

Conzelmann, H. "χάρις, κτλ." In *TDNT* 9:372–76; 387–415.

Cousar, C. B. *Galatians*. IBC. Louisville: John Knox, 1982.

———. *A Theology of the Cross*. OBT 24. Minneapolis: Fortress, 1990.

Donaldson, T. L. "The 'Curse of the Law' and the Inclusion of the Gentiles." *NTS* 32 (1986) 94–112.

Dunn, James D. G. *Jesus and the Spirit*. London: SCM, 1975.

———. "Once More, ΠΙΣΤΙΣ ΧΡΙΣΟΥ." In *Pauline Theology*. Vol. 4, *Looking Back, Pressing On*, ed. E. E. Johnson and D. M. Hay, 61–81. Atlanta: Scholars, 1997.

———. "The New Perspective on Paul." In *Jesus, Paul and the Law: Studies in Mark and Galatians*, 183–214. Louisville: Westminster John Knox, 1990.

———. "The Theology of Galatians: The Issue of Covenantal Nomism." In *Pauline Theology*, ed. J. M. Bassler, 1:160–79. Minneapolis: Fortress, 1996.

———. *The Theology of Paul's Letter to the Galatians*. New Testament Theology. Cambridge: Cambridge University Press, 1993.

———. *The Theology of Paul the Apostle*. Grand Rapids: Eerdmans, 1997.

Eastmann, E. J. "The Significance of Grace in the Letters of Paul." PhD diss., McMaster University, 1995.

Eckstein, H.-J. *Verheißung und Gesetz. Eine exegetische Untersuchung zu Galater 2,15—4,7*. WUNT 86. Tübingen: Mohr/Siebeck, 1996.

Fung, R. Y. K. *The Epistle to the Galatians*. NICNT. Grand Rapids: Eerdmans, 1988.

Gaventa, B. R. "Galatians 1 and 2: Autobiography as Paradigm." *NovT* 28 (1986) 309–26.

Gordon, T. D. "The Problem at Galatia." *Int* 41 (1987) 32–43.

Guthrie, D. *Galatians*. New Century Bible Commentary. Grand Rapids: Eerdmans, 1973.

Hansen, G. W. *Abraham in Galatians: Epistolary and Rhetorical Contexts*. JSNTSup 29. Sheffield: JSOT Press, 1989.

Hays, Richard B. *Echoes of Scripture in the Letters of Paul*. New Haven: Yale University Press, 1989.

———. *The Faith of Jesus Christ*. SBLDS 56. Chico, CA: Scholars, 1983.

———. "ΠΙΣΤΙΣ and Pauline Christology: What Is at Stake?" In *Pauline Theology*, ed. E. E. Johnson and D. M. Hay, 4:35–60. Atlanta: Scholars, 1997.

Hong, I.-G. *The Law in Galatians*. JSNTSup 81. Sheffield: JSOT Press, 1993.

Hooker, Morna D. "ΠΙΣΤΙΣ ΧΡΙΣΟΥ." *NTS* 35 (1989) 321–42.

Howard, George. *Paul: Crisis in Galatia*. 2nd ed. Cambridge: Cambridge, 1990.

Kruger, M. A. "Law and Promise in Galatians." *Neot* 26 (1992) 311–27.

Lambrecht, J. "Transgressor by Nullifying God's Grace: A Study of Gal 2,18–21." *Bib* 72 (1991) 217–36.

Lightfoot, J. B. *St. Paul's Epistle to the Galatians*. 3rd rev. ed. London: Macmillan, 1869.

Longenecker, B. *The Triumph of Abraham's God: The Transformation of Identity in Galatians.* Edinburgh: T. & T. Clark, 1998.

Longenecker, R. N. *Galatians.* WBC 41. Dallas: Word, 1990.

Martyn, J. L. *Galatians: A New Translation with Introduction and Commentary.* AB 33A. New York: Doubleday, 1997.

———. *Theological Issues in the Letters of Paul.* Edinburgh: T. & T. Clark, 1997.

Matera, F. J. *Galatians.* SP 9. Collegeville, MN: Liturgical, 1992.

Matlock, R. Barry. "Detheologizing the ΠΙΣΤΙΣ ΧΡΙΣΟΥ Debate: Cautionary Remarks from a Lexical Semantic Perspective." *NovT* 42 (2000) 1–23.

———. "'Even the Demons Believe': Paul and πίστις Χριστοῦ." *CBQ* 64 (2002) 300–18.

Metzger, B. *A Textual Commentary on the Greek New Testament.* 2nd ed. Stuttgart: German Bible Society, 1994.

Moffatt, J. *Grace in the New Testament.* London: Hodder & Stoughton, 1932.

Mußner, F. *Der Galaterbrief.* HTKNT 9. Freiburg: Herder, 1977.

Nolland, J. "Grace as Power." *NovT* 38 (1986) 26–31.

Oepke, A. *Der Brief des Paulus an die Galater.* 3rd rev. ed. THKNT 9. Berlin: Evangelische, 1973.

Oropeza, B. J. *Paul and Apostasy: Eschatology, Perseverance and Falling Away in the Corinthian Congregation.* WUNT 2/115. Tübingen: Mohr/Siebeck, 2000.

Sampley, J. P. *Pauline Partnership in Christ.* Philadelphia: Fortress, 1980.

Sanders, E. P. *Paul and Palestinian Judaism: A Comparison of Patterns of Religion.* Philadelphia: Fortress, 1977.

———. *Paul, the Law, and the Jewish People.* Philadelphia: Fortress, 1983.

Schlier, H. *Der Brief an die Galater.* KEK 7. 5th rev. ed. Göttingen: Vandenhoeck & Ruprecht, 1971.

Schmidt, K. L. "καλέω, κτλ." In *TDNT* 3:487–536.

Schmithals, W. "γινώσκω." In *EDNT* 1:248–51.

Schmitz, E. D. "γινώσκω." In *NIDNTT* 2:392–406.

Schweizer, E. "Slaves of the Elements and Worshipers of Angels." *JBL* 107 (1988) 455–68.

Scott, J. M. *Adoption as Sons of God: An Exegetical Investigation into the Background of Huiothesia in the Pauline Corpus.* WUNT 2/48. Tübingen: Mohr/Siebeck, 1992.

Söding, T. "Verheißung und Erfüllung im Lichte paulinischer Theologie." *NTS* 47 (2001) 150–61.

Wallis, Ian G. *The Faith of Jesus Christ in Early Christian Traditions.* SNTSMS 84. Cambridge: Cambridge University Press, 1995.

Westerholm, Stephen. *Israel's Law and the Church's Faith: Paul and His Recent Interpreters.* Grand Rapids: Eerdmans, 1988.

Williams, Sam K. "Again *Pistis Christou*." *CBQ* 49 (1987) 431–47.

———. "*Promise* in Galatians." *JBL* 107 (1988) 709–20.

Wisdom, J. R. "Blessing for the Nations and the Curse of the Law." PhD diss., University of Durham, 1998.

Witherington, Ben, III. *Grace in Galatia: A Commentary of St Paul's Letter to the Galatians.* Edinburgh: T. & T. Clark, 1998. Reprint, 2004.

Ziesler, Z. A. *The Epistle to the Galatians.* Epworth Commentaries. London: Epworth, 1992.

6

The Internal Integrative Motive Running through 2 Cor 11:23—12:10[1]

CHULHONG BRIAN KIM

INTRODUCTION

In the middle of the controversy against his opponents, reaching its climax in 2 Cor 11:13, where he labels them false apostles and subsequently servants of Satan, Paul unexpectedly turns our attention to his sufferings (2 Cor 11:23–30), and then to his escape from officers of King Aretas (2 Cor 11:31–33), who tracked him down as far as Damascus, a city located in the outside of border of Nabatean Kingdom at the time. Right after that episode, in 12:1–10, he mentions his sojourn to the third heaven and suffering from the thorn in his flesh. What on the earth resides in Paul's mind when he mentions four seemingly unrelated topics? What would have been the integrating motive behind them, especially in relation to his debate against Corinthian opponents in 2 Corinthians?

---

1. With the exception of Paul's motive for writing the suffering list, the two enigmatic episodes, and the thorn in the flesh, all of which are newly researched here in this essay, the remaining issues in 2 Cor 11:23—12:10 are argued with greater detail in my doctoral dissertation "Paul—A False Prophet?"

This study attempts to answer these questions through reinterpreting the four passages (i.e., his catalogue of sufferings, his escape from Damascus, his trip to the third heaven, and finally, the physical problems ensuing from it) in the context of similar false prophet controversies in the Old Testament. Placing Paul's false apostle controversy in the context of OT false prophet traditions gives us an opportunity to discover a common thread between the four episodes, a dynamic dimension of 2 Corinthians often hidden from ordinary occasional readers of the letter, while also providing clues to viewing the letter as an integrated whole.

THE LIST OF SUFFERINGS

Paul records "signs, and wonders and mighty works" in an inventory of signs identifying a true apostle (2 Cor 12:12).[2] Paul performed miracles in his ministry (Rom 4:21; 15:18–19; Gal 3:5; 1 Cor 2:4–5; 2 Cor 10:11; Col 3:17; 1 Thess 1:5; 2 Thess 2:17)[3] and saw them as authentic features of his apostleship, just as prophets in the Old Testament carried out signs and wonders to prove their genuineness (Exod 4:6–9; 7:8–13; 15:22–26; Num 17:11–13; Deut 13:1; 34:11; 1 Sam 12:16–18; 1 Kgs 13:5; 17:8–24; 2 Kgs 4:1–7, 18–37, 42–44; 20:8–11). However, it would be a mistake if we only count his execution of miracles as the sign of true apostleship, as Paul adds the endurance of suffering as another significant standard. He makes this distinction because true apostles, just like true Hebrew prophets, would not stop fulfilling what they are commissioned to do and declaring the name of God regardless of whatever afflictions, hardships, and calamities wait before them.

Israelites persecuted prophets whom they discerned to be false, often to the extent of killing some of them (e.g., Jer 2:30) because the law required them to purge the evil from their midst (Deut. 13:5–10; 12–18; 17:2–7; 18:9–22; Num 25:1–13). However, if they fail to distinguish the true prophets from the false ones, their obedience to the law leads to the sacrifice of God's prophets. Later Jewish tradition is not silent about their sacrifices. Isaiah (*Liv. Pro.* 1:1; *Mart. Isa.* 5; Heb 11:37; *b. Yebam.* 49b), Jeremiah (*Liv. Pro.* 2:1), Ezekiel (*Liv. Pro.* 3:1), Micah (*Liv. Pro.* 7:1), Amos

---

2. Contra Jervell, "Signs of an Apostle," 171n35. The "sign of an apostle" is often regarded as a fixed formulaic expression; cf. Bultmann, *Second Letter to the Corinthians*, 231.

3. See also Acts 13:6–12; 14:3–4, 8–13; 14:3; 15:12; 19:11–12, 13–19. Miracles legitimize the message of the apostles as being approved by God (cf. Acts 2:19, 22, 43; 4:16, 22, 30; 5:12; 6:8; 7:36; 8:6, 13; 13:22; 15:8; 20:23). Elsewhere Paul is portrayed as a miracle worker with the power of the Spirit (Acts 9:17; 13:2, 4, 9; 16:6–7, 18; 19:1, 21; 20:22–23; 21:11).

(*Shalshelet ha-Kabbalah* 97),[4] and Zechariah (*Liv. Pro.* 23:1; 2 Chr 24:20-22; Matt 23:35; Luke 11:51) were all killed whether by being sawn into two, stoned, thrown from a cliff, beaten with a club, or struck on the forehead with a red-hot iron. The same tradition is also found in the New Testament (Matt 23:29-33; Luke 11:47-51; Acts 7:52; 1 Thess 2:15; Heb 11:37-38).

True prophets are betrayed even by their family and friends. Even Jeremiah's close friends ironically, say: "Perhaps he can be enticed, and we can prevail against him, and take our revenge on him" (Jer 20:10; NRSV).[5] However, from the viewpoint of his opponents, they are doing what Deut 13:6-11 commands. Even if it is "your most intimate friend" (Deut 13:7), your brother, or even your spouse, as long as a prophet is suspected to be false, it is an indisputable obligation to report the prophet to the authorities for further investigation and evaluation in the court (Deut 13:14-15; cf. 2 Cor 11:26). Judicial punishments from the court of the law as well as unofficial persecutions from fellow country men and women were parts of the burdens they had to bear (2 Cor 11:23-25).

A gag order is often given to prophets of Israel (Jer 11:21; cf. Acts 23:12-15). Rebellious people say to the seers: "Do not see!" and to the prophets: 'Do not prophesy to us what is right'" (Isa 30:10; Amos 2:12; 7:16; Mic 2:6). It is notable that Moses resists the attempt to suppress prophecy (Num 11:28; cf. 1 Thess 5:19-20). Likewise, true prophets throughout biblical history violate these orders, intensifying their sufferings, because of their commission to deliver the divine message (cf. Acts 5:44). The fate of the disciples of Jesus is not quite different from that of prophets of Israel, where people would "revile, persecute, and utter all kinds of evil against you [= Jesus' disciples]" (Matt 5:11; cf. Luke 6:22) and "in the same way they persecuted the prophets who were before you" (Matt 5:12).

Paul's logic in 2 Cor 11:23-27 is not so complicated. His point is that he is a true prophet or apostle because he has endlessly endured humiliation, suffering, and excommunication throughout his career (cf. 2 Cor 6:4-5; 1 Thess 2:15; 1 Cor 4:9-13). In effect, Paul is pointing to his perseverance as a sign of his authenticity. It would be no exaggeration to say that all the true prophets in the Old Testament experience sufferings throughout their prophetic career and endure. What is more, true prophets (and apostles) persevere because of their fidelity to God and his commission to them.

Despite continuing hardship, because Paul is "entrusted with a commission" (1 Cor 9:17), he cannot be silent. He has no other choice but to proclaim the message he received from God (Gal 1:12; cf. 1:1). When he

---

4. Ginzberg, *Legends of the Jews*, 4:262; 6:357.
5. Unless otherwise noted, all English translations of the Bible are from the NRSV.

exclaims: "Woe to me if I do not proclaim the gospel!" (1 Cor 9:16; Phil 3:12), his self-understanding exactly parallels that of Amos who says: "The lion has roared; who will not fear? The Lord God has spoken; who can but prophesy?" (Amos 3:8; cf. Jer 1:17; 20:7; cf. Ezek 3:11; 2:5, 7). It also echoes Jeremiah, who shouts: "My anguish, my anguish! I writhe in pain! Oh, the walls of my heart! My heart is beating wildly; I cannot keep silent; for I hear the sound of the trumpet, the alarm of war" (Jer 4:19; cf. Ps 39:3–4). In order to fulfill their commission, true prophets need tenacity, and Paul shows it in his ministry.

As an apostle of Christ, Paul endured afflictions, hardships, and calamities. His suffering decisively differentiated Paul from the false apostles. In the list of sufferings Paul is asking: "If I were a false apostle, how could I have been able to endure these diverse and unending sufferings for such a long period of time?" He endured them. And that is an undeniable sign of his authenticity. That is why Paul, in the middle of his controversy against false apostles, gives a long list of his sufferings and emphasizes his endurance of them.

ESCAPE FROM DAMASCUS

2 Cor 11:32–33 has been enigmatic to many NT readers. For what reason does Paul mention the decade-old past episode of his escape from the officials under King Aretas[6] who guarded Damascus[7] to seize him? This passage has been seen as a misplaced excerpt from Gal 1,[8] a gloss,[9] an added postscript,[10] or an illustration of problems Paul encountered in cities.[11] A plethora of solutions has surfaced,[12] but a convincing explanation is still needed. One facet to keep in mind is that Paul's debate with false apostles and his flight narrative from Damascus should be read as a part of his argument for his authenticity as an apostle (and prophet) of God. The point Paul

---

6. Aretas IV, who allegedly ruled his desert kingdom from 9 BCE to 40 CE, died between 38 and 40 CE, See Jewett, *Dating Paul's Life*, 30.

7. Damascus probably was under the Nabatean king's influence at the time of the incident in 2 Cor 11:32–33. See Jewett, *Dating Paul's Life*, 30–33; Turner, "Chronology of the New Testament," 1:416–17.

8. Bishop, "Does Aretas Belong in Second Corinthians or Galatians?" 188–89.

9. Goudge, *Second Epistle to the Corinthians*, 110.

10. Héring, *First Epistle to the Corinthians*, 87.

11. Plummer, *Second Epistle to the Corinthians*, 333.

12. For the possible interpretive options, see Martin, *2 Corinthians*, 384; Judge, "Paul's Boasting," 47; Travis, "Paul's Boasting," 530; Edwards, "Tyche at Corinth," 529–42; Witherington III, *Conflict and Community*, 458–59.

tries to make is that as a true apostle he was in great danger for his life, yet he was rescued, not by chance but by God.

In the Old Testament, God promises his prophets divine protection and deliverance from lethal threats (e.g., Exod 3:12; Deut 31:6; Josh 1:5; 1 Kgs 13:4ff.) whereas divine will for false prophets is destruction and death (e.g., Jer 8:1; 14:15; 23:9-15, 19-20; 28:15-16; Jer 29:31-32; 32:32; Ezek 13:9, 14; 14:9; 22:28; Hos 4:5-6). God's promise given to Deutero-Isaiah in Isa 41:10-13 is short but clear: "Do not fear, for I am with you" (Isa 41:10; cf. 43:5). The divine promise of protection at the time of Jeremiah's commission (Jer 1:8) is repeated in Jer 1:19: "They will fight against you; but they shall not prevail against you, for I am with you, says the Lord, to deliver you" (cf. Jer 15:20-21). Daniel's deliverance from the burning furnace (Dan 3:19-27) and from the jaws of lions (Dan 6:19-23) is in the same venue.

In 3 Macc 6:1-15 Eleazar, the pious priest-prophet, prays for God to rescue him and makes special reference to Daniel and Jonah. In later rabbinic writing, Jonah is identified with the son of the widow of Zarephath whom Elijah resuscitates (*Liv. Pro.* 10:1-6; *Gen. Rab.* 98 on 49:13; *y. Sukkah* 5, 55a; *Midr. Ps.* 26.7 on 26:9). At the deliverance of Jonah, the sailors see the signs and great wonders which the Holy One did to Jonah (*Pirqe R. El.* 1.10). These episodes are understandable if we consider them from God's perspective. God selects and sends prophets, and he must protect them from life-threatening situations. Otherwise, God has to go through the process of selecting and dispatching apostles all over again. To this logic, some would argue that in some cases a true prophet is martyred by the rebellious people, as Uriah son of Shemaiah (Jer 26:20-23). However, a true prophet is normally protected by God from the hostile people and dangerous settings. Therefore, divine protection is a sign of a true prophet.

Therefore, that Paul has been continuously delivered from the danger of death gives him an advantage in the fight with his opposition. According to Luke, Paul is given a divine promise of rescue from those who try to harm him (Acts 26:17). He evades the lethal plans of his opponents in Damascus (Acts 9:23-25), Iconium (Acts 14:5-6), Thessalonica (Acts 17:10), and Jerusalem (Acts 23:12ff.). He is delivered from prison in Philippi (Acts 16:26-40; cf. 5:17-21; 12:3-17), and saved from a shipwreck and survived a serpent's bite (Acts 28:2-6). Luke's reports of Paul's recurring salvation from danger corroborate Paul's own account of God's acts of deliverance which he experienced.

In the beginning of 2 Corinthians, Paul mentions the grave danger he underwent in Asia. He was "so utterly, unbearably crushed that we despaired of life itself" (2 Cor 1:8), going as far as to say that "we had received the sentence of death" (2 Cor 1:9) in a declaration of absolute hopelessness.

However, God delivers him from the deadly peril (2 Cor 1:10). That he is sure of God's future deliverance from other threats (2 Cor 1:10) points to the repeating experience of Paul. As a matter of fact, Paul in 2 Cor 4:8–9 recapitulates his experience of God's deliverance in summary form. Whereas v. 8, which declares "we are afflicted in every way, but not crushed; perplexed, but not driven to despair" might refer to his psychological state, v. 9, which argues he is "persecuted, but not forsaken; struck down, but not destroyed" describes historical events in his apostolic ministry. He was repeatedly delivered and revived by God from countless life-threatening situations. Paul unambiguously makes this point in 2 Cor 6:9:" "as unknown, and yet are well known; as dying, and see—we are alive, as punished, and yet not killed." Even after all of the hazardous and risky circumstances into which he was thrown, Paul is still alive—and still preaching the same message.

The passages discussed above are preambles of what Paul tries to say in 2 Cor 11:32–33 (cf. Acts 9:23–24). Right after his calling and conversion on the Damascus Road, Paul went to Arabia to convert Jews and residents of the Nabatean Kingdom, especially the descendants of Ishmael (Gal 1:17; Isa 42:11; 60:7) with the gospel,[13] with the result that the Nabatean ethnarch tried to seize Paul for punitive treatment.[14] The escape Paul makes in Damascus is probably the first life-threatening experience he ever had as an apostle of Christ. That Paul successfully escaped from the hands of the Nabatean officials dramatically illustrates God's timely deliverance of Paul from danger in his ministry.

Since the first deliverance of God in Damascus right until the time of the most recent lethal threat in Asia, God delivers him every time when he needs divine salvation. The argument Paul wants to make in 2 Cor 11:32–33 is this: "If I were a false apostle, why would God have saved me from these many dangers from the beginning of my career as apostle? If I were not a true apostle God would have removed me from the land. Yet, from the time of my Arabian ministry up to now, including the most recent danger in Asia, God has delivered me from peril. Is not God's repeated deliverance an indication that I am a true apostle and my message is reliable?" This kind of argument must have been effective to the ears of those whose conviction of Paul authenticity was swayed by Paul's opponents. Paul continues his claims for apostolic authenticity against his opponents' accusations of heresy with yet another Scriptural basis.

---

13. Kim, *Paul and the New Perspective*, 101–27; Kim, "Paul—A False Prophet?," 177–81.

14. Thrall, *Second Epistle to the Corinthians*, 770.

PAUL'S VISIT TO PARADISE

Prophets in the Old Testament frequently mention their visionary and auditory experiences and connect them to their claim for prophetic legitimacy.[15] Prophets receive their commission and prophetic messages from God through ecstatic experience.[16] In the context of false prophet controversy, true prophets might opt for giving a detailed description of their encounter with divinity (e.g., Isa 6; Jer 1; Ezek 1; 1 Kgs 22:17–23).[17] The most compelling argument for prophetic authenticity is the prophet's first-hand experience of an other-worldly visit to where God holds his heavenly council.

In 1 Kgs 22 (= 2 Chr 18), we can find a unique account of a prophet's attendance in the council of Yahweh, where God discusses the matters of the universe with celestial beings (Jer 23:18, 22; Job 1:6–12; 15:8; Ps 82:1–8; 89:6–9; Sir 24:2).[18] When Micaiah, a true prophet, is attacked by false prophets, he reveals his participation in the council of the Lord (1 Kgs 22:19–23). From his testimony, we learn that: 1) God is king on the throne, 2) heavenly creatures surround God, 3) Micaiah "saw" Yahweh, and 4) his oracle is merely relaying what he saw and heard about God.[19] What differentiates Micaiah from false prophets is his privileged firsthand ecstatic experience in the arena of "the gods," the source of his knowledge for the things hidden to ordinary people. By simply talking about his attendance to the divine council, he is able to make claims to his authentic prophetic status.

As God reveals secrets to Micaiah by allowing him to stand before the divine council, so does God to Isaiah (Isa 6:1–13). Isaiah's heavenly experience is similar to that of Micaiah. We read that: 1) Isaiah "saw" Yahweh sitting on the throne (6:1), 2) God is addressed as "the King" (6:5), 3) God is with heavenly creatures around him (6:2–3), 4) God discusses the matters of the destiny of Israel with those who are with him (6:8), and 5) Isaiah, who

---

15. Clement, *Old Testament Interpretation*, 54; Gunkel, "Secret Experiences of the Prophets," 427–32.

16. Robinson, *Prophecy and the Prophets*, 50–51; Robinson, "Ecstatic Element," 217–38; Mowinckel, "Ecstatic Experience," 264–91; Widengren, *Literary and Psychological Aspects*, 98–120; Lindblom, *Prophecy in Ancient Israel*, 47–65, 105–8, 122–37, 177–82, 197–202, 216–19.

17. Wilson, "Interpreting Israel's Religion," 334; contra Long, "Prophetic Authority," 3–20.

18. According to Robinson the divine assembly in early Semitic thought may have originated from Babylonian myths. See Mullen, *Divine Council*; Miller, *Genesis 1–11*, 9–26; Robinson, "Council of Yahweh," 151–57; Brown, "Pre-Christian Semitic Concept," 418.

19. Kingsbury, "Prophets and the Council of Yahweh," 280.

is admitted for a deliberation in the council, is sent to relay what he saw and heard there to the Israelites.

Another theophany happened to Ezekiel (Ezek 1:1—2:7; 10:1–22) when he "saw" God (Ezek 1:1, 4, 15, 18, 27, 28; 2:9; 10:1, 8, 9), and after a prolonged conversation with God, was commissioned to pass on what he heard from God (Ezek 3:10–11). Basically, God does nothing "without revealing his secret to his servants the prophets" (Amos 3:7, cf. Gen 18:17).[20] From the council of Yahweh, the "mystery" is unveiled to the prophets. Only those who attended the council of God and receive his secret divine decrees are commissioned to carry the mystery to their audience.[21]

In this sense Jeremiah's mention of the council of God in Jer 23:18, 22 is significant. "Who has stood in the council of the Lord so as to see and to hear his word?" (Jer 23:18) is the message of God given in the first person. God legitimates Jeremiah as a God-commissioned prophet. Unlike his opponents who do not have messages "from the mouth of the Lord" (Jer 23:16), Jeremiah does. Unlike false prophets whose vision is "from their own mind" (Jer 23:16), since Jeremiah saw God in the council of God, his vision is revelatory and true. Jeremiah's involvement in the heavenly council legitimizes his message (Jer 23:22). Therefore, one certain criterion for distinction between true and false prophets is whether they are ever admitted into the divine council, the ultimate ground for prophets' claim for their authenticity (cf. Deut 30:12ff.; Prov 30:3–4; Bar 3:29–37).[22]

If the above is true, can Paul be regarded as a true prophet or apostle? Paul often uses ἀποκάλυψις (Rom 2:5; 8:19; 16:25; Gal 1:12; 2:2; 1 Cor 1:7; 14:6, 26; 2 Cor 12:1, 7; 2 Thess 1:7; Eph 1:17; 3:3) and its verbal form ἀποκαλύπτω (Rom 1:17, 18; 8:18; Phil 3:15; 1 Cor 2:10; 3:13; 14:30; Gal 1:16; 3:23; 2 Thess 2:3, 6, 8; Eph 3:5)[23] to describe how he, like the OT prophets, has seen the glorified Lord in the person of Jesus Christ (1 Cor 9:1; cf. to Isaiah 6:1, 5). He clearly relates this experience of seeing Christ face-to-face to his apostleship (cf. 1 Cor 15:8).[24] Paul's experience on the Damascus Road is God's revelation to him, through which he comes to hold on to the message

---

20. The expression, "his servants, the prophets," is typical of the Deuteronomic school (e.g., 2 Kgs 9:7; 17:13, 23; 21:10; 24:2; Jer 7:25; 25:4; 26:5; 29:19; 35:15; 44:4; cf. Ezek 38:17; Zech 1:6; Dan 9:6, 10; Ezra 9:11); see Paul, *Amos*, 112.

21. Mays, *Amos*, 62.

22. Brown, "Pre-Christian Semitic Concept," 420; Grabbe, *Priests, Prophets, Diviners, Sages*, 114.

23. For a bibliography of this subject, see Camery-Hoggatt, "Visions, Ecstatic Experience," 965; Hanson, "Dreams and Visions," 1395–1427.

24. Bruce, *1 and 2 Corinthians*, 83.

he carries (Gal 1:12, 16; cf. Acts 9:1–9; 22:6–11; 26:13–19).[25] Apart from this experience, for which Paul does not reveal much more detailed description, in 2 Cor 12:1–10 he mentions his rapture to an out-of-body experience. He visits the highest place of heaven, as far as paradise,[26] where the abode of God lies (2 Cor 12:2, 3–4).

The question we need to ask is why he brings in this experience into the debate with his opponents. Most commentators of 2 Corinthians regard that Paul mentions it because his opponents laid claim to such experiences.[27] However, because of the lack of internal evidence in the text of 2 Corinthians the suggestion is not unanimously acceptable. According to Segal, the revelation Gal 1:16 is similar to the one in 2 Cor 12:1–4,[28] although they should be differentiated. Paul utilizes the language of Jewish mysticism such as "paradise" and "third heaven" in 2 Cor 12:1–4[29] and talks about the "mystery" he has been given (Rom 11:25; 1 Cor 2:1; 4:1; 13:2; 14:2; 15:51; 16:25–26; Col 1:26–27; 2:2; 4:3; 2 Thess 2:7; Eph 1:9; 3:4; 5:32; 6:19). This mystery, which was kept secret for ages (Rom 16:25; 1 Cor 2:7; Eph 3:9), is now disclosed (Rom 16:26) and known to Paul through a revelation from God (Rom 16:25; Eph 3:3). The mystery is what Paul calls "my gospel" (Rom 16:26).

The term "mystery" itself indicates that the message he proclaims was given by God through spiritual experiences like the rapture in 2 Cor 12:1–4, and at the same time that he participated in the council of the Lord since the council of the Lord is the only place where a mortal being can hear the mystery of God. In 2 Cor 2:16, Paul asks: "Who is sufficient for these things?" This question is quite equivalent to saying: "Who has stood in the council of the Lord so as to see and to hear his word?" (Jer 23:18). Paul's statement in

---

25. Kim, *Origin of Paul's Gospel*, 56–66; Barrett, *First Epistle*, 200; Conzelmann, *1 Corinthians*, 152; Fee, *First Epistle*, 395.

26. "Paradise," an old Persian loan word (*pairidaza*) can be understood to be referring to the "third heaven" in 2 Cor 12:2; Strachan, *Second Epistle*, 31; Barrett, *Second Epistle*, 310; Scott, "Coherence and Contingency," 64, 224. Paradise can also be regarded as included in the third heaven; see Harris, *Second Epistle*, 845; Lincoln, *Paradise Now and Not Yet*, 79; Thrall, *Second Epistle*, 791. In fact, *2 En.* 8:1, 31:1, *Apoc. Mos.* 37:5, and *3 Bar.* 4:8 place paradise in the third heaven; see Bruce, "Was Paul a Mystic?," 73; Schäfer, "New Testament and Hekhalot Literature," 22; Thrall, *Second Epistle*, 791.

27. For instance, Strachan, *Second Epistle*, 30; Tasker, *Second Epistle*, 169; Barrett, *Second Epistle*, 312; Barrett, "Paul's Opponents in II Corinthians," 251; Lincoln, *Paradise Now and Not Yet*, 74–75; Martin, *2 Corinthians*, 396; Furnish, *2 Corinthians*, 543; Thrall, *Second Epistle*, 773; Harris, *Second Epistle*, 832.

28. Since Galatians was written before 2 Corinthians, it is generally believed that those ecstatic experiences were discrete ones; see Segal, *Paul the Convert*, 37.

29. Quispel, "Ezekiel 1:26," 8.

2 Cor 12:2, 4 is the answer to this question: "I am qualified for the apostolic works since I have stood in the council of God."

THORN IN THE FLESH

Right after mentioning his rapture experience in 2 Cor 12:1–4, from v. 7 Paul moves to the issue of "the thorn in the flesh." We need to ask ourselves: why does he raise this subject right after his heavenly journey up to the third heaven? Does it have anything to do with his debate with false apostles? In order to answer the question, we need to observe the physical problem Paul has in the eyes of his opponents—i.e., his untreatable illness which his Jewish or Christian opponents may have seen as God's just punishment of Paul as a law-breaker.

According to Deut 28:15–68, a series of divine curses eventually will fall upon "anyone who does not uphold the law by observing them" (Deut 27:26; cf. Gal 3:10). Whether disease, famine, the loss of land, or the marginalization of God's people, these issues are all signs of a divine curse on the law-breaker. One of the most frequently repeated punishments in the list is physical affliction. God afflicts the transgressor "with consumption, and with fever, inflammation, and fiery heat, and with drought, and with blasting, and with mildew" (Deut 28:22) and "with the boils of Egypt, and with the ulcers and the scurvy and the itch, of which you cannot be healed" (Deut 28:27). Madness and ecstatic experience are included in the curse list (Deut 28:28, 34). He will be "driven mad by the sight that your eyes shall see" (Deut 28:34). One of the peculiar characteristics of such diseases is that they are incurable (Deut 28:35). All of these curses will be "signs and wonders" (Deut 28:46; cf. 2 Cor 12:12) for the Jews and their descendants. Incurable illness is a sign of God's curse upon the sinner who ignores God's law. He will serve his enemies "in hunger and thirst, in nakedness" (Deut 28:48; cf. 2 Cor 11:27).[30] He is cursed "in the city" as well as "in the field" (Deut 28:16; cf. 2 Cor 11:26). If a prophet or apostle had an incurable disease, opponents would have easily used the illness as an accusation of false apostleship.

Paul must have been ill (cf. 2 Cor 4:7–8; 6:3–10; 11:23–12:10; 1 Cor 4:9–12, 15:30, 32), though which illness he had is unknown to us. His illness is somehow related to what he calls "a thorn in the flesh" (2 Cor 12:7). In a sense he is an ailing miraculous healer.[31] The concept of an "ailing miracle

---

30. The phrase "in hunger and thirst, in nakedness" (ἐν λιμῷ καὶ ἐν δίψει καὶ ἐν γυμνότητι) in Deut 28:48 LXX is repeated in 2 Cor 11:27 (ἐν λιμῷ καὶ δίψει . . . ἐν ψύχει καὶ γυμνότητι).

31. Jervell, "Signs of an Apostle," 94.

worker" probably would not have been understood by his opponents: to them, his illness was a basis to indict Paul. The curse list in Deut 28:15–68 would have been foundation for Paul's opponents to label him as a false prophet, since by their logic Paul is cursed by God. The curse upon his body was powerful evidence for their claim. Paul's physical weakness and the theological interpretation his opponents gave to it must have been a powerful dissuasion for Paul's audience against his claim to true prophecy. That is what Paul meant by "my condition was a trial to you" in Gal 4:14.

Some textual evidence even indicates that Paul was mad as a result of his trance experience, or that Paul experienced his trance because he was mad. In 2 Cor 5:13 Paul says: "if we are beside ourselves, it is for God." The verb ἐξίστημι, denoting a state of "being beside oneself," describes his ecstasy with language similar to that of his other visionary experiences (12:2–4; cf. 11:23; Acts 22:17; Mark 3:21).[32]

In short, the thorn in the flesh harassed Paul, both physically and theologically. That is why he brings up the issue in vv. 7–10. It must have been used as a powerful attack by opponents against Paul because his illness denied the origin of his gospel, the authenticity of the gospel, and even his apostleship. If Paul's opponents had not attacked his physical weakness to invalidate his authenticity as God's prophet, Paul would not have suddenly turned the attention of his audience to the issue of his physical weakness in his controversy with false apostles (2 Cor 11:30; 12:7–10). Paul eventually had to develop his theology of weakness to deal with this heavy criticism.

CONCLUSION

The seemingly loosely-related four themes—i.e., the suffering catalogue (2 Cor 11:23–30), the episode of escape from the officers of King Aretas in Damascus (11:31–33), the rapture to the third heaven (12:1–4), and the argument about the thorn in the flesh (12:5–10)—are all closely interrelated. The unifying motive lying behind these issues is the controversy surrounding false apostles, prominent in the Old and New Testament alike. Paul's defense of his apostleship is best framed against the OT background that true prophets persevere through suffering, are rescued from harm by God himself, receive ecstatic visions, and experience weakness not as a divine punishment but as a gift.

---

32. Plummer mentions as a possibility that Paul's non-Christian fellow Jews might have held that Paul's conversion experience led him to madness (*Second Epistle*, 172). Thrall seems to consider the proposal possible; however, she does not pursue it (*Second Epistle*, 406).

BIBLIOGRAPHY

Barrett, C. K. *A Commentary on the First Epistle to the Corinthians*. HNTC. New York: Harper & Row, 1971. Reprint, Peabody, MA: Hendrickson, 1987.
———. *A Commentary on the Second Epistle to the Corinthians*. HNTC. New York: Harper & Row, 1974. Reprint, Peabody, MA: Hendrickson, 1987.
———. "Paul's Opponents in II Corinthians." *NTS* 17 (1970-71) 233-54.
Bishop, E. F. F. "Does Aretas Belong in 2 Corinthians or Galatians?" *ExpTim* 64 (1953) 188-89.
Brown, Raymond E. "The Pre-Christian Semitic Concept of 'Mystery.'" *CBQ* 20 (1958) 417-43.
Bruce, F. F. *1 and 2 Corinthians*. New Century Bible Commentary. London: Oliphants, 1971. Reprint, Grand Rapids: Eerdmans, 1980.
———. "Was Paul a Mystic?" *RTR* 34 (1975) 66-75.
Bultmann, Rudolf. *The Second Letter to the Corinthians*. Trans. R. A. Harrisville. Minneapolis: Augsburg, 1984.
Camery-Hoggatt, J. "Visions, Ecstatic Experience." In *DPL*, ed. G. F. Hawthorne et al., 963-65. Downers Grove, IL: IVP, 1993.
Clement, Ronald E. *One Hundred Years of Old Testament Interpretation*. Philadelphia: Westminster, 1976.
Conzelmann, Hans. *1 Corinthians: A Commentary on the First Epistle to the Corinthians*. Hermeneia. Philadelphia: Fortress, 1975.
Edwards, C. M. "Tyche at Corinth." *Hesperia* 59 (1990) 529-42.
Fee, Gordon D. *The First Epistle to the Corinthians*. NICNT. Grand Rapids: Eerdmans, 1987.
Furnish, Victor Paul. *2 Corinthians: A New Translation with Introduction and Commentary*. AB 32A. Garden City, NY: Doubleday, 1984.
Ginzberg, Louis. *The Legends of the Jews*. Trans. H. Szold. 7 vols. Philadelphia: Jewish Publication Society of America, 1909-38.
Goudge, H. L. *The Second Epistle to the Corinthians*. London: Methuen, 1927.
Grabbe, Lester L. *Priests, Prophets, Diviners, Sages: A Socio-Historical Study of Religious Specialists in Ancient Israel*. Valley Forge, PA: Trinity, 1995.
Gunkel, H. "The Secret Experiences of the Prophets." *Expositor* 9, no. 1 (1924) 427-32.
Hanson, J. S. "Dreams and Visions in the Graeco-Roman World and Early Christianity." In *ANRW* II.23.2 (1980) 1395-1427.
Harris, Murray J. *The Second Epistle to the Corinthians*. NIGTC. Grand Rapids: Eerdmans, 2005.
Héring, Jean. *The First Epistle of Saint Paul to the Corinthians*. Trans. A. W. Heathcote and P. J. Allcock. London: Epworth, 1962.
Jervell, Jacob. "The Signs of an Apostle: Paul's Miracles." In *The Unknown Paul: Essays on Luke-Acts and Early Christian History*, 77-95. Minneapolis: Augsburg, 1984.
Jewett, Robert. *Dating Paul's Life*. London: SCM, 1979.
Judge, E. A. "Paul's Boasting in Relation to Contemporary Professional Practice." *ABR* 16 (1968) 37-50.
Kim, Chulhong Brian. "Paul—A False Prophet?: False Prophet Accusations against Paul." PhD diss., Fuller Theological Seminary, 2007.
Kim, Seyoon. *The Origin of Paul's Gospel*. WUNT 2/4. Rev. ed. Tübingen: Mohr/Siebeck, 1984.

———. *Paul and the New Perspective: Second Thoughts on the Origin of Paul's Gospel.* Grand Rapids: Eerdmans, 2002.
Kingsbury, Edwin C. "The Prophets and the Council of Yahweh." *JBL* 83 (1964) 279–86.
Lincoln, Andrew T. *Paradise Now and Not Yet.* SNTSMS 43. Cambridge: Cambridge University Press, 1981.
Lindblom, J. *Prophecy in Ancient Israel.* Philadelphia: Muhlenberg, 1962.
Long, B. O. "Prophetic Authority as Social Reality." In *Canon and Authority*, ed. G. W. Coats and B. O. Long, 3–20. Philadelphia: Fortress, 1977.
Martin, Ralph P. *2 Corinthians.* WBC 40. Waco: Word, 1986.
Mays, James L. *Amos.* OTL. Philadelphia: Westminster, 1969.
Miller, Patrick D., Jr. *Genesis 1–11: Studies in Structure & Theme.* JSOTSup 8. Sheffield: Department of Biblical Studies, 1978.
Mowinckel, Sigmund. "Ecstatic Experience and Rational Elaboration in Old Testament Prophecy." *AcOr* 13 (1935) 264–91.
Mullen, E. T., Jr. *The Divine Council in Canaanite and Early Hebrew Literature.* Chico, CA: Scholars, 1980.
Paul, Shalom M. *Amos.* Hermeneia. Minneapolis: Fortress, 1991.
Plummer, Alfred. *A Critical and Exegetical Commentary on the Second Epistle of St. Paul to the Corinthians.* ICC. Edinburgh: T. & T. Clark, 1915.
Quispel, Gilles. "Ezekiel 1:26 in Jewish Mysticism and Gnosis." *VC* 34 (1980) 1–13.
Robinson, H. Wheeler. "The Council of Yahweh." *JTS* 45 (1944) 151–57.
Robinson, T. H. "The Ecstatic Element in Old Testament Prophecy." *The Expositor* (8th series) 21, no. 123 (1921) 217–38.
———. *Prophecy and the Prophets in Ancient Israel.* London: Duckworth, 1953.
Schäfer, Peter. "New Testament and Hekhalot Literature: The Journey into Heaven in Paul and in Merkavah Mysticism." *JJS* 35 (1984) 19–35.
Scott, J. M. "Coherence and Contingency: The Function of Scripture in 2 Corinthians 6:14—7:1." In *Paul and the Scriptures of Israel*, ed. C. A. Evans and J. A. Sanders, 187–220. JSNTSup 83. Sheffield: JSOT Press, 1993.
Segal, Alan. *Paul the Convert: The Apostolate and Apostasy of Saul the Pharisee.* New Haven: Yale University Press, 1990.
Strachan, Robert H. *The Second Epistle of Paul to the Corinthians.* MNTC. London: Hodder and Stoughton, 1935.
Tasker, Randolph V. G. *The Second Epistle of Paul to the Corinthians.* TNTC. Grand Rapids: Eerdmans, 1958.
Thrall, Margaret E. *A Critical and Exegetical Commentary on the Second Epistle to the Corinthians.* 2 vols. ICC. Edinburgh: T. & T. Clark, 1994–2000.
Travis, S. H. "Paul's Boasting in 2 Corinthians 10–12." *SE* 6 (1973) 527–32.
Turner, C. H. "Chronology of the New Testament." In *Dictionary of the Bible*, ed. J. Hastings, rev. F. C. Grant and H. H. Rowley, 1:403–25. New York: Scribner, 1963.
Widengren, G. *Literary and Psychological Aspects of the Hebrew Prophets.* Uppsala: Lundequist, 1948.
Wilson, R. R. "Interpreting Israel's Religion: An Anthropological Perspective on the Problem of False Prophecy." In *The Place Is Too Small for Us: The Israelite Prophets in Recent Scholarship*, ed. R. P. Gordon, 332–44. Winona Lake, IN: Eisenbrauns, 1995.
Witherington, Ben, III. *Conflict and Community in Corinth: A Socio-Rhetorical Commentary on 1 and 2 Corinthians.* Grand Rapids: Eerdmans, 1995.

Part Two

Essays on the Gospels and Gospel Hermeneutics

7

Matthew's Use of the Septuagint and Its Implications[1]

JIN KI HWANG

INTRODUCTION

It is generally acknowledged that Matthew intended his Gospel for Jewish Christian readers. Given this understanding, it is interesting to observe that Matthew sometimes translates a transliterated Hebrew / Aramaic word or phrase into Greek (e.g., Matt 1:21, 23; 27:46 // Mark 15:22; cf. Matt 15:5 // Mark 7:11). He makes explicit scriptural quotations from the Septuagint text not only when other Evangelists (Mark in particular) do the same, but also when they do not appear to do so (e.g., Matt 13:10-17 // Mark 4:10-12; Luke 8:9-10). The present paper will (1) investigate Matthew's own knowledge of the Septuagint text(s) and (2) examine how he consciously uses the Septuagint for his purposes in his Gospel.

---

1. This article is a revision of the paper presented at the Society of Biblical Literature Annual Meeting in San Francisco on November 20, 2011.

SOME OBSERVATIONS ON MATTHEW'S EXPLICIT SCRIPTURAL QUOTATIONS

According to NA[27],[2] Matthew explicitly quotes the Scriptures in at least 53 different places.[3] This is remarkable when compared to the frequency of the formal scriptural quotations in the other Synoptic Gospels (e.g., 29 different places in Mark). The peculiarities of Matthew's scriptural quotations can be summarized as follows.

1. Matthew frequently uses the πληρόω verb and its cognates to introduce a formal scriptural quotation (1:22-23; 2:15, 17-18; 4:14-16; 8:17; 12:17-21; 13:14-15; 13:35; 21:4-5; 27:9-10; cf. 2:23; 26:54, 56). For instance, in 1:22-23, Matthew explicitly cites Isa 7:13 in terms of the πληρόω verb (ἵνα πληρωθῇ τὸ ῥηθὲν ὑπὸ κυρίου διὰ τοῦ προφήτου λέγοντος).[4] Matthew also introduces his scriptural quotations with γέγραπται (2:5-6; 4:4, 6, 7, 10; 11:10; 21:13; 26:31).[5] This phrase, "it is written," is actually the most popular quotation formula used by the New Testament writers (e.g., Luke 2:23; 3:4; Mark 1:2; 7:6; 11:17; 14:27; John 8:17; Rom 12:19; 14:11; 1 Cor 1:19; 9:9; Gal 4:22, 27).[6]

2. Matthew attests most of the scriptural quotations made by Mark, as demonstrated in the table below (cf. Mark 6:3, 4; 8:18; 9:48; 12:32-33), while he seldom shares a scriptural quotation with Luke against Mark.[7] Matthew's scriptural quotations almost always correspond to those in the Markan parallels in both their wording and length. Mark's scriptural texts are predominantly Septuagintal,[8] and likewise those in the Matthean parallels.

---

2. Unless otherwise noted, the Greek text for the New Testament is based on the NA[27].

3. Boring catalogues 61 OT quotations in the Gospel of Matthew ("Matthew," 151): 24 of these quotations shared with Mark, 9 with Q, and 28 unique to Matthew.

4. The πληρόω verb is also used as a quotation formula both in Luke (4:17-21; cf. 24:44) and John (12:38; 13:18; 15:25; 18:9; 19:24, 36), but interestingly not at all in Mark (cf. 14:49).

5. Γέγραπται γάρ: Matt 2:5; 4:6, 10; 26:31; γέγραπται: Matt 4:4, 7; 21:13; cf. λέγων: Matt 15:7.

6. A similar use can also be found in the Septuagint (ὡς γέγραπται: 4 Kdgms 23:21; 2 Chr 23:18; 25:4; 35:12; Dan 9:13; cf. 2 Chr 32:32; 33:19), Philo (γέγραπται γάρ: Post. 1.102; Decal. 1.147), and the writings of the apostolic fathers (1 Clem 4:1; 14:4; 29:2; 39:3; 46:2; 50:4, 6; Barn. 4:3; Ign. Eph. 5:3).

7. See, e.g., Q: Matt 4:1-11//Luke 4:1-13 (temptation account) though in a different order; and Matt 11:10//Luke 7:27 (Exod 23:20; Mal 3:1). Gundry finds Matthew's formal quotations in common with Luke only in Matt 4//Luke 4 (Use of the Old Testament, 66-69).

8. Ibid., 9.

Jin Ki Hwang   *Matthew's Use of the Septuagint and Its Implications*   133

But at times Matthew diverges from Mark in the wording and/or length of the scriptural quotation (e.g., Matt 19:18 // Mark 10:19; Matt 22:37 // Mark 12:29–30). Table 1 below summarizes the comparisons between Mark's and Matthew's quotation of Scripture.

Table 1: Scriptural Citations Shared by Matthew and Mark

Quotation formula in Mark?	Mark	Old Testament	Matt	Old Testament	Remark
Yes	1:2–3	Isa 40:3 LXX ("Isaiah")	3:3	Isa 40:3 LXX ("Isaiah")	also Luke 3:4–6 (Isa 40:3–5; "Isaiah")
Yes	1:2–3	Exod 23:20; Mal 3:1 ("Isaiah")	11:10	Exod 23:20; Mal 3:1 ("γέγραπται")	also Luke 7:27 ("γέγραπται")
No	4:12	[Isa 6:9–10] (allusive quotation)	13:14–15	Isa 6:9–10 LXX ("Isaiah")	
No	4:32	Ps 103:12 LXX	13:31	Ps 103:12 LXX	
No	6:34	Num 27:17	14:14	–	cf. Matt 9:36 [Num 27:17]
Yes	7:6–7	Isa 29:13 LXX ("Isaiah")	15:7–8	Isa 29:13 LXX ("Isaiah")	identical (cf. the order of ὁ λαὸς οὗτος)
No	8:18	Jer 5:21	16:9	–	cf. Matt 13:13 (allusion)
No	9:11	Mal 3:23	17:10	Mal 3:23	identical
No	9:48	Isa 66:24	5:9	–	
No	10:6–7	Gen 1:27; 2:24 LXX	19:4–5	Gen 1:27; 2:24 LXX	identical (cf. αὐτοῦ); no citation formula
No	10:19	Exod 20:12–16; Deut 5:16–20; Sir 4:1 LXX	19:18	Exod 20:12–16 LXX; Deut 5:16–20 + Lev 19:18 LXX	also Luke 18:20 (order / content different)
No	11:9	Ps 118:25–26	21:9	Ps 118:25–26	also Luke 19:38; John 12:13
No	11:10	Ps 148:1	21:9	Ps 148:1	

Table 1: Scriptural Citations Shared by Matthew and Mark (cont.)					
Quotation formula in Mark?	Mark	Old Testament	Matt	Old Testament	Remark
Yes	11:17	Isa 56:7 (includes LXX's πᾶσιν τοῖς ἔθνεσιν; cf. MT) + Jer 7:11	21:13	Isa 56:7 (drops Mark's/LXX's πᾶσιν τοῖς ἔθνεσιν) + Jer 7:11	also Luke 19:46 (adds ἔσται, omits πᾶσιν τοῖς ἔθνεσιν, and different order)
Yes	12:10–11	Ps 117:22–23 LXX (= 118:22–23 MT)	21:42	Ps 117:22–23 LXX	identical; also Luke 20:17 (Ps 117:22 only)
Yes	12:19	Deut 25:5–6	22:24	Deut 25:5	
Yes	12:19	Gen 38:8	22:24	Gen 38:8	
Yes	12:26	Exod 3:6	22:31	Exod 3:6	also Luke 20:37
No	12:29–30	Deut 6:4 (= LXX), 6:5 (almost LXX); Josh 22:5 LXX	22:37	Deut 6:5; Josh 22:5 LXX (drops *shema* saying)	also Luke 10:27 / Deut 6:5 (quotation formula)
No	12:31	Lev 19:18	22:39	Lev 19:18	also Luke 10:27
No	12:32	Deut 6:4; 4:35; Isa 45:21	22:40	–	
No	12:33	Deut 6:5; Josh 22:5 LXX (scribe's retelling)	22:40	–	cf. Matt 22:37
Yes	12:36	Ps 110:1 ("David")	22:43–44	Ps 110:1 ("David")	identical; also Luke 20:42–43
No	13:14	Dan 12:11	24:15	Dan 12:11 ("Daniel")	Matt specifies Daniel's name
No	13:24–25	Isa 14:10; 34:4	24:29	Isa 14:10; 34:4	also Luke 21:25–26
No	13:26	Dan 7:13–14	24:30	Dan 7:13–14	also Luke 21:27
No	14:27	Zech 13:7	26:31	Zech 13:7	identical, except order and τῆς ποίμνης in Matt
No	14:34	Ps 42:6, 12; 43:5	26:38	Ps 42:6, 12; 43:5	Identical
No	14:62	Dan 7:13	26:64	Dan 7:13	
No	15:24	Ps 22:19	27:35	Ps 22:19	
No	15:34	Ps 22:2	27:46	Ps 22:2	

3. Matthew also explicitly quotes scriptural texts that are not attested in other Gospels in order to prove the fulfillment of certain OT prophecies in Jesus (e.g., Matt 1:23; 2:6, 15, 17–18, 23; 4:14–16; 8:17; 12:17–21; 13:14–15, 35; 21:4–5; 27:9–10). O'Leary points out that most of Matthew's so-called "fulfillment quotations" do not "arise out of Mark's narrative." According to her, Matt 21:4–5 is the only exception.[9] But when we also consider all the other scriptural quotations that Matthew introduces with the πληρόω verb, Matt 13:14–15 can be another such exception.[10] These texts (i.e., Matt 13:14–15 and 21:4–5) can therefore be helpful in understanding how Matthew consciously uses scriptural texts for his own purposes even while depending, in the main, on the Markan narrative.

4. Isaiah is one of the scriptural books Matthew quotes most frequently (1:23; 3:3; 4:15; 8:17; 11:5; 12:18; 13:14; 15:8–9; 21:5, 13; 24:29).[11] Matthew specifically mentions the name "Isaiah" six times when he introduces a formal scriptural quotation (3:3; 4:14; 8:17; 12:17; 13:14; 15:7). In two cases, Matthew simply mentions "the prophet" as a reference to Isaiah (1:23; 21:4). Similarly, Mark and Luke mention "Isaiah" along with γέγραπται, though less frequently than Matthew does (Matt 3:3 // Mark 1:2 // Luke 3:4; Matt 15:7 // Mark 7:6; cf. also John 1:23; 12:38).

Table 2: Quotations from Isaiah in Matthew				
Isaiah	Text type	Matthew	Quotation Formula	Matthean Contexts
6:9–10	LXX	13:14–15	καὶ ἀναπληροῦται αὐτοῖς ἡ προφητεία Ἡσαΐου ἡ λέγουσα	Jesus' logia
7:14	LXX	1:23	ἵνα πληρωθῇ τὸ ῥηθὲν ὑπὸ κυρίου διὰ τοῦ προφήτου λέγοντος	Commentary
8:10	LXX	1:23	ἵνα πληρωθῇ τὸ ῥηθὲν ὑπὸ κυρίου διὰ τοῦ προφήτου λέγοντος	Commentary
8:23—9:1		4:15	ἵνα πληρωθῇ τὸ ῥηθὲν διὰ Ἡσαΐου τοῦ προφήτου λέγοντος	Commentary

9. O'Leary, *Matthew's Judaization of Mark*, 137; see also Menken ("Source of the Quotation," 313), who states: "The fulfillment quotations can be omitted without a loss of flow of the storyline."

10. There are some scriptural quotations peculiar to Luke: 2:23 (Exod 13:2, 12, 15); 2:24 (Lev 5:11; 12:8); 4:17–19 (Isa 61:1–2 LXX: read in a synagogue at Galilee).

11. See Boring ("Matthew," 151), who states: "As in the other Gospels and the New Testament as a whole, Matthew cites most often the Psalms, Isaiah, and Deuteronomy."

| Table 2: Quotations from Isaiah in Matthew (cont.) |||||
Isaiah	Text type	Matthew	Quotation Formula	Matthean Contexts
13:10		24:29	–	Jesus' logia
26:19		11:5	–	Jesus' logia
29:13	LXX	15:8–9	καλῶς ἐπροφήτευσεν περὶ ὑμῶν Ἡσαΐας λέγων	Jesus' logia
29:18		11:5	–	Jesus' logia
34:4		24:29	–	Jesus' logia
35:5–6		11:5	–	Jesus' logia
40:3	LXX	3:3	οὗτος γάρ ἐστιν ὁ ῥηθεὶς διὰ Ἡσαΐου τοῦ προφήτου λέγοντος	Commentary
42:18		11:5	–	Jesus' logia
42:1–4		12:18–21	ἵνα πληρωθῇ τὸ ῥηθὲν διὰ Ἡσαΐου τοῦ προφήτου λέγοντος	Commentary
53:4		8:17	ὅπως πληρωθῇ τὸ ῥηθὲν διὰ Ἡσαΐου τοῦ προφήτου λέγοντος	Commentary
56:7	close to LXX	21:13	Γέγραπται	Jesus' logia
62:11	close to LXX	21:5	Τοῦτο δὲ γέγονεν ἵνα πληρωθῇ τὸ ῥηθὲν διὰ τοῦ προφήτου λέγοντος	Commentary

When Matthew explicitly quotes Isaiah, Matthew does not always exactly follow the Septuagint. O'Leary contends that in all of the "fulfillment quotations" (definitely including the Isaiah quotations in Table 2) Matthew does not follow the Septuagint.[12] But this is an overstatement because in at least two places Matthew seems to consciously use an Isaiah text that is identical to the Septuagint (Matt 1:23 [Isa 7:14; 8:10]; 13:14–15 [Isa 6:9–10]; cf. Matt 3:3 [Isa 40:3]; 15:8–9 [Isa 29:13]).

The above survey gives us three groups of passages by which we can determine Matthew's own knowledge and use of Septuagint texts.

Group A: Matthew's Scriptural Quotations That Diverge from Mark's (Matt 19:18; 22:37)

---

12. O'Leary, *Matthew's Judaization of Mark*, 137.

Group B: Matthew's Scriptural Quotations Added to the Markan Narrative (Matt 13:14–15; 21:4–5)

Group C: Matthew's Independent Use of Quotations from Isaiah (Matt 1:23; 13:14–15)

To better appreciate Matthew's intertextuality with the Old Testament, it would be helpful to examine how other Jewish exegetes like Philo quote from, and allude to, Israel's Scriptures. Philo's use of the Old Testament might provide analogues by which to compare with Matthew's quotation practices.

PHILO'S USE OF SEPTUAGINT TEXTS

As a Hellenistic Jewish theologian, Philo reveres the Septuagint (especially the five books of the Torah) just as highly as the Hebrew Bible. He makes this clear in the following statement:

> And there is a very evident proof of this; for if Chaldaeans were to learn the Greek language, and if Greeks were to learn Chaldaean, and if each were to meet with those Scriptures in both languages, namely, the Chaldaic and the translated version [ἀμφοτέραις ταῖς γραφαῖς ἐντύχωσι, τῇ τε Χαλδαϊκῇ καὶ τῇ ἑρμηνευθείσῃ], they would admire and reverence them both as sisters, or rather as one and the same both in their facts and in their language; considering these translators not mere interpreters but hierophants and prophets [ἑρμηνέας ἐκείνους ἀλλ' ἱεροφάντας καὶ προφήτας προσαγορεύοντες] to whom it had been granted it their honest and guileless minds to go along with the most pure spirit of Moses (*Mos.* 2.40).[13]

It is, therefore, no wonder that Philo consciously quotes from the Septuagint in his exegetical works. When he makes an explicit scriptural quotation, Philo indicates this with a quotation formula.[14]

Philo, at a given time, takes any one of the following five approaches to the Septuagint text, with which we may compare with Matthew's. This, of course, is not an exhaustive list of the kinds of the scriptural quotations

---

13. ET by Yonge; see also Goulder, *Midrash and Lection in Matthew*, 136. For Philo, the Chaldean Scriptures means the Hebrew Bible (*Mos.* 2.26), which was translated into Greek by the order of Ptolemy Philanthropos (2.29, 31, 38).

14. Philo often uses verbal expressions such as φησί, λέγει, and γέγραπται in order to introduce a scriptural quotation. He sometimes even specifically mentions the book from which he will cite a passage (e.g., *Leg.* 3.174: Δευτερονομίῳ; *Leg.* 2.105: ὁ ἱερὸς λόγος ἐν Λευιτικῷ; *Her.*1.251: ἐν Ἐξαγωγῇ).

that Philo makes in his writings. More complex uses of the scriptures do appear in Philo. But the five kinds of scriptural quotations in Philo presented here are enough to show his attitude towards the Septuagint texts and demonstrate some similarities between Philo and Matthew in their use of the Septuagint.

1. First of all, Philo *cites Scripture exactly as we also have it in the Septuagint*.[15] In *Aet.* 1.19, Philo cites Gen 1:1–2a, whose wording exactly corresponds to that of the Septuagint (ἐν ἀρχῇ ἐποίησεν ὁ θεὸς τὸν οὐρανὸν καὶ τὴν γῆν· ἡ δὲ γῆ ἦν ἀόρατος καὶ ἀκατασκεύαστος).[16] In *Mut.* 1.139, Philo cites Hos 14:9–10 almost exactly from the Septuagint (ἐξ ἐμοῦ ὁ καρπός σου εὕρηται. τίς σοφὸς καὶ συνήσει ταῦτα; συνετὸς καὶ γνώσεται αὐτά, with the exception that where Philo uses γνώσεται the LXX reads <u>ἐπι</u>γνώσεται.

2. Second, Philo *replaces certain words or phrases in the Septuagint text with some other expressions*.[17] In *Leg.* 3.8, Philo explicitly cites Num 5:2–3 but makes a slight modification in wording (διό φησι καὶ ὁ θεῖος λόγος· ἐξαποστειλάτωσαν ἐκ τῆς ἁγίου ψυχῆς πάντα λεπρὸν καὶ πάντα γονορρυῆ καὶ πάντα ἀκάθαρτον ἐν ψυχῇ, ἀπὸ ἀρσενικοῦ ἕως θηλυκοῦ [cf. LXX: ἐξαποστειλάτωσαν ἐκ τῆς <u>παρεμβολῆς</u> . . . <u>ἐπὶ</u> ψυχῇ ἀπὸ ἀρσενικοῦ ἕως θηλυκοῦ]). Philo's replacement of παρεμβολῆς (tent) with ἁγίου ψυχῆς (holy soul) may have been grounded on his identification of πολίς (city) with ψυχῇ (soul), because the soul—as the city of the living creatures—gives laws and customs (*Leg.* 3.43). In *Mut.*1.169, Philo cites Isa 57:21 from the Septuagint but instead of the somewhat redundant κύριος ὁ θεός in the LXX simplifies it to ὁ θεός (= MT) and slightly modifies the word order: καθάπερ καὶ ἐν προφητικαῖς ᾄδεται ῥήσεσι·χαίρειν οὐκ ἔστι τοῖς ἀσεβέσιν, εἶπεν ὁ θεός (cf. LXX: οὐκ ἔστιν χαίρειν τοῖς ἀσεβέσιν).[18]

---

15. Unless specified otherwise, the Septuagintal texts to be compared with Philo's scriptural quotations will be taken from Alfred Rahlfs's 1935 edition.

16. In *Leg.* 2.94, Philo cites a longer passage from Gen 49 (i.e., 49:16–18), and again his scriptural text exactly matches the LXX, word for word. See also *Gig.* 1.49 [Deut 5:31]; *Leg.* 3.110 [Lev 27:33]; 3.162 [Exod 16:4]; *Somn.* 1.133 [Gen 28:12]; *Her.* 1:68 [Gen 15:14].

17. Although it is difficult to prove, Philo may reflect a variant reading of the Septuagint when his scriptural text slightly diverges from the Septuagint.

18. In all other passages in Isaiah, *shalom* is rendered as εἰρήνη (e.g., Isa 27:5). See also *Leg.* 1.53 (τίς οὖν ἐστιν, ἐφ᾿ οὗ ὕστερόν φησιν ὅτι ἔλαβε κύριος ὁ θεὸς τὸν ἄνθρωπον ὃν ἐποίησε καὶ ἔθετο αὐτὸν ἐν τῷ παραδείσῳ, ἐργάζεσθαι αὐτὸν καὶ φυλάσσειν); cf. τὸν ἄνθρωπον ὃν <u>ἔπλασεν</u> in Gen 2:15 LXX, but note: there is no reference to the verb in MT. See also *Her.* 1.258 (ζήσεις; cf. ζήσῃ in Gen 20:7 LXX); 1.94 (λογισθῆναι τὴν πίστιν εἰς δικαιοσύνην αὐτῷ; cf. καὶ ἐπίστευσεν Αβραμ τῷ θεῷ καὶ ἐλογίσθη αὐτῷ εἰς δικαιοσύνην in Gen 15:6 LXX).

3. *Philo drops some words or phrases that are attested in the Septuagint.* In *Leg.* 3.174, Philo cites Deut 8:3 from the Septuagint but omits ζήσεται ὁ ἄνθρωπος at the end (λέγει δὲ καὶ ἐν Δευτερονομίῳ· καὶ ἐκάκωσέ σε καὶ ἐλιμαγχόνησέ σε, καὶ ἐψώμισέ σε τὸ μάννα, ὃ οὐκ ᾔδεισαν οἱ πατέρες σου, ἵνα ἀναγγείλῃ σοι, ὅτι οὐκ ἐπ' ἄρτῳ μόνῳ ζήσεται ἄνθρωπος, ἀλλ' ἐπὶ παντὶ ῥήματι τῷ ἐκπορευομένῳ διὰ στόματος θεοῦ).[19] Maybe he thought it would suffice to cite "one will live" only once, albeit this is repeated twice in both the Hebrew and Septuagint texts. In *Her.* 1.262, Philo drops ἐν Ισραηλ when he quotes Deut 34:10 (καὶ πάλιν οὐκ ἀνέστη ἔτι προφήτης ὡς Μωυσῆς, ὃν ἔγνω κύριος αὐτὸν πρόσωπον πρὸς πρόσωπον; cf. LXX: καὶ οὐκ ἀνέστη ἔτι προφήτης ἐν Ισραηλ ὡς Μωυσῆς ὃν ἔγνω κύριος αὐτὸν πρόσωπον κατὰ πρόσωπον).[20]

4. *Philo shortens a longer scriptural text selectively or paraphrases as necessary to make his point clear.* For example, in *Her.* 1.262, when Philo cites Num 12:6–8, he takes a few words with slight modifications from v. 6 (λέγει γάρ· ἐὰν γένηται ὑμῶν προφήτης κυρίου, ἐν ὁράματι αὐτῷ γνωσθήσομαι; cf. LXX: ἐὰν γένηται προφήτης ὑμῶν κυρίῳ ἐν ὁράματι αὐτῷ γνωσθήσομαι καὶ ἐν ὕπνῳ λαλήσω αὐτῷ), draws Moses' name from v. 7 (Μωυσῇ δέ), and then cites a phrase from v. 8 (ἐν εἴδει, καὶ οὐ δι' αἰνιγμάτων).

5. *Philo bases his scriptural quotation on the Septuagint but assimilates it to the Hebrew text.*[21] In *Leg.* 1.51, Philo cites Exod 20:23 from the Septuagint but changes the wording in an attempt to assimilate the LXX to the Hebrew text (οὐ ποιήσετε μετ' ἐμοῦ θεοὺς ἀργυροῦς, καὶ θεοὺς χρυσοῦς οὐ ποιήσετε ὑμῖν ἑαυτοῖς; cf. LXX: οὐ ποιήσετε ἑαυτοῖς θεοὺς ἀργυροῦς καὶ θεοὺς χρυσοῦς οὐ ποιήσετε ὑμῖν αὐτοῖς; MT: 'itti ... lakem).[22]

---

19. Matt 4:4 omits the last ζήσεται ὁ ἄνθρωπος when Luke omits ἀλλ' ἐπὶ παντὶ ῥήματι ἐκπορευομένῳ διὰ στόματος θεοῦ.

20. Cf. also *Somn.* 1.183 (ἐξηγέρθη γάρ φησιν Ιακὼβ καὶ εἶπεν ὅτι ἔστι κύριος ἐν τῷ τόπῳ τούτῳ ἐγὼ δὲ οὐκ ᾔδειν; cf. Gen 28:16 LXX: καὶ ἐξηγέρθη Ιακωβ ἀπὸ τοῦ ὕπνου αὐτοῦ καὶ εἶπεν ὅτι ...).

21. Marcos states: "Although it is possible that he consulted learned Jews who knew some Hebrew, it is preferable to attribute the divergences of his text from the LXX to his own exegesis" (*Septuagint in Context*, 264). See also O'Leary, who points out: "Philo, who writes in Greek for Greek-speaking people, obviously draws on the Greek version of the Scriptures which was in use among his readers, but he might well have known Hebrew, even thoroughly" (*Matthew's Judaization of Mark*, 35).

22. Cited in Dell'Acqua, "Philo's Biblical Text and the Septuagint," 48. See also *Conf.* 1.44 (ὦ μῆτερ, ἡλίκον με ἔτεκες, ἄνθρωπον μάχης καὶ ἄνθρωπον ἀηδίας πάσης τῆς γῆς; οὐκ ὠφέλησα, οὐδὲ ὠφείλησάν μοι, οὐδὲ ἡ ἰσχύς μου ἐξέλιπεν ἀπὸ καταρῶν αὐτῶν; cf. Jer 15:10 LXX: οἴμμοι ἐγὼ μῆτερ ὡς τίνα με ἔτεκες ἄνδρα δικαζόμενον καὶ διακρινόμενον πάσῃ τῇ γῇ οὔτε ὠφέλησα οὔτε ὠφέλησέν με οὐδείς ἡ ἰσχύς μου ἐξέλιπεν ἐν τοῖς καταρωμένοις με; MT: 'ish rib we'ish madon).

MATTHEW'S USE OF THE SEPTUAGINT

Group A: Matthew's Scriptural Quotations That Diverge from Mark's (Matt 19:18; 22:37)

In 19:18, Matthew explicitly quotes the commandments as summarily presented in Exod 20:12–16 and/or Deut 5:16–20 (cf. Philo, *Spec.* 4.1: περὶ τοῦ μὴ κλεπτεῖν [Exod 20:13]; note that he introduces a scriptural quotation with τό as in Rom 13:9). Although Mark also quotes the same scriptural texts as a simplified list of the commandments, their wording in Matthew is quite different from that in Mark. Matthew aligns the verbal forms of each commandment with the Septuagint (οὐ . . . -σεις [future indicative]), while Mark deviates from the Septuagint (μὴ . . . -σῃς [aorist subjunctive]). I would identify Matthew's use of the LXX here with Philo Type 1, albeit with a different word order (cf. also Philo, *Decal.*1.36).

With regard to the order of the commandments, neither Matthew nor Mark follow Exod 20:12–16 or Deut 5:16–20.[23] Matthew does not mention a commandment that is comparable to Mark's μὴ ἀποστερήσῃς, which is definitely not a part of Exod 20:12–16 or of Deut 5:16–20 (see Mark 10:19; Sir 4:1; Lev 19:13;[24] cf. Exod 21:10). Instead, he uses an additional scriptural quotation from Lev 19:18 (καὶ ἀγαπήσεις τὸν πλησίον σου ὡς σεαυτόν) to emphasize one's duty to his/her neighbor. The wording of this quotation in Matt 19:19 corresponds exactly to the Septuagint (Philo Type 1; cf. also Rom 13:9; Mark 12:31).

Matthew 22:37 is an interesting passage because all three Synoptic Gospels explicitly quote Deut 6:4–5, but they differ from one another in the wording and extent of the quoted scriptural text. The scope of Mark's quotation is wider than Matthew in that he even cites Deut 6:4–5. Mark follows the Septuagint when he quotes v. 4 (the *shema* saying) in 12:29, and yet he slightly deviates from the Septuagint when he quotes v. 5 (note his references to ἐξ ὅλης τῆς διανοίας σου and ἐξ ὅλης τῆς ἰσχύος σου instead of ἐξ ὅλης τῆς δυνάμεώς σου; 12:30).

In contrast, Matthew does *not* quote the *shema* saying in Deut 6:4, and this lack of attestation is surprising because his Gospel is generally known as targeting Jewish Christian readers. Although he has three prepositional phrases as does the Septuagint, Matthew's third word does not come from the Septuagint (Matt: ἐν ὅλῃ τῇ διανοίᾳ σου; Deut 6:5 LXX: ἐξ ὅλης τῆς δυνάμεώς σου). Matthew also introduces each of these three with the

---

23. Even in Exod 20:12–16 and Deut 5:16–20, the order of the commandments are not the same.

24. Gundry, *Use of the Old Testament*, 18.

preposition ἐν (a literal translation of the Hebrew preposition *be*) rather than with ἐξ as in the Septuagint and Mark. By doing this, Matthew seems to correct the Septuagint text quoted in his source (probably Mark) based on his knowledge of the Hebrew text (Philo Type 5).

Group B: Matthew's Scriptural Quotations Added to the Markan Narrative (Matt 13:14–15; 21:4–5)

In 21:1–9, Matthew describes Jesus' entry to the city of Jerusalem. Matthew follows Mark's story line closely: the account begins with Jesus' approaching Jerusalem and ends with the crowd's singing hosanna to Jesus who was entering the city riding on a colt. But Matthew differs from Mark in some details. First of all, Matthew makes it clear that the disciples have brought both a female-ass (ὄνος) and a colt (πῶλος) to Jesus so that he might sit on them (Matt 21:2–3; cf. Mark 11:20; Luke 19:30). Second, Matthew gives an explicit scriptural quotation to prove that what Jesus did was to fulfill the prophecies in the Scriptures. Matthew quotes Isa 62:11 and Zech 9:9 in a conflated form. The form of the Isa 62:11 text that Matthew quotes exactly corresponds to the Septuagint (εἴπατε τῇ θυγατρὶ Σιων) (Philo Type 1). But Matthew appends a scriptural quotation from Zech 9:9 (ἰδοὺ ὁ βασιλεύς σου ἔρχεταί σοι πραῢς καὶ ἐπιβεβηκὼς ἐπὶ ὄνον καὶ ἐπὶ πῶλον υἱὸν ὑποζυγίου). This quotation virtually corresponds to the Septuagint text (Χαῖρε σφόδρα θύγατερ Σιων κήρυσσε θύγατερ Ιερουσαλημ ἰδοὺ ὁ βασιλεύς σου ἔρχεταί σοι <u>δίκαιος καὶ σῴζων αὐτός</u> πραῢς καὶ ἐπιβεβηκὼς ἐπὶ <u>ὑποζύγιον</u> καὶ πῶλον <u>νέον</u>). But Matthew drops δίκαιος καὶ σῴζων αὐτός in his scriptural quotation (Philo Type 3) and changes the wording of the Septuagint, particularly with reference to the animals on which the king will ride (ἐπὶ ὄνον καὶ ἐπὶ πῶλον υἱὸν ὑποζυγίου) in accordance with the Hebrew text (*ʿal-hamor weʿal-ʿayir ben-ʾatonot*: "on a male ass (*hamor*), on a young male ass (*ʿayir*), the son of a female donkey (*ʾaton*)" (Philo Type 5). Although the Septuagint's πῶλον νέον may indicate that the colt was young enough that no one else had ever ridden on it (Mark 11:2; 19:30), Matthew seems to find a literal translation from the Hebrew text more suitable to connect the female-ass and her young colt on which Jesus rode with the prophecy in Zech 9:9 (Matt 21:7).[25]

---

25. Cf. Menken, "Source of the Quotation," 327, who believes that Matthew derives Zech 9:9 from a revised Septuagint because Matthew makes the anarthrous ὄνον into a she-donkey, whereas the Hebrew counterpart indicates a he-donkey.

Group C: Matthew's Independent Use of Quotations from Isaiah (Matt 1:23, 13:14–15)

Matthew 13:14–15 is one of the most obvious cases that shows Matthew's own knowledge and conscious use of the Septuagint text of Isaiah. As this passage also belongs to Group B, we will here consider Matt 13:14–15 first.

The wording of Matthew's scriptural quotation in 13:14–15 almost exactly corresponds to Isa 6:9–10 in the Septuagint. The only exception is his omission of αὐτῶν after τοῖς ὠσίν. While some early NT manuscripts have αὐτῶν in this passage (ℵ, C, 33, 1241), the reading without αὐτῶν is probably more original than the alternative reading (Philo Type 3).

Table 3: Isaiah 6:9–10 in Matt, LXX, and MT		
Matt 13:14–15	Isaiah 6 (LXX)	Isaiah 6 (MT)
14 καὶ ἀναπληροῦται αὐτοῖς ἡ προφητεία Ἠσαΐου ἡ λέγουσα·	9 καὶ εἶπεν πορεύθητι καὶ εἰπὸν τῷ λαῷ τούτῳ	9 wayyo'mer lek we'amarta la'am hazzeh
Ἀκοῇ ἀκούσετε καὶ οὐ μὴ συνῆτε, καὶ βλέποντες βλέψετε καὶ οὐ μὴ ἴδητε.	ἀκοῇ ἀκούσετε καὶ οὐ μὴ συνῆτε καὶ βλέποντες βλέψετε καὶ οὐ μὴ ἴδητε	shim'u shamoa' we'al-tabinu ure'u ra'o we'al-teda'u
15 ἐπαχύνθη γὰρ ἡ καρδία τοῦ λαοῦ τούτου, καὶ τοῖς ὠσὶν βαρέως ἤκουσαν, καὶ τοὺς ὀφθαλμοὺς αὐτῶν ἐκάμμυσαν· μήποτε ἴδωσιν τοῖς ὀφθαλμοῖς καὶ τοῖς ὠσὶν ἀκούσωσιν καὶ τῇ καρδίᾳ συνῶσιν καὶ ἐπιστρέψωσιν, καὶ ἰάσομαι αὐτούς.	10 ἐπαχύνθη γὰρ ἡ καρδία τοῦ λαοῦ τούτου καὶ τοῖς ὠσὶν <u>αὐτῶν</u> βαρέως ἤκουσαν καὶ τοὺς ὀφθαλμοὺς αὐτῶν ἐκάμμυσαν μήποτε ἴδωσιν τοῖς ὀφθαλμοῖς καὶ τοῖς ὠσὶν ἀκούσωσιν καὶ τῇ καρδίᾳ συνῶσιν καὶ ἐπιστρέψωσιν καὶ ἰάσομαι αὐτούς	10 hashmen leb-ha'am hazzeh we'oznayw hakbed we'enayw hasha' pen-yir'eh be'enayw ube'oznayw yishma' ulebabo yabin washab werapa' lo

The Septuagint text of Isaiah 6:9–10 differs from the MT in several ways. First, the verbs in the Septuagint text are predominantly in the future indicative forms (-σετε), while they are in the masculine imperatival forms in the MT text (the suffix *u*). Second, the reason behind Isaiah's is explained differently. In the Septuagint, the message is intended so that God may not heal them, while in the MT, it is intended for them not to turn (repent) and be healed.[26]

The wording of Matthew's scriptural quotation corresponds to the Septuagint rather than the Hebrew text. In a parallel passage, Mark 4:12 quotes Isa 6:9–10, but his wording is quite different from that of the Septuagint. Mark mentions seeing first, then hearing, then understanding, then repenting, and finally being forgiven (by God), whereas in the Septuagint, hearing comes first, then understanding, then seeing, and healing comes last (cf. Matt 13:13).

It is interesting that Matthew, after having alluded to Isa 6:9–10 in 13:13, finds it necessary to use an explicit quotation of the same text from the Septuagint. Why does he quote from the Septuagint (against the Hebrew text)? As Gundry points out, the Septuagint text of these prophetic statements may have been more suitable than the Hebrew text (with its many imperatives) for Matthew to explain what has already become a reality in Jesus' ministry.[27] The direct quotation of Isa 6:9–10 from the Septuagint with its two references to ἡ καρδία also provided a chance for Matthew to introduce Jesus' explanation of the parable, according to which the seed is identified with the word of the kingdom of God sown in the heart of the hearers (ἐν τῇ καρδίᾳ αὐτοῦ; Matt 13:19; cf. Luke 8:11, 15).

In 1:23, Matthew explicitly quotes Isa 7:14 to prove the fulfillment of the prophecy in Isaiah (τοῦτο δὲ ὅλον γέγονεν ἵνα πληρωθῇ τὸ ῥηθὲν ὑπὸ κυρίου διὰ τοῦ προφήτου λέγοντος· ἰδοὺ ἡ παρθένος ἐν γαστρὶ ἕξει καὶ τέξεται υἱόν, καὶ καλέσουσιν τὸ ὄνομα αὐτοῦ Ἐμμανουήλ). His scriptural quotation almost exactly corresponds to the Septuagint (ἰδοὺ ἡ παρθένος ἐν γαστρὶ ἕξει καὶ τέξεται υἱόν καὶ καλέσεις τὸ ὄνομα αὐτοῦ Εμμανουηλ). The unusual rendering of *ha'almah* as ἡ παρθένος is attested only in Isaiah 7:14 in the Septuagint. Matthew changes the person of the καλέω verb, from the second-person singular (καλέσεις) to the third person plural (καλέσουσιν) (Philo Type 2). This is odd because the Septuagint text provides a real parallel to Matthew's account for Jesus' birth in vv. 18 and 21 (πρὶν ἢ συνελθεῖν αὐτοὺς εὑρέθη ἐν γαστρὶ ἔχουσα ἐκ πνεύματος ἁγίου. . . τέξεται δὲ υἱόν, καὶ καλέσεις τὸ ὄνομα αὐτοῦ Ἰησοῦν).[28] The third-person plural form of the verb may have come from the variant reading of *weqara't* ("it [impersonal] shall be called" or "one will call") attested by 1QIsa[a] and reflected in LXX Aleph.[29]

---

26. See Symmachus: ἰαθῇ for the passive reading; cf. JPS Tanakh: "And repent and save itself."

27. Gundry, *Use of the Old Testament*, 118.

28. See also Menken, "Textual Form of the Quotation," 156; 15–60.

29. Gundry, *Use of the Old Testament*, 90. Menken claims that Matthew did not change the wording but quotes Isa 7:13 from a revised LXX ("Textual Form of the Quotation," 160).

Matthew's dependence on the Septuagint is again made clear by his quotation of Isa 8:8 and 10 along with an explanatory comment on Ἐμμανουήλ at the end of 1:23 (ὅ ἐστιν μεθερμηνευόμενον μεθ' ἡμῶν ὁ θεός; cf.1:21: Ἰησοῦν· αὐτὸς γὰρ σώσει τὸν λαὸν αὐτοῦ ἀπὸ τῶν ἁμαρτιῶν αὐτῶν). The μεθερμηνεύω verb is used seven times elsewhere in the New Testament to provide a translation of either an Aramaic (Mark 5:41; 15:22; 15:34) or a Hebrew expression (John 1:38, 41; Acts 4:36; 13:8).[30] This translation may have been intended to help readers who are not familiar with the meaning of the transliterated Hebrew word or to stress certain aspects of the lexical meaning of the Hebrew / Aramaic word (cf. Philo, *Abr.* 1.201: Ἰσαάκ being translated into Greek as γέλως; *Legat.* 1.4: Ἰσραήλ being translated into Greek as ὁρῶν θεόν).

MATTHEW'S RECASTING OF HEBREW AND ARAMAIC WORDS FOR HIS READERS

Matthew sometimes provides a translation for a Hebrew or Aramaic word or phrase, as we can see in 1:21 and 23. In some cases both the Hebrew or Aramaic phrase and its translation together may have come from his source (Matt 27:46: ηλι ηλι λεμα σαβαχθανι; τοῦτ' ἔστιν· Θεέ μου θεέ μου, ἱνατί με ἐγκατέλιπες; cf. Mark 15:34). But it should be noted that in other cases Matthew also tries to either recast those words to make them comprehensible enough to his readers or he removes them.

In the following five particular cases Matthew preserves the transliterated Hebrew expressions but accommodates them for his readers.

1. Σατανᾶς: Although he does not give the details of Jesus' temptations, Mark names Jesus' tempter ὁ σατανᾶς (1:13). In his temptation account, however, Matthew identifies the tempter (ὁ πειράζων) with ὁ διάβολος (3:3, 5, 8). But he also retains ὁ σατανᾶς—if only on Jesus' lips[31]—as a reference to this tempter (Matt 3:10), while Luke drops it altogether (Luke 4:8). In the Septuagint, *satan* is often translated as ὁ διάβολος (1 Chr 21:1; Job 1:6; Zech 3:1), although it is also transliterated as σαταν (3 Kdgms 11:14).

2. Βεελζεβούλ: Matthew retains βεελζεβούλ, a transliterated word for Satan, along with an explanatory comment (ἄρχοντι τῶν δαιμονίων) in

---

30. Josephus uses the same verb to provide the literal meaning of a transliterated Hebrew personal name (*Ant.* 1.52). Philo uses the verb ἑρμηνεύω to provide the meaning (*Leg.*1.68; 3.231; *Her.* 1.58).

31. Cf. also Matt 12:26; 16:23.

his account of the exorcism controversy (12:24, 27) just as Mark does (3:22; cf. also Luke 11:15; Βεελζεβούλ in *T. Sol.* 3:1-7; *beba'al zebub* [= ἐν τῇ Βααλ μυῖαν θεὸν Ακκαρων] in 2 Kings 1:2-3; Str-B 1:631). In the Lukan account, Jesus identifies this βεελζεβούλ with ὁ σατανᾶς (11:18).

3. Ἠλὶ ἠλὶ λεμὰ σαβαχθάνι: Matthew retains an Aramaic or Hebrew expression in Jesus' last words on the cross (27:46) just as Mark does (15:34: ελωι ελωι λεμα σαβαχθανι). Although they have the first two words spelled differently, both Matthew and Mark provide a translation for the entire phrase and go on to mention people's misunderstanding of, and puzzled reaction to, this saying (Matt: τοῦτ' ἔστιν· Θεέ μου θεέ μου, ἱνατί με ἐγκατέλιπες; Mark: ὅ ἐστιν μεθερμηνευόμενον· ὁ θεός μου ὁ θεός μου, εἰς τί ἐγκατέλιπές με). This transliterated Hebrew phrase may have been needed to indicate a possible ground for people's misunderstanding that Jesus was calling Elijah. In both places, however, the translation does not match the Septuagint text of the psalm (21:1-2 LXX = 21:1-2 MT).

4. Ὡσαννά: Matthew retains ὡσαννά, a transliteration of *hoshi'ah nna'* from Psalm 118:25 and 148:1 as Mark does (Matt 21:9; Mark 11:9). The Septuagint translates this Hebrew phrase as σῶσον δή (Psalm 117:25 LXX = 118:25 MT). But Matthew, like Mark, does not provide a translation for the phrase, probably because "hosanna" not only had been a liturgical word commonly used for Jewish temple worship but also became one of the liturgical words for Christian worship at a very early stage (cf. Didache 10:6: ἐλθέτω χάρις καὶ παρελθέτω ὁ κόσμος οὗτος Ὡσαννὰ τῷ θεῷ Δαυείδ εἴ τις ἅγιός ἐστιν ἐρχέσθω εἴ τις οὐκ ἔστι μετανοείτω μαρὰν ἀθά ἀμήν).

5. Γολγοθᾶ: Matthew retains Γολγοθᾶ along with its translation, Κρανίου Τόπος from Mark (Matt 27:33 [ὅ ἐστιν]; cf. Mark 15:22 [ὅ ἐστιν μεθερμηνευόμενον]).

But there are also five other cases in which Matthew removes the transliterated Hebrew or Aramaic words that are attested in the Markan parallels:

1. Βοαρνηργές: Mark mentions an Aramaic nickname of James and John and provides its translation (3:17: ὅ ἐστιν υἱοὶ βροντῆς). Matthew notes Simon's other name, Πέτρος, but he shows no interest in James and John's nickname.

2. Ταλιθα κουμ: Mark has a transliterated Aramaic phrase, ταλιθα κουμ, and its Greek translation (ὅ ἐστιν μεθερμηνευόμενον· τὸ κοράσιον, σοὶ λέγω, ἔγειρε; 5:41), but Matthew only mentions that the little girl has been raised by Jesus (ἠγέρθη τὸ κοράσιον; 9:25). Luke does not put

Jesus' command in Aramaic but translates it into Greek (ἡ παῖς, ἔγειρε; 8:54).

3. Κορβᾶν: Unlike Mark, Matthew does not mention the transliterated Aramaic word κορβᾶν (Matt 15:5: Δῶρον ὃ ἐὰν ἐξ ἐμοῦ ὠφεληθῇς; Mark 7:11: κορβᾶν, ὅ ἐστιν δῶρον, ὃ ἐὰν ἐξ ἐμοῦ ὠφεληθῇς; cf. Josephus, *Ant.* 4.73: καὶ οἱ κορβᾶν αὐτοὺς ὀνομάσαντες τῷ θεῷ δῶρον δὲ τοῦτο σημαίνει κατὰ Ἑλλήνων γλῶτταν; *C. Ap.* 1.167).[32]

4. Εφφαθα: Matthew does not have εφφαθα (cf. Mark 7:34: ὅ ἐστιν διανοίχθητι).

5. Αββα: Mark 14:36 has αββα ὁ πατήρ in Jesus' prayer, while Matt 26:39–57 does omits αββα (likewise with Luke), but πάτερ μου is used (Matt 26:39; cf. Rom 8:15; Gal 4:6).

CONCLUSION

After some preliminary observations on Matthew's explicit scriptural quotations, we examined six Matthean passages with explicit scriptural quotations using three different categories to determine his own knowledge and conscious use of the Septuagint. The study shows that in most of those passages Matthew consciously quotes the Isaiah texts almost exactly as we have them in the Septuagint. But Matthew also sometimes changes the words and phrases in his scriptural quotation in order to make it align with the Hebrew text. This is largely a practice we can also find in Philo, who depends heavily on the Septuagint in his scriptural quotations. The primary purpose of Matthew's own scriptural quotations is to highlight the fulfillment of prophecies in Jesus, particularly in his birth, ministry of teaching in parables, and entry to Jerusalem during the last week before his crucifixion.

We have also observed that Matthew translates or rephrases Hebrew or Aramaic words that he has taken from his sources into plain Greek language and even removes them when the passage makes sense without mentioning those words. Matthew's knowledge and conscious use of the Septuagint and his tendency to recast Hebrew or Aramaic words that he has probably taken from his sources all indicate that his readers were not so much Jewish Christians in Palestine as Jewish Christians in the Diaspora who were at home

---

32. Κορβανᾶς, a name for the temple treasury, is mentioned in Matt 27:6. Cf. also Josephus, *Bell.* 2.175 (Μετὰ δὲ ταῦτα ταραχὴν ἑτέραν ἐκίνει τὸν ἱερὸν θησαυρὸν καλεῖται δὲ κορβωνᾶς εἰς καταγωγὴν ὑδάτων ἐξαναλίσκων κατῆγεν δὲ ἀπὸ τετρακοσίων σταδίων πρὸς τοῦτο τοῦ πλήθους ἀγανάκτησις ἦν καὶ τοῦ Πιλάτου παρόντος εἰς Ἱεροσόλυμα περιστάντες τὸ βῆμα κατεβόων).

with the Greek language but not so familiar with the Hebrew or Aramaic words or phrases.

There is, of course, no *a priori* reason to exclude the Gentile Christians among the targeted audience. But the very Jewish nature of Matthew (e.g., the characteristic presentation of Jesus as the Davidic King Messiah who has come to fulfill the Scriptures; emphasis on Jesus' role for the Jews; and Jewish symbolism associated with the numbers such as 12, 14, and 40) makes it difficult to see them as the primary audience. It may be impossible to specify Matthew's provenance precisely. However, the affinities between Matthew and Philo in their scriptural citations noted above indicate to us that Alexandria, the Hellenistic Jewish center in Egypt and Philo's hometown, may also be considered a possible place for Matthew's primary readers just as much as Antioch of Syria.

BIBLIOGRAPHY

Boring, Eugene. "Matthew." In *NIB*, ed. L. E. Keck et al., 8:87–506. Nashville: Abingdon, 1995.

Dell'Acqua, Anna Passoni. "Upon Philo's Biblical Text and the Septuagint." In *Italian Studies on Philo of Alexandria*, ed. Francesca Calabi, 25–52. Ancient Mediterranean and Medieval Texts and Contexts 1. Leiden: Brill, 2003.

Goulder, M. D. *Midrash and Lection in Matthew: The Speaker's Lectures in Biblical Studies 1969–71*. London: SPCK, 1974.

Gundry, Robert H. *The Use of the Old Testament in St. Matthew's Gospel: With Special Reference to the Messianic Hope*. NovTSup 18. Leiden: Brill, 1967.

Marcos, Natalio Fernández. *The Septuagint in Context: Introduction to the Greek Version of the Bible*. Atlanta: SBL, 2010.

Menken, Maarten J. J. "The Source of the Quotation from Isaiah 53:4 in Matthew 8:17." *NovT* 39/4 (1997) 313–27.

———. "The Textual Form of the Quotation from Isaiah 7:14 in Matthew 1:23." *NovT* 43/2 (2001) 144–60.

O'Leary, Anne M. *Matthew's Judaization of Mark: Examined in the Context of the Use of Sources in Graeco-Roman Antiquity*. LNTS 323. Edinburgh: T. & T. Clark, 2006.

8

The Understanding of στηρίζειν τὸ πρόσωπον in Luke 9:51[1]

SOON BONG CHOI

INTRODUCTION

The general order of the Gospel of Luke is, for the most part, consistent with that of Mark's gospel,[2] except for the content of the so-called "Travel Narrative" in Luke 9:50—18:15.[3] As a matter of fact the order in the aforementioned passage of Luke parallels not Mark but a section from the Gospel of Matthew.[4] Although the corresponding passages of Luke and Matthew both account for the same content, they exhibit different styles of writing. The narrative styles identified in these two gospels point to different communicative purposes. As we compare the evangelists' varying methods of description for the portrayal of Jesus' journey or march to Jerusalem, we

---

1. An earlier version of this article was published in *Kwangshin Nonban* (2011). I am grateful to Kwangshin University for permission to reprint this essay here in revised form.

2. Jeremias, *Die Sprache des Lukasevangeliums*, 178; Jeremias, "Perikopen-Umstellungen bei Lukas?," 115-17. Cf. Marshall, *The Gospel of Luke*, 399. It is possible the author (of Luke) used "other sources." Cf. Goulder, "From Ministry to Passion," 562-67.

3. Cf. Ogg, "The Central Section," 39-53.

4. See Aland, *Synopsis Quattuor Evangeliorium*, 255.

must also carefully examine the perspective each author had regarding Jesus' passage to Jerusalem.

Matt 19:1-2	Mark 10:1	Luke 9:51
1 Καὶ ἐγένετο ὅτε ἐτέλεσεν ὁ Ἰησοῦς τοὺς λόγους τούτους, μετῆρεν ἀπὸ τῆς Γαλιλαίας καὶ ἦλθεν εἰς τὰ ὅρια τῆς Ἰουδαίας πέραν τοῦ Ἰορδάνου. 2 καὶ ἠκολούθησαν αὐτῷ ὄχλοι πολλοί, καὶ ἐθεράπευσεν αὐτοὺς ἐκεῖ.	Καὶ ἐκεῖθεν ἀναστὰς ἔρχεται εἰς τὰ ὅρια τῆς Ἰουδαίας ⌜καὶ πέραν τοῦ Ἰορδάνου, καὶ συμπορεύονται πάλιν ὄχλοι πρὸς αὐτόν, καὶ ὡς εἰώθει πάλιν ἐδίδασκεν αὐτούς.	Ἐγένετο δὲ ἐν τῷ συμπληροῦσθαι τὰς ἡμέρας τῆς ἀναλήμψεως αὐτοῦ καὶ αὐτὸς τὸ πρόσωπον ἐστήρισεν τοῦ πορεύεσθαι εἰς Ἰερουσαλήμ,

In 9:51–56, Luke recounts the start of Jesus' journey to Jerusalem but also describes the Samaritans' rejection of Jesus when he tried to enter their village.[5] There are many accounts of the hostilities shared between the Samaritans and Jews, the latter of whom often traveled from Galilee to Jerusalem.[6] Jesus' motive for intentionally wanting to cross through Samaria despite knowing about the existing hostilities suggests that he had a particular plan and purpose for the visit.[7] Notably, the Gospel of Luke at this juncture in the narrative begins to employ a different method for describing Jesus' deeds than the Gospel of Matthew. In the text of 9:51, Luke unveils to his readers the 'implied intention' of Jesus by narrating particular actions taken by Jesus. In particular, Jesus "set his face to Jerusalem." This idiomatic expression "στηρίζειν τὸ πρόσωπον" is not found in the other two gospels and stands as a key to Luke's unique perspective on Jesus' mission in the holy city.[8]

---

5. Cf. Gasse, "Zum Reisebericht des Lukas," 293–99.

6. In the time of Jesus, people from Galilee generally had to go through Samaria in order to go to Jerusalem. But this route's usage was not easily permitted. John 4 also describes the substantial conflict that existed between these two people groups. In reality, the inhabitants of Samaria rejected many of the Jewish pilgrims who traveled through the province of Samaria on their way from Galilee to Jerusalem. Josephus illustrates this occurrence more explicitly in his *Jewish Antiquities* (see *Ant.* 4.20).

7. Schürmann, *Das Lukasevangelium*, 2.26–30. In Acts 8:1–25, the author depicts how the gospel has already reached Samaria. It is one of the signs that the mission in Samaria was fulfilled earlier than we think.

8. Cf. Baarlink, "Die zyklische Struktur," 485. It is also very plausible that Luke begins "die zyklische Structure" with v. 51.

POSSIBLE INTERPRETATIONS OF THE PHRASE "ΣΤΗΡΙΖΕΙΝ ΤΟ ΠΡΟΣΩΠΟΝ"

In the context of Jesus' beginning journey to Jerusalem, Luke uses the following unique expression in the first sentence: "He *set his face* to go to Jerusalem" (αὐτὸς τὸ πρόσωπον ἐστήρισεν τοῦ πορεύεσθαι εἰς Ἰερουσαλήμ; 9:51). Generally, this expression has been understood by past scholarship as having two interpretations: 1) it describes the self-determination of Jesus to his own immutable plan, and 2) it expresses Jesus' commitment to do the will of God.[9] Certainly the idiom makes the reader aware that Jesus is not simply traveling to Jerusalem haphazardly. Yet, Luke chose to describe Jesus' intentions using the distinctive expression: "to set one's face" (στηρίζειν τὸ πρόσωπον) to offer other reasons for Jesus' sojourn to Jerusalem.

So what does the Lukan author hope to communicate regarding Jesus' intention through the use of "στηρίζειν τὸ πρόσωπον"? Is his purpose simply to inform us of Jesus' advance and the expansion of his ministry into Jerusalem? Or, does he allude to Jesus' impending death? Or, can we draw an inference to a completely different purpose not previously mentioned? Does this expression attempt to communicate some other intention? These inquiries have been discussed extensively in the past.[10]

It is possible that Luke interacts with OT and Jewish traditions on the ascended Elijah to foreshadow the death and resurrection of Jesus. As Schweitzer points out, the narrative description of Jesus' ascension to Jerusalem and the disciples' reference of fire coming down from heaven could function as textual clues that point to the the ascended Elijah tradition. When Jesus goes to Jerusalem, his journey can be interpreted as meaning: "going home" (*Heimgang*).[11] Besides Luke 9:51–56, there are many other episodes in the Lukan narrative that describe Jesus' comings and goings into the holy city (10:1, 38; 11:53; 13:22, 33; 17:11; 18:31, 35; 19:1). These forms of expression utilized in Luke point to the fact that Jesus' end, i.e., the destination and *telos* of his mission, is Jerusalem.[12] Yet, the above explanations are not satisfying. There still remains another area of inquiry on the origins of the expression "στηρίζειν τὸ πρόσωπον."

---

9. Harder, στηρίζω κτλ., 655. See also Str-B 2.165. The expression designates the command of God, although the person wants to go somewhere else. We find similar examples in Jer 42:15; 44:12; 2 Kgs 12:18.

10. Evans, "He Set His Face," 80–84.

11. Schweizer, *Das Evangelium nach Lukas*, 110.

12. Cf. Schürmann, *Das Lukasevangelium*, 24–25.

THE ORIGIN OF THE PHRASE "ΣΤΗΡΙΖΕΙΝ ΤΟ ΠΡΟΣΩΠΟΝ" FROM THE JUDGMENT ORACLES OF OT PROPHETIC LITERATURE

Preliminary Comments on Luke's Use of the Old Testament

It has been determined by many that the Gospel of Luke is much more closely related to the LXX translation than to the MT of the Old Testament.[13] Since many of the terms which appear in Luke's gospel are not directly cited from the Hebrew, Luke likely draws any technical terms in the Old Testament from the wording and idiolect of the Greek Septuagint. In fact, the terminology "στηρίζειν τὸ πρόσωπον" appears in the LXX.[14] In the LXX, it is a technical phrase to denote judgment against someone. So then, does Jesus use the phrase "στηρίζειν τὸ πρόσωπον" as a Septuagintal idiom to pronounce judgment against the city of Jerusalem in his day? If the answer is "yes," then Luke does not simply view Jesus' action of setting his face toward Jerusalem as a personal commitment to die according to the will of God. He has an additional purpose. To understand this purpose, we need to examine, then, how the phrase was used by the OT prophets to pronounce a message of judgment in various socio-historical settings.

Interpreting "στηρίζειν τὸ πρόσωπον" in the Book of Jeremiah

The message that God proclaims to Israel through the prophets is repentance. Jeremiah calls the rebellious Israelites to repentance and announces judgment against those who refuse to repent.

Turning to the Book of Jeremiah, we see these intertwining themes of repentance and judgment repeated throughout his oracles. In Jer 3, for example, YHWH calls the rebellious Israelites to repentance so that God could spare them from an impending judgment. Verses 12–13 constitute an independent paragraph. The expression "στηρίζειν τὸ πρόσωπον" is here employed by Jeremiah in v. 12 as follows:

> Go and read these words toward the north, and you shall say: "Return to me, O house of Israel," says the Lord, "and I will not set my face against you: for I am merciful," says the Lord, "and

---

13. Cf. Turner, "The Relation of Luke I and II," 100–109.

14. Nolland, *Luke 9:21–18:34*, 534. The use of this expression στηρίζειν τὸ πρόσωπον is obviously different than its Hebrew equivalent in the MT. Cf. Ellis, *The Gospel of Luke*, 152. It is also comparable with Isa 50:7 in the LXX.

I will not be angry with you for ever."[15] (πορεύου καὶ ἀνάγωθι τοὺς λόγους τούτους πρὸς βορρᾶν καὶ ἐρεῖς ἐπιστάφητι πρός με ἡ κατοικία τοῦ Ισραηλ λέγει κύριος καὶ <u>οὐ στηριῶ τὸ πρόσωπόν μου</u> ἐφ᾽ ὑμᾶς ὅτι ἐλεήμων ἐγώ εἰμι λέγει κύριος καὶ οὐ μηνιῶ ὑμῖν εἰς τὸν αἰῶνα)

Here the oracle focuses upon YHWH's urgent call for Israel to repentance, and it is rendered in the LXX translation with different nuances from the MT. God states: "I will not set my (angered) face towards you" (οὐ στηριῶ τὸ πρόσωπόν μου ἐφ᾽ ὑμᾶς [LXX] = *lo'-'appil panay bakem* [MT].[16] The language used to express God's anger is the same expression "στηρίζειν τὸ πρόσωπον" that we find in Luke 9:51. Although Jeremiah made his proclamation to Israel with the presumption that God does not harbor any anger, this is a *conditional* proclamation that is founded on the response of Israel. The prophet therefore warns of an imminent judgment that will result if the condition of repentance remains unfulfilled. This text suggests that the concept of judgment is intrinsically tied to the terminology "στηρίζειν τὸ πρόσωπον."

Another illustration is found in Jer 21:10 LXX. This text is not an account that seeks repentance from the rebellious (house of) Israel, but rather Jer 21:10 pronounces judgment as an already foregone conclusion. Here the Lord declares:

> For *I have turned my face* against this city for evil, and not for good. It will be delivered into the hands of the king of Babylon, and he will consume it with fire. (διότι <u>ἐστρικα τὸ πρόσωπόν μου</u> ἐπὶ τὴν πόλιν ταύτην εἰς κακὰ καὶ οὐκ εἰς ἀγαθὰ εἰς χεῖρας βασιλέως Βαβυλῶνος παραδοθήσεται καὶ κατακαύσει αὐτήν ἐν <u>πυρί</u>)

The paragraph of 21:1–10 is an oracle aimed at Zedekiah and Jerusalem.[17] Verse 10 seeks a definite response to what was expressed in God's prophecy. Namely, would the inhabitants of the city and their king follow the Lord their God and His prophet Jeremiah, or would they follow the king of Babylon? Though there is an appeal for a decision, the outcome sounds pre-determined as if God foreknew how Israel would reject his call to repentance. The reference to fire (πῦρ) anticipates how the king of Babylon would destroy the city and burn down its walls and the temple. The warning

---

15. Unless otherwise noted, all English translations from the LXX have been modified slightly to reflect more modern idiom from Brenton, *The Septuagint with Apocrypha*.

16. Craigie et al., *Jeremiah 1–25*, 56n12a.

17. Ibid., 289.

of 21:10 ultimately marks the commencement of judgment. This message of warning proclaimed by God through Jeremiah against Jerusalem, like Jer 3:12–13, ties the concept of God's anger with the expression: "ἔστρικα τὸ πρόσωπόν μου ἐπὶ τὴν πόλιν ταύτην" (I have turned my face towards this city/castle) but also associates it with judgment by fire (πῦρ).

Interpreting "στηρίζειν τὸ πρόσωπον" in the Book of Ezekiel

The terminology "στηρίζειν τὸ πρόσωπον" has been shown to designate God's judgment in the Book of Jeremiah. The same thesis can be demonstrated for Ezekiel. This expression actually appears more frequently in Ezekiel (6:2, 13:17; 21:2; 21:7; 25:2; 28:21; 29:2; 35:2), and their citations reveal similar theological implications for Luke's usage of the same phrase in 9:51. Let us examine the following select four out of eight texts.

1. Ezek 6:2 is the opening line of an introductory segment found in vv. 1–14. The text warns of "the death of Israel's mountains," or, as Zimmerli puts it, "Der Tod über den Bergen Israels."[18] Ezekiel is commissioned by YHWH to prophesy against the mountains of Israel:

> Son of man, set your face against the mountains of Israel, and prophesy against them. (υἱὲ ἀνθρώπου στήρισον τὸ πρόσωπόν σου ἐπὶ τά ὄρη Ισραηλ καὶ προφήυσον ἐπ' αὐτὰ)

2. Ezek 13:17 is a pronouncement of warning and judgment to the false prophets. In v. 17, which begins a new paragraph, God commands the 'son of man,' i.e., Ezekiel, to set his face against "the daughters of your people who prophecy":

> And son of man, set your face against the daughters of your people who prophesy out of their own heart; and prophesy against them. (καὶ υἱὲ ἀνθρώπου στήρισον τὸ πρόσωπόν σου ἐπὶ τὰς θυγαέρτέρας τοῦ λαοῦ σου τὰς προφητευούσας ἀπὸ καρδίας αὐτῶν καὶ προφήτευσον ἐπ' αὐτὰς)[19]

Verse 18 revisits God's prophecy contained in verse 17. The prophecy deals with divine judgment directed towards them.[20] The LXX employs "στηρίζειν τὸ πρόσωπον" as a set formula of judgment and often as the dramatic

---

18. Zimmerli, *Ezechiel 1–24*, 139.

19. The MT uses the same metaphor: "set your face (*sim paneyka*)," and this Hebrew idiom likewise expresses the prophecy or the judgment of God.

20. Cf. Zimmerli, *Ezechiel 1–24*, 295–96. It is the choice between life or death.

opening announcement made by the prophet against those whom God has called to repentance or has already judged.

3. Ezek 15:7 offers a difference nuance to the phrase. It reads as follows:

> And I will set my face against them; they will come out of the fire, and yet fire will devour them; and they will know that I am the Lord, when I have set my face against them. (καὶ δώσω τὸ πρόσωπόν μου ἐπ' αὐτούς ἐκ τοῦ πυρὸς ἐξελεύσονται καὶ πῦρ αὐτοὺς καταφάγεται καὶ ἐπιγνώσονται ὅτι ἐγὼ κύριος ἐν τῷ στηρίσαι με τὸ πρόσωπόν μου ἐπ' αὐτούς)

In this text, God seeks to have a conversation with the prophet through the parable of the useless vine branch. The branch was useless before, but it has become even more useless as a result of having been burnt. The fire (πῦρ; v. 4) represents the judgment of God and at the conclusion of the conversation, God executes his wrath, that is, his judgment against the apostates living in Jerusalem.

Noteworthy is the fact that God judges with fire (πῦρ). The Gospel of Luke employs fire as a metaphor for judgment. God uses fire as an instrument for judgment and according to Luke's account, Jesus likewise announces that he has come to this earth to bring fire (Πῦρ ἦλθον βαλεῖν ἐπὶ τὴν γῆν, καὶ τί θέλω εἰ ἤδη ἀνήφθη; Luke 12:49). The interpretation of the fire which Jesus brings as a metaphor for judgment is supported by Ezekiel (cf. Jer 3:13 LXX).[21]

In Ezekiel the phrase "στηρίζειν τὸ πρόσωπον" emerges as the introductory statement for the prophecy of judgment. The judgment aimed at the apostates (v. 8) makes use of a similar expression "καὶ δώσω τὸ πρόσωπόν μου ἐπ' αὐτούς" in v. 7, where διδόναι replaces στηρίζειν. But once again, YHWH uses the exact expression "στηρίζειν τὸ πρόσωπον" in the next clause and ties the act of judgment with the acknowledgment that the God of Israel is Lord over all (καὶ ἐπιγνώσονται ὅτι ἐγὼ κύριος).

4. Ezekiel 21:2 delivers a prophecy stating that everyone from Jerusalem, both the just and the evil will be judged by the sword.

> Son of man, set your face against Thaeman, and look toward Darom, and prophesy against the forest land ruling over Negeb (υἱὲ ἀνθρώπου στήρισον τὸ πρόσωπόν σου ἐπὶ Θαιμαν καὶ ἐπίβλεψον ἐπὶ Δαρωμ καὶ προφήυσον ἐπὶ δρυμὸν ἡγούμενον Ναγεβ)

Here we have a change in the agency of the expression. Up until now, all examples in Ezekiel have God himself as the one who sets his face against

---

21. Bovon, *Das Evangelium nach Lukas*, 349–51. Cf. Zimmerli, *Ezechiel 1–24*, 295–96.

Israel or other nations. Here, the prophet Ezekiel, whose frequent designation is "the son of man," is the one who sets his face against the regions just south of Jerusalem *on behalf of* God. The prophet here represents God as he sets his face against Thaeman, Darom, and those who rule over the Negeb (i.e., the southern forest lands surrounding Jerusalem, if Zimmerli is correct in locating these regions in the south).[22] This text especially constitutes a very good analogy with Jesus' prophetic actions as the Son of Man who sets his face, in the name of God, against Jerusalem (Luke 9:51).

Until now, we have examined the expression as it is found in Ezekiel. The common language of expression for proclaiming judgment after having received an oracle from God is "στηρίζειν τὸ πρόσωπον" (with some verbal substitutions for στηρίζειν; e.g., διδόναι [15:7]; cf. ἐπιστρέφειν [35:2]). This expression is not simply a result of habitual usage, but rather it demonstrates an intentional denotation of judgment. Therefore, the expression "στηρίζειν τὸ πρόσωπον" functions as special terminology that is utilized in the process of transmitting YHWH's message of judgment against a non-repentant people.

The remaining examples of Ezek 25:2, 28:21, 29:2, and 38:2 need not be rehearsed here as they also employ the phrase "στηρίζειν τὸ πρόσωπον" (or its near equivalent: e.g., "ἐπίστρεψον τὸ πρόσωπόν σου;" 35:2) as an introductory formula for a prophetic judgment oracle. Instead, to summarize and conclude our study of Septuagintal usages in Ezekiel, I highlight the following observations.

The phrase "στηρίζειν τὸ πρόσωπον" (and its near equivalents) occurs eight times as words of warning in Ezekiel LXX in the following contexts: 1. against the mountains of Israel (6:2), 2. against false women prophets (13:17), 3. against Thaeman, Darom, and "the forest land ruling Negeb" (21:2), 4. against Jerusalem (21:7), 5. against the Ammonites (25:2), 6. against Sidon (28:21), 7. against Pharaoh of Egypt (29:2), and 8. against Mount Seir (35:2). In each case, the phrase functions as an introductory formula to proclaim judgment. Of these eight total occurrences, two employ the mountain metaphor (6:2; 35:2), and if we widen the metaphor to include geographic locations or cities that function as complex metonymies for a particular people group, then the number expands to seven out of eight (with the exception being 13:17 against the "daughters of Israel" who prophesy). Thus in Ezekiel we have examples where to "set / give / turn one's face against" someone is a proclamation of divine judgment, and often the

---

22. Zimmerli, *Ezechiel 1–24*, 464–65. It is very interesting to see where this designation Θαιμαν fits into the discussion. After going through various alternatives, Zimmerli reaches the conclusion that Θαιμαν is "Jerusalem" or "Forest in the south (*Wald im Süden*)," that is, Israel.

recipients of the warning or oracle are addressed as geographic metonymies, especially as mountains or cities.

FINAL WORDS CONCERNING THE PHRASE "ΣΤΗΡΙΖΕΙΝ ΤΟ ΠΡΟΣΩΠΟΝ" IN THE GOSPEL OF LUKE

It has been demonstrated that the expression στηρίζειν τὸ πρόσωπον in Ezekiel exhibit a higher resemblance to Luke's usage than in all the other Old Testament texts. It is unlikely that this unique expression of the Gospel of Luke was written simply because it was part of the author's *cultural* idiom, but rather it reveals that the author was well aware of the important *theological* implications recorded in the LXX. These uses of this expression in the Gospel of Luke suggest a close connection with the expressions found in the book of Ezekiel.

Luke 9:51 begins with the expression: "ἐγένετο . . . καὶ . . ." (which is also used in Luke 5:1).[23] Since the expression is frequently found in the Gospel of Luke,[24] it appears to indicate that it was part of the author's preferred style of writing.[25] The text of 9:51, which begins with a similar style, shifts our attention to things related to Jesus' prophetic work. The Gospel of Luke demonstrates that Jesus' intention in advancing to Jerusalem is to consummate his death and comply to God's calling.[26] Here we also add that the intertextual ties with Ezekiel point to Jesus' imminent judgment against the city whose inhabitants will reject and crucify him.

The Lukan text alludes to Jerusalem's destruction. The text communicates Jesus' expression of sadness for the city of Jerusalem in 19:41–44, which is only found in Luke's gospel. Both the Gospels of Matthew and Mark are silent regarding this subject.[27] What does the Gospel of Luke intend to communicate by describing Jesus' sadness? The answer is his remorse for the lack of repentance he will encounter in the city. Jesus' intention for going to Jerusalem was not merely to die, but that it held the significance of judgment for those who fail to respond to his message. Previously, Luke had observed that the mission of Jesus includes bringing to the earth the fire of

---

23. The full text reads: Ἐγένετο δὲ ἐν τῷ τὸν ὄχλον ἐπικεῖσθαι αὐτῷ καὶ . . . παρὰ τὴν λίμνην Γεννησαρὲτ (Luke 5:1).
24. Marshall, *The Gospel of Luke*, 405.
25. Nolland, *Luke 9:21–18:34*, 534.
26. Cf. Schlatter, *Erläuterungen zum Neuen Testament*, 1:254.
27. Cf. Aland, *Synopsis Quattuor Evangeliorum*, 369.

judgment (12:49). This section shows the tension between Jesus' sadness for the city of Jerusalem with the judgment that will come through Jesus.

This type of tension in Luke's narrative, regardless of whether his identity was Jewish Christian or a Gentile Christian, demonstrates that Luke, as an interpreter, had a deep understanding of Judaism and the interpretive traditions of the Old Testament. He used the idioms of the LXX to express Jesus' role as "the son of man," who like the prophet Ezekiel, set his face against the ancient city of Jerusalem to proclaim a message of repentance, all the while knowing that her inhabitants would not respond and the city would therefore be judged by fire. His was a prophetic act with a long-standing history in the prophetic oracles of Israel's Scriptures.

BIBLIOGRAPHY

Aland, Kurt, ed. *Synopsis Quattuor Evangeliorum*. 12th ed. Stuttgart: Deutsche Bibelgesellschaft, 1982.

Baarlink, Heinrich. "Die zyklische Struktur von Lukas 9.43b–19.28." *NTS* 38 (1992) 481–506.

Bovon, François. *Das Evangelium nach Lukas (Lk 9, 51–14, 35)*. EKK 3/2. Benzinger: Neukirchen, 1996.

Brenton, Sir Lancelot C. L. *The Septuagint with Apocrypha*. London: Bagster and Sons, 1851. Reprint, Peabody, MA: Hendrickson, 1986.

Choi, Soon Bong. "The Understanding of 'στηρίζειν τὸ πρόσωπον' in Luke 9:51." *Kwangshin Nondan* (2011) 83–94.

Craigie, P., et al. *Jeremiah 1–25*. WBC 26. Dallas: Word, 1991.

Ellis, E. Earle. *The Gospel of Luke*. New Century Bible Commentary. Grand Rapids: Eerdmans, 1987.

Evans, C. A., "'He Set His Face': A Note on Luke 9,51." *Bib* 63 (1982) 80–84.

Gasse, W. "Zum Reisebericht des Lukas." *ZNW* 34 (1935) 293–99.

Goulder, M. "From Ministry to Passion in John and Luke." *NTS* 29 (1983) 561–68.

Harder, G. στηρίζω κτλ. In *TWNT* 7:653–57.

Josephus, Flavius. *Antiquitates / Jüdische Altertümer*. Ed. W. G. Kümmel. Trans. H. Clementz and O. J. Wiesbaden. Jüdische Schriften aus helleistisch-römischer Zeit. Gütersloh: Gütersloher, 1973.

Jeremias, Joachim. "Perikopen-Umstellungen bei Lukas?" *NTS* (1958) 115–17.

———. *Die Sprache des Lukasevangeliums. Redaktion und Tradition im Nicht-Markusstoff des dritten Evangeliums*. KEK. Göttingen: Vandenhoeck & Ruprecht, 1980.

Marshall, I. H. *The Gospel of Luke: A Commentary on the Greek Text*. NIGTC. Grand Rapids: Eerdmanns, 1992.

Nolland, John. *Luke 9:21—18:34*. WBC 35B. Dallas: Word, 1993.

Ogg, George. "The Central Section of the Gospel according to St. Luke." *NTS* 18 (1971) 39–53.

Schlatter, Adolf. *Die Evangelien und die Apostelgeshichte*. Erkläuterungen zum Neuen Testament 1. Stuttgart: Calwer Vereinsbuchhandlung, 1928.

Schürmann, Heinz. *Das Lukasevangelium* (9,51–11,54). HTKNT 3/2. Freiburg: Herder 1994.

Schweizer, Eduard. *Das Evangelium nach Lukas*. Das Neu Testament Deutsch 3. Göttingen: Vandenhoeck & Ruprecht, 2000.

Turner, Nigel. "The Relation of Luke I and II to Hebraic Sources and to the Rest of Luke-Acts." *NTS* 2 (1956) 100–109.

Zimmerli, Walther. *Ezechiel 1–24*. BKAT 13/1. Neukirchen-Vluyn: Neukirchen, 1969.

9

Re-examining the Ironical Interpretation of the Parable of the Unjust Steward in Luke 16[1]

CHANG WOOK JUNG

INTRODUCTION

Almost every New Testament scholar agrees that the parable of the unjust steward represents one of the more difficult parables in the gospels.[2] The history of NT interpretation on the parable illustrates that it has been the *crux interpretum*. Over half a century ago, Bretscher titled his article concerning the parable as "The Parable of the Unjust Steward—A *New* Approach to Luke 16:1-9."[3] Surprisingly, Arnott published an article entitled:

1. This article was originally published in the journal *Korean Evangelical New Testament Studies* (2012). I am grateful to the editors of *KENTS* for permission to reprint this essay here.

2. See Forbes, *The God of Old*, 152. He introduces Bultmann's assessment that "the original meaning is irrecoverable." Almost every commentator admits that the parable is the most difficult of Jesus' parables, or "notoriously difficult." See Liefeld and Pao, "Luke," 256. Young also describes the parable "as one of the most, if not the most, perplexing of the parables of Jesus" (*The Parables*, 232).

3. Bretscher, "Unjust Steward," 756–62. Derrett published an article ten years after Bretscher's publication and titled it as "Fresh Light on St. Luke xvi.1," 198–219.

"The Unjust Steward in a *New* Light" about half a century before Bretscher's publication.[4] Two more scholars co-authored an article at the dawn of this century concerning the parable whose title includes the word "new" as well: "Honor Restored: *New* Light on the Parable of the Prudent Steward (Luke 16:1–8a)."[5] This trend demonstrates that the parable has been drawing fresh attention repeatedly. It is therefore not surprising at all that numerous scholars have been writing to resolve the puzzles in the parable of the unjust steward.[6]

Opinions are first divided concerning even the title of the parable, whether it is "the unjust steward," "the prudent steward," "the crafty steward," or even "the dishonored master." Each title reflects its basic interpretation of the parable.[7] Scholarly views also vary as to where the parable proper ends and the application of the parable begins (vv. 7, 8a, 8b, 9).[8] Due to such difficulties, scholars have suggested various ways of interpreting the parable: i.e., the traditional interpretation, the eschatological interpretation, the social-economic interpretation, the sociological interpretation, and the ironical interpretation.[9] The debate is still ongoing and will certainly con-

---

4. Arnott, "The Unjust Steward in a New Light," 508–11.

5. Landry and May, "Honor Restored," 287–309.

6. For the works concerning the parable until 1990, see Ireland, *Stewardship and The Kingdom of God*. Many works have been published since then. Schellenberg lists about fourteen works, except for his own article, on the parable since 1990 ("Which Master? Whose Steward?," 283–88).

7. As listed above, Bretscher and Arnott title the parable as "the unjust steward." Topel employs the same adjective "unjust" as they do (Topel, "Injustice," 216–27). Fletcher and Bock call the parable "parable of the dishonest steward" and "parable of the crafty steward" respectively (Fletcher, "The Riddle," 15; and Bock, *Luke 9:51—24:53*, 1323). In contrast, Marshall and deSilva title the parable as "the parable of the prudent steward" (Marshall, *Gospel of Luke*, 614; deSilva, "Prudent Steward," 255–68). Shifting the main character from the steward to the master, Kloppenborg entitles his article as "The Dishonoured Master." Dormandy's title includes both steward and master (Dormandy, "Converted Master," 512–27). English Bibles also name the parable variously; e.g., NRSV as "The Parable of the Dishonest Manager," but the NIV as "The Parable of the Shrewd Manager."

8. For details, see Fitzmyer, *Luke X–XXIIII*, 1096–97; Bock, *Luke 9:51—24:53*, 1340–43; and Parrott, "Dishonest Steward," 512–14. As Landry and May point out, the vast majority of recent scholars agree that the parable proper ends in 16:8a ("Honor Restored," 288). deSilva notes that scholars who regard 8a as the end of the parable "have the strongest arguments on their side" ("Prudent Steward," 257).

9. Division of scholarly views varies from scholar to scholar. Some of the major views listed here may be named differently, and others may be put into more specific subcategories (e.g., traditional interpretation as monetary interpretation, or ironical interpretation as belonging to the subcategory of "negative example interpretation"). For details, see Ireland, *Stewardship and the Kingdom of God*, 5–49.

tinue among the advocates of each view, since "it is relatively easy to raise objections to most of the solutions offered."[10] Any interpretations, more positively speaking, cannot be discarded easily, since each of them offers a "particular insight for the interpretation of this difficult parable."[11]

While the majority of recent scholars still uphold the traditional view and many suggest the social-economic and the sociological interpretations, some are inclined to accept the ironical interpretation. An interesting phenomenon also needs to be pointed out: whereas the social-economic, sociological, and ironical interpretations have been claimed by many scholars in their works, few commentaries accept their views even though some aspects of the social-economic and the sociological interpretations are adopted.[12] Especially, no commentary follows the advocates of the ironical interpretation, probably because it is difficult to find any ironical factors in the passage in Luke 16:1–13.

Now this study seeks to re-examine the ironical interpretation and demonstrate that the parable of the unjust steward involves ironical force and is thus to be interpreted ironically.[13] Before re-examining the ironical interpretation, the major views—i.e., the traditional, the socioeconomic, and the sociological interpretations—need to be first re-evaluated. It is unnecessary to reiterate other scholars' arguments for and against these views. It will suffice to summarize the interpretations in brief and point out the main criticisms of each and the flaws which other scholars did not treat or have overlooked.

---

10. Snodgrass, *Stories with Intent*, 409.

11. Ireland, *Stewardship and the Kingdom of God*, 47.

12. See, e.g., Bock who, though taking an ambiguous attitude toward the socioeconomic interpretation, appears to give some credit to the interpretation (*Luke 9:51—24:53*, 1339). Young accepts the shame-based interpretation of the parable, although he believes the parable reflects the criticism of the Essenes (*The Parables*, 239–44).

13. The function of the passage vv. 14–18 also requires inspection, since it bridges the parable of the unjust steward with the parable of the rich man and Lazarus. Due to the limit of space, however, this study will not treat vv. 14–18, but see Nolland, who notes that vv. 14–15 bind the whole chapter together (*Luke 9:21—18:34*, 809).

THE MAJOR VIEWS FOR INTERPRETING THE PARABLE OF THE UNJUST STEWARD

The Traditional Interpretation: Its Critical Deficiency

As stated above, most recent commentators regard the traditional interpretation as the most probable. Is their decision conclusive and convincing?[14] According to the traditional view, the emphasis of the parable is laid on the prudent attitude of the steward, regardless of whether the steward's conduct in vv. 5–7 is legal or illegal.[15] The parable of the unjust steward intends to highlight the shrewd attitude in general or the prudent use of the earthly wealth to enter the kingdom of God. Some scholars add an eschatological aspect to this view. The parable, according to them, is also designed to urge Jesus' disciples to imitate the urgent and prudent response of the unjust steward in the face of the eschatological crisis.[16] The traditional interpretation, whether including the eschatological element or not, should depend on the *a fortiori* argument or *a minore ad maius*, i.e., from-lesser-to-greater argument.[17] If the unjust steward resolves a crisis by means of dishonesty and making friends, *how much more* the children of the light should act wisely by means of honesty in the eschatological crisis! More simply, the parable shows that if the unjust steward behaves shrewdly at a crisis, *how much more* righteous believers should conduct themselves wisely in the last days!

It is admitted that Luke adopts this "how much more" argument in two parables in the Gospel of Luke, i.e., the parable of the friend at midnight in

---

14. See Porter's discussion of the traditional view in "Unjust Steward," 130–32; also Loader, "Jesus and the Rogue," 518–32. According to these scholars, the core problem for the traditional interpretation is how it distinguishes between the dishonest action of the steward and yet his prudence. Such a distinction is very arbitrary. If the steward's deed is dishonest, as the advocates of the standard interpretation claim, the steward does not accomplish his goal since "who would hire dishonest manager, especially if it might jeopardize one's relationship with his former employer?" (Kloppenborg, "Dishonored Master," 478).

15. To explain which conduct of the steward causes him to be called dishonest is one of the key issues in understanding the parable. Some scholars regard the action in vv. 5–7 as the unjust action while others consider "squandering" in v. 1 to be. These issues will be explored further below.

16. Snodgrass, *Stories with Intent*, 416.

17. Mathewson, "Unjust Steward," 33; Bailey, *Poet and Peasant*, 105. See also Williams, who understands the *a fortiori* argument is the key to resolve the puzzle by asserting that the deficiency of the traditional theory "disappears, once it is realized that we are dealing here with a sort of a fortiori argument" ("Almsgiving," 294–95). Snodgrass also recognizes the parable as a "how much more parable" (*Stories with Intent*, 416).

ch. 11 and the parable of the unjust judge in ch. 18, both of which are found only in the Gospel of Luke.[18] This observation suggests the use of *a fortiori* argument in the parable of the unjust steward to be a Lukan convention.

The problem, however, rests on the fact that whereas the *a fortiori* argument is clearly suggested in the two parables, its presence is not obvious in the parable of the unjust steward. In the case of the parable of the friend at midnight in Luke 11:5–8, the expression in v. 8 implicitly and the expression in v.13 explicitly represents the *a minore ad maius* argument: "If you then, though you are evil, know how to give good gifts to your children, *how much more* will your Father in heaven . . . !"[19] In the parable of the unjust judge in Luke 18:1–8, the clear idea of "how much more" in v. 7 demonstrates that the same argument is applied to the parable: "If the unjust judge vindicates the widow lest she wears him out, *how much more* the righteous God will grant justice to his chosen ones, who cry out day and night to Him."[20]

In contrast, there is no such element in the parable of the unjust steward. Scholars like Forbes assume that "the parable argues *a fortiori*" and "16:10–13 makes essentially the same point" of *a fortiori* argument.[21] It is uncertain, however, that the passage 16:1–13 substantially betrays the force of *a fortiori* argument.[22] Although the *a fortiori* argument could be perceived with the glasses of the traditional view, it is doubtful that the passage in 16:1–13 itself evokes the argument.[23] If this parable were intended to give such a lesson, the *a fortiori* argument would be clearly expressed by some syntagm as the phrase "how much more" in Luke 11:7.[24]

---

18. For more details, see Ireland who argues that the two parables involve a from-lesser-to-greater argument (*Stewardship and the Kingdom of God*, 76).

19. Bailey, *Poet and Peasant*, 125–28; Green, *Luke*, 448–49, esp. n46.

20. Concerning the meaning of the Greek verb for "wear out," scholars suggest various interpretations. For details, see Hedrick, *Parables as Poetic Fictions*, 200–202, who interprets the verb as indicating physical violence.

21. Forbes, *The God of Old*, 178; Williams, "Almsgiving," 293–97.

22. Topel simply states in the footnote of his article that he finds no hint of the *a fortiori* argument "in text and context." He does not explain why in detail ("Injustice," 226n48).

23. Ireland is cautious to argue for the parallel between the parable of the unjust steward and the parables in chs. 11 and 18, though he asserts that the uniqueness of the parable of the unjust steward does not constitute the decisive counterargument for the presence of *a fortiori* argument within the parable (*Stewardship and the Kingdom of God*, 76n115).

24. Schellenberg observes that though negative characters are used as positive examples in the Gospel of Luke, "their actions are endorsed without reservation." "Nowhere in Luke's Gospel," he insists, "do we have an example of abstracting a praiseworthy quality from an action that is itself reprehensible" ("Which Master? Whose Master?," 266–67).

The Socioeconomic and the Sociological Interpretations: A Critical Re-Evaluation

Since the traditional (or standard) view does not resolve all the problems and raises questions, it is reasonable that other alternative explanations have been offered. Of such views, the socioeconomic interpretation tries to answer the question which the traditional view cannot solve: the character of the steward's action in vv. 5–7. The praise of the lord in v. 8, whether he is the master of the parable or Jesus, is a stumbling block, if the action in vv. 5–7 represents an unjust deed, since: 1) Jesus never counsels his audiences to perform a dishonest action to accomplish their goals, and 2) the master, if he loses his own money, cannot recommend the steward in general. This difficulty, in fact, forces the traditional view to apply the *a fortiori* argument to the parable.

Recognizing such problems, the advocates of the socioeconomic view attempt to make the steward a positive model. Derrett introduces the concept of usurious loan which points to master's illegal profit in the sense that the Mosaic Law prohibits the interest.[25] The steward remitted the unlawful interest which may belong to both the steward and the master. Then, the master, having recognized what the steward had done, decided to ratify the steward's action of reduction of the illegal interest, though reluctantly, and the steward became a hero who forgave the illegal interest. Now the steward's action in vv. 5–7 is not defined as "dishonest" but "righteous," and he becomes a positive model.

Despite the ingenuity of Derrett's view, Fitzmyer is not completely satisfied with it, most probably because the steward's action may be counted still illegal, if the interest, even a portion of it, is of the master, which makes it also difficult to understand the master's applause.[26] Thus, Fitzmyer attempts to completely eliminate the illegal aspect by positing that the reduced amount is not the interest (which may belong to both the master and the manager) but the steward's commission (which belongs only to the

---

25. Derrett, "Fresh Light," 198–219.

26. Fitzmyer, "Dishonest Manager," 23–45. Concerning Derrett's understanding of the character of usury, Ireland considers the remitted amount as belonging to the steward (*Stewardship and the Kingdom of God*, 46–47). In contrast, Kloppenborg regards the usury as the master's interest (Kloppenborg, "Dishonoured Master," 480). Loader also notes that "when the manager reduces the bills by subtracting the usury fee, he is, on Derrett's reading, depriving the master of gain" ("Jesus and the Rogue," 480). Derrett's position is rather ambiguous as he does not clearly define the character of the renounced fee of usury. At least a part of the interest, however, must belong to the master according to his explanation.

steward).²⁷ In this way, the steward is justified to receive the praise of the lord in v. 8. As a result, the main thrust of the parable should be "the proper management of God's wealth entrusted to disciples."²⁸ The problem is, however, that if the amounts belonged to the steward, as Fitzmyer assumes, he would not need to change the contract. In addition, the text clearly states that the steward asked the debtors how much they owed to the master not to the steward (vv. 5, 7).²⁹

Different from the socioeconomic interpretation, the sociological interpretation understands honor and shame as the most important element to be considered for the parable of the unjust steward, though both interpretations have in common that they rely on the contemporary social background. Since Landry and May provides the most thoroughly and recently argued case for this view, their work needs to be analyzed here.

The honor and shame framework, according to Landry and May, is the key to unlock the puzzle of the parable.³⁰ Kloppenborg is on right tract, they claim, when he pays attention to the value of honor in the world of the New Testament. He fails, however, to properly explicate the steward's action in vv. 3–7 when he defines it as "outright fraud" motivated merely for his own benefit. The steward, they continue, does not remit the portion of the amount mainly for his own selfish advantage but for the restoration of the master's honor.

The core of their argument lies on the delineation of the accusation in vv. 1–2. Landry and May, like Derrett and Fitzmyer, try to define the steward's action in vv. 5–7 as legitimate. Following Beavis's suggestion, they maintain that the steward is a slave rather than a free man, though they add that his status does not matter much.³¹ The slave steward, they claim,

---

27. Different from Derrett, Fitzmyer makes it clear that the manager owns all of the remitted commission. He points out this repeatedly ("Dishonest Manager," 33, 35, 36, 41). Refuting that the steward was labeled "unjust" due to the action in vv. 5–7, he emphasizes that the manager's conduct in vv. 5–7 is neither dishonest nor wrong. Ibid., 31–32.

28. Fitzmyer, *Luke IX–XXIV*, 1099.

29. Upkong, "Shrewd Manager," 203. For the detailed criticism on Derrett's and Fitzmyer's argument, see Kloppenborg, "Dishonoured Master," 481–86. See also Bindemann who claims that "der Text selbst keinen Hinweis auf etwaigen Wucher seitens des Herrn, der durch den Schulderlab des Verwalters korrigiert wuerde, enthael" ("Ungerechte als Vorbilder?," 962).

30. Landry and May, "Honor Restored," 293.

31. Ibid., 296. Scholars like Baergen believe the manager was a slave ("Servant, Manager, or Slave?," 34). He argues that the slave had no power at all but "discovered the power which lies within his group and uses it effectively to win the day." The position of the poor and that of the rich are reversed. Different from Landry and May, however, Baergen clearly understands that the status of the steward deeply influences

is falsely accused without any reliable facts, and the steward's "crime might best be described as misappropriation of funds."[32] In contrast, his action in vv. 5–7 cannot be labeled as "unjust" since his main purpose was to restore his master's honor. As the advocates of the socioeconomic interpretation, Landry and May endeavor to eliminate the illegal aspect of the steward's deed in vv. 5–7 so that the *a fortiori* argument does not need to be applied. The master was dishonored since he could not control his own steward properly, which they assume is supported by ancient literature. Honor takes an important place in both Jewish and Greco-Roman worlds. The steward aims to restore his master's honor by reducing part or all of the interest charge in order that the steward may "salvage his reputation as a good, loyal steward" and the debtors may employ him as a manager if he is fired.[33]

In spite of the brilliant effort of Landry and May, the following makes their argument less plausible. First, their presupposition that the steward was labeled as "unjust" because of his conduct in vv. 1–2 is dubious. Remarkably, the steward is called "unjust" after his deed in vv. 5–7, which probably indicates that his act in these verses causes him to be defined "unjust."[34] If the steward was accused falsely, as they claim, why then is the steward called "unjust" because of the very same conduct? Second, they provide few instances from contemporary Jewish literature which support their argument that "honor was at stake if it was known that the master could not control his servants."[35] Almost all the references, if not all, derive from scattered Greco-Roman sources.[36]

Finally, if the master was stirred up by the unreliable hearsay and fired the steward hastily, as they suggest, how could he not be upset by the

---

the interpretation of the parable.

32. Landry and May, "Honor Restored," 298.

33. Ibid., 301–2.

34. Stein, *Luke*, 414. Interestingly, Landry and May cite Derrett that numerous scholars think the steward is "unjust" because of his deed in v. 1 ("Honor Restored," 304). However, Derrett's view does not represent the majority view as less have accepted it, at least in recent years. Forbes adopts Stein's argument that the unjust deed is found in vv. 5–6 and lists scholars who follow this understanding (*The God of Old*, 162–63; cf. 159). We may add more names: Williams ("Almsgiving," 294); Gagnon ("Second Look," 3); Ireland (*Stewardship and the Kingdom of God*, 82); Porter ("Unjust Steward," 143–44); Green (*Luke*, 594); Schellenberg ("Which Master? Whose Steward?," 279); Ukpong ("Shrewd Manager," 206). Snodgrass asserts that "it is his (steward) actions in vv. 5–7 that qualify him for this (unjust) label, not his squandering of goods in v. 1" (*Stories with Intent*, 410). Meanwhile, other scholars believe the adjective "unjust" simply indicates a common character of this world (deSilva, "Prudent Steward," 265).

35. Landry and May, "Honor Restored," 298.

36. Ibid., 298–99.

steward's deed in vv. 5–7? The master was not a generous or thoughtful figure according to their analysis, since he fired the manager for a trivial misconduct whose basis of accusation was unreliable. It was widespread news, according to them, that the steward was not loyal to his master and the master lost face mostly due to his own failure to control his steward. The only way for the manager to recover his master's honor is to demonstrate that the master really controls him. It is not clear how the master restored his own honor and how the manager betrays his own loyalty. Landry and May turned the master into an impulsive man at first who fired his slave based upon unreliable hearsay and a careless person who did not realize what was happening concerning his property.[37] Then they described the master as a thoughtful figure who suddenly perceives the very core of the problem. They would argue that honor was so important that the master recognized everything at once. Their explanation, however, is too arbitrary and speculative. In fact, the context of the parable does not indicate that the rich man is fickle as much as fortunate.[38]

Landry and May justify their approach by making the steward look sympathetic. The text itself, however, presents nothing that supports this reading. The steward never appealed to the master about the accusation, and the master's attitude reflected in his questions in vv. 3–4 does not betray any sympathy. In addition, one can hardly perceive that the steward achieves his goal through employment by the debtors. Moreover, the application of the parable in vv. 8b–13 does not fit the argument that the restoration of the master's honor constitutes the primary lesson of the parable.[39] With all these considerations, it becomes clear that their argument is not convincing.

In sum, the critical problem of the socioeconomic and the sociological views, both of which rely on the ancient social background, is that no one can reconstruct with certainty the social-economic and sociological background of the parable in first-century Palestine. The advocates of these interpretations, as Porter concludes, assume too much which the text itself does not explain.[40] So far, we re-evaluated the traditional, the socioeconomic, and the

---

37. Ibid., 305.

38. As Michael Wolter points out, there may be a connection between this parable and the parable of the rich fool in Luke 12 (*Das Lukasevangelium*, 544). The rich man in Luke 16, however, is not defined as "foolish" as in the parable of the rich fool.

39. Greene claims that the restoration of the master's honor is not the main concern of the parable. "The issue of the threatened honour may be on the periphery," he postulates, "but it certainly is not the explicit focus of the stated text" ("Question and Challenge," 84).

40. Porter, "Unjust Steward," 133. For the detailed explanation and criticism of the socioeconomic interpretation, see Ireland, *Stewardship and the Kingdom of God*, 40–47 and 80–82. See also Mathewson, who introduces and criticizes the interpretation

sociological interpretations. Now we turn to the main subject, i.e., the re-examination of the ironical interpretation.

THE IRONICAL INTERPRETATION: PAST PROPOSALS AND A NEW WAY FORWARD

The Crucial Difficulty of the Ironical Interpretation[41]

Different from the above three views, the ironical interpretation understands the parable as conveying sarcasm or irony.[42] The applause for the steward's action in v. 8 and Jesus' saying in v. 9 should be understood ironically. Even the passage in vv. 10–13, according to scholars like Porter, should be interpreted ironically.[43] To act like the steward does not secure the future and thus he could not accomplish his goal. This parable gives a lesson that no one can obtain true rest and security by means of the unjust actions and the prudent use of the unrighteous wealth.

In rebuttal to the ironical interpretation, however, the advocates of other views postulate that no irony exists in vv. 1–13 at all.[44] The difficulty of understanding the recommendation in v. 8, according to them, causes scholars to assume wrongly an ironical force in the parable. Ireland succinctly summarizes the crucial deficiency of the ironical interpretation:

("Unjust Steward," 31–33).

41. Quoting Forbes's words, the ironical interpretation is "the best argued alternative to the traditional view" (*The God of Old*, 174).

42. It is not easy to define the term "irony." As Booth confesses, "there is no agreement among critics about what irony is" (*A Rhetoric of Irony*, Preface, ix). We may follow, however, the simple definition which Porter suggests. Irony, according to him, is "defined as an interpretative situation in which an explanation discrepancy perceived by the reader between what is said and/or done by the characters in a dramatic story, and what is the established state of affairs in the contextual world" ("Unjust Steward," 129). It is also noteworthy that distinction between irony and satire needs to be maintained: "irony is used in some satire, not in all; some irony is satiric, much is not" (Booth, *Rhetoric of Irony*, 30).

43. For details, see Porter who persuasively argues that the parable should be interpreted ironically ("Unjust Steward," 127–53). Mathewson evaluates Porter's argument in his article, "Unjust Steward," 29–39. Fletcher adds that the key word φρόνιμος indicates "a slight irony" ("The Riddle," 23).

44. See, e.g., Ireland, *Stewardship and the Kingdom of God*, 78–79; Bock, *Luke 9:51—24:53*, 1343. Williams remarks that the irony is too subtle to be easily grasped ("Almsgiving," 293–97). Forbes also raises questions about the ironical interpretation by pointing out that "vv. 8–9 do not appear to indicate irony in their present form" (*The God of Old*, 176).

> There is nothing in the context itself to point to irony. Instead irony seems to have suggested itself because of the difficulty of explaining the praise in v. 8 or Jesus' exhortation in v. 9. Difficulty alone, however, is no proof of irony if, as I am arguing, other plausible explanations are available. Such explanations make resorting to irony unnecessary.[45]

The ironical interpretation, Ireland assumes, arose solely due to the difficulty in understanding the applause in v. 8 and Jesus' admonition in v. 9. Now the issue, therefore, centers on whether the text and the context of the parable of the unjust steward include ironical elements apart from "difficulty of explaining the praise."

Possible Irony in Luke 16: The Awkward Combination between the Two Words "Eternal" and "Tents"

Concerning the present matter, some scholars' views on the phrase "eternal habitations" in v. 9 warrant our attention. McFayden, already in 1926, discerned the awkward combination of the two words, "eternal" and "tents" and regards the parable as including an ironical nuance.[46] The praise in v. 9, according to him, is simply a satiric remark which indicates a mock for the unjust steward. Fletcher also perceives "the juxtaposition of antithetical ideas about the 'eternal tents.'"[47] In a similar way, Bowen observes that the basic meaning of the Greek expression for "eternal habitations" should be "eternal tents."[48] He goes one step further by paying attention to the alternation of the Greek words for habitation in Luke 15–16. The Greek noun οἶκος or οἰκία for "house" is used in the three parables in Luke 15 (vv. 6, 8, 25) as well as in 16:4, whereas another Greek noun σκηνή ("tent") is found in 16:9. Though tents cannot be eternal in nature, Bowen claims, the author intends to convey the ironical meaning by adding the modifying adjective "eternal" to the noun "tent." The manager assumed that he acted shrewdly in order for people to receive him into their "houses" or "habitations," which are not "houses" but "tents" in reality. He failed thus to gain what he intended to obtain. The parable, Bowen concludes, has to be read ironically.

---

45. Ireland, *Steward and the Kingdom of God*, 78–79.

46. McFayden, "Unjust Steward," 535–39. Snodgrass also admits that the phrase "eternal tents" "has little precedent and is odd enough to be suspected of being irony," although he disputes the ironical interpretation by suggesting a couple of Jewish texts which he believes show a similar idea (*Stories with Intent*, 415).

47. Fletcher, "The Riddle," 28–29.

48. Bowen, "*Oikos*," 314–15.

Philological Support for the Ironical Interpretation

However attractive the above three scholars' views are, they do not undertake an investigation into the Greek word σκηνή, and the expression "αἰωνίους σκηνάς" ("eternal tents"). Now we turn to the examination of these two phrases.

The Noun σκηνή

The Greek word for "tent": σκηνή occurs twenty times in the New Testament. Of twenty instances, ten take place in Hebrews where the earthly tabernacle of the Old Testament is compared with the heavenly tabernacle made by Jesus (8:2, 5; 9:2, 3, 6, 8, 11, 21; 11:9; 13:10). The noun σκηνή means "a temporary dwelling" in all instances except for those in 8:2, 9:11, in which the noun denotes the transcendent heavenly dwelling, compared with the earthly tabernacle of the Old Testament. The noun appears three times also in Revelation where it points to a heavenly dwelling place (Rev. 15:5; 13:6; 21:3).[49]

In Luke-Acts, the noun σκηνή occurs four times, excluding the instance in Luke 16:9. Peter employs the noun at the event of the transfiguration in Luke 9:33, suggesting that he will make three "tents." He tries to prolong the stay of the visitors, Moses and Elijah, by making temporary habitations because it does not seem probable that Peter wants to stay there permanently.[50] The remaining three instances are found in Acts 7:43, 7:44, and 15:16.[51] In the first and second examples, the noun points to a temporary dwelling, i.e., "tent" or ""tabernacle." The sentence in the last instance quotes Amos 9:11 which includes the expression "the tabernacle (tent) of David" (τὴν σκηνὴν Δαυὶδ). This expression used also in Isa 16:5 LXX metaphorically describes the Davidic kingdom or Davidic line in Act 15:16, which will be restored or rebuilt through Jesus.[52] It is noteworthy that in the Gospel of Luke, another expression "house of David" is employed in 1:27, 1:69, and 2:4 where the Greek word οἶκος is used for "house." Luke thus adopts the noun σκηνή in

---

49. BDAG, s.v. σκηνή, 928. In Rev 21:3, the tabernacle is described as being among people; this tabernacle points to the place where God is among them.

50. For details, see Liefeld and Pao, "Luke," 180; Bock, *Luke 1:1—9:50*, 871; Godet, *Luke*, 273. In contrast, Marshall insists that Peter wished to erect "everlasting dwellings." His argument is not convincing, since he depends on the use of the noun in Luke 16:9 to support his argument.

51. The remaining two instances are found in the parallels of Luke 9:33; Matt 17:4; Mark 9:5.

52. Bock, *Acts*, 503–4; Johnson, *Acts*, 265.

Acts 15:16, since he relies on Amos 9:11 LXX where the Greek noun σκηνή is found.[53]

All recent English versions adopt "habitation," "dwelling," or "home" for the Greek word σκηνή in Luke 16:9, which may reflect the influence of BDAG, which suggests the meaning of the noun with the adjective αἰώνιος as "permanent house." BDAG's explanation, however, is imprecise concerning the usage of the noun. It is accepted, as noted previously, that in some instances in Hebrews (8:2; 9:11) and Revelation (15:5; 13:6; 21:3), the noun denotes the transcendent heavenly habitation. Putting Luke 16:9 into this category, BDAG notes that the noun signifies the heavenly dwelling. In the instances of Hebrews and Revelation, however, the noun obviously refers to the heavenly place which Jesus made (two instances in Hebrews) or the transcendent realm where God stays (three instances in Revelation). In other words, the context with explanatory remarks indicates that the noun does not mean a temporary dwelling, "tent," or "tabernacle" but an "eternal habitation." In contrast, the context of Luke 16:9, where no explanatory expressions appear, does not guarantee the meaning of the heavenly habitation at all.

Remarkably, Luke avoids the noun "tent" even in the eschatological context. As pointed out above, Luke employs the noun "house" for the expression "the house of David." Why did Luke, who utilizes the noun "house" for the locution "house of David" in the eschatological context, especially in 1:69, not employ "eternal house" but "eternal tents," which probably conveys an ambiguous implication without any modifying explanation?[54] If Luke had intended to point to the real eternal habitation, he should have modified the noun with an expositional remark or adopted the noun which delivers his intention manifestly, i.e., "house," not "tent," as he did in other parts of the Gospel. As pointed out by Bowen, the shift of the word for the habitation from οἶκος to σκηνή in Luke 15–16 also lends support to that Luke's use of the word σκηνή in 16:9 is deliberate and ought to be translated as "tent." If

---

53. Scholars agree that Luke relies on the LXX for the quotation in Acts; see Steyn, *Septuagint Quotations*.

54. It is recognized that the context of 1:27, 69 clearly suggests the eschatological connotation. The text after 1:27 follows the annunciation of Mary where the eschatological color is very strong. See Evans, who notes that vv. 32–33 "echoes the great Davidic covenant of 2 Sam 7 in which King David is promised that his throne and kingdom would be established forever" (*Luke*, 25). This everlasting aspect is eschatological in character. In 1:69, the eschatological connotation emerges prominently, as Strauss explains: "The hymn (Benedictus) begins with the horn of salvation who is raised up in the house of David and ends with the Davidic ἀνατολή, the eschatological rising light" (*Davidic Messiah*, 108).

he meant for an eternal dwelling place, Luke would have changed σκηνή to οἶκος as he did in other passages.

The Nouns οἰκία and σκῆνος in the Pauline Letters

The usage of the synonym noun σκῆνος (which includes the identical stem to σκηνή except for the ending) occurs twice in Pauline letters (2 Cor 5:1; 5:4) and supports my argument. In 2 Cor 5:4, the noun refers to a temporary lodging, i.e., the human body emphasizing its temporary nature and mortality.

The example in 2 Cor 5:1, which also includes the adjective "αἰώνιος," warrants a close reading:

> For we know that if the earthly tent we live in is destroyed, we have a building from God, a house not made with hands, eternal in the heavens.[55] (ἐὰν ἡ ἐπίγειος ἡμῶν οἰκία τοῦ σκήνους καταλυθῇ, οἰκοδομὴν ἐκ θεοῦ ἔχομεν, οἰκίαν ἀχειροποίητον αἰώνιον ἐν τοῖς οὐρανοῖς)

As in 2 Cor. 5:4, the noun σκῆνος refers to the human body here. Intriguingly, the genitive of the noun "tent" (σκήνους) is added to the noun οἰκία for the expression "earthly house" (οἰκία τοῦ σκήνους) compared with "eternal house in heaven" (οἰκίαν . . . αἰώνιον ἐν τοῖς οὐρανοῖς). The earthly house renders a temporary habitation which is identified as the tent. The Greek noun "οἰκία" occurs here both for the earthly "house" and the eternal "house" but the noun σκῆνος is added as an expositional word for the earthly house so that the phrase "the earthly house" conveys a rather clear meaning for a temporary habitation.

The use of οἰκοδομὴν which contains the same stem with οἰκία for the heavenly house also draws our attention. It clearly denotes the house which is from God in this verse. These observations may indicate that the noun σκῆνος is inserted since the noun οἰκία may cause the reader to misunderstand that it implies a permanent or stable habitation. The comparison between tent and house appears prominent, and the temporary quality of the tent is emphasized. Given these considerations, the noun manifestly conveys the meaning of "temporary habitation" in the Pauline letters.[56]

---

55. All English translations of the Bible, unless otherwise noted, are from the NRSV.

56. Though suggesting the "tent" as the basic meaning of the noun σκηνή, Louw and Nida point out that such a tent was a permanent dwelling in the Old Testament, which indicates that the noun may refer to a permanent habitation in some contexts (Louw and Nida, *Greek-English Lexicon*, 82). It is not clear why Louw and Nida delineate the word as denoting a permanent habitation in the NT. The basic meaning of the noun,

In sum, considering the meaning of σκηνή and its synonym σκῆνος in light of its usage in Luke-Acts and other NT books, it is to be interpreted more probably as "tent" or "temporary dwelling" than a permanent "home" or "habitation" in Luke 16:9.[57]

Eschatological Implications of "(Eternal) Tents?"

In rebuttal to this argument, one could point out that the expression "eternal tents" certainly has "an eschatological connotation, and thus the expression refers to everlasting dwellings which believers enter in the last days."[58] The presence of the following parable of the rich man and Lazarus (Luke 16:19–31) may strengthen this suggestion, since that parable may deal with such eternal habitations. The evidence is not convincing, however.

First, the Septuagint does not support the argument for the presence of the eschatological connotation for the phrase "αἰωνίους σκηνάς." In the LXX, the expression for "eternal habitation" occurs in Eccl 12:5 and Tob 3:6 but does not use the lexemes σκηνή / σκῆνος. The Greek word οἶκος is employed with the adjective αἰώνιος in Tob 3:6 (εἰς οἶκον αἰώνος) and another Greek word τοπός occurs with the adjective in Eccl 12:5 (εἰς τὸν αἰώνιον τόπον).[59] The locution "eternal house" or "eternal place" in these two verses refers to a real and permanent habitation. The noun σκηνή is not used but

---

however, is a "tent" which does not refer to a permanent dwelling even in the OT where οἶκος is used to denote "house." More importantly, whereas it clearly signifies an eternal heavenly dwelling in Hebrews and Revelation, the context of the parable of the unjust steward does not provide any clear reason to interpret the noun as such a permanent place; rather it points to the "tent" in Luke-Acts. Louw and Nida emphasize that the context decides the meaning of the noun, but the context of the parable itself does not suggest its meaning as "permanent dwellings."

57. Its usage in the LXX lends support to this argument, where σκηνή always means a temporal dwelling at least in the Pentateuch and the Prophets in which another noun οἶκος is adopted for the eternal dwelling. Concerning the meanings of these words in the LXX, this study relies on Muraoka, *Greek-English Lexicon*. As mentioned above, the phrase "tabernacle of David" in Amos and Isaiah metaphorically refer to the kingdom of David or Davidic line.

58. Forbes, *The God of Old*, 168. Snodgrass suggests that the parable clearly reveals the eschatological connotation, especially with the expression "with their own generation" (*Stories with Intent*, 724n129).

59. Eccl 12:5: "[W]hen one is afraid of heights, and terrors are in the road; the almond tree blossoms, the grasshopper drags itself along and desire fails; because all must go to their *eternal home*, and the mourners will go about the streets" (NRSV). See also Tob 3:6: "Command, O Lord, that I be released from this distress; release me to go to the *eternal home*, and do not, O Lord, turn your face away from me. For it is better for me to die than to see so much distress in my life and to listen to insults" (NRSV).

other lexemes like οἶκος and τοπός are employed to describe the real eternal dwelling in the Septuagint.

Second, the occurrence of the "eternal habitation" in the later Christian literatures warrants our attention. It appears in 4 Ezra 2:11 LXX which was composed in the third century AD and whose Greek text has not survived.[60] The Latin phrase *tabernacula aeterna* corresponding to the Greek expression αἰώνιοι σκηναί occurs in this verse: "Moreover, I will take back to myself their glory, and will give to these others the *everlasting habitations*, which I (God) had prepared for Israel (et sumam mihi gloriam illorum et dabo eis *tabernacula aeterna*, quae praeparaveram illis).[61] The Latin phrase "tabernacula aeterna" can be translated "everlasting tabernacles" or "eternal habitations."[62] Also, the Greek version αἰώνιοι σκηναί does take place four times in second- to third-century Christian literature and twenty-seven times in fourth-century Christian literature.[63]

These observations lend support to the argument that the locution "eternal tents" can have eschatological connotations. Even though the instances occur in second- to fourth-century AD post-New Testament documents, it reveals how later Christian authors understood the phrase. Noteworthy, however, is the explicit eschatological context of 4 Ezra and other early Christian literature. The author of 4 Ezra, for example, adds an expositional explanation: "which I (God) had prepared for Israel" to the phrase "eternal tabernacles" in 2:11. By contrast, no explanation is attached to a different phrase "celestial kingdoms" (caelestia regna) in the

---

60. Interestingly, Snodgrass suggests the possibility that the phrase in 4 Ezra probably reflects the influence of the Gospel of Luke (*Stories with Intent*, 724n129). His suggestion is possible but not necessarily correct. For details, see below.

61. For the Latin text of 4 Ezra, this study depends on Ralph's edition of the LXX. The ET is from the NRSV.

62. Another instance suggested by scholars is 1 Enoch 39:4 ("There I saw another vision; I saw the habitations and resting places of the saints") in which only the noun for "habitation" occurs. This should not be included for this study since no Greek text remains (only the Ethiopic version includes most parts of 1 Enoch), and more importantly only the noun "habitation" occurs.

63. Of the four occurrences in second- and third-century literature, two instances are the quotation of Luke 16:9 (Clement of Alexandria, *Quis Dives Salvetur* 13.3.2; 31.6.1) and the date of the composition of the book for the other two is uncertain (both in Physiologus). This indicates that the later authors are cautious to interpret the meaning of the phrase. Of twenty-seven instances in fourth-century literature, one-third of which are from John Chrysostom, four instances are the quotation of the Lukan text. The twenty-seven examples are found in Gregory Nyssen (3X), Gregory Nazianzen (1X), Athanasius (2X), Basil (1X), Didymus the Blind (3X), Cyril of Alexandria (2X), Ephrem of Syria (6X), and John Chrysostom (9X). For the above, statistics and citation conventions follow the *TLG*.

same chapter (2:37) which has the virtually the same meaning as "eternal tabernacles."

This phenomenon may indicate that the locution "eternal tabernacles" requires a clarification by the Christian author whereas the expression "celestial kingdom" is clear enough without any explanation. In other words, the author explains the phrase "eternal tents" unusually as a heavenly permanent abode simply because the eschatological context itself demands this meaning. Likewise, early church fathers inserted "God" or other words or phrases which make it clear to the reader that the locution "(eternal) tents" points to real eternal houses.[64] In all these instances, the context manifestly requires that the expression be rendered as "eternal habitations."[65] In short, the locution "eternal tents" itself dose not guarantee the eschatological connotation unless the context itself, or the syntagms which frame the use of the term, demand an eschatological reading. Otherwise, the locution "tent" normally designates something temporary and non-permanent.

The parable of the unjust steward itself does not promote any eschatological atmosphere as scholars assume.[66] The broader context of the parable may supply the eschatological connotation, but the expression αἰωνίους σκηνάς itself does not intrinsically convey eschatological implications in the parable. Evidently, even in the eschatological context, the locution without any exposition provides no evidence for the eschatological connotation. It is less plausible, therefore, that the combination of the two words "eternal tents" itself clearly delivers an eschatological force and indicates "heavenly habitations." Instead, the awkward combination of two words with dialectical meanings—i.e., eternal (αἰώνιοι) vs. temporary (σκηναί)—is the linguistic unit that marks a sense of irony.

---

64. This was the case even for the instances in Hebrews and Revelation where only the noun for "tent" is used.

65. If scholars insist that the phrase itself reveals the eschatological connotation, though the context does not explicitly support such understanding, this may betray "parallelomania." See Sandmel, "Parallelomania," and Kim's critique of anti-imperial readings of Paul in his *Christ and Caesar*, 28–33.

66. Kloppenborg explains that "nothing in the parable evokes an apocalyptic situation" ("The Crisis," 478). See also Crossan, 46; Landry and May, "Honor Restored," 293. Fletcher raises a question about the eschatological understanding suggested by Jeremias ("The Riddle," 18). Greene also posits that the parable itself does not explicitly betray an eschatological component: "Such an eschatological reading of the Parable of the Unjust Steward," Greene concludes, "must depend on a series of assumptions external to the immediate narrative itself" ("Unjust Steward," 86).

The Structure of the Broader Unit Framing the Parable

How does the broader context support the ironical interpretation? How does the interpretation fit in the broader context? The ironical force may be sensed in different ways, depending on who the audience was and how they responded to the parable.

The Audience of the Parable

Luke describes the audience of the parable of the unjust steward as Jesus' disciples in 16:1. Luke begins ch. 15 by narrating that the following parables were a response to the Pharisees' accusation, and then he alters the audience to his disciples in ch.16. As a result, the parable in Luke 16:1–13 seems to be primarily addressed to disciples. The targeted audiences, however, probably include the Pharisees as well as his disciples. Due attention should be also placed on the relationship between 16:1 (where the disciples are addressed) and 16:14 (where the Pharisees respond to Jesus' parable). Below is a table showing the audience structure of Luke 15–16.

Lukan Text	Jesus' Audience in the Narrative World of Luke's Gospel
14:7	Parables Directed toward the Pharisees
15:1	Parables as Response to the Pharisees' Accusation
15:25–32	Jesus' Partial Accusation against the Pharisees in the Parable of the Prodigal Son
16:1	Audience Altered to Jesus' Disciples
16:14	Pharisees' Reaction
16:19–31	Another Audience Change: The Parable of Lazarus and the Rich Man Directed to the Pharisees
16:28–31	Directly against the Pharisees' Disobedience to the Law

It seems that though Jesus' eyes looked at his disciples in 16:1, his teaching was not only overheard by the Pharisees but also directed to them (cf. Luke 11:45 where a similar phenomenon happens).[67] The Pharisees' reaction in

---

67. Bailey suggests a chiastic structure for the central section of the Gospel of Luke (9:51—19:48). Luke 16:1–8, 16, according to his analysis, is paralleled with the passage 12:35–59 where not only his disciples but also the Pharisees are included in the audience, especially in vv. 41–48 and 54–59 (*Poet and Peasant*, 80–81). See also Talbert who finds the chiastic pattern between Luke 16 and 12:1–48 (*Literary Patterns*, 51–55). Cf. Kamlah who observes the close relation between the parable of the unjust steward and the parable of the wise steward in 12:41–48 ("Die Parabel vom Ungerechten Verwalter," 292).

16:14 and the concluding part of the parable of the rich man and Lazarus in 16:28–31 confirm that the primary audience in ch. 15–16 is consistently the Pharisees rather than his disciples, though the disciples are not excluded. Clearly, the Pharisees are not excluded from the audience.[68]

The Pharisees' Ridicule toward Jesus

In this context, the Pharisees' response in 16:14 requires a close investigation. The primary question is: "Why did the Pharisees (described as money-lovers) sneer at Jesus?" The verb for "ridicule," ἐκμυκρίζω, conveys a very strong condemnation, literally "turn up one's nose (toward someone)."[69] In the whole New Testament, the verb appears only here and Luke 23:35 where the rulers ridicule Jesus saying that: "He saved others; let him save himself if he is the Messiah of God, his chosen one!" (NRSV). Intriguingly, Luke adopted a different verb in ch. 23 from the parallel verses in Matt 27:41 and Mark 15:31 where a milder verb ἐμπαίζω denotes "mocking." Its context and Luke's alternation of the verb in ch.23 indicate that the verb conveys a very strong sense of ridicule. Luke could have used the Markan verb ἐμπαίζω in 16:14 which he employed four times in his gospel (Luke 14:29; 22:63; 23:11, 36) or ἐξουθενέω which he adopted three times in Luke-Acts (Luke 18:9, 23:11; Acts 4:11).[70] It is very probable that Luke intended to present a stronger sense of ridicule in the scene of Luke 16:14 by using a harsher word.

The imperfect tense of the verbs in v. 14 also implies the harshness of the Pharisees' response. The tense signifies that the Pharisees were hearing

---

68. See Brown, who notes that 15:1–2 is part of the context for the parables in Luke 16 as well as Luke 15 ("A New Twist?," 139). He admits that the parable is addressed to the Pharisees as well as the disciples (Ibid, 142). Loader also recognizes that the Pharisees are the audience ("Jesus and the Rogue," 530). Bailey claims that "the parable does not fit as a parable spoken only to the disciples, nor does it fit as a parable spoken only to outsiders," which denies that the parable was solely or mainly directed to Jesus' disciples (*Poet and Peasant*, 108).

69. Earle, *Word Meanings*, 249. See also Bock who notes that the verb "indicates strong contempt" (*Luke 9:51—24:53*, 1359). *Contra* Bailey, *Jesus through the Middle Eastern Eyes*, 380, who regards English words like "scoff" or "ridicule" as "too strong." He overlooks, however, that Luke uses the same word in 23:35 where Luke probably altered ἐμπαίζω into this verb to indicate a stronger meaning.

70. Both verbs ἐμπαίζω and ἐξουθενέω have a similar meaning to the verb ἐκμυκρίζω and occur in the New Testament. The former is the most frequently used verb, which means "mock," while the second one signifies the meaning "despise" or "treat with contempt" (cf. BDAG, s.v. ἐμπαίζω, 323; BDAG, s.v. ἐξουθενέω / ἐξουθενόω, 352). It is at least very plausible that Luke intended to present a strong sense of ridicule in this scene by using a very strong verb.

Jesus and kept on sneering at him.[71] The Pharisees did not simply ridicule Jesus once, but also kept on scoffing at him in public. All these considerations demonstrate that the ridicule or sneering of the Pharisees was severe and serious. What then caused the Pharisees, "the lovers of money," to scoff at him seriously and continuously in this scene?

The participial phrase "φιλάργυροι ὑπάρχοντες" may be translated in a causal sense and mean: *because* they were lovers of money, they sneered at Jesus. How can we explain this sentence? The Pharisees sneered at Jesus probably because they perceived the ironical force of the parable.[72] It is hard to understand why they bitterly scoffed at Jesus if the parable presents the lesson described by the traditional view. This is probably why Porter insists that the ironical force of the passage, especially the sentence in v. 13, made the Pharisees ridicule Jesus.[73] Noteworthy is that the Pharisees scoffed at Jesus not only because of the content of v. 13 but also because of the parable's message itself.[74] Their response probably reflects their offense at the ironical force of the parable. At this point, we need to think about the power of Jesus' parables. Most scholars agree that the parable is primarily provocative and polemical rather than irenic or teasing.[75] The parable of the unjust steward, if directed toward the Pharisees, certainly contains the provocative force by the use of irony.[76]

---

71. Robertson understands the first imperfect tense as a progressive one and the second one as inchoative: "the Pharisees had been listening to all this, being fond of money, and they began to sneer at him" (*Luke's Gospel*, 94, 208). While his suggestion is possible, both imperfect's may be understood as progressive. The result is that the inchoative imperfect connotes some duration of the action indicating "began sneering at him."

72. It does not necessarily signify, however, that Jesus tells the parable only sarcastically or vindictively, directed only to the Pharisees. His irony may be also a "teasing kind" (Dawsey, *The Lukan Voice*, 154). Jesus probably intends to make both His disciples change their perspective and the Pharisees to repent. Cf. Booth who notes concerning the use of the irony in Mark that "Mark may in part intend an irony against the original ironists, but surely his chief point is to build, through ironic pathos, a sense of brotherly cohesion among those who see the essential truth" (*A Rhetoric of Irony*, 28).

73. He persuasively argues that the Pharisees ridiculed Jesus since they perceived the ironical force of the sentence in v. 13, which should be a question beginning with οὖν and expecting an affirmative answer ("Unjust Steward," 152–53).

74. The phrase "ταῦτα πάντα" (all these things) clearly indicates that the Pharisees responded to Jesus' sayings in the preceding verses including the parable (cf. Luke 1:65; 18:21; 21:36; 24:9; Acts 7:50).

75. Beavis argues that the purpose of the parable is not polemical but irenic ("Power of Jesus' Parables," 3–30). She also admits, however, that the majority of scholars consider polemic as the primary goal of the parable.

76. It is intriguing to observe that "John uses irony as a critical polemic against the Jewish religious hierarchy" (Hamid-Khani, *Revelation and Concealment*, 83).

Jesus' Instruction to Perform Generous Actions

In this parable, Jesus appears to instruct the audience to do a favor for others in order to receive reciprocation, which appears explicitly in v. 4 and v. 9 ("in order to receive me into their houses" and "in order to receive you into an everlasting tent" respectively).[77] This contradicts Jesus' teaching in Luke since he encourages his disciples to perform giving without expecting return in 6:34–35 and 14:12–14.[78] If the targeted audiences are his disciples, he now recommends his own disciples practice something different from his teaching. In contrast, if the targeted audiences are the Pharisees, he asks them to do something considered to be unattainable by them, but not necessarily contradicting to their practice. One thing becomes clear: Jesus must never have intended for his disciples to take his instructions in v. 9 at face value. Jesus might have given such instructions to the Pharisees in order to scoff back at them and to his disciples to deliver an ironical teaching moment. Considering these factors, the only way to avoid the dilemma is to interpret the exhortation in v. 9 ironically.

Jesus' Use of Irony as a Prophet

The use of irony to criticize the unfaithful Israelites and urge them to repent in the Old Testament prophetic books may provide the background of Jesus' use of irony to warn the Pharisees, who do not faithfully obey God and his words because of their love of money. In the Gospel of Luke, Jesus understands himself as a prophet (4:24; 13:33) and thus the form of his speech was mainly prophetic.[79] The prophets of the Old Testament employ irony not only to criticize unfaithful Israel but also "to accentuate their spiritual dullness."[80]

The spiritual dullness of the Pharisees emerges as a prominent theme in the context of Luke 14–16. The parables in Luke 15 were directed to the Pharisees who did not listen to Jesus and would not repent of their sins. These parables, and the parable of the rich man and Lazarus (16:19–31) aim to urge them to repent. The older son in the parable of the prodigal son (15:25–32) represents the Pharisees who, believing themselves to be

---

77. Shellard, *New Light*, 121.
78. Green, *Gospel of Luke*, 594.
79. Dawsey, *Lukan Voice*, 41, 43. See also Brodie who points out that Jesus is presented as the prophet "more than in other gospels" (*Birthing of the New Testament*, 85).
80. Hamid-Khani, *Revelation and Concealment*, 79.

righteous, did not realize the Father's gracious forgiveness.[81] In the parable of the rich man and Lazarus, the rich man may point to the Pharisees, where the main thrust of the parable is listening and obeying Jesus' words. The "characterization of Jesus as a prophet who will not be received by his own" is emphasized in 16:31.[82]

As many scholars argue, the wise management of the wealth is certainly accentuated in this broader context.[83] Money is presented as the main obstacle to obeying God and Jesus' words in two parables in ch. 16. The spiritual dullness and refusal of Pharisees to hear Jesus is emphasized in the context of Luke 15–16 and thus, the obedience of the Law and the teachable attitude toward Jesus' words constitute the main thrust of the parables in ch. 16.[84] In other words, obedience and repentance mark the core lesson of becoming his disciples against which money could be the main barrier.

CONCLUSION

It becomes evident that a lexical analysis on the usage of the noun σκηνή, and the phrase σκηνή αἰώνιος refreshes the ironical interpretation of the parable of the unjust steward in Luke 16. An ironical element emerges with the careful investigation into the usage of the Greek word σκηνή and the expression σκηνή αἰώνιος. A close look at the Pharisees' reaction in v. 14, especially the Greek verb for "ridicule," i.e., ἐκμυκρίζω also lends support to the ironical interpretation of the parable. Considering the findings of this study, we should interpret the parable of the unjust steward ironically. Illustrating how foolish it is to assume that one could enter the heavenly kingdom by means of the unjust wealth, this parable teaches that one should not rely on earthly wealth, but listen to and obey Jesus' words and serve God

---

81. Brown argues that "the parable presents the grim challenge of rejection and stark choice." The older son in the parable of the prodigal son should make a decision. For details, see his article, "Unjust Steward," 138, 140.

82. Liefeld and Pao, "Luke," 265. See also Jeremias who argues that the parable intends to urge the audience to hear the word of God (*The Parable of Jesus*, 182–87).

83. Fitzmyer, "Dishonest Manager," 20; Green, *Luke*, 589. See also Arndt, who claims that the two parables in ch. 16 deal with "the use of earthly possession" (*St. Luke*, 354). Cf. Bailey who asserts that the subject of the parable of the unjust steward is not "honesty in dealing with money" but rather the same subject as the parable of the prodigal son, i.e., "God, sin, grace and salvation" (*Jesus through Middle Eastern Eyes*, 332).

84. Parrot "Dishonest Steward," 499. He claims that the main thrust of the parable of the unjust steward is "repentance and it should be understood as a contrary example." See also Fletcher who points out that the main thrust of the parable is "a demand for faithfulness and obedience" ("The Riddle," 30).

faithfully to enter eternal houses.[85] Only in this context can the wise use of wealth, like charity, become an important lesson. Having provided this lesson ironically, Jesus next told the parable of the rich man and Lazarus rather straightforwardly promoting the same instruction.

BIBLIOGRAPHY

Arndt, William F. *The Gospel according to St. Luke*. Saint Louis: Concordia, 1956.
Arnott, W. "The Unjust Steward in a New Light." *ExpTim* 24 (1913) 508–11.
Baergen, Rene A. "Servant, Manager, or Slave? Reading the Parable of the Rich Man and His Steward (Luke 16:1–8a) through the Lens of Ancient Slavery." *SR* 35/1(2006) 25–38.
Bailey, Kenneth E. *Jesus through Middle Eastern Eyes: Cultural Studies in the Gospels*. Downers Grove, IL: IVP Academic, 2008.
———. *Poet & Peasant and Through Peasant Eyes: A Literary-Cultural Approach to the Parables in Luke*. Combined ed. Grand Rapids: Eerdmans, 1983.
Beavis, Mary Ann. "The Power of Jesus' Parables: Were They Polemical or Irenic?" *JSNT* 82 (2001) 3–30.
Bindemann, Walter. "Ungerechte als Vorbilder? Gottesreich und Gottesrecht in den Gleichnissen vom 'ungerechten Verwalter' und 'ungerechten Richter.'" *TLZ* 120 (1995) 955–70.
Bock, Darrell L. *Acts*. BECNT 5. Grand Rapids: Baker Academic, 2007.
———. *Luke 9:51—24:53*. BECNT 3B. Grand Rapids: Baker Academic, 1996.
Booth, Wayne C. *A Rhetoric of Irony*. Chicago: University of Chicago Press, 1974.
Bowen, C. E. "The Parable of the Unjust Steward: *Oikos* as the Interpretative Key." *ExpTim* 112 (2001) 314–15.
Bretscher, Paul G. "The Parable of the Unjust Steward: A New Approach to Luke 16:1–9." *CTM* 22 (1951) 756–62.
Brodie, Thomas L. *The Birthing of the New Testament: The Intertextual Development of the New Testament Writings*. New Testament Monographs 1. Sheffield: Sheffield Phoenix Press, 2004.
Brown, Colin. "The Unjust Steward: A New Twist?" In *Worship, Theology and Ministry in the Early Church: Essays in Honor of Ralph P. Martin*, ed. M. J. Wilkins and T. Paige. JSNTSup 87. Sheffield: JSOT Press, 1992.
Dawsey, James M. *The Lukan Voice: Confusion and Irony in the Gospel of Luke*. Macon, GA: Mercer University Press, 1986.
Derrett, J. Duncan M. "Fresh Light on St. Luke xvi.1: The Parable of the Unjust Steward." *NTS* 7 (1960–1961) 198–219.
deSilva, David A. "The Parable of the Prudent Steward and Its Lucan Context." *CTR* 6, no. 2 (1993) 255–68.

---

85. The sayings in vv. 10–11 are also interpreted ironically: "If you have not been faithful in the unrighteous mammon, who will commit to your trust the true *riches*?" This means: "if you are unfaithful with the unrighteous mammon, do you really believe that someone will commit to your trust true riches?" Verse 13 is the conclusion of the parable: no man can serve both God and Mammon. The parable is aimed at the Pharisees. Because they believed in Mammon, they sneered at him.

Dormandy, Richard. "Unjust Steward or Converted Master?" *RB* 109, no. 4 (2002) 512–27.
Earle, Ralph. *Word Meanings in the New Testament*. Vol. 1: *Matthew, Mark and Luke*. Grand Rapids: Baker, 1980.
Evans, Craig A. *Luke*. NIBC 3. Peabody, MA: Hendrickson, 1990.
Fitzmyer, Joseph A. *The Gospel According to Luke X–XXIIII: Introduction, Translation, and Notes*. AB 28a. Garden City, NY: Doubleday, 1985.
———. "The Story of the Dishonest Manager (Lk 16:1–13)." *TS* 25 (1964) 23–45.
Fletcher, D. R. "The Riddle of the Unjust Steward: Is Irony the Key?" *JBL* 82 (1963) 15–30.
Forbes, Greg W. *The God of Old: The Role of the Lukan Parables in the Purpose of Luke's Gospel*. Sheffield: Sheffield Academic, 2000.
Gagnon, Robert A. J. "A Second Look at Two Lukan Parables: Reflections on the Unjust Steward and the Good Samaritan." *Horizon in Biblical Theology* 20 (1998) 1–11.
Green, Joel B. *The Gospel of Luke*. NICNT. Grand Rapids: Eerdmans, 1997.
Greene, M. Dwaine. "The Parable of the Unjust Steward As Question and Challenge." *ExpTim* 112, no. 3 (2000) 82–87.
Hamid-Khani, Saeed. *Revelation and Concealment of Christ: A Theological Inquiry into the Elusive Language of the Fourth Gospel*. Tübingen: Mohr/Siebeck, 2000.
Hedrick, Charles W. *Parables as Poetic Fictions: The Creative Voice of Jesus*. Peabody, MA: Hendrickson, 1994. Reprint, Eugene, OR: Wipf & Stock, 2005.
Ireland, Dennis J. *Stewardship and the Kingdom of God: A Historical, Exegetical Study of the Parable of the Unjust Steward in Luke 16:1–13*. NovTSup 70. Leiden: Brill, 1992.
Jeremias, J. *The Parables of Jesus*. Trans. S. H. Hooke. Philadelphia: Westminster, 1963.
Johnson, Luke Timothy. *The Acts of the Apostles*. SP 5. Collegeville, MN: Liturgical, 1992.
Jung, Chang Wook. "Reexamination of the Ironical Interpretation of the Parable of the Unjust Steward in Luke 16." *Korean Evangelical New Testament Studies* 11, no. 4 (2012) 793–828.
Kamlah, E. "Die Parabel vom Ungerechten Verwalter (Luk 16,1ff.) im Rahmen der Knechtsgleichnisse." In *Abraham unser Vater: Juden und Christen in Gespräch über die Bibel*, ed. Otto Betz et al., 276–94. Leiden: Brill, 1963.
Kim, Seyoon. *Christ and Caesar: The Gospel and Roman Empire in the Writings of Paul and Luke*. Grand Rapids: Eerdmans, 2008.
Kloppenborg, John S. "The Dishonoured Master (Luke 16:1–8a)." *Bib* 70 (1989) 474–95.
Landry, David and Ben May. "Honor Restored: New Light on the Parable of the Prudent Steward (Luke 16:1–8a)." *JBL* 119 (2000) 287–309.
Liefeld, Walter L. and David Pao. "Luke." In *The Expositor's Bible Commentary*, ed. T. Longman III and D. E. Garland, 10:9–355. Rev. ed. Grand Rapids: Zondervan, 2007.
Loader, William. "Jesus and the Rogue in Luke 16,1–8A: The Parable of the Unjust Steward." *RB* 96 (1989) 518–32.
Louw, J. P. and E. A. Nida. *Greek-English Lexicon of the New Testament: Based on Semantic Domains*. 2 vols. New York: United Bible Societies, 1988–1989.
Marshall, I. Howard. *The Gospel of Luke: A Commentary on the Greek Text*. NIGTC 3. Grand Rapids: Eerdmans, 1978.

Mathewson, Dave L. T. "The Parable of the Unjust Steward (Luke 16:1–13): A Reexamination of the Traditional View in Light of Recent Challenges." *JETS* 38 (1995) 29–39.

McFayden, J. F. "The Parable of the Unjust Steward." *ExpTim* 37 (1925–1926) 535–39.

Muraoka, T. *A Greek-English Lexicon of the Septuagint: Chiefly of the Pentateuch and the Twelve Prophets.* Louvain: Peeters, 2002.

Nolland, John. *Luke 9:21—18:34.* WBC 35B. Dallas: Word Books, 1993.

Parrott, D. M. "The Dishonest Steward (Luke 16.1–8a) and Luke's Special Parable Collection." *NTS* 37 (1991) 499–515.

Porter, Stanley E. "The Parable of the Unjust Steward (Luke 16:1–13): Irony *is* the Key." In *The Bible in Three Dimensions: Essays in Celebration of Forty Years of Biblical Studies in the University of Sheffield*, ed. D. J. A. Clines et al., 127–53. Sheffield: JSOT Press, 1990.

Robertson, A. T. *A Translation of Luke's Gospel: With Grammatical Notes.* New York: Doran, 1923.

Sandmel, Samuel "Parallelomania." *JBL* 81 (1962) 1–13.

Schellenberg, Ryan S. "Which Master? Whose Steward? Metalepsis and Lordship in the Parable of the Prudent Steward (Lk 16.1–13)." *JSNT* 30 (2008) 263–88.

Shellard, Barbara. *New Light on Luke: Its Purpose, Sources and Literary Context.* Sheffield: Sheffield Academic, 2002.

Snodgrass, Klyne *Stories with Intent: A Comprehensive Guide to the Parables of Jesus.* Grand Rapids: Eerdmans, 2008.

Stein, Robert H. *Luke.* NAC 24. Nashville: Broadman & Holman, 1992.

Steyn, Gert J. *Septuagint Quotations in the Context of the Petrine and Pauline Speeches of the Acta Apostolorum.* Kampen: Kok Pharos, 1995.

Strauss, Mark L. *The Davidic Messiah in Luke-Acts: The Promise and Its Fulfillment in Lukan Christology.* Sheffield: Sheffield Academic, 1995.

Talbert, Charles H. *Literary Patterns, Theological Themes and the Genre of Luke-Acts.* SBLMS 20. Missoula: Scholars, 1975.

Topel, L. John. "On the Injustice of the Unjust Steward: Lk 16:1–13." *CBQ* 37 (1975) 216–27.

Upkong, Justin S. "The Parable of the Shrewd Manager (Lk 16:1–13): An Essay in Inculturation Biblical Hermeneutic." *Semeia* 73 (1996) 189–210.

Williams, Francis E. "Is Almsgiving the Point of the 'Unjust Steward'?" *JBL* 83 (1964) 293–97.

Wolter, Michael. *Das Lukasevangelium.* HNT 5. Tübingen: Mohr/Siebeck, 2008.

Young, Brad H. *The Parables: Jewish Tradition and Christian Interpretation.* Peabody, MA: Hendrickson, 1998.

10

Forgiveness, Faith, and the Lordship of Jesus

A Contextual Reading of Luke 17:1–10[1]

YON-GYONG KWON

INTRODUCTION

The present text, Luke 17:1–10, does not usually receive as much attention from commentators as it deserves.[2] There are, however, strong reasons to believe that it commends itself as a very interesting, indeed highly significant, collection of sayings of Jesus where the nature of Christian life, characterized by unconditional forgiveness (vv. 3–4), is explained in terms of eschatology (vv. 1–2), faith (vv. 5–6), and the disciples' relationship with the Lord (vv. 7–10). It may not be possible to say that the whole passage is distinctively Lukan, since much of what we have in our text also occurs in Mark and Matthew. But a change in context can generate a fresh shade

---

1. This essay first appeared in *Korea Evangelical New Testament Studies* (2012). I am grateful to the editors of *KENTS* for permission to reprint this essay here in a revised form.

2. Bibliographies in most commentaries easily show the relative lack of interest in our passage.

of meaning out of the same tradition, or at least, a new way of applying it to the life of its hearers. Bringing out the unique perspective of Luke will be the main focus of the present study. What is offered here is a *contextual* reading of Luke 17:1–10 as a whole, a text usually taken to be a collection of three disparate and mutually unrelated sayings, with a view to find the logic which runs through the whole passage.

CONTEXT AND REDACTIONAL CONSIDERATIONS

As it now stands, Luke 17:1–10 comes as part of a larger sayings section which commences at 15:1: "Now all the tax-collectors and sinners were coming near to listen to him,"[3] and continues until the last phase of the Travel Narrative (19:27). In this extensive collection Luke introduces such significant themes as the repentance and restoration of the lost (repeated 3X in the form of memorable parables; ch. 15), the accountability of the disciples and the need for faithfulness (16:1–14), single-minded service to God over against the love of money (addressed chiefly to the Pharisees; 16:15–18), and the importance of compassion (16:19–31). The passage under study is also placed right before the explicitly eschatological sayings concerning the Kingdom of God which is also addressed to the Pharisees (17:20–21), and the coming day of the Son of Man, which is addressed to the disciples (17:22–37).

Concerning Luke 17:1–3a, though Mark also contains part of the section (i.e., the "millstone" saying in Mark 9:42), the somewhat unusual coming of the σκάνδαλον (Matthew) or σκάνδαλα (Luke) which Matthew and Luke share (Matt 18:6–7 // Luke 17:1) over against Mark strongly suggests that it probably comes from Q. Among the two, it seems that Luke has appended his own introduction: Εἶπεν δὲ πρὸς τοὺς μαθητὰς αὐτοῦ to his source and omitted οὐαὶ τῷ κόσμῳ ἀπὸ τῶν σκανδάλων found in Matthew (18:7), probably to make the saying more focused on the disciples.

The next section about the need for forgiveness (vv. 3–4) also seems to be based on Q. Here, while Matthew introduces the saying as part of a rather detailed manual for Christian conduct in the church (Matt 18:15, 21–22), Luke focuses more faithfully on the original theme of forgiveness itself. The disciples' response in v. 5 is a Lukan addition, which serves to bridge the preceding words about forgiveness to the following lesson on faith. It also has the effect of turning Jesus' saying in v. 6 into a corrective to their (mis) conception about faith. The redactional background of v. 6 is not at all clear.

---

3. Here the NIV 2011. Unless otherwise noted, all English translations of the Bible are the author's own. Cf. Nolland (*Luke*, 835) who sees a new setting at 16:1.

The reference to "a mustard seed" at least indicates the influence of Q.[4] The next saying about "the unprofitable servant" (vv. 7–10) is Lukan, and has no parallel in the other gospels. It will be argued in the following that this saying is appended as a further explication of the nature of faith, and thus it does reveal an intrinsic connection to the preceding sayings.

ΣΚΑΝΔΑΛΟΝ: INEVITABLE AND TRAGIC (LUKE 17:1–2)

The first saying begins with Luke's own introductory formula: Εἶπεν δὲ πρὸς τοὺς μαθητὰς αὐτοῦ (v. 1), which makes the words explicitly addressed to the disciples. The conjunction δέ indicates a transition of thought.[5] This formula, distinct from other sayings addressed either to the general audience or to Jesus' adversaries, usually introduces more specifically Christian and practical lessons for the followers of Jesus.[6] It is uncertain whether τοὺς μαθητὰς αὐτοῦ refers to the Twelve, as is implied by "the apostles" in v. 5, or more generally to all the followers of Jesus as indicated by "all the sinners and tax-collectors" in 15:1, which provides the broader setting for the present saying. In either case, it seems probable that the apostles function as the main actors in the scene while the teaching itself is directed to all disciples of Jesus.

The actual teaching of Jesus begins with the statement: ἀνένδεκτόν ἐστιν τοῦ τὰ σκάνδαλα μὴ ἐλθεῖν. The construction, a definite article in the genitive (τοῦ) and an infinitive (ἐλθεῖν), is quite frequent in Luke and used here substantivally as the subject of the preceding ἀνένδεκτόν ἐστιν.[7] Thus, with a negative particle μή in it, the phrase translates as "for τὰ σκάνδαλα not to come." The verb ἔρχομαι, coupled with τὰ σκάνδαλα, carries an eschatological note. Apart from cases of its regular unmarked usage (e.g., the coming of people, the devil, rain/cloud, or time), the word ἔρχομαι is almost exclusively applied to the coming of the eschatological entities, such as the coming of the Kingdom (11:2; 22:27), the end-day (23:29), the new age (18:30), or salvation (19:10), which is, of course, ultimately grounded on the coming of Jesus (3:16; 7:20; 19:38; cf. 4:43; 19:10). The same eschatological thrust

---

4. Marshall suggests that here Matthew has been assimilated to Mark by substituting "mountain" for "tree." See his *The Gospel of Luke*, 643.

5. BDAG, s.v. δέ, 213.

6. For example, see Luke 9:43; 17:22; 18:31 where the formula introduces his passion predictions, and 6:20; 10:23; 12:1; 12:22; 16:1 in which it introduces various themes related to discipleship.

7. See, e.g., 1:57; 2:6; 4:42; 10:19; Zerwick, *Biblical Greek*, 133.

also seems to be present in the rather unusual combination: the "coming" of τὰ σκάνδαλα. If this is the case, we can further infer that ἀνένδεκτον, which usually means "impossible," goes beyond mere inescapability. Rather, it approaches the idea of divine necessity, an idea deeply imbedded in Luke's understanding of history.[8] The effect is that τὰ σκάνδαλα, whatever it may refer to, is bound to come as part of the eschatological divine-human drama of the coming of Jesus.

This eschatological drama provides the framework for the sayings that follow. More specifically, it means that both τὰ σκάνδαλα and forgiveness, things that happen in the community of disciples, are essentially eschatological nature in that they will have eternal consequences on those individuals involved. This text also reveals an important aspect of Lucan perspective, i.e., that the everyday life of the disciples cannot be separated from the broader, eschatological dimension of history. In addition, this eschatological thrust of the sayings may explain, at least in part, why they are placed here before the teachings concerning the Day of the Son of Man which are more explicitly eschatological (vv. 20–37).

Given the eschatological tenor of the saying, what then is the precise meaning of τὰ σκάνδαλα? Its cognate σκανδαλίσῃ also occurs as a transitive verb in v. 2, but without any sign of change in its meaning. The customary meaning given by the commentators is: "causing somebody to sin" in the sense that a person causes another to sin and thereby falls away from one's relationship with God.[9] From its uses in LXX as "trap," "snare" (Ps 68:22; Josh 23:13), "something over which one could stumble" (Ps 140:5), or from such meanings as "to lead to sin or apostasy" (*Pss. Sol.* 16.7; Wis 14:11), the typical rendering seems quite legitimate. If so, then, the next saying on forgiveness (vv. 3–4) becomes a kind of "follow-up lesson" for the case of

---

8. Luke is well known for his frequent use of δεῖ to communicate the idea that God is in charge of all things in history; see, e.g., Luke 4:43; 21:9; Acts 1:16; 3:21; 4:12. We may say that here ἀνένδεκτον is something of a functional equivalent of δεῖ. Matthew conveys the idea with ἀνάγκη (18:7).

9. Evans, *Saint Luke*, 619; Marshall, *The Gospel of Luke*, 640; Johnson, *The Gospel of Luke*, 258; Fitzmyer, *The Gospel according to Luke*, 1137. Bovon (*Das Evangelium nach Lukas*, 138) interprets the whole text in an ecclesial context, and takes the phrase in a "Pauline" way to mean an officeholder's misbehavior which causes others to sin in the sense that they, on seeing such a σκάνδαλον, either ignore it or begin to doubt God's power or pass judgment on their neighbor with excessive rage. One wonders, however, why Jesus would warn against such misbehavior indirectly (Does such misbehavior not count as problematic, as long as no one sees it?). The subject matter of Paul's discussion is not "misbehavior" but an action which is perfectly permissible in itself but becomes problematic in specific situations (1 Cor 8:1–13). It would also be odd to suppose that such a misconduct causes a σκάνδαλον only for "one of these little ones" rather than the church as a whole.

such an inescapable σκάνδαλον, if we are to find any connection between the two at all.[10]

The problem of this interpretation, however, is that the notion of causing someone to sin or to fall from God does not sit comfortably with the major theological concern of Luke-Acts. A survey of Luke-Acts provides quite substantial ground for a different, even opposite, understanding of the term σκάνδαλον. First, in Luke-Acts, we do not see much interest in the idea of "turning away from God." Luke's interest lies rather in the opposite movement, namely, the idea of "turning from the state of sinfulness to the merciful God," which he calls "repentance." A quick survey of Luke shows the following cases: John's preparation for the Lord is to call people unto repentance (Luke 3:3; Acts 13:24; 19:4); Jesus came to seek the lost and call them to repentance (Luke 5:32; Acts 5:31) which is open even to the Gentiles (Acts 11:18); this generation will be judged because of their unrepentant attitude (Luke 10:13; 11:32; 13:3, 5); there will be joy in heaven over those who return with repentance (Luke 15:7, 10); repentance is central to apostolic preaching (Acts 2:38; 8:22; 17:30; 26:20).

Closely related to this motif is the concept of hindrances or barriers to this repentance. For example, the theme of repentance and restoration receives an unusual emphasis in the three well-known Lucan parables: the lost sheep (vv. 3–7); the lost coin (vv. 8–10); and the lost son (vv. 11–32). The common emphasis of all three parables is the necessity of joyful acceptance of the lost ones who repent (vv. 7, 10, 34, 32), a theme considerably expanded and more poignantly expressed in the third parable. Here we notice the presence of "hindrances" to Jesus' work of restoring the lost. This discourse on hindrances functions as a polemic against the complaining Pharisees who do not like Jesus' work of welcoming the "sinner and the tax collectors" (15:1; also 5:31–32) due to their attitude of self-righteousness (18:9–14). They are those who try to prevent "the lost ones" from coming to God through repentance. They are "stumbling blocks" on the sinners' way back to God, hindering God's work of restoration through Jesus. Within this broad *theological* context, an extended meaning of σκάνδαλον in this particular logion is: "preventing someone from returning to God through repentance."

---

10. Most commentators regard vv. 1–2 and vv. 3–4 as two distinct sayings; see Evans, *Saint Luke*, 618; Johnson, *The Gospel of Luke*, 261; Marshall, The Gospel of Luke, 641. Even Bovon (*Das Evangelium nach Lukas*, 138) finds the transition from vv. 1–3a to vv. 3b–4 "abrupt." He thinks that both parts have the responsibility of an officeholder as a common theme. The position taken in the present study is to consider the whole of vv. 1–4 as a single *logion*, which is, in turn, closely related to the following vv. 5–10.

Second, this σκάνδαλον is so serious that the one who causes it cannot escape Jesus' condemnation. In other places, Luke tells us that the hypocritical exclusivism of Jewish religious leaders is severely criticized and condemned by Jesus as an act of hindering others from entering the Kingdom (11:46; 11:52). They receive the same judgment as those who cause σκάνδαλον: "Woe to you scribes!" Here, what Jesus condemns is not the act of causing somebody to sin or fall away from God, but the act of keeping a person from entering the Kingdom through repentance. Their judgment is inevitable, because this is in outright opposition to what God is doing through Jesus (cf. 5:21; 6:7; 7:39, 49; 13:14; 14:1–6; 19:7). Since it is so serious a sin, even the disciples need to be frequently warned against such danger (9:49–50; 18:15–16).

Third, there is a special concern against "stumbling these little ones" (σκανδαλίζειν τῶν μικρῶν τούτων ἕνα; v. 2). The phrase "these little ones" clearly refers to the people present at the scene, and in this particular context, the best choice seems to be "the sinners and the tax-collectors" who are there to hear Jesus teach alongside with the disciples, the Pharisees, and the scribes (15:1).[11]

Since the idea of "causing the sinner to fall away from God" does not make much sense within the Lukan theological perspective, a much better option is to consider them as those who, having already fallen from God, need to return to him in repentance. Then, scandalizing these sinners most likely refers to the act of making them stumble in such a way that they cannot be restored to God, the kind of behavior which the Pharisees and the scribes are apt to do (15:1). Based on these considerations, we can safely conclude that in this particular context "causing someone to stumble" primarily means "preventing someone from coming to God in repentance."[12]

This understanding of the saying makes a nice connection with the following saying about the need to forgive those who are repentant. Refusing to forgive the one who says "I repent," is to prevent him or her from being fully restored to the right relationship with God. Such actions constitute a σκάνδαλον. This must not happen in the community of disciples since such

11. Since 15:1, where a new setting begins, we do not have any definite mark for a different setting until 17:11 where Jesus resumes his journey. My view receives further support from the fact that other synoptic gospels have "to believe" at the end of "these little ones," while Luke omits it. Nolland (*Luke*, 837) renders it more generally "the weak, the lowly, the vulnerable" but does not ask further who these people would be *in the context of the Gospel*.

12. Much closer to our interpretation is Green (*The Gospel of Luke*, 612), who sums up Jesus' demand as "Do not act like the Pharisees" and renders the σκάνδαλον as "the injustice and indifference of inhospitality on behalf of those in need." So Jesus' warning is also one "against dispositions that obstruct the restoration of sinners to community."

an attitude stands as an outright challenge to the mission of Jesus who has come "to call not the righteous but sinners to repentance" (5:32). To the one who is repentant, then, forgiveness is to be extended whole-heartedly.

The coming of Jesus inevitably divides the world into two distinct groups of people: those who proclaim and accept the message of repentance vs. those who refuse and cause others to refuse it (11:52!). Thus, as it is impossible for Jesus not to come, it is also impossible (ἀνένδεκτον) for the tragedy of this σκάνδαλον not to come. Within a Lukan perspective, the inevitability of such tragic incidents can ultimately be traced back to God's sovereign plan. That does not mean, however, that those who cause it to happen are exempt from their guilt. Necessary as it may be, through the divine and mysterious "but" (πλήν),[13] they still have to bear the dire consequences of their misconduct (22:22; Acts 2:23, 38). This receives a more detailed explication in the following verse.

The comparative construction of v. 2: λυσιτελεῖ . . . ἤ, together with the emphatic ἕνα, implies that the statement is not a description of actual judgment, but a rhetorical way of accentuating the seriousness of the judgment for those who cause the σκάνδαλον.[14] The thought of a millstone hanging around the neck refers to weighing down a person so that he or she may not overcome its weight.[15] Thus, drowning (ἔρριπται) into the sea in that way means nothing less than a complete destruction of the person. Still, even such a terrible consequence is better (λυσιτελεῖ) than the woe (οὐαί) which falls upon the one who causes the σκάνδαλον among "one of these little ones." What is more serious than complete destruction? How dreadful then is it to cause a σκάνδαλον!

Beyond the *gravitas* of the situation, we can even detect a note of absoluteness which emerges from comparing it with the incomparable. So the effect of the saying is a strong warning that the disciples should make every effort to avoid σκάνδαλον, the force of which is also reflected in the following admonition: προσέχετε ἑαυτοῖς.[16] We, in fact, see that this absoluteness is one of the threads which run through all of the three sayings: absolutely

---

13. Some manuscripts (A, W, etc.) omit the word, but it is to be read as original.

14. Cf. Marshall's interpretation (*The Gospel of Luke*, 641), who states: "So fearful is the judgment that it would be better for a man to die before he can act as a stumbling block," which is very strange and unacceptable. If he were right, the result would be that every single one of the community would have to die, for the possibility is open to every one of Jesus' disciples. See also Evans, *Saint Luke*, 619–20. The idea expressed here is not death as a way of escaping the occasion but as a complete judgment.

15. See Marshall (*The Gospel of Luke*, 641) who points out some relevant parallels: Jer 51:63; Josephus, *Ag. Ap.* 1.307.

16. Similar warnings are frequently found in New Testament: σκοπῶν σεαυτόν, μὴ καὶ σὺ πειρασθῇς (Gal 6:1); "Ὥστε ὁ δοκῶν ἑστάναι βλεπέτω μὴ πέσῃ (1 Cor 10:12).

unconditional forgiveness (vv. 3–4), the absolute effectiveness of faith (vv. 5–6), and the absolute commitment required of the servant (7–10).

The construction: ἵνα σκανδαλίσῃ τῶν μικρῶν τούτων ἕνα at the end of v. 2 (ἵνα + an aorist subjunctive), unlike its typical usage to denote purpose or result, is employed here substantivally to denote content.[17] So it reads: "[better than] that he should cause one of these little ones stumble." Again, this does not refer to causing a little one to fall away from his / her initially healthy relationship with God, but to keeping him / her from being fully restored to God by refusing to grant the person the unconditional forgiveness which God himself offers.

It is also noteworthy that Luke here replaces the eschatologically-loaded word "coming" or arrival of the σκάνδαλον in v. 1 by a functionally identical, yet more practically oriented, verbal phrase: "causing one of these little ones to stumble." He thereby prepares the following lesson in which he provides his readers with more specific instructions for avoiding the σκάνδαλον. Luke makes a similar connection with προσέχετε ἑαυτοῖς ("be careful for yourselves") in v. 3. The basic meaning of the phrase, which is found in other cases of the same expression (21:34; Acts 20:28), is "to maintain a certain attitude or behavior" appropriate for the disciples or ministers, such as persevering in faithful prayer in eager anticipation of the *parousia*.[18] Thus, this phrase not only reinforces the gravity of the matter just expressed (vv. 1–2) but also makes the disciples (or, readers) more attentive to the following directive (vv. 3–4). So, the effect of this phrase seems to be something like this: "Listen carefully to what I am telling you, if you want to avoid the σκάνδαλον, of which the consequences are simply fatal."[19]

UNLIMITED FORGIVENESS (LUKE 17:3-4)

The teaching given in Luke 17:3–4 does not pose any serious interpretive problems: repentance should be met by immediate forgiveness. Here ὁ ἀδελφός means the brothers and sisters in the community of believers as in Luke 6:41, 42; 22:32.[20] Ἐὰν ἁμάρτῃ ὁ ἀδελφός σου, as is clear from the

---

17. Moule, *An Idiom Book of New Testament Greek*, 145. Another similar example is found in 1:43.

18. In four places in Acts, the word is used without a reflexive pronoun to mean "to obey" or "to follow" (8:6, 10, 11; 16:14). These examples confirm that the sense of "actual practice" in contradistinction to "mere inner posture" is certainly present in the phrase, albeit not explicitly.

19. Thus, the question whether the phrase belongs to the preceding saying or to the following is in fact missing the point. See also Evans, *Saint Luke*, 620.

20. In Acts, the term is more widely used to denote "fellow Israelites." This usage,

εἰς σέ in v. 4,[21] refers to the act of sinning against a fellow believer, with the construction (ἐάν+ aorist subjunctive) denoting a future possibility: "From now on, if your brother sins. . ." Luke's view of sin is not easy to formulate, since he tends to refrain himself from referring to it explicitly, even though he definitely acknowledges its reality and seriousness. The only other occurrence of the verb ἁμαρτάνειν in Luke's Gospel is found in the parable of the prodigal son where the remorseful son twice says that he has "sinned against the heaven and against you" (15:18, 21).[22]

What is interesting here is that the son's sin is not only regarded as sinning against his father, but also against "the heaven," namely God. If this is really what Luke thinks of the nature of sin, there is no reason why we should not interpret sin in Luke 17 in the same way.[23] Perhaps this is the reason why Luke can simply say "if your brother sins" even when he means "if your brother sins against you." This perception points to another dimension of the Christian life, namely, the disciples' relation with the heavenly God, which is in fact closely related to their relationship with one another. We may say that this idea is already present in the strong eschatological thrust of vv. 1–2. The sinning and forgiving among the community is not just a matter of mundane everyday life. Rather, it also touches upon their relationship with God, and thus becomes "a present process with an eschatological effect."[24]

If a brother or sister sins against another, the first responsibility of the wronged is to rebuke the wrong-doer (ἐπιτίμησον αὐτῷ; v. 3). The word ἐπιτιμῶν, in this context, means: "to rebuke or warn the one who has sinned in order to prevent an action or bring one to an end."[25] Thus, just as we see in Lev 19:17, such a rebuke is a necessary for guiding the sinner to repentance. Rebuke is thus legitimate in so far as it is used in this way. But criticizing others with no intention of restoring them, namely, the uncompassionate act

---

however, is not found in Luke's Gospel. The present saying is explicitly directed to the disciples of Jesus.

21. Ἐἰς σέ in v. 3 is a later addition, most likely the result of an attempt to harmonize the phrase with v. 4. See Metzger, *A Textual Commentary on the Greek New Testament*, 141.

22. Luke's conspicuous silence about the nature of sinning is striking. The noun ἁμαρτία occurs 19X in Luke-Acts and, very significantly, always in conjunction with "forgiveness," except in 4:18, which is a quotation from Isaiah. Luke never talks about sin for its own sake, but always to point out the new gift of forgiveness. The same goes for the present passage, too.

23. This generalization can be justified by the fact that the parable is designed to show the nature of sin, repentance, and God's joyful response of forgiveness.

24. Stählin, "σκάνδαλον, κτλ.," 351.

25. BDAG, s.v. ἐπιτιμάω, 384.

of passing judgment upon others or defaming them, is not for the disciples to practice (6:37). This focus on repentance and restoration is also detected clearly from the swift movement of thought from rebuke to forgiveness in 17:3, as well as from the absence of the former in the next verse (17:4) where the subject remains the same. Thus, we see that Luke's primary interest does not lie in rebuke itself, but in the repentance and forgiveness such a rebuke would hopefully accomplish.[26]

The second part of v. 3 expresses the kind of result which should be happening in the disciples' community: καὶ ἐὰν μετανοήσῃ ἄφες αὐτῷ. Here καί is to be taken consequentially to mean "and then,"[27] that is, "as the result of your rebuking," or "as you had intended." In fact, the expected result is quite obvious: "and, as the result of your rebuking, if he repents, forgive him." Unlike in our many real-life situations, Luke here does not show any concern at all about the possibility of the person's not repenting. Neither is he concerned about examining the genuineness of that person's repentance. Jesus' point here is straightforward, leaving the disciples with no other choice. "If he repents, then, you, who are my disciples, have no other choice but to forgive him."

The force of Jesus' command is further explicated in the following verse (v. 4). This verse is led by another καί which seems to have the meaning of "in other words" or "what I am saying is." Here, compared to the preceding v. 3, the act of sinning and especially repenting is more specifically described. Concerning the sinning part, Luke, while deleting the obvious subject, ὁ ἀδελφός σου, adds instead: ἑπτάκις τῆς ἡμέρας and εἰς σέ. The genitive here is that of time, and the phrase means "seven times within the period of a day," which may be rendered more naturally, "seven times a day." The addition of εἰς σέ specifies the situation as one between two disciples, and that corresponds nicely to πρὸς σέ in the next part. The simple μετανοήσῃ in the preceding verse is now expanded as ἐπιστρέψῃ πρὸς σὲ λέγων μετανοῶ to which an emphatic ἑπτάκις is also appended: "seven times [he] returns to you and says: 'I repent'. . . ." As Marshall points out, the phrase "and says: 'I repent'" does not need to imply the superficiality of repentance.[28] Rather it serves as a warning that it is not the offended person's role to investigate

---

26. In contrast to this, the Matthean parallel (18:15) puts more emphasis on the responsibility of the offender to listen to the rebuke by the offended, and also, naturally, more on the act of rebuking itself. Luke seems to better reflect the atmosphere of Leviticus where the act of rebuke is viewed within the larger context of loving one's neighbor. Paul's admonition that one should "restore" the offender "in a spirit of gentleness" also conveys the same idea (Gal 6:1).

27. BDAG, s.v. καί, 495.

28. Marshall, *The Gospel of Luke*, 643.

whether the other's repentance is genuine or not. The implication is: "If he says: 'I repent,' that should be enough for you. Do not try to play the judge by trying to test the genuineness of his repentance. Your job is to simply forgive him."[29]

Now the sinning and repentance, which constitutes two separate conditions in v. 3 (ἐὰν ἁμάρτῃ ὁ ἀδελφός σου ἐπιτίμησον αὐτῷ; and καὶ ἐὰν μετανοήσῃ) are combined into a single protasis in v. 4: ἐὰν ... ἁμαρτήσῃ ... ἐπιστρέψῃ. And the disciples are commanded to offer forgiveness: ἀφήσεις αὐτῷ. The future indicative, "you will forgive," clearly used as a command, seems to imply the idea that once repentance is made, forgiveness should be a matter of course, thereby carrying a much stronger force than a simple imperative. Here the use of ἑπτάκις, implying the idea of "boundlessness," or "totality,"[30] renders this command still stronger or even absolute. The force of this interpretation may seem somewhat mitigated by its use in Matthew where it is Peter who suggests "seven times" only to be corrected by Jesus, "seventy-seven times" (18:22). But Luke retains the note of absoluteness by adding τῆς ἡμέρας, that is, "seven times *within a single day*." So the point Jesus wants to make here is: "Even if your brother offends you as many times as seven within a single day, that is, however many times he sins against you, it makes no difference. As soon as he says, 'I repent,' you just have to forgive him." As Bovon puts it, "Die zentrale Idee dabei ist natürlich, daß der Vergebung keine Grenzen gesetzt sind."[31]

Within the community of disciples, the importance of this injunction can hardly be overemphasized since the dynamic of repentance and forgiveness is precisely the summary of what God is doing through Christ, as we have noted above. The significance of this command would then be that this activity of God through Jesus is now being extended to the life of his followers. As the two commission stories indicate, the disciples are those who are called to carry on the same kind of activity which Jesus himself does (9:1–6; 10:1–21). The ground of their ministry as Jesus' disciples, in turn, lies in the fact that their sin has been forgiven and they are now fully restored to a right relationship with God. This right relationship is clearly indicated by both the calling and the commissioning stories (5:8–10; 10:20).

---

29. This reminds us of the younger son in the third parable of Luke 15 whose return to his father is more motivated by his desire to escape from his dire predicament than by his sense of wrongdoing (15:17). His father, of course, has no intention of investigating into the genuineness of his repentance, a fact indicated by his cutting the rehearsed confession of the son short.

30. Fitzmyer, *The Gospel according to Luke*, 1140. The symbolic sacredness of the number seven is particularly important in Revelation.

31. Bovon, *Das Evangelium nach Lukas*, 139.

The absolute nature of Jesus' command becomes evident: the disciples are those who, grounded on the forgiveness of their own sin by God, are now sent to call other people into repentance and forgiveness. So they are instructed by their "Lord" to pray: "And forgive us our sins, for *we ourselves* forgive *everyone* indebted to us" (11:4). Likewise, the converse is true: refusing to extend God's forgiveness toward other members of the community means refusing to do the very mission they have been called to do. Such behavior amounts to deserting God who first forgave them upon their repentance and wrote their names in heaven. No wonder Jesus has to pronounce: οὐαὶ δι' οὗ [τὰ σκάνδαλα] ἔρχεται.³² Once again, this reflection reminds us of the heavy eschatological note which colors Jesus' teaching here: λυσιτελεῖ αὐτῷ εἰ λίθος μυλικὸς περίκειται περὶ τὸν τράχηλον αὐτοῦ καὶ ἔρριπται εἰς τὴν θάλασσαν (17:2).

THE NATURE OF FAITH (LUKE 17:5-6)

The following request of faith, found only in Luke, is best understood as the disciples' response to what Jesus has just commanded them. The sheer weight of Jesus' demand for unconditional and unlimited forgiveness must have burdened them tremendously.³³ So in response to such a demand which far exceeds the limits of normal expectations, the disciples ask that they might have a greater faith if they are to perform such an absolute, super-human act of forgiveness.³⁴

Luke introduces the disciples' response with an introduction: Καὶ εἶπαν οἱ ἀπόστολοι τῷ κυρίῳ (v. 5). Here, as we have noted above, the conjunction καί is taken to mean: "then, in response to what Jesus has said." What is

---

32. In the Matthean parallel, the failure to extend God's merciful forgiveness to one's fellow disciples who humbly ask for it results in the revoke of the forgiveness previously given (18:21-35).

33. Nolland, *Luke*, 837.

34. The connection of this section either to the preceding or the following context is considered to be out of the question by most commentators. As the possible reason for the placement of the present *logion* in this context, Johnson (*The Gospel of Luke*, 259) suggests the presence of the same word "sea" both in v. 2 and here. Evans (*Saint Luke*, 621) tries to discern a thematic balance between the teaching on faith and work. For Marshall (*The Gospel of Luke*, 643) Luke here follows the order of his source, which simply lists his sayings. In contrast to this, Ellis (*The Gospel of Luke*, 207-8) suggests that this saying is the disciples' response to Jesus' saying in the preceding verses, which, so we argue, is the right way to go. Perhaps we need to remember the generally acknowledged tendency of Luke to provide good contexts to many of Jesus' sayings, as is seen in the case of the Lord's Prayer (11:1-4). Anyway, this is a matter to be decided through an actual examination of the saying itself, which seems to support our stance.

particularly interesting here is Luke's use of οἱ ἀπόστολοι for the disciples and κύριος for Jesus. The former, used six times in the Gospel (6:13; 9:10; 11:49; 22:14; 24:10), is a very formal designation for "the Twelve" (6:13; 8:1, 41, 43; 9:1, 12, etc.). The latter is a "post-resurrection" title the disciples applied to Jesus.

Luke's choice of these titles does not seem accidental. Evans nicely captures one possible effect of such a choice, when he says that "this invests the request and the reply with a solemn, perhaps official character."[35] So the weight of the preceding saying is carried over to this section, thereby inviting us to read both together. Another aim of using the "apostles–Lord" pairing instead of the usual "disciples–Jesus" can be seen in the following parable in which the nature of faith is explicated in terms of a slave–master relationship. Repetition of the term "Lord" in v. 6 makes this connection even stronger.

To their Lord, the disciples requested: πρόσθες ἡμῖν πίστιν. In the Gospel of Luke the word προστίθημι means either "to give something" (12:31; 19:11) or "to add to something which already exists" (3:20; 12:25; 20:12). So the phrase can be translated either: "Grant us faith," with the implication that the disciples do not have such faith at all, or "Increase our faith," meaning that they do have faith but just not enough. Although the former seems to be supported by the use of dative pronoun ἡμῖν,[36] as well as the improbability that the disciples think of themselves as those who have no faith at all, I argue for the latter. As far as the disciples' intention is concerned, "increase our faith" seems to fit the context better. They need more faith if they are to obey Jesus' command of unconditional forgiveness. So they ask their Lord to add more to their existing faith.[37] It is, then, this "quantitative" understanding of faith that is corrected by Jesus in his response, a point accentuated by the reference to a "mustard seed."[38]

The following conditional construction is rather curious: the present ἔχετε in the protasis and an imperfect plus ἄν in the apodosis, followed by another apodosis with the aorist ὑπήκουσεν ἄν. It is evident that κόκκον σινάπεως ("a mustard seed") conveys the idea of "smallness" as it does in 13:19.[39] The clause: "even if you have faith as small as a mustard seed" virtually means: "if you have any faith at all." Here commentators often empha-

---

35. Evans, *Saint Luke*, 621

36. Johnson, *The Gospel of Luke*, 59.

37. Nolland, *Luke*, 838; Bovon, *Das Evangelium nach Lukas*, 140.

38. The parable of the mustard seed and its relation to faith will be discussed further below.

39. In Matt 13:31–32, the idea of smallness is explicitly expressed: "It is the smallest of all the seeds."

size the hypothetical nature of the saying in such a way that they interpret the sentence as saying that the disciples do not have faith. (i.e., "if you *had* the faith . . . "). For this meaning, however, the construction, which begins with a "real" condition, is rather ineffective and confusing. Moreover, we have already pointed out the unlikelihood that Luke portrays the disciples as those who do not have any faith at all. Their weakness is certainly unmistakable, especially when they failed to cast out the demon-possessed boy (9:40–41), but it is also clear that they have been given the authority of Jesus and have actually done much the same thing as Jesus has been doing since his commission (9:1, 10; 10:17). That is, from the information that we can glean from the preceding stories, it is very hard to understand why Luke would say that the disciples do not have any faith.[40]

It seems more reasonable to suppose that the hypothetical nature of the saying does not concern itself with the disciples' absence of faith, but the following illustration in which the sycamore tree is commanded to perform such a marvelous feat points to a level of faith which the disciples had yet to experience or practice. Thus, though forming part of the apodosis, the following clause: ἐλέγετε ἂν τῇ συκαμίνῳ ("If you say to this sycamore tree . . ..") is best to be taken to be another protasis within a bigger apodosis (i.e., the following καὶ ὑπήκουσεν ἂν ὑμῖν). Both these elements are combined together to serve as the apodosis of the original conditional clause so that the structure of the sentence would be:

> Protasis A: "If you have even such small faith as a mustard seed"
>
> Apodosis B: "Then if you say to this syncamore tree: 'Be uprooted . . .' it will obey you" (= protasis a + apodosis b).

The difficulty of rooting out (ἐκριζώθητι) a sycamore tree, which is known to be very deep-rooted, is proverbial,[41] and to this already impossible demand a far more ridiculous command, καὶ φυτεύθητι ἐν τῇ θαλάσσῃ, is added.[42] This hypothetical condition evidently refers to something which is considered completely impossible. Then the meaning of the whole verse would be: "If you have even such small faith as a mustard seed, that is, if you have any faith at all, there is nothing impossible. Even if you say to this

---

40. Bovon, *Das Evangelium nach Lukas*, 140. In Matthew Jesus declares that the disciples could not cast out the demon διὰ τὴν ὀλιγοπιστίαν ὑμῶν (17:20).

41. Evans, *Saint Luke*, 621; Marshall, *The Gospel of Luke*, 644. The parallel passages in both Mark and Matthew have "mountain" instead.

42. Thus, Luke replaces the Markan/Matthean βλήθητι with a far more stronger word.

sycamore tree, 'Be uprooted and be planted in the sea,' it would obey you."[43] The effect of this hypothetical and hyperbolic juxtaposition of "faith like a mustard seed" and "uprooting a sycamore tree and planting it in the sea" is the absolute effectiveness or power of faith regardless of its "amount." So what they need is "not the increase of faith, but the *exercise* of faith."[44]

This saying is Jesus' response to the disciples' request for the increase of their faith. Thus, the point he wants to drive at is this: "The first thing you disciples have to realize is the absolute nature of faith. Faith is not something that works by the amount. To exercise unlimited forgiveness is not a matter of having more faith but a proper understanding of it." What the disciples should realize about faith is the very lesson which they are to learn in the following saying (vv. 7–10).

THE MEANING OF FAITH (LUKE 17:7-10)

Space precludes a detailed examination of Luke 17:7–10.[45] But a brief review will suffice to show its main point. The saying consists of two main parts: the parable (vv. 7–9) and its application to the disciples (v. 10). As we have noted earlier with respect to the double use of the title "Lord," it is already clear that even before Jesus says οὕτως καὶ ὑμεῖς, the parable is intended as a corrective to the disciples' misguided view of faith. As the story of the parable clearly shows, what the disciples need to lean is the precise nature of their relationship to their Lord. With effective use of three poignant rhetorical questions, Jesus provides a situation-based exposition of what it means for a servant to serve his master.[46] Needless to say, the point borne out of such rhetorical questions is the *absolute superiority* of the master to whom the servant is supposed to render complete and self-disregarding obedience. If the master commands, the servant simply does it, since he knows that that is the only proper disposition a servant can assume before his master. It is simply absurd for the servant to do less than obey, and expect a better treatment from, his master.

---

43. In Matthean parallel we find such a conclusion explicitly stated by Jesus: "And nothing will be impossible for you" (17:20).

44. Nolland, *Luke*, 838; italics original.

45. Concerning the passage, there are some discussions on the unnatural connection between the parable (vv. 7–9) and its application (v. 10). See, Fitzmyer, *The Gospel according to Luke*, 1145. Our brief discussion, however, will show that this question is a wrong one. The disciples' request is answered in terms of who Jesus is to them, which is in turn applied to the command to forgive.

46. Cf. Jeremias, *The Parables of Jesus*, 103.

After repeating an emphatic "No!" three times to such an absurd notion, Jesus goes on to apply the obvious lesson to the disciples: "so *you* also!"[47] The point cannot be clearer: the necessity for the disciples to realize the nature of their relationship with Jesus. The one who demands unlimited forgiveness is none other than their κύριος and they are his δοῦλοι. We know that this is not a strange lesson at all for Luke, since throughout the narrative we have already been reminded of exactly the same point many times over (6:46–49; 8:19–21; 11:27–28; 12:47). As Luke implied in the preceding section, Jesus is in fact "the Lord" and they are his apostles, that is, those who are selected to do what Jesus commands them to do. This is exactly what the disciples, as those who are commanded to live a life of forgiveness, should never forget.

The conclusion, then, cannot be stated better: "So you also, when you have done all that is commanded to you (i.e., when you have practiced unconditional forgiveness just as I had commanded you) say: 'We are unworthy servants; we have only done what was our duty.'" It is not that they need more faith; they just need to have a full grasp of the meaning of their calling Jesus "Lord."[48] Lordship includes a renewed awareness of their identity as "unworthy servants," an insight brought about by nothing less than God's merciful and unconditional grace bestowed upon them.[49] So behind the life of forgiveness lies genuine faith; behind the genuine faith lies a clear recognition of their being servants of their Lord obedient to his commands. If they fail to forgive others, this means that they have not yet understood the nature of their relationship with their Lord. If they have no clear understanding of Jesus as their Lord, it means that their faith is not geniune yet. This Luke calls a σκάνδαλον, which the disciples have to avoid at all cost. This is why the command to forgive others can never be separated from the gift of forgiveness from God.

---

47. Minear, "A Note on Luke 17:7–10," 82, 87, who sees a gap between vv. 7–9 and v. 10 and assigns the latter to a later addition. However, this seems to be the result of ignoring the simple fact that Jesus talks about faith in terms of a *relationship* between him as the Lord and his disciples as his servants. Bovon, *Das Evangelium nach Lukas*, 136, also speaks of "[d]ie moralisierende Perspektive" of v. 10, which is the result of "eine sekundäre Entwicklung." The present author is very pessimistic about modern scholars' ability to discern different layers of tradition behind the text; cf. Lewis, "Modern Theology and Biblical Criticism," 152–66.

48. Bovon, *Das Evangelium nach Lukas*, 135, while detecting the connection between vv. 3–4 and vv. 5–6, fails to relate vv. 7–10 to the preceding lesson on forgiveness and faith.

49. Cf. Shelton, "Luke 17:1–10," 280–85.

CONCLUDING REMARKS

We have thus far examined Luke 17:1–10, a passage which has usually been considered as a loose collection of three, or, four, disparate *logia* of Jesus. The result of our study, however, shows that each section can make excellent sense as an integral part of a single periscope: the eschatological aspect of the matter (vv. 1–2), the necessity of unlimited forgiveness (vv. 3–4); the nature of faith, which is enough to fulfill Jesus' command of forgiveness (vv. 5–6); the essence of faith as acknowledging the absolute Lordship of Jesus (vv. 7–10). Taken together, the whole passage reveals how such crucial themes as eschatology, faith, Lordship can be related to one another around the subject of forgiveness, arguably one of the most important ingredients in restoring and maintaining a harmonious community. This indicates that for Luke Christian forgiveness is not just an isolated virtue in the life of the believer, but a positive result of their whole vision of God and His world, and His work of restoration which each believer carries out through the Lord Jesus Christ.

Our reading does not necessarily mean to invalidate interpreting these sayings individually, as is typically done. It does, however, invite readers to reflect how a tradition can be used to maintain one's identity as a member of Jesus' community and help generate appropriate responses to one's changing life context. If our reading above makes any sense, Luke is not just a mere collector of Jesus' sayings, but also a perceptive and responsible theologian who was able to see things within the framework of the whole reality of "what has been accomplished among us" (Luke 1:1) through Jesus Christ, whom he also calls "Lord" (Acts 1:1). Loyalty to the tradition does not necessarily hinder a creative response to the demand of ever-changing situations but rather encourages it, by forcing us to remember and reflect faithfully the meaning of the tradition handed down to us. Luke provides us with an excellent example of such a response of faith, as our reading of Luke 17:1–10 illustrates.

BIBLIOGRAPHY

Bovon, Francois. *Das Evangelium nach Lukas*. Vol. 3, *Lukas 15,1—19,27*. EKK 3/3. Zürich: Benziger, 2001.

Ellis, E. Earle. *The Gospel of Luke*. New Century Bible Commentary. London: Marshall, Morgan & Scott, 1981. Reprint, Grand Rapids: Eerdmans, 1987.

Evans, C. F. *Saint Luke*. London: SCM, 1990.

Fitzmyer, J. A. *The Gospel according to Luke X–XXIV*. AB 28A. Garden City, NY: Doubleday, 1985.

Green, J. *The Gospel of Luke*. NICNT. Grand Rapids: Eerdmans, 1997.

Jeremias, J. *The Parables of Jesus*. New York: Scribner's Sons, 1963.
Johnson, L. T. *The Gospel of Luke*. SP 3. Collegeville, MN: Liturgical, 1991.
Kwon, Yon-Gyong. "Forgiveness, Faith, and the Lordship of Jesus: A Contextual Reading of Luke 17:1–10." *Korean Evangelical New Testament Studies* 11, no. 3 (2012) 613–42.
Lewis, C. S. "Modern Theology and Biblical Criticism." In *Christian Reflections*, ed. W. Hooper, 152–66. Grand Rapids: Eerdmans, 1967.
Marshall, I. H. *The Gospel of Luke*. NIGTC. Grand Rapids: Eerdmans, 1978.
Metzger, B. M. *A Textual Commentary on the Greek New Testament*. 2nd ed. United Bible Society, 1971. Reprint, 1994.
Minear, P. "A Note on Luke 17:7–10" *JBL* 93, no. 1 (1974) 82–87.
Moule, C. F. D. *An Idiom Book of New Testament Greek*. Cambridge: Cambridge University Press, 1959.
Nolland, J. *Luke 9:21—18:34*. WBC 35B. Dallas: Word, 1993.
Shelton, R. M. "Luke 17:1–10." *Int* 31, no. 3 (1977) 280–85.
Stählin, G. "σκάνδαλον, κτλ." In *TDNT* 7:339–58.
Zerwick, M. *Biblical Greek*. Trans. and ed. J. Smith. Scripta Pontificii Instituti Biblici 114. Rome: Editrice Pontificio Istituto Biblico, 1963. Reprint, 1994.

11

Was Johannine Christianity Sectarian?[1]

DONGSOO KIM

INTRODUCTION

It has widely been claimed among NT scholars that the Johannine community was sectarian.[2] First of all, the clarification of the word "sect" is required, in that the question of whether it was sectarian or not seems to depend on its definition. The word "sect" may refer to a group in possession, or in support, of some heresy in a theological sense. It also may mean a group which stands over against another religious body or over against society at large.

So far many scholars borrowed the definition of a sect from sociology. Many biblical scholars depend on Bryan R. Wilson, a sociologist, whose principal criterion for a sect consists in a movement's attitudes to the world.[3] What is important for our purpose, however, is the Johannine attitude towards other contemporary Christian groups rather than its attitude vis-à-vis the world. For in the former sense, most of the Christian groups in the first century could be judged as sects. In this essay, what I mean by "sect" is

---

1. Some parts of my dissertation, particularly ch. 9, are included in this work. See Kim, "The Church in the Gospel of John."

2. Beutler, "Kirche als Sekte," 21–32; Pryor, "Covenant and Community," 44–51.

3. Wilson, *Magic and the Millennium*, 19.

a group alienated and expelled from the other main groups of a like kind. If we judge Johannine Christianity as sectarian in this sense, it must be a Christian group removed from other Christian groups at the end of the first century.

The purpose of this study is to investigate the nature of Christian sectarianism and to redefine Johannine Christianity. This study will show that Johannine Christianity was neither sectarian in a sociological sense nor in a theological sense. Rather, Johannine Christianity was a kind of prophetic voice in early Christianity.

WAS JOHANNINE CHRISTIANITY SECTARIAN IN A SOCIOLOGICAL SENSE?

The simple question this study asks is whether Johannine Christianity was sectarian or not under (modern) sociological categories. Rebell answers in the affirmative. For him, the belief that the Johannine community was not detached from the early Christian churches is fiction.[4] Rensberger, however, hesitates to apply Johannine sectarianism in relation to other Christian groups, although he admits that it was sectarian in its attitude towards contemporary Judaism.[5]

If one attempts to judge a Christian group as a sect in early Christianity, at least three criteria must be met by the group. First of all, the group must show its self-consciousness as a distinctive group from other groups. Second, it must include considerable peculiarities from other Christian groups with regard to its ideology or theology. The peculiarity, however, does not necessarily form a sectarian character of a group. Third, the more important criterion should be its hostility to the other groups, because a sectarian group tends to stand over against a generally accepted religious tradition. If the Johannine group meets the above three criteria, it can be judged as sectarian.

First, there is no objection that Johannine community was acutely aware of its identity as a Christian group distinct from the main Christian movement stemming from Jerusalem at the end of the first century. Second, did the distinctiveness of the Johannine mindset lead it to its hostile relationship vis-à-vis against other apostolic forms of Christianity? What seems to be an initial difficulty here is the fact that John does not include

---

4. Rebell, *Gemeinde als Gengenwelt*, 113. So Bogart, *Orthodox and Heretical Perfectionism*, 140; Neyrey, *An Ideology of Revolt*, 115.

5. Rensberger, *Johannine Faith*, 28.

any directly confrontational or critical claims against the contemporary Christian groups of his day.

The Johannine attitude to the other forms of Christianity in the first century can be detected partly by comparing the Johannine theology with that in the other NT writings. This undertaking will not be easy methodologically, especially if there is no direct literary interdependence between John and any NT writings. However, the results can be fruitful if we find more similarities than are often expected. Did the Johannine theology deviate from the theologies of the other NT writings in such a way that its inclusion in the New Testament happened because of human error and God's providence (Käsemann)? or do the similarities in terms of their theology between John and the other NT authors suggest that John can be regarded as a voice harmonious with the diverse Christian movements of the first century AD?

Barrett in the *Festschrift* for D. Moody Smooth compares Acts with John in regard to their eschatology, pneumatology, ecclesiology, and christology. He draws a conclusion that the parallels between the two writings are more substantial than are often presupposed. This leads Barrett further to state:

> It is important to place John correctly within the general stream of Christian tradition. Perhaps the evangelist was not quite such a lonely figure as has sometimes been maintained. There is a good deal to be said for the view that Johannine Christianity was an isolated dissenting sect, but not all dissenters are badly informed about main lines of Christian tradition . . . it is important to chart John's positions as clearly as we can within the Christian history and literature for the first and second centuries.[6]

Smith also tries to include John among the Gospels. He simply asks a question: Is John an apocryphal gospel in the sense that John does not conform to the Synoptic Gospels either in sequence or in content? Initially, on the criteria of sequence and content, John has something in common with the apocryphal gospels. Accordingly for Smith, John is, in a sense, the first apocryphal gospel. However, as Smith notes, John is also quite different from the apocryphal gospels in the sense that it is "controlled, determined, or guided by a distinctive theological position and perspective."[7] This leads Smith to conclude: "Distinctive and different as it may be, the Gospel of John presents a Jesus who makes a certain theological sense of the Jesus of

---

6. Barrett, "The Parallels between Acts and John," 175–76.
7. Smith, "The Problem of John," 161.

the other gospels, and the New Testament generally."[8] It is noteworthy that Barrett and Smith, two renowned Johannine scholars, reach similar conclusions on the nature of Johannine Christianity by the comparison between John with other NT writings.

The above evidences lead me to doubt the claim that Johannine Christianity was sectarian vis-à-vis other forms of Christianity, although it could be claimed that it was sectarian with regard to the world at large.

WAS JOHANNINE CHRISTIANITY HERETICAL?

The Testament of Jesus is a provocative work by Ernst Käsemann on the issue of Johannine sectarianism in a theological sense. It has always been the center of the debates on the origin and the nature of Johannine Christianity. What prevented him from receiving John as one of the orthodox Christian works was, he believed, that the Johannine voice was so distinct from the rest of early Christianity.[9] It was against the stream of contemporary orthodox Christianity which was directed to early Catholicism. His thesis is that Johannine Christianity was "the relic of a conventicle" which was pushed to the periphery of early Christianity.[10] So for Käsemann, Johannine Christianity was heretical.

Käsemann attempts to prove his thesis by analyzing key themes in John 17. He argues that the Christology of glory, which is one of key themes in John, can hardly be harmonized with the view that Jesus was a human being. In John, Jesus was "God going about on the earth."[11] The so-called realized eschatology found in John 3:36; 5:24; 6:47; 8:51 demonstrate "what the enthusiasts in Corinth and heretics of 2 Tim 2:18 had proclaimed, namely that the reality of the general resurrection of the dead is already present."[12] These beliefs led Käsemann to claim that from a Christological point of view, Johannine Christianity was characterized by docetism, even if it was in a naive (not-fully fledged) form.[13]

Further, Käsemann believed that John's understanding of community was typically a heretical or sectarian type. Against the institutionalizing tendency of early Christian orthodoxy, John did not show any explicit idea of formal offices or ecclesial structure. He did not employ any traditional

---

8. Ibid., 162.
9. Käsemann, *The Testament of Jesus*, 2.
10. Ibid., 39.
11. Ibid.
12. Ibid., 15–16.
13. Ibid., 51–52.

terms for the church. John's community did not include formal liturgical elements such as worship, sacraments, and offices. Its democratic church order, characterized by priesthood of all believers and women disciples, appeared heretical. Finally, John's concept of love is a sectarian type in that it directs love exclusively within the confines of Johannine membership. In essence, for Käsemann, Johannine Christianity was heretical, sectarian, and docetic in nature. Its enthusiastic tendencies led it to be in tension or conflict with the other forms of the early church. Thus the acceptance of John's Gospel into the canon by the church of early Christian orthodoxy was a mistake. In Käsemann's words: "it's acceptance into the Church's canon took place through man's error and God's providence."[14]

The value of the Gospel of John is not to be underestimated in the debates of "orthodox and heresy." Käsemann applies the question of orthodox and heresy to the Johannine Christianity, whose question was first raised by Bauer.[15] Käsemann had already reached a conclusion that Johannine Christianity was sectarian in his investigation of the Johannine epistles.[16]

Although Käsemann helps us to ask appropriate questions on the origin and the nature of Johannine Christianity, I am not entirely convinced by his conclusions. First of all, his interpretations of Johannine theology seem to be one-sided. Even if it is possible to regard Johannine Christology as docetic, most scholars are more convinced by the anti-docetic reading of Johannine theology. Bornkamm is right when he says that "even from the point of view of history, the thesis that the Christology of John is naively docetic seems to me be false."[17]

Further, Käsemann's understanding of Johannine ecclesiology is arbitrary. His anti-ecclesiastical reading of John cannot be sustained. It seems to me that he overemphasized one aspect of Johannine eschatology, i.e., the concept of love exclusive to the membership within the community and the community's stance toward the world. While certainly there are clear emphases on realized eschatology in John: i.e., brotherly love and hatred of the world, it is also a mistake to disregard aspects of a futuristic eschatology: i.e., universal love and love for a lost world (John 3:16).

What seems to be most problematic is that the Johannine movement was posited as an enthusiastic or heretic type of Christianity in direct conflict with early catholicism. Admittedly, Johannine community was one of

14. Ibid., 75.

15. Bauer, *Orthodox and Heresy in Earliest Christianity*.

16. Käsemann, "Ketzer aud Zeuge," 291–311.

17. Bornkamm, "Towards the Interpretation of John's Gospel." Cf. Schnelle, *Anti-docetic Christology*.

the so-called pneumatic movements of early Christianity. However, were pneumatic movements necessarily hostile to the institutional church? Even Käsemann's preferred term "early catholicism," on which Käsemann's thesis is so heavily dependent, is anachronistic.[18] If there was such a phenomenon as early catholicism, one can interpret the reasons of the emergence differently from him. It could have found impetus from the passing of the apostles and charismatic leaders, from the rapid growth of the Church, or from "persecution from outside the Church."[19] Harrington is correct when he asks: "Why does Käsemann see 'Early Catholicism' as a retrogression rather than a development?"[20]

Thus Hengel challenges Käsemann's thesis from the second-century Christian history. If Johannine Christianity was seen as heretic from the viewpoint of an emerging orthodoxy, how could the Johannine writings "be accepted by the other communities of the mainstream church and gain such broad and deep influence in it as early as the second century ... ?"[21] Another weakness of Käsemann's argument is that it is based on the presupposition that there was a single normative Christianity in the late first century AD, by which another type of Christianity could be judged as a sect. Dunn gives us an alternative historical reconstruction.[22] He begins with Bauer's question of orthodoxy and heresy in earliest Christianity but argues that earliest Christianity was diverse in its character and that "there was no single normative form of Christianity in the first century" by which other forms of Christianity could be judged.[23] If Dunn is right (and I believe he is), it would be hard to regard Johannine Christianity as sectarian because of its theological peculiarity.

JOHANNINE CHRISTIANITY WITHIN THE STREAM OF EARLY CHRISTIANITY

Against any attempt to place Johannine Christianity on the fringe of early Christianity, Cullmann views the Johannine type of Christianity as an integral part of church's growth and history. He traces the origin of Johannine Christianity from the Hellenists in Acts 6.[24] He finds many common ele-

18. See Bornkamm, "Towards the Interpretation of John's Gospel," 94.
19. Harrington, "Ernst Käsemann on the Church," 366.
20. Ibid.
21. Hengel, *The Johannine Question*.
22. Dunn, *Unity and Diversity in the New Testament*.
23. Ibid., 373.
24. Cullmann, *The Johannine Circle*, 54.

ments between the Johannine circle and the Hellenists. The most notable one is the opposition to the temple, which is commonly found in heterodox Judaism. An interest in the mission to Samaria is another common factor. This leads him to conclude that the historical origin of the Johannine community is in heterodox marginal Judaism, particularly a Hellenist group in Jerusalem.[25]

If the Johannine circle was posited as a distinctive movement within early Christianity, what was its relation to the rest of the Christianity? First, it is clear to Cullmann that "the Johannine circle was aware of being fundamentally different from the rest of Christianity."[26] Second, however, "this awareness was never led to direct polemic against the other Christians."[27] The Johannine circle did not break off communion with the rest of the Church. Third, more importantly, the ambivalent relationship between Peter and the beloved disciple in John's Gospel reflects the attitudes of the Johannine circle to the rest of the early Christian community. On "the one hand it deliberately maintains its own independence, but on the other it is convinced of the need for mutual supplementation in the common interest."[28]

Cullmann traces the further development of the Johannine circle. Simply put, the majority of Johannine circle was assimilated to the rest of the Christianity, whereas some members in the group joined up with the Gnostics. Cullmann's endeavor to identify Johannine Christianity within early Christianity helps us to place the Johannine movement within the heart of early Christian history. The similarities between the Johannine circle and the Hellenists in Acts suggests a certain link between the two movements. Although I do not fully agree with him when he connects the Hellenists to the Johannine circle historically, I do agree that Johannine Christianity was one of several types of Christian groups in early Christianity that contributed to the movement's identity as a whole.

How can the historian, however, describe the peculiarities of Johannine Christianity without positing it as a heretical or separate sect? There are several ways to explain the peculiarity of Johannine theology without mislabeling it as sectarian. Scholars typically explain it with regard to its religious background such as Gnosticism (Bultmann), Hellenism (Dodd), or Judaism (Charlesworth).[29] I am more convinced by Brodie's explanation that Johannine Christianity was "a prophetic voice from within early

25. Ibid., 87.
26. Ibid., 58.
27. Ibid., 55.
28. Ibid.
29. Charlesworth, "Reinterpreting John," 8–25; 54.

Christianity."[30] In other words, it was a corrective, although implicitly, to other forms of Christianity in the first century AD. It was a refreshing corrective that challenged mainline traditions.

Take, for example, the ecclesiology of John versus those found in other NT writings. On the identity and mission of the church, Johannine theology offers a corrective voice. One distinctive character of Johannine images of the church is John's christological orientation. Expressed by the centrality of Jesus and by the emphasis of the union of each believer with Jesus, John's ecclesiology is distinct from those found in the Synoptics and in the Pauline letters because in John the vertical relationship with Christ, rather than the horizontal one among one another, is the point of focus. At that time the early church was directed to the institutionalization. The pastorals in particular evinced a development towards the church offices. The Johannine shepherd discourse (John 10:1–18) could be read against this background. Here the core element of the church was none other than Jesus himself. Concerning the members of the church, the close individual union of each member with Christ was indeed the *sine qua non* of ecclesial life. For John, the vertical relationship must be the basis for the horizontal one in the church. Accordingly, this voice was critical to the tendency of the contemporary churches whose direction was headed unfortunately towards institutionalization.

The Johannine voice, however, was not so excessively critical as to derail the mission of the mainline churches. It was similar to the voice of the prophets in the Old Testament who had served as a corrective to contemporary Jewish tendencies. So the prophetic role of John's ecclesiology can be an explanation why Johannine Christianity was easily incorporated into the Great Church of the second century. Prophets tends to disappear after their missions are completed. I believe that Johannine Christianity was such a case.

CONCLUSION

In this essay, I have attempted to prove that Johannine Christianity was not sectarian. It does not constitute a sect in either the sociological or theological sense. In addition, I have argued that Johannine Christianity was a prophetic voice or corrective to the mainline churches in early Christianity. In a sense, the Johannine voice was a challenge to the other forms of Christianity. John was critical of other Christian groups. However, John's challenge did not hinder their work. John's role was similar to that of the prophets in

30. Brodie, *The Quest for the Origin of John's Gospel*, 150.

the Old Testament, one of whose main roles was to challenge the contemporary religious tendencies of their day and awaken the complacent mass from their slowly fossilizing religiosity. What John had done was to challenge the church to place the living union with Jesus, not only above the fellowship among fellow Christians, but also above church organization. Thus, John's challenging voice, in the tradition of the OT prophets, was "from within the heart of the Christian Church" and consistent with the church's doctrines.[31]

BIBLIOGRAPHY

Barrett, C. K. "Parallels between Acts and John." In *Exploring the Gospel of John: In Honor of D. Moody Smith*, ed. R. Alan Culpepper and C. Clifton Black, 175–76. Louisville: Westminster John Knox, 1996.

Bauer, Walter. *Orthodox and Heresy in Earliest Christianity*. London: SCM, 1971.

Beutler, Johannes. "Kirche als Sekte? Zum Kirchenbild der johanneischen Abschiedreden." In *Studien zu den johanneischen Schriften*, 21–32. SBAB 25. Stuttgart: Katholisches Bibelwerk, 1988.

Bogart, John. *Orthodox and Heretical Perfectionism in the Johannine Community as Evident in the First Epistle of John*. Missoula, MT: Scholars, 1977.

Bornkamm, G. "Towards the Interpretation of John's Gospel: A Discussion of the Testament of Jesus by Ernst Käsemann." In *The Interpretation of John*, ed. J. Ashton, 79–98. London: SPCK, 1986.

Brodie, Thomas. *The Quest for the Origin of John's Gospel: A Source-Oriented Approach*. New York: Paulist, 1979.

Charlesworth, James H. "Reinterpreting John: How the Dead Sea Scrolls Have Revolutionized Our Understanding of the Gospel of John." *BRev* 9, no. 1 (1993) 8–24, 54.

Cullmann, Oscar. *The Johannine Circle: Its Place in Judaism among the Disciples of Jesus and in Early Christianity*. London: SCM, 1976.

Dunn, James D. G. *Unity and Diversity in the New Testament: An Inquiry into the Character of Earliest Christianity*. London: SCM, 1990.

Harrington, Daniel. "Ernst Käsemann on the Church in the New Testament." *HeyJ* 12 (1971) 246–57.

Hengel, Martin. *The Johannine Question*. Trans. J. Bowden. London: SCM, 1989.

Käsemann, Ernst. "Ketzer und Zeuge. Zum johanneischen Verfasserproblem." *ZTK* 48 (1951) 291–311.

———. *The Testament of Jesus: A Study of the Gospel of John in the Light of Chapter 17*. Trans. G. Krodel. London: SCM, 1968.

Kim, Dongsoo. "The Church in the Gospel of John." PhD diss., University of Cambridge, 1999.

Rebell, W. *Gemeinde als Gegenwelt. Zur soziologischen und didakischen Funktion des Johannesevangeliums*. Frankfurt: Lang, 1987.

Rensberger, David. *Johannine Faith and Liberating Community*. Philadelphia: Westminster, 1988.

---

31. Ibid., 150.

Schnelle, Udo. *Antidocetic Christology in the Gospel of John: An Investigation of the Place of the Fourth Gospel in the Johannine School.* Trans. L. Maloney. Minneapolis: Fortress, 1992.

Smith, D. Moody. "The Problem of John and the Synoptic Gospels in Light of the Relation between Apocryphal and Canonical Gospels." In *John and the Synoptics*, ed. A. Denaux, 147–62. Leuven: Leuven University Press, 1992.

Wilson, B. R. *Magic and the Millennium: A Sociological Study of Religious Movements of Protest among Tribal Third-World Peoples.* London: Heinemann, 1973.

12

The "Son of Man" in Johannine Eschatology

STEPHEN E. YOUNG

INTRODUCTION

The coexistence within the Gospel of John of texts that support a "realized eschatology"[1] with those that support a "future eschatology"[2] has been amply documented. Passages which support the former far outnumber those which support the latter, as the overall emphasis within the Gospel is clearly one of realized eschatology. In the ongoing struggle over how to interpret the existence of these two sets of texts in the same document, it appears that the past scholarly tendency to excise the references to future eschatology[3] has been replaced by a growing consensus that allows for the legitimacy of both. This is a positive trend. Work, however, remains to be done: while various theories have been proposed to explain the historical background

---

1. Meaning, with Aune, "the realization in present experience of blessings normally regarded as belonging to the eschatological future" ("Early Christian," 606).

2. Or "temporal eschatology," meaning that it will take place within time (or at the end of time) as opposed to giving way to mysticism; see Cullmann, *Salvation*, 289.

3. Associated especially with Bultmann; see his "Eschatology," 166 and n2; Bultmann, *John*, 219–20; Bultmann, *Theology*, 2:38–39.

for the coexistence of these two sets of eschatological texts in John, the relationship between the two, as they now stand in the Gospel of John, has received less attention and remains an open question.[4] This relationship is the focus of the present essay.

This essay will argue that there is a reciprocal relationship of support between these two sets of texts, those that contain the idea of realized eschatology finding support in those that are oriented toward the future, and vice versa.[5] Given that an essay of this length could not possibly address all the relevant material, it will focus upon a sub-set of texts that identify Jesus as "the Son of Man" (ὁ υἱὸς τοῦ ἀνθρώπου), as this identification is one of the means by which the above-mentioned reciprocal relationship of support is achieved.[6]

It might seem foolhardy to attempt to solve one complicated problem by appeal to another, the Son of Man having been the center of a long and as-yet-unresolved debate for well over a century. Much of that debate, however, has addressed such issues as the origin of the phrase ὁ υἱὸς τοῦ ἀνθρώπου; whether Jesus used it as a self-designation or to refer to another; the implications of the phrase for Jesus' self-understanding (*if* it originated on the lips of the historical Jesus); and/or the distinction to be made between its use by Jesus and the meaning of the phrase in the creativity of the early church.[7] This paper is not concerned with these issues, but rather with how the phrase is used within the Fourth Gospel in its final form. Here the phrase clearly functions either as a title Jesus uses of himself,[8] or perhaps more correctly as a way to point to a *particular* son of man, the "one

---

4. For a summary of scholarly trends on Johannine eschatology, see Frey, *Johanneische Eschatologie*, reviewed and summarized in Beasley-Murray, *John*, cxxvii–cxlii.

5. In general terms, my position is aligned with those who see the coexistence of these two sets of texts in the Gospel of John as evidence that the Gospel shares in the "already/not yet" understanding of eschatology found in other NT documents; see, e.g., Beasley-Murray, *John*, lxxxv–lxxxvii; Barrett, *John*, 67–70 et passim; Cullmann, *Salvation*, 268–91; de Jonge, *Jesus*, 169–91; Howard, *Christianity*, 106–28, esp. 121–28; Kümmel, *Theology*, 293–95, 327–30; Kysar, *John*, 125; Ladd, *Theology*, 334–44.

6. It is my hope that Dr. Seyoon Kim will appreciate this choice of subject matter for this essay written in his honor, given his own important work on the Son of Man (see his *Son of Man as the Son of God*).

7. The scope of this study does not allow for even a cursory treatment of the many complex, debated issues surrounding the "Son of Man." For a survey see Burkett, *Debate*, and more recently Hurtado and Owen, eds., "*Who Is This?*"; and further Nickelsburg, "Son of Man," 137–50; Lindars, *Jesus*, 1–16; Lindars, "Son of Man," 639–42; Colpe, "ὁ υἱὸς τοῦ ἀνθρώπου," 400–477; specifically related to John, see Burkett, *Son of the Man*, 16–50; Reynolds, *Apocalyptic*, 2–10; and more briefly Reynolds, "Son of Man."

8. For both Burkett (*Son of the Man*, 16) and Dunn (*Christology*, 66) this is beyond dispute.

like a son of man" in Dan 7:13,[9] as symbolic of Jesus' own vocation.[10] Dan 7:13–14 reads as follows:

> In my vision at night I looked,
> and there before me was one like a son of man,
> coming with the clouds of heaven. He
> > approached the Ancient of Days and was led into his presence.
> He was given authority, glory and sovereign power;
> > all peoples, nations and [people] of every language worshiped him.
> His dominion is an everlasting dominion that will not pass away,
> > and his kingdom is one that will never be destroyed (NIV).

What C. F. D. Moule states regarding the use of the phrase in Christian and Jewish literature in antiquity, as it applies to Jesus' self-understanding, can also be applied to the phrase within the finished Gospels:

> [T]he simplest explanation of the almost entire consistency with which the definite singular is confined to Christian sayings is to postulate that Jesus did refer to Daniel 7, speaking of "*the* Son of man [whom you know from that vision]," and that he used Daniel's human figure as not primarily a title so much as a symbol for the vocation to victory through obedience and martyrdom to which he was called and to which he summoned his followers (so that they would together constitute "the people of the saints of the Most High").[11]

This paper's findings will both support the above points and build on them, to shed new light upon the eschatology of the Fourth Gospel.

---

9. I use this transliteration of the Aramaic instead of the translation "one like a human being" found in certain translations precisely because here is where the wooden Greek transliteration ὁ υἱὸς τοῦ ἀνθρώπου relates back to the Aramaic.

10. As pointed out by Burkett in his survey of Johannine scholarship on the Son of Man, the majority of scholars have argued for one of two views regarding the intended referent for the phrase: it is either (1) a direct reference to an apocalyptic Son of Man derived from interpretations of Dan 7; or (2) a reference to an originally apocalyptic Son of Man, "but the ideas associated with it have been modified under the influence of some non-apocalyptic figure" (*Son of the Man*, 16–20, 26–37, esp. 16). A minority has argued for a referent altogether outside of apocalyptic, but Burkett's objections to these positions suffice to discount them (see ibid., 20–26). Burkett himself argues for "the Man" in Proverbs 30:1–4 as the intended referent (ibid., 38–178).

11. Moule, "Son of Man," 278 (for supporting points see his whole article), and more fully idem, "Neglected Features," 75–90. Given this approach, the ongoing discussion regarding an Aramaic *Vorlage* for the phrase ὁ υἱὸς τοῦ ἀνθρώπου in the Gospels has little relevance for the present study. On the history of scholarship on this issue, see Lukaszewski, "Issues," 1–13.

THE SON OF MAN IN JOHN

The phrase "the Son of Man" is found thirteen times in John, in 1:51; 3:13, 14; 5:27; 6:27, 53, 62; 8:28; 9:35; 12:23, 34 (twice); and 13:31.[12] In what follows, one of the basic presuppositions that will guide the investigation of these texts will be the "normative process of reading": the assumption that material that comes earlier in the Gospel informs material that comes later, because narratives are to be read sequentially.[13] This means, e.g., that insights gained from the study of the Son of Man saying in John 1:51 will inform one's reading of the saying in 3:13, which will cumulatively affect the reading of 5:27, and so forth.

The Johannine Son of Man as the Locus of God's Revelation

Turning to an examination of these Son of Man texts, the first contains Jesus' statement in 1:51: "Truly I tell you, you will see heaven open, and the angels of God going up and going down on the Son of Man."[14] John's narrative leaves this statement hanging, with no further explanation of its meaning or any description of a reaction on the part of the hearers. Its meaning most likely derives from its intertextual allusion to Jacob's dream in Gen 28:12: "in which he saw a stairway resting on the earth, with its top reaching to heaven, and the angels of God were ascending and descending on it" (NIV). Upon waking, Jacob interprets his dream in part with the words: "How awesome is this place! This is none other than the house of God; this is the gate of heaven" (Gen 28:17; NIV). By means of this intertextual allusion, John transfers to a person what Jacob had concluded about a place: the Son of Man, Jesus, is the locus of revelation.[15]

The next two mentions of the Son of Man in John are found close together in 3:13-15: "No one has gone up into heaven except the one who came down out of heaven, the Son of Man; and just as Moses lifted up the snake in the desert, so it is necessary for the Son of Man to be lifted up, so that everyone who believes in him may have eternal life." Here the uniqueness of the role of the Son of Man as the locus of revelation, established in the first Son of Man saying in 1:51, is explained: Jesus is uniquely qualified

---

12. All of these contain the article with the exception of 5:27, on which see below.

13. Powell, "Narrative Criticism," 244.

14. All English translations from the Greek, unless otherwise indicated, are by the author.

15. Ashton, *Understanding*, 244-51; Lincoln, *John*, 122-23.

to speak of heavenly things (see 3:12) because he knows of them first hand as the Son of Man who came down from heaven (3:13).

Verses 14–15 also introduce some new elements of the Son of Man's role. The mention of Moses lifting up the snake in the desert in v. 14 is a clear reference to Num 21:9. To set it in context, Num 21:4–9 narrates how God sent poisonous snakes among the people as punishment for speaking against him and against Moses, and many died when bitten by the snakes. Following the people's repentance and Moses' intercession for them, God commanded Moses to make a serpent and place it on a pole, so that those who were bitten could look at it and live. The reference to this story in John 3:14–15 serves to add urgency and immediacy to the role of the Son of Man: people are perishing (see 3:16), but through his "lifting up" (in 12:33 explained as a reference to the crucifixion, but here left ambiguous[16]) the Son of Man gives eternal life to those who believe.

The following verses expand upon this saving role of the Son of Man: "For God loved the world in such a way that he gave his one and only Son, in order that whoever believes in him should not perish, but should have eternal life. For God did not send his Son into the world in order to condemn the world, but in order to save the world through him. Whoever believes in him is not condemned, but whoever does not believe is already condemned because he did not believe in the name of God's one and only Son" (3:16–18). These verses associate a new theme, that of judgment, with the figure of the Son of Man in John, a theme that will recur as a unifying factor of the Johannine Son of Man texts.[17] The emphasis here is on the present time, in which the role of the Son of Man is not to condemn, but to save. And yet in the contrast between "*eternal* life" and "condemnation" or "judgment" (both possible renderings of the Greek κρίνω) is an implied "*eternal* condemnation"; i.e., here the final judgment is in view.[18]

The Son of Man texts examined so far, then, serve to establish the unique relationship of Jesus to the heavenly world as the locus of revelation (1:51), and as the only bearer of firsthand knowledge of heavenly things (3:13). They also serve to present him as the one sent by God to provide eternal life (3:14–17), while hinting at his eschatological role as judge (3:18). When the next saying clearly identifies the Son of Man as the eschatological judge, these earlier sayings have prepared a foundation for it by establishing

---

16. Michaels, *John*, 197–98.

17. See Maddox, "Function," 186–204 (who analyzes this theme in John 3:13–14; 5:27; 8:25–28; 9:35–41; and 12:31–35); Schnackenburg, *John*, 1:535–38.

18. Cf. Schnackenburg, *John*, 1:402–3.

the heavenly source of Jesus' judgment, and that he is in his own person the source of present and future salvation.

The Johannine Son of Man as Eschatological Judge

The fourth Son of Man text, in John 5:27, continues the trajectory of the first three by further defining the identity of the Son of Man as heaven-appointed judge. The theme of judgment is introduced already in 5:22, where Jesus states that "the Father judges no one, on the contrary, all judgment he has given to the Son," and developed further when in 5:24 Jesus echoes his own words from 3:18: "the one who hears my word and believes in him who sent me has eternal life and does not come under judgment, but has gone over from death to life." The next text reads:

> In truth I tell you that a time is coming, and it is now, when the dead will hear the voice of the Son of God, and those who hear will live. For just as the Father has life in himself, so also he has granted the Son to have life in himself; and he has given him authority to execute judgment because he is the Son of Man. Do not be amazed at this, because a time is coming when all those who are in the graves will hear his voice and will rise: those who practiced good to a resurrection of life, but those who practiced evil to a resurrection of judgment. (vv. 25–29)

These verses almost certainly connect the Johannine Son of Man to the figure "like a son of man" of Daniel 7. That the phrase in v. 27 is anarthrous (ὅτι υἱὸς ἀνθρώπου ἐστίν, the only such use of the phrase in the Gospels) is probably meant to allude to the anarthrous "one like a son of man" in the Aramaic of Dan 7:13.[19] More importantly, that Daniel is in view is especially clear from the verses that follow, which echo Dan 12:2:

---

19. This view is shared by Brown, *John*, 1:220; Barrett, *John*, 262; Davies, *Rhetoric*, 190; Lindars, *John*, 226; Smalley, "Johannine," 292. For dissenting opinions see Borsch, *Son of Man*, 293–94; Burkett, *Son of the Man*, 43; Casey, *Son of Man*, 198–99.

Dan 12:2	John 5:28-29
Many of those who sleep	All those who are
in the dust of the earth	in the graves
will awake:	will hear his voice and will rise
some	those who practiced good
to everlasting life,	to a resurrection of life,
and some	but those who practiced evil
to shame and everlasting contempt	to a resurrection of judgment[A]

A. Based on Dahl, "Do Not Wonder," 326 (ET of Dan 12:2 from the NRSV). Collins has shown that the figure of the Son of Man in Dan 7 is related to that of Michael in Dan 12 (*Apocalyptic Vision*, 144–46), so the midrashic relating of Dan 7:13-14 and 12:2 in John 5:27-29 should cause no surprise; cf. Brown, *John*, 1:220; Michaels, *John*, 322 n. 74. That the expectations associated with the Son of Man as eschatological judge in John arose from interpretations of Dan 7 is argued effectively by Reynolds, *Apocalyptic*; see also Ashton, *Understanding*, 259-66; Collins, "Son of Man," 449-51; Dunn, *Christology*, 68-82; idem, "Danielic," 532-33; Nickelsburg, "Son of Man," 137-38. In Casey's view, however, in the Fourth Gospel "there is no certain trace of Dan. 7 at all" (Casey, *Son of Man*, 163).

John's use of Danielic material in this text should come as no surprise, as other works of Jewish literature of the period similarly contain a strong emphasis on eschatological judgment in their expectations concerning the Son of Man figure.[20] This is the case with the Synoptic Gospels, where the future element of the judgment associated with Jesus as Son of Man is more pronounced than in John.[21] Other contemporary texts that speak of a Son of Man figure and eschatological judgment with language and imagery derived from Dan 7 include *1 Enoch*, *4 Ezra*, and less clearly, *2 Baruch*.[22] These texts

---

20. See Higgins, *Jesus*, 167-68; Barrett, *John*, 262. The final editing of John in the mid-80s to mid-90s allows for it to have been influenced by these works even if the latter were written fairly late. As Hannah notes, "most [scholars] would place the *Parables* at the turn of the eras, while a significant minority would argue for later in the first century A.D." ("Elect," 134, with literature cited in his notes 13-14). Nickelsburg also dates the *Similitudes of Enoch* between the late first century BCE and sometime in the first century CE, and *IV Ezra* and *Baruch* roughly near the end of the first century CE ("Son of Man," 138-41).

21. The Synoptic texts which portray Jesus the Son of Man as eschatological judge are well known; see, e.g., Matt 13:37-43; 19:28; 25:31-46; Mark 13:24-27; Luke 17:22-35; 21:27. John 5:27 is the clearest link to this tradition (Schnackenburg, *John*, 1:535). Reynolds concludes his comparison of the Son of Man material in the Synoptics and John as follows: "[T]he Son of Man has a number of similar functions and characteristics in each of the Gospels. There are some clear differences between John and the Synoptic portrayals, but these differences tend to be differences of nuance or timing rather than contradictory features" ("Son of Man," 127).

22. Ashton's conclusion is well worded: "With some caution, then, it may be said

together attest to the use of Dan 7 as a model for portraying this type of figure in the writings of the period.[23]

While the expectation of the Son of Man as eschatological judge in John 5:24–29 is similar to that found in the above-mentioned literature, it also differs from that literature in one important way: in vv. 24–27 Jesus as Son of Man is *exercising judgment in the present*, while vv. 28–29 make clear that *this does not discount his role as judge at the final resurrection*. But these present and future roles do not simply coexist. Dahl has shown that, in keeping with other Johannine examples and with rabbinic materials, the warning: "Do not be amazed" of v. 28a introduces what follows in 28b–29 as a warrant for what had been expressed in 25–27.[24]

For the purposes of this paper it is important to note that the reference in v. 27 to Jesus' authority to judge *as Son of Man* is included in what is being substantiated by vv. 28–29. To paraphrase Dahl's conclusion: The Evangelist argues that those who believe that the Son of Man will bring about a future resurrection and a final separation of those who have done good from those who have done evil ought not to be surprised that Jesus *as* this Son of Man even now gives life and exercises judgment.[25] For Dahl, the "most striking feature" of this form of argumentation "is that a christianized version [*Jesus as judge*] of the doctrine of future resurrection and judgment provides the warrant for the credibility of the preceding sayings."[26] The identification of

---

that by the end of the first century AD two originally distinct figures, the one like a man in Daniel and the messianic redeemer, had started to coalesce, hesitantly in *2 Baruch*, more perceptibly in *4 Ezra*, and most clearly of all in *4 Enoch*" (*Understanding*, 264).

23. See especially *1 En.* 37–71, regarding which Longenecker is justified in stating that ch. 46 "is virtually a midrash on Dan 7:13" (*Christology*, 90n120). On the Son of Man in all these texts see further Ashton, *Understanding*, 261 65; Bock, "Use of Daniel 7," 85–87; Collins, "Son of Man;" Nickelsburg, "Son of Man," 138–46; Owen, "Problems," 46–47; Russell, *Method*, 289, 294–95, 327–31; Smalley, "Johannine," 281–87; Yarbro Collins, "Apocalyptic," 220–28. Casey has sought to dismiss any significant relationship between these texts and Dan 7 in a number of publications (see the list of his own works in his *Solution*, 327–28), but see the cogent criticisms of his arguments in Owen, "Problems." Perhaps previous generations of scholars too quickly assumed that these writings implied a widely held messianic expectation of a heavenly Son of Man in first century Judaism (see critique in Hooker, "Son of Man Problem," 155–68). The expectation need not have been widespread, however, for its presence to be significant in the above-mentioned documents, dating from the decades surrounding the editing of the Fourth Gospel.

24. Dahl, "Do Not Wonder," 323–25.

25. My paraphrase of Dahl, "Do Not Wonder," 334, which is Dahl's paraphrase (with some revision in light of his article) of Hoskyns's interpretation of this text in *The Fourth Gospel*, 291.

26. Dahl, "Do Not Wonder," 334; cf. Michaels, *John*, 321: "Jesus, Son of God and Lord of the present, is Lord of the future as well."

Jesus as Son of Man thus serves to bring together the present reality with the future expectation on a Christological basis, i.e., based on Jesus' very identity as Son of Man.

In short, one finds in John 5:24–29 neither that a future eschatology has been replaced by a realized eschatology, nor even that they simply coexist, but rather that the presupposition of a future eschatology is called upon to *support* a claim of realized eschatology. The hinge that holds the present and the future together is Jesus' identity as Son of Man, in John's present as a source of eternal life, and yet having a future role at the final judgment. In 5:27–29 the future element of this judgment is at its most explicit, but the future element is also brought to bear explicitly or implicitly in other texts, as will be seen below.

The next three references to the Son of Man in John are found in 6:27, 53, and 62. The prominence of these Son of Man texts within the discourse in 6:26–65 is shown by their placement at its beginning, middle and end.[27] The first two texts have to do with the Son of Man as the source of food that brings eternal life (the theme of food having carried over from the miraculous feeding of the 5,000 narrated in 6:1–15). The general reference to food in Jesus' statement, "Do not work for food that spoils, but for food that remains for eternal life, which the Son of man will give you" (v. 27a), is interpreted by his words, "unless you eat the flesh of the Son of man and drink his blood, you do not have life in you. The one who eats my flesh and drinks my blood has eternal life, and I will raise that person up on the last day" (vv. 53–54). This reference to ingesting the flesh and blood of the Son of Man is shocking, but its fundamental meaning is clear: Jesus' death will be a source of eternal life for others,[28] echoing the main theme of the Son of Man saying in 3:14. The phrase "I will raise that person up on the last day" (v. 54), found three other times in the wider discourse (6:39, 40, 44), is a clear reference to the final judgment.[29] So the identification on the Son of Man with future judgment, found already in 5:24–30, is here again made explicit.[30] It is as the Son of Man who has been entrusted by God with the

---

27. Maddox, "Function," 196, who also notes the importance in this regard of the repeated "raised up at the last day" in vv. 39, 40, 44, 54, on which see below. On the role of the three Son of Man *logia* in unifying this pericope, see Schnackenburg, *John*, 1:530–31.

28. Michaels, *John*, 395.

29. Lincoln, *John*, 230; Michaels, *John*, 381.

30. Verses 39, 40, 44, and 54 tie the mention of the Son of Man in vv. 27, 53, and 62 to the idea of an apocalyptic, heavenly judge (*pace* Hare, *Son of Man*, 96–98). That these verses do not mention judgment, but only "raising up on the last day" is because they function not as warning but as promise.

final raising of the dead for judgment that Jesus can promise that he will raise his own for eternal life.

Those who wished to excise these references to the future as not fitting John's emphasis on realized eschatology[31] missed the function they have in substantiating Jesus' claims for the present life of those who follow him. The many promises Jesus makes in this passage all have to do with eschatology: that those who come to him will never be hungry or thirsty (v. 35) echoes his offer of "food of eternal life" (v. 27), namely himself; those who eat of him will never die (v. 50) but live for ever (v. 52). That he will never turn away any who come to him (v. 37) or lose any of those the Father has given him (v. 39) have as their end goal that he may give them all eternal life (vv. 40, 47). In the final analysis, then, this discourse is all about eternal life, or more correctly about the One who *gives* eternal life. Here, as in 5:24–29, the future is called upon to substantiate a claim in the present: Jesus can give his hearers life in the present because he is the Son of Man who in the future will "raise them up at the last day" (vv. 39, 40, 44, 54). The claim to be the one who in the future would raise them at the last day ultimately under-girds his claim to be in his own person the very bread of life in the present (vv. 35, 48), and that only in eating his flesh and drinking his blood can life be found (vv. 53–58; also 50–51). The promise of life is inextricably bound to the person of Jesus in the present, just as it is—and *because* it is—inextricably bound to his person in the future.

To turn to the last Son of Man saying in this discourse, when many of Jesus' disciples were offended at his teaching, Jesus replied, "Does this shock you? Then what if you were to see the Son of Man going up to where he was before?" (6:61b–62). The reader, aware that Jesus has "gone up into heaven" (3:13), and even more fundamentally, aware of his heavenly origin (1:2), would know "where he was before" (6:62).[32] This awareness would serve as a warrant for the truth of Jesus' claims regarding the present and the future in the preceding verses.

The above two texts, John 5:24–30 and 6:26–65, when combined offer a strong precedent for reading the references to the Son of Man in subsequent chapters against the background of future eschatological judgment. As noted early on in this paper, following the normative process of reading implies that insights given earlier in the Gospel inform the reading of texts that come later.[33] New possibilities emerge for interpreting texts in John

---

31. E.g., Bultmann, *John*, 218–20ff. Against this approach Beasley-Murray rightly states: "There is no contradiction between the gift of life now and resurrection in the future" (*John*, 92).

32. Michaels, *John*, 407; Schnackenburg, *John*, 2:71.

33. Powell, "Narrative Criticism," 244.

7–21 when one reads them in light of future eschatological judgment, which the reader knows is implicit in the mention of the Son of Man due to having read John 1–6.

One can apply this insight to John 9:1–41, which unites once again the Son of Man and judgment, but does not make the future element of this judgment explicit.[34] In 9:35 Jesus asks the blind man whom he had healed, "Do you believe in the Son of Man?"[35] In answer to the man's question concerning the identity of the Son of Man, Jesus replies: "Not only have you seen him, but the one speaking with you is him" (v. 37).

What is one to make of Jesus' question? The blind man had just been "cast out" (perhaps from the synagogue, though this is not stated explicitly) by the Pharisees (v. 34), a theme central to the idea of persecution within the Gospel of John (9:22; 16:2).[36] The irony of the situation should not be lost on the reader, who knows that in spite of the charges leveled against the man by the Pharisees, he had been cast out for speaking the truth about Jesus. For Jesus to question the man at that point as to his belief in the Son of Man, identifying himself as such, might suggest to the mind of the reader that the wrong suffered by the man (and by the First Century readers who had suffered a like fate!) would be set right by Jesus the Son of Man at the eschatological judgment. This association with the future was set in place by the Son of Man texts in John 5 and 6, and informs the reading of the verses now under consideration. The language of judgment is found later in this pericope when in 9:39 Jesus says, "For judgment I have come into this world . . ." Even this reference to present judgment points to a future judgment by Jesus as Son of Man, when this passage is read in conjunction with such statements as: "For I have come not in order to judge the world, but in order to save the world" (12:47); that is, the judgment that takes place in the present is the division among peoples in terms of their acceptance or rejection of Jesus, so that their fate is already cast for the future judgment.

In light of all of the above, one may interpret Jesus' statement in 9:41: "because you declare that you see, your guilt remains" as implying: "your guilt remains *until the final judgment*." As Barnabas Lindars rightly states: "it may well be that [John] is thinking of the future judgment, which is

---

34. The Son of Man text in 8:28 will be addressed out of order together with the one in 13:31 below.

35. Some MSS read "Son of God" in place of "Son of Man" in 9:35, but the weight of MSS support leans heavily toward the originality of "Son of Man," and following the rule of the most difficult reading, "Son of Man" is to be preferred; see Metzger, *Textual Commentary*, 194.

36. For a reconstruction of the historical situation see Brown, *Community*, 22–23, 66–69; cf. Meeks, "Man from Heaven," 192–95.

anticipated in the confrontation with Jesus in his incarnate life; the response to Jesus *now* determines his verdict as Son of Man in the future."[37] This reading is supported by John 3:36, the closest Johannine parallel to 9:41: "Whoever believes in the Son has eternal life, but whoever does not believe in the Son will not see life, and God's wrath remains on them."[38] This contrast between having eternal life, and not seeing life but remaining under God's wrath, may imply that not only is life eternal, but also the not seeing life and the wrath are eternal, as all have to do with eschatological judgment.

In the above one finds once again that the future is brought to bear on the present and the present on the future. Jesus' claim to have come into the world so that "those who do not see may see, and those who see might become blind" (9:39), which will ultimately be corroborated at the final judgment, is substantiated in the present on the one hand by his power to give sight to the physically blind, and on the other by the spiritual blindness of the Pharisees who claimed to see but fail to recognize Jesus' identity. But it is in part the knowledge of his identity as Son of Man who will exercise judgment on the final day that leaves the reader in no doubt regarding Jesus' authority to speak judgment in the present.

The Johannine Son of Man and the Call to Discipleship

The next two Son of Man sayings, in 12:23 and 34, are best treated together within the larger discourse unit of 12:20–50. Jesus' discourse begins with the statement: "The time has come for the Son of Man to be glorified" (v. 23), a clear reference to his passion in light of the wider context of vv. 24–33. In the corresponding cotext one finds two references to a future eschatology in vv. 25–26: "Whoever loves their life will lose it, but whoever hates their life in this world will keep it for eternal life. If anyone would serve me, they must follow me, and where I am, there also my servant will be. If anyone serves me my Father will honor them." The contrast of "for eternal life" (εἰς ζωὴν αἰώνιον) with "in this world" (ἐν τῷ κόσμῳ τούτῳ) indicates that "eternal life" here does not pertain to the present but to the eschatological future.[39] Jesus' statement that those who would serve him must follow him, spoken in the context of references to his own death, implies that the

---

37. Lindars, *John*, 351; author's own italics. This statement still holds true, regardless of whether or not Lindars would have wanted to revise it in light of his later understanding of the Son of Man in John (see his *Jesus*, 145–57; Lindars, *John*, 82–84).

38. Michaels, *John*, 576n18.

39. Lincoln, *John*, 350.

following includes death, with the further implication that the honor given by the Father is in post-resurrection life.[40]

Here the future is impacted by the present in a different way than what has been noted so far in this essay: those who are willing to join the suffering of the Son of Man in the present will also be joined to him "for eternal life."[41] In light of all that has been argued above, the following may be implied: the Son of Man who calls to discipleship in the present can guarantee that it will result in honor and life at the final resurrection because he is the very one entrusted with raising the dead and carrying out that judgment.

Later on in this passage Jesus states:

> "Now is the judgment of this world, now will the ruler of this world be cast out. And when I am lifted up from the earth I will draw all people to myself." He said this to indicate what kind of death he was about to die. The crowd answered him, "We have heard from the law that the Messiah remains for ever. Why do you say that it is necessary to lift up the Son of Man? Who is this 'the Son of Man'?" (12:31–34)

With this portrayal of the people's difficulty in understanding a Son of Man who would not remain forever, John may imply that they held the expectation of a Son of Man who would inaugurate an eternal kingdom after judging the nations.[42] The irony implicit in their questioning is that, as the reader knows, Jesus the Son of Man *would* live forever, but by first experiencing death he would make eternal life available to all (v. 32).

The people also failed to realize that as hearers they were included in the time of judgment upon the world. As Brown states, "The crowd ponders about the nature and identity of the Son of Man; but it is more important that they face up to the judgment that is associated with the Son of Man, the judgment of coming to the light and walking in it lest they be swallowed up in darkness."[43] Of those who reject his word and remain in darkness (12:46) Jesus says, "But if anyone should hear my words and not obey them, I do not judge them. For I did not come in order to judge the world, but in order to save the world. Anyone who rejects me and does not receive my words has a judge: the word that I spoke will be their judge on the last day" (12:47–48).

---

40. Brown, *John*, 1:474–5.

41. De Jonge speaks of the already/not yet dynamic in these texts in terms of a "prolepsis" and a "*futurum continuum*" (*Jesus*, 176).

42. As reflected in *1 En.* 49:2–4, a text roughly contemporary with the Fourth Gospel.

43. Brown, *John*, 1:479.

Jesus' word spoken to the people in the present would be their future judge on the last day.

These statements by Jesus need to be understood in the context of other statements such as those in 5:22–29 and 9:39, already discussed above. It is only that aspect of the judging work of the Son of Man reserved for the *future* that explains the apparent contradiction between the statements: "for judgment I have come into this world" (9:39; cf. 5:22–29) and "I did not come in order to judge the world, but in order to save the world" (12:47; cf. 3:17–21). This future element is made explicit for the statement in 12:47 when in 12:48 Jesus continues: "Anyone who rejects me and does not receive my words has a judge: the word that I spoke will be their judge on the last day." Jesus' role in the present is to provide salvation (12:47), but how his hearers respond to his word constitutes the basis upon which Jesus as the Son of Man will judge them "on the last day." In this way, although John makes clear that Jesus is the Son of Man in the present, his role as such is proleptic in the sense that the full work of Jesus as the Son of Man will only be completed on the final day.[44]

When Martyn states that the "judgment by the Son of Man takes place essentially on earth and in the present,"[45] this is true to the extent that humans (both Jesus' contemporaries and John's readers) only have the present within which to respond to Jesus' word addressed to them.[46] Those who heed his word and put their trust in the Father already have eternal life; they will not see judgment but have "gone from death to life" (5:24). Although in this sense the final judgment upon Jesus' hearers "on the last day" will be already decided, that does not bring the future judgment itself fully into the present, but does so only proleptically.[47] Finally, Jesus' statement in 9:39, "for judgment I have come into this world," finds its deepest present meaning in the once-for-all nature of the presence of Jesus on earth as the revelation of the Father.[48] His continued presence in the Paraclete does not supersede his word delivered as he walked the earth, but rather serves to

---

44. Pace Martyn, *History*, 134.

45. Ibid.

46. To this extent Bultmann's emphasis on Johannine eschatology as the existential moment of decision was justified, but incomplete. In order to hold that view in exclusion of a future judgment he was forced to excise the "on the last day" from the end of 12:47, attributing it to the hand of a redactor (*Theology*, 2:38–39).

47. Based on a number of texts: John 5:24; 3:18; 5:29; and 11:25b. One could argue that the final judgment in John is reserved only for those who reject Jesus. However, this does not materially affect the present argument.

48. Cf. Hare, "the incarnation is the locus of judgment" (*Son of Man*, 96).

point back to it and explain its significance (14:26).[49] Jesus' word as it was spoken will stand in judgment of his contemporaries and of John's readers until the very last day.

In the above, one sees once more the dynamic by which the present determines the future and the future the present. The criterion by which the Son of Man will judge at the eschaton is the people's response to his word and person in the present. And yet he is present even now as the Son of Man, his future role as judge of his hearers providing a basis for his present claims.

The two Johannine Son of Man sayings that remain, which will be considered only briefly, are found in 8:28 and 13:31 (treated together here because of their similarity). Here once again one finds that the present impacts the future, in that both sayings have to do with the present choices of Jesus' hearers determining their future destiny. In the verses leading up to 8:28 Jesus tells "the Jews" that where he is going they cannot go (v. 21), that they are "from below" and "of this world," but he is "from above" and "not of this world" (v. 23), and that if they do not believe in him they will die in their sins (v. 24).[50] Then Jesus states, "When you have lifted up the Son of Man, then you will know that I am,[51] and that I do nothing of my own accord, but speak only those things the Father has instructed me" (v. 28). Here one finds reflected several themes cumulatively present in previous Son of Man sayings: Jesus' insider knowledge of the things of God, his origin "from above," and the fate of Jesus' hearers in the future judgment having already been determined by their response to him in the present.[52]

The saying in John 13:31 is similar to the one in 8:28, but in this case Jesus' hearers are not "the Jews" but his disciples. When Jesus says to them: "Now is the Son of man glorified" (13:31b), this is a reference to his certain and imminent crucifixion, given that Judas has just gone out to betray him (vv 30–31a).[53] Jesus then refers back to the cotext of 8:28 in stating: "You will look for me, and I say to you now the same thing that I told the Jews before, 'Where I go you are not able to go'" (13:33b). Shortly after, Peter asks

---

49. Cf. Cullmann, *Salvation*, 272–73.

50. The meaning of the phrase "if you do not believe that I am [ἐγώ εἰμι] you will die in your sins" (v. 24b) is ambiguous. It seems best to interpret the "I am" as a reference to Jesus having come from the Father, doing nothing on his own, and speaking only those things that the Father instructs him (vv. 26–28); see Michaels, *John*, 488.

51. On this "I am" (ἐγώ εἰμι) see the immediately preceding note.

52. The contrast with 13:31 (see below) makes it likely that 8:28 is about judgment rather than salvation; that the "then you will know that I am" refers to a saving knowledge, however, remains a possibility; see Schnackenburg, *John*, 2:202–3.

53. Michaels, *John*, 756.

where he is going, to which Jesus replies, "Where I am going you cannot follow me now, but you will follow me later" (v. 36). Jesus' death implies his imminent departure, and the reader has already been told that Jesus' hour has come "to depart this world towards the Father" (13:1), and that "he had come from God and was departing to God" (13:3). This final Johannine Son of Man text serves as the climax for those texts that spoke of his heavenly origin, his relation to the Father, and that people's response to him in the present predetermined their future destiny. The text sounds a clear note of hope, a promise to those who have believed in Jesus that they will join him where he will go after being lifted up.

CONCLUSION

The above note of hope is a fitting place at which to conclude this study of the Son of Man in John, as the emphasis within this Gospel is upon his role in providing present salvation. Yet this study has shown that there is another side to John's portrayal of the Son of Man, admittedly not an emphasis, and yet discernible as part of the intricate weaving of themes in this Gospel. The claims of Jesus the Son of Man in the present to be the revealer of heavenly things and the bearer of eternal life are supported in part by his identity *as* the Son of Man, given that as such he is not only of heavenly origin but also will play a role in determining the eternal destiny of his hearers in the eschatological future. Likewise, that he is the one who will play this role in the future is attested by his identity in the present as the bearer of divine revelation and eternal life. He is the watershed who judges human beings in the present and divides them between those who will see eternal life and those who will experience a future condemnation. One could say that the Son of Man material in John thus provides another example of the Evangelist's masterful use of irony.[54] Just as John presents as profoundly ironic such ideas as God becoming human,[55] or of the Jews rejecting their eagerly awaited Messiah,[56] so also there is a strong element of irony in the Son of Man retaining his role as eschatological judge even while being revealed in the present as Savior.

---

54. Culpepper identifies six themes that are treated ironically in John: "(1) the rejection of Jesus, (2) the origin of Jesus, (3) Jesus' identity, (4) Jesus' ministry, (5) Jesus' death, and (6) discipleship" ("Johannine Irony," 195, treated at length in Culpepper, *Anatomy*, 169–75); on irony in John, see further Smith, *John*, 102–4.

55. Culpepper, "Johannine Irony," 200.

56. Culpepper, *Anatomy*, 169.

BIBLIOGRAPHY

Ashton, John. *Understanding the Fourth Gospel*. 2nd ed. Oxford: Oxford University Press, 2007.
Aune, David E. "Early Christian Eschatology." In *ABD*, 2:594–609.
Barrett, C. K. *The Gospel According to St. John*. 2nd ed. Philadelphia: Westminster, 1978.
Beasley-Murray, G. R. *John*. 2nd ed. WBC 36. Nashville: Nelson, 1999.
Bock, Darrell L. "The Use of Daniel 7 in Jesus' Trial, with Implications for His Self-Understanding." In *"Who Is This Son of Man?": The Latest Scholarship on a Puzzling Expression of the Historical Jesus*, ed. L. W. Hurtado and P. Owen, 78–100. LNTS 390. London: T. & T. Clark, 2010.
Borsch, Frederick Houk. *The Son of Man in Myth and History*. NTL. Philadelphia: Westminster, 1967.
Brown, Raymond E. *The Community of the Beloved Disciple*. New York: Paulist, 1979.
———. *The Gospel According to John*. Vol. 1, *I–XII*. AB 29. New York: Doubleday, 1966.
Bultmann, Rudolf. "The Eschatology of the Gospel of John." In *Faith and Understanding*, ed. R. W. Funk, 165–83. Trans. L. P. Smith. Philadelphia: Fortress, 1987.
———. *The Gospel of John: A Commentary*. Ed. and trans. G. R. Beasley-Murray et al. Philadelphia: Westminster, 1971.
———. *Theology of the New Testament*. Trans. K. Grobel. 2 vols. London: SCM, 1952–1955.
Burkett, Delbert. *The Son of Man Debate: A History and Evaluation*. SNTSMS 107. Cambridge: Cambridge University Press, 1999.
———. *The Son of Man in the Gospel of John*. JSNTSup 56. Sheffield: JSOT Press, 1991.
Casey, Maurice. *The Solution to the "Son of Man" Problem*. LNTS 343. London: T. & T. Clark, 2007.
———. *Son of Man: The Interpretation and Influence of Daniel 7*. London: SPCK, 1979.
Collins, John J. *The Apocalyptic Vision of the Book of Daniel*. HSM 16. Missoula, MT: Scholars, 1977.
———. "The Son of Man in First-Century Judaism." *NTS* 38 (1992) 448–66.
Colpe, Carsten. "ὁ υἱὸς τοῦ ἀνθρώπου." In *TDNT* 8:400–477.
Cullmann, Oscar. *Salvation in History*. Trans. S. G. Sowers et al. London: SCM, 1967.
Culpepper, R. Alan. *Anatomy of the Fourth Gospel: A Study in Literary Design*. Philadelphia: Fortress, 1983.
———. "Reading Johannine Irony." In *Exploring the Gospel of John: In Honor of D. Moody Smith*, ed. R. A. Culpepper and C. C. Black, 193–207. Louisville: Westminster John Knox, 1996.
Dahl, Nils A. "'Do Not Wonder!' John 5:28–29 and Johannine Eschatology Once More." In *The Conversation Continues: Studies in Paul and John in Honor of J. Louis Martyn*, ed. R. T. Fortna and B. R. Gaventa, 322–36. Nashville: Abingdon, 1990.
Davies, Margaret. *Rhetoric and Reference in the Fourth Gospel*. JSNTSup 69. Sheffield: JSOT Press, 1992.
de Jonge, Marinus. *Jesus: Stranger from Heaven and Son of God: Jesus Christ and the Christians in Johannine Perspective*. SBLSBS 11. Ed. and trans. J. E. Steely. Missoula, MT: Scholars, 1977.
Dunn, James D. G. *Christology in the Making: A New Testament Inquiry into the Origins of the Doctrine of the Incarnation*. 2nd ed. Grand Rapids: Eerdmans, 1996.

———. "The Danielic Son of Man in the New Testament." In *The Book of Daniel: Composition and Reception*, ed. J. J. Collins and P. W. Flint, 2:528–49. VTSup 83. Formation and Interpretation of Old Testament Literature 2. Leiden: Brill, 2001.

Frey, Jörg. *Die johanneische Eschatologie*. Vol. 1, *Ihre Probleme im Spiegel der Forschung seit Reimarus*. WUNT 96. Tübingen: Mohr/Siebeck, 1997.

Hannah, Darrell D. "The Elect Son of Man of the *Parables of Enoch*." In *"Who Is This Son of Man?": The Latest Scholarship on a Puzzling Expression of the Historical Jesus*, ed. L. W. Hurtado and P. Owen, 130–58. LNTS 390. London: T. & T. Clark, 2010.

Hare, Douglas R. A. *The Son of Man Tradition*. Minneapolis: Fortress, 1990.

Higgins, A. J. B. *Jesus and the Son of Man*. Philadelphia: Fortress, 1964.

Hooker, M. D. "Is the Son of Man Problem Really Insoluble?" In *Text and Interpretation: Studies in the New Testament Presented to Matthew Black*, ed. E. Best and R. McL. Wilson, 155–68. Cambridge: Cambridge University Press, 1979.

Hoskyns, Edwyn C. *The Fourth Gospel*. Ed. F. N. Davey. Rev. ed. London: Faber and Faber, 1947.

Howard, W. F. *Christianity According to St. John*. Philadelphia: Westminster, 1946.

Hurtado, Larry W., and Paul Owen, eds. *"Who Is This Son of Man?": The Latest Scholarship on a Puzzling Expression of the Historical Jesus*. LNTS 390. London: T. & T. Clark, 2010.

Kim, Seyoon. *"The 'Son of Man'" as the Son of God*. WUNT 30. Tübingen: Mohr/Siebeck, 1983.

Kümmel, W. G. *The Theology of the New Testament according to Its Major Witnesses: Jesus, Paul, John*. Trans. J. E. Steely. Nashville: Abingdon, 1973.

Kysar, Robert. *John: The Maverick Gospel*. 3rd ed. Louisville: Westminster John Knox, 2007.

Ladd, George E. *A Theology of the New Testament*. Ed. Donald A. Hagner. Rev. ed. Grand Rapids: Eerdmans, 1993.

Lindars, Barnabas. *The Gospel of John*. New Century Bible Commentary. Grand Rapids: Eerdmans, 1981.

———. *Jesus, Son of Man: A Fresh Examination of the Son of Man Sayings in the Gospels in the Light of Recent Research*. Grand Rapids: Eerdmans, 1984.

———. *John*. NTG. Sheffield: JSOT Press, 1990.

———. "Son of Man." In *A Dictionary of Biblical Interpretation*, ed. R. J. Coggins and J. L. Houlden, 639–42. Philadelphia: Trinity, 1990.

Longenecker, Richard N. *The Christology of Early Jewish Christianity*. London: SCM, 1970.

Lukaszewski, Albert L. "Issues Concerning the Aramaic Behind ὁ υἱὸς τοῦ ἀνθρώπου: A Critical Review of Scholarship." In *"Who Is This Son of Man?": The Latest Scholarship on a Puzzling Expression of the Historical Jesus*, ed. L. W. Hurtado and P. Owen, 1–27. LNTS 390. London: T. & T. Clark, 2010.

Maddox, Robert. "The Function of the Son of Man in the Gospel of John." In *Reconciliation and Hope: New Testament Essays on Atonement and Eschatology Presented to L. L. Morris on his 60th Birthday*, ed. R. Banks, 186–204. Grand Rapids: Eerdmans, 1974.

Martyn, J. Louis. *History and Theology in the Fourth Gospel*. 3rd ed. NTL. Louisville: Westminster John Knox, 2003.

Meeks, Wayne A. "The Man from Heaven in Johannine Sectarianism." In *The Interpretation of John*, ed. John Ashton, 169–205. 2nd ed. Studies in New Testament Interpretation. Edinburgh: T. & T. Clark, 1997.

Metzger, Bruce M. *A Textual Commentary on the Greek New Testament*. 2nd ed. New York: United Bible Societies, 1994.

Michaels, J. Ramsey. *The Gospel of John*. NICNT. Grand Rapids: Eerdmans, 2010.

Moule, C. F. D. "Neglected Features in the Problem of 'the Son of Man.'" In *Essays in New Testament Interpretation*, 75–90. Cambridge: Cambridge University Press, 1982.

———. "'The Son of Man': Some of the Facts." *NTS* 41 (1995) 277–279.

Nickelsburg, George W.E. "Son of Man." In *ABD*, 6:137–50.

Owen, Paul L. "Problems with Casey's 'Solution.'" In *"Who Is This Son of Man?": The Latest Scholarship on a Puzzling Expression of the Historical Jesus*, ed. L. W. Hurtado and P. Owen, 28–49. LNTS 390. London: T. & T. Clark, 2010.

Powell, Mark Allan. "Narrative Criticism." In *Hearing the New Testament: Strategies for Interpretation*, ed. Joel B. Green, 240–58. 2nd ed. Grand Rapids: Eerdmans, 2010.

Reynolds, Benjamin E. *The Apocalyptic Son of Man in the Gospel of John*. WUNT 2/249. Tübingen: Mohr/Siebeck, 2008.

———. "The Use of the Son of Man Idiom in the Gospel of John." In *"Who Is This Son of Man?": The Latest Scholarship on a Puzzling Expression of the Historical Jesus*, ed. L. W. Hurtado and P. Owen, 101–29. LNTS 390. London: T. & T. Clark, 2010.

Russell, D. S. *The Method and Message of Jewish Apocalyptic*. OTL. Philadelphia: Westminster, 1974.

Schnackenburg, Rudolf. *The Gospel According to St. John*. 3 vols. HTKNT. Trans. Kevin Smyth et al. New York: Herder and Herder, 1968–1990.

Smalley, Stephen S. "The Johannine Son of Man Sayings." *NTS* 15 (1968–1969) 278–301.

Smith, D. Moody. *John*. 2nd rev. enlarged ed. Proclamation Commentaries. Philadelphia: Fortress, 1986.

Yarbro Collins, Adela. "The Apocalyptic Son of Man Sayings." In *The Future of Early Christianity: Essays in Honor of Helmut Koester*, ed. Birger A. Pearson et al., 220–28. Minneapolis: Fortress, 1991.

13

The Bilingualism of the Hebrews and the Hellenists in the Jerusalem Church[1]

SANG-IL LEE

INTRODUCTION

Who are the Hebrews and the Hellenists in the earliest church in Jerusalem at Acts 6:1? In reply to this old and complicated question, scholars have proposed various opinions. It has generally been accepted, however, that Hengel's suggestion is the most persuasive and influential. He proposes that the Hebrews refer to Palestinian Jewish Christians who spoke Aramaic and some Greek, whereas the Hellenists refer to Diaspora Jewish Christians who spoke only Greek.

Although he tried to apply bilingualism to solving the problem, he could not work out the details of his theory completely. The difficulty is that his view is still based on monolingualism. In this essay, I apply sociolinguistic theory to the linguistic milieu of the Jerusalem church and propose that the Hebrews were Aramaic-matrix Christians and the Hellenists were Greek-matrix Christians.

---

1. This article is a slightly revised version of ch. 5 in my monograph *Jesus and Gospel Traditions*. I am grateful to the publisher Walter de Gruyter for permission to reprint this essay here in a revised form.

THE STATE OF AFFAIRS

Since Baur, the identities of the Hebrews and the Hellenists (Acts 6:1) have provoked endless controversies.[2] Scholars have suggested various ways to define their identities, which include such views as: the linguistic distinction between Aramaic-speaking and Greek-speaking Jews, the geographical distinction between Palestinian and Diaspora Jews, the theological distinction between conservative and radical Jews, or the ethnic distinction between Jews and Gentiles.[3] At present, it would appear that scholars have almost reached a consensus that the two terms stem from the linguistic-geographical distinction on the basis of an assumption that both of them were Jews. That is, the Hebrews refer to Aramaic-speaking Palestinian Jews and the Hellenists refer to Greek-speaking Diaspora Jews.

There have been two approaches to the Hellenists. The first is a bilingual approach and the other a monolingual one. More than 250 years ago, Bengel proposed that the Hellenists refer to bilinguals in Greek and Hebrew (i.e., Aramaic). He insisted that the Hellenists "were Jews born outside of Palestine, to whom it seems the Greek tongue, besides the Hebrew, was vernacular."[4] In modern linguistic terms, this means that the Hellenists were *primary* bilinguals. Bengel also mentioned that "there is no doubt but that these Jews of all nations, who moreover were *dwelling* at Jerusalem, knew Hebrew."[5] This means that the Hellenists *acquired* Hebrew (i.e., Aramaic) while living in Jerusalem. His suggestion that there were two kinds of bilingual Hellenists who used Greek and Hebrew (i.e., Aramaic) respectively remained convincing for two reasons: (1) the Hellenists from all nations were *primary* bilinguals in Greek and Aramaic because Jews who spoke Aramaic were born in Greek-speaking regions; and (2) some were acquired bilinguals learned Aramaic when they lived in Jerusalem or other Aramaic-speaking regions. It is regrettable that Bengel's suggestions in this regard have not continued to be debated by the academy.

---

2. Baur, *Paul, the Apostle*, 1:39. According to Baur, there were two groups in the Jerusalem church: one is the Hellenists whose leader was Stephen, and the other is the Hebraists including the apostles of Jesus. The former rejects Judaism and is in opposition to the existing Temple worship, whereas the latter more closely adheres to Temple worship.

3. For the history of the debate, see Penner, *Christian Origins*, 69–72; Hill, *Hellenists and Hebrews*, 5–17; Hengel, *Between Jesus and Paul*, 1–11. Concerning the discussion over one hundred years ago, Roberts (*Greek the Language*, 187–89n1) epitomized the history of research of the Hellenists and the Hebrews in detail.

4. Bengel, *Gnomon*, 2:564; italics author's own.

5. Ibid., 2:525.

A number of scholars have given consideration to a monolingual-geographical view of the Hellenists, as suggested by Hengel. Hill's opinion is justified when he writes that "the most influential contemporary advocate of a view of the Hellenists consistent with that of F. C. Baur is Martin Hengel."[6] In light of the position of Hengel's argument in the current debate, he serves as the primary counterpart below.

Hengel suggests that the Hebrews refer to Palestinian Jewish Christians who spoke Aramaic and some Greek, while the Hellenists refer to Diaspora Jewish Christians who spoke *only Greek*, having returned from the Diaspora.[7] The Hellenists' monolingualism quickly led them to separate their community from worship with the Aramaic-speaking Jerusalem church.[8] The formation of the Greek-speaking Jewish Christian community is noteworthy because the Hellenists made an essential contribution to the translation of the Jesus tradition from Aramaic to Greek. In other words, some parts of the Jesus tradition, including at least the passion narrative and the development of significant theological terms, were most likely translated by the Hellenists.

The Hellenists may have had vivid memoirs of the activities, death, and the resurrection of Jesus on which the Greek-speaking Christian community in the Jerusalem church was based.[9] The Greek tradition of Jesus could have given impetus to the propagation of the message of Jesus to non-Jews by the

---

6. Hill, *Hellenists and Hebrews*, 15. Penner (*Christian Origins*, 23) also notes that "the trajectory of scholarship on the Hellenists that begins with Baur culminates in Hengel's work on Acts 6:1—8:1. Hengel not only provides the most systematic interpretation of the Hellenists in the tradition of Baur; he also fuels the debate over the reconstruction of early Christian origins." To date, Hengel has persistently held his position; see Hengel, "Eye-witness Memory," 83–90.

7. Hengel and Schwemer, *Paul between Damascus and Antioch*, 32–35; Hengel, *Acts*, 79; Hengel, *Between Jesus and Paul*, 8–11. In fact, Hengel and Schwemer rejected the sharp distinction between Judaism and Hellenism. Hengel (*Judaism and Hellenism*, 104) upholds the view that "a better differentiation could be made between the Greek-speaking Judaism of the Western Diaspora and the Aramaic/Hebrew speaking Judaism of Palestine and Babylonia." He (*Hellenization*, 7) also argues that "'Hellenistic' Jews and Jewish Christians are . . . those whose mother tongue was Greek, in contrast to the Jews in Palestine and in the Babylonian Diaspora who originally spoke Aramaic." Hengel's arguments are not persuasive in two points: (1) his definition of the "Western Diaspora" is not clear. Does, for instance, the Antiochene Christian community, one of the most important Christian communities, belong to the Western Diaspora? (2) Diaspora Jews do not always refer to Greek-speaking Jews.

8. Hengel, *Between Jesus and Paul*, 14–15; Hengel, *Pre-Christian Paul*, 56, 68. Hengel (*Between Jesus and Paul*, 55) notes: "The separation of two groups in Jerusalem had become necessary because of the language of their liturgy." This view is further developed by Esler (*Community*, 135–59, esp. 143, 159).

9. Hengel, *Between Jesus and Paul*, 27.

earliest missionaries such as the Hellenists, including the Seven.[10] On this account, Hengel asserts that "we owe the real bridge between Jesus and Paul to those almost unknown Jewish-Christian 'Hellenists' of the group around Stephen and the first Greek-speaking community in Jerusalem which they founded; this was the first to translate the Jesus tradition into Greek."[11]

But how was it possible for the Hellenists, who spoke only Greek, to translate the tradition of Jesus from Aramaic to Greek? Hengel assigns the translation duty to *bilinguals*. The bilinguals played the role of translators-transmitters of the Jesus tradition between Aramaic-speaking Palestinian Jewish Christians (i.e., the Hebrews) and Greek-speaking Diaspora Jewish Christians (i.e., the Hellenists) in the Jerusalem church.[12] At points he calls the bilinguals *"jüdische 'Graekopalästiner'"*[13] and at a later point develops the designation *"zweisprachige 'Graekopalästiner.'"*[14] He provides examples of many bilinguals,[15] such as Mary and her son John Mark (Acts 12:12, 25; 13:5, 13; 15:37), Silas-Silvanus (Acts 15:22, 27, 32; 1 Thess.1:1; 2 Cor.1:19), Judas Barsabbas (Acts 15:22, 32), Menahem (i.e., the younger contemporary of Herod Antipas; Acts13:1), Matthew,[16] and Peter.[17] Hengel includes in this list "Jews who themselves came from the Diaspora but whose families were closely associated with Palestine and spent a great part of their life there."[18] These were bilinguals such as Jason of Cyrene and later the Levite Joseph Barnabas from Cyprus, the "cousin" of John Mark (Acts 4:36 etc; cf. Col 4:10), and the Pharisee Saul-Paul from Tarsus.[19]

10. Ibid., 26–27.

11. Hengel, *Between Jesus and Paul*, 29; cf. Hengel and Schwemer, *Paul between Damascus and Antioch*, 34.

12. Hengel, *Between Jesus and Paul*, 14. He presumes: "The Hellenists may have been converted by the preaching of bilingual disciples and conversation with them" (ibid., 14).

13. Hengel, *Judaism and Hellenism*, 104–5.

14. Hengel, *Between Jesus and Paul*, 11. First, Hengel calls them *"jüdische 'Graekopalästiner'"* in his *Judentum und Hellenismus*, 193 (in English: *Judaism and Hellenism*, 1–5); later, he takes up *"zweisprachige 'Graekopalästiner'"* in his "Zwischen Jesus und Paulus," 151–206 (in English: *Between Jesus and Paul*, 1–29). He mixes the two terms. However, the problem lies in that he does not define the terms clearly, as will be discussed.

15. The lists of bilinguals of the earliest Christian community in Jerusalem come from Hengel, *Judaism and Hellenism*, 104–5; Hengel, *Between Jesus and Paul*, 10–11; idem, *Hellenization*, 14–18.

16. Hengel, *Judaism and Hellenism*, 105n359; cf. Jeremias, "Muttersprache," 270–74.

17. Hengel, *Between Jesus and Paul*, 37; 162n39; 170n26.

18. Hengel, *Judaism and Hellenism*, 105.

19. Ibid., 105. For Paul's bilinguality, see Lee, *Jesus and the Gospel Traditions*, 120–29.

In addition, Hengel adds more names to his list of the bilinguals later: Johanna (the wife of Chuza, ἐπιτρόπου of Herod Antipas, i.e., his steward; Luke 8:3), the tax farmers (e.g., the ἀρχιτελώνης Zacchaeus in Jericho; Luke 19:2), and then men like Nicodemus (John 3:1) and Joseph of Arimathaea (Matt 27:57).[20] Hengel also believes that "these bilingual 'Palestinian Greeks' are of decisive significance for the development of early Christianity."[21] According to him, they take an *active* and important role in the translation of the Jesus tradition, thereby bridging the linguistic gap between the groups of the Hebrews and the Hellenists. This can be called the Jerusalem church translation theory. The bilingualism of first-century Palestine, however, could have led to the Galilee translation theory (i.e., the simultaneous translation theory) rather than the Jerusalem church translation theory.[22]

Many scholars have criticized Hengel's arguments. However, those who disagree with him have also based their comments upon a monolingual approach.[23] Furthermore, it is interesting that when Hengel criticizes other scholars' positions, he also proposes that they fail to consider the bilinguals who took a significant part in the transmission of the Jesus tradition.[24] For nearly thirty years, Hengel has been discussing this issue from the perspective of bilingualism.[25] More recently, he has emphasized that "we should not forget, especially in Jerusalem but also in Galilee or Syria and Babylonia, the bilingual Jews, who are so important for the beginnings of Christianity."[26]

Despite these remarks, a fundamental problem remains in that his own work does not clearly or comprehensively engage with the phenomena of bilingualism. The fact that Hengel does not take the bilingualism of Diaspora Jews and Gentile Christians of the Roman Empire seriously is apparent, although he accepts the following three points: (1) the bilingualism of first-century Jerusalem,[27] (2) the bilingualism of Jewish Graeco-Palestinians,

---

20. Hengel, "*Hellenization*," 17-18.

21. Hengel, *Between Jesus and Paul*, 11, 29.

22. For a detailed discussion, see Lee, *Jesus and the Gospel Traditions*, 58-61; 133.

23. Hill, *Hellenists and Hebrews*, 462-69; Hurtado, *Lord*, 207-14; Witherington, *Acts*, 243-47; Watson, *Paul, Judaism and the Gentiles*, 26; Räisänen, *Jesus*, 149-58.

24. Hengel criticizes Heitmüller's ("Problem," 320-37) and Kramer's (*Christ*) arguments of the Greek-speaking Jewish-Christian community and the Aramaic-speaking primitive community and claims that they fail to take account of bilingual Palestinian Greeks (*Between Jesus and Paul*, 32-37; and *Studies in Early Christology*, 381n52).

25. See his *Judaism and Hellenism*, 104-5, and recently in his "Judaism and Hellenism Revisited," 6-37.

26. Hengel, "Judaism and Hellenism Revisited," 7.

27. Hengel, *Between Jesus and Paul*, 10.

including some of Jesus' disciples in the Jerusalem church,[28] and (3) the bilingual "Jews who themselves came from the Diaspora but whose families were closely associated with Palestine and spent a great part of their life there."[29] His suggestion that the Hellenists spoke *only* Greek, while the Hebrews spoke Aramaic and *some Greek*, seems to be an important starting point for the interpretation of the linguistic transmission of the Jesus tradition in earliest Christianity.

At the same time, Hengel misinterpreted the entire situation. The two terms, "Hellenists" and "Hebrews," are used together only by Luke ("Hebrews" by itself is used by Paul).[30] If Luke designates the Hebrews as those who speak Aramaic and some Greek, why do we not think that he uses the Hellenists as those who speak Greek and some Aramaic? The counterpart of the two-language speakers (i.e., the Hebrews) should be the two-language speakers (i.e., the Hellenists). Therefore, the bilingualism of the Hebrews and the Hellenists of the community in Jerusalem as well as the bilingual Seven needs to be considered from the perspective of bilingualism theory.[31]

BILINGUALISM OF THE HEBREWS AND HELLENISTS

Hengel designates the Hebrews as Aramaic-speaking Palestinian Jewish Christians and the Hellenists as Greek-speaking Diaspora Jewish Christians; that is, he provides a monolingual, geographical, and ethnic distinction between the two groups. It seems that his geographical and ethnic designations are based on his monolingual approach. Hengel's conception of bilinguals is not clear for five reasons.

(1) He neither adequately defines *"jüdischen 'Graekopalätiner'"* and *"zweisprachige 'Graekopalästiner,'"* nor explains the difference between them although these two designations can be used differently to some degree. The relevance of this distinction becomes clear when one asks whether Matthew or Peter is to be designated a bilingual Palestinian *Greek*.

(2) It is not certain that bilinguals belong to either the Hebrews or the Hellenists. Also not clear is whether the bilingual group should be considered as "third parties."[32]

---

28. Hengel, *Judaism and Hellenism*, 104–5; Hengel, *Between Jesus and Paul*, 11.
29. Hengel, *Judaism and Hellenism*, 105.
30. See Lee, *Jesus and the Gospel Traditions*, 120–29.
31. Concerning my detailed argument of the bilingualism of the Seven, see Lee, *Jesus and the Gospel Traditions*, 197–208.
32. Hengel and Schwemer, *Paul between Damascus and Antioch*, 35.

(3) If the bilinguals belong to the Hellenists, how can "bilinguals like Paul from Tarsus and Joseph Barnabas from Cyprus" be distinguished from the Hellenists who spoke only Greek?

(4) If the bilinguals belong to the Hebrews, how can "Jews who themselves came from the Diaspora but whose families were closely associated with Palestine and spent a great part of their life there"[33] be labeled as the Hebrews who spoke Aramaic as their matrix language? Some of them appear to be the Hellenists who spoke Greek as their matrix language. If anyone learns a second language after the ages of 11–12, they cannot use the second language with the same adeptness as their primary language.[34] This means that unless we have their personal language acquisition details, it is difficult to classify them as the Hebrews.

(5) Can bilinguals like Peter from Bethsaida (an Aramaic-matrix bilingual) and Joseph Barnabas from Cyprus (a Greek-matrix bilingual) be categorized as belonging to the same group of "*zweisprachigen 'Graekopalästinern'*"?[35] Hengel seeks to introduce bilinguals as a bridge between two linguistic communities in the Jerusalem church; however, there is no place for bilinguals in his hypothesis because he recognizes a strict dichotomy between the two groups on the basis of monolingual-geographical distinction.[36]

It is noteworthy, however, that Marshall argues that "members of each group might know the other's language and both linguistic groups were to be found in Palestine and in the Diaspora."[37] He convincingly insists: "In Jerusalem and elsewhere, the early Christian communities included bilingual members,"[38] and "this makes the thesis of a completely separate

---

33. Hengel, *Judaism and Hellenism*, 105.
34. Lee, *Jesus and the Gospel Traditions*, 81–82.
35. It has been discussed among some scholars that the monolingual approach to the Hebrews and the Hellenists is faced with the difficulty to which category Paul and Barnabas as bilinguals belong. For instance, in terms of Paul and Barnabas, Haenchen (*Acts*, 365–66) assumes that Paul and Barnabas belong to the Hellenists. However, Barrett (*Acts*, 548) mentions that "though the witness of Acts is complicated by the fact that Luke seems to regard Paul and Barnabas as standing in succession from Stephen, Barnabas seems on the whole to belong to 'the Hebrews' rather than to 'the Hellenists.'" Rather, the fact that the monolingualists have different views hints that the bilingual approach to them should be required. Brown ("Not Jewish Christianity," 74–79) argues that it is hard to make a simple distinction between Jewish Christianity and Gentile Christianity in the first century AD.
36. Hengel, *Pre-Christian Paul*, 56, 68; Hengel, *Between Jesus and Paul*, 14.
37. Marshall, "Palestinian Christianity," 277–78.
38. Ibid., 280.

Aramaic-speaking church in Jerusalem all the less likely."[39] His suggestion leads us to consider the bilingualism of the earliest Christian community in Jerusalem.

If the bilingualism of Jerusalem and the Jewish Diaspora is taken seriously into account, the "bilingual distinction" of the two designations should be investigated for three reasons.

(1) Above all, the bilingual distinction can better explain the situation of the Jerusalem church. Whereas, in a sense, Aramaic-speakers and Greek-speakers can be associated with monolingual terminology, Aramaic-matrix speakers and Greek-matrix speakers are better described with bilingual terminology. Aramaic-matrix speakers refer to those who speak Aramaic as their matrix language and their linguistic competencies open the possibility that they can speak another language(s) as their embedded language(s).[40]

(2) The monolingual distinction does not cover all members of the Jerusalem church, especially bilinguals. Aramaic-matrix Christians in the Jerusalem church mean those who spoke Aramaic as their matrix language and Greek as their embedded language. Greek-matrix Christians mean those who spoke Greek as their matrix language and Aramaic as their embedded language.

(3) As will be discussed, Luke seems to find it difficult to group the members of the Jerusalem church into Aramaic-speakers and Greek-speakers (monolingual distinction), Palestinian and Diaspora persons (geographical distinction), or Jews and Gentiles (ethnic distinction) in a clear-cut way. It is because the members of the earliest Christian community in Jerusalem were mixed linguistically, geographically, and ethnically. Accordingly, Luke seems to divide the church members into the two groups, the Hebrews and the Hellenists, on the basis of the bilingual context of the Jerusalem church.

On the basis of this bilingual context, it will be proposed that the distinction between the Hebrews and the Hellenists does not refer to a monolingual, geographical, or ethnic distinction but a bilingual distinction in Aramaic-matrix Christians and in Greek-matrix Christians.

---

39. However, it is noteworthy to consider Cadbury's argument. Cadbury regards the Hebrews as Aramaic-speaking Diaspora Jews. Citing the inscriptions of "synagogue of Hebrews" found at Corinth, Rome, and Philadelphia in Lydia, he ("Hellenists," 5:59–74; esp. 62n4) asserts that the "Jews of the dispersion, whether at Rome, Corinth, Tarsus, or even at Jerusalem, might distinguish from members of the older dispersion the more recent Jewish emigrants from Palestine." The former are Greek-speaking Diaspora Jews and the latter are Aramaic-speaking Diaspora Jews without regard to geographical distinction.

40. Lee, *Jesus and the Gospel Traditions*, 84–85.

Hebrews: Aramaic-Matrix Christians

Hengel considers the Hebrews as Aramaic-speaking Palestinian Jews. However, bilingualism in the Jewish Diaspora and the Roman Near East in the first century suggests that the Hebrews refer to Aramaic-matrix Christians in the earliest Christian church in Jerusalem without regard to geographical or ethnic distinction. According to my sociolinguistic analysis of the linguistic milieu of Diaspora Jews,[41] most Diaspora Jews and Gentiles in the Jerusalem church who were from Aramaic-speaking areas could have spoken Aramaic as their matrix language.[42] If this is the correct model, the Greek-speaking Diaspora Jews hypothesis, that is, that the Diaspora Jews who spread throughout the Roman Near East spoke only Greek, would have been the exception to the norm. The Greek-speaking Gentile Christians hypothesis, that is, that Gentile Christians spoke Greek, should be reexamined because not all Gentiles do speak Greek as their matrix language. Accordingly, although some Christians are Gentiles or come from outside of Palestine, they should be called the Hebrews because they spoke Aramaic.

Hengel's monolingual-geographical distinction has also been questioned by some scholars, most often in connection to Paul's competence in Aramaic.[43] The occurrences of the term "Hebrew" in 2 Cor. 11:22 and Phil. 3:5 point to Paul's linguistic competence despite the fact that he is a Diaspora Jew. Scholars argue that the Hebrews refer to Aramaic-speaking Jews both in Palestine and *in the Diaspora* without respect to geographical distinction. Marshall concludes that "even, then, if there was a linguistic difference between 'Hebrews' and 'Hellenists,' this was not necessarily the same thing as a difference between Palestinian and Diaspora Jews or between Palestinian and Hellenistic Jews."[44] The fact that Paul, who is a bilingual, calls himself a Hebrew strongly indicates that the Hebrews refer to a bilingual term deserves serious consideration. Accordingly, if Paul's usage is the same

---

41. The reasons most Diaspora Jews were bilinguals are four points, as follows: (1) bilingualism of the Roman Empire; (2) successive immigration; (3) periodic connection with Jerusalem; (4) learning Aramaic in Jerusalem. In light of the strong interaction between Hellenism and Semitism in the Roman Near East (cf. Lee, *Jesus and the Gospel Traditions*, 147–50), it is likely that some Greek-matrix Jewish Christians in the Jerusalem church may have tried to learn or relearn Aramaic because the Jerusalem church was a bilingual community.

42. Millar puts forward that "various dialects of the Semitic language which we call 'Aramaic' were spoken all the way round the Fertile Crescent, from Babylonia to Arabia" ("Empire," 144). See also Millar, *Roman*, 503–4; Taylor, "Bilingualism," 298–331.

43. Lee, *Jesus and the Gospel Traditions*, 120–29; Michael, *Philippians*, 142; Beare, *Philippians*, 107; Fitzmyer, *Acts*, 347; Richardson, *Israel*, 118n2.

44. Marshall, "Palestinian Christianity," 278.

as Luke's, the Hebrews of the Jerusalem church refer to Aramaic-matrix Christians both in Palestine and from the Diaspora without geographical distinction.

The language lists of Josephus and Acts 2:9–11 support the view that the designations, the Hebrews and the Hellenists refer to the bilingual distinction and not the monolingual-geographical-ethnic distinction. Josephus implies that Aramaic was the matrix language for some Diaspora Jews. In *Jewish Wars* he states in the introduction (*J.W.* 1.3–6) that this was originally an Aramaic work translated into Greek at a later time. Josephus explains that it was intended for Diaspora Jews who lived among "the Parthians, and the Babylonians, and the remotest Arabians, and those of our nation beyond the Euphrates, with the Adiabeni." Josephus implies that his Palestinian Aramaic work could be understood well by Diaspora Jews spread throughout these regions.[45]

Comparisons should be made with the Lukan linguistic list of Diaspora Jews who visited Jerusalem (Acts 2:9–11): "*Parthians and Medes and Elamites and residents of Mesopotamia, Judea*[46] and Cappadocia,[47] Pontus and Asia, Phrygia[48] and Pamphylia, Egypt[49] and the parts of Libya belonging to Cyrene, and visitors from Rome, both Jews and proselytes, Cretans and Arabians*" (italics added).[50] It is noteworthy that most nations from Luke's

---

45. Sevenster (*Do You Know Greek?*, 61) also mentions that "the first impression given by the scattered comments made by Josephus on the language problems is that Aramaic was the language most familiar to the Jewish people in the first century CE."

46. In terms of the Lukan geographical horizon, there has been no consensus about why the Lukan list includes "Judea" in the list of the nations. However, it seems that the problem results from a different view of the distinction between dialect and language. There was not a clearer distinction between dialect and language in ancient times than in modern times (cf. Lee, *Jesus and the Gospel Traditions*, 77–79). In other words, Luke seems to distinguish "Judaean Aramaic" from "Galilean Aramaic" (cf. Janse, "Aspects of Bilingualism," 349). In fact, most Jews who came from Parthia, Media, Elam, Mesopotamia and Arabia also used Aramaic dialects that are sister languages of Galilean Aramaic. Luke seems to classify "Judean Aramaic" as a dialect of the Aramaic language family like Galilean, Syriac, Palmyrene or Nabatean. Accordingly, in comparison with Galilean Aramaic, Luke seems to add Judea to the list.

47. Cappadocia was multilingual; see Lee, *Jesus and the Gospel Traditions*, 138–41.

48. Phrygians used Phrygian and Greek; see ibid.

49. For the bilingualism of Egypt, see ibid., 150–62.

50. Quoting a letter from Agrippa I to Caligula, Philo (*Legat.* 281–82) mentions that Jerusalem is the mother city not only for Judaean Jews, but also those of Egypt, Phoenicia, Syria, Coele-Syria, Pamphylia, Cilicia, Asia, Bithynia, Pontus, Europe, Thessaly, Boeotia, Macedonia, Aeolia, Attica, Argos, Corinth, the Peloponnese, the isles of Euboea, Cyprus, Crete, the lands beyond the Euphrates, Babylonia, and its neighboring satrapies. See also Van der Horst, *Jews*, 12–36.

linguistic list are those of known bilingual regions.[51] Janse observes that "what is interesting about the 'nations' (Acts 2:5) . . . is that most of them are known to be bilingual in the first century A.D., speaking either Greek or Aramaic as a second language (as opposed to their 'own *native* language')."[52] In comparison with these two ethnic lists, it seems that most Diaspora Jews in Jerusalem who came from the overlapped countries (see italicized names above) spoke Aramaic as their matrix language.[53]

Acts 2:8 explains that the reason they were bewildered and marveled lies in the fact that they heard the Galileans employ "our own native languages." This means that the Diaspora Jews discerned their own native language and that they distinguished their languages from the Galilean Aramaic, which Diaspora Jews had expected to hear from the Galileans. Even though the apostles spoke Galilean Aramaic, most Diaspora Jews who used a language from the Aramaic family[54] could have understood what the disciples were speaking about to a great extent.[55] Taylor tabulates morphological and lexical differences and agreements among Aramaic sister languages. Table 1 is helpful in the present discussion:[56]

---

51. Janse ("Aspects of Bilingualism," 357) also suggests that "in the easternmost parts of Asia Minor a number of non-indigenous languages coexisted with Greek."

52. Ibid., 349.

53. Cf. Millar, *Roman*, 503-4; Bruce, *The Book of Acts*, 61-62.

54. Aramaic can be called an ancestor language. Galilean, Judean, Syriac, Nabatean, and Palmyrene can be called daughter languages of Aramaic, and those languages can be called sister languages to each other; see Lee, *Jesus and the Gospel Traditions*, 85-86; Taylor, "Bilingualism," 302.

55. Cf. Taylor, "Bilingualism," 302-3; Cotton, "Language," 162. Tcherikover (*CPJ* 1:5) states that "though differing from Jews in their religion, they [Syrians and Jews in Egypt] had a common language with them (Aramaic) . . . No wonder, then, that the Egyptian population confused all peoples coming from 'Syria' and called them all 'Syrians'; even the Hebrew language was sometimes mistaken for 'Syrian,' i.e. Aramaic."

56. Taylor, "Bilingualism," 303. See also Yardeni, *Textbook*, 11; 216-17; Naveh, *History*, 112-14; 162-64; Rahmani, *Catalogue*, 12n6.

Table 1: Differences and Agreements among Aramaic Sister Languages				
Aramaic Dialects	S₃M imperfect: 'he will write'	P₁ pronoun: 'we'	SM demonst. Pronoun: 'this'	(Vocabulary): 'he saw'
Palmyrene	yktb (=yiktob?)	'nhnw	dnh	hz'
Hatran	lktb (=liktob?)	–	hdyn / 'dyn	hz'
Syriac	nktwb (nekob)ᴬ	'nhnn/hnn	hn'	hz
Christian Palestinian	yktwb (=yiktob)	'nh / 'nn	hdn / hdyn	hm'
Samaritan	yktb (=yiktab)	'nn	hdn / 'hn	hm', 'm', hz'

A. Early Syriac inscriptions have the form *yktb*.

As Table 1 demonstrates, although the Aramaic family consists of diverse dialects both within and outside of Palestine, Aramaic language family speakers would have understood the Aramaic dialects of others.[57] Clearly, most Diaspora Jews in Jerusalem who came from Aramaic-speaking countries spoke Aramaic as their matrix language just like Palestinian Jews. The fact that many Aramaic-matrix Diaspora Jews resided in first-century Jerusalem (Acts 2:9–11) leads to the conclusion that there were many Aramaic-matrix Diaspora Christians in the earliest Christian church in Jerusalem. Furthermore, as will be discussed in detail below, most proselytes (ethnically, Gentiles; Acts 2:5, 11; 6:5) who came from Aramaic-speaking regions would have spoken Aramaic as their matrix language. In other words, most Gentiles who were from Aramaic-speaking regions should have spoken Aramaic as their matrix language.[58] That most Gentiles of the Roman Near East spoke Aramaic as their matrix language means that many Gentile Christians in the Jerusalem church and churches in the Roman Near East spoke Aramaic as their matrix language.

Accordingly, Aramaic-matrix Diaspora Jewish Christians and Gentile Christians should be classified as the Hebrews in spite of their name tags such as "Diaspora" or "Gentile." It is evident that the distinction between the Hebrews and the Hellenists is not made through monolingual, geographical, or ethnic distinctions but by bilingual distinction. The Hebrews at Acts 6:1 refer to Aramaic-matrix Christians, that is, Aramaic-matrix

57. Millar (*Roman*, 9) rightly suggests that "the use of the term 'Semitic' is harmless and unavoidable; the mutual resemblances in vocabulary and grammatical form, the identity of alphabet and the similarities of script of all the languages concerned are unmistakable."

58. For a detailed discussion, see Lee, *Jesus and the Gospel Traditions*, 135–73.

Jewish and Gentile Christians, and Aramaic-matrix Palestinian and Diaspora Christians.

Hellenists: Greek-Matrix Christians

As mentioned before, Hengel holds that the Hellenists refer to Greek-speaking Diaspora Jews, that is, he makes a monolingual, geographical, and ethnic distinction. However, when the bilingualism of the first-century Roman Near East is taken into account seriously, the Hellenists (Acts 6:1) mean Greek-matrix Christians. The bilingual approach will be made by considering three points: textual, ethnic, and geographical arguments.

When we deal with the referent of Hellenists (Acts 6:1), special attention should be given to Luke because the Hellenists occurs on only three occasions (Acts 6:1; 9:29; 11:20) in the New Testament literature. In the case of the Hellenists (9:29), there is a general consensus that the Hellenists in 9:29 refer to Greek-speaking Jewish non-Christians.[59] Furthermore, there is no textual problem because the designation Ἑλληνιστάς has no variants except for Codex A.

The term Ἑλληνιστάς in Acts 11:20, on the other hand, is very complicated because some manuscripts like $\mathfrak{P}^{74}$, ℵ², A, and D* read Ἕλληνας.[60] Some scholars prefer to read Ἕλληνας rather than Ἑλληνιστάς.[61] They suggest three main reasons for preferring the Ἕλληνας variant. First, Luke makes an ethnic contrast between Ἰουδαίοις in v. 19 and Ἕλληνας in v. 20. Second, the Lukan focus at 11:19-20 moves toward a Gentile mission. Third, the strongest argument is the assumption that Luke uses the Hellenists to designate Greek-speaking *Jews*, as the other two occurrences (6:1; 9:29) show. For these reasons, it is assumed that Ἕλληνας (i.e., Gentiles) is a better reading.

Other scholars consider that the Ἑλληνιστάς is the proper reading.[62] Two major reasons have been suggested. First, Ἕλλην occurs in Acts ten times. Whenever an ethnic contrast is made, Ἕλλην is coupled with Ἰουδαῖος.[63] It is obvious that Luke makes an ethnic contrast between Ἰουδαῖος

---

59. Foakes Jackson, *Acts*, 99; Simon, *Stephen*, 14–15; Fitzmyer, *Acts*, 440.

60. Codex A shows the same tendency to alter Ἑλληνιστάς into Ἕλληνας (Acts 9:29).

61. Bengel, *Gnomon*, 2:611; Hort, "Notes," 94; Warfield, "Readings," 120–25; Rackham, *Acts*, 166; Foakes Jackson, *Acts*, 99–100; Moule, "Once More," 100; Haenchen, *Acts*, 365; Neil, *Acts*, 144; Conzelmann, *Acts*, 87; Johnson, *Acts*, 203; Dunn, *Acts*, 154; Fitzmyer, *Acts*, 476.

62. Ropes, *Text of Acts*, 3.106; Cadbury, "Hellenists," 5:71; Williams, *Acts*, 142; Bruce, *The Acts of the Apostles*, 151, 235; Bruce, *The Book of Acts*, 237; Barrett, *Acts*, 550–51; Metzger, *Textual Commentary*, 340–42; Witherington, *Acts*, 242.

63. Acts 14:1; 18:4; 19:10, 17; and 20:21. All the occurrences in Acts are related to

and Ἕλλην in Acts.⁶⁴ Rather, in this sense, the reading Ἑλληνιστάς is better because it is *lectio difficilior*. Second, although the Hellenists in Acts 6:1, 9:29, for example, refer to Greek-speaking *Jews*, the same term Hellenists in 11:20 refers to Greek-speaking *persons*. For instance, Barrett claims: "It is thus by no means impossible that the word should have a third meaning here: at 6.1, Greek-speaking Jewish Christians; at 9.29, Greek-speaking Jews; at 11.20, Greek-speaking Gentiles."⁶⁵ Accordingly, there is a scholarly consensus that Ἑλληνιστάς (11:20) is improperly used and that the Hellenists at 6:1 and 9:29 refer to Greek-speaking *Jews*.

However, it seems that Luke intentionally uses Ἑλληνιστής three times in his narrative because the Hellenists at 6:1 and 9:29 as well as at 11:19 refer to Greek-speaking *persons*. In other words, like the term Hebrews, Hellenists refer to Greek-speaking persons who were Jews and Gentiles without regard to the ethnic distinction. As will be discussed, Luke recognizes that the earliest church in Jerusalem includes Greek-speaking Gentiles from the start. He intentionally indicates the existence of Gentiles in the Jerusalem church from the beginning. This argument leads us into the issue of the ethnicity of the members of the Jerusalem church at 2:5, 2:11 and 6:5.

The term Ἰουδαῖοι (Acts 2:5) has variants. The fact that Ἰουδαῖοι was absent in the majority of texts may indicate that it was added later.⁶⁶ Metzger points out: "Since Jews were already an ἔθνος, to say that these were from another ἔθνος is tantamount to a contradiction of terms."⁶⁷ If the Ἰουδαῖοι is inserted later, it can be said that the residents of Jerusalem are composed of both Jews and proselytes from every nation under heaven, not only Jews. This view is strongly supported by the internal evidence which includes the explicit phrase: Ἰουδαῖοί τε καὶ προσήλυτοι (Acts 2:11). Johnson proposes that "this (both Jews and proselytes) is a summary rather than a separate

---

the dissemination of the gospel. Luke states that the gospel was preached to Jews and Greeks, that is, to all people.

64. In this regard, Johnson (*Acts*, 105) argues that when Luke intends to make an ethnic distinction between Jews and Greeks, he employs Ἰουδαῖος and Ἕλλην. Johnson prefers to read Ἕλληνας.

65. Barrett, *Acts*, 550. Bruce (*The Acts of the Apostles*, 151) also proposes: "[H]ere (vi. 1), Greek-speaking Jewish Christians; in ix. 29 probably Greek-speaking Jews in the synagogues; in xi. 20, probably Gentiles."

66. Ropes (*Text of Acts*, 3:12) suggests that the original text including Sinaiticus omits Ἰουδαῖοι, that the Western text holds Ἰουδαῖοι, and that the Old Uncials inserts it again; also see Cadbury, "Hellenists," 5:113–14; Williams, *Acts*, 64.

67. Metzger, *Textual Commentary*, 251.

ethnic entry."⁶⁸ So the residers in Jerusalem refer to Diaspora Jews and proselytes.

On the other hand, Lake proposes: "In vs. 10 'Jews and proselytes' are treated as one of the component parts of the crowd. If so, obviously the rest of the crowd was not composed of Jews."⁶⁹ Lake suggests that most of the residents in Jerusalem are Gentiles including some Diaspora Jews and proselytes. Whether Johnson or Lake might be right, Luke considers some residents in Jerusalem as Gentiles because proselytes mean ethnic Gentiles. Luke (2:41; 4:4) reports that Peter's sermon converted 3,000 and 5,000 persons to Christianity. The Christians should have included the Jews as well as the proselytes in Jerusalem. In this sense, Luke seems to have in mind that the earliest Christian church in Jerusalem includes both Jews and Gentiles from the start.

Furthermore, the possibility that Luke insinuates that there were some Gentiles in the Jerusalem church can be shown at Acts 6:5. It is of interest that the origin of Nicolas, one of the Seven (Acts 6:5), was a Gentile who came from Antioch.⁷⁰ The introduction of the Seven resulted from the practical purpose to solve the problem of the alienation of Greek widows. The Seven served tables although they, of course, were leaders of the Jerusalem church. Why was an Antiochene Gentile chosen as one of the Seven representatives by the church members? Why, in an ethnic sense, does the Jerusalem church need a Gentile leader to serve tables? The fact that a Gentile leader was selected implies that there were some Gentile Christians in the earliest Christian community in Jerusalem.⁷¹ In this sense, some scholars consider that the Hellenists (6:1) refer to proselytes⁷² or Gentiles.⁷³

68. Johnson, *Acts*, 44; cf. Fitzmyer, *Acts*, 243.

69. So noted by Cadbury, "Hellenists," 5:113–14. Cadbury assumes: "Probably Ἰουδαῖοι in vs. 5 was originally a mistaken gloss on εὐλαβεῖς." He argues: "The desire of the writer was . . . to show that from the beginning the Gentiles heard and the Jews refused the testimony of the Spirit."

70. Only the origin of Nicolas is mentioned in the present verse. This implies that the other six were born Jews; see Haenchen, *Acts*, 264; Barrett, *Acts*, 315. Even Kraeling ("Jewish Community," 147) considers Nicolas as a Greek. However, there is no information that he is a Greek.

71. Some scholars, in the same vein, consider that the Seven were composed of the Hebrews and the Hellenists, lest they disregard the Hebrew widows; for a detailed discussion, see Lee, *Jesus and the Gospel Traditions*, 204–8.

72. Blackman, "Hellenists," 524–25; Grundmann, "Problem," 45–73; Reicke, *Glaube*, 116–17, 121; Schwartz, "Chronologie," 146–47; Schmithals, *Paul*, 34n71; Bauer, "Jesus," 107–8.

73. Warfield, "Readings," 113–27; Wetter, "Christentum," 411–12, 404–5; Cadbury, "Hellenists," 5:68. As a consequence, Cadbury ("Hellenists," 5:65, 71–72) assumes that the Ἑλληνιστάς of 11:20 refer to Greek-speaking Gentiles because he supposes that the

Others (including Hengel) challenge the ethnic distinction and propose that the Hellenists (6:1) refer to only Jews, especially Diaspora Jews. The most significant reason is that Luke intends to unfold his story toward the Gentile mission step by step. In this respect, they consider that the appearance of Gentiles in Acts 6:1 is a gross anachronism, let alone in 2:5.[74] Fitzmyer mentions that "the Lucan story disregards any others in Jerusalem who might not be Jews."[75] Johnson also asserts that "Luke takes such pains to show the *gradual development of the Gentile mission* after the close of the Jerusalem narrative."[76]

Although many of the scholars mentioned above consider that the residents in Jerusalem (2:5) were ethnically composed of *Jews and Gentiles*, they suggest that the Hellenists (6:1) refer to only Diaspora *Jews*.[77] Given this fact, where are the Christian Gentiles prior to the time at which Peter appears for the Gentile missions? In reply to this, two points mentioned above can be suggested: (1) Luke recognizes that the Jerusalem church includes Gentiles from the start. (2) Luke intends to unfold his story in the direction of the Gentile mission. Barrett persuasively concludes that Luke regards the Jerusalem church as a universal church including Gentiles from the start: "from the beginning the Christian church was an inspired community and a universal community. It therefore included both Jews and 'pious men' of every kind."[78] It seems that Luke depicts his narrative about the Gentile mission not in a unilinear but in a spiral way. The literary style is supported by the fact that he repeatedly introduces the Gentile mission.[79]

As a consequence, it seems that Luke intimates to his readers that the Jerusalem church includes Gentile Christians from the start, as Acts

---

Ἑλληνιστής is synonymous with Ἕλλην, such as the relationship between the two Greek spellings of Jerusalem.

74. Witherington, *Acts*, 241.

75. Fitzmyer, *Acts*, 239.

76. Johnson, *Acts*, 105; emphasis added. See also Barrett, *Acts*, 309; Haenchen, *Acts*, 260; Bruce, *The Acts of the Apostles*, 83; Bruce, *The Book of Acts*, 61; Simon, *Stephen*, 15; Moule, "Once More," 100–102; Güting, "Horizont," 149–69.

77. Bruce, *The Book of Acts*, 60, 128; Haenchen, *Acts*, 171, 260; Marshall, *Acts*, 70, 125–26; cf. Fitzmyer, *Acts*, 239, 347; Schnabel, *Early Christian Mission*, 654–55.

78. Barrett, *Acts*, 118.

79. Cadbury ("Hellenists," 5:66–68) considers that Luke repeats the beginnings of Gentile Christianity several times. He cites the missionary journey of Paul and Barnabas (Acts 13–14), the first conversion of Gentiles (Acts 11:19–20), the story of Cornelius (Acts 10–11), Philip and the Ethiopian (Acts 8), and the story of Pentecost (Acts 2). In relation to the Lukan focus on the Gentile mission, some scholars suggest that Acts is a response concerning the identity of Gentile Christianity; see Jervell, *Luke*, 41–69; Franklin, *Christ*, 116–44; Maddox, *Purpose*, 183–86.

2:5, 2:11, and 6:5 imply. The use of the terms Hebrews and Hellenists (i.e., Aramaic-matrix speakers and Greek-matrix speakers, including both Jews and Gentiles) seems to be placed in the medial stage between Ἰουδαῖοι (i.e., Jews) and Ἕλλην (i.e., Gentiles). Concerning the expansion of the gospel, Luke intends to dilute the ethnic border line between Jews and Gentiles by means of using the linguistic distinction as a bridge. Accordingly, it can be concluded that Luke uses the Hellenists for Greek-speaking persons at Acts 6:1, 9:29 and 11:20 without regard to ethnic distinction.[80] Therefore, the reading Ἕλληνας (11:20) does not seem appropriate because the ethnic distinction that the other two occurrences (6:5; 9:29) refer to only Jews is not persuasive.

Here, it is noteworthy to mention Hill's argument. He insists that those who were persecuted were both the Hebrews and the Hellenists.[81] If those who were scattered were composed of Greek-matrix as well as Aramaic-matrix Christians, then the fact that those who were scattered travelled and preached the word only to Jews (μόνον Ἰουδαίοις) in Phoenicia, Cyprus and Antioch is more understandable. It seems that the term Ἰουδαίοις at 11:19 means an ethnic distinction.[82]

On the other hand, Luke seems to draw a linguistic distinction by using the Hellenists at 11:20. "Some of them" who were from Cyprus and Cyrene preached even to Ἑλληνιστάς, that is, Greek-matrix speakers. Did the people, who are referred to as "some of them," *intentionally* preach to only Greek-speaking Gentiles? Rather, it seems that "some of them" preached the word to Greek-matrix speakers, Jews as well as Gentiles in Antioch. The implied audience entails two ethnic groups, Jews and Gentiles.

There are good reasons to infer a mixed audience. For one thing, the population of the Antiochene Jews may be between 30,000 and 50,000 out of 300,000, the total population of Antioch.[83] It is unlikely that the Christians intentionally avoided preaching the word to Antiochene Jews. Also, not all Antiochene Gentiles spoke Greek as their matrix language. Rather, most Antiochene Gentiles in the first century spoke Aramaic as their matrix language.[84] "Some of them" from Cyprus and Cyrene preached to ethnically

---

80. Cf. Barrett, *Acts*, 550; Metzger, *Textual Commentary*, 342; Witherington, *Acts*, 242.

81. See Lee, *Jesus and the Gospel Traditions*, 120–29; Hengel, *Hellenization*, 17–18; Witherington, *Acts*, 243–47.

82. Johnson, *Acts*, 105.

83. Hengel and Schwemer, *Paul between Damascus and Antioch*, 186, 196; for a detailed discussion, see Lee, *Jesus and the Gospel Traditions*, 163–67.

84. It is interesting that Parker ("Readings," 168) suggests: "Ἑλληνιστάς is correct. Luke probably meant to indicate that some Jews at Antioch spoke Greek, others

mixed Greek-matrix inhabitants, both Greek-matrix Jews and Gentiles. Metzger convincingly suggests that "the word (Ἑλληνιστάς) is to be understood in the broad sense of 'Greek-speaking persons,' meaning thereby the mixed population of Antioch in contrast to the Ἰουδαῖοι of ver. 19."[85] In this sense, it seems that Luke intentionally chooses to use the linguistic term Ἑλληνιστάς rather than the ethnic term Ἕλληνας at 11:20. Luke finds it difficult to group the inhabitants of Antioch, to whom the Christians preached, into Gentiles on the basis of the ethnic distinction like the case of the Hebrews. Accordingly, Luke seems to select the linguistic term (Ἑλληνιστάς) rather than the ethnic term (Ἕλληνας).

Hengel's position of the geographical distinction in relation to the Ἑλληνιστής will now be challenged. It is not persuasive. Some scholars, including Mann,[86] Meier,[87] Johnson,[88] and Barrett[89] throw doubt upon the strict geographical distinction between Aramaic-speaking *Palestinian* Jews and Greek-speaking *Diaspora* Jews. They have proposed the possibility that some Hellenists were Greek-speaking Diaspora Jews and others Greek-speaking Palestinian Jews. Recently, Schnabel criticizes Baur and Hengel's view that there was an early schism in the Jerusalem church. He rightly suggests that the Hellenists who resided in Jerusalem spoke Aramaic as well because: "They hardly would have settled in the Jewish capital if they were unable or unwilling to communicate in Aramaic."[90] For this reason, he concludes that "we must remember that presumably the majority of Palestinian Jewish Christians were bilingual, speaking both Aramaic and Greek."[91]

Aramaic—which was the case—and that the wandering missionaries addressed themselves to both of the Jewish groups in that city."

85. Metzger, *Textual Commentary*, 342.

86. Mann ("Hellenists," 301) mentions that "many Jews in Palestine, unless living far from cities, would be more or less at home in the vernacular Greek of the time (koine)."

87. Meier (*Marginal Jew*, 267) asserts that "Probably some of these Diaspora Jews were bilingual, but others (e.g., recent émigrés from the Diaspora) may have spoken nothing but Greek.

88. Johnson (*Acts*, 105) also states that "*hellenistes* refers to a Jew who predominantly speaks Greek. *Some* of them were probably from the Diaspora (see Acts 2:7–12; 4:36; 6:9), although Greek was widely spoken in Palestine as well" (emphasis added).

89. Barrett (*Acts*, 315) suggests that "Luke's usage of the word Hellenist must not be taken to mean that they were necessarily Diaspora Jews."

90. Schnabel, *Early Christian Mission*, 654.

91. Frommel (*Poetry*, 18) also considers the Jerusalem church as a bilingual community from the beginning "so that in public assemblies the Words of Jesus may have been communicated in Greek as well as in Aramaic." However, he assumes that an Aramaic Gospel was an oral gospel on the basis of uni-directionality.

Some Palestinian Jews would have used Greek as their matrix language and Aramaic as their embedded language from the perspective of regional and personal bilingualism. As for the regional bilingualism of first-century Palestine,[92] it can be summarized in three points: (1) In relation to language choice and inscriptions, the statistical data about the inscriptional languages from first-century Palestine leads to the conclusion that some Palestinian Jews used Greek as their matrix language, at least to the extent that they chose Greek as the appropriate language for the linguistic domain of sublime inscriptional language. (2) Greek papyri excavated from Palestine such as the Babatha archive, Waddis Murabaat and Seiyal, Nahal Hever, and DSS suggest that the linguistic milieu of first-century Palestine is largely bilingual. The papyrological evidence also persuasively supports the assertion that some Palestinian Jews could speak Greek as their matrix language. (3) Population geographical evidence indicates that Jews and Gentiles mixed in many cities throughout the Levant. Living in a border area or among different language groups would have brought about bilingualism. These regional bilingualism factors point to the causes of the personal bilingualism, such as bilingual parents and region, formal education, and occupation. Personal bilingualism factors of first-century Palestine strongly support the idea that some Palestinian Jews in early Christianity used Greek as their matrix language. Therefore, it can be concluded that Greek-matrix *Palestinian* Jews and Greek-matrix *Palestinian* Jewish Christians should be classified as Hellenists. The Hellenists refer to Greek-matrix persons, whether they were Jews or not.

CONCLUSIONS

In summary, Hengel suggests that the Hebrews refer to Aramaic-speaking Palestinian Jewish Christians and the Hellenists Greek-speaking Diaspora Jewish Christians in the Jerusalem church on the basis of a monolingual, geographical, and ethnic distinction. This suggestion then becomes the starting point for a far-reaching theological program about how the Jesus tradition was transmitted. Contrary to Hengel's opinion, an evaluation of bilingualism within the Roman Near East and Judaeo-Palestine in the first century results in a much more complex picture than what he conceives. The most significant aspects of this linguistic view may be summarized as follows.

(1) It is clear that Luke's designations, the Hebrews and the Hellenists, are based not upon monolingual-geographical-ethnic but bilingual

---

92. For a detailed explanation, see Lee, *Jesus and the Gospel Traditions*, 105–12.

distinctions. Both groups could have included Jews and Gentiles and residents in and out of Judaeo-Palestine.

(2) The bilingualism of first-century Jews in both Palestine and the Diaspora implies that the Jerusalem church was a bilingual community and that many bilingual Christians were in the Jerusalem church.

(3) The Hebrews in Acts 6:1 were Aramaic-matrix Christians (both Jews and Gentiles) who were in Palestine or came from the Diaspora. Aramaic-matrix Christians (i.e., dominant bilinguals in Aramaic) used Aramaic as their matrix language and Greek as their embedded language. One can easily support the notion that early or primary bilinguals spoke Greek as much as they would have spoken Aramaic. On the contrary, late or acquired bilinguals spoke Greek less than they spoke Aramaic and to varying degrees. Aramaic-matrix Christian semi-bilinguals used Greek for special purposes.

(4) The Hellenists in Acts 6:1 were Greek-matrix Christians (both Jews and Gentiles) who were in Palestine or came from the Diaspora. Greek-matrix Christians (i.e., dominant bilinguals in Greek) used Greek as their matrix language and Aramaic as their embedded language. For instance, early or primary bilinguals spoke Aramaic just as much as Greek. On the contrary, late or acquired bilinguals spoke Aramaic less than they spoke Greek and to varying degrees. Greek-matrix Christian semi-bilinguals used Aramaic for special purposes.

(5) Lastly, many monolinguals may have tried to acquire Aramaic or Greek as their secondary language in the bilingual Jerusalem church.

BIBLIOGRAPHY

Barrett, C. K. *The Acts of the Apostles*. ICC. 2 vols. Edinburgh: T. & T. Clark, 1994–98.
Bauer, Walter. "Jesus der Galiläer." In *Aufsätze und kleine Schriften*, ed. G. Strecker, 91–108. Tübingen: Mohr, 1967.
Baur, F. C. *Paul, the Apostle of Jesus Christ: His Life and Work, His Epistles and Doctrine*. Rev. E. Zeller. Trans. A. Menzies. 2 vols. London: Williams & Norgate, 1873–1875.
Beare, Francis W. *A Commentary on the Epistle to the Philippians*. BNTC. 2nd ed. London: A. & C. Black, 1969.
Bengel, Johann. *Gnomon of the New Testament*. Rev. and ed. by A.R. Faussel. 5 vols. Edinburgh: T. & T. Clark, 1858–1859.
Blackman, E. C. "The Hellenists of Acts VI.1." *ExpTim* 48 (1936–1937) 524–25.
Brown, Raymond. "Not Jewish Christianity and Gentile Christianity but Types of Jewish/Gentile Christianity." *CBQ* 45(1983) 74–79.
Bruce, F. F. *The Acts of the Apostles: The Greek Text with Introduction and Commentary*. 3rd. rev. ed. Grand Rapids: Eerdmans, 1990.

———. *The Book of the Acts*. NICNT. Rev. ed. Grand Rapids: Eerdmans, 1988.
Cadbury, Henry. "The Hellenists." In *The Beginnings of Christianity, Part I: The Acts of the Apostles*, ed. F. J. Foakes Jackson and K. Lake, 5:59–74. London: Macmillan, 1933.
Conzelmann, Hans. *Acts of the Apostles: A Commentary on the Acts of the Apostles*. Hermeneia. Philadelphia: Fortress, 1987.
Cotton, Hannah. "Language Gaps in Roman Palestine and the Roman Near East." In *Medien im antiken Palästina: Materielle Kommunikation und Medialität als Thema der Palästinaarchäologie*, ed. C. Frevel, 151–69. FAT 2/10; Tübingen: Mohr/Siebeck, 2005.
Dunn, James D. G. *The Acts of the Apostles*. Epworth Commentaries. Peterborough: Epworth, 1996.
Esler, Philip. *Community and Gospel in Luke-Acts: The Social and Political Motivations of Lucan Theology*. SNTSMS 57. Cambridge: Cambridge University Press, 1987.
Fitzmyer, Joseph. *The Acts of the Apostles: A New Translation with Introduction and Commentary*. AB 31. New York: Doubleday, 1998.
Foakes Jackson, F. J. *The Acts of the Apostles*. MNTC. London: Hodder & Stoughton, 1931.
Franklin, Eric. *Christ the Lord: The Study in the Purpose and Theology of Luke-Acts*. London: SPCK, 1975.
Frommel, Otto. *The Poetry of the Gospel of Jesus*. London: Nutt, 1908.
Grundmann, Walter. "Das Problem des hellenistischen Christentums innerhalb der Jerusalemer Urgemeinde." *ZNW* 38 (1939) 45–73.
Güting, E. "Der geographische Horizont der sogenannten Völkerliste des Lukas (Acta 2, 9–11)." *ZNW* 66 (1975) 149–69.
Haenchen, Ernst. *The Acts of the Apostles*. Oxford: Blackwell, 1971.
Heitmüller, Wilhelm. "Zum Problem Paulus und Jesus." *ZNW* 13 (1912) 320–37.
Hengel, Martin. *Acts and the History of Earliest Christianity*. Trans. J. Bowden. London: SCM, 1979.
———. *Between Jesus and Paul: Studies in the Earliest History of Christianity*. Trans. Bowden. London: SCM, 1983.
———. "Eye-witness Memory and the Writing of the Gospels: Form Criticism, Community Tradition and the Authority of the Authors." In *The Written Gospel*, ed. M. Bockmuehl and D. Hagner, 70–96. Cambridge: Cambridge University Press, 2005.
———. *The "Hellenization" of Judaea in the First Century After Christ*. Trans. and ed. C. Markschies. London: SCM, 1989.
———. *Jews, Greek and Barbarians: Aspects of the Hellenization of Judaism in the Pre-Christian Period*. Trans. Bowden. London: SCM, 1980.
———. "Judaism and Hellenism Revisited." In *Hellenism in the Land of Israel*, ed. J. Collins and G. Sterling, 6–37. Christianity and Judaism in Antiquity 13. Notre Dame: University of Notre Dame Press, 2001.
———. *Judaism and Hellenism: Studies in their Encounter in Palestine during the Early Hellenistic Period*. Trans. Bowden. London: SCM, 1974. 2 vols. in 1. Reprint, 2012.
———. *The Pre-Christian Paul*. Trans. and ed. R. Deines. London: SCM, 1991.
———. *Studies in Early Christology*. Edinburgh: T. & T. Clark, 1995.
Hengel, Martin, and Anna Maria Schwemer. *Paul between Damascus and Antioch: The Unknown Years*. London: SCM, 1997.

Hill, Craig C. *Hellenists and Hebrews: Reappraising Division within the Earliest Church*. Minneapolis: Fortress, 1992.

Hort, Fenton. "Notes on Select Readings." In *The New Testament in the Original Greek*, ed. B. F. Westcott and F. Hort, 1–180. 2nd ed. London: Macmillan, 1896.

Hurtado, Larry. *Lord Jesus Christ: Devotion to Jesus in Earliest Christianity*. Grand Rapids: Eerdmans, 2003.

Janse, Mark. "Aspects of Bilingualism in the History of the Greek." In *Bilingualism in Ancient Society: Language Contact and the Written Text*, ed. J. Adams et al., 332–90. Oxford: Oxford University Press, 2002.

Jeremias, Joachim. "Die Muttersprache des Evangelisten Matthäus." *ZNW* 50 (1959) 270–74.

Jervell, Jacob. *Luke and the People of God: A New Look at Luke-Acts*. Minneapolis: Augsburg, 1972.

Johnson, Luke Timothy. *The Acts of the Apostles*. SP 5. Collegeville, MN: Liturgical, 1992.

Kraeling, C. H. "The Jewish Community at Antioch." *JBL* 51 (1932) 130–60.

Kramer, Werner. *Christ, Lord, Son of God*. SBT 50. London: SCM, 1966.

Lee, Sang-Il. *Jesus and Gospel Traditions in Bilingual Context: A Study in the Interdirectionality of Language*. BZNW 186. Berlin: de Gruyter, 2012.

Maddox, Robert. *The Purpose of Luke-Acts*. FRLANT 126. Göttingen: Vandenhoeck & Ruprecht, 1982.

Mann, C. S. "'Hellenists' and 'Hebrews' in Acts VI 1." In *The Acts of the Apostles* by J. Munck, 301–4. AB 31. New York: Doubleday, 1967.

Marshall, I. Howard. *The Acts of the Apostles*. TNTC. Grand Rapids: Eerdmans, 1980.

———. "Palestinian and Hellenistic Christianity: Some Critical Comments." *NTS* 19 (1972–1973) 271–87.

Meier, John P. *A Marginal Jew: Rethinking the Historical Jesus*. Vol. 1, *The Roots of the Problem and the Person*. ABRL. New York: Doubleday, 1991.

Metzger, Bruce. *A Textual Commentary on the Greek New Testament*. 2nd ed. New York: American Bible Society, 1994.

Michael, John H. *The Epistle of Paul to the Philippians*. MNTC. London: Hodder & Stoughton, 1928.

Millar, Fergus. "Empire, Community and Culture in the Roman Near East: Greeks, Syrians, Jews and Arabs." *JJS* 38 (1987) 143–64.

———. *The Roman Near East 31 BC–AD 337*. Cambridge, MA: Harvard University Press, 1993.

Moule, C. F. D. "Once More, Who Were the Hellenists?" *ExpTim* 60 (1958–1959) 100–102.

Naveh, Joseph. *Early History of the Alphabet: An Introduction to West Semitic Epigraphy and Palaeography*. Leiden: Brill, 1982.

Neil, William. *The Acts of the Apostles*. New Century Bible Commentary. London: Marshall, Morgan & Scott, 1973.

Parker, Pierson. "Three Variant Readings in Luke-Acts." *JBL* 83 (1964) 165–70.

Penner, Todd. *In Praise of Christian Origins: Stephen and the Hellenists in Lukan Apologetic Historiography*. Emory Studies in Early Christianity 10. London: T. & T. Clark, 2004.

Rackham, Richard. *The Acts of the Apostles*. London: Methuen, 1901. Reprint, 1951.

Rahmani, L. Y. *A Catalogue of Jewish Ossuaries in the Collections of the State of Israel*, Jerusalem: Israel Academy of Sciences and Humanities, 1994.
Räisänen, Heikki. *Jesus, Paul and Torah: Collected Essays*. JSNTSup 43. Sheffield: Sheffield Academic, 1992.
Reicke, Bo. *Glaube und Leben der Urgemeinde. Bemerkungen zu Apg. 1–7*. ATANT 32. Zürich: Zwingli, 1957.
Richardson, Peter. *Israel in the Apostolic Church*. SNTSMS 10. Cambridge: Cambridge University Press, 1969.
Roberts, Alexander. *Greek: The Language of Christ and his Apostles*. London: Longmans, 1888.
Ropes, James H. *The Text of Acts*. Vol. 3 of *The Beginnings of Christianity, Part I: The Acts of the Apostles*. Ed. F. J. Foakes Jackson and K. Lake. London: Macmillan, 1926.
Schmithals, Walter. *Paul and James*. SBT 46. London: SCM, 1965.
Schnabel, Eckhard. *Early Christian Mission*. Vol. 2, *Paul and the Early Church*. Downers Grove, IL: IVP Academic, 2004.
Schwartz, Eduard. "Zur Chronologie des Paulus." In *Zum Neuen Testament und zum frühen Christentum*, Vol. 5 of *Gesammelte Schriften*, ed. W. Eltester and H.-D. Altendorf, 124–69. Berlin: de Gruyter, 1907. Reprint, 1963.
Sevenster, J. N. *Do You Know Greek?: How Much Greek Could the First Jewish Christians Have Known*. NovT Sup 19. Leiden: Brill, 1968.
Simon, Marcel. *St Stephen and the Hellenists in the Primitive Church*. London: Longmans, 1958.
Taylor, David. "Bilingualism and Diglossia in Late Antique Syria and Mesopotamia." In *Bilingualism in Ancient Society: Language Contact and the Written Text*, ed. J. Adams et al., 298–331. Oxford: Oxford University Press, 2002.
Tcherikover, Victor and A. Fuks, eds. *Corpus Papyrorum Judaicarum III*. 3 vols. Cambridge, MA: Harvard University Press, 1957–1963.
Van der Horst, Pieter W. *Jews and Christians in their Graeco-Roman Context*. WUNT 196. Tübingen: Mohr/Siebeck, 2006.
Warfield, B. B. "The Readings Ἕλληνας and Ἑλληνιστάς, Acts xi. 20." *JBL* 3 (1883) 113–27.
Watson, Francis. *Paul, Judaism and the Gentiles: A Sociological Approach*. SNTSMS 56. Cambridge: Cambridge University Press, 1986.
Weiss, Johannes. *The History of Primitive Christianity*. 2 vols. London: Macmillan, 1937.
Wetter, G. P. "Das älteste hellenistische Christentum nach der Apostelgeschichte." *AR* 21 (1922) 397–429.
Williams, C. S. C. *A Commentary on the Acts of the Apostles*. BNTC. 2nd ed. London: A. & C. Black, 1964.
Witherington, Ben, III. *The Acts of Apostles: A Socio-Rhetorical Commentary*. Grand Rapids: Eerdmans, 1998.
Yardeni, Ada. *Textbook of Aramaic, Hebrew, and Nabataean Documentary Texts from the Judaean Desert and Related Material B*. The Ben-Zion Dinur Center for Research in Jewish History. Jerusalem: Hebrew University, 2000.

14

"The Word of God" as a New Testament Term

An Investigation into Its Terminological Origin

SUNG-JONG OH

INTRODUCTION

A theme like "a study on the concept of the word of God" is probably more pertinent to an essay belonging to systematic theology than NT studies. In reality dogmatic theologians begin their textbooks with the section: "The Doctrine of the Word of God."[1] This title naturally would mean a doctrine of Scripture. It was Karl Barth who emphasized "the word of God" as the ultimate criterion of dogmatics (i.e., the notion of *Deus dixit*). He spoke of the three-fold form of the word of God as "the proclaimed word of God," "the written word of God," and "the revealed word of God."[2] But though this conception is theologically appropriate, such an interpretation of "the word of God" goes well beyond the terminological usage of the same phrase in the New Testament.

In almost every book of the New Testament, we can indeed find the term "word of God" or its equivalent (e.g., the "word of the LORD," "word,"

---

1. See, e.g., Grudem, *Systematic Theology*, 45.
2. Barth, *KD* 1/1:89–128.

"word of the kingdom," "word of the truth," "word of the gospel").[3] This frequency of the term "word," some ninety-six times, is more than that of its synonymous term: "gospel" (εὐαγγέλιον, which appears seventy-five times in the New Testament).[4] Despite its frequency, studies on the conceptual history of the term "word of God" occur rarely.[5] By comparison, studies on the term εὐαγγέλιον have been a subject of much debate among NT scholars.

A quick look at a few Bible dictionaries demonstrate a general neglect of the "word of God" as a technical term in Scripture. In the *New Bible Dictionary*, Taylor spends only one-eighth of a page on the use of the term in the New Testament.[6] In the *Exegetisches Wörterbuch*, Ritt spends considerable space dealing with the Greek word λόγος in the NT books, but he limits his analysis to the "words" (plural) of Jesus and his proclamation (Matt 7:24, 28 par.; Mark 13:31; Luke 4:32, 36), or discusses what relations there are between the word of God and the preacher (1 Cor 2:1; 14:36; 1 Thess 2:13).[7] In reality, Ritt discusses the technical use of λόγος only in a short space of twenty lines.[8] The *Dictionary of Paul and His Letters* does not even have an entry for the "word" or "word of God." A study on the origin and conception of the NT technical term "word of God" is desperately overdue. The key question seems to be whether the usage of our term "word of God" finds its origin in the Old Testament, early Judaism, Hellenistic Greek religions, the historical Jesus, the early church, or some matrix of the above.

---

3. Unless otherwise noted, all English translations from biblical texts or phrases are my own.

4. See Table 1 below and Aland, *Vollständige Konkordanz*, 2:118–19.

5. Instead of the "word of God and its related terms," I hereafter refer to the "word of God" or "word" for short. The "word (of God)" in the original is λόγος or ῥῆμα. In reality the two Greek nouns are used for the same meaning in the New Testament and in the LXX. Since in the New Testament ῥῆμα referring to the "word of God" is used only in a few cases, in our study I prefer to take λόγος as the representative Greek word among them.

6. Taylor, "Word of God," 1259.

7. Ritt, "λόγος," 880–87.

8. Ibid., 884. In contrast to Ritt's article, Kittel has provided a superior analysis in *TWNT* concerning the phrase "the word of God" as the gospel message in the New Testament; see Kittel, "λέγω, λόγος, κτλ.," 115–26.

OCCURRENCES OF THE TERM "WORD OF GOD" IN THE NEW TESTAMENT

Preliminary Remarks

There are two distinct uses of the same phrase "word of God": (1) the "word of God" as the message about the eschatological salvation established by God's Messiah; and (2) the "word of God" with other meanings. Case (1) is the subject of our concern. Case (2) will largely be excluded as a subject of exegetical analysis. The following groups of texts belong to case (2):

1. Texts where the "word of God" refers to a commandment or general statement from the God of the Old Testament,[9] or a general word from the exalted Christ:

    - ὁ λόγος τοῦ θεοῦ: Mark 7:13; Matt 15:6; John 10:35; 15:25; Rom 9:6, 9; 13:9; 1 Cor 14:36; 15:54; Gal 5:14 ; 2 Pet 3:5, 7
    - τὸ ῥῆμα τοῦ θεοῦ: Matt 4:4; Luke 3:2; John 3:34; 8:47; Rom 10:8; Heb 1:3, 11:3; 1 Pet 1:25

2. Texts where the "word of the Lord" is referring to a word or words spoken by Jesus to specific persons in an occasioned historical setting:[10]

    - ὁ λόγος τοῦ κυρίου: Acts 20:35; 1 Thess 4:15
    - τὸ ῥῆμα τοῦ κυρίου: Luke 22:61; Acts 11:16

3. Texts where the "word of God" is referring to a word or words spoken in a vision of Jesus or an angel:

    - ὁ λόγος of God: Rev 1:2;[11] 17:17; 19:9

Here it is also necessary to discuss whether the unique concept of the λόγος of the prologue in John 1:1–18 and the several times repeated phrase "the word of the Father, who sent me" terminologically fit case (1), i.e., the word of God in the sense of the gospel message, or should be excluded as belonging to case (2).

---

9. Ibid., 110–13.

10. Ibid., 105–10.

11. The phrase "the word of God and the testimony of Jesus Christ" in Rev 1:2 appears at first to be identical in form and meaning with the phrases the author uses in 1:9 ("the word of God and the testimony of Jesus Christ"); 6:9 ("the word of God and the testimony"); 20:4 ("for the testimony of Jesus and for the word of God"). But from the context of 1:1–2, the phrase of 1:2 must refer to what was revealed to the author by God and Jesus, so it is different from the other phrases in meaning. See Lohmeyer, *Die Offenbarung des Johannes*, 8; Mounce, *The Book of Revelation*, 42n18.

Regarding the prologue, John describes Jesus as the only Son of God, who was with God in the beginning and became flesh, as "the Word" (1:1, 14). Why, and in which background, did the author designate the Son of God as "the Word"? In spite of the long debate over this question, it is generally recognized that the words and images in John 1:1–5 unmistakably echo Gen 1:1–3.[12] Here the author is presenting the Son of God as the agent of God's creation and revelation through the Son's designation as "the Word," against the background where "the word of the Lord" (*dabar YHWH*) bears a creative, life-giving, and revelatory function. In the same manner 1 John 1:1–2 describes "the Word of life," as one who "was with the Father and was revealed to us," and Rev 19:13 describes "the Word of God" as one who "is clothed in a robe dipped in blood."

But here the question remains: is this personified Johannine designation "the Word (of God)" the equivalent to the gospel message? It seems to be best to answer the question negatively. For except in Johannine literature nowhere is Jesus Christ ever called "the Word." The Johannine personified Word would scarcely have been used in other first-century Christian circles. The Word as the person of Jesus Christ, the Son of God, as the revealer and savior sent from God the Father, is a Christological title unique to the Johannine community.[13] Consequently, the use of "the Word (of God)" in the Johannine writings is out of our scope of interest.

Concerning the other phrases "his word" (5:38), "(the word) of the Father who sent me" (14:24), and "your [= the Father's] word" (17:6, 14, 17) also found in the Gospel of John, these Johannine texts do not designate the gospel message in a general sense but are also tied to the Christology of Jesus as the Son who has been sent by the Father. So strictly speaking I conclude that a technical use of "the word of God" for the gospel message is not found in the Gospel of John.

In 1 John, the phrase referring to "the word of God" is mentioned three times: "his (= God's) word" (1:10; 2:5) and "the word of God" (2:14). In 1 John 1:10, 2:5, "his word" is a reference to the revelation of God's will, but not as an equivalent to the gospel. On the other hand the concept of "the word of God" in 2:14 stands as a unique usage distinct from 1 John 1:10 and 2:5. The reason is twofold. First, in 2:14, "the word of God" is virtually synonymous with the gospel, for the readers are spoken to as true and strong believers holding to "the word of God" versus a heretical docetic group who denied that Jesus Christ had come in the flesh (4:2–3).[14] Second, the phrase

---

12. Brown, *John I–XII*, 519–24.
13. Morris, *John*, 124–25; Barrett, *John*, 154; Lincoln, *John*, 96–97.
14. Such a use of our phrase parallels the descriptions of the living and dynamic

"the word of God," which does not refer to Jesus Christ the Son of God, appears in the Johannine literature singularly here. In this one instance, "the word of God" in 1 John 2:14 reflects gospel terminology.[15]

Data and Analysis for the Technical Use of "Word of God" as Gospel Terminology

We now turn to those texts in which we clearly see the New Testament employing "the word of God" and its equivalents as technical term for the gospel message:[16] Examples of case (2) uses include:

1. ὁ λόγος τοῦ θεοῦ: Luke 5:1; 8:11, 21; 11:28; Acts 4:31; 6:2, 7; 12:24; 13:5, 7, 44, 46; 17:13; 2 Cor 2:17; 4:2; Col 1:25; 1 Thess 2:13 (twice!);[17] 1 Tim 4:5;[18] 2 Tim 2:9; Tit 2:5; Heb 4:12; 13:7; 1 Pet 1:23; 1 John 2:14; Rev 1:9; 6:9; 20:4

2. ὁ λόγος τοῦ αὐτοῦ/σου (= τοῦ θεοῦ): Tit 1:3; Acts 4:29

3. ῥῆμα τοῦ θεοῦ: Eph 6:17; Heb 6:5

4. ὁ λόγος τοῦ κυρίου: Acts 8:25; 13:48, 49; 15:35, 36; 16:32; 19:10, 20; 1 Thess 1:8; 2 Thess 3:1

5. ὁ λόγος Χριστοῦ: Col 3:16

---

character of "the word of God" in Luke 8:11, 15; Acts 19:20; 20:32; Phil 2:16; Col 1:6; 1 Thess 2:13; Heb 4:12-13; 1 Pet 1:23.

15. Westcott, *John*, 61; Smalley, *1, 2, 3 John*, 48.

16. See Schmoller, *Handkonkordanz*, 314-16; Moulton et al., *Concordance*, 601-5; BAGD, s.v. λόγος, 477-79; Kittel, "λέγω, λόγος, κτλ.," 115-26.

17. In 1 Thess 2:13 the phrase "the word of God" is mentioned twice. But whether the two references are both used here in the meaning of the gospel message is ambiguous. Here Paul states: "[W]hen you received the word of God, which you heard from us, you accepted it not as the word of a human being but as what it really is, the word of God, which is also at work in you believers." On the basis of the evangelistic expression "the word of God, which you heard from us" this first reference must belong to our "word of God" terminology. But is the second reference also to be regarded as well as the first one? If Paul's statement was his answer on the question whether "what is heard" from him and his co-workers was a human word or God's word, then the latter phrase "the word of God" might not be used in the meaning of the gospel message. So Dibelius, *Die Briefe*, 9: "göttliches Wort (a *divine word*)." But here Paul is dealing with the question about the divine origin of "the word of God" heard from him and his co-workers. And he continues to mention: "the word of God, which is also at work in you believers." Just this expression "the word of God, which is also at work in you believers" seems rather to denote our NT technical term, as Col 1:6, 8; Heb 4:12-13; Acts 20:32; Luke 8:11, 15. So Wanamaker, *Thessalonians*, 111-12.

18. For our understanding and categorization of the "word of God" in 1 Tim 4:5, see Roloff, *Timotheus*, 227; Johnson, *Timothy*, 242.

6. τὸ ῥῆμα Χριστοῦ: Rom 10:17

7. ὁ λόγος: Mark 2:2; 4:14, 15a, 15b, 16, 17, 18, 19, 20, 33; Matt 13:20, 21, 22a, 22b, 23; Luke 1:2;[19] 8:12, 13, 15; Acts 4:4; 6:4; 8:4; 10:36, 44; 11:19; 14:25; 16:6; 18:5; Gal 6:6; Phil 1:14; Col 4:3; 1 Thess 1:6; 2 Tim 4:2; Jas 1:21, 22, 23;[20] 1 Pet 2:8; 3:1

8. ὁ λόγος + an attributive genitive: "the word of the *kingdom*" (Matt 13:19); "the word of the *gospel*" (Acts 15:7); "the word of *salvation*" (Acts 13:26); "the word of *truth*" (Eph 1:13; Col 1:5; 2 Tim 2:15; Jas 1:18); "the word of *grace*" (Acts 14:3; 20:32); "the word of the *cross*" (1 Cor 1:18); "the word of *reconciliation*" (2 Cor 5:19); "the word of *life*" (Phil 2:16)

9. τὸ ῥῆμα + an attributive genitive: "the word of *faith*" (Rom 10:8); "the word of *Christ*" (Rom 10:17)

I offer below a table of listing the terminology for "the word (of God)" and its frequency in the New Testament:

Table 1: Case (2) Uses of "the Word of God" in the New Testament		
Forms of Expression	Occurrence	Frequency by Book
ὁ λόγος τοῦ θεοῦ (inclusive of αὐτοῦ / σου = τοῦ θεοῦ)	30	Luke (4); Acts (10); Rev (3); 2 Cor (2); 1 Thess (2); Tit (2); Heb (2); Col (1); 1 Tim (1); 2 Tim (1); 1 Pet (1); 1 John (1)
ὁ λόγος τοῦ κυρίου	10	Acts (8); 1 Thess (1); 2 Thess (1)
ῥῆμα θεοῦ/ θεοῦ ῥῆμα	2	Eph (1); Heb (1)
ὁ λόγος Χριστοῦ / ῥῆμα Χριστοῦ	2	Rom (1); Col (1);
ὁ λόγος	38	Synoptic Gospels (19); Acts (9); Pauline epistles (5); Jas (3); 1 Pet (2). Note: "the parable of the sower" alone contains 16 of the 19 synoptic occurrences [Matt (5); Mark (8); Luke (3)]
ὁ λόγος + attrib. genitive	12	Acts (4); Rom (2); Matt (1); 1 Cor (1); 2 Cor (1); Eph (1); Phil (1); Col (1); 2 Tim (1); Jas (1)
τὸ ῥῆμα + attrib. genitive	2	
Total	96	

19. With Fitzmyer (*Luke I–IX*, 295), I am inclined to regard the absolute form ὁ λόγος in Luke 1:2 not merely as a "general term applicable to the story of Christian origins" but as a term used for the gospel message or the salvation history realized in Jesus Christ.

20. For the understanding of λόγος in Jas 1:21, 22 as the gospel message, see Davids, *James*, 95–97.

As we have seen from the survey above, terminology for "the word of God" in the New Testament is widespread, but it is characterized by the following general features:

1. Its use is found in almost all the NT books (except John, Philemon, 2 Peter, 2 John, 3 John, and Jude) for a total occurrence of 96 times.

2. Though there are variegated forms,[21] the several ways to express "the word of God" are nevertheless conceptually non-variegated since all the terms mentioned above are in the immediate or broad context virtually interchangeable.

3. The terms for "the word (of God)" were already in general use during the period of the primitive church. It argued here that "the word (of God)" and its equivalents functioned as a NT *terminus technicus*.

4. The term ὁ λόγος τοῦ θεοῦ [κυρίου[22] / Χριστοῦ] and its abridged form ὁ λόγος appear respectively 44X and 51X in the New Testament, and nearly in equal dispersion and frequency. This terminological feature seems to strongly indicate that they were simultaneously in currency at relatively the same time.

5. It is to be noted that particularly in Acts our terminology appears frequently and intensively (31X). Acts on the whole describes the various

---

21. In 1 Thess: ὁ λόγος (1:6), ὁ λόγος τοῦ κυρίου (1:8), λόγος τοῦ θεοῦ (2:13); in Col: ὁ λόγος τῆς ἀληθείας (1:5), ὁ λόγος τοῦ θεοῦ (1:25), ὁ λόγος τοῦ Χριστοῦ (3:16), ὁ λόγος (4:3); in 2 Tim: ὁ λόγος τοῦ θεοῦ (2:9), ὁ λόγος τῆς ἀληθείας (2:15), ὁ λόγος (4:2); in James: λόγος ἀληθείας (1:18), ὁ λόγος (1:21); in Acts: ὁ λόγος σου (4:29), ὁ λόγος τοῦ θεοῦ (4:31), ὁ λόγος τοῦ θεοῦ (6:2, 7), ὁ λόγος (6:4), ὁ λόγος (18:5), ὁ λόγος τοῦ θεοῦ (18:11); in the parable of the sower in the Synoptics: ὁ λόγος (Mark 4:14, 15; Matt 20; Luke 8:12), ὁ λόγος τῆς βασιλείας (Matt 13:19), ὁ λόγος τοῦ θεοῦ (Luke 8:11).

22. It can be questioned whether in the phrase ὁ λόγος τοῦ κυρίου the possessive τοῦ κυρίου refers to τοῦ θεοῦ or Χριστοῦ, since in Acts ὁ κύριος is used with reference to God and to Christ at the same time. As Foerster and Quell ("κύριος," 1086) rightly observe, "there is no substantial difference between κύριος with and without the article." And as Fitzmyer ("κύριος," 816) has demonstrated through the evidence from the Aramaic and Hebrew Qumran documents and from the Josephus's writings that Palestinian Jews in the last two pre-Christian centuries referred to God as "(the) LORD." Compared with the frequent occurrence of the phrase of ὁ κύριος Ἰησοῦς [Χριστός], it is to be noted that a connection like ὁ λόγος τοῦ κυρίου Ἰησοῦ [Χριστοῦ] is wholly lacking in the Acts and also in the whole New Testament. Therefore, the phrase ὁ λόγος τοῦ κυρίου is best understood in the sense of "the word of Yahweh," that is, in connection with the usage of the title (ὁ) κύριος substituted for the Tetragrammaton *YHWH* in the LXX. See Foerster and Quell, "κύριος," 1081–87; Fitzmyer, "κύριος," 815. The phrase ὁ λόγος τοῦ κυρίου appears also in 1 Thess 1:8 and 2 Thess 3:1. Here the phrase is associated with the living and working character of the OT word of Yahweh (Ps 18:4 LXX; 147:4, 7 LXX); see Trilling, *Thessalonicher*, 135; Wanamaker, *Thessalonians*, 83, 274, whose reference, however, of the genitive τοῦ κυρίου to Christ seems to be erroneous.

accounts of preaching "the word of God" to unbelieving Jews and Gentiles. In Acts "the word of God" appears often (11X) in connection with typical verbs describing evangelistic activities.[23] Similar usages are found (19X) from other five other NT books.[24]

Given the above cursory observations, we are left with the question: how did the technical term "the word of God" as a synonym for the gospel originate? Now let us search a possible answer to this question in the remaining sections below. But here it is helpful to offer a brief explanation of whether there is any material difference between the two terms ὁ λόγος τοῦ θεοῦ and τὸ ῥῆμα τοῦ θεοῦ. The latter one appears only 4X in the New Testament.

The root of ῥῆμα is ερ-/ρη- and is seen in its verbal forms: the future (ἐρῶ), the aorist passive (ἐρρήθην), and the present perfect (εἴρηκα) of the verb λέγω. So ῥῆμα represents 'what is definitely spoken.'[25] While λόγος and ῥῆμα together mean "word," or "speech," they are characterized by the fact that the former denotes a "rationally connected and understood expression" and the latter connotes an 'individual, more emotionally charged expression.'[26] Since those two Greek nouns can be used as the rendering of the *dabar*, in reality there is little semantic difference between them. Rendering the Hebrew *dabar*, two words λόγος and ῥῆμα in the LXX have share a ratio of approximately 2:1 in the occurrences of the canonical books.[27] They are used interchangeably also in the New Testament, as Col 3:16; Rom 10:17; 1 Pet 1:23-25 demonstrates.

HISTORY OF NT RESEARCH ON THE ORIGIN OF THE NT TERM "THE WORD OF GOD"

"The Word of God": A Term of the *Missionssprache* of the Early Church?

Almost all the form-critically minded commentators[28] take "the word of God" as a missionary language used by the early church. It is a *terminus*

---

23. Acts 4:4; 8:14; 10:44; 11:1; 13:5, 7, 44; 15:35, 36; 17:11, 13.

24. Mark 4:18, 20; Matt 13:19, 22, 23; Luke 8:13, 15; Rom 10:17; Eph 1:13; Col 1:5; 4:3; 1 Thess 1:6; 2:13; 2 Tim 4:2; Tit 1:3; 2:5; Jas 1:21; 1 Pet 2:8; 3:1.

25. Debrunner, "λέγω, κτλ," 74.

26. Kleinknecht, "λόγος," 78.

27. See HRCS, 881-86, 1249-51; Gerleman, "*dābār* Wort," 438.

28. E.g., Bultmann, *Geschichte*, 202; Taylor, *Mark*, 258-59; Jeremias, *The Parables of Jesus*, 77-79; Pesch, *Markusevangelium*, 242-47; Gnilka, *Markus*, 173; Schweizer, *Markus*, 48; Bovon, *Lukas*, 405-6; Lührmann, *Markusevangelium*, 88-89; Luz, *Matthäus*,

technicus referring to the message of the gospel preached to Jewish and Gentile people. The term "the word (of God)" is normally constructed with the verbs like to speak, proclaim, hear, and receive as shown typically in the explanation of the parable of the sower (Mark 4:14–20 par.). Its vocabulary belongs to the "*christliche Missionssprache / Terminologie*," which reflects the manifold missionary situation of some existing Christian communities (*Sitz im Leben*).

Is the term "the word (of God)" really to be reckoned as the "*christliche Missionsprache*"? Is its origin to be attributed to its invention in the early church? And is the phrase to be understood as formed in analogy to "the word of the LORD" frequently occurring in the prophetic writings of the Old Testament? In my view, the grounds for an affirmative answer to these questions are not self-evident. Here are at least four reasons why I would answer the above questions in the negative.

1. The phrase "the word of God" has been never used as any missionary language either in the Hebrew Bible or the LXX. Apart from Acts, in which the phrase here describes what the apostles and evangelists preached to unbelieving people, "the word of God" in the rest of the New Testament is normally used more frequently rather not as a missionary term but more broadly as "gospel," which encompasses both non-believers (as a call to faith) and believers (as a call to continually live by faith). So the Acts definition of "word of God" appears to a derivation or specialization of meaning rather than its semantic origin.

2. Even though "the word of the LORD" occurs over a hundred times in the prophetic writings of the Old Testament, in all these occurrences this phrase is never used as referring to any good news about an eschatological salvation.[29] This fact exhibits an explicit and decisive contrast with the frequent occurrence of "the word (of God)" in the New Testament, in which this technical term is used in parallel or as an apposition to the "gospel," or in construction with the verb εὐαγγελίζεσθαι.[30] Therefore it unlikely our NT term is formally or theologically derived from the familiar phrase "the word of the LORD" in the Old Testament.

314–20. See also Haenchen (*Apostelgeschichte*, 185), who states: "Der Sprachgebrauch entspicht der LXX. Λαλεῖν τὸν λόγον ist ein term. techn. der frühchristlichen Missionssprache und bezeichnet die Missionspredigt"; Fitzmyer (*Acts*, 311), who states: "The phrase is derived from the Old Testament (LXX of Jer 1:2; 9:19), where *logos Kyriou*, 'the word of the LORD,' is far more frequent"; and Ritt ("λόγος," 883), who states: "Missionssprache ist ὁ λ[όγος] zum t.t. für die missionarische Verkündigung geworden."

29. Cf. Jer 49:14; Obad 1:1; Isa 40:9; 41:27; 61:1; Nah 1:15.

30. Acts 8:4, 25; 15:35; Col 1:5; Eph 1:13; 1 Pet 1:25. Cf. also Gal 1:11; 1 Cor 15:1; 2 Cor 11:7.

3. All commentators who regard "the word of God" in the New Testament as belonging to the Christian missionary language suppose that they could see in the shorter designation "the word" the same definition. But how has "the word" as an abridged form of "the word of God / the Lord" come into being in the early church? How do we account for the fact the our term in the New Testament appears in six different authors and eleven different books? The absolute form "the word" is used with an attributive genitive construction thirteen times, and indeed in ten different books. The NT term "the word" could scarcely been originated by the early church but rather in an earlier stage, probably the historical Jesus himself.

4. It is often said without much consideration that "the word of God" was a technical term of the early church, but in what sense? Haenchen thinks: "The λόγος τοῦ θεοῦ is 'word of God': namely the Good News about Jesus, which God lets proclaim through the apostles."[31] When Bock maintains that "an oral message about Jesus ... can be called God's word because the message about Jesus is from God, describing God's work,"[32] he seems to be not far from Haenchen's understanding. But our question is this: why could a divinely given oral message about Jesus have been called "the word of God" or "the word"? In other terms, how could the early church uniformly have come to understand "the word (of God)" in such an eschatological and messianic meaning? In the exegetical scholarship, in so far as I know it, there has been no persuasive solution to this question and it deserves a closer examination here.

Early Judaism and 'the Word of God'?

The tradition of using the concept of "the word of God / Yahweh" as a technical term of the OT prophetic literature may have continued in early Judaism.[33] But the early Jewish literature shows that the term appeared very frequently in the Old Testament has been significantly reduced in early Judaism. These features can be probably explained from the fact that such an active prophetic ministry as in the OT times has almost stopped in the period of the Second Temple.[34]

Early Judaism, regardless of the sects, was enthusiastic in learning and keeping the Torah, and for the Jewish people the Torah was "joy and crown

---

31. Haenchen, *Apostelgeschichte*, 185.
32. Bock, *Acts,* 210.
33. See, e.g., Sir 42:15; 48:3; Wis 9:1; 16:12.
34. The rabbis taught that the spirit of prophecy in Israel had disappeared after the death of the last prophets, that is, Haggai, Zechariah, and Malachi. See Str-B 1:125–27.

of existence" and "substance of life."³⁵ The rabbis were less interested in the fulfillment of the prophecies written in the Old Testament. While expectations for the various eschatological or apocalyptic "age to come" (*'olam habba'*), the Messianic era (*yemot hammashiakh*), and the restoration of the kingdom of David (cf. Acts 1:6) appear frequently,³⁶ expectations about the Messiah based on any specific prophecies from the Old Testament were rarely found except the Qumran community.³⁷ The two Messiahs awaited by the Qumran community were described as the leaders for the Jewish people, who would contribute to the thorough observance of the law and the renewal of the sacrificial system.³⁸ According to Neusner, "the sages of the Mishnah . . . most needed: a rabbi-Messiah, who will save an Israel sanctified through Torah."³⁹

In the literature of early Judaism there seldom appears the phrase "*dabar* / λόγος of YHWH," which so frequently occurred in the Old Testament. Of the 79 pages in the *TWNT* article on "λέγω, κτλ.," any reference to early Judaism is in fact wholly lacking, except for those which deal with the peculiar *logos* concept of Philo.⁴⁰ The term "the word of the LORD / God" is scarcely found in the Mishnah.⁴¹ There is therefore little possibility that the NT term "the word of God" originates in early Judaism.

ONCE AGAIN: HOW DID THE NT TERM "THE WORD OF GOD" ORIGINATE?

Then, should it remain impossible to search for any solution to the question on the origin of the NT term "the word of God"? To answer, it pays to take up the following related questions: 1. What are the common characteristics of our NT term? In other words, how much does its use have eschatological and Messianic implications? 2. Are there any OT texts where particularly the two themes—the word of God and the eschatological good news—are at the same time mentioned in the immediate context, and are they intentionally related together in the New Testament? If the answer to these questions is affirmative, what does the juxtaposition of the word of God with the good news mean? 3. If the parable of the sower in the Synoptics is a genuine

35. Bousset, *Die Religion des Judentums*, 119; Schürer, *History*, 498–99.
36. Str-B 4:799–976.
37. Green, "Introduction," 2; Sandmel, *Judaism*, 206.
38. Lohse, *Die Texte aus Qumran*, xiii–xx.
39. Neusner, "Mishnah and Messiah," 282.
40. Kleinknecht, "λόγος," 86–88.
41. See the indices by Darby, *The Mishnah*, 844.

saying of Jesus, how does the parable contribute to the investigation into the origin of the term "word of God"?

Common Characteristics of "the Word of God" in the Old Testament and the New

The word λόγος in the phrase λόγος τοῦ θεοῦ used in the New Testament as a *terminus technicus* was originally in the ancient Greek a common noun representing a variety of meanings. According to LSJ, λόγος has had about fifty semantic categories.[42] The basic meanings of the root: λεγ-, whose nominal form is λόγος, are *choose, count, say / speak*.[43] But as examples referring to the "Word" or "Wisdom of God," LSJ mentions only instances from the LXX and New Testament. It is likely that such a theological use of λόγος is a marked usage not common in ancient Greek. Kleinknecht rightly remarks in his explanation of the Hellenistic logos-speculation that while the stress on the word of God in the Old Testament and New Testament was on God's speaking to humans and the expression of his will in history, the emphasis of the Hellenistic λόγος-conception was on their rational intellect of humans and the internal law of the nature.[44] We should therefore not resort to the use of the Greek word λόγος in the ancient Greek literature and Hellenism, but to the Hebrew word *dabar* (of the LORD / God) in the Old Testament.

We should admit that in the New Testament the noun λόγος is used according to several semantic categories found in Hellenistic literature.[45] But such uses are the exception rather than the rule, since they apply to only 14 cases among the 330 occurrences of our Greek word in the New Testament.[46] Further, in the LXX λόγος almost always renders *dabar* (or its Aramaic equivalent *milla*),[47] a term whose range of meaning overlaps with that of λόγος but is not co-extensive with it. The Hebrew noun *dabar* is derived from the root *dbr* which means "to speak." In the LXX *dbr* (piel) is mostly translated into λαλεῖν.[48] As rightly emphasized by Gerleman, the synonymous Hebrew verb '*mr* (qal) stands in explicit contrast with *dbr* (piel): "While in the former ['*mr* (qal)] the consideration for the content

42. LSJ, s.v. λόγος, 1057–59.
43. Debrunner, "λέγω, κτλ.," 71–74.
44. Kleinknecht, "λόγος," 88–89.
45. BAGD, s.v. λόγος, 478.
46. Aland, *Konkordanz*, 170–71.
47. HRCS 881–86.
48. HRCS 841–46. As HRCS (863–71) shows clearly, in the LXX the Greek verb λέγω renders the Hebrew verb '*m'r* (qal).

of what is spoken is important, with *dbr* (piel) the activity of speaking, the uttering of words and sentences, is first of all marked."[49] So in the Old Testament, prophets claim: "Now the *dabar* of the LORD came to me, saying . . . "[50] A true prophet, to whom the *dabar* of the LORD came, cannot cease to preach in spite of terror and derision, since he feels "a burning fire" in his heart and bones (Jer 20:8–9). The *dabar* of the LORD, which is found 242 times in the Old Testament, of which 225 times refer to prophetic oracles,[51] is distinctively shown as divine, living, personal, and dynamic, as follows:

- creative and powerful: Lev 1:9–10; 23:28–29; Jer 23:28–29; Ezek 37:4; Ps 33:6, 9
- self-living and personal: Isa 9:8; 55:11; Jer 15:16; 23:9; Ps 105:19; 107:20; 147:15–18; cf. Acts 10:36
- irrevocable and faithful until its realization: Jer 28:9; 1 Kgs 2:27; 15:29; 16:12, 34; 2 Kgs 1:17; 9:36; 22:16; Ps 105:42
- having divine authority: 1 Sam 15:26; 1 Kgs 12:24; Ps 119:89
- eternal and effective: Isa 40:8

Moreover, when the word of the LORD came to the prophets whom the LORD himself had selected as his servants to preach it and to whom he personally entrusted its contents,[52] the word was accompanied by the descent and inspiration of the Spirit of YHWH on them.[53] All of this evidence points to a linguistic and conceptual tie between "the *dabar* of Yahweh" in the Old Testament and "the λόγος of God" in the New Testament although the terms are not perfectly equivalent to each other.

"The Word of God" and Isa 40:3–11 as the Background to its Concept

The phrase "the word of God" in the New Testament follows the tradition of "the *dabar* of Yahweh" in the Old Testament. However, the terms are not semantically identical. For "the word of God" as a NT technical term refers to God's eschatological message about the crucified and resurrected Jesus Christ, that is, the gospel of God. In this sense "the word of the LORD,"

---

49. Gerleman, "*dabar* Wort," 435.
50. Jer 1:4, 13; 16:1; 18:5; 25:3; 33:1; 34:1; 35:1; 43:8.
51. Gerleman, "*dabar* Wort," 439.
52. Amos 3:8; 8:14–15; Joel 1:1–2; Jer 1:5–10; 23:9, 16–40; 28:9.
53. Num 11:17, 25, 26; 24:2; 1 Sam 23:1–2; 1 Chr 12:18; 2 Chr 15:1; 20:14; 24:20; Hos 9:7; Ezek 11:5. See also 1 Sam 10:10; 19:20–24. Cf. Kittel, "λέγω, λόγος, κτλ." 93.

the phrase so often used in the Old Testament, has no direct conceptual relationship with that NT term "the word of God."

Are there then no texts in the New Testament which quote or echo the phrase 'the word of YHWH as it refers to a prophecy about the eschatological Messiah and / or the gospel? There are indeed four texts in the New Testament which do: namely 1 Pet 1:23-25; Mark 1:1-15; 4:14-20; and Rom 10:5-17. These texts find their source material in a specific OT passage: Isaiah 40:3-11, where "the word of the LORD" and the eschatological gospel are explicitly linked.

"The Word of God" in Isa 40:3-11 and 1 Pet 1:23-25

In 1 Pet 1:22-23, "the living and abiding word of God" is described metaphorically as an "imperishable seed" (1:23). The juxtaposition of "seed" and "word of God," along with their syntagms 'imperishable' and "living and abiding," extend the meaning of "word of God" to include its life-producing, creative power. The use of "seed" metaphor is also interpreted in the same way by Jesus when he explains the message behind the parable of the sower (Luke 8:11; cf. Mark 4:14).[54]

In the following v. 24 (διότι, 'for'), 1 Peter grounds the character of God's word by the quotation from Isa 40:6, 8, where the everlasting nature of the "word of the Lord" stands in contrast with perishability of "all flesh."[55] In the Old Testament the word "flesh" (Hebrew *basar* / LXX σάρξ) indicates humanity but especially humanity's mortality and powerlessness. For the Petrine author (henceforth simply as "Peter") this supernatural "word of God" described in Isa 40:6-8 is the OT background for the "living and abiding word of God" bringing rebirth to fragile and sinful humanity (1 Pet 1:23-24). In the broad context of 1 Peter (1:3, 18-22; 2:24-25; 4:1) the author affirms the vulnerability of *basar* / σάρξ and humanity's need for salvation in his quoting of Isa 40:6.[56]

In 1 Pet 1:25, Peter can identify the "word of the Lord" with the "good news that was preached to you." But on which ground could he venture to make this identification? It is the most natural for Peter to have read Isaiah 40:6-8 in relation the following verses 40:9-11, where the latter is an exposition of "announcing the good news" (MT: *mebasseret*, participle of *bsr* (piel) = LXX: ὁ εὐαγγελιζόμενος) of Yahweh's impending return to his

---

54. Elliott, *1 Peter*, 388-89.

55. See Gerleman, "*bāśār* Fleisch," 377-79.

56. See Elliger, *Deuterojesaja*, 22-23: "In spite of the sin of the nation and the futility of its faith, (God realizes) his own promise of salvation."

people.[57] It is significant that in the Old Testament the two ideas—i.e., "announcing the good news" (of the eschatological kingly reign of God)[58] and the (life-giving) "word of our God"—stand side by side only in Isa 40:6–11.

Special attention should be paid to the use of "the word" (short for "the word of God") in sense of the gospel at two other places in 1 Peter. In 2:8 and 3:1, Peter speaks of "those who *do not obey the word*" meaning "unbelievers." Similarly in 4:17, unbelievers are referred to "those that *do not obey the gospel of God*." Peter shares with a unique understanding of "the word (of God)" as "the gospel (of God)" with the Jesus traditions in Mark. If it is valid that the Gospel of Mark essentially reflects Peter's eyewitness testimony and the authorship of 1 Peter is to be ascribed to Peter himself, then the usage of "the word (of God)" as "the gospel" shared by both Mark and 1 Peter can be attributed to a common author or traditions source.[59]

In 1:23–25, Peter equates the "word of God" with the "gospel" and sees in Isa 40:6–11 the biblical basis for this understanding. Then, was Peter the originator of this interpretive understanding? Highly unlikely. For there are many other NT writers who also use the image of the growing, life-bringing and fruit-bearing seed as referring to the word of God and thus also identify "the word" / "the word of God" with "the gospel."[60] It cannot be simply a strange coincidence that the common conception and usage of the term "the word (of God)" is universally found in 1 Peter, Mark, and other NT books. They share a common traditions source, i.e., Isaiah 40:3–11.

"The Word of God" in Isaiah 40:3–11 and Mark 1:1–15

John the Baptist appeared in the wilderness, proclaiming a baptism of repentance for the forgiveness of sins, whereby the prophecy of Isa 40:3 came to be fulfilled. After the baptism by John, Jesus as "the Son of God" began

---

57. Selwyn, *St. Peter*, 133; Jobes, *1 Peter*, 124–29.

58. There are only four instances, where in the MT and the LXX the prophecies about the eschatological salvation are written with the verb *bsr* (piel) meaning to "preach the good news." See Ps 96:2 (LXX 95:2); Isa 40:9; 52:7; 61:1.

59. Concerning the view of Mark as the recognized records of the essentially Petrine eyewitness tradition, see Hengel, *Saint Peter*, 36–47; Hengel, "Eye-witness Memory," 70–96; Burridge, *What Are the Gospels?*, 337–40; Bauckham, *Jesus and the Eyewitnesses*, 114–201. For the argument for the Petrine authorship of 1 Peter through Silvanus, see Reicke, *James, Peter, and Jude*, 69–72, 133; Davids, *The First Epistle of Peter*, 3–7, 197–99. For the view that 1 Peter is "'Petrine' in the secondary sense," see Elliot, *1 Peter*, 124–30.

60. Mark 4:20 // Matt 13:23 // Luke 8:15; Acts 20:32; Col 1:5–6; 1 Thess 2:13; 2 Thess 3:1; 2 Tim 2:9; Heb 4:12–13; Jas 1:18.

to preach the message of the good news about the impending presence of God's eschatological kingly reign. This narrative is unanimously testified by the evangelists.[61] Especially Mark makes it unmistakably clear in his prologue (1:1–15)[62] that John was sent to "prepare the way of *the Lord*," that is, the way for *Jesus the Messiah, the Son of God*. Quoting Isa 40:3, Mark changed "a highway for *our God*" into "*his* paths"(1:3) and showed that Jesus the Son came in the name of God the LORD. In 1:14–15, Mark narrates that Jesus "preached the good news of God," saying: "The kingly reign of God has come near; repent, and believe in the good news" In what sense should the "good news of God's kingly reign preached by Jesus" be reckoned as the "good news about Jesus Christ the Son of God"? In my opinion, the only possible answer to these questions is that Jesus himself understood his preaching ministry as the realization of the prophecy of Isaiah 40:6–11. The reason is twofold:

1. Indeed, John as forerunner of the Messiah did say not without significance: "*After me* comes he who is mightier than I" (1:7). Mark seems unmistakably to signify that the end of the Baptist's mission as Isaiah's voice in the desert marks the beginning of Jesus' preaching ministry: "Now *after John was arrested*, Jesus came into Galilee, proclaiming the gospel of God, and saying, 'The time is fulfilled, and . . . '" (1:14–15). Like John, Jesus' mission follows the Isaianic script.

2. In Isa 40:3–11, the prophecy about the herald who comes to prepare the way of the LORD who comes in glory (vv. 3–5; cf. Luke 3:4–6) is followed by the prophecy about "the word of our God" (v. 6–8) and preaching the good news of YHWH's arrival (vv. 9–11). The prophecy in Isa 40:6–8, that the "word of our God" will impart life to the hopeless and perishable people due to their sins, stands appositionally parallel to the prophecy in following vv. 9–11, that the Lord God will come as a conquering king and a gentle shepherd to bring the Jewish exiles back to the Judea. According to the Markan Prologue, Jesus came in the name of the LORD and preached "the word of our God," that is, "the good news" about the coming kingly reign of the Lord God, to fulfill the prophecy of Isa 40:6–11. Jesus was conscious of how his ministry of preaching the good news of God's kingly reign realized the Isaiah prophecy of how Yahweh himself will rule and shepherd his people.[63]

---

61. Mark 1:1–15; Luke 3:1–22; 4:14–19; Matt 3:1–17; 4:17; cf. John 1:6–8, 19–34.

62. For the division of 1:1–15 instead of 1:1–13, see Keck, "The Introduction to Mark's Gospel," 352–70; Pesch, *Markusevangelium*, 71–73; Guelich, *Mark 1—8:26*, 4–5.

63. Or we may say, as sharply expressed by Lohmeyer (*Markus*, 30): "So now when

This interpretation of Mark 1:1–15[64] corresponds to that of 1 Pet 1:22–25. In both passages "the word of God" and "the gospel" appear as equivalents. The act of preaching the word of God / the gospel performs a necessary function in bringing eschatological salvation. The OT background for this usage of God's word is the soteriology described by the Isaiah prophecies.

"The Word of God" in Isa 40:3–11 and Rom 10:5–17

The common terminology, christology, and soteriology in Mark 1:1–15 and 1 Pet 1:22–25 are again found in Rom 10:5–17. In Rom 10:9–13, Paul demonstrates a daring identification of the YHWH (LXX: κύριος) as the One who saves in Joel 2:32 with the resurrected Lord Jesus Christ. As the biblical basis for salvation through faith in the Lord Jesus, Paul offers the quote from Joel 2:32: "Everyone who calls on the name of the LORD (MT: YHWH) shall be saved."

In Rom 10:5–17, Paul explicitly uses the terms "the word (of faith)" (v. 8) and "the word of Christ" (v. 17) as synonyms for "the gospel" (vv. 15–16). Here "the word" as the gospel message needs to be preached, heard, and believed (vv. 8–17). In vv. 15–16 Paul describes this gospel as the message about the eschatological kingly reign of God (Isa 52:7) and the suffering servant of the Lord (Isa 53:1). The central content of "the word" / "the gospel" is the crucified and resurrected Savior and Lord Jesus Christ. Paul's usage of "the word / gospel (of God)" as referring the gospel about (the Lord) Jesus Christ the Son of God, along with parallel usages in Mark and 1 Peter, points to the possibility that the technical use of "word (of God)" as gospel was already in place among the apostles and the early church. Its origin can be traced back to the historical Jesus himself.

"The Word of God" in Isa 40:3–11 and Mark 4:14–20 (Par.)

In the parable of the sower, the referent of the seed varies slightly in the synoptic tradition between "the word" (ὁ λόγος, Mark 4:14), "the word of God"

Jesus announces the fulfillment [of the prophecy of God's kingly reign], then either to the ears of the Jews his saying is a blasphemy or for the ears of the early Christians it is God's own voice, and God's own word. Then the carrier of this announcement is so closely with God united that his word and God's word are one and the same." See also Taylor, *St. Mark*, 382; Hengel, *Studies in the Gospel of Mark*, 54.

64. Concerning the understanding of Isa 40:3–11 as the background of Mark 1:1–15, see Watts, "Mark," 113–20.

(Luke 8:11), and "the word of the kingdom" (Matt 13:19). But once Jesus has explained the parable, the phrase for the seed is uniformly shortened in the synoptic gospels as simply "the word." The synoptic tradition bears evidence for the common understanding and use of the term "the word (of God)" as the gospel of Jesus.

If the explanation of the parable of the sower originates with the historical Jesus, so too its usage of "the word (of God)." Since this term appears concentrated in the parable of the sower but rarely elsewhere in the canonical gospels points to likely authenticity. However, many scholars, who read the synoptic gospels from the standpoint of form criticism, argue that the "allegorizing" explanation of the parable of the sower can not be traced back to the historical Jesus.[65] Instead the pericope with Jesus' explanation of the parable would have derived from the situations and experience (*Sitz im Leben*) of the preachers and their Christian communities.[66]

When form critics assert that the allegorizing explanation of the parable of the sower is a late addition and may have derived from the patristic fathers, they are depending upon Adolf Jülicher's theories of interpretation for the parables of Jesus. In his view, a parable is an "enlarged simile" (*Gleichnis*) and to be thoroughly differentiated from allegory as an "enlarged metaphor" which is a late practice and not original to the historical Jesus. For a long time, following Jülicher, NT scholars viewed the parables as focusing on a single point of comparison (*tertium comparationis*) and can not have any allegorizing interpretation (*Allegorese*).[67] So the majority of current redaction-critical scholars believe that the allegorical explanation of the four kinds of soils into which the seed is sown is proof that the parable's explanation originates from the *Sitz im Leben* of the Christian communities.

But recently other NT gospel specialists consider the sharp distinction between allegory and parable to be false.[68] They criticize that Jülicher's theory has functioned too long as a religious dogma.[69] Many examples for the story-type parable (in Hebrew: *mashal*) include narrative sections

65. Theissen, *Studien zur Soziologie des Urchristentums*, 9.

66. Jülicher, *Gleichnisreden Jesu*, 2:514–38; Bultmann, *Geschichte*, 202; Taylor, *St. Mark*, 258–59; Jeremias, *Parables of Jesus*, 77–79; Gnilka, *Markus*, 173; Schweizer, *Markus*, 48; Ritt, "λόγος," 883; Bovon, *Lukas*, 405–6; Luz, *Matthäus (Matt 8–17)*, 314–20.

67. Jülicher, *Die Gleichnisreden Jesu*, 1:60–81.

68. See Cranfield, *Mark*, 158–61; Guelich, *Mark 1—8:26*, 217–19; Stein, *Mark*, 213–15; France, *Mark*, 202–7; Snodgrass, *Stories with Intent*, 4–7, 31–35; Lemicio, "External Evidence," 323–38; Payne, "The Authenticity of the Parables of Jesus," 329–44. For the *mashal*-interpretations of some early Jewish rabbis, see Str-B, 1:664–65.

69. Snodgrass, *Stories with Intent*, 6: "Today most of Jülicher's argument has been set aside. Hardly anyone today follows Jülicher."

of questions and explanation. These are found in the Old Testament, the Apocrypha, and the rabbinic writings. Most likely Jesus' parable of the sower with his explanation can be attributed to this category of parables. The explanation of the parable of the sower does not intend any application to a particular pastoral situation in the growing later church. It is best read in its context as a teaching by Jesus on the responsiveness or non-responsiveness of his audience to the message of God's kingly reign.

Depending on recent arguments for the authenticity of the parable's explanation,[70] I now turn to the question of a possible relation between Jesus' interpretation of the parable with Isa 40:3–11. In Mark 1:1–15, I argued that Mark equates the prophecy of Yahweh's arrival in Zion as the king and shepherd of Israel in Isa 40:3–11 with the coming of Jesus Christ the Son of God as a powerful king and the realization of that Isaianic prophecy through his preaching ministry.

The Isaianic prophecy also contributes to the interpretation of parable in Mark 4:14–20. Jesus' interpretation of "the word (of God)" as the gospel message of God's kingly reign is symbolized in the growing and fruit-bearing seed. The message about sowing the seed is twofold: 1) it assures the reader of the dynamic and divine power of God's word, which brings growth and abundant fruit-bearing among the subjects of God's kingly reign; and 2) it exhorts the reader to respond to God's word. Hearing and heeding God's word is essential to the successful realization of God's kingly reign. So in Mark 4:14–20 the verb to "hear" can be found four times, and the verb to "receive" twice.

Only in Isa 40:3–11 does the configuration of the three motifs: "coming of Yahweh," "preaching the (life-giving, dynamic) word of God," and "good news of God's kingly reign" appear together. Just as this Isaiah prophecy in the Markan prologue (1:1–10) was fulfilled as Jesus began his preaching ministry, the same Isaiah prophecy in the parable of the sower is realized as the hearer receives and acts on the word of God.

"The Word of God" in Isaiah 40:3–11 and Other Related NT Verses

The word of God described in Isa 40:3–11 as preaching, life-giving power, and the good news of salvation is not only quoted in 1 Pet 1:23–25; Mark 1:1–15; 4:14–20; and Rom 10:5–17, but also is echoed in other NT verses in these contexts:

---

70. See, e.g., Moule, *The Birth of the NT*, 115–17; Gundry, *Matthew*, 261; France, *Mark*, 204; Bock, *Luke 1:1—9:50*, 731–32.

- having vitality and self-activity that is able to work out a solid faith: Acts 20:32; Col 3:16; 1 Thess 2:13; 2 Thess 3:1; 2 Tim 2:9; Heb 4:12–13
- bearing fruit abundantly: Mark 4:26–29; Rom 1:13; Col 1:5–10
- giving birth to a new creation: Jas 1:18; 1 Pet 1:23
- being received with great delight and eagerness: Acts 8:14; 11:1; 17:11; 1 Thess 1:6; 2:13a; Jas 1:21
- having divine authority, not merely human speech: 1 Thess 1:5; 2:13b; Titus 2:5
- so powerful that even obstinate sinners convert eventually: Acts 6:7; 12:24; 19:20
- preaching the good news (εὐαγγελίζομαι): Acts 8:4, 25; 15:35; 1 Pet 1:25
- preaching for the sake of solemn and divine imperative: Acts 4:29, 31; 6:2, 4; 13:46; 18:5; Eph 6:19; Phil 1:14; Col 4:3; 2 Thess 3:1; 2 Tim 4:2
- by hearing one comes to faith: Luke 5:1; Acts 4:4; 10:44; 13:7, 44, 48; 15:7; 19:10; Rom 10:14–18; Eph 1:13; Col 1:5

CONCLUSION

The NT technical term "the word (of God)," as an equivalent to the gospel message but not as a reference to Scripture or a particular scriptural passage, appears 96 times in the New Testament. Its philological background is the phrase "*dabar* of Yahweh," which is frequently found in the OT prophetic writings. But its conceptual background has little relationship with that OT phrase.

In the prologue of Mark (1:1–15), Jesus as the Son of God applied the prophecy of Isa 40:3–11 to himself. In the explanation of the parable of the sower (Mark 4:14–20 par.) Jesus identifies the the "word of God" as the "seed" or the effective divine agent for the successful realization of God's kingly reign. Since in the Old Testament there is no passage where such motifs as "the life-giving word of God," "the good news," and "God's kingly reign" appear together, except in Isa 40:3–11, Jesus' use of the phrase "the word (of God)" in the sense of the gospel message derives from this Isaiah passage.

In 1 Pet 1:23–25, quoting Isa 40:6–8, Peter speaks of the "living and abiding word of God" as being the agent of rebirth. Here the Petrine author is representing Jesus' interpretive understanding of Isa 40:3–11, especially if he indeed is the historic Peter who functioned as an eyewitness of Jesus' public ministry.

In conclusion, the technical term "the word of God" (in the sense of the good news of God's kingly reign and salvation through Jesus Christ) derives its meaning from Jesus' own use of this phrase in Isaiah 40. There are about fifty instances in the New Testament in which "the word (of God)" carries such motifs as self-activity, bearing fruit abundantly, giving rebirth, receiving with great delight, growth, dynamic power, and good news. But the most explicit dependence on Isa 40:3–11 for the technical use of "the word (of God)" as the gospel message is found in 1 Pet 1:23–25, Mark 1:1–15, Mark 4:14–20, and Rom 10:5–17.

BIBLIOGRAPHY

Aland, K., ed. *Vollständige Konkordanz zum griechischen Neuen Testament*. 2 Vols. *Spezialübersichten*. ANTF 4/1–2. Berlin: de Gruyter, 1978.
Barrett, C. K. *The Gospel according to John*. Philadelphia: Westminster, 1978.
Barth, K. *Die Kirchliche Dogmatik*. 1/1, *Die Lehre vom Wort Gottes*. Zollikon-Zürich: Evangelischer, 1955.
Bauckham, R. *Jesus and the Eyewitnesses: The Gospels as Eyewitness Testimony*. Grand Rapids: Eerdmans, 2006.
Bock, D. L. *Acts*. BECNT. Grand Rapids: Baker Academic, 2007.
———. *Luke 1:1—9:50*. BECNT. Grand Rapids: Baker Academic, 1994.
Bousset, W. *Die Religion des Judentums im späthellenistischen Zeitalter*. Ed. H. Ressmann. HNT 21. Tübingen: Mohr, 1966.
Bovon, F. *Das Evangelium nach Lukas (Luke 1,1—9,50)*. EKK 3/1. Zürich: Benziger, 1989.
Brown, R. E. *The Gospel according to John I–XII*. AB 29. New York: Doubleday, 1970.
Bultmann, R. *Die Geschichte der synoptischen Tradition*. Göttingen: Vandenhoeck & Ruprecht, 1964.
Burridge, R. A. *What Are the Gospels? A Comparison with Graeco-Roman Biography*. Grand Rapids: Eerdmans, 2004.
Cranfield, C. E. B. *The Gospel according to Saint Mark*. Cambridge: Cambridge University Press, 1959.
Danby, H., Trans. and Ed. *The Mishnah*. Oxford: Oxford University Press, 1933.
Davids, P. H. *The Epistle of James*. NIGTC. Grand Rapids: Eerdmans, 1982.
———. *The First Epistle of Peter*. NICNT. Grand Rapids: Eerdmans, 1990.
Debrunner, A. "λέγω, κτλ." In *TWNT* 4:69–76.
Dibelius, M. *Die Briefe des Apostels Paulus II. Die Neun Kleinen Briefe*. HNT. Tübingen: Mohr, 1913.
Elliger, K. *Deuterojesaja*. Vol. 1, *Jesaja 40,1—45,7*. BKAT 11/1. Neukirchen-Vluyn: Neukirchener, 1978.
Elliot, J. H. *1 Peter*. AB 37B. New Haven: Yale University Press, 2000.
Fitzmyer, J. A. *The Acts of the Apostles*. AB 31. New Haven: Yale University Press, 1998.
———. *The Gospel according to Luke I–IX*. AB 28. New York: Doubleday, 1981.

———. "κύριος." In *EWNT* 2:811–19.
Foerster, W., and G. Quell. "κύριος." In *TWNT* 3:1038–98.
France, R. T. *The Gospel of Mark*. NIGTC. Grand Rapids: Eerdmans, 2002.
Friedrich, Gerhard. "εὐαγγελίζομαι, κτλ." In *TWNT* 2:705–35.
Gerleman, G. "*bāśār* Fleisch." In *THAT* 1:77–79.
———. "*dābār* Wort." In *THAT* 1:33–43.
Gnilka, J. *Das Evangelium nach Markus (Mark 1–8,26)*. EKK 2/1. Köln: Benziger, 1978.
Goppelt, L. *Der erste Petrusbrief*. Göttingen: Vandenhoeck & Ruprecht, 1978.
Green, W. S. "Introduction: Messiah in Judaism: Rethinking the Question." In *Judaisms and their Messiahs at the Turn of the Christian Era*, ed. J. Neusner et al., 1–14. Cambridge: Cambridge University Press, 1987.
Grudem, W. *Systematic Theology: An Introduction to Biblical Doctrine*. Grand Rapids: Zondervan, 1994.
Guelich, R. A. *Mark 1—8:26*. WBC 34A. Waco: Word, 1989.
Gundry, R. H. *Matthew: A Commentary on His Handbook for a Mixed Church under Persecution*. Grand Rapids: Eerdmans, 1993.
Haenchen, E. *Die Apostelgeschichte*. Göttingen: Vandenhoeck & Ruprecht, 1961.
Hengel, M. "Eye-witness Memory and the Writing of the Gospels." In *The Written Gospel*, ed. M. Bockmuehl and D. A. Hagner, 70–96. Cambridge: Cambridge University Press, 2007.
———. *Saint Peter: The Underestimated Apostle*. Trans. T. H. Trapp. Grand Rapids: Eerdmans, 2010.
———. *Studies in the Gospel of Mark*. Trans. J. Bowden. Philadelphia: Fortress, 1985.
Jeremias, J. *The Parables of Jesus*. Trans. S. H. Hooke. NTL. New York: Scribner, 1955. Reprint, 1972.
Jobes, K. H. *1 Peter*. BECNT. Grand Rapids: Baker Academic, 2005.
Johnson, L. T. *The First and Second Letters to Timothy*. AB 35A. New York: Doubleday, 2001.
Jülicher, A. *Die Gleichnisreden Jesu*. Vol 2, *Auslegung der Gleichnisreden der Drei ersten Evangelien*. Tübingen: Mohr, 1910.
Keck, L. E. "The Introduction to Mark's Gospel." *NTS* 12 (1965–1966) 352–70.
Kittel, G. "λέγω, λόγος, κτλ." In *TWNT* 4:100–147.
Kleinknecht, H. "λόγος." In *TWNT* 4:76–89.
Lemicio, E. E. "External Evidence for the Structure and Function of Mark iv. 1–20, vii. 14–23 and viii. 14–21." *JTS* 29 (1978) 323–38.
Lincoln, A. T. *The Gospel according to Saint John*. BNTC. Peabody, MA: Hendrickson, 2005.
Lohmeyer, E. *Das Evangelium nach Markus*. KEK 1/2. Göttingen: Vandenhoeck & Ruprecht, 1963.
———. *Die Offenbarung des Johannes*. Tübingen: Mohr, 1953.
Lohse, E. *Die Texte aus Qumran: Hebräisch und Deutsch*. Darmstadt: Wissenschaftliche Buchgesellschaft, 1981.
Lührmann, D. *Das Markusevangelium*. Tübingen: Mohr, 1987.
Luz, U. *Das Evangelium nach Matthäus (Matt 8–17)*. Zürich: Benziger, 1990.
Morris, L. *The Gospel according to John*. NICNT. Grand Rapids: Eerdmans, 1971.
Moule, C. F. D. *The Birth of the New Testament*. 3rd ed. London: A. & C. Black, 1981.

Moulton, W. F., et al. *A Concordance to the Greek Testament according to the Texts of Westcott and Hort, Tischendorf, and the English Revisers*. 5th ed. Edinburgh: T. & T. Clark, 1978.

Mounce, R. H. *The Book of Revelation*. Rev. ed. NICNT. Grand Rapids: Eerdmans, 1997.

Neusner, J. "Mishnah and Messiah." In *Judaisms and Their Messiahs at the Turn of the Christian Era*, ed. J. Neusner et al., 265–82. Cambridge: Cambridge University Press, 1987.

Payne, P. B. "The Authenticity of the Parables of Jesus." In vol. 2 of *Gospel Perspectives: Studies in Midrash and Historiography*, ed. R. T. France and D. Wenham, 329–44. Sheffield: JSOT Press, 1981.

Pesch, R. *Das Markusevangelium*. Wege der Forschung 411. Freiburg: Herder, 1976.

Reicke, B. *The Epistles of James, Peter, and Jude*. AB 37. New York: Doubleday, 1964.

Ritt, H. "λόγος." In *EWNT* 2:880–87.

Roloff, J. *Der erste Brief an Timotheus*. Neukirchen-Vluyn: Neukirchener, 1988.

Sandmel, S. *Judaism and Christian Beginnings*. New York: Oxford University Press, 1978.

Schmoller, A. *Handkonkordanz zum griechischen NT*. Stuttgart: Deutsche Bibelgesellschaft, 1990.

Schreiner, T. R. *Romans*. BECNT. Grand Rapids: Baker Academic, 1988.

Schürer, E. *The History of the Jewish People in the Age of Jesus Christ (175 B.C.–A.D. 135)*. Vol. 2. Rev. and ed. G. Vermes et al. Edinburgh: T. & T. Clark, 1991.

Schweizer, E. *Das Evangelium nach Markus*. Göttingen: Vandenhoeck & Ruprecht, 1967.

Selwyn, E. G. *The First Epistle of St. Peter*. London: Macmillan, 1961.

Smalley, S. S. *1, 2, 3 John*. WBC 51. Waco: Word, 1984.

Snodgrass, K. R. *Stories with Intent: A Comprehensive Guide to the Parables of Jesus*. Grand Rapids: Eerdmans, 2008.

Stein, R. H. *Mark*. BECNT. Grand Rapids: Baker Academic, 2008.

Strecker, Georg. "εὐαγγέλιον." In *EWNT* 2:176–86.

Taylor, J. B. "Word of God." In *New Bible Dictionary*, ed. J. D. Douglas and N. Hillyer, 1258–59. 2nd ed. Downers Grove, 1982.

Taylor, V. *The Gospel according to St. Mark*. London: Macmillan, 1953.

Theissen, G. *Studen zur Soziologie des Urchristentums*. Tübingen: Mohr, 1979.

Trilling, W. *Der zweite Brief an die Thessalonicher*. Zürich: Benziger, 1980.

Wanamaker, C. A. *The Epistles to the Thessalonians*. NIGTC. Grand Rapids: Eerdmans, 1990.

Watts, R. E. "Mark." In *Commentary on the New Testament Use of the Old Testament*, ed. G. K. Beale and D. A. Carson, 111–250. Grand Rapids: Baker Academic, 2007.

Westcott, B. F. *The Epistles of John*. Reprint, Grand Rapids: Eerdmans, 1976.

15

Methodological Similarity between *Xunguxue* and Biblical Exegesis[1]

HYEON WOO SHIN

INTRODUCTION

Though there have been a few attempts to read the Bible in Chinese philosophical frameworks such as *Yin Yang*,[2] there has been no attempt to compare the methods of biblical exegesis with that of traditional Chinese exegetical linguistics. The closest example of a methodological study on Asian hermeneutics was by Moonjang Lee, but his study did not analyze the history of academic work on linguistic exegesis in Asia, although he did mention the hermeneutics of non-critical and self-transforming readings of the sacred texts in the culture of Asian people.[3]

---

1. This article has originally been published in a slightly different form in the journal *Korean Evangelical New Testament Studies* (2012). I am grateful to the editors of *KENTS* for permission to reprint this essay here in a revised form. Thanks also to Prof. Dr. Martinus de Boer who has commented on an earlier draft of this article.

2. See Kim, "Interpretative Modes of Yin-Yang Dynamics," 287–308; Yeo, *What Has Jerusalem to Do With Beijing?*

3. Lee, "Identifying an Asian Theology," 256–75; Lee, "A Post Critical Reading of the Bible," 272–85.

China, however, has a long academic tradition of scholarly exegesis of more than 2000 years. In the course of such a long history of exegesis, Chinese people have developed very systematic methods of interpreting ancient texts. This tradition of critical exegesis in China is called *Xunguxue*. Its goal is to attain the meaning of the text intended by the author, just as the (traditional) goal of biblical exegesis "is to determine the author's intended meaning."[4] A comparative study between *Xunguxue* and biblical exegesis is worth pursuing and may expose the strengths and weaknesses of each approach. This article aims to describe the methodology of *Xunguxue* and ask whether there exists a methodological similarity between Western biblical exegesis (especially New Testament exegesis) and *Xunguxue*. If analogues between the two approaches exist, they could help Western interpreters understand traditional Chinese exegesis and help Chinese scholars understand biblical exegesis. Also, the exegetical tools of *Xunguxue* can provide insights into the biblical text that Western methods may have missed.

EXEGESIS BY STRUCTURAL ANALYSIS: PARALLELISM

Since the structure of the text reflects its content, structural analysis helps the reader to understand the text. Structure can be analyzed at the sentence and phrase level. The most common structure in any body of literature is parallelism, where two sentences or phrases have similar syntax. If the elements in the parallel sentences have similar content as well, it is called "synonymous parallelism." If the parallel elements involve a contrast, it is called "antithetical parallelism." In both cases, one element of the parallelism helps to interpret the other element.

Understanding how parallel structure works is an important part of the exegetical enterprise for both biblical interpretation and *Xunguxue*. Berkhof notes: "Parallelism may aid in determining the meaning of a word."[5] Klein adds: "Actually, parallelism is that phenomenon whereby two or more successive poetic lines strengthen, reinforce, and develop each other's thought. As a kind of emphatic additional thought, the follow-up lines further define, specify, expand, intensify, or contrast the first."[6] Even in synonymous parallelism, the succeeding sentence (or phrase) does not merely repeat the same content but deepens it.[7]

---

4. McQuilkin, *Understanding and Applying the Bible*, 67.
5. Berkhof, *Principles of Biblical Interpretation*, 79.
6. Klein, *Introduction to Biblical Interpretation*, 225.
7. Ibid., 226: "The succeeding lines do not simply restate the opening line; rather, they add to or expand its thought."

Synonymous Parallelism

In *Xunguxue*, scholars have recognized the importance of parallelism for exegesis. They called synonymous parallelism "*huwen*." Scholars in the period of the *Han* dynasty (206 BC–AD 220) often used *huwen* as a way of analyzing structure for exegesis.[8] Jia (seventh century) helpfully defined *huwen* in his book *Yilizhushu* as follows:[9]

> *Fanyanhuwenzhe, gejuyishi.*
>
> Generally speaking, *huwen* mentions the same thing several times.[10]

Huwen is characterized by mutual supplementation. For example, the following structure is *huwen*.[11]

> *Dongtiandi, ganguishen.*
>
> It moves heaven and earth, and impresses divine beings.
>
> (= It impresses not only heaven and earth but also divine beings.)

In this sentence, *dong* (move) and *gan* (impress) supplement each other. These words combined together make one sense: *gandong* (impress) has both *tiandi* (heaven and earth) and *guishen* (divine beings) as objects in the sentence.

A similar *huwen* is found in Han's *Zhanchengnan*.

> *Zhanchengnan, siguobei.*
>
> He fought at the south of the city, and died at the north of the wall.
>
> (= He fought and died outside of the city wall.[12])

In this sentence, *cheng* (city) and *guo* (wall) supplement each other and make the meaning *chengguo* (city wall).[13] *Nan* (south) and *bei* (north) supplement each other to generate the meaning of *nanbei* (north and south, i.e., outside of).[14]

---

8. Zhou, *Xunguxue Chugao*, 282.

9. Ibid., 284.

10. Unless otherwise noted, all English translations from Chinese literature and biblical texts are the author's own.

11. Zhou, *Xunguxue Chugao*, 284.

12. Sun, "Sanjushidehuwen," 198.

13. Ibid.

14. Ibid.

Sun mentions another example of *huwen*. It is *"Zhaogeyexian"* in Du's (803–52) *Afanggongfu*. In this sentence, *zhao* (morning) and *ye* (night), *ge* (sing) and *xian* (play the string), supplement each other. Accordingly, though this sentence literally means: "In the morning they sing, at night they play the string," it actually means: "They sing and play the musical instrument all day long."[15]

We observe another *huwen* sentence *"Dongquanxifei"* in Gui's (1506–71) *Xiangjixuanzhi*. Since *dong* (east) and *xi* (west), *quan* (dog) and *fei* (bark), supplement each other, this sentence means "Dogs bark in east and west."[16]

Stylistic authors sometimes avoid repetition of the same word and choose a synonym. This is a kind of *huwen*, and is called '*bianwen*.'[17] Xu mentions an example of *bianwen* found in *Shangshu, Taijia*.[18]

> *Tianzuonieyou kewei*
> *Zizuonie bukehuan.*
>
> Disasters made by nature can still be avoided,
> but disasters made by oneself cannot be avoided.

Here *wei* and *huan* have the same sense of "avoid."[19]

He provides another example found in *Shiji, Huozhizhuan* as follows:

> *Zhibuzu yuquanbian*
> *Yongbuzu yijueduan.*
>
> Though wisdom is lacking, an emergency is managed.
> Though courage is lacking, a decision is made.

Here the two sentences make *bianwen*. *Yu* and *yi* are used to avoid repetition of the same word.

Huwen is also found in the New Testament as well as in the Old Testament. For example, Mark 9:43 and 9:47 make use of *huwen*, especially *bianwen*.

> Καὶ ἐὰν σκανδαλίζῃ σε ἡ χείρ σου, ἀπόκοψον αὐτήν·
> καλόν ἐστίν σε κυλλὸν εἰσελθεῖν εἰς <u>τὴν ζωὴν</u>
> ἢ τὰς δύο χεῖρας ἔχοντα ἀπελθεῖν εἰς τὴν γέενναν. (Mark 9:43)
> καὶ ἐὰν ὁ ὀφθαλμός σου σκανδαλίζῃ σε, ἔκβαλε αὐτόν·
> καλόν σέ ἐστιν μονόφθαλμον εἰσελθεῖν εἰς <u>τὴν βασιλείαν τοῦ θεοῦ</u>
> ἢ δύο ὀφθαλμοὺς ἔχοντα βληθῆναι εἰς τὴν γέενναν. (Mark 9:47)

15. Ibid.
16. Fu, *Xunguxue Shuolüe*, 184.
17. Zhao, *Xunguxue Gangyao*, 287.
18. Xu, *Xunguxue Daolun*, 115.
19. Ibid.

> And if your hand causes you to sin, cut it off.
> It is better for you to enter *life* crippled
> than go away into hell with two hands. (Mark 9:43)
> And if your eye causes you to sin, pluck it out.
> It is better for you to enter *the Kingdom of God* with one eye
> than to be thrown into hell with two eyes. (Mark 9:47)

The repetition of καὶ ἐὰν (and if), σκανδαλίζῃ σε (causes you to sin), καλόν ἐστιν (it is better), εἰσελθεῖν εἰς (enter), ἢ (than), δύο (two), ἔχοντα (having), εἰς τὴν γέενναν (into hell) constitutes a parallelism. From this structure we can recognize that τὴν ζωὴν ("life") and τὴν βασιλείαν τοῦ θεοῦ ("the Kingdom of God") mean the same thing. Mark demonstrates *bianwen* by using two different words to avoid repetition.

Bianwen is also observed in Matt. 19:23–24. Here we can recognize that τὴν βασιλείαν τῶν οὐρανῶν ("the Kingdom of Heaven") has the same meaning as τὴν βασιλείαν τοῦ θεοῦ ("the Kingdom of God").[20]

> πλούσιος δυσκόλως εἰσελεύσεται εἰς <u>τὴν βασιλείαν τῶν οὐρανῶν</u>. (v. 23)
> εὐκοπώτερόν ἐστιν κάμηλον διὰ τρυπήματος ῥαφίδος διελθεῖν
> ἢ πλούσιον εἰς <u>τὴν βασιλείαν τοῦ θεοῦ</u>. (v. 24)
>
> It is difficult for a rich person to enter *the Kingdom of Heaven*. (v. 23)
> It is easier for a camel go through the eye of a needle
> than a rich person go into *the Kingdom of God*. (v. 24)

In Chinese texts, another form of *huwen*, which Li calls *hexu*,[21] is often observed. In *hexu*, instead of the common word order AB'A'B', a variation of this word order is used: AA'BB'. Li mentions an example found in Ouyang's (1007–1073) *Zuiwengtingji*.[22]

> *Fengshuanggaojie.*
>
> The wind and frost are high and clean.
> (= The wind blows high, the frost freezes cleanly.)

In *Shuijingzhu* vol. 34, another good example of *hexu* is found in this example:[23]

> *Sutuanlutan, huiqingdaoying.*

If the sentence is literally translated, it reads: "The white rapids and the green pond, flow round and reflects inversely." However, *sutuan* is the subject of

---

20. Yang, *How to Read Matthew*, 82.
21. Li, *Xiandai Xunguxue Daolun*, 235.
22. Ibid.
23. Zhou, *Xunguxue Chugao*, 291.

huiqing, and *lutan* is the subject of *daoying*.[24] Being more precise about the semantic connections, it is best to translate the sentence non-literally because it means: "The white rapids flow around, and the green pond reflects inversely."

Hexu is also found in the New Testament. One example is Mark 4:27: καθεύδῃ καὶ ἐγείρηται νύκτα καὶ ἡμέραν ("He sleeps and gets up night and day"). This sentence is a *hexu* form of καθεύδῃ νύκτα καὶ ἐγείρηται ἡμέραν ("He sleeps at night and get up at the daytime"). Mark 2:21 also has an instance of *hexu*: αἴρει τὸ πλήρωμα ἀπ' αὐτοῦ τὸ καινὸν τοῦ παλαιοῦ ("The patch pulls away from it, the new from the old."). This is AB A'B' form of the more natural word order AA'BB': αἴρει τὸ πλήρωμα τὸ καινὸν ἀπ' αὐτοῦ τοῦ παλαιοῦ ("The new patch pulls away from the old [garment]").

Parallel sentences have similarities in grammatical structure and word order. On account of such similarities, parallel sentences help inform one another in the process of exegesis. Zhou mentions the following example.[25]

> *Qiruiganpi*
> *Aiganwanyan.*
>
> Grief enters the liver and the spleen.
> Sorrow moves the foolish and the wise.

If the two sentences above are parallel to each other, the second sentence has the word order of "subject + verb + object." Thus, *gan* seems to mean "to move" as a verb.[26]

Antithetical Parallelism

In *Xunguxue*, general parallelism can be described as "*duiwen*," but it is mostly used as the specific designation for antithetical parallelism. As an example of *duiwen*, the following sentence in *Dufushiji* has been mentioned by Zhou.[27]

> *Wanjie xiyou jian, pingju xiaoyi chen.*
>
> In his old age his amusement was simple;
> in ordinary days his filial duty and righteousness were proper.

---

24. Ibid.
25. Ibid., 290.
26. Ibid.
27. Ibid., 286.

Since *wanjie* and *pingju* are in parallelism, *pingju* may also refer to time. It may be that the phrase "in ordinary days" is being contrasted to "in old age" (*wanjie*) rather than "the place for usual residence."²⁸

Zhou also mentions the following example of *duiwen* observed in *Hanshu, Zhaodiji*.²⁹

> *Pingju fazhe ershiyishang zhiwushi weijiazu,*
> *jinzhe wushiyishang liushiyixia weibenming.*
>
> In ordinary days, those from 20 to 50 years old were sent as soldiers.
> This time, those from 50 to 60 years old were sent.

Here, as Zhou has pointed out, *pingju* means "in ordinary days" since it is contrasted to *jinzhe* ("this time").

Duiwen is also found in *Laozi*.³⁰ In the following sentence of *Laozi*, *ju* is contrasted to *yongbing* ("using soldiers"), and thus means "in ordinary days."

> *Junzi ju ze guizuo,*
> *yongbing ze guiyou.*
>
> In ordinary days, a noble man considers those who are on the
> left to be important,
> but while using soldiers, he considers those who are on the right
> to be important.

Duiwen structure helps exegesis. Lu calls the exegetical method that uses *duiwen* by the designation '*liyong duiwen qiuyi*,'³¹ and points out that this method was already used long ago by Chinese exegetes.³² In biblical interpretation, Camery-Hoggatt uses *duiwen* structure for understanding πληρῶσαι (normally: "to fulfill") in Matt. 5:17: οὐκ ἦλθον καταλῦσαι ἀλλ ἀ πληρῶσαι ("I have not come to abolish but to establish [the Law and the Prophets]"). Without calling it *duiwen*, Camery-Hoggatt explains: "From the negative parallel, it's a fair guess that here it [=πληρῶσαι] has to mean the opposite of *abolish*, so we might translate, *establish* [not its unmarked translation of 'fulfill']."³³

---

28. Ibid.
29. Ibid., 288.
30. Ibid.
31. Lu, *Xiandai Xunguxue Shenlun*, 111.
32. Ibid.
33. Camery-Hoggatt, *Reading the Good Book Well*, 101. Likewise, the phrase ἀποκάλυψιν ἐθνῶν ("revelation to the Gentiles") in Luke 2:32 may also be understood by *duiwen* structure. In Luke-Acts, the word ἀποκάλυψις occurs only here, and thus

THE AUTHOR'S USAGE

"Words change in usage over a period of time."[34] The meaning of the same word can be different according to the authors and times. The root of a word often helps discern the meaning of the word, but it cannot help understand its derivative meanings. If we depend on the root in discerning the meaning of a word, we commit an etymological fallacy (root fallacy).[35] Cotterell and Turner explains this aspect of lexical semantics as follows:

> In practice, all languages change gradually with time, and words come to have new meanings, older meanings often becoming obsolete. Hence the appeal to "original" meaning as authoritative or normative involves fundamental misunderstanding.[36]

The root, or what the constituting elements of a word refer to, does not safely lead us to the meaning of the word.[37] For example, the meaning of "enthusiasm" cannot be perceived by its roots "*en*" (in) and "*theos*" (God).[38] Carson mentions another example. The root of "good-bye" is an Anglo-Saxon contraction of "God be with you," but nowadays "good-bye" does not contain such a meaning.[39]

The meaning of a word is perceived by its usage. In *Xunguxue*, usages of words are called "*cili*." Observing the specific in-context usage or *cili* of a word is important for the meaning of the word, since the same word can be used differently in different times and contexts. For example, "*xingli*" used to meant "diplomatic delegation" in ancient days, but later came to mean "wandering around" in the middle age, but it is translated as "baggage" in modern times.[40]

The changes to the meaning(s) of a word is well known in biblical exegesis. Gorman points out: "A 'biblical' word ... should not be treated as an

---

one may not observe the author's usage elsewhere. However, the *duiwen* structure reveals the meaning of ἀποκάλυψις in Luke 2:32: φῶς εἰς ἀποκάλυψιν ἐθνῶν καὶ δόξαν λαοῦ σου Ἰσραήλ ("a light for revelation to the Gentiles and for glory to your people Israel" [NIV]). Here since "Israel" (Ἰσραήλ) and "the Gentiles" (ἐθνῶν) are contrasted, ἀποκάλυψις may also be contrasted to δόξα. So ἀποκάλυψις should be translated as a "revelation or exposure of one's sins" in contrast to "glory." This meaning is supported by the use of the verb ἀποκαλύπτω in v. 35 for the revelation of evil thought.

34. Barackman, *How to Interpret the Bible*, 29.
35. Gorman, *Elements of Biblical Exegesis*, 108; Carson, *Exegetical Fallacies*, 26.
36. Cotterell and Turner, *Linguistics and Biblical Interpretation*, 131.
37. Gorman, *Elements of Biblical Exegesis*, 108.
38. Ibid.
39. Carson, *Exegetical Fallacies*, 27.
40. Zhou, *Xunguxue Chugao*, 371.

unchanging, homogeneous unit of meaning."⁴¹ Camery-Hoggatt provides an example: "[D]uring the period of the NT the word *martyrein* originally meant "to bear witness," and it didn't acquire the meaning "to die for one's faith" until later, after the period of the New Testament has closed."⁴²

On account of diachronic shifts in the meaning(s) of a word, the interpreter should avoid exegeting a word in the ancient text according to its current modern meaning. Chisholm remarks: "When a word develops a new, specialized use, one must be careful not to read this later specialized meaning into chronologically earlier occurrences of the word."⁴³ Camery-Hoggatt also points this out: "[W]e have to be careful not to read later understanding back into earlier contexts."⁴⁴ The exegetical fallacy of interpreting an ancient word in terms of the modern meaning is called 'semantic anachronism.'⁴⁵ Interpreting a word with an older meaning that was not used in the day of composition can also take place, and this exegetical fallacy is called 'semantic obsolescence.'⁴⁶

In China, ancient scholars already perceived the alteration of word meanings over time.⁴⁷ Zhou mentioned *jing* as an example. "*Zijingyugouduzhizhong*" is attested in *Lunyu, Xianwen*. Here *jing* means "to kill oneself," though it originally means "to die by strangling oneself."⁴⁸ He also mentioned "*zhengnu*" (women of the country *Zheng*) which later became to mean "beautiful women."⁴⁹ In consideration of such an alteration of meaning, Chisholm proposes the following principle of exegesis. "Don't assume there is a concrete word picture behind every abstract use of a word or phrase."⁵⁰ He remarks: "For example, to most English speakers the idiomatic expression 'right from the horse's mouth' simply means 'direct from the source.'"⁵¹

The meaning of a word can also vary from author to author. Walton explains: "Different authors may use the same word in different ways."⁵²

41. Gorman, *Elements of Biblical Exegesis*, 107.
42. Camery-Hoggatt, *Reading the Good Book Well*, 104.
43. Chisholm, *From Exegesis to Exposition*, 40.
44. Camery-Hoggatt, *Reading the Good Book Well*, 147.
45. Carson, *Exegetical Fallacies*, 32.
46. Ibid., 34.
47. Fu, *Xunguxue Shuolüe*, 155.
48. Zhou, *Xunguxue Chugao*, 395.
49. Ibid., 394.
50. Chisholm, *From Exegesis to Exposition*, 38.
51. Ibid.
52. Walton, "Principles of Productive Word Study," 161.

For example, in Luke 7:17, "Judea" does not seem to fit with the immediate context in its original meaning. Since Nain is located in Galilee, the news about Jesus probably spread throughout Galilee (not Judea). Here "Judea," however, reflects Luke's characteristic usage. Luke's "Judea" includes Galilee as in Luke 4:44; 6:17; 23:5; Acts 2:9; 10:37.[53]

Likewise in *Xunguxue*, Zhao correctly points out that each author has his own tendencies in using words.[54]

> *Tongyigerende zuopin zaiyongci zaojufangmian zongyou yixiezijidetedian.*
>
> The same author's work generally has some of one's own characteristics in making a sentence by using words.

On account of such characteristics, we need to observe the (sometimes specialized) usage of a word by the author to perceive the meaning of the word. We need to avoid perceiving the meaning of a word by relying on other authors' usages. To know the meaning of *A* in Mark, we need to observe *A*'s usage in Mark, not in other books (say Romans, Galatians).

In *Xunguxue*, scholars perceived this and considered observing word usage by the same book to be important.[55] Li calls such a method '*yinwenliyujingqiuyi*.'[56] *Wenliyyjing* refers to the usage of words or grammar observed in the same book.[57] Pi (1850–1908) called this method "*yijingzhengjing*" ("Interpret the scripture by the scripture").[58] This principle is also used in biblical exegesis. "The interpreter must understand that Scripture interprets Scripture."[59] This principle should not be misunderstood as allowing just any book in the Bible to interpret another random passage from the Bible. A passage in each book of the Bible needs primarily to be interpreted by using the same (author's) book (not the other books of the Bible).

In contrast, some exegetes like Barackman have proposed a different principle: "Interpret the passage in the light of all that the Bible teaches."[60] This principle, however, is misleading. Though the Bible is combined in one volume, each book of the Bible still reflects its author's style. Especially the parallel passages in the same book (or author) help exegesis. Berkhof

---

53. Bock, *Luke*, 654.
54. Zhao, *Xunguxue Gangyao*, 164.
55. Zhou, *Xunguxue Chugao*, 362.
56. Li, *Xiandai Xunguxue Daolun*, 231.
57. Ibid., 232.
58. Zhou, *Xunguxue Chugao*, 362.
59. Couch, *Evangelical Hermeneutics*, 57.
60. Barackman, *How to Interpret the Bible*, 26.

explains: "Parallel passages also constitute an important help. . . ."[61] The interpreter should seek for parallels, first of all, in the writings of the same author."[62] Mickelsen likewise proposed: "Observe carefully any parallels in the same book to the materials in the passage being interpreted."[63]

Dunnett calls usages found in the same book or the same author's books "a broader context" in the sense that it is broader than the immediate context.[64] The broader context helps the interpreter to understand Mark 2:17, which reads: οὐκ ἦλθον καλέσαι δικαίους ἀλλὰ ἁμαρτωλούς ("I have not come to call the righteous but sinners"). This saying is better understood against the expression of a similar structure in Mark 9:37: ὃς ἂν ἐμὲ δέχηται, οὐκ ἐμὲ δέχεται ἀλλ᾽ ἀ τὸν ἀποστείλαντά με ("Whoever receives me does not receive me but him who sent me"). Here οὐκ ἐμὲ δέχεται ("he does not receive me") does not mean a negation on account of the preceding ἐμὲ δέχηται ("he receives me"). By "not A but B" structure, Mark conveys the notion of: "not merely A but rather B." Accordingly, οὐκ ἦλθον καλέσαι δικαίους ἀλλὰ ἁμαρτωλούς means: "I have come to call not merely the righteous but rather the sinners."[65]

LITERARY CONTEXT

Dictionaries enable us to know the semantic range of a word, but in order to be able to choose the specific meaning of the word we need to observe the literary context. The meaning that best fits the literary context may be the meaning intended by the author.

Barackman remarks: "Of the various meanings a word may have in its biblical usage, select the one that best fits the passage being interpreted, its context."[66] Chisholm similarly has pointed out: "When determining meaning, it is also essential to consider linguistic factors within the framework of context."[67] Erickson also mentions the relationship between meaning and context: "The meaning of a word, a text, a "thing" or an event, is partly a function of its place in a context."[68] Bock's statement is simpler: "Words op-

---

61. Berkhof, *Principles of Biblical Interpretation*, 80.
62. Ibid.
63. Mickelsen, *Interpreting the Bible*, 113.
64. Dunnett, *The Interpretation of Holy Scripture*, 99.
65. This interpretation is also supported by other examples found in Gen 45:8; Exod 16:8; Jer 7:22–23; John 12:44; see the discussion by France, *Mark*, 135.
66. Barackman, *How to Interpret the Bible*, 31.
67. Chisholm, *From Exegesis to Exposition*, 38.
68. Erickson, *A Beginner's Guide to New Testament Exegesis*, 95.

erate in a context and receives meaning from that context."[69] Reed likewise explains that: "words acquire meaning when they are used in a context."[70] Finally, Gorman makes the most succinct formation when he says that "meaning is context-dependent."[71]

The meaning of a word depends on the literary context, as the value of x depends on its connections to other constituent parts in an equation such as $3 + x = 5$. In this context, x has only one value: two. Likewise, in a specific context the meaning of a word is only one, unless the author intends a *double entrendre*. Chisholm states: "When determining the meaning of a word in a specific context, the interpreter should choose one, and only one, of the available nuances."[72] Likewise Walton has remarked: "Individual occurrences of a word generally do not carry all of the different elements found in the semantic range."[73] Barr calls such an exegetical fallacy which includes all or several meanings of a word into a single occurrence of the word within a specific literary context 'illegitimate totality transfer.'[74]

Of course, a word or a phrase may also have a figurative meaning instead of a literal meaning. Such usages are simile, metaphor, symbol, idiom, synecdoche, metonymy, hyperbole, irony, sarcasm, euphemism, among other literary devices.[75] Such rhetorical usages may be perceived by the context. Yet even in these cases, the meaning of a word is basically one.

In *Xunguxue*, the context (especially the literary context) is called "*yanyuhuanjing*" and the method of interpreting the text by observing the context is called "*guanjingweixun*."[76] This method of context-dependent interpretation is also called "*yinyujingqiuyi*,"[77] or simply "*jingxun*."[78]

Li calls the literary context "*shangxiawenyujing*," and the interpretation of a word by using the literary context "*yinshangxiawenyujingqiuyi*."[79] Chinese literary theorists have employed a variety of terms to describe this

---

69. Bock, "Lexical Analysis," 138.

70. Reed, "Modern Linguistics and the New Testament," 232.

71. Gorman, *Elements of Biblical Exegesis*, 106.

72. Chisholm, *From Exegesis to Exposition*, 38.

73. Walton, "Principles of Productive Word Study," 167.

74. Gorman, *Elements of Biblical Exegesis*, 108.

75. Barackman, *How to Interpret the Bible*, 52–57. As an example of symbol, "fig tree" in Luke 13:6 may be mentioned. As in the Old Testament (Hos 9:10; Mic 7:1; Jer 8:13; 24:5, 8), it refers to Israel. Fitzmyer, *Luke X–XXIV*, 1008.

76. Zhou, *Xunguxue Chugao*, 252.

77. Li, *Xiandai Xunguxue Daolun*, 229.

78. Sun and Jingzhong, *Xinpian Xunguxue Gangyao*, 97.

79. Li, *Xiandai Xunguxue Daolun*, 230.

method of interpretation: *'juwendingyi,'*[80] *'yinwendingyi,'*[81] *'yinwenzuojie,'*[82] *"suiwenlixun,"* or *"yiwenweiyi."*[83] In the *Qing* dynasty, Wang and Duan called context-dependent exegesis *"yinwenqiuyi."*[84] This *yinwenqiuyi* method tries to interpret the unknown value or meaning of a word on the basis of the known meanings of surrounding words or phrases to which the unknown word is attached. In the same way a person can get the value of x in the equation $3 + x = 5$, here $x = 2$, one may know the value of an unknown word on the basis of what is known. So the one basic principle of *Xunguxue* is *yinwenqiuyi* or interpreting the unknown (or difficult) part of a text on the basis of the known (or easier) part of the text.[85]

Since a word often has various meanings, we need to observe the literary context to determine the meaning of a particular instantiation of the word in a sentence. For example, in sentence (1): *"fa"* means "to send" in *"Wang hebufajiang erjizhi"* (Why the king does not send a general and attack it?).[86] But in sentence (2): *"fa"* means "to open (a map)" in *"Qinwangfatu, tuqiongerbixian."*[87] In sentence (3): *"Miyinzhizhi erbufaqishi," "fa"* means "to expose."[88] In sentence (4): *"Shishi yingjian Nanjing guanshi, dafa Hedong, Xiaxi caimu"* (Then for building a government office in Nanjing, they recruited people from Hedong, and gathered woods from Xiaxi.), *"fa"* means "to recruit."[89]

A good example of using *yinwenqiuyi* is found in the interpretation of *"Juefeixuanxunjizu"* by Wang. In his *Jingyishuwen*, vol. 3, Wang (1766–1834) pointed out that *ji* does not fit the literary context if it refers to a kind of bead, a reading which the traditional commentary *Zhuan* supports.[90] Since *"xuan," "xun,"* and *"zu"* all refer to "making hemp cloth," "bead" does not fit the immediate context.[91] Hence he proposed to define *ji* as "together with."[92]

---

80. Huang, *Xunguxue Jichu*, 84.
81. Bai, *Jianming Xunguxue*, 176.
82. Ibid., 177.
83. Huang, *Xunguxue Jiaocheng*, 274.
84. Li, *Xiandai Xunguxue Daolun*, 229.
85. Zhao, *Xunguxue Shilue*, 312.
86. Sun and Kan, *Xinpian Xunguxue Gangyao*, 100.
87. Ibid.
88. Ibid.
89. Ibid.
90. Zhou, *Xunguxue Chugao*, 255.
91. Ibid.
92. Ibid.

USAGE IN OTHER BOOKS

After we perceive the meaning of a word by the help of its literary context, the validity of this meaning needs to be tested according to how the same word is used in other chapters or books within the same body of literature. The usage of the word in the same book or by the same author needs to be examined. Wang formulated this principle of exegesis in his work *Jingzhuanshici, Xu*.[93]

> *Kuizhi benwen erxie, Yanzhi taquan ertong.*
>
> Examine whether [the meaning] fits with the text or not, and test whether it is so used in other books.

Of course, a word may also be used in various meanings in the same book. Especially in these cases the immediate literary context cannot be neglected. Usage and literary context complement each other in exegesis.[94] If the usage observed in the same book is not enough to perceive the exact meaning of a word (or an expression), we may depend on the usage in other books that may have influenced the author. For example, New Testament authors knew, read, and even quoted from the Septuagint. The usage of lexemes in the Septuagint may help us to discern how those same lexemes are deployed in the NT writings.[95]

At times even literature that does not exhibit direct literary relationships with the New Testament books may also be helpful. Comparisons can be made with intertestamental literature such as the Dead Sea Scrolls, the Apocrypha, the Pseudepigrapha, and even the later literature of the rabbis such as the *Mishnah, Tosefta, Talmud,* and *Midrashim*. Since these books and the New Testament belong to a common linguistic, cultural, religious world, they can help us to understand the New Testament. Berkhof pointed out: "[T]he works of contemporaries should be consulted before those of others."[96] Chisholm has pointed this out: "The meaning of a word

---

93. Li, *Xiandai Xunguxue Daolun*, 246.

94. For example, σὺ λέγεις in Matt 27:11 does not seem to function as an affirmative. If it has such an affirmative meaning, the chief priests and the elders do not need to accuse Jesus further, which occurs in v. 12. Here σὺ λέγεις seems to indicate that Jesus is not a military king of the Jews as Pilate supposes but a different kind of king. The usage of σὺ εἶπας in Matt 26:25, 64 for a restrictive affirmative also supports this interpretation.

95. New, *Old Testament Quotation in the Synoptic Gospels*, 122; Shin, *Textual Criticism and the Synoptic Problem*, 104.

96. Berkhof, *Principles of Biblical Interpretation*, 80.

is established by usage among a community of speakers in a given time period."⁹⁷ Cotterell and Turner have also pointed this out: "[I]n order to find out *what* a lexeme means at that particular time we have only to look at the contemporary *usage*."⁹⁸ We, nevertheless, have to avoid verbal parallelomania, which "refers to the practice of some biblical exegetes who claim that the presence of the same term in several different, often extrabiblical, contexts automatically indicates conceptual parallelism, borrowing of terms, or literal dependency."⁹⁹

In *Xunguxue*, Zhou also points out that the study of writings of the same or adjacent period may help to understand words and phrases found in them since authors' linguistic styles necessarily depend on common use in society.¹⁰⁰ Such an exegetical approach is called "*leibihuzheng*"¹⁰¹ or "*bijiaohuzheng*."¹⁰² When we use this method, we first need to study the same book or the same author's books. If the same book or author does not provide enough clues for interpretation, one may examine other books that are (nearly) contemporaneous to the work under study.

Zhou refers to various books to interpret the meaning of "*houqixing*" in *Guoyu, Zhouyushang*. He found parallel expressions as follows.

> *Tiandizhe, shengzhibenye.* (*Xunzi, Lilun*)
>
> *Tiandizhe, xingzhibenye.* (*Dadaili, Lisanben*)
>
> *Shengmingshouchang.* (*Zhanguoce, Qincesan*)
>
> *Xingmingshouchang.* (*Shiji, Caizezhuan*)

From these parallel expressions, he concludes that "*xing*" refers to "*sheng*," and thus "*houqixing*" is the same as "*houqisheng*" which means "make their lives comfortable."¹⁰³

This exegetical method had already been used in the period of *Qing* dynasty by Wang (1766–1834) in his *Jingzhuanshici*. In the period of *Qing* dynasty, Qian (?–1844) explained this way of exegesis in his book *Ba*.¹⁰⁴ Using parallel expressions (which are similar but slightly different) in the other books, editions, or manuscripts can help the reader discern the meaning of

97. Chisholm, *From Exegesis to Exposition*, 32.
98. Cotterell and Turner, *Linguistics and Biblical Interpretation*, 132.
99. Bock, "Lexical Analysis," 152.
100. Zhou, *Xunguxue Chugao*, 364.
101. Ibid., 119.
102. Cheng and Liang, *Yingyong Xunguxue*, 132.
103. Zhou, *Xunguxue Chugao*, 364.
104. Ibid., 118–19.

rare or difficult lexical expressions. For example, Qian proved that *"yan"* and *"shi"* have the same meaning on the basis of the following example.[105]

> Jin, zhengyanyi. (*Zuozhuan*)
> Jin, zhengshiyi. (*Zhouyu*)

Qian also proved that *"shuyu"* and *"heru"* have the same meaning ("what about?") on the basis of the following usage.[106]

> Yuqincheng herubuyu. (*Zhanguoce, Zhaoce*)
> Shall we turning back the castle of *Qin*? What about not turning it back?
>
> Jiuzhao shuyuwujiu. (*Qice*)
> Shall we save *Zhao*? What about not saving it?

Readings of the same words or phrases attested in other books may also be used for exegesis. For example, instead of *"moranyoujian"* in *Zhuangzi*, *Shiwen* has *"moranweijian."* On the basis of the variant, Qian argued that *"wei"* here means *"you"* ("to have").

Together with parallel expressions, usages of a word in other books are helpful for determining the meaning of the word. Wang in his *Jingyishuwen* (vol. 5: *Maoshi*) interprets the meaning of *"Zhongfengqiebao"* as follows. "The wind already blows and it is violent."[107] For such an interpretation, he illustrates that *"zhong"* may mean "already" on the basis of the following instances.[108]

> Zhongwenqiehui, shushenqishen. (*Yanyan*)
> "When one is already warm and merciful, be quiet and take care of oneself."
>
> Zhongjuqiepin, mozhiwonan. (*Beimen*)
> "I am already needy and poor, but they do not know my trouble."
>
> Shenzhitingzhi, zhongheqieping. (*Xiaoya, Famu*)
> "Since God hears it, there are already harmony and peace."
>
> Heyichangmu, zhongshanqieyou. (*Futian*)
> "The rice plants have grown well, and they are already good and abundant."
>
> Zhongqieyonghuai, youjiongyinyu. (*Zhengyue*)

---

105. Ibid., 118.
106. Ibid., 118–19.
107. Ibid., 105.
108. Ibid., 105–6.

"Already I miss a long time, but the gloomy rain further troubles me."

PERSONAL AND CULTURAL CONTEXTS

For exegesis, the personal context is also useful. "The personal context" refers to "personal information shared between author and reader."[109] Dunnett calls it "the situation context," and it involves the place where the text was formed.[110] In text linguistics, it is called "context of situation," and it refers to "the immediate situation" where the discourse takes place.[111]

"The general cultural context" is also useful for exegesis. It is "the knowledge of the world the reader is expected to have in hand just by virtue of being part of the culture in which the text is written."[112] Reed calls it "context of culture" and defines it as "shared world view."[113] In text linguistics the cultural context is simply called "context," whereas the literary context is called "co-text."[114]

The author often presupposes background knowledge on part of his or her recipients. To understand the text, the audience needs to share a certain base of cultural knowledge with the author. Barackman states this principle of exegesis as follows: "Interpret the passage in the light of its background."[115] Klein, Blomberg, and Hubbard also formulate this principle: "The correct interpretation of a biblical passage will be consistent with the historical-cultural background of the passage."[116]

For example, a study of the cultural context helps us interpret Mark 10:1–12. In the first century husbands had rights to divorce wives, whereas wives had no right for divorce. Further, the cause for divorce was easy to find. Deut 24:1 supposes "what is shameful" as a cause of divorce. The school of Shammai interpreted it as "bad behaviors" (unfaithfulness, i.e., sexual immorality), but the school of Hillel considered failure in preparing a meal to be grounds for divorce (*m. Gittin* 9:10). Philo's opinion is the same as that of the school of Hillel (Philo, *Spec. Laws* 1.30).[117] With regard

---

109. Camery-Hoggatt, *Reading the Good Book Well*, 157.
110. Dunnett, *The Interpretation of Holy Scripture*, 99.
111. Reed, "Modern Linguistics and the New Testament," 232.
112. Camery-Hoggatt, *Reading the Good Book Well*, 157.
113. Reed, "Modern Linguistics and the New Testament," 232.
114. Ibid., 228, 232.
115. Barackman, *How to Interpret the Bible*, 48.
116. Klein, *Introduction to Biblical Interpretation*, 172.
117. Safrai, "Home and Family," 790.

to divorce, the school of Hillel's view was popular.[118] Accordingly, not only disobedience (Sir 25:26; cf. Josephus, *Life* 426) but also making burned bread (*Sifre Deut.* 269.1.1) became a reason for divorce.[119] According to the *Mishnah* (*m. Ketub.* 7:6), talking with another man, cursing parents in front of them, walking around the street, and other reasons were sufficient for divorce. Josephus reported that in Palestine Jewish husbands could in fact divorce their wives for any reason (*Ant.* 4.253). In the first century, Jewish husbands had the right to divorce and could freely abuse this right. In such a situation, Jesus' prohibition of divorce could function for the protection of the weak. In such a society, women were the absolutely weak party and Jesus intended to protect them by his teaching on divorce.

Jesus' teaching on divorce in Mark 10:9-12 was not conservative but radically revolutionary. This can be perceived on the basis of the cultural context. In the Old Testament and the intertestamental literature, we cannot find any teaching which explicitly prohibits divorce. Deut 24:1-4 presupposes a society where divorce is possible and prohibits reunion with a divorced wife who has married another man. Mal 2:16 also does not prohibit divorce but only means: "for he hated to send away."[120] Philo, Josephus, and the Rabbis do not prohibit divorce.[121] According to Meir, even the Qumran literature does not completely prohibit divorce.[122] Sir 7:56 discourages divorce. "Even though you have a detestable wife, do not divorce her." Sirach, however, does not prohibit the practice, but means shows disdain for the process. Sir 25:26 commands that a husband can divorce a disobedient wife. "If she does not follow your guidance, separate her from your flesh." In this cultural context, Jesus' teaching on divorce was a form of protection for the weak and a teaching which invited reformation of the Jewish tradition. In Jesus' teaching, prohibition of divorce was also limits the privileges of the strong.

The author and the first readers shared much information which did not need to be explained since they lived in the same culture. However, since later readers lack such information, they have difficulty in understanding the text. Such information can be historical facts, customs, religious traditions, geographic knowledge, or ways of cultural expression.

---

118. Ibid., 6.
119. Keener, "Adultery, Divorce," 6.
120. Meier, "The Historical Jesus," 76.
121. Evans, *Mark 8:27-16:20*, 81.
122. Meier, "The Historical Jesus," 75.

In *Xunguxue*, not only the linguistic context but also the social context, where the text is formed, is included in *yujing*.[123] *Zhanguoce Zhaoce* has the following passage.

> *Yuanling debu heiyizhishu, yiwei wanggong.*
>
> Please command to get and supplement the number of black clothes, and let them guard the royal palace.

Here, the meaning of "*heiyi*" (black clothes) may be understood in light of the knowledge that the warriors of the royal palace of *Zhao* wore black clothes.[124] "Black clothes" is a cultural metonymy that refers to the warriors of the royal palace.[125]

CONCLUSION

Xunguxue is similar to biblical exegesis, and biblical students and scholars can learn from the refined and systematized methods of *Xunguxue*. The Chinese academic tradition of linguistic exegesis has many analogues with the Western academic tradition of biblical exegesis. Those who are trained in one tradition can understand the other tradition well. The discovery of similarities can therefore help us understand the strengths and weaknesses of each exegetical approach when the other approach is used as a foil of comparison. Though different technical terms are used in biblical exegesis and the traditional Chinese exegesis, their methods are also quite analogous to each other. Though culture and language are different from area to area, their methods of overcoming the temporal, cultural, and conceptual gaps between the modern reader and the ancient text are similar.

Asian methods of reading the Bible can not only provide tools for understanding the biblical text but also reveal the presuppositions of the Western reader who engages with only one method of biblical interpretation. The reverse is also true. Western traditions of exegesis can help the Asian reader appreciate the history of exegesis in one's own cultural tradition and where the tradition needs to grow further. This short study on the exegetical practices of *Xunguxue* demonstrates that ancient Chinese hermeneutics, like the West, values attention to the author's intention, the polysemous meanings of a word and which meaning is employed in a given literary context, literary

---

123. Li, *Xiandai Xunguxue Daolun*, 230.
124. Sun and Kan, *Xinpian Xunguxue Gangyao*, 111.
125. Ibid.

devices such as structural parallelism, and reconstructing the historical setting of the work as an important means to biblical interpretation.

BIBLIOGRAPHY

Bai, Zhaolin. *Jianming Xunguxue*. Hangzhou: Zhejiang Education, 1984.
Barackman, F. H. *How to Interpret the Bible*. Grand Rapids: Kregel, 1989.
Berkhof, L. *Principles of Biblical Interpretation*. Grand Rapids: Baker, 1950.
Bock, Darrell L. "Lexical Analysis." In *Interpreting the New Testament*, ed. D. L. Bock and B. M. Fanning, 135–54. Wheaton, IL: Crossway, 2006.
———. *Luke 1:1—9:50*. BECNT. Grand Rapids: Baker Academic, 1996.
Camery-Hoggatt, Jerry. *Reading the Good Book Well*. Nashville: Abingdon, 2007.
Carson, D. A. *Exegetical Fallacies*. Grand Rapids: Baker, 1984.
Cheng, Junying, and Yongchang Liang, *Yingyong Xunguxue*. Shanghai: Huadong Normal University Press, 2008.
Chisholm, Robert B. *From Exegesis to Exposition: A Practical Guide to Using Biblical Hebrew*. Grand Rapids: Baker, 1998.
Cotterell, Peter, and Max Turner, *Linguistics and Biblical Interpretation*. Downers Grove, IL: IVP, 1989.
Couch, Mal., ed. *An Introduction to Classical Evangelical Hermeneutics*. Grand Rapids: Kregel, 2000.
Dunnett, Walter M. *The Interpretation of Holy Scripture*. Nashville: Nelson, 1984.
Erickson, Richard J. *A Beginner's Guide to New Testament Exegesis*. Downers Grove, IL: IVP, 2005.
Evans, C. A. *Mark 8:27—16:20*. WBC 34B. Nashville: Nelson, 2001.
Fitzmyer, J. *The Gospel According to Luke X–XXIV*. AB 28A. New York: Doubleday, 1985.
France, R. T. *The Gospel of Mark*. NIGTC. Grand Rapids: Eerdmans, 2002.
Fu, Jinbi. *Xunguxue Shuolüe*. Wuhan: Hubei Renmin, 2003.
Gorman, Michael J. *Elements of Biblical Exegesis*. Rev. exp. ed. Peabody, MA: Hendrickson, 2009.
Huang, Darong. *Xunguxue Jichu*. Guiyang: Guizhou Renmin, 1987.
Huang, Jianzhong. *Xunguxue Jiaocheng*. Wuhan: Jingchu, 1988.
Keener, C. S. "Adultery, Divorce." In *Dictionary of New Testament Background*, ed. C. A. Evans and S. E. Porter, 6–16. Downers Grove, IL: IVP, 2000.
Kim, Hyun Chul Paul. "Interpretative Modes of Yin-Yang Dynamics as an Asian Hermeneutics." *Biblical Interpretation* 9 (2001) 287–308.
Klein, William W., et al. *Introduction to Biblical Interpretation*. Dallas: Word, 1993.
Lee, Moonjang. "Identifying an Asian Theology: A Methodological Quest." *Asia Journal of Theology* 13 (1999) 256–75.
———. "A Post-Critical Reading of the Bible as a Religious Text." *Asia Journal of Theology* 14 (2000) 272–85.
Li, Qianju. *Xiandai Xunguxue Daolun*. Wuhan: Huazhong Normal University Press, 2008.
Lu, Zhongfa. *Xiandai Xunguxue Shenlun*. Hangzhou: Zhejiang University Press, 2008.
McQuilkin, Robertson. *Understanding and Applying the Bible*. Rev. ed. Chicago: Moody, 1992.

Meier, J. P. "The Historical Jesus and the Historical Law." *CBQ* 65 (2003) 52–79.
Mickelsen, A. Berkeley. *Interpreting the Bible*. Grand Rapids: Eerdmans, 1963.
New, David S. *Old Testament Quotation in the Synoptic Gospels, and the Two-Document Hypothesis*. SBLSCS 37. Atlanta: Scholars, 1993.
Reed, J. T. "Modern Linguistics and the New Testament: A Basic Guide to Theory, Terminology, and Literature." In *Approaches to New Testament Study*, ed. S. E. Porter and D. Tombs, 222–65. JSNTSup 120. Sheffield: Sheffield Academic, 1995.
Safrai, S. "Home and Family." In *The Jewish People in the First Century*, ed. S. Safrai et al., 2:728–92. CRINT 1. Assen: van Gorcum, 1976.
Shin, Hyeon Woo. "Methodological Similarity between Traditional Chinese Exegesis and Western Biblical Exegesis." *Korean Evangelical New Testament Studies* 11 (2012) 553–86.
———. *Textual Criticism and the Synoptic Problem in Historical Jesus Research*. CBET 36. Leuven: Peeters, 2004.
Sun, Yongchang. "Sanjushidehuwen." *Zhongguo Xunguxue Bao*, 1 (2009) 198–200.
Sun, Yongxuan, and Jingzhong Kan, eds. *Xinpian Xunguxue Gangyao*. Jinan: Qilu, 2007.
Walton, John H. "Principles of Productive Word Study." In *A Guide to Old Testament Theology and Exegesis*, ed. Willem A. VanGemeren, 158–68. Grand Rapids: Zondervan, 1997.
Xu, Weihan. *Xunguxue Daolun*. Corrected ed. Beijing: Beijing University Press, 2003.
Yang, Yong-Eui. *How to Read Matthew*. Seoul: Scripture Union, 2005.
Yeo, K. K. *What Has Jerusalem to Do With Beijing?* Harrisburg, PA: Trinity, 1998.
Zhao, Zhenduo. *Xunguxue Gangyao*. Corrected ed. Chengdou: Bashu, 2003.
———. *Xunguxue Shilue*. 1st ed. Zhengzhou: Zhongzhou Guli, 1988.
Zhou, Dapu. *Xunguxue Chugao*. 3rd ed. Wuhan: Wuhan University Press, 2007.

Dr. Seyoon Kim
A Comprehensive Bibliography

BOOKS

The Origin of Paul's Gospel. WUNT 2/4. Tübingen: Mohr/Siebeck, 1981. A Revision of "An Exposition of Paul's Gospel in the Light of the Damascus Christophany: An Investigation into the Origin of Paul's Gospel." PhD diss., University of Manchester, 1977.

———. American ed. Grand Rapids: Eerdmans, 1982.

———. 2nd enlarged ed. Tübingen: Mohr/Siebeck, 1984.

———. Korean trans. of the 2nd enlarged ed. with a new foreword. Seoul: Emmaus, 1994.

———. Reprint of the American ed. Eugene, OR: Wipf and Stock, 2007.

Salvation in Christ. Seoul: Scripture Reading, 1981 (in Korean).

———. 2nd exp. ed. Seoul: True Word, 1993.

———. New ed. Seoul: Tyrannus, 2001.

"The 'Son of Man'" as the Son of God. WUNT 30. Tübingen: Mohr/Siebeck, 1983.

———. The American ed. Grand Rapids: Eerdmans, 1985.

———. Korean trans. Seoul: Emmaus, 1992.

———. New Korean trans. Seoul: Duranno, 2012.

———. Reprint of the American ed. Eugene, OR: Wipf and Stock, 2011.

Christian Social Responsibility. Seoul: IVP, 1989 (in Korean).

Christianity and Korean Culture. Seoul: IVP, 1991 (in Korean).

Jesus and Paul. Seoul: The True Word, 1993 (in Korean).

———. 2nd ed. Seoul: The True Word, 1997.

———. New ed. Seoul: Tyrannus, 2001.

The Lord's Prayer Expounded. Seoul: Tyrannus, 2000 (in Korean).

The Gospel of John Expounded. Seoul: Tyrannus, 2001 (in Korean).

Lectures on 1 Thessalonians. Seoul: Tyrannus, 2002 (in Korean).

Paul and the New Perspective: Second Thoughts on the Origin of Paul's Gospel. WUNT 140. Tübingen: Mohr/Siebeck, 2002.

———. The American ed. Grand Rapids: Eerdmans, 2002.

———. Korean trans. Seoul: Tyrannus, 2002.

What is the Gospel? Seoul: Tyrannus, 2003 (in Korean).

Philippians Expounded. Seoul: Tyrannus, 2004 (in Korean).

Women Created and Redeemed by God. Seoul: Tyrannus, 2004 (in Korean).
1 Corinthians Expounded. Seoul: Tyrannus, 2007 (in Korean).
How Are We to Read the New Testament? Seoul: Scripture Union, 2008 (in Korean).
Win Caesar: A Lesson of a Pauline Missionary Strategy for Korean Christian Youth. Seoul: Knowing Him, 2008 (in Korean).
Christ and Caesar: The Gospel and the Roman Empire in the Writings of Paul and Luke. Grand Rapids: Eerdmans, 2008.
———. Korean trans. Seoul: Tyrannus, 2009.
The Theological World of Professor Seyoon Kim: Collected Essays and Interviews. Seoul: Jiireh, 2009 (in Korean).
Justification and Sanctification: Paul's Doctrine of Justification as a Soteriological Form of Jesus' Gospel of the Kingdom of God. Seoul: Duranno, 2013 (in Korean).

ARTICLES AND ESSAYS

"'The Grace That Was Given to Me . . .': Paul and the Grace of His Apostleship." Ed. G. Maier, *Die Hoffnung Festhalten: Festgabe für Walter Tlach zum 65,* 50–59. Stuttgart: Hanssler, 1978.
"The Cross of Our Lord Jesus Christ." *Asian Challenge* (Singapore, 1978) n.p.
"Theological Education in Asia and Korea." *Modern Thought* 17 (Seoul, 1979) 212–23 (in Korean).
"Yahweh, My Shepherd." In *The Biggest Heritage*, 153–55. Seoul: SungKwang, 1980 (in Korean).
"Life and Teaching of Jesus." In *Ewha*, 174–85. Seoul: Ewha University Press, 1981 (in Korean).
"The Background and Terminology of Jesus' Self-Designation the 'Son of Man.'" *Bible and Theology* 1 (Seoul, 1983) 83–116 (in Korean).
"The Missionary Vision of Paul the Apostle." In *The 60th Birthday Celebration of Dr. Han Chul-Ha, President of ACTS*, ed. Hyung-Ki Lee, 53–62. Seoul: Asia United Theological College, 1984.
"Criticism on Contemporary Mission Theology: Trends and Problems of Korea and World Church, a Panel Discussion." *Bible and Theology* 2 (Seoul, 1984) 256–62 (in Korean).
"Christianity and Culture in Korea: Nationalism, Dialogue and Contextualization." *ACTS Theological Journal* 2 (Seoul, 1986) 32–63 (in Korean).
"Is Minjung Theology a Christian Theology?" *Calvin Theological Journal* 22 (1987) 251–74.
"Jesus—the Son of God, the Stone, the Son of Man, and the Servant: the Role of Zechariah in the Self-Designations of Jesus." In *Tradition and Interpretation: Essays in Honor of E. Earle Ellis for his 60th Birthday*, ed. G. F. Hawthorne and O. Betz, 134–48. Grand Rapids: Eerdmans, 1987.
"The Purpose of Paul's Letter to the Romans." *Ashin* (Seoul, 1988) 115–29 (in Korean).
"The Baptism and Temptation of Jesus." *The World of the Bible* 5 (Seoul, 1989) 106–18 (in Korean).
"Zechariah and Jesus' Self-Understanding." *Reformed Thought* 1 (Seoul, 1989) 155–80 (in Korean).

"Die Vollmacht Jesu und der Tempel: der geschichtliche Zusammenhang und der theologische Sinn der 'Tempelreinigung' Jesu." *ANRW* II.26.6. Berlin: de Gruyter (completed in 1985 and still awaiting publication). Korean trans. "Jesus and the Temple." *Reformed Thought* 2 (Seoul, 1989) 121-64.

"Jesus' Proclamation of the Kingdom and Christian Political Existence." *Presbyterian Theological Quarterly* 222 (Seoul, 1989) 6-49 (in Korean).

"Grace and Call: A New Interpretation of Paul's Teaching on Divine 'Calling' and Its Implications for Christian Culture." In *What Can Christianity Offer to Korean Society?*, co-authored by Jin-Hong Kim, Manyeol Lee, Cheolsoo Park, and Seyoon Kim, 47-74. Seoul: Daejanggan, 1990 (in Korean).

"The Kingdom of God for Today: The Bible and the Kingdom of God." *A Study of Korean Church* 5 (Seoul, 1990) 11-102 (in Korean).

"The Kingdom of God for Today: A Panel Discussion." *A Study of Korean Church* 5 (Seoul, 1990) 201-9 (in Korean).

"Concept on Korea Christianity and Church Leadership: A Response." In *Korean Christianity toward Twenty-first Century*, 137-43. Seoul: Soongsil University, 1990 (in Korean). Also in *A Study on Korean Christianity* 10 (1990) 117-44 (in Korean).

"A Fresh Look at Paul's Understanding of Calling." *Gospel and Context* 1 (1991) 66-71.

"'Peace' in the New Testament." *Logos* (Seoul, 1991) 21-39 (in Korean).

"Once More: Jesus' Proclamation of the Kingdom and Christian Political Existence." In *Korean Christians and Democracy*, 1-21. Seoul: Christian Ethics Movement in Korea, 1992 (in Korean).

"Interpretations of Jesus' Death in the New Testament, Especially Concerning the Origin of Its Soteriological Interpretation." *Religion and Theology* 5 (Seoul, 1992) 77-121 (in Korean).

"Romans Expounded (1)." *Light and Salt* 83 (Seoul, 1992) 169-75 (in Korean).

"Romans Expounded (2)." *Light and Salt* 84 (Seoul, 1992) 185-93 (in Korean).

"Romans Expounded (3)." *Light and Salt* 85 (Seoul, 1992) 191-99 (in Korean).

"Romans Expounded (4)." *Light and Salt* 86 (Seoul, 1992) 193-202 (in Korean).

"'You are the Salt of the Earth': Paul's Application of Jesus' Teaching on the Christian Existence in the World." *Light and Salt* 100 (Seoul, 1993) 42-58 (in Korean).

"The Millennial Kingdom." *Ministry and Theology* 44 (1993) 194-204 (in Korean).

"Jesus, Sayings of." In the *Dictionary of Paul and His Letters*, ed. G. F. Hawthorne et al., 474-92. Downers Grove: IVP, 1993.

"Salvation and Suffering according to Jesus." *Presbyterian Theological Quarterly* 241 (1994) 128-44 (in Korean).

"New Heaven and New Earth." *Gospel and Context* 7 (1994) 71-81 (in Korean).

"Theology of Prosperity and Theology of Suffering: Jesus' Teaching on Christian's Salvation and Suffering." *Bible and Theology* 17 (Seoul, 1995) 69-82 (in Korean).

"In What Sense Is Jesus the Messiah? (1)." *Ministry and Theology* 67 (1995) 212-18 (in Korean).

"In What Sense Is Jesus the Messiah? (2)." *Ministry and Theology* 68 (1995) 192-98 (in Korean).

"In What Sense Is Jesus the Messiah? (3)." *Ministry and Theology* 69 (1995) 178-84 (in Korean).

"Salvation and Suffering according to Jesus." *EvQ* 68 (1996) 195-207.

"Jesus' Teaching on Salvation and Suffering." *Evangelical Review of Theology* 20, no. 1 (1996) 49-59.

"The 'Mystery' of Rom 11.25-26 Once More." *NTS* 43, no. 3 (1997) 412-29.

Ibid. Korean trans. *Ministry and Theology* 117 (1999) 182-94.

"God Reconciled His Enemy Paul to Himself: The Origin of Paul's Concept of Reconciliation." In *The Road from Damascus: The Impact of Paul's Conversion on His Life, Thought and Ministry*, ed. R. N. Longenecker, 102-24. Grand Rapids: Eerdmans, 1997.

"2 Cor 5:11-21 and the Origin of Paul's Concept of Reconciliation." *NovT* 39 (1997) 360-84.

"Kingdom of God." In the *Dictionary of the Later New Testament and Its Development*, ed. R. P. Martin and P. Davids, 629-38. Downers Grove: IVP, 1997.

"Paul as a Model of Christian Leadership." *KAFA (Korean Association of Fuller Alumni/ae)* (1997) 11-24 (in Korean).

"The Kingdom of God and the Church." *KAFA (Korean Association of Fuller Alumni/ae)* (1997) 36-42 (in Korean).

"The Future of Korean Churches in North America." *Ministry and Theology* 119 (1999) 124-28 (in Korean).

"Theological Confusions of Korean Church." *Ministry and Theology* 122 (1999) 38-48. (an interview article in Korean)

"The New Tübingen School, Tyndale Fellowship/IBR, Evangelicalism in the English-Speaking World, and the Korean Church." *Ministry and Theology* 126 (1999) 196-201 (in Korean).

"The Lord's Prayer Expounded (1): A Prayer That Reveals the Ideals and Hope of the Jesus Movement." *Light and Salt* 174 (1999) 60-63.

"The Lord's Prayer Expounded (2): He Knows What You Will Need." *Light and Salt* 174 (1999) 64-67.

"The Lord's Prayer Expounded (3): Pray Not Like the Hypocrites or the Gentiles." *Light and Salt* 176 (1999) 68-71.

"The Lord's Prayer Expounded (4): Abba Father Who Knows His Children's Needs." *Salt and Light* 178 (2000) 58-61.

"The Lord's Prayer Expounded (5): The Coming of God's Kingdom and Fulfillment of Shalom." *Light and Salt* 179 (2000) 66-69.

"The Lord's Prayer Expounded (6): Human Beings in Finitude." *Light and Salt* 180 (2000) 70-73.

"The Lord's Prayer Expounded (7): Why Is the Rule of God a Good News?" *Light and Salt* 181 (2000) 90-93.

"The Lord's Prayer Expounded (8): 'Give Us Our Daily Bread.'" *Light and Salt* 183 (2000) 72-75.

"Paul as a Model of Christian Leadership—What Is Biblical Leadership?" *Ministry and Theology* 134 (2000) 72-83 (in Korean).

"Suffering as a Sign of Christian Existence." *Ministry and Theology* 140 (2001) 38-51 (an interview article in Korean). Also in *The Disease of the Health and Wealth Gospels*. Essays by Gordon D. Fee, Walter C. Kaiser, Douglas J. Moo, David L. Larsen, Dennis P. Hollinger, and Seyoon Kim, 201-233. Seoul: Holy Wave Plus, 2011 (in Korean).

"Sabbath that Jesus Brings." *Ministry and Theology* 141 (2001) 84-93 (in Korean).

"The Resurrection of Jesus Christ—the Ground of Hope for Humankind." *Kidok Shinmun* (2001) (in Korean).

"Christian Civilization under Threat and the Responsibility of the Korean Churches." *Kidok Shinmun* (2001) (in Korean).

"The Doctrine of Justification in 1 Thessalonians." *Ministry and Theology* 151 (2002) 110–23 (in Korean).

"Salvation by God's Grace—a Theological Interview." *Ministry and Theology* 153 (2002) 200–213 (in Korean).

"The Jesus Tradition in 1 Thess 4.13—5.12." *NTS* 48, no. 2 (2002) 225–42.

"Taxi Drivers, Ko Sunghee and Han Sangjoon." *Light and Salt* 217 (2002) 26–27.

"*Imitatio Christi* (1 Corinthians 11:1): How Paul Imitates Jesus Christ in Dealing with Idol Food (1 Corinthians 8–10)." *BBR* 13 (2003) 193–226.

"The Education of Second-Generation Korean Pastors in America." In *Fuller Voices Then and Now*, ed. R. P. Spittler, 123–28. Pasadena: Fuller Theological Seminary, 2004.

"'*Imitatio Christi*' (1)." *Ministry and Theology* 176 (2004) 190–203 (in Korean).

"'*Imitatio Christi*' (2)." *Ministry and Theology* 177 (2004) 196–211 (in Korean).

"Women Redeemed by Christ." *Ministry and Theology* 179 (2004) 56–71 (in Korean).

"Again, Women Redeemed by Christ: A Reply to Rev. Suh's Critique." *Ministry and Theology* 185 (2004) 186–99 (in Korean).

"Win Caesar." *Diaspora Leadership: Monthly Magazine for Korean-American Pastors* 1 (2005) 190–203 (in Korean).

"To Win Caesar: A Lesson from the Missionary Strategy of the Apostle Paul." In *Theology and Higher Education in the Global Era: Festschrift for Professor Doctor Sang Chang*, ed. by Sung Jae Kim and Kyung Sook Lee, 218–29. Seoul: Korea Theological Study Institute, 2005 (in Korean).

"Paul's Entry (*Eisodos*) and the Thessalonians' Faith (1 Thessalonians 1–3)." *NTS* 51, no. 4 (2005) 519–42.

"The Structure and Function of 1 Thessalonians 1–3." In *History and Exegesis: New Testament Essays in Honor of Dr. E. Earle Ellis for his 80th Birthday*, ed. Sang-Won (Aaron) Son, 170–88. New York: T. & T. Clark, 2006.

"Hearing from Seyoon Kim—Quest for the Historical Jesus." *Gospel and Context* 7, no. 2 (Seoul, 2006) 36–38 (in Korean).

"Waiting for the Son of God (1 Thess 1:9–10): The Gospel That Paul Preached to the Thessalonians." In *Bible and Life: Ronald Fung Festschrift*, edited by L.-K. Lo et al., 32–50. Hong Kong: Chinese University of Hong Kong, 2007.

"The Atoning Death of Christ on the Cross." *Theology, News and Notes* 55, no. 1 (2008) 14–20.

"For a Proper Interpretation of Scripture and Maturity of Korean Church." *The Word* 226 (2008) 4–13. (an interview article)

"For a New Reformation of Korean Church." *Christian Thoughts* 600 (2008) 48–55.

"Dr. Seyoon Kim, the Theologian Who Represents Korea." *Ministry and Theology* 239 (2009) 132–37.

"Paul's Gospel: Was It Anti-Imperial?" *Gospel and Context* 223 (Seoul, 2009) 14–27. (an interview article)

"What is Spiritual Warfare?" *Newsnjoy.* November 5, 2010. http://www.newsnjoy.or.kr. (an interview article)

"Paul as an Eschatological Herald." In *Paul as Missionary: Identity, Activity, Theology, and Practice*, ed. T. J. Burke and B. S. Rosner, 9–24. LNTS 420. London: T. & T. Clark, 2011.

"Paul's Common Paraenesis [1 Thess.4–5; Phil. 2–4; and Rom. 12–13]: The Correspondence between Romans 1:18–32 and 12:1–2, and the Unity of Romans 12–13." *TynBul* 62, no. 1 (2011) 109–39.

"Korean Church and the Prosperity Gospel (1): Why Are We Poor and Sick Even When We Pray?" *Chosun Ilbo*, August 16, 2011. (an interview article with the largest circulating Korean newspaper)

"Korean Church and the Prosperity Gospel (2): You Will Become Rich If You Go to Church? It Is Idolatry." *Chosun Ilbo*, August 17, 2011. (an interview article in Korean)

"Jesus the Son of God as the Gospel (1 Thess 1:9-10 and Rom 1:3-4)." In *Earliest Christian History, Literature, and Theology: Essays from the Tyndale Fellowship in Honor of Martin Hengel*, ed. M. F. Bird and J. Maston, 117–41. Tübingen: Mohr/Siebeck, 2012.

"Theological Poverty as a Fundamental Cause for the Problems of Korean Church." In *The Road to a Reformation of Korean Church*, ed. by Youngan Kang et al., 17–36. Seoul: Holy Wave Plus, 2013 (in Korean).

"Paul's Gospel of God's Kingdom." In *The Gospel of God's Kingdom in the OT and NT*, co-authored by Hyun-Koo Chung, Hae-Kwon Kim, and Seyoon Kim, 273–332. Seoul: Holy Wave Plus, 2013 (in Korean).

BOOK REVIEWS

Review of *Who is This Christ?*, by R. H. Fuller and P. Perkins. *CTJ* 20, no. 1 (1985) 106–8.

Review of *The Thesis of Corinthians*, by Kyungyeon Jeon. *Christian Thought* 32, no. 8 (1988) 153–55 (in Korean).

Review of *Paul's Early Period*, by R. Riesner. *Them* 25 (1999) 105–8.

Review of *Paulus: Der Werdegang eines Apostels*, by K. Haacker. *JBL* 119, no. 1 (2000) 146–47.

Review of *Paul: In Fresh Perspective*, by N. T. Wright. *RBL* 06 (2006). http://www.bookreviews.org

WORKS IN PROGRESS

1 & 2 Thessalonians. WBC 45. Rev. ed. Nashville: Nelson. [Seyoon Kim is currently writing a completely revised edition of F. F. Bruce's 1982 commentary on 1–2 Thessalonians in the Word Biblical Commentary series.]

Epilogue
Words of Appreciation from Former Students and Colleagues of Dr. Seyoon Kim

Professor Seyoon Kim has been more than a mentor to me. Through him I have learned, of course, the way of biblical studies, but he has also shown me the way of biblical life. As one of his earliest pupils at the Asian Center for Theological Studies in Korea, I still so vividly remember his keen mind, academic excellence, eloquent and passionate lectures, amazing fluency in English and German, lucid explanations in interpreting the biblical text, honesty in answering questions, intensity in challenging his students, directness in reproving, wisdom in supervising, and warmth in counseling. Though an eminent scholar, he has a congenial personality, leading a simple life, getting along well with his students.

Dr. Kim continued to encourage me through my doctoral studies. Dr. Kim made possible my move to Tübingen, Germany, by recommending me to my *Doktorvater* as well as to the Albrecht-Bengel-Haus for financial and spiritual assistance. I spent seven years there, trying to follow his footsteps in every respect, wishing to be trained as a more useful instrument of God as he was. Dr. Kim continued to encourage me at a distance from Seoul as well as during his visits to Tübingen. He had done all this out of a sincere care and concern for me. It is this genuine Christian integrity that I have seen in him and tried to learn for myself.

Just before my homecoming back to Korea, however, he moved to the United States. His absence was a heavy loss for the whole Christian community in Korea and for me personally, too. For such a long time I could not see him but only on a few random occasions, none of which afforded an opportunity to express properly my gratitude for all that he had done. Here I am so delighted to express my deep appreciation for Dr. Kim, and I am truly honored to take part in a Festschrift that celebrates his life and work.

—*Hae-Kyung Chang*

It is widely recognized that Dr. Seyoon Kim is the foremost New Testament scholar of Korean descent who has made significant contributions to the academy and the church worldwide. I first met him at Asia United Theological University in South Korea. It was such a great privilege for me to take his classes and learn from him. It was his excellent scholarship and teaching which motivated my own pursuits in New Testament studies. His New Testament Christology class was an inspiration. His ground breaking work, *The Origin of Paul's Gospel*, expanded my breadth and depth of the New Testament text. He influenced me to pursue doctoral studies abroad and write my dissertation on the subject of Paul at the University of Durham. He has been, and remains, a role model professor to many Korean biblical scholars. It is my privilege and honor to contribute an article to Dr. Kim's Festschrift. It is a token of my appreciation for his legacy to me. I will remember him in my heart.

—*Hung-Sik Choi*

Professor Seyoon Kim is often known as a cool-headed, incisive scholar, but he is also a warm-hearted pastor. I learned this from my past experiences with him in, and outside of, the classroom. In his classes at the Asian Center for Theological Studies, he taught simple-minded college students like me with much patience and tenacity. He listened so attentively to us and answered even our foolish questions with such charity. I believe his care and guidance helped me stay on the right course in my academic endeavors. In my third year of the MDiv program at Chongshin Seminary, I was fortunate to become his research assistant. I did my best to assist him. But the reality is that I was the beneficiary. While I was typing the manuscripts of his articles word for word, I was introduced to the disciplines of biblical studies and learned how to craft arguments in academic papers. My passion for the study of Pauline theology was intensified by those experiences. In all my interactions with him Dr. Kim was actually preparing me for my *Tübinger Zeit*. But his care and support for me continued even after I started the doctorate at Tübingen Univeristy. When I was confused and frightened by a challenging situation, he sent me a letter from Korea to encourage me to work on the dissertation. Not only that, when I faced a difficult problem in my dissertation writing, he also visited me and prayed earnestly for me at the Waldhäuser-Ost (student dormitory). Miraculously, the problem was solved the next day before his departure for Tübingen. I would like to express my appreciation for his care and guidance. In this Festschrift, I honor him for what he has accomplished as a biblical scholar and pastor. "Gott segne und behüte meinen geeherten Lehrer, Prof. Dr. Seyoon Kim!"

—Soon Bong Choi

God set around me many teachers and mentors to help form Christ-like character in me and equip me for service in his kingdom. Among them, Dr. Seyoon Kim, my *Doktorvater*, is the most special as he left indelible marks on my identity, character, and ministry at almost every defining moment in my academic and ministry career. From the time I first met him at Chongshin University in 1993, and for over twenty years since, I have been his follower. I hoped to become like him. I read like him. I spoke like him. I wrote like him . . . I considered it an honor when my friends at Chongshin Seminary even gave me the nickname, "Little Seyoon!" I am grateful to him for loving me so faithfully, for being a good role model for me to follow, for helping me grow as a biblical scholar, and for handing over to me the baton of directing the Korean DMin program at Fuller Theological Seminary so that I may continue the noble task of educating Korean and Korean American pastors in North America, South Korea, and many other places in the world, a work which God began in Dr. Kim seventeen years ago. My sincere hope is that I can be his joy and crown when I stand with him before our Lord Jesus Christ (Phil 4:1).

—Jin Ki Hwang

Having finished the Master of Theology program at Calvin Theological Seminary in Grand Rapids in 1996, I moved to the Netherlands to continue my study at the Free University in Amsterdam. When I arrived in Holland in June 1996, I heard surprising news that Professor Seyoon Kim would give the key-note address at the SNTS annual meeting in Strasbourg. As far as I can tell he was the first Korean biblical scholar who was ever invited to read a main plenary paper at SNTS. I felt fortunate to witness with my own eyes my great hero presenting a paper in front of a multitude of internationally renowned theologians and biblical scholars from the Western world. This historic moment kindled in me a passion for biblical scholarship and inspired a prophetic hope that more Korean scholars including myself will make future contributions to global biblical scholarship at similar distinguished academic meetings. I am so grateful to him for the inspiration and encouragement he has left with me since my first encounter with him at Chongshin University.

—Chang Wook Jung

It was definitely through the overflowing grace of God that I met Dr. Seyoon Kim in 1995. Back then I was a student at Fuller Theological Seminary and just decided to change my major from missiology to New Testament. In my master's program, Dr. Kim did not shy from sparing his valuable time to teach me all of the fundamentals of writing a first-rate thesis paper. With my term paper in his hand, full of markings he had made with his red pen, he kindheartedly explained to me in detail all that I had to know. Sometimes he spent with me more than three hours. I am now in his shoes but find it very difficult to spare that many hours for my students. Dr. Kim also formed monthly *colloquia* for his doctoral students. The sessions are still fresh in my memory. The more I engaged various critical issues of Pauline studies with Dr. Kim and other fellow doctoral students, the more convinced I could be of my identity as a New Testament scholar. It is impossible for me to describe all that I owe to him in this short statement of remembrance. With respect and love I want to express my utmost gratitude to him for his passion for academic research and teaching as we celebrate his academic career and service for the Lord throughout his life.

—*Chulhong Brian Kim*

It was at one of the SBL annual meetings held in Nashville that I first met Professor Seyoon Kim. In a hotel room we talked about seminary education and biblical scholarship in Korea. I really enjoyed our conversation that day. Although he had been teaching at a North American institution (Fuller Theological Seminary) for many years by then, his concerns about seminary education in Korea were cogent and insightful. Since my first meeting with him, I have read many of his books and articles and learned that he fearlessly challenges contemporary trends in Pauline scholarship (e.g., the so-called "New Perspective on Paul") to defend biblical truth. He also loves the Korean Church and is dedicated to serve her. More often than not, New Testament scholars tend to engage ancient documents solely in their original historical settings. But as a pastor and teacher of the Church he also carefully makes the biblical message relevant to Christian life and ministry in the twenty-first century. I want to walk in his footsteps.

—*Dongsoo Kim*

I cannot think of Professor Seyoon Kim without mentioning his influence on my life and academic journey. When I was a university student I had a chance to hear his lectures at a conference hosted by a para-church ministry.

Appreciation from Former Students and Colleagues of Dr. Seyoon Kim

He was much praised as a famous scholar but I had no inkling to pursue further studies with him! But then I experienced a paradigm shift when I took his class on New Testament Theology. His lectures on the Kingdom of God and Christology were brilliant, powerful, and often times filled with humor. I was deeply absorbed in his books and lectures, which in turn made me desire to become a New Testament scholar myself, but the kind with a burning heart for the gospel like Dr. Kim. His research was also a source of inspiration to me during my doctoral studies. He made a huge impact on my life and career. I named my first son Sewon after Professor Seyoon Kim (these names are pronounced similarly in Korean). His influence did not end with my study abroad. He continues to inspire what I am now: a teacher of God's living Word. I thank God for Professor Kim whose leadership with Korean churches and theological students remains a source of inspiration. His work has raised the bar for academic excellence in New Testament studies. Professor Kim is to me what Paul was to Timothy!

—*Kyoung-Shik Kim*

I consider myself Dr. Kim's rightful pupil although I've never taken his class during my student years. I worked through my MDiv at Gordon-Conwell Theological Seminary and then at Fuller when he was teaching in Korea. Later Dr. Kim invited me to do doctoral studies at Fuller, but instead I ended up at King's College in London. So in a way, my academic training seems to have been virtually "free" from his influence. But in reality the opposite was the case. As I was preparing for doctoral studies in the UK, he suggested I contact four renowned British scholars, one of whom eventually became my *Doktorvater*, the late Professor Graham Stanton. Whenever I began conversations with other scholars at various *colloquia*, as soon as they learned about my nationality they would ask if I knew Dr. Seyoon Kim. What an ice-breaker and a fantastic way to set the whole conversation in motion!

Dr. Kim often speaks proudly of the remarkable advance in Korean New Testament scholarship, but I believe (and many Korean scholars would concur) that he himself is one of the most influential pioneers. I am grateful that he has become an excellent model to emulate, first as a teacher and now also as a fellow scholar. I pray that God's abundant grace be with him and his family, as he starts a new chapter in his fruitful life.

—*Yon-Gyong Kwon*

I first met Dr. Kim when he co-taught with Donald Hagner a doctoral seminar on recent Pauline studies during the Winter 1995 quarter at Fuller

Seminary. As a student in the seminar, I sat there astounded when Dr. Kim read fluently from the original German edition of Jürgen Becker's *Paulus: Der Apostel der Völker* while the rest of us opted for the English translation. I have to admit that I was intimidated by him in the beginning. But since then, after having served as his research assistant and having benefited from his guidance well beyond my graduation, I know Dr. Kim to be approachable, generous with his time, pastoral in demeanor, and an exemplary mentor. He pressed me to be a better scholar, but he was always more concerned with what kind of person I was becoming during my studies. This concern kept my head straight and my heart from straying.

Dr. Kim is also a man of commitment. I know of one occasion when he was asked to consider a position at another school, but he turned it down because his location in the Los Angeles area simply made him more accessible to Korean churches in the States and those in Korea. He has made concrete sacrifices in his career to teach and train the next generation of Korean Christian leaders. He has set for me an example of integrity and courage that will follow me for the rest of my life.

—*Max J. Lee*

It was in my first year of the MDiv program at Chongshin Theological Seminary when I first met Professor Seyoon Kim in one of his classes. When I heard his lectures I was just overwhelmed by his scholarly erudition, clarity, and confidence. He was no ordinary professor. He was, and still is, one of the greatest Pauline scholars. His passion for the gospel and devotion to New Testament studies inspired me to step into the world of New Testament scholarship myself. Since my seminary years Dr. Kim has always been my hero. During my studies abroad both in the UK and USA, he encouraged me whenever I was in need of encouragement. I really appreciate his caring heart and encouraging words. I hope that he will write prolifically during his retirement.

—*Sang-Il Lee*

In the Spring of 1983 I was originally preparing to study abroad in the United States, with an interest in systematic theology. Then Dr. Seyoon Kim made known to me opportunities at the University of Tübingen, West Germany, which I had not previously considered. He kindly explained that there were several internationally renowned professors in New Testament studies, and they took a theologically moderate stance. I made a decision and wrote a letter to the registrar of the Evangelisch-theologische Fakultät of Tübingen University. My letter was evaluated by Professor Otto Betz who had been the *Doktorvater* of Seyoon Kim, and this same Professor Betz accepted me as one of his *Doktoranden*. Thanks to Dr. Kim, I was able to finish writing my doctoral dissertation under the guidance of the friendly and, in Dr. Kim's terms, "saint-like" Professor. I would like to ask that Dr. Kim make more frequent visits to Korea after his retirement to contribute to the Korean Society of Evangelical New Testament Studies, of which I am serving as president this year.

—*Sung-Jong Oh*

Professor Seyoon Kim is one of the most influential Pauline scholars of our day. He is also the founding father of New Testament scholarship in South Korea. Although his missionary stay and teaching at seminaries in South Korea slowed down his own scholarly research, his work nevertheless accelerated the national development of New Testament studies in South Korea. His enthusiastic and insightful lectures encouraged many of his students to aspire to excellence in New Testament studies. It was because of his lectures at Chongshin University that I myself was converted from a philosophical interest in systematic theology to an exegetical interest in biblical studies. It is his unique combination of pioneering academic research and humble service for the Kingdom of God that has had a lasting impact on me throughout my academic journey. I would like to express my sincere gratitude to Professor Kim for his devotion to fostering excellence in Korean biblical scholarship. Without his sacrifice, Korean New Testament studies would not have reached its present level. He was, and still is, a great blessing not only to his students, myself included, but also to other biblical scholars who have been influenced by him in one way or another.

—*Hyeon Woo Shin*

When I think of Dr. Seyoon Kim the two things that consistently come to mind are rigorous scholarship and a generous heart. Dr. Kim's approach to studying the New Testament is characterized by diligent care and effort. No nuance of a word is to be overlooked, no detail of a cultural context to be ignored as irrelevant, and no scholarly view to be accepted without question. Behind this painstaking scholarship is an unflagging zeal for the truth. Dr. Kim is not allured by the novel idea or the latest fad, though his publications contain many fresh ideas. He is concerned with what is true, and the pursuit of truth often leads him to new insights. Dr. Kim, however, is no aloof academic. I have enjoyed his genuine concern and hospitality over the past ten years, first as his student and research assistant, and more recently as his colleague. On every visit to his office I can expect a warm welcome: he invariably invites me with a wave of his hand to take a seat in front of his desk, upon which he inquires regarding my research and the well-being of my family, and only after this do we address business. During my days as a cash-strapped doctoral student, there would also be the occasional holiday gift, always given unassumingly, with words about making sure my son had an enjoyable Christmas. I value Dr. Kim as a scholar, but I prize him even more for the quality of his person.

—*Stephen E. Young*

Subject Index

ancient philosophy, xix, 6–8, 14, 16–17, 23–24, 43
Aramaic words, 131, 144–46, 214, 217, 242, 260, 265
apocalyptic, 44, 85–86, 108, 175, 214, 220, 264
apostle/apostleship, ix, 55–56, 61, 63–64, 66, 68, 98, 115–16, 118, 120, 122, 124–25, 188, 203
atonement, see sacrifice

belief, see faith
bilingualism, xxi, xxiii, 4, 30, 231–32, 234–38, 239–42, 243, 248–50

Caesar, see emperor
Chinese exegesis, xxiii, 277–78, 295–96
    antithetical parallelism, 282–83
    synonymous parallelism, 279–82
Christology, x, 89, 204–6, 213, 218, 257, 270
church, x, xix, xx, xxi, 55–60, 61–63, 65–67, 71, 73, 99, 102, 185, 203, 206–10, 213, 231–36, 237–42, 244–46, 248–50, 255, 260, 261–63, 270, 272
covenant, xx, 31–32, 45–46, 81, 83–84, 87–88, 91, 95–96, 104–5, 107–8, 110–12, 171
creation, x, 31–32, 42, 44, 46, 48, 69, 71, 100, 103, 257, 273
cross/crucifixion, 145–46, 156, 216, 226, 259, 266, 270

Damascus, ix, xx, 115–16, 118–20, 122, 125, 299, 302
Dead Sea Scrolls, see Qumran
discipleship/disciple, xxi, 15, 19, 117, 141, 150, 162, 165, 176–79, 180, 184–87, 189–95, 196–99, 206, 208, 221, 223–24, 226–27, 234, 236, 241

ecclesiology, see church
epistle, see letter
emperor/empire, 10–11, 14, 17–19, 24, 43, 55–56, 175, 235, 239
eschatology, xxi, 45, 71, 103, 108, 111–12, 160, 162, 171, 173–75, 184–87, 191–92, 195, 200, 204–6, 256, 262–64, 266–70
    future, xxi, 206, 212–14, 216, 217–20, 221–23
    realized, xxi, 205–6, 212–14, 220–21
evangelists / evangelism, 62, 131, 148, 204, 219, 227, 258, 261–62, 269
evil, see sin
expiation, see sacrifice

faith, xxi, xxiii, 7, 18, 23, 32, 42, 45, 48, 62, 64–65, 70–72, 84, 104–7, 112, 179, 180–81, 184–86, 191–92, 195–200, 259, 262, 266–67, 270, 273, 285, 293
forgiveness, xxi, xxiii, 49, 143, 180, 184–85, 187, 189–95, 196, 198–200, 268

313

Subject Index

freedom, 8, 16, 20, 22–23, 25, 34, 37, 39, 40–42, 47, 102, 105–7, 165, 294

Gentiles, ix, xx, 55–59, 60–61, 63–67, 68–69, 71–72, 78–80, 81–84, 87–89, 92–93, 95–96, 98–100, 101–8, 109–12, 147, 157, 188, 232, 235, 237–39, 242–50, 261–62, 283–84
Gnosticism, see Greco-Roman religions
gospel/good news, ix, xx–xxii, 45, 54–57, 61–66, 68–73, 98, 101, 111, 118, 120, 123, 125, 131, 148–49, 151, 156, 159, 177, 179, 186, 189, 204–5, 244, 247, 255–59, 261–62, 264, 266–74
grace/gift, xx, 9, 32, 42, 45, 47, 65, 67, 72–73, 95–102, 104–5, 108–12, 125, 163, 180, 192, 199, 221, 259
Greco-Roman philosophy, see ancient philosophy
Greco-Roman religions, 7–9, 16, 19–20, 202–3, 208, 210, 241, 255, 290, 294
Greek language, 3–5, 35, 21, 26, 29–30, 31–36, 137, 146–47, 155, 236–38, 249–50, 284

Hebrew language, xxi, xxii, 3–4, 25, 30–32, 40, 47, 49, 70, 82–83, 109, 131, 137, 139, 142–47, 151, 153, 170, 232, 241–42, 249–50, 260–62, 265, 267, 271
Hebrews/Hebraists, see Judaism, Aramaic-matrix speakers
Hellenists, see Judaism, Greek-matrix speakers
heresy, 120, 201, 206–7

idiom, xxi, 13–14, 20, 149, 150–53, 155–57, 285, 288
imperial cult, see emperor/Empire
irony, xxi, xxiii, 32, 117, 159–61, 168–70, 175–76, 178–81, 222, 224, 227, 288
Israel, xx, 43, 45–46, 64, 68–69, 71, 78–84, 87–92, 98–99, 101–2, 105–6, 110, 116–17, 121–22, 137, 151–55, 157, 174, 179, 191, 263–64, 272, 284, 288

Jerusalem, xxi, 15, 53–54, 56, 66–67, 69, 73, 119, 141, 146, 148–49, 150–57, 203, 208, 231–36, 237–42, 244–46, 248–50
Jews, see Judaism
Johannine community, xxi, 202–3, 205–6, 208, 222
Judaism, xx–xxi, 15, 30, 33, 35, 40–41, 57–60, 62, 64–65, 67–69, 71–73, 78–81, 83, 85–89, 92–93, 101–2, 104–9, 111–12, 116, 120, 123–25, 131, 137, 140, 145, 149, 150, 157, 166, 169, 189, 203, 208–9, 214, 218–19, 226–27, 232–33, 255, 261–64, 269–70, 290, 294
  Aramaic-matrix speakers, xxi, 231–32, 239–43, 249–50
  Diaspora/Hellenistic Jews, xxi, 137–40, 146–47, 231, 233–36, 237–38
  Greek-matrix speakers, 232, 243–50
  Palestinian Jews, 146, 231–36, 260, 271, 294
Judaizers, 57, 73, 98
judgment/judge, xx–xxi, 5–7, 9–10, 12–14, 20–22, 25–26, 33, 37–39, 42, 46–48, 69, 81, 83–84, 87, 90, 92–93, 151–57, 163, 187–90, 193–94, 202–3, 207, 216–27
judicial, see lawcourt
juridicial, see lawcourt
justice, see righteousness
justification, x, xx, 26, 29–31, 33, 41–42, 47–48, 49, 68, 69, 71, 95, 99, 100–108, 110–12
  administer justice, putting to rights, 17–19, 22, 24–25, 38, 41, 43–45, 49
  declare just, 7, 9–12, 13, 22, 25–26, 32–33, 39, 47–48
  do justice for someone, penalize, 8, 10–12, 13–15, 22–23, 25, 37, 39, 42, 47, 88, 117, 124–25
  in the right, 7–8, 11–12, 22, 24–26, 37, 39–40, 43, 47–48

make ethically righteous, 19–20, 22, 26, 39, 47, 49
set free, acquit, 10, 22, 25–26, 32–33, 34, 37, 39, 40, 47–48

kingdom of God, ix, 143, 162, 170–71, 173–75, 180, 185–86, 189, 214, 224, 255, 259, 264, 271, 281
Koiné Greek, see Greek language
law, xx, xxiii, 4, 6–13, 15–16, 19–20, 22, 24–26, 33, 37–41, 46, 57, 59–60, 64–65, 67–69, 71–72, 81, 88, 90, 95, 98–112, 116–17, 124, 137–38, 162–64, 166, 176, 180, 224, 264–65, 283, 293
lawcourt, xx, 4, 6–7, 9–10, 11–12, 15, 20, 22, 25–26, 31, 38–40, 45–47
letter, xx, 4–5, 23, 25–26, 29–30, 32, 35–36, 41, 48–49, 53–60, 61–69, 70–73, 77, 80, 84, 92, 96, 100–101, 104, 108, 110–11, 116, 172, 206, 209, 259
lexicography, xx, 21–26, 31–36, 37–41
  BDAG, 37–41, 49, 171
  lexical meaning, 4, 15, 21, 25, 29, 30–33, 34–36, 41, 45, 47, 49, 173–74, 290
  syntagmatic meaning, 25–26, 30–35, 46, 49

miracles, 116, 124
mission/missionary, ix–x, xix–xx, 30–31, 54–57, 59–68, 72–73, 98, 116–19, 121–22, 149–50, 153, 156, 164–65, 190, 194–95, 197, 208–9, 234, 243, 246, 248, 261–63, 269
mystery, ix, 122–23
mystery cult, see Greco-Roman religions
mysticism, 123–25

New Perspective, x, 41, 112, 120

Pharisee, 99, 176–77, 178–81
Post-New Perspective, 41–42
prayer, ix, 67, 81, 119, 146, 191, 195

proclamation/preaching, ix, xix, 57, 61–66, 68, 98, 117–18, 120, 123, 151, 153, 155, 157, 188, 190, 205, 234, 244, 247–48, 254–55, 261–63, 266–72
prophecy/prophet, ix, xx–xxi, 41, 64, 70, 87–88, 101, 116–22, 124–25, 135, 137, 141, 143, 146, 151–55, 157, 173, 179–80, 203, 208–10, 262–64, 266–70, 272–73, 283
propitiation, see sacrifice

Qumran, 40, 89–92, 260, 264, 290, 294

repentance, xxi, 90–91, 143, 151–52, 154–57, 178–80, 185, 188–95, 216, 268–69
resurrection, 150, 196, 205, 217–19, 221, 224, 233, 266, 270
revelation, xxi, 45, 63, 106–8, 121–23, 215–16, 225, 227, 254, 256–57, 283–84
righteousness, xx, 3–5, 21–24, 29–31, 32–36, 38, 40–44, 45–49, 79–80, 81–84, 88–89, 90–93, 105–6, 108, 111, 162–64, 168, 180, 190, 282, 287
  distributive justice, 5–6, 7, 8–10, 12–15, 24, 37–38, 42–43, 45–46, 49, 163, 189
  moral uprightness, 6–7, 15–17, 19, 22, 24, 30–32, 37–39, 42–43, 47, 79, 81–82, 88, 160
  right, fitting, appropriate, 5–6, 10, 12, 22, 24, 37, 39
  rights, legal license, 7, 11–13, 22–23, 38–39, 293
  tsedeq, tsedaqah, tsadaq, 4, 30–31, 32, 34, 47, 49
Rome/Roman church, xx, 4, 18, 23, 26, 29, 53–73, 238, 240

sacrifice, 3, 42, 46, 105, 116, 264
salvation, xx, 3, 7, 18, 31–32, 38, 40–45, 49, 58, 68, 69, 71, 78, 84, 87–89, 92, 96, 98–102, 104–12, 119–20, 171, 180, 186, 216–17,

225–27, 256, 259, 262, 267–68, 270, 272, 274, 292
scandal/stumbling block, 164, 185, 187–91, 199
sectarianism, xxi, 202–9, 263
Septuagint, xx–xxi, 3–4, 26, 29–30, 35–36, 40–43, 47–49, 82–83, 109, 131–47, 151–53, 155–57, 170–74, 187, 255, 260–62, 265, 267–70, 290
signs and wonders, see miracles
sin/sinners, xx–xxi, 20, 34, 42, 46–49, 72, 77–84, 87–93, 105–6, 124, 179–80, 185–90, 192–95, 226, 267–69, 273, 281, 284, 287
social-scientific criticism, see sociology
sociology, xxi, 58, 160–61, 164–65, 167–68, 202–3, 209
Son of God, 70, 99, 213, 217, 222, 257–58, 268–70, 272
Son of Man, xxi, 153–55, 157, 185, 187, 212–27

soteriology, see salvation
suffering, xx, 14, 115–18, 125, 222, 224, 270

temple, 15, 81–82, 145–46, 152, 208, 232, 263

vice, 19–20
virtue, 6, 15-20, 41, 43, 200

weak/weakness, xx, xxii, 57, 65, 68–69, 73, 125, 189, 197, 207, 278, 294–95
wise/wisdom, ix, 15–17, 19, 39, 162, 176, 180–81, 265, 280, 282
word of God, ix, xxi, 180, 254–74
works of the law, see law

Xunguxue, see Chinese exegesis

Author Index

Aland, Kurt, 148, 156–57, 257, 265, 274
Allen, L. C., 82, 93
Anderson, A. A., 81–2, 93
Arndt, William F., 180–81
Arnold, C. E., 109, 111
Arnott, W., 159–60, 181
Ashton, John, 210, 215, 218–19, 228, 230
Aune, David E., 212, 228

Baarlink, Heinrich, 149, 157
Baergen, Rene A., 165, 181
Bai, Zhaolin, 289, 296
Bailey, Kenneth E., 51, 162–63, 176–77, 180–81
Bandstra, A. J., 109, 112
Barackman, F. H., 284, 286–88, 293, 296
Barr, James, 33, 50, 288
Barrett, C. K., 107, 112, 123, 126, 204–5, 210, 213, 217–18, 228, 243–48, 250, 257, 274
Barth, K., xiv, 254, 274
Bauckham, R., 268, 274
Bauer, Walter, xiii, 206–7, 210, 245, 250
Baur, F. C., 53, 74, 232–33, 248, 250
Beare, Francis W., 216, 227, 239, 250
Beasley-Murray, G. R., 213, 221, 228
Beavis, Mary Ann, 165, 178, 181
Beker, J. C., 32, 50, 74
Bengel, Johann, 232, 243, 250
Berger, K., 96, 112
Berkhof, L., 278, 286–87, 290, 296

Betz, H. D., 96–99, 101, 103–5, 112
Beutler, Johannes, 202, 210
Billings, J. Todd, 48, 50
Bindemann, Walter, 181
Bird, Michael, 26, 31–32, 43–44, 48, 40
Birkeland, H., 93
Bishop, E. F. F., 118, 126
Blackman, E. C., 245, 250
Bock, Darrell L., 160–61, 168, 170, 177, 181, 219, 228, 263, 272, 274, 286–88, 291, 296
Bogart, John, 203, 210
Booth, Wayne C., 168, 178, 181
Boring, Eugene, 132, 135, 147
Bornkamm, G., 206–7, 210
Borsch, Frederick Houk, 217, 228
Bousset, W., 264, 274
Bovon, François, 154, 157, 187–88, 194, 196–97, 199–200, 261, 271, 274
Bowen, C. E., 169, 171, 181
Brenton, Sir Lancelot C. L., 152, 157
Bretscher, Paul G., 159–60, 181
Briggs, C. A., 81, 84, 93
Briggs, E. G., 81, 84, 93
Brodie, Thomas L., 179, 181, 208–10
Brown, Colin, xvi, 177, 180–81
Brown, Raymond E., 60, 74, 121–22, 126, 217–18, 222, 224, 228, 237, 250, 257, 274
Bruce, F. F., 97–99, 101, 103–4, 110, 112, 122–23, 126, 241, 243–44, 246, 250
Bruckner, James, 31, 50
Brueggemann, Walter, 88, 93

Bultmann, Rudolf, 31–33, 50, 109–10, 112, 116, 126, 159, 208, 212, 221, 225, 228, 261, 271, 274
Bundrick, D. R., 109, 112
Burkett, Delbert, 213–14, 217, 228
Burridge, R. A., 268, 274
Burton, E. D., 96–98, 101, 103, 112
Byrne, B., 65, 74

Cadbury, Henry, 238, 243–46, 251
Camery-Hoggatt, Jerry, 122, 126, 283, 285, 293, 296
Campbell, Douglas A., 34, 43–48, 50, 68–69, 74, 106, 112
Campbell, Jonathan G., 89–91, 93
Campbell, W. S., 54, 74
Carson, D. A., 54–55, 65, 74, 284–85, 296
Casey, Maurice, 217–19, 228
Chang, H.-K., 70, 71, 74
Charlesworth, James H., 208, 210
Cheng, Junying, 291, 296
Chester, Stephen, 48, 50
Chisholm, Robert B., 285, 287–88, 290–91, 296
Chlup, Radek, 19, 27
Choi, Hung-Sik, 106, 113
Choi, Soon Bong, 157
Clement, Ronald E., 121, 126
Cole, R., 99, 113
Collins, John J., 218–19, 228
Colpe, Carsten, 213, 228
Comrie, Bernard, 21, 27, 35, 50
Conzelmann, Hans, 96, 113, 123, 126, 243, 251
Cooley, Alison E., 17–18, 27
Copenhaver, Brian P., 19–20, 27
Cotterell, Peter, 284, 291, 296
Cotton, Hannah, 241, 251
Couch, Mal, 286, 296
Court, John M., 78, 93
Cousar, C. B., 99, 106, 113
Craigie, Peter C., 82, 84, 93, 152, 157
Cranfield, C. E. B., 271, 274
Cremer, Hermann, 30, 32–33, 50
Croft, Steven J. L., 82, 93
Cruse, D. A., 31, 50

Cullmann, Oscar, 207–8, 210, 212–13, 226, 228
Culpepper, R. Alan, 227, 228

Dahl, Nils A., 218–19, 228
Danby, H., 274
Danker, Frederick, 21, 30, 34, 50
Davids, P. H., 259, 268, 274
Davies, Glenn N., 78–79, 84, 93
Davies, Margaret, 217, 228
Davies, Philip R., 90, 93
Dawsey, James M., 178–79, 181
Debrunner, A., 261, 265, 274
Deissmann, Adolf, 35, 50
Deissmann, G. A., 61, 74
Dell'Acqua, Anna Passoni, 139, 147
Derrett, J. Duncan M., 159, 164–66, 181
deSilva, David A., 160, 166, 181
Dibelius, M., 258, 274
Dodd, C. H., 20, 27, 208
Donaldson, T. L., 106, 113
Donfried, K. P., 53, 58–59, 74
Dormandy, Richard, 160, 182
Drane, J. W., 54, 74
Drummond, J., 54, 74
Dunn, James D. G., 34, 47, 50, 54, 74, 79–80, 93, 96–101, 103–6, 109, 112–13, 207, 210, 213, 218, 228, 243, 251
Dunnett, Walter M., 287, 293, 296

Earle, Ralph, 177, 182
Eastmann, E. J., 96, 113
Eckstein, H. J., 103, 105, 113
Edwards, C. M., 118, 126
Edwards, J. R., 54, 59–60, 65, 68, 74
Elliger, K., 267, 274
Elliot, J. H., 267–68, 274
Ellis, E. Earle, 86, 93, 151, 157, 195, 200
Erickson, Richard J., 287, 296
Esler, Philip, 233, 251
Evans, C. F. 187, 190–91, 195–97, 200
Evans, Craig. A., 150, 157, 171, 182, 294, 296
Evans, Vyvyan, 24, 27

Fee, Gordon D., 123, 126
Feine, P., 67, 74
Fitzmyer, Joseph A., 46, 50, 65, 74, 160, 164-65, 180, 182, 187, 194, 198, 200, 239, 243, 245-46, 251, 259-60, 262, 274, 288, 296
Fletcher, D. R., 160, 168-69, 175, 180, 182
Foakes Jackson, F. J., 243, 251
Foerster, W., 260, 275
Forbes, Greg W., 159, 163, 166, 168, 173, 182
France, R. T., 271-72, 275, 287, 296
Franklin, Eric, 246, 251
Frey, Jörg, 213, 229
Friedrich, Gerhard, xvii, 275
Frommel, Otto, 248, 251
Fu, Jinbi, 280, 285, 296
Fuks, A., 253
Fung, R. Y. K., 96-98, 101, 113
Furnish, Victor Paul, 123, 126

Gagnon, Robert A. J., 166, 182
Gamble, H. Y., 62, 74
Garlington, Don, 26-27, 34, 50
Gasse, W., 149, 157
Gaventa, B. R., 54, 66, 74, 98, 113
Geeraerts, Dirk, 31, 50
Georgi, D., 67, 75
Gerleman, G., 261, 265-67, 275
Ginzberg, Louis, 117, 126
Gnilka, J., 261, 271, 275
Goppelt, L., 275
Gordon, T. D., 98, 113
Gorman, Michael J., 32, 45, 50, 284-85, 288, 296
Goudge, H. L., 118, 126
Goulder, M. D., 137, 147-48, 157
Grabbe, Lester L., 122, 126
Grafe, E., 54, 75
Green, Joel B., 163, 166, 179-80, 182, 200
Green, Melanie, 24, 27
Green, W. S., 264, 275
Greene, M. Dwaine, 167, 175, 182
Grenfell, B. P., 11, 13, 27
Grudem, W., 254, 275
Grundmann, Walter, 245, 251

Guelich, R. A., 269, 271, 275
Güting, E., 246, 251
Gundry, Robert H., 132, 140, 143, 147, 272, 275
Gunkel, H., 121, 126
Guthrie, D., 75, 99, 113

Haacker, K., 54, 59-60, 66, 73, 75
Haenchen, Ernst, 237, 243, 245-46, 251, 262-63, 275
Hamid-Khani, Saeed, 178-79, 182
Hannah, Darrell D., 218, 229
Hansen, G. W., 107, 113
Hanson, J. S., 122, 126
Harder, G., 54, 75, 150, 157
Hare, Douglas R. A., 220, 225, 229
Harrington, Daniel, 207, 210
Harris, Murray J., 123, 126
Harrison, E. F., 59, 75
Havelock, E. A., 5, 15, 27
Hays, Richard B., 104, 106, 113
Hedrick, Charles W., 163, 182
Heitmüller, Wilhelm, 235, 251
Hengel, Martin, 207, 210, 232-37, 239, 243, 246-47, 249, 251, 268, 270, 275
Héring, Jean, 118, 126
Higgins, A. J. B., 218, 229
Hill, Craig C., 232-33, 235, 247, 252
Hill, David, 3-5, 10, 15, 22, 27, 32-33, 49-50
Hong, I. G., 105, 109, 113
Hooker, Morna D., 106, 113, 219, 229
Hort, Fenton, 243, 252
Hoskyns, Edwyn C., 219, 229
Howard, George, 103, 106-7, 113
Howard, W. F., 213, 229
Huang, Darong, 289, 296
Huang, Jianzhong, 289, 296
Hüber, Hans, 86, 94
Hultgren, A. J., 55, 59-60, 68, 72, 75
Hunt, A. S., 11, 13, 27
Hurtado, Larry W., 213, 235, 252

Ireland, Dennis J., 160-61, 163-64, 166-69, 182

Jacobson, Rolf A., 84, 94

Author Index

Jamison, Leland, 32, 50
Janse, Mark, 240–41, 252
Jeremias, Joachim, 148, 157, 175, 180, 182, 198, 201, 234, 252, 261, 271, 275
Jervell, Jacob, 116, 124, 126, 246, 252
Jervis, L. A., 54–55, 61, 63, 75
Jewett, Robert, 54, 75, 85, 94, 118, 126
Jobes, K. H., 268, 275
Johnson, J. de M., 11–12, 27
Johnson, Luke Timothy, 170, 182, 187–88, 195–96, 201, 243–48, 252, 258, 275
Jonge, Marinus de, 213, 224, 228
Jouget, Pierre, 10, 27
Judge, E. A., 118, 126
Jülicher, A., 271, 275
Jüngel, Ebehard, 32, 50
Jung, Chang Wook, 182

Käsemann, Ernst, xxi, 32, 40, 43–44, 50, 204–7, 210
Kamlah, E., 176, 182
Kan, Jingzhong, 289, 295, 297
Kearsley, R. A., 7, 28
Keck, L. E., 59–60, 75, 79, 85–86, 94, 269, 275
Keener, C. S., 294, 296
Kertelege, K., 5, 27
Kettunen, M., 54, 75
Kim, Chulhong Brian, 120, 126
Kim, Dongsoo, 202, 210
Kim, Hyun Chul Paul, 277, 296
Kim, Kyoung-Shik, 87, 94
Kim, Seyoon, 120, 123, 126, 175, 182, 213, 229
Kingsbury, Edwin C., 121, 127
Kissane, E. J., 81, 83, 94
Kittel, G., xvii, 33–34, 255, 258, 266, 275
Klein, William W., 278, 293, 296
Kleinknecht, H., 261, 264–65, 275
Kloppenborg, John S., 160, 162, 164–65, 175, 182
Koch, D. A., 70, 75
Kornemann, E., 11, 27
Kraeling, C. H., 245, 252
Kramer, Werner, 235, 252

Krueger, Paul, 9, 28
Kruger, M. A., 105, 113
Kruse, C. G., 54–55, 59, 65, 68, 75, 101
Kümmel, W. G., 213, 229
Kwon, Yon-Gyong, 201
Kysar, Robert, 213, 229

Laato, Timo, 31–32, 41–46, 48, 51
Lacey, W. K., 17, 27
Ladd, George E., 213, 229
Lakoff, George, 21, 24, 28, 35, 51
Lambrecht, J., 99, 113
Lampe, P., 60, 68, 75
Landry, David, 160, 165–67, 175, 182
Lane, Anthony N. S., 34, 51
Lee, Moonjang, 277, 296
Lee, Sang-Il, 234–42, 245, 247, 249, 252
Leithart, Peter, 48, 51
Lemicio, E. E., 271, 275
Lewis, C. S., 199, 201
Li, Qianju, 281, 286, 288–90, 295–96
Liang, Yongchang, 291, 296
Liefeld, Walter L., 159, 170, 180, 182
Lightfoot, J. B., 99, 104, 113
Lincoln, Andrew T., 123, 127, 215, 220, 223, 257, 275
Lindars, Barnabas, 213, 217, 222–23, 229
Lindblom, J., 121, 127
Llewelyn, R., xvi, 7, 28
Loader, William, 162, 164, 177, 182
Lohmeyer, E., 256, 269, 275
Lohse, E., 264, 275
Long, B. O., 127
Longenecker, Bruce, 108–9, 114
Longenecker, Richard N., 55, 59–61, 63, 68, 70, 75, 97–98, 101, 103–4, 114, 219, 229
Louw, Johannes P., 33, 35, 51, 172–73, 182
Lu, Zhongfa, 283, 296
Lührmann, D., 261, 275
Lukaszewski, Albert L., 214, 229
Lutz, Cora E., 16, 23–24, 28
Luz, U., 261, 271, 275
Lyons, John, 31, 51

Maddox, Robert, 216, 220, 229, 246, 252
Mann, C. S., 248, 252
Mannermaa, Tuomo, 48, 51
Marcos, Natalio Fernández, 139, 147
Marshall, I. Howard, 148, 156–57, 160, 170, 182, 186–88, 190, 193, 195, 197, 201, 237, 239, 246, 252
Martin, Ralph P., xiv, 118, 123, 127
Martyn, J. Louis, 32, 51, 97–104, 108–10, 114, 225, 229
Matera, F. J., 97–98, 101, 103–4, 114
Mathewson, Dave L. T., 162, 167–68, 183
Matlock, R. Barry, 106, 114
May, Ben, 160, 165–67, 175, 182
Mays, James L., 122, 127
McFayden, J. F., 169, 183
McQuilkin, Robertson, 278, 296
Meeks, Wayne A., 222, 230
Meier, John P., 248, 252, 294, 297
Menken, Maarten J. J., 135, 141, 143, 147
Metzger, Bruce M., 97, 114, 192, 201, 222, 230, 243–44, 247–48, 252
Meyer, P. M., 11, 27
Michael, John H., 239, 252
Michaels, J. Ramsey, 216, 218–21, 223, 226, 230
Mickelsen, A., 287, 297
Millar, Fergus, 239, 241–42, 252
Miller, J. C., 54, 75
Miller, Patrick D., 121, 127
Minear, P. S., 54, 75, 199, 201
Moffatt, J., xv, 96, 114
Mohrlang, R., 59, 75
Mommsen, Theodor, 9, 28
Moo, Douglas J., 4, 28, 32, 34, 43, 45, 47, 51, 55, 59, 64–65, 68, 75
Morris, L., 257, 275
Motyer, J. A., 87, 89, 94
Moule, C. F. D., 191, 201, 214, 230, 243, 246, 252, 272, 275
Moulton, W. F., xv, 11–12, 258, 276
Mounce, R. H., 256, 276
Mowinckel, Sigmund, 81, 94, 121, 127
Mullen, E. T., Jr., 121, 127
Muraoka, T., 173, 183

Murphy, M. Lynne, 31, 51
Mußner, F., 96–99, 101, 103–4, 110, 114

Naveh, Joseph, 241, 252
Neil, William, 243, 252
Neusner, J., 264, 276
New, David S., 290, 297
Nickelsburg, George W. E., 218–19, 230
Nida, E. A., 172–73, 182
Nolland, John, 100, 114, 151, 156–57, 161, 183, 185, 189, 195–96, 198, 201

O'Brien, P., 61, 75
O'Leary, Anne M., 135–36, 139, 147
Oepke, A., 96, 114
Oesterley, W. O. E., 81–83, 94
Ogg, George, 148, 157
Olley, John W., 10, 12, 15, 22, 28
Oropeza, B. J., 101, 114
Osborne, G. R., 59, 65–66, 75
Oss, Douglas A., 77, 94
Oswalt, John N., 87–88, 94
Owen, Paul L., 213, 219, 229–30

Pao, David, 159, 170, 180, 182
Parker, Pierson, 247, 252
Parrott, D. M., 160, 183
Paul, Shalom M., 122, 127
Payne, P. B., 271, 276
Penner, Todd, 232–33, 252
Pesch, R., 261, 269, 276
Pietersma, Albert, 83, 94
Piper, John, 34, 42, 44, 51
Plummer, Alfred, 118, 126–27
Porter, Stanley E., 72, 75, 162, 166–68, 178, 183
Powell, Mark Allan, 215, 221, 230

Quell, G., 260, 275
Quispel, Gilles, 123, 127

Rackham, Richard, 6, 26, 276
Räisänen, Heikki, 235, 253
Rahmani, L. Y., 241, 253
Rebell, W., 203, 210

Reed, J. T., 288, 293, 297
Reicke, Bo, 245, 253, 268, 276
Rensberger, David, 203, 210
Reumann, John, 5-6, 10, 16, 22, 28, 30, 40, 47, 51
Reynolds, Benjamin E., 213, 218, 230
Richardson, Peter, 239, 253
Ritt, H., 255-56, 262, 271, 276
Roberts, Alexander, 232, 253
Robertson, A. T., 35, 51, 178, 183
Robinson, H. Wheeler, 121, 127
Robinson, T. H., 121, 127
Roloff, J., 258, 276
Ropes, James H., 243-44, 253
Russell, D. S., 219, 230
Russell, W. B., 54, 75
Ryle, Gilbert, 34-35, 51

Safrai, S., 293-94, 297
Sampley, J. P., 98, 114
Sanders, E. P., 105, 112, 114
Sandmel, Samuel, 175, 183, 264, 275
Schäfer, Peter, 123, 127
Schellenberg, Ryan S., 160, 163, 166, 183
Schlatter, Adolf, 156-57
Schlier, H., 97-98, 101, 114
Schmeller, T., 72, 75
Schmidt, K. L., 101, 114
Schmithals, Walter, 64, 76, 110, 114, 245, 253
Schmitz, E. D., 109, 114
Schmoller, A., 258, 276
Schnabel, Eckhard, 246, 248, 253
Schnackenburg, Rudolf, 216, 218, 220-21, 226, 230
Schnelle, Udo, 206, 211
Schreiner, Thomas. R., 59-60, 62, 64-65, 68-70, 76, 79-80, 94, 276
Schrenk, Gottlob, 5, 10, 13, 15, 19-20, 22, 28, 54, 76
Schubert, P., 61, 76
Schürer, E., 264, 276
Schürmann, Heinz, 149-50, 158
Schwartz, Eduard, 245, 253
Schweizer, Eduard, 109, 114, 150, 158, 261, 271, 276

Schwemer, Anna Maria, 233-34, 236, 247, 251
Scott, J. M., 106, 108, 114, 123, 127
Scott, Walter, 19-20, 28
Scullion, J. J., 47, 51
Seebass, H., 5, 15, 28
Segal, Alan, 123, 127
Seifrid, Mark A., 5, 13-15, 28, 30-31, 33, 51, 70, 76
Selwyn, E. G., 268, 276
Sevenster, J. N., 240, 253
Shellard, Barbara, 179, 183
Shelton, R. M., 199, 201
Shin, Hyeon Woo, 290, 297
Shum, Shiu-Lun, 85-86, 94
Simon, Marcel, 243, 246, 253
Smalley, Stephen S., 217, 219, 230, 258, 276
Smiga, G., 54, 76
Smith, D. Moody, 70, 76, 204-5, 211, 227, 230
Smith, W. B., 54, 76
Snodgrass, Klyne, 161-62, 166, 169, 173-74, 183, 271, 276
Söding, T., 107, 114
Spicq, Ceslas, xvii, 5, 7-8, 10, 13, 15-16, 22, 28
Stählin, G., 192, 201
Stanley, Christopher D., 71, 76, 84-85, 94
Stein, Robert H., 166, 183, 271, 276
Steyn, Gert J., 171, 183
Stowers, S. K., 72, 76
Strachan, Robert H., 123, 127
Strauss, Mark L., 171, 183
Strecker, Georg, 250, 276
Stuhlmacher, Peter, 32, 43-44, 51, 62, 64-65, 68, 76
Suhl, A., 54, 76
Sun, Yongchang, 279-80, 297
Sun, Yongxuan, 288-89, 295, 297

Talbert, Charles H., 176, 183
Tasker, Randolph V. G., 123, 127
Taylor, David, 239, 241, 253
Taylor, J. B., 255, 276
Taylor, John R., 24, 28, 31, 51
Taylor, V., 261, 270-71, 276

Tcherikover, Victor, 241, 253
Theissen, G., 271, 276
Thrall, Margaret E., 120, 123, 125, 127
Topel, L. John, 160, 163, 183
Travis, S. H., 118, 127
Trilling, W., 260, 276
Turner, C. H., 118, 127
Turner, Max, 284, 291, 296
Turner, Nigel, 151, 158

Upkong, Justin S., 165, 183

Van der Horst, Pieter W., 240, 253
Van der Minde, H. J., 71, 76
VanLandingham, Chris, 32–33, 47–48, 52

Wagner, J., 94
Wallace, Daniel, 35, 52
Wallis, Ian G., 106, 114
Walton, John H., 285, 288, 297
Wanamaker, C. A., 258, 260, 276
Warfield, B. B., 243, 245, 253
Watson, D. F., 72, 76
Watson, Francis, 79–80, 94, 235, 253
Watts, John D., 87, 94
Watts, R. E., 270, 276
Way, David, 32, 52
Wedderburn, A. J. M., 76
Weima, J. A. D., 54, 61, 64, 76
Weiser, A., 82, 94
Weiss, Johannes, 253
Westcott, B. F., 258, 276
Westerholm, Stephen, 96, 114
Wetter, G. P., 245, 253
Widengren, G., 121, 127

Wilcken, U., 7, 28, 54, 64, 76
Williams, C. S. C., 243–44, 250, 253
Williams, Francis E., 163, 166, 168, 183
Williams, P. R., 54, 76
Williams, Sam K., 102–4, 106, 114
Wilson, B. R., 202, 211
Wilson, R. R., 121, 127
Winger, Michael, 35, 52
Wisdom, J. R., 103, 114
Witherington, Ben, 97, 99, 114, 118, 127, 235, 243, 246–47, 253
Wolter, Michael, 167, 183
Wood, J., 54, 76
Wright, Benjamin G., 83, 94
Wright, N. T., 32, 34, 43–46, 52, 59, 76

Xu, Weihan, 280, 297

Yang, Yong-Eui, 281, 297
Yarbro Collins, Adela, 219, 230
Yardeni, Ada, 241, 253
Yeo, K. K., 277, 297
Young, Brad H., 159, 161, 183

Zeller, D., 65, 76
Zerwick, M., 186, 201
Ziesler, John, 10, 15, 19–20, 22, 26, 28, 32–33, 35–36, 47, 52
Ziesler, Z. A., 104, 114
Zhao, Zhenduo, 280, 286, 289, 292, 295, 297
Zhou, Dapu, 279, 281–86, 288–89, 291–92, 297
Zimmerli, Walther, 153–55, 158

Ancient Document Index

OLD TESTAMENT

Genesis

1:1–3	257
1:1–2a	138
1:27	133
2:15	138
2:24	133
12:3	xx, 103–4, 107
15:2–4	104
15:6	45, 138
15:7–8	104
15:14	138
16—21	107
17:5	86, 103
18:17	122
18:18	xx, 103–4, 107
18:19	109–10
20:7	138
21:10	104
22:18	103–4
26:4	103–4
28:4	104
28:12	138, 215
28:14	103–4
28:16	139
28:17	215
38:8	134

Exodus

3:6	134
3:12	119
4:6–9	116
13:2	135
13:12	135
13:15	135
16:4	138
16:8	287
20:12–16	133, 140
20:13	140
20:23	139
21:10	140
21:23	15
23:7	40, 47
23:20	132–33

Leviticus

1:9–10	266
5:11	135
12:8	135
18:5	105
19:13	140
19:17	192
19:18	133–34, 140
23:28–29	266
27:33	138

Numbers

5:2–3	138
11:17	266
11:25–26	266
11:28	117

Numbers (continued)

12:6–8	139
16:5	110
17:11–13	116
21:4–9	216
21:9	216
24:2	266
25:1–13	116
27:17	133

Deuteronomy

1:39	104
2:12	104
4:35	134
5:16–20	133, 140
5:31	138
6:4	134, 140
6:5	134, 140
6:24	105
8:3	139
13:1	116
13:5–10	116
13:6–11	117
13:7	117
13:12–18	116
13:14–15	117
17:2–7	116
18:9–22	116
24:1–4	294
24:1	293
25:1	47
25:5–6	134
27:26	124
28:15–68	124–25
28:16	124
28:22	124
28:27	124
28:28	124
28:34	124
28:35	124
28:46	124
28:48	124
30	45
30:12	122
31:6	119
34:10	139
34:11	116

Joshua

1:5	119
22:5	134
23:13	187

1 Samuel

10:10	266
12:16–18	116
15:26	266
23:1–2	266

2 Samuel

7	171

1 Kings

2:27	266
8:32	47
12:24	266
13:4	119
13:5	116
15:29	266
16:12	266
16:34	266
17:8–24	116
22	121
22:17–23	121
22:19–23	121

2 Kings

1:2–3	145
1:17	266
4:1–7	116
4:18–37	116
4:42–44	116
5:7	105
9:7	122
9:36	266
12:18	150
17:13	122
17:23	122
20:8–11	116
21:10	122
22:16	266
23:21 (LXX)	132

24:2	122	9:5	83
		9:16	83
1 Chronicles		9:18	83
		9:20	83
12:18	266	9:21	83
21:1	144	9—10	83
		10	47, 82–83
2 Chronicles		10:1-18 (9:22-39 LXX)	83
		10:3 (9:24 LXX)	83
6:23	47	10:4	83
15:1	266	10:7 (9:28 LXX)	80, 82
18	121	10:13 (9:34 LXX)	83
20:14	266	12	47
23:18	132	13	92
24:20-22	117	14 (13 LXX)	81
24:20	266	14:1-3 (13:1-3 LXX)	80
25:4	132	16	47
32:32	132	17	47
33:19	132	18	47
35:12	132	19:3 (18:4 LXX)	260
		22:2	134
Ezra		22:19	134
		25:27-28	45
9:11	122	31:1	45
		33:6	266
Nehemiah		33:9	266
		35	93
9:6	105	36 (35 LXX)	84
		36:1 (35:2 LXX)	80, 84
Job		36:5-6 (35:6-7 LXX)	84, 89
		37:18	110
1:6-12	121	39:3 4	118
1:6	144	42:6	134
11:2	47	42:12	134
13:18	47	43:5	134
15:8	121	44:21	110
36:6	105	44:22 (43:23 LXX)	86
		51:4 (50:6 LXX)	47
Psalms		51:14	45
		68:22	187
1:6	110	71:20	105
3:1	81	73:13 (72:13 LXX)	39, 41, 48
3:4	81	82:1-8	121
3:7	81	89:5-14	30
5	47, 81, 93	89:6-9	121
5:10	80-81	94:11	110
7	47	96:2 (95:2 LXX)	268
9	82-83, 93	97:1-12	30
9:1-20	30		

Psalms (continued)

99:1–5 (98:1–5 LXX)	44
99:4–5	30
103:6	30
104:12 (103:12 LXX)	133
105:19	266
105:42	266
107:20	266
110:1	134
118:22–23 (117:22–23 LXX)	134
118:25–26	133
118:25 (117:25 LXX)	145
119:7	45
119:54	45
119:62	45
119:89	266
119:160	45
139	93, 110
140 (139 LXX)	81–82
140:1 (139:2 LXX)	81–82
140:3 (139:4 LXX)	80–82
140:4 (139:5 LXX)	82
140:5	187
140:7 (139:8 LXX)	82
140:8 (139:9 LXX)	82
140:11 (139:12 LXX)	82
140:13 (139:14 LXX)	82
142:2	39–40
143:1–2	45
147:15 (147:4 LXX)	260
147:18 (147:7 LXX)	260
147:15–18	266
148:1	133

Proverbs

1:16	86
3:1–2	105
6:17	40
6:23	105
25:21–22	86
30:1–4	214
30:3–4	122

Isaiah

5:23	40
6	121
6:1–13	121
6:1	122
6:5	122
6:9–10	133, 136, 142–43
7:13	132, 143
7:14	136, 143
8:8	144
8:10	136, 144
9:8	266
14:10	134
16:5	170
27:5	138
28	78
29	78
29:13	133, 136
30:10	117
32:14	103
34:4	134
40	274
40:3–11	xxi, 266–70, 272–74
40:3	133, 136, 269
40:6–11	268–69
40:6–8	267, 269, 273
40:6	267
41:8–9	101
40:8	266–67
40:9	262
41:10–13	119
41:10	119
41:27	262
42:11	120
43:1	101
43:5	119
44:3	103
45	78
45:3–4	101
45:21	134
46:13	44–45
48:12	101
48:15	101
49:1	98
50:7	151
50:8	47
50:11	91
51:5–8	44
52	78
52:7	268, 270
53:1	270

54:17	44	9:23–24	30
55:11	266	11:21	117
56:1	44	14:15	119
56:7	134	15:10	139
57:7	86	15:16	266
57:21	138	15:20–21	119
59	xx, 77–79, 84–93	20:7	118
59:1–11a	87	20:8–9	266
59:5	90–91	20:9	xix
59:6–17	89	20:10	117
59:7–8	80, 84–86	21:10	152
59:10	90	23:9–15	119
59:12	90	23:9	266
59:15b–21	88	23:16–40	266
59:16	88, 92	23:16	122
59:19	92	23:18	121–23
59:20–21	92	23:19–20	119
59:20	90	23:22	121–22
59:21	103	23:28–29	266
60:7	120	24:5	288
61:1–2	135	24:8	288
61:1	262, 268	25:4	122
61:10–11	44	26:5	122
62:1	44	26:20–23	119
62:11	141	28:9	266
66:24	133	28:15–16	119
		29:19	122
		29:31–32	119
		32:32	119

Jeremiah

1	121	35:15	122
1:2	262	42:15	150
1:5 10	266	44:4	122
1:5	98, 110	44:12	150
1:8	119	49:14	262
1:17	118	51:63	190
1:19	119		
2:30	116		

Lamentations

3:12–13	151, 153	4:13	40
3:13	154		
4:2	104		

Ezekiel

4:19	118		
5:23	133	1	121
7:11	134	1:1—2:7	122
7:22–23	287	1:1	122
7:25	122	1:4	122
8:1	119	1:15	122
8:13	288	1:18	122
9:19	262		

Ezekiel (continued)

1:27	122
1:28	122
2:5	118
2:7	118
2:9	122
3:10–11	122
3:11	118
6:2	153
10:1–22	122
10:1	122
10:8	122
10:9	122
11:5	266
11:19	103
13:9	119
13:14	119
13:17	153
14:9	119
15:7	154–55
21:2	154
22:28	119
25:2	155
28:21	155
29:2	155
35:2	155
36:26–27	103
37:4	266
37:14	103
38:2	155
38:17	122
39:29	103

Daniel

3:19–27	119
6:19–23	119
7	214, 217–19
7:13–14	134, 214, 218
7:13	134, 214, 217, 219
9	45
9:6	122
9:10	122
9:13	132
9:16–28	44
9:17–19	45
12	218
12:2	217–18
12:11	134

Hosea

1:10	101
2:23	101
4:5–6	119
9:7	266
9:10	288
14:9–10	138

Joel

1:1–2	266
2:28–29	103
2:32	270
4:19	40

Amos

2:12	117
3:2	110
3:7	122
3:8	118, 266
7:16	117
8:14–15	266
9:11	170–71

Obadiah

1:1	262

Micah

2:6	117
7:1	288

Nahum

1:15	262

Habakkuk

2:4	30, 45

Zechariah

1:6	122
3:1	144

9:9	141
13:7	134

Malachi

2:16	294
3:1	132–33
3:23	133

APOCRYPHA

Baruch

3:9	105
3:29–37	122
4:1	105

2 Esdras (= 4 Ezra)

2:11	174
7:21	85
7:22–24	89
8:34–36	44

3 Maccabees

6:1–15	119

Sirach

4:1	133, 140
7:56	294
17:11	105
24:2	121
25:26	294
26:29	39, 41, 48
42:15	263
48:3	263

Tobit

3:6	173

Wisdom of Solomon

9:1	263
14:11	187
16:12	253

PSEUDEPIGRAPHA

Apocalypse of Moses

37:5	123

Assumption of Moses

5:2–6	85

3 Baruch

4:8	123

1 Enoch

37–71	219
39:4	174
49:2–4	224

2 Enoch

8:1	123
31:1	123

Joseph and Asenath

8:3	105
8:9	105
12:1	105
20:7	105

Letter of Aristeas

16	105

Lives of the Prophets

1:1	116
2:1	116
3:1	116
7:1	116
10:1–6	119
23:1	117

Martyrdom and Ascension of Isaiah

5	116

Psalms of Solomon

16:7	187
24:2	105

Testament of Simeon

6:1	39, 41, 48

Testament of Solomon

3:1–7	145

NEW TESTAMENT

Matthew

1:18	143
1:21	131, 143–44
1:22–23	132
1:23	131, 135–37, 142–44
2:5–6	132
2:5	132
2:6	135
2:15	132, 135
2:17–18	132, 135
2:23	132, 135
3:1–17	269
3:3	133, 135–36, 144
3:5	144
3:8	144
3:10	144
4	132
4:4	132, 139, 256
4:6	132
4:7	132
4:10	132
4:14–16	132, 135
4:14	135
4:15	135
4:17	269
5:9	133
5:11	117
5:12	117
5:17	283
7:24	255
7:28	255
8:17	132, 135–36
9:25	145
9:51–56	149
11:5	135–36
11:10	132–33
12:17–21	132, 135
12:17	135
12:18–21	136
12:18	135
12:24	145
12:26	144
12:27	145
13:10–17	131
13:13	143
13:14–15	132–33, 135–37, 141–42
13:14	135
13:19	143, 259–61, 271
13:22	261
13:23	261
13:31	133
13:35	132, 135
13:37–43	218
14:14	133
15:5	131, 146
15:6	256
15:7–8	133
15:7	132, 135
15:8–9	135–36
16:9	133
16:23	144
17:4	170
17:10	133
17:20	197
18:6–7	185
18:7	187
18:15	185
18:21–22	185
18:22	194
19:1–2	149
19:4–5	133
19:18	133, 136, 140
19:19	140
19:23–24	281
19:28	218
20	260
21:1–9	141
21:2–3	141
21:4–5	132, 135, 137, 141
21:5	135–36

21:7	141	4:14	260, 267, 270
21:9	133, 145	4:15	260
21:13	132, 134–36	4:18	261
21:42	134	4:20	261
22:24	134	4:26–29	273
22:31	134	4:27	282
22:37	133–34, 136, 140	4:32	133
22:39	134	5:41	144–45
22:40	134	6:3	132
22:43–44	134	6:4	132
23:29–33	117	6:34	133
23:35	117	7:6–7	133
24:15	134	7:6	132, 135
24:29	134–36	7:11	131, 146
24:30	134	7:13	256
25:31–46	218	7:34	146
26:25	290	8:18	132–33
26:31	132, 134	9:5	170
26:38	134	9:11	133
26:39–57	146	9:37	287
26:39	146	9:42	185
26:54	132	9:43	280
26:56	132	9:47	280
26:64	134, 290	9:48	132–33
27:9–10	132, 135	10:1–12	293
27:11	290	10:1	149
27:33	145	10:6–7	133
27:35	134	10:9–12	294
27:41	177	10:9	133
27:46	131, 134, 144–45	10:19	133, 140
27:57	235	11:2	141
		11:9	133, 145
		11:10	133
		11:17	132, 134

Mark

		11:20	141
1:1–15	267–70, 272–74	12:10–11	134
1:2–3	133	12:19	134
1:2	132, 135	12:26	134
1:3	269	12:29–30	133–34, 140
1:7	269	12:31	134, 140
1:13	144	12:32–33	132
1:14–15	269	12:33	134
2:17	287	12:36	134
2:21	282	13:14	134
3:21	125	13:24–27	218
3:22	145	13:24–25	134
4:10–12	131	13:26	134
4:12	133, 143	13:31	255
4:14–20	262, 267, 270, 272–74		

Mark (continued)

14:27	132
14:34	134
14:36	146
14:49	132
14:62	134
15:22	131, 144–45
15:24	134
15:31	177
15:34	134, 144–45
19:30	141

Luke

1:1	200
1:2	259
1:27	170
1:57	186
1:65	178
1:69	170–71
2:4	170
2:6	186
2:23	132, 135
2:24	135
2:32	283–84
3:1–22	269
3:2	256
3:3	188
3:4–6	133, 269
3:4	132, 135
3:20	196
4	132
4:8	144
4:14–19	269
4:17–19	135
4:17–22	132
4:24	179
4:32	255
4:36	255
4:42	186
4:43	187
4:44	286
5:1	156, 273
5:8–10	194
5:21	189
5:31–32	188
5:32	188, 190
6:7	189
6:13	196
6:17	286
6:20	186
6:22	117
6:34–35	179
6:37	193
6:41	191
6:42	191
6:46–49	199
7:17	286
7:27	132–33
7:39	189
7:49	189
8:1	196
8:3	235
8:9–10	131
8:11	143, 258, 260, 267, 271
8:12	259–60
8:13	259, 261
8:15	143, 258–59, 261
8:19–21	199
8:41	196
8:43	196
9:1–6	194
9:1	196–97
9:10	196–97
9:12	196
9:33	170
9:40–41	197
9:43	186
9:49–50	189
9:50—18:15	148
9:51—19:48	176
9:51–56	149–50
9:51	xxi, 148–50, 152, 155–56
10:1–21	194
10:1	150
10:13	188
10:17	197
10:19	186
10:20	194
10:23	186
10:27	134
10:38	150
11:1–4	195
11:2	186
11:4	195
11:5–8	163

11:7	163	15:25–32	176, 179
11:8	163	15:25	169
11:15	145	15:32	188
11:27–28	199	15:34	188
11:32	188	16	159, 167, 169, 176, 180
11:45	176	16:1–14	185
11:46	189	16:1–13	161, 176
11:47–51	117	16:1–9	159
11:49	196	16:1–8	160, 176
11:51	117	16:1	176, 186
11:52	189–90	16:4	169, 179
11:53	150	16:7	160
12:1–48	176	16:8a	160
12:1	186	16:8b	160
12:22	186	16:9	160, 170–71, 173–74, 179
12:25	196	16:14–15	161
12:31	196	16:14	176–77, 180
12:35–59	176	16:15–18	185
12:41–48	176	16:16	176
12:47	199	16:19–31	173, 176, 179, 185
12:49	154, 157	16:28–31	176
12:54–59	176	16:31	180
13:3	188	17	192
13:5	188	17:1–10	xxi, 184–85, 200
13:6	288	17:1–3a	185
13:14	189	17:1–2	184, 186, 191, 200
13:19	196	17:1	185–86
13:22	150	17:2	187, 191, 195
13:33	150, 179	17:3–4	184, 187, 191, 199–200
14–16	179	17:3	191, 193–94
14:1–6	189	17:4	192–94
14:7	176	17:5–6	184, 191, 195, 199–200
14:12–14	179	17:5	185–86, 195
14:29	177	17:6	185, 196
15–16	169, 171, 176, 180	17:7–10	184–85, 191, 198–200
15	179, 185	17:7–9	198
15:1–2	177	17:10	198
15:1	176, 185, 188–89	17:11	150, 189
15:2	189–90	17:20–37	187
15:3–7	188	17:20–21	185
15:6	169	17:22–37	185
15:7	188	17:22–35	218
15:8–10	188	17:22	186
15:8	169	18:1–8	163
15:10	188	18:7	187
15:11–32	188	18:9	177
15:18	192	18:15–16	189
15:21	192	18:20	133

Luke (continued)

18:21–35	195
18:21	178
18:30	186
18:31	150, 186
18:35	150
19:1	150
19:2	235
19:7	189
19:10	186
19:11	196
19:27	185
19:30	141
19:38	133
19:41–44	156
19:46	134
20:12	196
20:16	72
20:17	134
20:37	134
20:42–43	134
21:9	187
21:25–26	134
21:27	134, 218
21:34	191
21:36	178
22:14	196
22:22	190
22:27	186
22:32	191
22:61	256
22:63	177
23:5	286
23:11	177
23:29	186
23:35	177
23:36	177
24:9	178
24:10	196
24:44	132
24:49	103

John

1–6	222
1:1	257
1:1–5	257
1:1–18	256
1:2	221
1:6–8	269
1:14	257
1:19–34	269
1:23	135
1:38	144
1:41	144
1:51	215–16
2:9–10	98
2:9	98
3:1	235
3:13–15	215
3:13	215–16, 221
3:14–17	216
3:14–15	216
3:14	215–16, 220
3:16–18	216
3:16	206, 216
3:17–21	225
3:18	216–217, 225
3:34	256
3:36	205, 223
4	149
5	222
5:21	105
5:22–29	225
5:22	217
5:24–30	220–21
5:24–29	219–221
5:24–27	219
5:24	205, 217, 225
5:25–29	217
5:25–27	219
5:27–29	218, 220
5:27	215, 217–19
5:28–29	218–19
5:28a	219
5:28b–29	219
5:29	225
5:38	257
6	222
6:1–15	220
6:26–65	220–21
6:27	215, 220–21
6:27a	220
6:35	221
6:37	221
6:39	220–21

6:40	220–21	13:18	132
6:44	220–21	13:30–31a	226
6:47	205, 221	13:31	215, 226
6:48	221	13:31b	226
6:50–51	221	13:33b	226
6:50	221	13:36	227
6:52	221	14:24	257
6:53–58	221	14:26	226
6:53–54	220	15:25	132, 256
6:53	215, 220	16:2	222
6:54	220–21	17	205
6:61b–62	221	17:6	257
6:62	215, 220–21	17:14	257
7–21	222	17:17	257
8:17	132	18:9	132
8:21	226	19:24	132
8:23	226	19:36	132
8:24	226		
8:28	215, 226	Acts	
8:47	256		
8:51	205	1:1	200
9:1–41	222	1:4	103
9:22	222	1:16	187
9:34	222	2:17	103
9:35	215, 222	2:19	116
9:37	222	2:22	116
9:39	222–23, 225	2:23	190
9:41	222–23	2:33	103
10:1–18	209	2:38	188, 190
10:35	256	2:43	116
11:25b	225	3:21	187
12:13	133	4:11	177
12:20–50	223	4:12	187
12:23	215, 223	4:16	116
12:24–33	223	4:22	116
12:25–26	223	4:30	116
12:31–34	224	4:36	144, 234
12:32	224	5:12	116
12:33	216	5:17–21	119
12:34	215, 223	5:31	188
12:38	132, 135	5:44	117
12:44	287	6	207
12:46	224	6:1—8:1	233
12:47–48	224	6:1	231–32
12:47	222, 225	6:8	116
12:48	225	7:36	116
13:1	227	7:43	170
13:3	227	7:44	170

Acts (continued)

7:50	178
7:52	117
8:1–25	149
8:6	116, 191
8:10	191
8:11	191
8:13	116
8:22	188
9:1–9	123
9:17	116
9:23–25	119
9:23–24	120
9:29–30	67
11:18	188
12:3–17	119
12:12	234
12:25	234
13:2	116
13:4	116
13:5	234
13:6–12	116
13:8	144
13:8–41	71
13:9	116
13:13	234
13:22	116
13:24	188
13:43	98
13:45–50	71
14:1–2	71
14:3–4	116
14:3	116
14:5–6	119
14:8–13	116
14:19	71
15:3	66
15:8	116
15:12	116
15:16	170–71
15:22	234
15:27	234
15:32	234
15:37	234
16:6–7	116
16:14	191
16:18	116
16:26–40	119
17:2–5	71
17:10	119
17:30	188
18:1–3	62
18:2	60
18:18	62
18:26	62
19:1	116
19:4	188
19:11–12	116
19:13–19	116
19:21	116
20:3b	67
20:22–25	67
20:22–23	116
20:23	116
20:28	191
21:10–13	67
21:11	116
21:17–28	71
21:19–21	67
21:20–21	69
22:6–11	123
22:17	125
22:19–23	71
23:12–15	117
23:12	119
26:13–19	123
26:17	119
26:20	188
28:2–6	119

Romans

1–14	56
1–3	85
1:1–15	54, 59, 73
1:1–7	61, 63
1:1	63–64, 101
1:2–4	63
1:2	64, 70
1:3	64
1:5–6	63, 66–67
1:5	61, 64, 98
1:7	56, 63, 96, 101
1:8—2:29	70
1:8–15	61, 65
1:9	64

1:10–13	65	3:11–18	92
1:11–15	66	3:11–12	80, 92
1:11–12	73	3:11	81
1:11	65	3:12	81
1:12	65	3:13	80–81, 93
1:13–15	67	3:13a	81
1:13	56, 61, 65–66, 73, 273	3:14–17	80
1:14–15	64	3:14	80–81, 93
1:15	56, 61, 64, 66	3:15–17	78, 84–86, 89, 92–93
1:16—15:13	54, 59, 61	3:15	84, 86
1:16–17	44, 64	3:16–17	86
1:16	64	3:16	85
1:16a	58, 64	3:17	85
1:17–18	79, 122	3:18	80, 84, 93
1:17	30, 45, 70, 79	3:19	46, 92
1:18—11:36	56	3:20–24	111
1:18—3:20	78	3:20	39, 40, 46, 106, 111
1:18—3:9	86	3:21–26	26, 30, 41–42, 45–46, 48–49, 112
1:18—3:8	85		
1:18	79, 81	3:21	41–43, 46, 64, 70
2–3	68	3:22–26	46
2:1–5	71–72	3:22	42, 45–46
2:5	122	3:23–24	47
2:16	58, 63	3:23	42, 106
2:17–29	72	3:24	39, 40, 42, 46, 111
2:17–24	71–72	3:25–26	47
2:17–20	65	3:25	42, 46
2:24	70	3:26	39, 42, 46
3–4	71	3:27—4:2	71–72
3	46, 79, 83, 85, 87–88, 90–92	3:27–31	71
3:1–20	84	3:27	46
3:1–9	71–72	3:28	39, 46
3:1–8	71, 80	3:29	111
3:1	65	3:30	39
3:1a	80	3:31	46, 58, 64, 70, 72
3:4–18	70	4	64, 68
3:4	46, 72	4:1–25	70
3:6–7	46	4:1	58, 72
3:6	72, 81	4:2	39
3:7	81	4:5	47
3:8	58, 68, 81	4:9	111
3:9–18	xx, 77–80, 84–85, 92	4:16–25	102
3:9–11	87	4:17	86, 101, 105
3:9	46, 78–81, 106	4:21	116
3:9b	86	4:23–24	70
3:10–18	77–80, 84–86, 88–89, 92	5:1—8:30	70
3:10–12	81	5:1	39
3:10	80, 86	5:2	98

Romans (continued)

5:15–17	111
6:1–3	72
6:1	58
6:2	72
6:7	26, 34, 39, 41
6:14	111
6:15–16	72
6:15	58, 72, 111
7	68
7:6	106
7:7	58, 70, 72
7:12	58, 72
7:13	72
7:14,	58, 72
8:4	64
8:15	146
8:18	122
8:19	122
8:28–30	101
8:29	110
8:30	39, 102
8:33	39
8:36	70, 86
9–11	58, 64, 68, 70–71, 77–78, 111
9:4–26	101
9:6—11:36	70
9:6	70
9:10–12	102
9:11	101
9:12	101
9:14	72
9:19–21	71–72
9:19–20	72
9:24–33	70
9:24	101
9:25–26	101–2
10:5–17	xxii, 267, 270, 272, 274
10:8–17	270
10:8	259
10:9–13	270
10:14–18	273
10:15–16	270
10:16–21	70
10:17	259, 261, 270
10:18	79
11	86
11:1	72
11:2	110
11:7–10	70
11:11–32	59
11:11	72
11:13	67
11:17–24	67, 71–72
11:18	65
11:19–20	72
11:25	123
11:26–27	70
11:26	78, 84, 111
11:28–29	101
11:28	67
11:30–31	67
11:32	106
12:1—14:23	70
12:9–21	57
12:19	70, 132
12:20	86
13:1–7	57, 73
13:8–10	57
13:9	140
13:9a	70
13:9b	70
14–15	68–69
14:1—15:13	65, 68
14:1—15:12	57, 73
14:4–11	71
14:4	72
14:10	72
14:11	70, 132
15	71
15:1–12	70
15:7–13	59
15:7–9	67
15:8–12	70
15:14—16:27	54, 59, 73
15:14–33	56, 61, 65–66
15:14–16,	66
15:14–15	65
15:15–16	65, 67, 98
15:15	66
15:16–28	59
15:16	64
15:17–21	66
15:17–19a	66
15:18–19	116

15:18	67	1:19	132
15:19	64	1:24	101–2
15:19b	66	1:26–29	101
15:20–21	66	1:26	101
15:20	64	1:30	38, 48
15:21	70	2:1	123, 255
15:22–24	65, 66	2:4–5	116
15:22	61, 73	2:7	123
15:23–24	61	2:10	122
15:23a	66	2:17	102
15:23b	67	3:13	122
15:24	66	4:1	123
15:24a	66	4:4	39
15:24b	66–67, 73	4:9–13	117
15:24c	66	4:9–12	124
15:25–33	67	6:6	39
15:25–26	67	6:12–13	71
15:28–29	73	6:15	72
15:28	61	7:15	97, 101
15:30–31	67	7:17	101
15:32	73	8:1–13	188
16	58	8:3	110
16:1–27	61	9:1	122
16:1–24	56	9:9	132
16:1–23	62	9:16	118
16:3	60, 62	9:17	117
16:5	62	10:12	190
16:7	62	13:2	123
16:13	62	13:12	110
16:16	62	14:2	123
16:17–20	58	14:6	122
16:17 19	68	14:26	122
16:20	96	14:30	122
16:21	63	14:36	255–56
16:23	97	15:1	262
16:25–27	64	15:8	122
16:25–26	63	15:9	101
16:25	63–64, 122–23	15:22	105
16:26	64, 123	15:30	124
		15:32	124
		15:35–38	71

1 Corinthians

		15:51	123
1:1	101	15:54	256
1:2	101	16:6	67
1:3	96	16:11	67
1:7	122	16:19	62
1:9	101–2	16:23	97
1:18	259	16:25–26	123

2 Corinthians

1:1	63
1:2	96
1:8	119
1:9	119
1:10	120
1:16	66
1:19	234
2:16	123
2:17	258
4:2	258
4:7–8	124
4:7	124
4:8–9	120
4:8	120
4:9	120
5:1	172
5:4	172
5:13	125
5:19	259
5:21	38
6:3–10	124
6:4–5	117
6:9	120
8:4	67
9:13	67
10:11	116
11:7	262
11:13	115
11:22	239
11:23—12:10	XX, 115, 124
11:23–30	XX, 115, 125
11:23–27	117
11:23–25	117
11:23	125
11:26	117, 124
11:27	124
11:30	125
11:31–33	XX, 115, 125
11:32–33	118, 120
12:1–10	115, 123
12:1–4	XX, 123–25
12:1	122
12:2–4	125
12:2	123–24
12:3–4	123
12:4	124
12:5–10	XX, 125
12:7–10	125
12:7	122, 124
12:12	116, 124
13:1	97

Galatians

1	118
1:1—5:1	99
1:1	117
1:3	96–97
1:6	96–97, 99–101
1:7	111
1:8–9	111
1:11	63, 262
1:12	117, 122–23
1:13	99
1:15	96–99, 101
1:16	122–23
1:17	120
1:23	99
2:2	64, 122
2:7	98
2:9–10	98–99
2:9	96, 98
2:15–17	106
2:16	39, 95, 105
2:17	72
2:20	99
2:21	95–96, 98–100, 105, 111
2:21a	99
3:2–5	109
3:5	100, 116
3:8	39, 100, 103–4, 106
3:10—4:7	103
3:10–29	106
3:10	124
3:11	39, 95
3:14	102–3, 108
3:15–26	102
3:15–18	100, 104–5
3:15	104
3:16	102–3
3:17	102–4
3:18	95, 102–3
3:19–22	105
3:21	72, 95, 100, 102–3, 105
3:22	102–3, 105–6

Ancient Document Index 343

3:22b	106
3:23–29	106–7
3:23–25	106
3:23	100, 106, 122
3:24	39
3:25–26	106
3:26–29	107
3:28	107
3:29	100, 102–3, 107–8
4:2	108
4:3–5	108
4:3	108
4:3b	109
4:4–7	108–9
4:4–6	108
4:5–7	108
4:5b	106
4:6	100, 106, 109, 146
4:6a	106
4:6b–7	106
4:6b	106
4:7	108
4:7a	106
4:9	100, 109
4:14	125
4:21–31	108
4:21	107
4:22	132
4:23	102–3, 107
4:27	132
4:28	100, 102–3, 107–8
4:29	108
4:31	102
5:1	102, 106
5:4	39, 95–96, 100
5:4b	95
5:4c	95, 99
5:5	106
5:8	100–101
5:13	100, 102
5:14	256
6:1	190, 193
6:6	259
6:11–16	68
6:14	72
6:18	96–97

Ephesians

1:2	96
1:9	123
1:13	259, 262, 273
1:17	122
1:18	101
3:3	122–23
3:4	123
3:5	122
3:9	123
4:4	97
5:32	123
6:14	84
6:17	84
6:19	123, 273
6:24	97

Philippians

1:1	64
1:14	259, 273
1:2	96
2:16	258–59
3:5	239
3:12	39, 118
3:15	122
3:17–21	68
4:23	98

Colossians

1:1	64
1:2	96
1:5–10	273
1:5–6	268
1:5	260–62, 273
1:6	258
1:7–8	61
1:8	258
1:25	258, 260
1:26–27	123
2:1	61
2:2	123
3:15	97
3:16	258, 260–61, 273
3:17	116
4:3	123, 259–61, 273
4:10	234

Colossians (continued)

4:12–13	61
4:18	97

1 Thessalonians

1:1	63, 234
1:2	96
1:5	116, 273
1:6	259, 261, 273
1:8	258, 260
2:12	101
2:13	255, 258, 261, 268, 273
2:13a	273
2:13b	273
2:15	117
4:7	97, 101
4:15	256
5:19–20	117
5:24	101
5:28	97

2 Thessalonians

1:1	63
1:2	96
1:7	122
2:3	122
2:6	122
2:7	123
2:8	122
2:14	101
2:16	97
2:17	116
3:1	258, 260, 268, 273
3:18	97

1 Timothy

1:2	96
4:5	258
6:12	101
6:21	97

2 Timothy

1:2	96
1:9	98
2:1	98
2:9	258–60, 268, 273
2:15	259–60
2:18	205
2:19	110
4:2	259–61, 273
4:22	97

Titus

1:4	96
2:5	273
3:13	66
3:15	97

Philemon

1:1	63
1:3	96

Hebrews

1:3	256
4:12–13	258, 268
4:12	258
6:5	258
11:3	256
11:37–38	117
11:37	116
13:7	258

James

1:18	259–60, 258, 273
1:21	259–61, 273
1:22	259
1:23	259

1 Peter

1:3	267
1:18–22	267
1:22–25	270
1:22–23	267
1:23–25	xxii, 261, 267–68, 272–74
1:23–24	267
1:23	258, 267, 273
1:24	267
1:25	256, 262, 267, 273

2:8	259, 261, 268
2:24–25	267
3:1	259, 261, 268
4:1	267
4:17	268
5:12	98

2 Peter

3:5	256
3:7	256
3:18	98

1 John

1:1–2	257
1:10	257
2:5	257
2:14	257–58
4:2–3	257

Revelation

1:2	256
13:6	170
15:5	170
17:17	256
19:9	256
19:13	257
21:3	170

DEAD SEA SCROLLS

1QH

4:30–37	38

1QS

11:9–15	38
11:12–15	44

CD

1–8	89–90
1	91
1:1—2:1	90
1:3–12	90

1:3–5	90
1:3	91
1:4	91
1:5	90
1:8–9	90
1:8	90
1:8b–9	90–91
1:9	90
1:10	90–91
2:2–13	90
2:14—4:12a	90
4:12b—5:15a	90
5	92
5:12	91
5:13–17	85
5:13–14	91–92
5:13	91
5:15b—6:11a	90
6:11b—8:21	90
19–20	89–90
19:33—20:34	90

Philo

De Abrahamo

1.201	144

De aeternitate mundi

1.19	138

De confusione linguarum

1.44	139

De decalogo

1.36	140
1.147	132

De mutatione nominum

1.139	138
1.169	138

De posteritate Caini

1.102	132

De somniis

1.183	139
1.333	138

De specialibus legibus

1.30	293
4.1	140

De vita Mosis

2.26	137
2.29	137
2.31	137
2.38	137
2.40	137

Legatio ad Gaium

1.4	144
1.281–82	240

Legum allegoriae

1.51	139
1.53	138
1.68	144
1.258	138
2.94	138
2.105	137
3.8	138
3.43	138
3.110	138
3.162	138
3.174	137, 139

Quis rerum divinarum heres sit

1.58	144
1.68	138
1.251	137
1.262	139

Josephus

Against Apion

1.167	146
1.307	190

Jewish Antiquities

1.52	144
4.20	150
4.73	146
4.253	294
4.278	15, 23
14.288	14, 23
15.213	23
16.151–67	15
16.206	15, 23
18.178	15, 23
20.135	14, 23

Jewish War

1.3–6	240
2.175	146

Vita

426	294

RABBINIC WRITINGS

Mishnah

m. Gittin

9:10	293

m. Ketubbot

7:6	294

Jerusalem Talmud

y. Sukkah

5	119
55a	119

Babylonian Talmud

b. Yebamot

49b	116

Other Works

Genesis Rabbah

98	119

Midrash Psalms

26.7	119

Pirqe Rabbi Eliezer

1.10	119

Sifre Deuteronomy

269.1.1	294

Shalshelet ha-Kabbalah

97	117

GRECO-ROMAN LITERATURE

Appian

The Civil Wars

2.8.51	19

Aristotle

Nichomachean Ethics

1129a6–9	6, 23
1129a34–1129b1	6, 23
1136b32–1137a4	6
1137a10–12	6, 23
1138b10–11	6, 23

Politics

1291a26–29	6, 23

Caesar Augustus

Res Gestae Divi Augusti

25.1	17–18
26.1–3	18
26.3	19
32.3	18
34	17, 24
34.1–2	23, 18
34.1	18
34.2	18

Corpus hermeticum

13	19–20
13.1	19
13.7–9b	20
13.7a	19
13.8b	19
13.9	20, 24, 26, 39, 41, 47

Demosthenes

Orations

3.21	7, 23
3.26	7
44.4	7, 23

Dio Cassius

Roman History

37.12.2	13
37.23.3	23
37.41.2	13, 23
38.11.3	13, 23
40.19.2	11, 23
41.28.4	13, 23
43.24.4	13, 23
48.46.4	11, 23
49.12.1	10
49.12.5	13–14, 23
52.24.2–3	23
52.24.3–4	13, 23
52.25.3–4	23
54.15.4	13–14, 23
54.19.2	14, 23
54.24.6–7	12, 23
55.14.3	13, 23
56.4.5	23
60.6	60

Diodorus Siculus

The Library of History

5.71.1	9, 23
12.45.1	10, 23
19.85.4	10, 23
40.11.1–2	10, 23
40.11.1	10
40.11.2	10
49.12.1	10

Diogenes Laertius

Lives of Eminent Philosophers

3.80	16
7.92	16, 23
7.126	17

Dionysius of Halicarnassus

Roman Antiquities

10.2–3	12, 23
10.2	12, 23
10.3	12

Epictetus

Dissertationes

3.14.13–14	16, 23
3.24.4–5	8, 24
3.26.32	8, 23

Fragments

14	16
28b	16

Herodotus

Histories

1.96	5, 23

Hesiod

Opera et dies

213–24	5, 24

Homer

Odyssey

6.120–21	5, 22
9.172–76	5, 22
13.209–12	5, 22
14.89–92	5, 22

Justinian

Digest

3.2	9

Ancient Document Index   349

Musonius Rufus

Fr. 11	16, 23
Fr. 13B	16, 23
Fr. 14	16, 23
Fr. 16	16, 23
Fr. 17	16, 23
Fr. 38	16, 24

Pindar

Fr. 16.9	5, 23

Plato

Gorgias

484B	5, 23

Plutarch

Ad principem ineruditum

780E	8, 24
781B	8, 24

Aemilius Paullus

2.6	16, 23

Comparatio Demosthenis et Ciceronis

3.4	16

De curiositate

522B	17

De fortuna

87E	17

De sera numinis vindicta

565B	14, 23–24

De virtute morali

440E–441B	16

On Listening to Lectures

48C	xix

Polybius

Histories

3.31.9	8, 13, 23

Stobaeus

Eclogae

1.49.44	9, 23

Stoicorum veterum fragmenta

3.314	9

Thucydides

History of the Peloponnesian War

2.71.2–4	6
2.71.2	23
2.71.4	23

OSTRACA, PAPYRI, AND INSCRIPTIONS

BGU

1138.4	10, 23
1824.30	10, 23

P. Giss

I.47.14–17	11
I.47.16	11, 23

P. Oslo

128.10	10, 23
1873.15	23

P. Oxy.

III.653	13, 23
VI.905.9	11, 23
1873.15	10

P. Ryl.

II.119.14–16	11–12, 23

P. Tebt.

II.444	12, 23

P. Thead.

23.9–11	10, 23
23.12–21	10

UPZ

II.16, col. 7 lines 2–27	6, 23

EARLY CHRISTIAN WRITINGS

Barnabas

4:3	132

1 Clement

4:1	132
14:4	132
29:2	132
39:3	132
46:2	132
50:4	132
50:6	132

Clement of Alexandria

Salvation of the Rich

13.3.2	174
31.6.1	174

Didache

10:6	145

Ignatius

Letter to the Ephesians

5:3	132

Justin

Dialogue with Trypho

27:3	85

www.ingramcontent.com/pod-product-compliance
Lightning Source LLC
Chambersburg PA
CBHW071147300426
44113CB00009B/1117